Stalin's Peasants

Resistance and Survival in the Russian Village after Collectivization

Sheila Fitzpatrick

New York   Oxford

OXFORD UNIVERSITY PRESS

1994

Oxford University Press

Oxford   New York   Toronto
Delhi   Bombay   Calcutta   Madras   Karachi
Kuala Lumpur   Singapore   Hong Kong   Tokyo
Nairobi   Dar es Salaam   Cape Town
Melbourne   Auckland   Madrid

and associated companies in
Berlin   Ibadan

Library of Congress Cataloging-in-Publication Data
Fitzpatrick, Sheila.
Stalin's peasants : resistance and survival in the Russian village
after collectivization / Sheila Fitzpatrick.
p. cm.   Includes bibliographical references (p.   ) and index.
ISBN 0-19-506982-X
1. Collectivization of agriculture—Soviet Union.
2. Agriculture and state—Soviet Union.
3. Soviet Union—Rural conditions.
I. Title.   HD1492.S65F58 1994   306.3'64'0947—dc20
93-4786

1 3 5 7 9 8 6 4 2

Printed in the United States of America
on acid-free paper

To
MD *and* DMF
with love

Acknowledgments

This book was a long time in the making, and there are many people to thank. I am particularly grateful to those who generously read the entire manuscript and gave me detailed and extremely useful critiques: John Bushnell, Michael Danos, David Fitzpatrick, Richard Hellie, Steven Hoch, Lynne Viola, and Allan Wildman. For helpful comments on individual chapters, I thank Jonathan Bone, Lorraine Daston, Julie Hessler, Jerry Hough, and Roberta Manning.

I presented papers based on chapters of the book at the University of Michigan at Ann Arbor, Bard College, Cornell University, Tübingen University, the University of Toronto, Monash University, the Australian National University, the Ruhr-Universität in Bochum, Cologne University, Freiburg University, and at the University of Chicago's Workshop in Russian and Soviet Studies Workshop and Workshop in Comparative Politics and Historical Sociology. For their comments and insights on these and other occasions I would particularly like to acknowledge Leora Auslander, Katerina Clark, Ranajit Guha, Steven L. Kaplan, David Laitin, Colin Lucas, Nellie Ohr, William Parrish, T. H. Rigby, William Rosenberg, Yuri Slezkine, Peter Solomon, Susan Solomon, Ronald Suny, and Andrew Verner.

All my Chicago graduate students contributed to the development of this book in various ways, but special thanks are due to those who were my research assistants at various times: Golfo Alexopoulos (who helped with archival work in Moscow), James Andrews, Jonathan Bone, Nicholas Glossop, and Joshua Sanborn.

For sundry assistance in obtaining references, materials, and access, I thank V. V. Alekseev, G. A. Bordiugov, V. P. Danilov (to whom I owe particular gratitude for telling me of the existence of the *Krest'ianskaia gazeta* archive), the late V. Z. Drobizhev, June Farris, Beate Fieseler, Arch Getty, Konstantin Gurevich, James Harris, A. Kapustin, A. Kirin, V. A. Kozlov, Hiroaki Kuromiya, Harry Leich, T. Mironova, Jane Ormrod, E. I. Pivovar, and T. I. Slavko. For helping to locate the illustration used on the jacket of this book, I am grateful to Edward Kasinec, Chief of the Slavonic and Baltic Division at the New York Public Library.

The early part of this work was done when I was at the University of Texas at Austin, and I would like to express my gratitude to all my colleagues in Austin, particularly Myron Gutmann, Michael Katz, Robert King, William Livingston, Standish Meacham, Jagat Mehta, Janet Meisel, Sidney Monas, and Walt Rostow for friendship and support beyond the call of duty.

I was aided in this work by support from the Guggenheim Foundation, the John C. and Catherine D. MacArthur Foundation, the University Research Institute of the University of Texas at Austin, IREX, the Russian State Humanities' University, and the University of Chicago (with special acknowledgement to Edward Laumann as Dean of Social Sciences, John Boyer in his many roles, and John Coatsworth as Chairman of the History Department).

A section of "The Mice Bury the Cat" first appeared in a longer version in *Russian Review* 52:3 (July 1993); the journal's permission to publish it here is gratefully acknowledged.

Contents

Glossary

aktiv informal group of Soviet activists (i.e., peasants associating themselves with Soviet regime) in village

artel form of collective farm (with collective cultivation, marketing, and ownership of means of production)

barshchina labor obligation under serfdom

batrak (f. batrachka) agricultural laborer

bedniak (pl. bednota) poor peasant(s)

brigade (brigada) main kolkhoz work unit

Central Committee central decision-making body of Communist Party of the Soviet Union, elected by periodic national congresses of party

chastushka (pl. chastushki) satirical or light-hearted verse on a topical theme, popular in villages and towns

Cheka political police during Civil War period

dekulakization expropriation of kulaks

desiatina old measure of size (equals 1 hectare or 2.7 acres)

dvor peasant household

edinolichnik independent (non-collectivized) peasant

feldsher paramedic

First Five-Year Plan industrialization program, 1929–1932

GPU (Gosudarstvennoe politicheskoe upravlenie) political police, successor to Cheka (1921–28)

gulag labor camp system

hectare measure of size (equals 2.7 acres)

izba peasant hut

khutor enclosed farm with farmhouse, or group of farms (separate from the village)

kolkhoz (pl. kolkhozy) collective farm

kolkhoznik (f. kolkhoznitsa) collective farm member

kommuna commune (form of collective farm)

Komsomol Union of Communist Youth

krai province containing ethnically distinct autonomous oblasts

kraikom provincial party committee

kulak prosperous peasant (regarded by Bolsheviks as exploiter of poor peasants)

labordays (trudodni) unit of payment for kolkhoz work based on time worked, weighted according to job

lapti bast sandals

mekhanizator machine operator

mir peasant land commune (obshchina)

MTS Machine-Tractor Station

muzhik Russian peasant (male)

NEP New Economic Policy (1921–1928)

NKVD (Narodnyi Komissariat Vnutrennikh Del) political police, successor to OGPU (1934 on)

oblast administrative unit, province

obkom provincial party committee

OGPU (Obyedinennoe gosudarstvennoe politicheskoe upravlenie) political police, successor to GPU (1928–1932)

Old Believers schismatics who split from Orthodox Church in late seventeenth century

orgnabor organized labor recruitment (based on contract between industrial enterprise and the kolkhoz)

otkhodnik peasant working for wages outside the village

otkhod seasonal or temporary departure for off-farm wage work

People's Commissar head of a government ministry (People's Commissariat)

Pioneer member of Soviet youth organization for ten- to fourteen-year olds, the Young Pioneers

politotdel political department of MTS

Politburo political bureau of party's Central Committee

pud old measure of weight (equals 16.38 kilograms)

raion administrative district, subordinate to oblast or krai

raikom district party committee

rural soviet (sel'sovet) lowest-level administrative unit

samogon home-distilled vodka

sel'kor unpaid, voluntary newspaper correspondent in village

seredniak middle peasant (economic category)

shef sponsoring organization, patron

skhod village assembly

Solovki islands in White Sea, used as prison

soviet elected body with administrative functions

sovkhoz state farm, employing wage labor

Stakhanovite peasant or worker recognized for outstanding production record (used from 1935)

stanitsa Cossack settlement

starosta elder (of mir; also of parish council of church)

TOZ (tovarishchestvo po obshchestvennoi obrabotki zemli) form of collective farm (only land and major equipment collectivized)

tverdozadanets fixed-quota peasant (early 1930s)

udarnik (f. udarnitsa) peasant or worker with outstanding production achievements (mainly used in early 1930s)

util'syryë scrap, recyclable for industrial purposes

valenki felt boots

vlast' power (of state)

znakharka wise woman, folk healer

zveno link, subunit of a brigade

Chronology

26 October 1917	Decree on land "*O zemle*," *SU RSFSR*, 1917 no. 1, art. 3
November 1929	Mobilization of worker "25,000-ers" begins
27 December 1929	Stalin announces policy of "liquidating kulaks as a class" "*K voprosam agrarnoi politiki v SSSR*," in Stalin, *Soch.* 12:141–72
5 January 1930	Central Committee resolution on increased tempo of collectivization and dekulakization "*O tempe kollektivizatsii i merakh pomoshchi gosudarstva kolkhoznomu stroitel'stvu*," *KPSSvR* 4:383–86
January 1930	All-out collectivization drive, closing of churches in countryside
1 March 1930	Stalin, "Dizzy with Success" "*Golovokruzhenie ot uspekhov*," in Stalin, *Soch.* 12:191–99
1 March 1930	First Kolkhoz Charter "*Primernyi ustav sel'skokhoziaistvennoi arteli. . .*," *SZ SSSR*, 1930 no. 24, art. 255
30 July 1930	Mir abolished in Russia

"*O likvidatsii zemel'nykh obshchestv v raionakh
sploshnoi kollektivizatsii,*" *SU RSFSR*, 1930 no. 51,
art. 621

11 August 1930   Central Committee resolution mandating
universal compulsory elementary education
"*O vseobshchem obiazatel'nom nachal'nom obuchenii,*"
KPSSvR 4:473–76

30 June 1931   Law on otkhod
"*Ob otkhodnichestve,*" *SZ SSSR*, 1931 no. 46, art. 312

20 May 1932   Law allowing peasants to trade
"*O poriadke proizvodstva torgovli kolkhozov,
kolkhoznikov i trudiashchikhsia edinolichnykh krest'ian.
. . ,*" *SZ SSSR*, 1932 no. 38, art. 233

7 August 1932   Law on protection of socialist property
"*Ob okhrane imushchestva gosudarstvennykh
predpriiatii, kolkhozov i kooperatsii i ukreplenii
obshchestvennoi (sotsialisticheskoi) sobstvennosti,*" *SZ
SSSR*, 1932 no. 62, art. 360

winter 1932   Onset of famine in major grain-growing regions of
USSR

27 December 1932   Law establishing an internal passport system
"*Ob ustanovlenii edinoi pasportnoi sistemy po Soiuzu
SSR i obiazatel'noi propiske pasportov,*" *SZ SSSR*,
1932 no. 84, art. 516

January 1933   Central Committee resolution creating political
departments of MTS
"*Tseli i zadachi politicheskikh otdelov MTS i
sovkhozov,*" *KPSSvR* 5:78–89

February 1933   First Congress of Outstanding Kolkhozniks
(*kolkhoznikov-udarnikov*)

17 March 1933   New law on otkhod
"*O poriadke otkhodnichestva iz kolkhozov,*" *SZ SSSR*,
1933 no. 21, art. 116

November 1934   Central Committee resolution liquidating political
departments of MTS
"*O politotdelakh v sel'skom khoziaistve,*" *KPSSvR*
5:198–204

February 1935   Second Congress of Outstanding Kolkhozniks

17 February 1935   Second Kolkhoz Charter
"*Primernyi ustav sel'skokhoziaistvennoi arteli. . . ,*" *SZ
SSSR*, 1935 no. 11, art. 82

7 July 1935	Law granting titles of "eternal use" of land to collective farms "*O vydache sel'skokhoziaistvennym arteliam gosudarstvennykh aktov na bessrochnoe (vechnoe) pol'zovanie zemlei*," SZ SSSR, 1935 no. 34, art. 300
November 1935	Conference of Stakhanovites "500-ers" in sugar-beet production
December 1935	Conference of Stakhanovite combine-operators
December 1935	Conference of Stakhanovite grain harvesters, scene of Stalin's remark that "A son does not answer for his father"
19 December 1935	Law on strengthening collective farms in the non-Black Earth belt "*Ob organizatsionno-khoziaistvennom ukreplenii kolkhozov i podyëme sel'skogo khoziaistva v oblastiakh, kraiiakh, i respublikakh nechernozemnoi polosy*," SZ SSSR, 1935 no. 65, art. 250
February 1936	Conference of Stakhanovites in animal husbandry
27 February 1937	Laws giving some lands from state farms to collective farms in various regions "*Ob otrezke zemel' ot sovkhozov, khoziaistv orsov i podsobnykh prepriiatiikh . . . i ob uvelichenii za etot schët zemel' kolkhozov*," SZ SSSR, 1937 no. 16, arts. 49–58
Autumn, 1936	Harvest failure in many regions, leading to hunger in winter and spring of 1937
20 March 1937	Forgiveness of arrears on agricultural procurements for 1936 "*O sniatii nedoimok po zernopostavkam za 1936 g.*," SZ SSSR, 1937 no. 21, art. 79
July 1937	Secret instruction from Stalin on roundup of returned kulak deportees and criminals
Autumn, 1937	Show trials of former raion leaders for mistreatment of kolkhozniks, violation of Kolkhoz Charter, and sabotage of agriculture
19 April 1938	Law forbidding mass expulsions from collective farms "*O zapreshchenii iskliuchenii kolkhoznikov iz kolkhozov*," SZ SSSR, 1938 no. 18, art. 115
19 April 1938	Law on improper distribution of kolkhoz income

*"O nepravil'nom raspredelenii dokhodov v
kolkhozakh,"* SZ SSSR, 1938 no. 18, art. 116

27 May 1939   Decree "On measures to protect the public lands
                       of the collective farms from being squandered"
                       *"O merakh okhrany obshchestvennykh zemel' ot
                       razbazarivaniia,"* SZ SSSR, 1939 no. 34, art. 235

28 December 1939   Decree on sowing
                       *"O poriadke planirovaniia posevov zernovykh kul'tur v
                       kolkhozakh,"* SZ SSSR, 1940 no. 1, art. 3

21 April 1940   Law allowing payment of monthly salary to
                       kolkhoz chairmen (in eastern regions of USSR,
                       later extended to other regions)
                       *"Ob oplate predsedatelei kolkhozov v vostochnykh
                       raionakh SSSR,"* SZ SSSR, 1940 no. 11, art. 271

Stalin's Peasants

Introduction

In the winter of 1929–30, the Soviet regime launched a drive for all-out collectivization of peasant agriculture. There was little support for this in the village (do peasants ever actively support programs of radical change advocated by the state?), but in any case the regime did not seem overly concerned about securing peasant support. The drive to collectivize came not from within the village, but from without. The state was the initiator of the collectivization drive, and the new collective farms were organized at village level by outsiders—Soviet rural officials, supplemented by tens of thousands of urban Communists, workers, and students whom the regime sent out into the countryside for the purpose.

In the spirit of the Cultural Revolution then in progress, many of these urban outsiders were imbued with a militant zeal for change and contempt for peasant backwardness. This led them to interpret their mission of socialist modernization in the most extreme terms, with the result that the establishment of a *kolkhoz* was often accompanied by forcible closing of the village church and public destruction of icons. But the violence involved in the collectivization drive was not only symbolic, and local executants were not its only initiators. The regime's own strategy for collectivization involved violence, namely the expropriation and deportation of hundreds of thousands of *kulak* (prosperous peasant) households. The policy of wholesale dekulakization was launched simultaneously with the collectivization drive in the winter of 1929–30. Although joining the kolkhoz was supposedly a voluntary act, it was clear from the beginning of the collectivization drive that troublemakers who refused to sign up might find themselves slated for expropriation and deportation under the elastic category of kulak.

The first, tumultuous phase of collectivization, January and February 1930, coincided with the inactive period of the agricultural cycle. What collectivization meant in an immediate sense, therefore, was seizure and removal of the peasants' livestock (horses, cows, pigs, sheep, and even chickens in some cases) by state agents, who declared the animals to be the property of the kolkhoz. At the beginning of March, Stalin announced that this wholesale seizure of livestock was a mistake, and that peasants were entitled to keep a cow and small animals as part of their noncollectivized household economies. But the damage had been done, both in economic terms (as the threat of seizure led to massive peasant slaughter of livestock, and many collectivized animals died of mistreatment and neglect) and in terms of the peasants' attitude to the kolkhoz. As far as the peasants were concerned, collectivization was based on an original act of robbery that the regime subsequently repudiated only partially (since horses remained the property of the kolkhoz), and for which it never gave compensation.

Collectivization was a traumatic experience for Russian peasants. True, it was not the first time in living memory that the state had decided to reorganize the structure of peasant agriculture in the name of progress and social betterment. The first occasion followed the Emancipation proclamation of 1861, when the state often had to call in troops to get peasants to sign the charters that obligated the peasants to pay for the land. The second occasion was the Stolypin agrarian reform initiated in 1906–7, which—in violation of tradition and the peasants' preference for structures that inhibited economic differentiation and minimized risk—encouraged entrepreneurial peasants to leave the traditional land commune, the *mir*, and set up as independent small farmers. But no previous state reform had been conducted so violently and coercively, involved such a direct and all-encompassing assault on peasant values, or taken so much while offering so little.

The main purpose of collectivization was to increase state grain procurements and reduce the peasants' ability to withhold grain from the market. This purpose was obvious to peasants from the start, since the collectivization drive of the winter of 1929–30 was the culmination of more than two years of bitter struggle between peasants and the state over grain procurements. Collectivized, mechanized farming might, as the state promised, increase the total crop; but even if it did, the peasants were unlikely to benefit. Many peasants called collectivization a "second serfdom"; they did so because they perceived it as a mechanism of economic exploitation by which the state could force peasants to hand over (for a nominal payment) a much larger proportion of the crop than they would have sold under market conditions.

My subject in this book is the range of strategies Russian peasants used to cope with the state-inflicted trauma of collectivization, and the way they tried to modify the kolkhoz so that it served their purposes as well as the state's. These strategies may be called "subaltern"[1] because they were inextricably linked with the peasants' subordinate status in society and their position as objects of aggression and exploitation by superordinate institutions and individuals. In my understanding, however, subaltern strategies are not limited to the varieties of resistance to domination.[2] They are the ploys by which weak people try to protect or assert themselves against each other, as well as against the strong. They involve projects of individual advancement as well as collective protest. In sum, they are the ways in which a person who is supposed to take orders rather than give them tries to get what he wants.

Resistance Strategies

Among the strategies Russian peasants used to cope with collectivization were those forms of "everyday resistance" (in James C. Scott's phrase) that are standard for unfree and coerced labor all over the world, viz.: foot dragging, failure to understand instructions, refusal to take initiative, pilfering, unwillingness to go out to the fields in the morning, and so on.[3] This was a behavioral repertoire familiar to Russian peasants from serfdom; and in the early 1930s there was certainly an element of conscious role-playing in their reversion to the work habits appropriate to serfs who had to perform *barshchina* (labor obligations) for a master. In 1931–32, as it became clear to the new kolkhozniks just how large a proportion of the crop the state was determined to take, the peasants' passive resistance—expressed particularly in demonstrative apathy and inertia, unwillingness to sow, and reduction of the acreage under cultivation—reached levels so high that Stalin called it a "go-slow strike." The famine of 1933 was the consequence of an irresistible force (the state's demands for set quotas of grain) meeting an immovable object (the peasants' stubborn passive resistance to these demands).

Violent uprisings against collectivization were comparatively rare in the Russian heartland. This was partly because of the state's ruthlessness in suppressing it (any troublemaker could become a "kulak" and be shipped off to gulag or deported to Siberia), and partly because the young peasant males who constituted the main potential fighting force were leaving the village en masse to work in the towns or on the new industrial construction sites.

Flight, one of the standard forms of everyday resistance, had an important place among the strategies of Russian peasants responding to collectivization. But this was not the standard situation in which slaves or serfs flee from a master who wants to keep their labor. It is true that the kolkhoz often tried to impede the departure of individual peasants, much as the peasant mir had done in the long period of collective responsibility for redemption payments after the 1861 Emancipation. But the Soviet state, which was presumably the peasants' ultimate master, opposed peasant departure from the kolkhoz only in a hesitant, ambiguous fashion, when it did so at all. The Communist leaders' underlying assumption at the time of collectivization was that the countryside had a surplus population of at least ten million people that must sooner or later be drawn into the urban labor force. By expropriating and deporting kulaks, the regime itself removed well over a million peasants from Russian villages and encouraged an even larger number to flee out of fear of suffering a similar fate. Even after the introduction of an internal passport system in 1933, the outflow of peasants from village to town continued, and was tolerated and sometimes actively encouraged by the regime.

As the kolkhoz stabilized in the mid-1930s, peasant strategies changed. To many peasants, outright departure from the kolkhoz came to seem less attractive than the more ambiguous *otkhod*, that is, departure for outside work that was temporary or seasonal (at least in theory) and did not involve abandonment of kolkhoz membership. By the late 1930s, to the government's chagrin, surprisingly large numbers of kolkhozniks had found ways of maintaining kolkhoz membership—and the private plots of land that went with it—while doing little or no work for the kolkhoz.

The apocalyptic and antiregime rumors that circulated in the Russian countryside constituted another strategy of resistance. This was recognized by the Soviet authorities, whose careful monitoring of the "conversation of rumors"[4] turns out to be a boon for historians. In the first flush of collectivization, the main thrust of the rumors was to suggest that it was dangerous, foolhardy, or against God's law to join the kolkhoz: Collectivization was a new serfdom, the old landowners were coming back, those who joined the kolkhoz would starve, the children of kolkhozniks would be branded with the Devil's mark, the Last Judgement was at hand, God would punish those who joined the kolkhoz, and so on. Throughout the 1930s, one of the most persistent rumors was that there would soon be war, and then foreign armies would invade Russia and the kolkhoz would be abolished.

The profession of religious faith, too, had some relationship to peasant resistance to the state. Orthodoxy was in the doldrums in the Russian village of the 1920s, with the church in disarray as a result of its disestablishment in the revolution, Protestant sects gaining converts, and demonstrative expressions of religious skepticism and contempt for priests in vogue among young male peasants, especially returned soldiers. But collectivization—or, to be more exact, the mass closing of churches, burning of icons, and arrests of priests that accompanied it—effected an instantaneous revival of Orthodox piety. The collectivizers' footsteps in the village were often dogged by weeping peasant women chanting "Lord have mercy" and accompanied by the village priest; and the same techniques of protest were used in demonstrations outside rural soviet offices. The trope of peasant religious belief and its violation by the state won a central place in the imagery of peasant resistance to collectivization.

This framing of conflict between peasants and the state in religious terms had a long history in Russia, including the Old Believers' identification of Peter the Great with Antichrist and the state's persecution of sectarians in the late Imperial period. At the time of collectivization, the peasants drew on the symbolism of Orthodoxy to express their protest. Later in the 1930s, however, the Orthodox referent was often lost, or at least became highly unorthodox, while the interwoven strands of Old Belief, sectarianism, and folk religion became increasingly prominent. Peasants developed their own homemade religious observances and drifted in and out of the influence of the multitude of charismatic and Protestant sects that maintained a semiunderground existence in the countryside.[5]

As far as we can tell, the great majority of Russian peasants regarded themselves as believers (*veruiushchie*) in the 1930s, and more than half took the risk of publicly identifying themselves as such in response to a question in the 1937 population census (after a flurry of rumors in the village about the political significance of the question, and the likely political consequences of replying affirmatively and negatively). In a situation where the state was committed to nonbelief, public assertions of belief inevitably had a flavor of protest. The converse may also have been true as far as peasants were concerned: that is, protest almost inevitably assumed a religious coloration. Examples can be taken from many different arenas of peasant-state interaction. What the authorities called evasion of fieldwork by kolkhozniks was often justified by the kolkhozniks in terms of religious holidays (often not to be found on any church calendar) that they were required to celebrate. In 1937, when the state briefly experimented with multicandidate elections to the Supreme Soviet, the "church people and believers" in the villages who, according to the Soviet press, tried to take unfair advantage of the new rules could probably be described with equal accuracy as ordinary peasants, carrying the religious banners that were conventionally used in the village for political protest.

Defining the Terms of Collectivization

Not all the subaltern strategies of Russian peasants were associated with resistance. Many of their strategies had to do with establishing the terms of collectivization—that is, the process of working out what collectivization would mean in practice. There were no blueprints, no position papers, hardly any real discussion, no systematic instructions about collectivization prepared before the fact. Grain procurement was almost the only mechanism associated with collectivization that had been tested in advance. Even dekulakization, for all its magnitude as an organizational task and its enormous political and social consequences, was undertaken with little preparation or thought, almost improvised.

The party leaders had one firm conviction about the kolkhoz, which was that its basic function was fulfilling state orders (procurements quotas) for grain and other agricultural products. Beyond that, however, *the kolkhoz* was a relatively empty concept at the beginning of 1930. What it meant had to be defined by practice, in a kind of three-way negotiation between the central leadership, local officials, and the peasantry. As far as its internal arrangements were concerned, the kolkhoz was what peasants and local officials made of it; it was not a given, but something that was in the process of being invented. Was the kolkhoz to be a commune (*kommuna*), in which all property was held in common, or was it to be an artel, in which peasants cultivated the kolkhoz fields collectively but retained their individual household economies? Was the kolkhoz to be coextensive with the village and the mir? Could kolkhozniks depart freely for work outside the village? Were kolkhozniks entitled to grow vegetables and run chickens in their yards? Could they sell its products in the market? Could they have a cow, two cows, or a horse? How was kolkhoz income to be distributed among peasant members? These and many other questions remained.

Communists initially imagined that the kolkhoz would be a large agricultural unit (substantially larger than the old village) in which basic farming processes would be modernized and mechanized. At the local level, officials and urban collectivizers often assumed that they should press for the highest possible degree of collectivization and objected to the peasants retaining any individual property. Beyond that, ideas were very hazy. Any manifestation of the old village, from strip farming to patriarchal authority, was the object of automatic disapproval. Since the village was assumed to have been a class-differentiated society, containing exploiting kulaks and exploited poor peasants (*bedniaks*), the collectivizers also tried to enforce the principle that "the last shall be the first," which meant favoring bedniaks as well as punishing kulaks.

Most peasants did not want a kolkhoz at all. But as the kolkhoz became a reality, the peasants developed ideas about what the minimum requirements of kolkhoz life must be. They wanted a cow, and thought the state should give a cow to any kolkhoz household without one. They wanted their horses back from the kolkhoz. They wanted to be able to cultivate their yards (which the state called "private plots") as they saw fit, and without being taxed on the produce. They thought the kolkhoz, and beyond it the state, should help peasants in bad years. When the crops were harvested, they wanted peasants' needs to be met first, before state procurements quotas. These broad generalizations, of course, conceal many divergences of interest and preference among peasants along lines of region, age, gender, capacity for outside earnings, and so on.

Much of what happened in the 1930s can be seen as a process of pushing and pulling as the various interested parties strove to define the kolkhoz to serve their purposes. In the first years, the great issue was the struggle over compulsory procurements levels that culminated disastrously for both sides in the 1932–33 famine. Although quotas had to be lowered temporarily in response to the famine, the state did not abandon its determination to take a much larger share of the harvest than peasants would willingly have marketed, a situation that was to define the nature of the Soviet kolkhoz and the peasants' view of it throughout the Stalin period.

On other issues there was more room for compromise and the kind of everyday negotiation that is part of most human transactions. On some questions, such as the size of the kolkhoz, the state modified its original preferences. On other questions, such as the obligatory collectivization of horses, the state held its ground despite persistent peasant pressure. Still other questions, such as the size of the private plot and the extent of the kolkhoznik's labor obligations, became subjects of endless contestation, with the boundaries of permissible practice shifting back and forth.

The metaphor of negotiation raises the question of what private image of "the good life" underlay the peasants' demands and preferences. This is not a simple question. More than one image of the good life was circulating in the private discourse of the Russian village. There was probably regional variation as well as variation arising from gender, age, and position in village society. Beyond that, however, it seems that Russian peasants simply had a repertoire of images of the good life on which to draw, just as they had a repertoire of proverbs and precepts, and that at any given time they chose the image they thought most appropriate to the circumstances.

For some peasants, and in some circumstances, the good life seemed to be a return to what scholars sometimes call the "traditional" village, meaning a self-contained agricultural community, indifferent or hostile to the outside world of states and cities, governed by notions of "moral economy" and "limited good." Needless to say, this traditional village is an imaginative construct rather than historical reality; but it was a construct that existed in the minds of Russian peasants, not just the minds of anthropologists. This had been dramatically demonstrated in 1917–18 when, to the surprise of many Russian intellectuals, the peasant mir revived, supervised the seizure and allocation of manorial lands, and forced the return of many of those peasants who had "separated" from the mir as a result of the prewar Stolypin reforms. It was demonstrated again, though less forcefully, in the early years of collectivization when peasants often demanded that the kolkhoz distribute grain among households on an egalitarian basis, adjusting for household size ("by eaters") but not for the amount of work that household members had done for the kolkhoz.[6]

A competing image of the good life, drawing on the experience of the Soviet New Economic Policy (NEP) in the 1920s and the prewar Stolypin reforms, was that of a small-farming independent peasantry left largely to its own devices by the state, producing for the market, and aiming at more than a subsistence economy. It was in pursuit of this aim that some entrepreneurial kolkhozniks—close relatives of Popkin's "rational peasants"[7]—were always trying to find ways of increasing their private-plot acreage and marketings; and it is in this general context that we can understand the often-deplored tendency of kolkhozniks to treat the plots as private property (a concept allegedly alien to "traditional" Russian peasants) that could be leased, rented, bought, or sold by individuals as they saw fit.

A third image of the good life, perhaps the most surprising of the three, was that of a kolkhoz in which the peasants' security was guaranteed by a range of state-backed welfare provisions, such as pensions, a guaranteed minimum income, an eight-hour day, sick leave, maternity benefits, and even paid vacations. These demands were articulated in statements and letters to the authorities from individual peasants (in contrast to the demands of "traditional" and "rational" peasants, which were conveyed by actions rather than words). They drew in part on an idealized version of the "good master" under serfdom, who would help peasants in time of hardship and di-saster. But the main inspiration seems to have come from Russian peasants' reading of the new Soviet Constitution—which was the subject of an orga-nized national discussion in 1936—and their knowledge of the benefits avail-able to wage and salary earners in the cities. The benefits they wanted were those that urban workers already had, at least in principle, and that the Con-stitution promised to Soviet citizens. In their requests for such benefits, peas-ants usually treated them as rights or entitlements, citing the Constitution. This could be interpreted as implicit recognition that, on one question at least, peasants and the socialist regime had values in common; or it could simply mean that the peasants were sufficiently alert to ask for something the regime seemed to think it should give. I call this the *welfare-state* image of the good life that developed along with the kolkhoz in Russian villages.

Strategies of Active Accommodation

The "hidden transcripts" of Russian peasant life[8]—that is, what peasants said to each other, as fellow subalterns out of the earshot (or so they thought) of the powerful—contain a bitter and consistent rejection of the kolkhoz throughout the 1930s. That, at any rate, is what the Soviet police reports on the peasants tell us. Of course, hidden transcripts, like their public counter-parts, give only part of the story. A peasant may routinely curse the kolkhoz in the presence of his fellows, the fraternity of the insulted and injured, just as he routinely accedes in the presence of the powerful to the convention that the kolkhoz has brought all sorts of benefits. But neither of these two rhetorical positions may accurately represent his real opinion, the one he holds as an individual who presumably has his own private accounting of the costs and benefits of the kolkhoz to him personally, as well as his own pri-vate grievances and aspirations.

Just as peasants had a variety of images of the good life, so they also had a variety of strategies for dealing with their situation after collectivization. Passive resistance was a strategy that most peasants used to a greater or lesser extent. So was passive accommodation, meaning an acceptance, however grudging, of the new rules of the game associated with the kolkhoz, and an effort to use them to one's own best advantage. But there were also strate-gies of active accommodation. These were unpopular with other villagers, on the familiar "limited good" premise (that is, that if one member of the community claims a larger slice of the pie, other members get smaller slices).

The three main avenues of active accommodation were to become a kolkhoz officeholder, to become a machine operator working part of the year for the local Machine-Tractor Station (MTS), and to become a Stakhanovite. The first was a practical option mainly for men of relatively mature age. The second was an option mainly for young men, although the regime did its best to open the ranks of machine operator to women. The third option was open in principle to any kolkhoznik who did not hold a managerial position in the kolkhoz. In practice, it was available mainly to young machine operators and, perhaps most significantly, to women who were ordinary fieldworkers, milkmaids, and caretakers of kolkhoz livestock.

Officeholding was more important in the kolkhoz than it had been in the old mir. The rewards were greater, both formally and informally, especially for the kolkhoz chairman, and to a lesser degree the kolkhoz brigade leaders and accountant. Still, after a brief period of confusion in the early 1930s, the degree of continuity between the mir (officially abolished in Russia in 1930) and the kolkhoz was considerable. In the first place, the kolkhoz was often coextensive with the mir, and thus its direct successor as an administrative and organizational entity. In the second place, the kolkhoz and the mir served a similar function of brokering relations between peasants and the state. There was a particular resemblance to the mir in the half century after Emancipation, when the mir's collective responsibility for redemption payments paralleled the kolkhoz's collective responsibility for compulsory procurements.

As far as leadership was concerned, the expulsion of kulaks and the temporary reign of urban outsiders produced a sharp break in continuity in the early 1930s. By the mid 1930s, however, the solid farming families that had earlier been alienated and intimidated by collectivization and bullied by the state's bedniak allies in the early 1930s were tending to move back into center stage and starting to holding office in the kolkhoz, as they had previously done in the mir.

The chairman's position was comparable in many ways to the old position of village elder (*starosta*), but with more power, significant economic rewards, and bigger risks. Parallels could also be drawn between the role of the kolkhoz chairman and brigade leaders, on the one hand, and, on the other hand, that of the *bol'shaks* (heads of households) on a big manorial estate under serfdom, who have been described as a privileged group collaborating with the estate bailiffs in disciplining other peasants.[9] The kolkhoz chairman was the chief broker in the kolkhoz-village's relationship with the state. He mediated between the village and the district authorities; it was his job to tell the district that the procurements target on such-and-such a crop was too high and try to get it lowered; to convey to the peasants that the *raion* (district administration) was serious about clamping down on pilfering or individual use of kolkhoz horses without payment; to try to provide excuses for any failures to meet procurements targets, and so on.

Both outsider and local chairmen performed this role, although in different ways. The outsider chairman had the advantage of greater credibility and prestige in dealing with the outside world; he could speak to the raion on more equal terms and in the same Soviet language. But the local chairman was likely to know more about the village and its real productive capacities, and to enjoy the confidence of his fellow villagers. By the mid-1930s, most kolkhoz chairmen were locals—peasants who came from that particular village or the surrounding district—and only a minority of them (about a third) were party members.

Substantial material rewards were available to kolkhoz chairmen. In the first place, they were paid much better than other kolkhozniks, even before they won the coveted prize of a regular monthly salary in cash at the beginning of the 1940s. In the second place, they had extensive perks and patronage opportunities, including de facto control over the kolkhoz assets like horses and the disposition of the kolkhoz's cash income. But there were also risks attached to officeholding, notably the risk of being arrested if the kolkhoz failed to meet its procurement quotas. In addition, the office of kolkhoz chairman in the 1930s was not part of a bureaucratic ladder that the ambitious peasant could try to climb. A kolkhoz chairman might be moved by district (raion) authorities to head another kolkhoz, or appointed chairman of the rural soviet. But these two rural offices were cut off from the regular administrative structure; kolkhoz and rural soviet chairmen had little chance of promotion to administrative posts in the raion.

The young kolkhozniks who became machine operators (mainly tractor drivers and combine operators) were another privileged group, much better paid than ordinary kolkhozniks for their six months work for the MTS during the growing season, and with opportunities for mobility and advancement that were far superior than those of other peasants. But they were essentially marginal in kolkhoz life, not only because they worked for the MTS but also because the chances were high that they would soon use their mechanical skills as a ticket out of the countryside into urban employment.

It was a given in kolkhoz life of the 1930s that young peasants were likely to leave because the only real opportunities lay outside the village. This was an area of intergenerational difference, because it was easy for young people to leave and difficult for the old, but it was not apparently a cause of intergenerational hostility. Collectivization changed the relations between peasant parents and children. The clash of values and conspicuous defiance of parental authority by young men that was characteristic of the 1920s was no longer in evidence. Instead, parents and children seemed to agree that departure was the best chance for their children, especially their sons.

Stakhanovism was a movement to encourage individual initiative in raising production that was born in industry and transferred to the countryside in the mid-1930s. On the kolkhoz, as in industry, the Stakhanovite was a normbuster—someone who was willing to work harder or longer than the others, thus earning a reward as an individual, but giving the bosses an excuse to raise the norms for everyone. Stakhanovites in all fields including agriculture were resented by fellow workers and were often targets of spiteful retaliation. But the kolkhoz Stakhanovites fell into a special category because they were often women, rank-and-file fieldworkers or livestock tenders, whose self-assertion on the work front was coupled with a flouting of male authority (fathers and husbands) at home. The rhetoric of women's liberation from patriarchal oppression that accompanied the Stakhanovite movement in the countryside evidently had genuine appeal to some village women—mainly the young, but also some older women who had been widowed or abandoned by their husbands—as well as being genuinely offensive to the majority of peasants.

In general, the peasant woman who sought to take advantages of the opportunities offered under the new dispensation, whether by becoming a kolkhoz officeholder, a tractor driver, or a Stakhanovite, was much more harshly judged by her fellow peasants than the peasant man who did the same thing. As far as men were concerned, there was a fair amount of tolerance for individual (household) strategies of accommodation. But this was not true of women, especially those who did not bear the burden of being head of a household. The female Stakhanovite, in particular, was often treated as a collaborator who deserved public shaming—even though such behavior might be punished quite severely by the authorities.

It remains an open question to what degree the adoption of strategies of active accommodation by some kolkhozniks should be taken as an index of "sovietization," that is, the acceptance and internalization of regime values in the village. Acceptance, such as it was, always had a provisional quality in the 1930s; it was probably only the postwar restoration of the kolkhoz (in the face of widespread hope of decollectivization) that convinced peasants that the kolkhoz was really there to stay. The extremely heavy burden of compulsory procurements quotas throughout the 1930s also militated against acceptance.

One of the factors inhibiting sovietization was that peasants who were most disposed to accept Soviet values were also peasants who were most likely to leave the village and make their life in the towns. This process quickly drained the kolkhoz of much of its small cohort of original supporters (young men willing to challenge the wisdom of the elders, worker-peasants with a foot in two worlds, former Red Army men); and it continued to carry away a steady stream of young kolkhozniks who left the village for the army, the mines, and the new industrial construction sites, or to continue their education, and never returned. In the early years of the kolkhoz, when half to a third of the villagers were still uncollectivized and attacks on the kolkhoz by bandits (often expropriated kulaks) were common, there were some indications that a kind of kolkhoz patriotism, based on rivalry between kolkhozniks and "independent" peasants, was developing. Within a few years, however, almost all the independents were forced into the kolkhoz by punitive taxation, and this source of kolkhoz identity and patriotism disappeared.

Strategies of Manipulation

The Russian village was a factious place in the 1930s. It is true that the villagers mainly agreed on some basic propositions, for example, that collectivization was a bad thing, that the state's demands for grain and taxes were far too high, and the raion should stop interfering by giving ignorant instructions about agricultural practices such as sowing and harvest. But that did not mean that state interference produced heightened village solidarity. Probably the contrary was true, although to what extent depends on whether we judge the village of the 1920s to have been highly factious (as Soviet observers believed) or comparatively united (as some Western historians suggest).[10]

Collectivization worsened the economic situation of most peasants and thus intensified their chronic tendency to envy their neighbors. Dekulakization, which victimized some peasants and enabled others to profit from their misfortune, added enormously to the sum of village grievance, as well as removing natural leaders from the villages. The liquidation of the mir surely weakened the ability of the village community to discipline its members and control feuding—at least until the kolkhoz solidified its position as the mir's successor. The collective principle that was formally embodied in the kolkhoz structure seemed to have no resonance at all with Russia's peasants, despite the legacy of communalism. Peasants never admitted that they were in any sense co-owners of kolkhoz land and property. They made a point of describing themselves as a mere workforce, toiling in the kolkhoz fields for somebody else's benefit.

Possibly Russian peasants had the capacity for generosity, mutual aid, and communal solidarity described so nostalgically by Russian Slavophiles and Populists, though it seems prudent to treat these accounts with skepticism.[11] In any case, there were few signs of it in the decade after collectivization, when the dominant mood among peasants seemed to be a mixture of resentment, malice, and lethargy. The Russian village of the 1930s resembled Oscar Lewis's faction-ridden Mexican village, not Robert Redfield's idyllic one. Perhaps even more, it resembled the gloomy and malicious villages of southern Italy in the 1950s, where (as described by one sociologist) poverty and a sense of inferiority and exploitation by the north combined to produce the belief that the only possible way to achieve the good life was by emigrating.[12]

A major faultline in the Russian village of the 1930s lay between former bedniaks and former kulaks (or relatives of kulaks). This distinction was based partly on a peasant's precollectivization economic position. But it also reflected the ascribed status that peasants had acquired during collectivization, when some households had been tarred with the kulak brush as a result of the dekulakization of a relative, while others had joined the bedniak group that cooperated with the collectivizers, often acquiring property confiscated from kulaks in the process. Resentments between these two groups were bitter, complex, and long lasting.

Slavophile assertions to the contrary, factiousness and feuding were scarcely novelties in the Russian village. In recent memory, antagonisms within the village had been fanned by the Stolypin reforms and the Civil War. It was nothing new, either, for peasants to take their grievances outside the village, complaining to local authorities and writing petitions and denunciations. In the 1930s, however, the great volume of complaints and denunciations coming from the village was almost certainly without earlier precedent. This was not only a tribute to the rising literacy rates in the countryside (less than 70 percent of rural men under 50 and less than 40 percent of rural women in the Soviet Union were literate at the beginning of the decade, compared to 85–90 percent of rural men and more than 70 percent of rural women at the end). It also reflected the strong encouragement given by the regime to the writing of individual petitions, complaints, and denunciations. The Soviet leaders of the 1930s regarded this as an important channel of information from the grassroots, and used it to compensate for the weakness of the state's administrative presence in the countryside. This was one area in which the Stalinist regime, usually neglectful (at best) of peasants' interests and needs, showed itself to be extremely responsive. The authorities read the peasants' letters, investigated their complaints, and often acted on their denunciations.

While there was a long tradition in Russian villages of writing petitions and complaints, both collective and individual, to state authorities, the practices of the 1930s had several distinctive characteristics. In the first place, the majority of petitions were individual, not collective. It was extremely rare for a kolkhoz to petition or complain collectively, as the mir had often done, since that might lead Soviet authorities to suspect conspiracy or punish the village for engaging in organized protest. In the second place, the majority of complaints and denunciations from the village in the 1930s were written by peasants who did not hold office in the kolkhoz against peasants who did.

The denunciations of officeholders, especially kolkhoz chairmen, that kolkhozniks sent so freely to newspapers and provincial and central authorities had a precedent in the complaints against bailiffs on the old serf estates that peasants sent to the estate owners in Petersburg and Moscow. But there was also a specifically Soviet antecedent for this type of complaint. In the 1920s, when Soviet leaders were still uneasy about encouraging anything that reminded them of old-regime practices such as informing and denouncing, they nevertheless promoted the institution of "rural correspondents" (*sel'kory*), unpaid village volunteers who regularly wrote to Soviet newspapers exposing wrongdoing by local kulaks, corrupt officials, and priests. The sel'kory of the 1920s, often teachers or others with marginal status in the village, were people who chose to associate themselves with the Soviet regime (and, implicitly, to dissociate themselves from the "backward" village) out of ideological conviction. In the 1930s, however, the term sel'kor was used increasingly loosely, until the distinction between sel'kory and ordinary peasant letter writers was almost completely lost. Detached from ideological conviction, the act of writing a letter exposing wrongdoing in the village became virtually synonymous with the act of writing a denunciation, and was adopted as one of the standard weapons used in village feuds.

Peasants were quick to learn the kind of accusation that produced a reflex response from Soviet authorities. "Links with kulaks" was the clear favorite for village accusations and counteraccusations until the Great Purges, when "links with enemies of the people" and unspecified suggestions of "Trotskyite counter-revolutionary" became commonplace. Such "ideological" accusations were generally accompanied by more concrete charges, such as theft or misuse of kolkhoz funds. The investigations provoked by such letters frequently ended in arrests, criminal prosecutions, and the removal of kolkhoz officeholders and low-level rural officials from their posts.

While the constant stream of denunciations of kolkhoz officeholders may have served some state interests, they were very detrimental to other interests such as administrative stability and the development of a cadre of experienced, efficient rural managers. It was not the state but the peasant denouncers who really benefited from this practice. True, there was a risk involved: Sometimes it was the denouncer rather than the object of denunciation who was condemned by the investigators and subsequently punished. But there was a reasonable chance that the outcome would be favorable. In the context of the 1930s, denunciation functioned as an important subaltern strategy of Russian peasants—not a strategy of resistance, but one of manipulation of the state, which could be induced by this mechanism not only to protect peasants from abusive local bosses (which was probably in the interest of the state as well as the peasant) but also to intervene in village feuds (which was only in the interest of the peasant complainant).

The Potemkin Village

In the 1930s, Russian peasants needed strategies to cope not only with the actual kolkhoz but also with the Potemkin village, that is, the state's idealized and distorted representation of rural life.

Potemkinism was a Stalinist discourse in which the defects and contradictions of the present were overlooked and the world was described not as it was but as it was becoming, as Soviet Marxists believed it necessarily *would be* in the future. It was the real-life counterpart of the discourse of socialist realism in literature and the arts. Thus, the Potemkin village had all the amenities and culture that was lacking in the real Russian village; its peasants were happy and not resentful of the Soviet regime; there was always an atmosphere of celebration; the sun always shone. It was the Potemkin village that could be seen in movies—Stalin's only source of information about village life, Khrushchev later claimed[13]—but this was not its only manifestation.

Many public rituals occasions involving real peasant participants, such as national Congresses of Outstanding Kolkhozniks and Stakhanovites, were in fact representations of the Potemkin village. The peasant roles in these spectacles were played not by professional actors but by what might be called professional peasants—peasants who specialized in the public representation of Soviet peasanthood. Among the peasants who were sent to Stakhanovite congresses or elected as soviet deputies, some won celebrity status. These were the ones like the Stakhanovites Pasha Angelina or Maria Demchenko, who had the personality to play the peasant role opposite Stalin and the other real-life political leaders who regularly attended these conferences. But at lower levels, too, there was a demand for Potemkin peasants: Stakhanovites of provincial status (*oblastnogo masshtaba*) who could make a speech expressing gratitude for the *obkom* secretary's gift of a sewing machine; Stakhanovites of district status (*raionnogo masshtaba*) who could be photographed by the local newspaper milking cows on the kolkhoz or listening intently to a speech at a district meeting.

Potemkinism also had its place in actual practices of everyday life in the village, notably the plethora of formally conducted kolkhoz meetings that constituted the major cultural innovation associated with collectivization. But the village was often hard on those of its members who became too deeply involved in Potemkin representation; and the representation itself became a great staple of peasant jokes and anecdotes. Nevertheless, Potemkinism created opportunities for manipulation by peasants, too. On the positive side, an energetic kolkhoz chairman might train up a Stakhanovite milkmaid for her publicity value in the raion or oblast. But there were more opportunities on the negative side for peasant criticism of officials and kolkhoz officeholders under whose stewardship the village failed to reach the proper Potemkin level.

During the Great Purges in 1937, when show trials of disgraced officials were held in many raion centers, scores of peasant witnesses provided testimony to support the state's indictment of the officials' cruel extortion, ignorance of agriculture, and indifference to peasant suffering. This was political theater, thus a part of the Potemkin world—but the peasant witnesses were playing themselves (not playing Potemkin peasants) and expressing their own real grievances. The trials could almost be described as expressions of peasant protest legitimized by the Potemkin facade. That was a dangerous combination from the regime's standpoint, and it is not surprising that this genre of show trial lasted only a few months before disappearing from the repertoire.

In the Potemkin world, kolkhozniks were "Stalin's peasants," characterized by the special affection and even intimacy with the leader displayed by speakers at congresses of peasant Stakhanovites. This is one aspect of the Potemkin village that has often been taken at face value by outside observers, especially those impressed by the tradition of "naive monarchism" alleged to exist in the Russian peasantry. Whether the protestations of loyalty to the tsar made by peasants caught rebelling against local officials in the 1860s should be taken at face value is a question in itself,[14] but certainly their Potemkin equivalents in the Stalin period should not be taken at face value. The latter might be described dialectically (to borrow a favorite heuristic device of Soviet Marxism) as the antithesis rather than the thesis of Soviet reality; and readers should note that my title, "Stalin's Peasants," is intended to convey that irony.

Judging by the police reports, Russian peasants strongly disliked Stalin, blamed him personally for collectivization and the famine, and regarded his every subsequent overture to them with deep suspicion, always looking for the hook hidden in the bait. This hostility carried over, although to a lesser degree, to all other political leaders, including the *muzhik* Kalinin, except for those like Zinoviev who were officially declared enemies of Soviet power and became by the same token honorary friends of the peasantry. When Sergei Kirov, reputedly the most popular of Soviet leaders, was murdered in 1934, peasants wept in the Potemkin village. But in its real-life counterpart, if we are to believe Soviet police reports, the peasants' satisfaction that *any* Communist leader should die at an assassin's hand was tempered only by regret that the victim had not been Stalin.

Scope of This Study

This is a study of the 1930s, bounded chronologically by collectivization in 1929–30 and the Soviet entry into the Second World War in 1941. The period is distinctive in the history of the Russian kolkhoz for several reasons. In the first place, the kolkhoz of the 1930s was generally coextensive with the old village. This was no longer the case after the kolkhoz amalgamations of the early 1950s. In the second place, the initial trauma of collectivization and famine hung over the Russian village throughout the 1930s. The kolkhoz was not yet fully accepted as a fact of life; the peasants' anger with the Soviet regime was still unmitigated by the passage of time and the complex experiences of German invasion and the Second World War.

The book is about Russian peasants. "The Russian peasant" is a problematic construct, since peasants in Russia usually identified themselves by village and region rather than by nation. it is appropriate for my purposes, however, because I am primarily interested in peasant responses to an experience all Russian peasants shared, namely collectivization. Collectivization, imposed by the state with little regard for specific local conditions, not only gave peasants throughout Russia the same basic institutional structure (the kolkhoz), but also generated similar cultural patterns of resistance and adaptation. To a lesser degree, this commonality extended to peasants in the non-Russian Soviet republics, especially Ukraine and Belorussia. Of course, there were important differences, too, in the experience of collectivization and the cultural construction of the kolkhoz in different regions. But they lie beyond my scope in this book.

1

The Village of the 1920s

The Setting

Russia's population—about 140 million on the eve of the First World War—was still four-fifths rural and predominantly peasant at the time of the Bolsheviks' October 1917 revolution. In European Russia, just under half of the rural population was literate, but this masked a broad divergence between the almost universal literacy of young males and the much lower literacy of women and older men. The oldest peasants still had memories of serfdom, which was abolished only in 1861, and vestiges of this institution affected many aspects of the peasants' lives up to the early twentieth century.[1]

The old serf categories were still often used in official documents to identify a peasant's social position. The 1897 population census required respondents who were of the peasant estate to list their pre-1861 serf category: "manorial peasant," "state peasant," "monastery peasant," and so on. Many peasants claimed in 1897 that they were unable to remember this status, according to a census taker. Whether this was genuine forgetfulness or a form of protest, peasants at the turn of the century were more likely to be able to identify themselves according to these categories than in terms of the older, more diverse social categories such as "single-homesteader" and "free cultivator" that Peter the Great had condensed into the single category of state peasant; serfdom had imposed at least superficial homogeneity on Russian peasants. The other mode of identification that had official significance was the land commune (mir, *sel'skoe obshchestvo*) to which a peasant belonged.[2]

The general terms that Russian rural folk most often used of themselves were peasants (*krest'iane*, a word derived from the word for Christians), grain cultivators and plowmen (*khleboroby, khlebopashtsy*), and Orthodox (*pravoslavnye*). The last term, of course, applied only to Slavic Christians, who constituted the great majority of the rural population in central European Russia. In the north, east, south, and west of European Russia, however, there were many *inorodtsy* and *inovertsy*, as Slavic Russians called peoples of non-Slavic ethnicity and non-Orthodox faith: Finns in the north, Turkic-speaking Muslim Tatars and Bashkirs along the Volga in the east; Catholic Poles and Jews (excluded from agricultural occupations) in the west; not to mention Cossacks (ethnically a mixture of Slav and Tatar; Orthodox) and German colonists (mainly Protestant) in the south.[3]

Russia was a country that accommodated a great deal of diversity. In European Russia, the situation of peasants in the fertile but overpopulated Black Earth belt to the south differed in many important respects from that of peasants in the less fertile non-Black Earth belt to the north, where crafts and trade were more developed, although manorial serfdom was part of the historical experience for both groups.[4] But that experience itself could be very different, depending whether a serf's obligation to the master was paid in labor (barshchina) or in cash (obrok). The barshchina obligation was generally regarded as the more burdensome and restrictive. A cash obligation, common in the non-Black Earth belt, put the manorial serf in a position closer to that of a state peasant.

In Siberia, peasants had never been enserfed to private masters; and in the Don and Kuban areas above the Caspian and Black seas, Cossack communities of the Don and the Kuban had originally been formed by peasants fleeing serfdom in the central provinces. Land hunger and rural overpopulation were prevalent in the Ukraine and Russia's Central Agricultural region, while in Siberia and the Far Eastern region land was abundant and people were scarce. In the north of European Russia, villages of 20–25 households were the norm, but in the central Black Earth region villages typically had 100–200 households, while the population of Cossack settlements (*stanitsy*) on the southern borders of Russia and the Northern Caucasus was often in the range of 5,000 to 10,000 persons, or upwards of 1,000 households.

At the beginning of the twentieth century, peasants were still repaying the redemption debts they had incurred under the 1861 Emancipation. The Emancipation settlement had been most onerous for manorial serfs, a slightly smaller and considerably more disadvantaged group than the state peasants. The peasants were emancipated with land, but had to pay for it. The payments (made to the state, which compensated the landowners) were spread over a forty-nine-year span following an interim period of "temporary obligation," sometimes of many years, when the former serfs continued to render labor or cash obligations to the lords.

The form of the Emancipation created many grievances. Although intended to bring benefits to the peasants, the complex provisions that were ultimately worked out clearly favored the interests of the landowners and the state treasury over those of the former serfs. Peasants felt cheated by the Emancipation because they had to pay for land they had traditionally regarded as theirs by virtue of the fact that they tilled it. Peasants in the fertile Black Earth belt also resented the fact that part of the land they had previously cultivated for themselves was cut off and given to the landowners. Peasant protest was expressed in various ways. There were a few uprisings in which peasants claimed that the document read to them by local officials was not the real Emancipation, and that evil local officials and landowners were conspiring to hide from them the true intentions of the benevolent tsar. There were many cases in which peasants refused, sometimes violently, to sign the charters establishing the financial obligations and land settlement of a particular peasant commune.[5]

In many Russian villages owned by private masters under serfdom, the master's land and that of the village were adjacent or intermingled, and the peasants tilled both. In the 1860s, the peasants' protests did not usually include the claim that the landowners' land was also rightfully theirs, although this later became a cause of grievance.

During the redemption period (which was finally ended by the 1905 Revolution), peasants had many things to remind them of serfdom. Collective responsibility for redemption payments inhibited the departure from the village of individual peasants or households, thus perpetuating the restriction on mobility that serfdom had earlier imposed. The nobles who were the peasants' former masters retained their estate lands (often hiring peasants to cultivate them), as well as having considerable residual authority over the local peasants. Even the mir, the peasants' own self-governing institution, which mediated between the village and the state and organized the distribution of communal land among the peasant households, was shaped by the experience of serfdom: For example, if a single village contained peasants who had been enserfed to two different masters, or if it contained former manorial serfs as well as state peasants, the two categories of peasant would belong to two different mirs.

Rapid industrialization and urban growth began in Russia in the 1890s. In European Russia, the urban population rose from six million in 1863 to twelve million in 1897 and to more than eighteen million by the beginning of 1914. This, of course, meant that large numbers of peasants were going to work in towns, despite the continuing restrictions on peasant mobility. In addition to permanent migrants, many of whom kept their land allotments and still had family in the villages, there were many peasant otkhodniks (literally, people who go away) who commuted between village and town, working part of the year as wage-laborers. Otkhod was a traditional phenomenon, but the burden of redemption payments coupled with the economic development of the post-Emancipation era produced a five-fold increase in the annual numbers of otkhodniks between 1860 and 1900. In the immediate prewar years, almost nine million passports were issued each year to peasant otkhodniks.[6]

Peasants in the non-Black Earth belt—which included St. Petersburg,

Moscow, Ivanovo, and other major industrial centers—were most affected by the rapid industrialization of the late nineteenth and early twentieth centuries. But its influence was also felt in the central agricultural region of Russia, for in the crowded provinces of Tambov and Voronezh many peasant households had a family member who was an otkhodnik in the mines of the Ukrainian Donbass. Ethnographers, who collected a great deal of data on the Russian peasantry in the period from the 1890s to the beginning of the 1930s, noted that urban mores and artefacts were beginning to enter the lives of peasants in many regions of central Russia, sometimes producing bitter conflicts between the more conservative older generation (especially the household patriarch) and the younger generation.

In 1905, a revolution broke out in the major cities of the Russian Empire and spread to the villages. The peasants burned manor houses and tried to drive the landlords out of the countryside, and it was two years before the village was fully "pacified" by the government, which had to resort to large-scale coercion and repression. A revolutionary Peasants' Union was formed and demanded "land to the tiller." Many liberals were convinced that the peasants could only be appeased by some form of compulsory alienation and transfer of the nobles' lands. In the aftermath of the 1905 revolution, however, the Imperial government, headed by Prime Minister Petr Stolypin, chose a different solution.

With the Stolypin reforms, initiated in 1906, the state withdrew its support from the peasant mir, hitherto valued for its administrative utility and roots in the Russian past, and started to dismantle the traditional system of communal land tenure. Under the old system, the land allotment of a peasant household, consisting of a number of strips scattered throughout the village lands, was not considered private property and could not be bought or sold (a principle that the Peasants' Union still upheld in 1905). In many villages, equality between households was still maintained, as it had traditionally been, by periodic redistribution of strips by the mir. This removed the peasant's incentive to improve land and was acknowledged to be a major impediment to any modernization of Russian peasant agriculture.

The reforms were aimed at extracting peasant households from the mir, encouraging "sober and strong" peasants to develop into a new class of independent small rural proprietors, capable of agricultural modernization and uninterested in revolution, while allowing weaker peasants to sell their holdings and become wage laborers in agriculture or industry. The process was complicated. First, the household obtained legal separation from the mir. Then its strips were consolidated into a block that was called an *otrub*. Finally, the household was supposed to move out of the village—in which peasant *izbas* were clustered in most of Russia—and build a homestead in the midst of its own independent farm (*khutor*).

The reforms, incomplete when the First World War broke out and halted in 1915, were introduced cautiously, with a large cohort of agronomists and surveyors available to advise and assist, but they still caused major disruptions in the villages. A minority of entrepreneurial peasants—those with the capitalist instincts approved by Stolypin, whom the Bolsheviks would later call kulaks—welcomed the reforms. Some poor peasants were also glad of the opportunity to sell, but others viewed the reforms with great apprehension because they would be forced to sink or swim on their own, without the life jacket of the mir. Many peasants saw the Stolypin "separators" as traitors to the mir and peasant tradition and condemned them for grasping greedily at the chance to live better than their fellow peasants.

The crises that brought down the tsarist regime in the February Revolution of 1917, when Russia was still a belligerent in the European war, did not directly involve the villages, but, as in 1905, it was not long before the impact of urban revolution was felt in the countryside. Peasant land seizures began in the spring of 1917, and by the summer peasant soldiers were deserting en masse from the armed forces to return to their villages and take part. The Provisional Government set up in the aftermath of the February Revolution temporized on the land issue. In the elections to the national Constituent Assembly, held in November, the majority of peasants voted for the party that had been their champion over the past fifteen years, the Socialist Revolutionaries, known as SRs. The Bolsheviks, an urban workers' party, were less well known to peasants. But they had been the first to sanction peasant land seizures; and, as they gathered popular support in the cities and the armed forces, the villages started to hear something of them from returning otkhodniks and Army deserters.

After the Bolsheviks seized power in October (soon joined, though not for long, by the left wing of the SR Party), one of their first actions in power was to issue a decree on land honoring "the peasant mandate" on the question: immediate expropriation of noble estates; distribution of their lands (and those of the Imperial family, the church, monasteries, state institutions, and so on) to the people; abolition of private property in land; recognition of the principles of egalitarian distribution and land to the tiller. Each village would decide for itself whether its land should be held in traditional communal tenure or some alternative form, including collective farms (artels) and khutors.[7]

During the land redistributions carried out locally in 1917–18, the mirs played a dominant role, surprising many educated Russians who believed their day was past. Communal land tenure and strip farming were firmly reestablished in many places, and Stolypin separators were often forced by other peasants to rejoin the mir. In the central Volga provinces, for example, the percentage of peasant households in otrubs and khutors dropped from 16 percent in 1916 to almost zero in 1922. Opinions differ as to whether this should be regarded as part of a class struggle against entrepreneurial peasants (kulaks) as a group. But the word *dekulakization*, meaning forcible expropriation of kulaks, makes its first appearance at this time; and it seems clear that incidents of expropriation and confiscation of kulak property did occur at the local level, perhaps as the result of spontaneous peasant initiatives but more likely usually with the encouragement of outsiders from the towns or the Red Army. In any event, bitter feuds and grievances within the village were often later explained in terms of clashes between poorer and richer (or pro- and anti-Soviet) peasants during the Civil War.[8]

The peasants' initially favorable attitude to the new Soviet regime was strained during the Civil War (which broke out in mid 1918 and continued through 1920) because of grain requisitions. Both Red and White armies requisitioned grain, and peasants usually regarded Reds as the lesser of two evils because of the fear that the Whites, if victorious, would reinstate the landowners. But the increasing ruthlessness and thoroughness with which the Bolsheviks requisitioned grain alienated peasants, especially in the major grain-producing areas such as the Central Black Earth and Central Volga regions. Another cause of peasant dissatisfaction were the Bolsheviks' attempts to split the village by enlisting bedniaks—often regarded as ne'er-do-wells and idlers by solid farming peasants—as their allies. The Committees of the Poor, set up under Bolshevik auspices to facilitate collection of grain from kulaks (and, implicitly, to challenge the authority of the mir) were highly unpopular in Russia and had to be abandoned, although their counterparts in the Ukraine survived into the 1920s.

The end of the Civil War brought peasant revolts against the Soviet regime in Tambov and the Ukraine; and in 1921–22 the Volga region was hit by a devastating famine and typhus epidemics. Both the revolts and the famine were at least partly caused by ruthless grain requisitioning during the war.[9] Early in 1921, with the economy in a state of collapse, the Soviet regime was forced to make major concessions to the peasantry, abandoning requisitions and substituting a fixed tax in kind (later converted to a money tax), as well as reopening markets that had been closed in most places during the era of War Communism. Discarding (at least for the moment) the idea of an alliance with the bedniaks, the Bolsheviks announced a new policy of alliance (*smychka*) with the "toiling peasantry" as a whole—that is, with all peasants but kulaks, whom the Bolsheviks still saw as dangerous capitalist exploiters who were natural opponents of Soviet power. These policy changes, collectively known as the New Economic Policy (NEP), remained in force until collectivization at the end of the 1920s.

With the introduction of NEP, a relatively benign period for the Russian peasantry began. Thus far, the revolution had brought certain benefits to the peasants, but there had also been enormous costs associated with the ravages of war, civil war, and famine. The main benefits were that the old landowners had fled the countryside (and many fled the country also, emigrating at the end of the Civil War) and that the peasants had acquired land from the nobles' estates, as well as lands formerly belonging to the church, monasteries, the Imperial family, and the state. The total amount of land acquired, often exaggerated by Soviet propagandists, is estimated at 40-50 million hectares (110–40 million acres). In European Russia, the average peasant household probably acquired 1–5 acres of arable land (some of which would previously have been leased), as well as the use of meadows and forest lands that had previously belonged to the nobles.[10]

On the debit side, the population of European Russia dropped in absolute terms from 72 million in 1914 to 66 million in 1920, and the total population deficit for the Soviet Union over the period 1915–23 has been estimated at 25–29 million. Young men bore a disproportionate share of the casualties; and this affected the ratio of women to men in the villages even more than in the towns. In the rural population of forty-five provinces of European Russia, there were 230 women in the nineteen-to-twenty-nine age group for every 100 men in 1920. Demobilization only slightly improved the situation because of the tendency of the demobilized to settle in towns. Six years later, in the age group twenty-five to thirty-five years, there were still 129 women for every 100 men in the villages of European Russia.[11]

In addition to the loss of human life, there were crippling losses of livestock, especially draft animals (horses, like men, being liable for military conscription in time of war). The number of horses in the territory that became the Soviet Union dropped from 34 million in 1916 to a low point of 23 million in 1923, and it still had not reached the prewar level on the eve of collectivization. In 1922, more than a third of all peasant households in the Russian Republic (37 percent) lacked a draft animal of any kind.[12]

Russian agriculture was still at a very primitive level: The iron plow had not completely replaced the traditional wooden one, scythes and sickles were the basic harvesting tools, and the age-old picture of parallel columns of men, women, and adolescents from the various households working the narrow strips at sowing and harvesttime remained part of rural reality in the 1920s. For would-be agricultural modernizers, the picture was gloomy. The undoing of the Stolypin reforms meant that in the basic agricultural regions of Russia, 98–99 percent of peasant land was divided into strips and held in communal tenure, often still subject to frequent repartition.

The 1922 Land Code allowed individual peasant households to withdraw at will from the mir. But here was a real dilemma for the Bolsheviks: if they encouraged peasants to remain within the communal framework, they implicitly abandoned hope of significant agricultural improvement, but if they encouraged them to leave, they would presumably be opening the gates to rural capitalism à la Stolypin. In fact, some local land departments—perhaps influenced by land surveyors from the Stolypin era who had entered Soviet service—followed a policy of cautiously encouraging separation to otrubs and khutors, and their numbers gradually climbed in the western provinces, as well as in the central industrial region (for example, Leningrad, Ivanovo, and Tver provinces), where worker-peasants were among the leaders of the trend. Still, by 1927 otrub and khutor farming constituted a significant proportion of all peasant farming in the Russian Republic only in the northwestern and western regions (respectively 11 percent and 19 percent of households).[13]

Peasant earnings from off-farm work and crafts were sharply reduced by the revolution. The collapse of urban industry during the Civil War forced otkhodniks and peasant-workers—including many in the latter category who had seemed fully assimilated into the urban working class—to return to their native villages. The workers mainly left again as factories and mines reopened in the first half of the 1920s; but jobs were in short supply, and the unions did their best to restrict industrial recruitment of peasants. Another important form of prerevolutionary otkhod, seasonal employment of agricultural laborers on the big commercial farms in the south, ended with the disappearance of commercial farming. The situation improved in the course of the 1920s and the number of otkhodniks more than doubled between 1923–34 and 1927–28. But the level of otkhod in the latter year, with fewer than four million otkhodniks, was was still way below the prewar level of around nine million otkhodniks a year.[14]

Village crafts and small-scale rural manufacturing were also in the doldrums, particularly in the early years of NEP, because of the disruption of established trading patterns during the Civil War. In Penza province, for example, the main local craft of cooperage (making casks and barrels for the fishing industry) collapsed with the disappearance of the middleman who had earlier supplied the materials and distributed the finished products. The only rural industry that was really flourishing was the production of home-brew (*samogon*), which sprang up in response to the tsarist state's patriotic ban on vodka production, imposed in 1914. The Bolsheviks maintained the ban for some years but then lifted it for fiscal reasons in 1925. The authorities waged energetic campaigns against samogon producers but the results were disappointing. Soviet statisticians estimated that in 1928 more than 40 percent of all Russian peasant households made samogon, with a total volume of production for the year of 6.15 million liters.[15]

The tax in kind introduced at the beginning of NEP was later converted to a money tax known as the agricultural tax. This was a major source of state revenue, and there was no equivalent taxation of the urban population. Although the agricultural tax was differentiated (kulaks paid more, and a small group of the poorest peasants was free of the tax altogether), it was a burden borne by the great majority of peasants. The peasants' nonagricultural earnings were also taxed from 1926 on. According to Iurii Larin, a noted Bolshevik economist, the total tax burden on the peasants (including indirect taxes) was lower than before the revolution. But direct taxes were higher, so that the peasants undoubtedly felt that they were being more heavily taxed than before. In Novgorod province, for example, the tax on an average peasant's household rose from around twelve rubles (4 percent of net profits) in the period 1905–12 to around twenty-four prewar rubles (14 percent of net profits) in 1922–23. This taxation structure, which made peasants the prime source of revenue, was matched by the Soviet pricing strategy of the NEP period, which aimed to turn the terms of trade against the peasant by keeping prices for manufactured goods high and those for agricultural products low.[16]

After the predatory incursions of Bolshevik requisitioning brigades during the Civil War, the NEP period was characterized by relative calm and a subdued, even minimal, administrative presence of the new regime in the villages. Communists were rare birds in the countryside of the 1920s. The rural organizations of the Communist Party of the Soviet Union had a total of 160,000 members at the beginning of 1925, although admittedly the number almost doubled in the next three years. Most of these were peasants by origin, but fewer than half were currently working as peasants in agriculture. The others were mainly in administrative positions.[17]

The Soviet administrative unit closest to village level was the rural soviet. But this was a skeletal institution, often consisting only of a chairman, paid an average of twenty rubles a month in the 1920s (which was not enough to live on), and a secretary, sometimes paid, who was often the same man who had been district scribe (*volostnoi pisar'*) before the revolution. The rural soviets generally had no budget and no resources in the 1920s; if the chairman had no horse of his own, he might have to beg a ride from a peasant every time he had to go in to the district center. Only about one in six rural soviet chairmen was a Communist in the mid 1920s. Virtually all were peasants, and the most common qualification for the position was having served with the Red Army during the Civil War.[18]

The village mirs, perhaps six or eight of which would be under the jurisdiction of a typical rural soviet, were much more effective and respected institutions. They had the power to impose levies on their members and might also have other sources of income from leasing of land and suchlike. The mirs were legal entities, able to enter into contracts, initiate court actions, and have official dealings with government agencies; and their leaders were generally "businesslike and influential people," experienced in dealing with the state on a variety of issues. The Bolsheviks regarded the mir with increasing suspicion because of its status as a competitor of the rural soviet: These two institutions were described by one Bolshevik commentator in 1928 as the rival centers of "two peasant *aktivs* in the village." It is likely, however, that many peasants would not have recognized this picture because, as far as they were concerned, the local authority was the mir.[19]

During NEP, the peasants' main complaint against the Bolsheviks had to do with taxation. Peasants sometimes referred to the agricultural tax as obrok, using the term for money dues under serfdom, and rumors circulated that the real reason the state had to generate this revenue was to compensate the landowners and industrialists for the property they had lost in the revolution. According to one rumor from Tambov (an area where anti-Soviet feeling still ran high), there had actually been a secret change of regime, the bourgeoisie had taken power again "and now they are adding tax after tax."[20]

Another cause of dissatisfaction was the Bolsheviks' favoritism towards urban workers. The Bolsheviks, as Marxists, identified themselves as a workers' party and described their regime as a dictatorship of the proletariat. Although they recognized that peasants were part of the "toiling masses" that had been oppressed under tsarism, and thus part of their natural constituency, there was still a sharp distinction between their attitudes to and treatment of the two groups. Although peasants were historic victims in the Bolsheviks' eyes, they were not proletarian but "petty-bourgeois" in essence, saved from capitalism only by their backwardness. For the Bolsheviks, the village exemplified the sluggish, tradition-bound, superstitious, non-Western, nonmodern Russia that needed to undergo revolutionary socialist modernization.

Among the peasants' complaints about preference to workers was the fact that workers' earnings were not taxed, although from 1926–27 those of peasant otkhodniks were. Student teachers sent to the villages for teaching practice reported that peasants were saying that "everything is for the worker, and the peasants have been deceived," complaining about workers' preferential access to education, and speculating that "finally there will be only workers in party positions." There were other similar reports of complaints that workers had trade unions to defend their interest, whereas peasants did not, and workers had better medical care. "With us the worker is in the first place, and no figures and words will hide it." "There are many more workers in power than peasants. But in our country, after all, it's really peasants who are the larger group." There were even complaints that the Bolsheviks' vodka policies and the criminalization of samogon production were antipeasant.[21]

Most reports suggest that the typical peasant attitude to Soviet power in the 1920s was neither strongly approving nor strongly disapproving. In most contexts, they saw it as a government like any other rather than a revolutionary people's regime. Some criticized the Communists for their atheism and said they were "Yids"; some said they were careerists; others said they were utopians who had only temporarily discarded the fantasies of War Communism. Observers (mainly Communists, it should be noted) saw few signs of regret for the tsar or residual SR loyalties in the village, and thought that most peasants had a respectful attitude toward Lenin and other political leaders, reserving their sharpest criticisms for local officials. In rural areas close to big industrial centers, where there was a lot of contact between peasants and urban workers, peasant feelings towards the Soviet regime were warmer: In the Moscow region, they even sang "Soviet chastushki" (couplets extemporized on contemporary themes). In the central agricultural provinces, where grain requisitioning had fallen hardest during the Civil War, the mood tended to be hostile (in Riazan, the chastushki were "clearly counter-revolutionary, biliously angry"). But most peasants had lost interest in politics.[22]

The Kulak Question

According to the Bolsheviks' Marxist analysis, capitalism was just beginning to take root in the Russian village at the beginning of the twentieth century. This was a "progressive" development in itself, since market-oriented small farming represented a higher stage than the subsistence economy of the traditional village, but in the context of socialist rule it was threatening. If a real capitalist stratum emerged in the Russian peasantry, it would necessarily oppose the socialist power of the soviets. The Bolsheviks were caught, theoretically speaking, between the Scylla of the tradition-bound mir and the

Charybdis of peasant capitalism. The kulak, seen both as a nascent capitalist and as a dominant influence in the mir, was the fulcrum of their fears.

According to Stalin, "ninety-nine out of a hundred Communists" would rather have been out fighting the kulak, as they had done during the Civil War in connection with grain requisitions, than following the NEP policy of avoiding confrontation and conciliating the middle peasant. The party had "introduced NEP knowing that it meant a revival of capitalism, a revival of the kulak," Stalin said in 1925. But Communists still instinctly regarded kulaks as the enemy.[23]

During the Civil War, many prerevolutionary kulaks had either been stripped of their property or fled with the Whites. Soviet statisticians estimated that at the end of the Civil War only 3 percent of peasant households could be categorized as kulak, compared to 15 percent before the revolution. But Communists feared that the process of dekulakization was very incomplete, especially in areas outside the central Russian provinces such as Siberia, the Northern Caucasus, the Crimea, and the Ukraine; and they were afraid that NEP would generate new kulaks. The process of expropriating kulaks in central Russia had only intensified the mutual antagonism between Bolsheviks and their peasant supporters, on the one hand, and kulaks on the other. A humiliated, impoverished, former kulak was actually more dangerous than a real kulak would have been. As one Bolshevik intellectual put it in 1924,

> Perhaps now a particular peasant has few animals and his farm is not large. But he is a dekulakized kulak whose wings were clipped by the revolution. In politics, he is an even more wild enemy of the revolution than that *burzhui* who has become prosperous now and is enjoying his prosperity.[24]

The dynamics of peasant agriculture and the future evolution of the peasantry were subjects of heated argument throughout the 1920s. The debate was a continuation of the arguments between Marxists and Populists on the inevitability of capitalist development and the socialist potential of the mir that had been going on since the 1880s. On one side were Marxist sociologists and economists, particularly those associated with the Agrarian Institute of the Communist Academy, who expected and feared an evolution towards rural capitalism, looked anxiously for signs of increasing class differentiation within the peasantry, and denied that the mir was anything but a brake on the village's emergence out of backwardness. On the other side was the group of non-Marxist scholars associated with the Timiriazev Agricultural Academy and headed by A. V. Chaianov, who denied that capitalist relations were developing in the countryside. Chaianov explained differentiation within the village in terms of the natural cyclical dynamics of peasant life; at any give time, some peasant households would prosper because they had many able-bodied members and few nonworking dependents, whereas others would decline because of an unfavorable ratio of workers to dependants, but this situation was neither permanent nor based on the exploitation of poorer households by richer ones.[25]

Among the Bolshevik Party leaders, there were disagreements as to the immediacy and intensity of the kulak threat. It was generally agreed, however, that class relations in the village ought to be carefully monitored, and that a peasant's attitude to Soviet power was likely to be related to his class position within the peasantry. In the statistics of the 1920s, peasants were not simply classified as "peasants" but as "bedniaks" (poor peasants), "seredniaks" (middle peasants), and "kulaks." The proportional weight of each group at the end of the Civil War in the country as a whole was calculated as follows: 35–40 percent bedniaks and *batraks* (agricultural laborers), 55–60 percent seredniaks, and 3 percent kulaks.[26]

But it turned out that monitoring rural class relations was no easy matter. It proved extremely difficult to find appropriate indices of class differentiation and exploitation. The initial assumption was that peasants who used hired labor were likely to be exploiters, but it turned out that the situation was more complicated. A horseless (therefore poor) peasant might have to pay a richer, horse-owning peasant to do his plowing. In addition, Bolshevik investigations were hampered by the peasants' tendency, developed over generations of dealings with the tax collector, to give misleading information. The peasants knew that the Bolsheviks disliked kulaks, and they had a fair idea of the signs by which the Bolsheviks hoped to distinguish them. Indeed, according to a report on rural reading habits in Siberia, kulaks bought "mainly juridical books" and knew more about the Land Code, the Criminal Code, and other relevant Soviet decrees than the local legal personnel.[27]

Identifying peasants according to their class position was more than an academic exercise in the 1920s. A person's class position affected his legal status and opportunities in many important respects. Kulaks and other "class enemies" of the proletariat were deprived of the vote from 1918 to 1936, as well as being liable to extra tax and subject to discrimination in educational admissions and a host of other areas. Local soviets had to keep lists of the names of the kulaks in each electoral district, adding and subtracting to it as required. Bedniaks, on the other hand, were released from the agricultural tax, and received preference in admission to secondary and higher education, the Komsomol, and the Communist Party.[28]

Over the period 1921–27, the economic statistics failed to show any striking trend towards class differentiation: as a proportion of all peasants, the kulak group grew by only one or two percentage points. Politically, however, the trends were much more alarming. The "kulak threat" had become a major issue in internal party politics, with the Left Opposition and the Stalinists vying with each other to take the tougher stand. In the soviet elections of 1927, as a result of instructions to local electoral committes to be more vigilant against kulaks and other class enemies, two or three times more people were disenfranchised than had been the case in 1925–26.[29]

Turning to peasant perspectives, the "strong" (*krepkii*) peasant—the kind the Bolsheviks often called a kulak—was an object of admiration in the village, as well as of envy and perhaps resentment. His voice had special weight in the mir. He was often the best informed and most competent peasant around, the best at dealing with outsiders and government officials. It was not in the interests of a weak peasant to cross him, because he might need his help, for example, with a loan of grain in the hard months before the new harvest. In time of misfortune, there was no other place the peasant could go but to a fellow villager who was better off. The conditions under which the more prosperous peasants gave help and loans might be more or less onerous, but this was often a relationship of dependence as well as (or rather than) exploitation.

As to the bedniak, village opinion seemed to make a distinction between those households that were poor through no fault of their own (but because of some accidental circumstance like the death of the father or the horse) and those that were poor because they were shiftless, headed by drunkards and idlers. Peasants frequently expressed annoyance and incomprehension with the Bolshevik preference for such "idlers" over good, hardworking peasants making their own way. They also perceived that the bedniaks had acquired assets—the range of opportunities and benefits associated with the Bolshevik preference—that often put them in a better situation than the seredniaks.

Consider this letter sent to the party's Central Committee in 1926 by a peasant in Kursk province who described himself as "a poor seredniak":

> I have a horse, a cow, and three sheep, for which the poor peasants call me a bourgeois, but nobody considers how much a seredniak has to work, harder than a bedniak. I don't have enough feed to keep my cattle, so I have to get it from the bedniaks in return for working their land. The main thing bedniaks do is sleep. . . . [The bedniak] walks along in a confident way, he is clean, [he wears] proper trousers, boots, a shirt, and a cap. . . . Yet a seredniak who is richer than he is has muddy boots whose tops are all out of shape like birds' nests, a shirt without buttons, and he probably only washed his face on Sunday, which reminded him how he looked. This seredniak gets tobacco and kerosene [from the store] and goes straight home so that the horse isn't hungry. A bedniak will visit the manager and get a 2-kopek cigarette on credit. There he sits and has a smoke, and I think how lucky he is. . . . He has no tax, no expenses for the horse, in a word no obligations; what he earns is all for himself, and I do his plowing. But it offends me that they call me a burzhui. . . . [30]

It would be a mistake to conclude that the Bolsheviks were single-handedly inventing the idea of conflict along class lines in the villages. As the letter suggests, peasants were often keenly aware of their identity as bedniaks, seredniaks, or strong (krepkii) peasants and felt hostility towards those with other identities. The term *burzhui* (a pejorative term for bourgeois), new to the village, acquired great popularity in the 1920s as was admitted even by those who disliked the whole notion of class differentiation of the peasantry.[31] But confusion arises because these were not purely economic categories, and because the exploitative relationship that the Bolsheviks depicted between kulaks and bedniaks did not fit the realities of the contemporary village. The "class" identities peasants recognized had as much to do with political allegiance and historical memory as they did with current economic status.

While some of the divisions in the village went back to the Stolypin period or even earlier, many could be traced to the Civil War period. Peasants who had been stripped of their cattle and horses by Bolshevik requisitions brigades, aided by local activists from the Committees of the Poor, did not quickly forget this, nor did the activist bedniaks who had pointed them out as proper targets. In areas that had changed hands between Red forces and White a number of times during the war, the permutations on the themes of betrayal, denunciation, confiscation and redistribution of assets, and retaliation were almost infinite.

When the peasant newspaper *Bednota* questioned its readers in 1924 on the burning question of "Who is a kulak?", a large number of letters cited specific Civil War experiences in the village. Many respondents (most but not all of whom were peasant activists) insisted that current economic status was not the best way to tell a kulak: What mattered, they said, was a peasant's past, his attitude to Soviet power, and his general mentalité. If he was grasping and avaricious, he was a kulak. If he turned to trade, no matter how small the trade or how great the need, he was also a kulak—a "parasite" on the village, as one respondent put it. A respondent from Gomel reached into history to say proudly that even in the hungry years after Emancipation, when peasants in his region had been given a bad deal and many had had to go away to the mines, not one peasant went into trade because "That is not our business, for that business there is a *shinkar'* (literally, tavernkeeper; by implication, a Jew)."[32]

A specific type of class antagonism often found in the villages was between otkhodniks and kulaks. This undoubtedly often had a prerevolutionary history. It was primarily bedniaks who were forced by poverty to go away and work in the mines, and when they returned to the village they were likely challengers of the prosperous, farming-oriented peasants who dominated the mir, by virtue both of longstanding resentment and newly acquired confidence and organizational savvy.[33]

In the years 1917–20, otkhodniks and even peasant workers who had been absent for years or decades returned to the villages in a flood, some drawn by the news that land was being distributed, others part of the great out-migration from the hungry towns during the Civil War. The returnees were generally given land; their problem was that they often lacked the other necessities for survival such as a horse, a cow, and a plow. These "bedniaks" often took the lead in confiscating "surplus" animals and equipment from peasants who were better off, cooperated with Bolshevik requisitions squads to get out the hoarded grain, and became activists in the Committees of the Poor. The Bolsheviks' image of bedniak allies in the village was to a large extent modelled on these returned otkhodniks and workers, literate and acquainted with a wider world, as well as on the peasant army veterans who returned at the same time or a few years later.

Conflict in the village between otkhodniks and kulaks during the Civil War is described in many sources. According to a report from the Smolensk area, for example,[34]

> There was some equalization in the volost [after the Revolution] . . . and yesterday's kulaks have now become seredniaks. One of these "unlucky ones" was the peasant V. from the village of Trostianki. He used to have three horses and a fine farm, but now "The miners have taken everything!"
>   By "miners" he means those peasants who, because they were poor, used to go to Iuzovka [the Donbass mining town later renamed Stalino, now Donetsk], but now they have got the same share per household as his own.

While many of the otkhodniks and worker returnees had gone back to the towns by the mid 1920s, others remained in the village, either by choice or because there were unable to find work outside. When otkhodniks in Saratov province were forced to stay in the village because of lack of employment outside, they not only suffered economically but "entered into sharp conflict with the kulak bosses (*verkhushka*)."[35]

Conflict Over Religion

The Bolsheviks were atheists, equating religion with superstition and the church with venality and hypocrisy. They were particularly hostile to the Orthodox church because of its long history of servile collaboration with the Tsarist regime. The new Soviet state formally cast off the church in a decree on the separation of church and state in January 1918, which ended state financial support to the church and nationalized church property (though allowing the church free use of buildings and religious objects necessary for celebration of rituals). Church schools were secularized and taken over by the state; registration of births, deaths, and marriages was transferred to civil authority; and divorce was legalized. The Constitution of the Russian Republic guaranteed both freedom of conscience and "freedom of religious and anti-religious propaganda."[36]

At the local level, the revolutionaries' treatment of the church and of priests was often much more violent and hostile than the judicious tone of central decrees might suggest. Local soviets often forcibly closed churches and sometimes plundered them. The ringing of church bells was often forbidden in towns during the Civil War, and priests were discouraged from appearing in public wearing clerical garb. Monks and priests (as well as pastors, rabbis, mullahs, and all other religious servitors) were deprived of the right to vote, along with other "exploiting classes," by the 1918 Constitution.

The Komsomol was particularly associated with active hostility to religion. There were many reports of Komsomols breaking up religious services in village churches, playing tricks on priests and worshippers, and staging parodies of the Orthodox service in the square outside the church. It should be noted that the Komsomol was much more of a presence in the village than the Communist Party in the 1920s: There were three to four times as many rural Komsomol members as rural party members at the end of the decade, and the movement had a broad attraction to peasant youth, especially male youth, that the party was unable to match for any rural group.[37]

Older peasants often called the Komsomols "hooligans"; and indeed, perhaps paradoxically, the village Komsomols of the 1920s seem in many ways to be the lineal descendants of the lads whose disruptive and disrespectful behavior—imitative of their urban counterparts—had drawn public attention in the prewar years. According to one Soviet ethnographer, the rural Komsomol, and particularly its antireligious activities, "attracted the mischief-maker (*ozornik*), those whom 'the fathers' have given up on long ago, and gives them a new intellectual quality (*ideinost'*) and new work to do. . . ."[38]

In 1923, in a somewhat belated extension of the NEP spirit of conciliation to the sphere of religion, the XII Party Congress emphasized, with special reference to peasants, the importance of avoiding unnecessary affronts to believers and mockery of their faith. It also noted and vigorously condemned "the Komsomol obsession with closing churches." The next year the XIII Party Congress warned against "any attempts to struggle with religious superstitions by administrative measures like closing churches, mosques, sinagogues, prayers houses, Catholic churches, and so on."[39] (These repeated calls for tolerance, it should be noted, are evidence not just of the party leaders' moderation and rationality on the question of religious but also—and perhaps more importantly—of the *lack* of tolerance and militant antireligious zest of the party's rank and file.)

The Orthodox church went through enormous convulsions in the decade after the revolution: Stripped of its position as an established church and most of its property, it was also rent by internal disagreements and uncertainty. A patriarch, Tikhon, was elected, the first in two hundred years, but had great difficulty managing either the church or his relations with the Soviet state. There was intense bitterness and recriminations when in 1922 the state seized gold, silver, and precious stones from the church to sell for relief of the Volga famine. At around the same time, the church split between followers of Tikhon and adherents of the "Living Church" (which later experienced further splits); and Patriarch Tikhon was briefly arrested and forced to sign a pledge to renounce all anti-Soviet activity.[40]

But all this was happening very far away from the village. The "white" clergy—parish priests who could marry and had no hope of preferment—had always been separated by a great gulf from the celibate "black" clergy and the church hierarchy. Parish priests traditionally received little if any financial support from the church (although efforts were under way to change this situation and put them on salary in the late Imperial period) but lived on what they received from parishioners, primarily on a fee-for-services basis. The rural parish clergy, indifferent to the rivalry between the Tikhonites and the Living Church supporters, had their own survival to worry about. In many cases, local soviets even took away their land and houses on the grounds that as parasitical persons "living off unearned income" they had no right to them.[41]

Many of them fled to territory controlled by the Whites. Large numbers of priests either renounced their vocation altogether or else started looking round for new full- or part-time occupations. There are many reports of priests becoming teachers, rural soviet secretaries, village scribes, journalists, atheist propagandists, peasant farmers, and even carpenters. One priest took charge of village theatricals, in which he himself acted ("His favorite roles were the roles of priests").[42]

The priest had a poor image in Russian popular lore, generally been depicted as idle, greedly, and drunken. As in Western Europe, peasants moving to cities during industrialization tended to lose their old religion on the way, or at least to cease observing it. In the early twentieth century, churchmen were alarmed at the growing indifference to religion in the villages and the increasing volume of complaints about the expense of supporting the parish priests and the exhorbitant fees they charges for performing various rites such as christenings, marriages, and funerals. One Orthodox cleric attributed it in part to the bad influence of the otkhodniks, since "people who spend time in cities and in factories regard religion coldly and even with hostility."[43]

Reports abound of the lukewarm attitude of peasants in the 1920s to the church and to priests: Ia. A. Iakovlev, the future Commissar of Agriculture, found a "contemptuous indifference (*naplevatel'skoe otnoshenie*)" common, especially among the men, and suggested wryly that the only way to rekindle religious fervor in the villages would be to close the churches by administrative fiat. Still, the mir was usually prepared to give some support to the parish priest, sometimes by giving him a plot of land or helping him till it. Iakovlev also noted that for all their expressed indifference to religion, peasants in one village were still "feeding eight persons who serve the church [yet] cannot feed one teacher for their children," even though they claimed to think schooling was important. With the sole exception of vodka, money for the priest (mainly for the celebration of various rites) was by far the largest single item in the budgets of peasant households in the late 1920s.[44]

One indicator of the peasants' attitude to the church was that civil marriage and divorce were starting to get a foothold in the villages in the 1920s. Of course, the majority of peasant weddings were still celebrated in church, but it was reported that marriages outside the church had become "a common event" in the village, at least in the non-Black Earth belt of European Russia. "In each village there are three or four couples who were not married in church," and other peasants had a tolerant (*nezlobnoe*) attitude to this. When Maurice Hindus returned to his native village in the Ukraine in 1929, he was startled at the degree to which the young people were both ignorant of church rituals and uninterested in them.[45]

Men who had served in the army and returned to the village were noted for their indifference to religion, and some even proclaimed themselves to be atheists. "In each village there are atheists, people who don't believe in God. They proclaim this openly. The peasants accept it without astonishment. . . ." It was generally agreed, however, that the pressures of village life tended to mute this attitude after a few years. For example:

> I came back from the Red Army, relates a demobilized veteran, and at first did not go to church. The priest ran into me one day and said: "Hey, soldier, why don't you go to church. I won't marry you." . . . And then my mother makes an issue of it. I thought of getting married, so I had to go to church. Now I have married and don't go to church.[46]

Older women, however, usually remained staunch believers. There were many reports of miraculous events such as renewal of icons in different parts of the countryside, and the faithful made pilgrimages to the sites. Various signs of God's anger at the Bolsheviks' blasphemies and intention to punish them were also seen. In Kursk province, the following rumor went around in the mid 1920s:

> A holy cross landed on one monastery. Many people including Communists saw the cross. The latter got in an aeroplane and tried to seize the cross. But it did not yield—the Communists could not catch up with it.[47]

Generational conflict was very evident in villages of the 1920s, particularly those in the industrialized non-Black Earth provinces. Young peasants "no longer wanted to wear the old village clothes, taking them as a symbol of age-old backwardness."

> Military dress, which many still had after the First World War and Civil War, enjoyed great popularity with men. . . . Former soldiers, rural activists, Komsomols—that is, all those who counted themselves as progressive people—went around in military and semimilitary uniform. Adolescent boys envied their fathers' clothes and also tried to dress up in greatcoats and *budënnovka* (Red Army cavalry cap).

For village girls, to the scandal of their mothers, powder and rouge were becoming common. Urban dances like the tango and the foxtrot were taking the place of the old folk dances in the recreations of the young.[48]

In some areas the bright lights of the city and the revolution had dazzled the young to the point where they despised the village, their parents, and agriculture as an occupation. In 1923 a young ethnography student summarized attitudes in his native village in Volokolamsk district, not far from Moscow, as follows:

> "The old people are fools. They knock themselves out endlessly and get nothing out of it. They just don't know anything except plowing. Which is to say they don't know anything," is what youth says about their fathers. . . . "Give up the farm. It is not profitable, does not justify the labor spent on it. The farm feeds only its own stomach," say young peasants.

What do the young people want?

To get away, get away as quickly as possible. Anywhere, if one can only get away—to the factory, to the army, to study or become an officer—it doesn't matter. To live as a free bird![49]

In this generational conflict, religion was almost always a key issue. The sons, and to a lesser extent the daughters, would refuse to wear a cross and would show disrespect for the church and the priest; the mothers, and to a much lesser extent the fathers, would scold and plead with them to no avail. In the opinion of the distinguished ethnographer Vladimir Bogoraz, this form of village iconoclasm had deep roots. Priest baiting and conspicuous irreverence for religion were not attitudes peasants picked up from urban Komsomols and Communists. More likely, he claimed, it was the other way round, with the new Marxist revolutionary taking on the characteristics of the traditional village freethinker, "the godfighter" (*bogoborets*).

The constant food of the village Communist cell is anecdotes about priests, sharp ones, highly spiced—in general, anecdotes "for smokers." ... But it's not only anecdotes. The whole thrust of the muckraking zest of [party] lectures and agitators is directed against the church.

In its popular version, Bogoraz implied, hostility to the church, priests, and religious "superstition" was the central tenet of Communism. Peasants seemed to have drawn the same conclusion: A linguist investigating peasant comprehension of new Soviet vocabulary reported that the new word "Communist" was often defined as "the ones who don't believe in God."[50]

On the Eve

The frenetic collectivization drive and mass expropriation of kulaks that burst forth in the winter of 1929–30 were the climax of two and a half years of rising political and social tension. This change of course was neither a response to developments within the peasantry nor the result of careful reconsideration of the party's agricultural policies. Indeed, the political leaders paid only spasmodic attention to agriculture and the peasantry in these years; their main attention was focused on internal party politics, international affairs, and preparation of the First Five-Year Plan that was to launch the Soviet Union into a new era of rapid, centrally planned industrial growth.

The 1927 war scare—a groundless but almost hysterical alarm about imminent military attack by the capitalist powers—set the tone. It was accompanied by an increase in police activity and public concern about spies, conspiracies, and internal enemies. Urban private entrepreneurs (*Nepmen*) were put out of business and many were arrested. Stalin, whose political predominance was increasingly visible, forced Trotsky and other opposition leaders out of the Communist Party and sent them into exile; then he began a cat-and-mouse game with the more moderate "Right Opposition" leaders in the Politburo that ended with their public humiliation and defeat early in 1929. The most ambitious version of the First Five-Year Plan was adopted: As Stalin said, using the characteristic Civil War rhetoric of the period,

"There are no fortresses Bolsheviks cannot storm." There were purges of "rightists" and "class enemies" in the Communist Party and the government bureaucracy. Militant young Communist radicals attacked the cultural hegemony of the old intelligentsia in the name of proletarian Cultural Revolution; and the Komsomol began an increasingly vigorous assault on religion.

In the countryside, problems started with the unexpectedly low level of state grain procurements after the 1927 harvest. The war scare was probably one reason that peasants were unwilling to sell. Another reason was that the state, intent on building capital reserves for the industrialization drive, had set prices too low. This need not have been a crisis, but Stalin—overruling the arguments of the future Right Opposition—decided to make it one. No doubt he expected a confrontation with the peasantry at some point, since it was generally accepted in the party's higher echelons that peasants would have to be "squeezed" to pay for First Five-Year Plan industrial expansion, and thought he should crack the whip early and show the peasants who was master.[51]

As usual, it was the kulaks who were blamed, but not only the kulaks suffered. Stalin said that kulaks were trying to sabotage state grain procurements by holding back grain, and recommended that hoarding should be punished as "speculation," a criminal offense under article 107 of the Criminal Code. But this reference to the Criminal Code was misleading: It was not primarily by law but rather by extra-legal methods of coercion and intimidation that the grain procurements crisis would be handled. The OGPU, the political police, played a prominent role. Tens of thousands of Communists were sent out to the countryside to help with procurements. Although Stalin denied it, it was obvious to everyone that the old Civil War methods, discarded with the introduction of NEP, were back. If the peasants would not sell their grain, the regime would go into the villages and requisition it.[52]

In the first months of 1928, and again in 1929, "emergency measures" of grain procurement were used. Procurements brigades and local authorities closed down markets, set up roadblocks to prevent peasants getting their grain to private dealers, searched barns, and arrested kulaks, millers, and other "hoarders," Grain was confiscated, as were horses, threshing machines, and other property. Failure to deliver grain procurements was treated as a political crime. State procurements agents harangued, threatened, and physically manhandled peasants. As in 1918, bedniaks were rewarded for informing on richer peasants who were hiding grain.

Sometimes peasant households were completely expropriated. The writer Mikhail Sholokhov told the story of a Cossack from his native region in the Kuban who was stripped of all his possessions down to the family's clothing and samovar in 1929 when he was unable to meet hefty extra levies in grain and cash, arbitrarily imposed after he had paid his regular agricultural tax and delivered 155 puds of grain to the state procurements agency. Moreover, Sholokhov reported, it was impossible for him or other peasants to appeal against unjust taxation because regional authorities had forbidden the post office to accept telegrams of complaint and were refusing travel authorization to those who tried to take their complaints to Moscow in person.[53]

Reports poured in that seredniaks and even bedniaks, not only kulaks, were being subjected to arrest and confiscation of property. But these random acts of repression were just part of the picture. In 1929, a contract system was introduced that obligated the whole village (strictly speaking, the whole land society or mir) to deliver specified quotas of grain to the state. When villages failed to meet their quotas, they too were liable to punishment. In the Central Volga region in 1929, for example, procurements brigades "blockaded" delinquent villages, conducting house-to-house searches for grain and holding "hoarders" under arrest for several days in an unheated village barn. They then organized a demonstration around the village, waving black flags and slogans such as "Death to the village of Griaznoe," "Boycott this village," and "Entrance and exit forbidden."[54]

Stalin raised the idea of large-scale collectivization in his speech on the grain procurements crisis in January 1928, hinting at the same time at the possibility of mass expropriation of kulaks. Despite the energetic measures that were being taken to bring in grain procurements, Stalin said, it was to be expected that the same kind of sabotage would take place next year, indeed that it would continue "as long as kulaks exist." But how to replace the kulaks as major grain marketers? Stalin's proposal was to expand the operations of both state farms and collective farms as quickly as possible, so that within "the next three or four years" they would be providing at least a third of total grain marketings and the state's vulnerability to kulak sabotage would be correspondingly reduced.[55]

Despite this verbal commitment, the meaning of collectivization was still extremely vague. It was unclear whether Stalin was talking about voluntary or compulsory collectivization; and he gave no indication as to whether the form of collectivization he had in mind was the kommuna, in which everything was collectivized; the artel, in which the means of production were collectivized; or the *TOZ*, in which only land and major agricultural equipment were collectively owned. The most perplexing aspect of Stalin's comments was that while the kolkhoz he was talking about seemed to be a quite different beast from the collective farms that actually existed in the Soviet Union, he was apparently unaware of the difference.

Stalin's kolkhoz was a large-scale, mechanized agricultural unit producing for the state in the same way as large commercial farms produce for the market in a capitalist system. He talked about the kolkhoz in the same breath as the *sovkhoz* (that is, a state farm employing hired labor), despite their basic structural difference from a Marxist standpoint, because he saw both of them as tools for the modernization of Soviet agriculture. The aim of collectivization, Stalin said in May 1928, was to "transfer from small, backward and fragmented peasant farms to consolidated, big, public farms, provided with machines, equipped with the data of science and capable of producing the greatest quantity of grain for market."[56]

The collective farms actually in existence in 1928 could scarcely have been further from this model. They were typically small, economically weak, unable to survive without state subsidies, and not significant producers for the market. In mid 1928, when fewer than 2 percent of peasant households belonged to the 33,000 collective farms in the Soviet Union, the average kolkhoz comprised a mere twelve households—roughly one-sixth the number in an average village or land society.[57]

Collective farms—or communes (*kommuny*) as they were usually called in the 1920s—were marginal social and economic entities, linked in popular perception with the utopianism of the Civil War. Neighboring peasants frequently claimed that the communards were city folk who did not know how to farm. Many communes had charismatic leaders without whom they could not function: Molotov later asserted (rather surprisingly) that he and Stalin deplored this characteristic and therefore chose the artel form of collectivization instead of the commune.[58] Perhaps one thing Molotov had in mind was that the charismatic figures leading communes were not invariably Communists. Some of the most successful communes were run by religious sectarians such as Churikov, well known in the 1920s for his crusade against alcohol, who had a flourishing dairy commune outside Leningrad.[59]

In the late 1920s, as collective farms came back into official favor, it became more common to find them farmed with modern techniques, perhaps even with a tractor they owned, and economically more successful than their predecessors. Alas, on closer examination many of these turned out to be bogus collectives (*lzhekolkhozy*) in Soviet eyes. In Sychevka raion in the Western oblast, for example, a group of traders and kulaks contributed 3,000 rubles a head to set up a kolkhoz that turned a healthy profit by operating an up-to-date oil-powered mill; in Roslavl raion, the "Comintern" kolkhoz was established on a former noble estate under the leadership of the pre-revolutionary estate manager. Another type of bogus kolkhoz often noted in the press in the late 1920s was the "sacred" kolkhoz, set up on the site of a former convent or monastery by a collective that turned out to be the former nuns and monks. In one such kolkhoz, which had even secured a state credit of 3,000 rubles for a chicken farm, hired laborers were "rapaciously exploited" by the nuns, according a Soviet newspaper report.[60]

In 1928, for the first time, Soviet officials conducted active propaganda among peasants about collective farms, encouraging peasants to join existing kolkhozy, which were often located on former noble or church estates with lands adjacent to those of the villagers. Progress was relatively slow, since peasants had to sign up voluntarily and on a household-by-household basis. But the goal of the First Five-Year Plan, inaugurated in 1929, was also quite modest in this area: Less than 15 percent of peasant agriculture was supposed to be collectivized by the end of the five-year period.[61]

The peasants' attitude, as expressed to officials, was that they needed time to see how the collectives worked and be convinced of their virtues. "Of course we are not against total collectivization," peasants told officials, "but for the time being we will abstain from joining the kolkhoz." But it is difficult to believe that most peasants were as open-minded as this diplomatic response suggests. An investigation of rural soviets in Shakhty raion towards the end of 1929 produced mainly negative findings on the population's readiness for collectivization: "There is no attraction to the kolkhoz," "The question of total collectivization has been discussed [in the rural soviets], but the population refuses to join the collective farms," "The mood against the collective farms is general, even among the bedniaks."[62]

Meanwhile, the continuing conflicts between peasants and the state over procurements were generating tension and violence in the village. It was not that a genuine class war between kulaks and bedniaks was bubbling up at the grass roots, as Soviet historians used to claim, but rather that a more or less phony class war espoused by Communists had genuine divisive effects. Organize actions against kulaks in such a way that they come "*as an initiative from below* [my emphasis], from the bedniaks," a regional party committee helpfully instructed district officials. But even phony initiatives could be divisive. Peasants in the Urals complained; "There's no need to call meetings of bedniaks; it only introduces disunity (*razmychka*) among the peasantry."[63]

The effect of such tensions in daily life may be illustrated by a trivial incident that occurred in a remote village in the Urals in the spring of 1929. The village's bedniaks and its solid citizens were holding separate Easter celebrations. Everyone was drunk. A bedniak who had recently joined the Communist Party wandered into the solid citizens' part of the village, bottle in hand. One of the solid citizens came out and abused him, calling him "a paper Communist." The bedniak then hit the solid citizen over the head with his bottle.[64]

Known kulaks—those who were so regarded in the village or had been so identified by local electoral commissions—found themselves in the position of lepers, shunned by other peasants who were anxious not to become kulaks by association (*podkulachniki*). Prosperous peasants of the solid-citizen type were increasingly frightened of being denounced as kulaks. Peasant activists encountered new levels of hostility from fellow villagers who blamed them for the regime's ruthlessness over procurements. Some bedniaks of the ne'er-do-well type were collaborating with officials to uncover hidden grain stores in order to receive a percentage of what was confiscated. Others were developing their own extortion tactics, of the kind reported early in 1930 from the Western oblast: "If you don't give me twenty rubles, I will tax you with the individual tax, confiscate all your property and deport you as a kulak: You know I am an activist kolkhoznik and I can do what I want."[65]

In the elections for rural soviets held early in 1929, bedniak status was emphasized more than ever before as a qualification for candidacy. The number of peasants who were disenfranchised as kulaks soared, and so did the number registering protests that they had been incorrectly classified. Although these were controlled elections, with lists of candidates prepared in advance, there was still scope for ridicule and rejection of candidates and voter boycotts. Sinister reports appeared in the Soviet press of political alliances being made in various regions between kulaks and middle peasants, kulaks and priests, kulaks and sectarians. Troublemakers displayed "caricatures and parodies" of the candidates at the voting places, and flourished slogans of their own that compared the "idlers and "ne'er-do-wells" on the official list with the "thrifty, self-supporting" (*khoziaistvennye, samostoiatel'nye*) peasants that the Bolsheviks vilified. Anti-Soviet leaflets were distributed, and one commentator noted that arguments about competence and intelligence were made much more often than in the past. ("Why am I rich? It means I am clever [*umnyi*]. And since I am clever, I could run the soviet in a competent manner.")[66]

The level of violence in the countryside was unusually high throughout 1929: Over a nine-month period, more than a thousand acts of violence by "class-alien elements," including 384 murders, were registered, and there were more than 1,400 cases of arson. The violence started to escalate in the summer and reached a peak during the procurements season in the fall. Almost daily reports appeared in the press of assaults and murders of rural officials, Communists, and village activists. Chairmen and secretaries of rural soviets were prime targets for violence, as were members of procurements brigades. In June, Sholokhov reported that armed gangs of bandits had reappeared in the Don Cossack region for the first time since the Civil War. Similar bands were observed in Siberia towards the end of the year.[67]

From the stories appearing in *Bednota*, the peasant activists' newspaper, in October, several categories of violence can be identified. The first was violence against Soviet officials who were outsiders to the village. Such acts might be committed by angry kulaks, or by other peasants recruited and directed by kulaks. In the Ukraine, for example, a kulak reportedly attacked a militiaman with an axe after his property was confiscated for nonpayment of the agricultural tax. In Kaluga, two Soviet propagandists sent out from the town were set upon in a village by kulaks and beaten. Other villagers ignored their calls for help. Finally, their assailants stripped them naked and dumped them on the road with the warning: "Don't look back or we'll shoot you."[68]

The second category was violence against local peasants who were Soviet activists. In the Central Volga region, for example, a female member of a rural soviet, Anastasia Semkina, was murdered and her body burned on a bonfire. In the central industrial region, a local peasant who was chairman of the rural soviet, A. N. Borisov, was killed by a shot through the window, evidently in revenge for his actions against kulaks. According to the newspaper, "Comrade Borisov was so popular and loved by the peasants that almost the whole population of six neighboring villages came to pay their last respects. 2,000 persons followed the coffin."[69]

A third category consisted of attacks on bedniaks who had informed on other peasants to the authorities. In Siberia, a bedniak was murdered after he told the authorities which of the villagers was hiding grain. In Georgia, a bedniak named Papashvili was murdered at night by a kulak and buried secretly, with the connivance of other villagers. Papashvili, dignified in death as an "activist" but not credited with any specific activities, had probably also been an informer.[70]

In addition to violence, other types of ostracism were also used against peasant activists. In a village in Irkutsk oblast, two peasant activists, Klimentev (a Communist) and Vakulenko, became objects of great resentment in the village. After the rumor spread that Klimentev was proposing to blow up the local church, villagers planned to murder him, but the plan was abandoned on the urging of the village teacher. Then a village meeting was called, and the peasants voted to expel Klimentev and Vakulenko from the mir and forbid them to graze their animals on the village pastures. The mir's resolution stated that Klimentev was expelled because he had "joined the party, did not christen his child, and took down icons and burnt them." The reason for Vakulenko's expulsion was stated simply and eloquently: "for active Soviet work."[71]

Bitter village conflicts erupted in connection with the establishment of collective farms. In the fall of 1929, when members of a new kolkhoz in the Western oblast went out to plow,

> a crowd of women armed with axes, forks and stakes appeared at the place where they were working and assaulted the kolkhozniks, beating a kolkhoznik and the wife of the chairman, destroying twelve plows, damaging harnesses and knocking out a horse's eye.

According to officials who investigated the incident, the attack had been planned and organized by kulaks, who watched the fight from a nearby hiding place.[72]

"The heroic period of our socialist construction has arrived," cried a repentant party Oppositionist, G. L. Piatakov, in October 1929.[73] Like the earlier "heroic period" of the Civil War, this was a time when even normally sober party members were liable to fling commonsense to the winds and succumb to the hope of a new Jerusalem just round the corner. Young Komsomol enthusiasts, like their Chinese Red Guard counterparts thirty-five years later, charged around in a state of wild excitement, unmasking Rightists and class enemies, intimidating bureaucrats, and destroying anything they could find of the old world. The passion for immediate revolutionary change was all the stronger because of the discomforts and uncertainties of the present, with continuing rumors of imminent war swirling around, Communists and state officials at a high pitch of anxiety under the scrutiny of purge commissions, and rationing of food and other basic goods already introduced in the towns.

Several important developments occurred in the second half of 1929. In the first place, the tempo of collectivization quickened. Over a four-month period (June to September, 1929) the number of collective farms almost doubled from a base of one million. In some major grain-growing regions, officials were reporting extraordinary results for the collectivization drive: 19 percent of all peasants collectivized in the Northern Caucasus by the end of the summer, for example; 18 percent in Lower Volga krai. By November, one district in the Lower Volga claimed that more than 50 percent of peasant households had been collectivized. "Reality is overtaking our plans," crowed a jubilant senior official responsible for collectivized agriculture.[74]

These extraordinary results were partly to be explained by the new zeal with which provincial and district officials were pursuing the task, and the fact that as Communist pressure on peasants grew, the voluntary element in collectivization was fast disappearing. Instead of asking the peasants "Who is for collectivization?" or even "Who is against collectivization?" officials were increasingly asking the ominous question: "Who is against Soviet power?"[75]

But there was also another reason for the collectivization successes: Officials had found a wonderful shortcut. Instead of trying to persuade individual households to join a kolkhoz, as they had done in the past, they had now adopted the strategy of signing up whole villages at a time—that is, turning an existing mir into a kolkhoz by the simple mechanism of taking a vote on it.[76] This might or might not be accompanied by any immediate real-life changes in the village, but it certainly produced impressive figures for official reports. There were even stories of young urban Pioneers going out to a village, making a passionate speech to the *skhod*, and then triumphantly announcing: "I collectivized it!"

Regardless of its window dressing possibilities, the new strategy had great substantive importance. In the past, peasants who joined the kolkhoz were, in effect, separators: Their decision to join the kolkhoz implied a decision to leave the mir. The new strategy meant collectivization without separation. Moreover, if a majority of members of the peasant commune signed up for the new kolkhoz and a minority resisted, the minority households found themselves in the position of involuntary separators.

The second major development of the latter half of 1929 was that expropriations of kulaks by local officials (dekulakization) began to be widely reported. There was, as yet, no central policy of mass dekulakization, although it is clear—if only from the repeated denials by Communist leaders over the previous two years that the party had any such intention—that the idea of a radical solution to "the kulak problem" was in the air. Individual acts of expropriation occurred in connection with procurements, however, and this trend was encouraged by a government decree of July 28, 1929, authorizing the seizure and sale of property of kulaks who were "malicious saboteurs of grain procurements." Throughout 1929, the secretariats of Mikhail Kalinin (the Soviet president) and Stalin received no less than 90,000 complaints from peasants about unlawful, arbitrary, and violent acts committed against them, including expropriation as kulaks.[77]

The new collectivization strategy gave greater urgency to the question of what to do about kulaks. In particular, it raised in acute form the issue of whether or not kulaks could join the kolkhoz. After all, they were members of the village mir. If the kolkhoz was now to be built on the basis of the mir, there was the possibility that they would become members almost automatically and dominate the new institution as they had dominated the mir in the past. This was highly undesirable from the Bolshevik standpoint, but it was hard to think of a feasible alternative. The kulaks could scarcely be sent away to "remote areas or a desert island," as a senior agricultural official put it sarcastically in the summer of 1929.[78] Or could they? That unspoken question was starting to reverberate quietly in the minds of Communists.

A final development that needs to be mentioned is the swiftly gathering momentum of the campaign against religion, associated primarily with the Komsomol. Rowdy and well attended antireligious "carnivals" had been organized in city streets by Komsomols at Easter, to the outrage of believers. In the fall, the newspapers carried a series of alarming stories about anti-Soviet conspiracies unmasked by the OGPU that involved church people and sectarians. There were also reports of conflicts in the countryside over procurements and collectivization in which priests and believers played a major role: In a village in Ivanovo oblast, for example, an outraged mob led by "priests and kulaks" tried to lynch local Communists and Komsomol members after they tried to turn an old cemetery into plowland and the rumor spread that they were desecrating the graves and intended to close the church.[79]

The closing of churches by municipal authorities was becoming increasingly frequent in the towns, along with a bizarre movement to "help the industrialization drive" by melting down churchbells. In the Ukraine, young enthusiasts from the towns fanned out into the countryside to take down the bells from village churches. All this reached a climax in an extraordinary episode in Gorlovka in the Donbass in December when 4,000 icons were ceremoniously burnt in a bonfire in the city square while a crowd of miners estimated at 15,000–18,000 danced and celebrated in the streets.[80]

Rumors of Apocalypse

As the pace of collectivization quickened and tensions rose, rumors swept the countryside.[81] It was said that the Day of Judgement was at hand, that the messengers of Antichrist had already appeared on earth, that a book had fallen from heaven forbidding peasants to enter the kolkhoz. When a workers' collectivization brigade appeared in a rural district of the Pskov region, evangelicals preached that Antichrist had come "to plant Satanic nests" and place "the Devil's mark" on peasants. In the Western oblast, collectivizers were rumored to be messengers of Antichrist, "promising [peasants] a better life but signing them up for Hell."[82]

These were the same apocalyptic terms in which Russian peasants more than two centuries earlier had expressed their fear and resentment of Peter the Great's reforms. But not all the rumors fit in this traditional pattern. We can hear a variety of voices and patterns of discourse in the peasant "conversation of rumors." Some rumors took the Apocalypse as a frame; others used imagery from Russian fairytales (*skazki*) and folk mythology; and yet others reflected the language of the Soviet press and even its contents—there are definite hints of a Marxist perspective in some of the rumors about politics and international relations.

In the collective conversation about collectivization, various hypotheses were advanced to explain the regime's actions. One hypothesis was that collectivization might be the product of a deal between the Soviet government and those foreign governments that had given shelter to expropriated landowners: perhaps a first step towards returning the lands that were seized in 1917–18 to their former owners, or even returning the peasants to their pre-1861 status as serfs. In Velikie Luki, peasants were saying in the summer of 1929 that collective farms were being organized because former landowners, now in emigration, had issued an ultimatum to the Soviet government that their estates be reconstituted and returned, "otherwise all the nations will go to war against Russia." A similar rumor was circulating in Leningrad oblast as late as 1931: "The collective farms have been organized so as to reestablish the lords' estates, after which the lord (*barin*) will appear and take over."[83]

The original rumors surely owed something to the report (published in the Soviet press in 1928) that Prince Petr Petrovich Volkonskii had sent a letter from Paris reaffirming his claim to his former estates in Riazan province. The letter was read at general meetings of peasants on his former estate, and they returned curses and messages of defiance, according to newspaper reports.[84] Less directly, it can be linked to allegations in the highly publicized Shakhty trial of 1928 that industrial officials had plotted to return certain industrial enterprises to their former owners under the guise of concessions.

Another hypothesis was that collectivization was indeed intended to serve the interests of the old landowners, but that it had been initiated from within the Soviet bureaucracy by former estate owners who had acquired influence in the Soviet Commissariat of Agriculture.[85] This was an elaboration of a theme very prominent in the press of the late 1920s—that of "class enemies" among the experts in the Soviet bureaucracy, who had used their positions to manipulate Communists and distort Communist policy.

The modern technological aspect of collectivization was the subject of a good deal of comment. Peasants were generally suspicious of the new technology when they first encountered it: There were angry demonstrations in the Ukrainian countryside in the fall of 1929 when the first tractors appeared. But their suspicions were formulated in a variety of ways, some archaic and some modern. One rumor of the archaic type deciphered the meaning of the initials "MTS" (Machine-Tractor Station) as follows: "*Mir Topit Satana* (Satan is ruining the world). Don't join the kolkhoz." Another offered the reasonable suggestion that the new MTS was the functional equivalent of the old landowner's estate: Its function was "to impose serfdom on the population, to transform tillers of the land into slaves." A third, which probably owed something to the Bolsheviks' support for popular science, asserted that "the tractor poisons the soil with its gases, and in five to ten years the land will cease to be fertile."[86]

Airplanes, an object of enormous interest in the Soviet Union in the 1920s, as in Germany and the United States at the same time, figured in some of the rumors about collectivization. One speculation was that the airplane's functions included the gathering of information on crop sowing that would help the state maximize procurements quotas: In the Duminichi district of the Western oblast, peasants were talking "about how an airplane flew through their area and sowed all the peasants' fields, [so] the state will know how much grain will be in their district. It flew [there] because the commune (kommuna) was organized, and therefore that commune has to be liquidated."[87]

Another aviation rumor turned the plane into a fairytale bird that would ultimately deliver the "real peasants" from the usurping kolkhozniks. "The kolkhozniks are all atheists; they will take the bells down from the churches and loot everything they can get from the real peasants. But then the peasants will be loosed on the kolkhozniks, and after that all the kolkhozniks will be put on an airplane and taken to [the prison island of] Solovki. . . . "[88]

The threat that collectivization represented to a traditional way of life was conveyed in the epidemic of hysterical rumors that all kolkhozniks would sleep under one blanket; that they would be forced to dress like convicts; that wives would become common property; that whole families would be made to wear "one cotton jacket for the whole family and . . . go around in it like convicts," and so on. Other comments thrown into the rumor mill were suggestions about modes of resistance: for example, "Why sow, if the end of the world is coming soon." Still other voices in the conversation offered various sober assessments and predictions: "They will put people on starvation rations in the kolkhoz and the state will take all the surplus;" "there will be whippings (*rozgi i palki*) in the kolkhoz."[89]

2

Collectivization

Bacchanalia

At the beginning of 1930, in the winter months that were usually times of inertia and isolation in the village, the storm that had been building for almost two years broke with a vengeance. Stimulated by Stalin's announcement in December that it was time to move towards "liquidation of the kulaks as a class," Communists and Komsomols descended on the countryside en masse to get rid of the kulaks, collectivize the village, close the churches, and generally kick the backward peasantry into the socialist twentieth century. Haranguing, browbeating, threatening, and arresting, the militant modernizers' approach had a basic underlying simplicity: Either you join the kolkhoz, they were in effect telling the peasants, or you risk joining the kulaks and going to Solovki or Siberia.

The peasants, for their part, responded with wailing and lamentations and all manner of passive and furtive resistance, but on the whole they bore it fatalistically, signed up for the kolkhoz when they saw no other choice, and did not erupt into outright rebellion. Of course many saw it as a return to serfdom, but that at least was an evil they knew, and one that the village suffered together, communally, not as individual lost souls like the unfortunate kulaks. The departure of the kulaks provoked pity in some peasants but indifference (or hidden hope of getting a bigger share of that finite peasant pie?) in many. The worst thing about dekulakization was that it had random qualities: Anyone might fall victim by bad luck or malice, although some were much more obvious and inevitable victims than others.

In all the extraordinary assaults on peasant values and tradition of January and February 1930, the one that seemed to sting the most was the onslaught on religion. Yet this may be misleading: Certainly the peasants did not persevere long in their newly found assertive reverence for the Orthodox church, but in many cases soon drifted off into nonobservance and apparent indifference or sectarianism. No doubt it was the safest of the Communists' three causes to resist (since they could afford to back off this one, and did); and perhaps also the peasants had in mind that it might be prudent to square oneself with God by registering an objection, just in case He was planning to send a thunderbolt in revenge for Soviet sacrilege and blasphemy.

Collectivization

There were no exact instructions on how to carry out collectivization. The government's order for "total (*sploshnaia*) collectivization" in some areas of the country indicated an upgrading of the urgency of the task, but it was not clearly explained what kind of collective farm the regime wanted, let alone how to achieve it. The Politburo approved a detailed set of prescriptions for the model kolkhoz only on March 1, 1930, the same day that the first big push for collectivization was halted by Stalin's article, "Dizzy with success." Even then, the Politburo did not let on—if indeed it knew—that the new Soviet kolkhoz was to be built on the basis of the old peasant commune, with the result that enthusiastic officials plunged into an orgy of "gigantomania," that is, infatuation with ever bigger and (on paper) better collective farms, which would have been even more damaging than it was if their plans had had more contact with reality.

The regime's failure to give adequate instructions on collectivization and dekulakization was not simply an oversight. Rather, it appears to have been a strategy whose main objective was to get local cadres pushing for the absolute maximum, thus providing both quick results and information on what the attainable maximum actually was. The cadres going out to collectivize may not know have known exactly what collectivization meant, but they knew very well that it was better (for their own careers, as well as for the cause) to go too far in collectivizing than not to go far enough ("*luchshe peregnut', chem nedognut'*"). They knew, too, that observing the letter of the law was not the way to achieve revolutionary social transformations. As the head of Kolkhoz Center (*Kolkhoztsentr*, the coordinating agency for national collectivization) admonished his troops as they set out for the great battle, "If you go overboard (*peregnete*) on some matter and they arrest you, remember that you were arrested for a revolutionary cause."[1]

As the Smolensk regional newspaper stated editorially in January 1930, Communist collectivizers and dekulakizers should not go whining to the center to ask how to carry out their tasks, because this was a form of rightism. Such "spinelessness, conciliationism, and attempts to put off practical implementation of . . . policy" constituted the "chief danger" at the present time—that is, they were *more* dangerous that any mistakes that might spring from excessive belligerence, haste, and zeal.[2]

This method of "unleashing" Communists to follow their own instincts, typical of the Cultural Revolution mentality of the period, explains a good deal about the chaotic mix of violence, frenzied persuasion, and utopianism observable on the Communist side of the confrontation. It also, of course, explains why so many egregious mistakes (misjudgements of practical possibilities, as well as misjudgements of the intentions of the party leadership) were made. Lacking exact instructions as to the nature of the kolkhoz they should be organizing, officials often preferred the kommuna, where everything was collectively owned and meals were taken communally, to any less radical form. Not only that, they sometimes managed to find even more maximal forms of communalization than were normal in the communes of the 1920s: In one raion in the Urals, they collectivized clothing, and peasants had to pick garments randomly from a common pile when they set out to work in the fields, "which provoked indignation among the kolkhozniks."[3]

Collectivizers often tried to socialize everything down to pigs and chickens, considering that there was more cachet in reporting that they had organized a commune than that they had organized an artel. In the Tatar Republic, some called for collectivization of "everything except houses." The same maximalism led some officials to deny the peasants' right to private plots once they had joined the kolkhoz, or their right to sell the produce of the plots at markets, or indeed the legitimacy of peasant markets at all. Markets and bazaars reported closed by administrative order in a number of places in the Central Black Earth oblast in the winter of 1929–30.[4]

While raion and rural soviet officials were deeply involved in the collectivization drive, the campaign was characterized by vast "mobilizations" of urban Communists, Komsomols, workers, and students for short- and long-term service in the countryside. The advantage of such people was that they had no local ties; their disadvantage was often that they knew nothing at all about agriculture or the village. From the peasants' point of view, they were "outsiders" to the nth degree. Some of them were on serious, long-term missions, like the "25,000-ers"—worker volunteers from major industrial plants who provided many of the kolkhoz chairmen of the early years. Others were evidently pure troublemakers, the young "Komsomol hooligan" types, out looking for some action (which usually involved drinking and attacking the church).

Sometimes several different brigades would descend at the same time on one village and stay for weeks. A specialist on preschool education who was drafted for one of these teams related that her brigade, representing the Leningrad Section of the Union of Scientific Workers, descended on one village in the Pskov region simultaneously with another brigade from the "Red Triangle" plant. There were at least eighteen people sleeping over each night, and many more coming in during the day, and the villagers submitted themselves somewhat bemusedly to a round of meetings and lectures on subjects as diverse as science and kindergartens: "As people explained to me, they are afraid of missing something, that something might be decided without them, and anyway there are no other demands on their time at the moment [since it was winter]. . . . "[5]

Meetings were indeed the essence of the initial process of collectivization. As we shall see, there was not much that was really voluntary about the collectivization drive of the winter of 1929–30. Nevertheless, as in many other situations involving Communist interaction with peasants, the Communists were anxious that the *forms* of democracy should be observed, which meant that by hook or by crook peasants had to be persuaded to put their signatures on the collectivization document. Hence the meetings of the whole village community (minus the kulaks, who had been declared ineligible for kolkhoz membership), which frequently lasted for many hours and were held many days in succession. The Communists explained, pleaded, threatened, and shouted themselves hoarse in the effort to get peasants to vote in favor of the kolkhoz. The peasants sometimes listened silently and skeptically, but often argued, raised objections, or tried to find ways of agreeing that would not really commit them to anything.

Peasants showed their mastery of evasive tactics in these meetings. There are reports of a wide variety of ploys to break up collectivization meetings before signatures were demanded. Old women would interrupt the meeting at crucial moments by singing "Christ Has Risen." Stoves were made to smoke. Someone would come running in with the news that houses in a nearby village were on fire. Or, for variety, "children run in shouting 'Uncle, uncle, they have stolen your horse' just before the vote is taken. As if on command, all present run out onto the street. The meeting is broken up."[6]

At times, the evasion clearly shaded over into mockery of the collectivizers. Peasants would sometimes seem to be quite happy to sign up to join the kolkhoz, then back off at the last minute. In one village, a brigade of urban workers come to hold a collectivization meeting was gratified when the village policeman "brought in an organized group of twenty-five peasants, who came in singing revolutionary songs. But at the meeting they all spoke against collectivization. . . . "[7]

There were many similar examples of mockery of officials, particularly outsiders from the towns, by peasants. In one village in Leningrad oblast, a village skhod passed a series of collectivization resolutions in impeccable Soviet form—except that each statement was negative instead of positive. In the Taganrog region, a meeting of poor and middle peasants voted for the following resolutions: "We will not join the kolkhoz, we will not give seed funds, since the grain procurements have crushed us, but we welcome the decision about total collectivization."[8]

The collectivizers used various threats in their efforts to induce peasants to join the kolkhoz. One of the most common was to suggest that the alternative to signing up for the kolkhoz was to be deported as a kulak. Thus, a raion chairman in the Urals collectivized by touring the rural soviets with his police chief and instructing peasants as follows: "Those who are joining the kolkhoz, sign up with me; those who do not want to join, sign up with the police chief." (Twelve peasants who did not join the kolkhoz were arrested on the spot.)[9]

Other collectivizers phrased the alternatives slightly differently: into the kolkhoz or to Solovki, the notorious prison island; into the kolkhoz or to Narym, a familiar place of exile in the north. In one village in the Central Black Earth oblast,[10] a *raikom* representative issued an order that all peasants join the kolkhoz within twenty-four hours. "Shirkers," even if they were poor or middle peasants, would be handed over to the Revolutionary Tribunal. These were not idle threats, since there were also many reported cases when peasants who refused to join the kolkhoz were in fact arrested or put on the list for deportation as kulaks.[11]

Sometimes the collectivizers would wave revolvers at the meetings, threatening to shoot peasants who refused to join.[12] In one village, peasants were terrorized by nocturnal summonses to the rural soviet office, where they were sometimes held for days at a time. An eyewitness wrote to the authorities that

> The night summonses, threats, and arrests produced an extreme degree of suppressed fear. I saw how the local bosses, Bersenev, Kopylov, and Riabtsev, insulted the people. They said: "Woe to you if you do not obey us." Nobody dared complain because they retaliated savagely for complaints.[13]

In another region, somewhat more benignly,

> "Collectivizers" went from house to house with a brass band. They called the peasants out onto the street. If they agreed to join the kolkhoz, the orchestra played a lively flourish. If they refused, the conductor waved his baton and the brass instruments frightened the undecided independent peasant (*edinolichnik*) with the "Funeral March."[14]

Officials also used violence and humiliation as means of persuasion, although the extent of this varied by region. In one case of brutality from the Urals, a region noted for violence, a collectivizer from the raion was found to have called individual peasants in for interrogation about their attitude to the kolkhoz and "hit them with his fists, burnt their bodies with cigarettes, made them kneel, pulled their beards, and staged a [mock] execution." There were many reports of recalcitrant peasants being put "in cold storage" (*v kholodnuiu*—that is, left overnight in an unheated izba or barn). In one village, collectivizers seized a woman peasant as she emerged with wet hair from the bathhouse, and took her off for immediate interrogation. During the interrogation, "her plait froze into an icicle."[15]

The humiliations devised by collectivizers were various, including forcing peasants to undress and to drink water from a bucket like a horse. But it is striking, as in the rumors, how important a part hair played in the humiliation game. A district agent was said to have pulled clutches of hair from peasants' beards and mocked them with the remark: "Here's some *util'syryë* (industrial scrap)—that's an export item." In an even more bizarre case that occurred during this collectivization bacchanalia, a group of Communists cut off the hair of 180 women after persuading the peasants to vote for the following resolution: That there is no point in women having long hair; the hair could be sold to buy a tractor, and then we would ride the tractor.[16]

Nakedness was a gambit that could be used by both sides. There were cases where officials used it as a means of humiliating peasants, as in the Cheliabinsk case where peasant women were forced to take off everything but their shifts for a body search in the presence of men. But from the Western oblast we have a counterexample of peasant defiance. When the authorities here were going from house to house taking precollectivization inventories of property, one peasant woman "met the inventory commission at her door completely naked, saying 'Well, take your inventory.'"[17]

In contrast to their concern over democratic forms in the gathering of signatures, officials often acted in an arbitrary manner once the signatures had been obtained, brusquely setting about the seizure of peasants' horses and cows for the kolkhoz without further consultation or warning. "I went to the [store] for kerosene, came home, and in that time they had already taken the cow," one peasant related. When peasants had put their animals under lock and key, as happened in one raion in the Urals, officials "broke the locks and led the cows away by force," although peasant women tried to hold them off "with knives and pitchforks."[18]

The manner in which animals were collected for the kolkhoz from newly collectivized households was clearly influenced by the method applied to dekulakized households, namely forcible confiscation. Seed grain was seized from individual households for the kolkhoz, despite the peasants' anguished protests, and sometimes other assets as well. In the Urals, a rural soviet chairman "took seven persons as witnesses and conducted a raid on aged women members of the commune [i.e., kolkhoz] living in one house and took 520 rubles in money and brought it into the commune writing a declaration in the name of the old women that they gave the money voluntarily."[19]

The result of all this was a high percentage of peasant houses collectivized, at least on paper, in a very short time, together with an enormous dissipation of the villages' economic assets. According to official figures, by February 20, 1930, 50 percent of all Soviet peasant households were collectivized, with the Central Black Earth oblast credited with 73–75 percent collectivization. But the peasants had started slaughtering and selling their livestock, either because they feared dekulakization if they had two horses or two cows or because they were unwilling to hand over the animals *gratis* to the kolkhoz. The slaughterhouses could not handle the increased traffic; and, although a number of organizations including the Cooperative Union and the state farms were buying from the peasants and trying to establish herds, large numbers of the animals they bought died for lack of proper care, feed, and shelter.[20]

Dekulakization

Mass expropriation of kulaks was formally carried out by commissions created under the rural soviets, headed by "officials from the raion executive committee" (presumably including an OGPU representative) and including representatives from the rural soviet, the local party organization, and the village's bedniaks and batraks.[21]

Once Stalin announced the policy of "liquidation of kulaks as a class" at a meeting with agricultural scholars in December 1929, it was not hard (at least in principle) to compile dekulakization lists. Such lists already existed in local electoral offices, for kulaks were among those deprived of the right to vote in soviet elections. But persons not on this list might also be at risk—for example, prosperous seredniaks, economically close to kulaks, or known village troublemakers in the village (especially those who made trouble about collectivization). "Kulaks and anti-Soviet elements are in a mood of panic—every hour awaiting their deportation," runs one winter report in the Smolensk Archive.[22]

The situation of a not-yet-dekulakized potential victim is vividly portrayed in this letter sent by a peasant in Novgorod province to a relative, a Moscow textile worker.

> Nastia, dear Nastia, we have very many problems and things are very bad. They took an inventory of all our property, *but did not deprive me of the vote* and I don't know if they are going to drive us out of our house or not. But they disenfranchised my brother Kolia, and on the night of March 28 somebody from the brigades drove up and took him from his house with his whole family to an unknown destination. His property and all his animals have been sequestered and we don't know where they have put them. Probably the *bednota* will take the animals. The *bednota* has tormented the whole village, they pick on whoever they choose and they are always believed. I beg you, Nastenka, couldn't you go to your boss there and find out whether such persecution of the people is the law. In one night they took away 60 families, we don't know where, so I am worried too, and if they drive me out then I and my family will have to die of hunger. . . .
>
> Please let me know as soon as you can whether I should come to petition myself or you can find out on your own. I would have come long ago *but they do not give me permission to go anywhere. They are forcing us into the kolkhoz by coercion,* but people don't want to go. Some people signed up, but then they signed out again. . . .[23]

A Politburo commission headed by V. M. Molotov drew up general guidelines for dekulakization in mid-January, including the instruction that about 60,000 kulaks should be sent to "concentration camps" and 150,000 kulak households deported to the North, Siberia, the Urals, and Kazakhstan. From then on it was up to the OGPU, which mobilized its entire apparat for the mammoth task, even calling in retired Chekists from the reserve and adding "1,000 bayonets and sabres" to its troops. According to the OGPU directive, 3–5 percent of all peasant households should be dekulakized.[24]

In Central Volga, the *kraikom* set its targets on 20 January: arrest 3,000 persons immediately, and organize a mass deportation of up to 10,000 kulak families to be conducted between February 5 and 15. (This was probably standard procedure, since the Moscow and Ivanovo authorities did likewise, though with slightly lower targets.) When the raion secretaries were called in on January 29 to receive their guidelines from the kraikom, the meeting revised the targets upwards: 5,000 kulaks should be arrested instead of 3,000, and up to 15,000 households should be deported instead of 10,000.[25] A number of regions exceeded their planned quotas, notably the Central Black Earth oblast, where an incredible 15 percent of all peasant households was dekulakized.[26]

In the Western oblast, observers reported that in many raions officials thought that the more households they dekulakized, the better, and were adding names to the list as they went along. Sometimes the names added were chosen arbitrarily, on the basis of personal spite or excessive concern about social origin. Many rural teachers were added to lists without (as was later established) due cause. There was a report from the Urals that activists in a rural factory settlement had dekulakized an old man who had been a village policemen in Tsarist times, despite the fact that he had "no land, no horse, [and] no cow." Others fell victim because they or their fathers had held local office before the revolution or under the Provisional Government.[27]

Anybody living in the same house as a kulak, even as a boarder or servant, was liable to dekulakization, or at least to share in the confiscation of all property that was part of the process. In Sverdlovsk raion, for example, Klavdiia Ushakova, daughter of an agricultural laborer, worked at a rural factory during the day, but also worked in the evenings for a kulak, Beliakov, in return for free lodging. When Beliakov was dekulakized, all Ushakova's possessions were confiscated as well.[28]

Sometimes victims were selected who seemed more likely to have been chosen for stigmatization by the village than by the Communist Party. Many unpopular village activists (teachers, former Red Army men) came into this category, as we know from their later successful appeals against dekulakization. In one village, a habitual thief ended up on the "kulak" list—just as he might have been selected by the village as an army recruit in the pre-Reform era of Tsarist Russia.[29]

The first step in dekulakization was to take an inventory of the kulaks' property. The point of this was to stop the kulaks from disposing of their property before the authorities had got round to confiscating it, but of course in many cases it simply caused the family or some of its members to make a furtive nocturnal departure from the village. The taking of an inventory caused panic and despair. For example:

> In the village of Maslovo, Rzhev district, a commission took an inventory of a 62-year-old woman, a widow, because her husband traded back in prerevolutionary times and died 25 years ago. That old women lives in poverty. Her children work as day laborers and are activists. As a result, this citizenness came

to the rural soviet in tears saying "Better to shoot me in my own home, where am I to go, I am 62 years old."[30]

Often the two processes of taking inventory and confiscation occurred simultaneously—or, in other cases, property was confiscated without any real inventory. A small group of officials from the raion or the rural soviet, with or without help from local bedniak and Komsomol activists in the village, usually constituted the dekulakization brigades. Sometimes workers from nearby towns lent a hand; and in the Western oblast, and probably elsewhere, military personnel from local garrisons were sometimes involved, although the practice was quickly repudiated by regional authorities. Even in the absence of military personnel, Komsomol dekulakizers, in particular, liked to behave as if they were on a search-and-destroy mission, going around the village flourishing rifles, "threatening people, shooting dogs."[31]

There were cases of rape and other acts of gratuitous violence. In Bashkiria, one volost party cell decided to follow "Trotsky's line" (sic) and liquidate the local kulaks in the course of five days:

> For this purpose they organized a shock group calling themselves "Red Fascists" . . . These 'Red Fascists' in fact turned into criminals, allowed outrages and drunkenness, and [personally] appropriating property of the people who were dekulakized. . . .[32]

The dekulakizers were supposed to be confiscating the kulaks' means of production and transferring it to the new collective farms as founding capital. In practice, however, they often took everything they could lay their hands on, and kept a good part for themselves. (Later, when some of the expropriations were reversed on appeal, one Communist official confessed that "We have a larger number of cases . . . when the property of incorrectly dekulakized is not fully returned only because it is in the personal possession of those who conducted the dekulakization."[33])

Sometimes there was scarcely a pretence that confiscation was anything more than sanctioned looting. In the Viazma region, "During the division of property taken from kulaks of Bukharin raion, one citizen got a bed and a sofa; he lay on the sofa and said: 'The priest used to take a nap here, now we are taking a nap.'" Personal clothing was taken, sometimes off the peasants' backs, and then worn by the dekulakizers. During a miller's dekulakization by workers from Ivanovo, his daughter's warm shirt was taken off with the words: "You've worn it long enough, now it's my turn." In the village of Kozelsk, officials conducting dekulakization wore the sheepskin jackets they had just confiscated from two kulaks. When dekulakizers found food and drink, they often consumed it on the spot. In Belyi raion, members of one brigade "took eggs and cooked themselves an omlet" while expropriating one prosperous peasant. A village brigade "dekulakizing" a priest took a quantity of honey "and at once ate it up, ate the whole thing. In general, the motto of dekulakization in [this] rural soviet was: 'Drink, eat—it's ours.'"[34]

To be sure, such behavior did not always pass unnoticed. The cases cited here were all, by definition, noticed by someone and listed as "excesses" when a halt was called in March with Stalin's "Dizzy with Success." That "someone" might be a neighbor who decided to send a denunciation to the authorities, as in the following example from the Perm region:

When . . . Ivan Andreevich Timshin was dekulakized, [those who did it] ate up his honey on the spot and put his cigarettes in their pockets. Also they did not include a silver watch in the inventory and it was put in the pocket of the policeman, Igashev. In the same way, the kulak's clock with gold trim fell to the share of comrade Ostanin, secretary of the Orda raikom. . . . [35]

While the reports of dekulakizers appropriating property for themselves are legion, there are comparatively few reports of them taking bribes and excluding someone from the list for dekulakization.[36] It seems likely, nevertheless, that some rural soviet chairmen (who had access to the dekulakization lists) gave private warnings to old friends to get out of the district quickly.

Dekulakized families were liable to deportation (out of the oblast, for first- and second-category kulaks; out of the raion, for third-category kulaks) as well as expropriation. Sometimes the deportation decision was taken with due formality, as in the rural soviet in Leningrad oblast that passed the following resolution:

As an unlawful exploiter of land, as [possessor of] a kulak farm which in pre-revolutionary days made a profit through various exploitative deals . . . , as the man who served as elder of the mir when the Whites were here, . . . in general as a socially dangerous element, to exile the kulak V. I. Egorov and his family (wife Ekaterina Vasilevna and sons Semen, Vasilii, and Ivan) beyond the limits of Novoselskii raion.[37]

But there was a lot of improvisation in dealing with expropriated kulaks, and the categories and rules on this matter were often developed after the fact. Dekulakization almost always meant immediate eviction. But what should happen after eviction was less clear. It sometimes seemed enough to the dekulakizers to take the moveable property, tear down the wallpaper and turn the kulak out on to the street. But it soon caused problems in the village when "dekulakized persons wander along the street and through the vegetable gardens, making the peasant masses nervous." In one district of the Tatar Republic, villagers were terrorized by dekulakized kulaks remaining in neighborhood, and were forced "to go to bed fully clothed and with forks in the hands" for fear of night raids. In response to this, local officials started to call for deportation of kulaks even if they were only third category. Some third-category kulaks even came close to requesting it in their despair: "On 14 February up to 20 kulaks came to the deputy prosecutor for Karachevskii raion [Western oblast] . . . with the questions 'Where are we to go, give us somewhere to live, arrest us, take our children.'"[38]

Arrest of kulaks was another means of dealing with the problem. The arrests might be conducted by raion officials, rural soviet officials, kolkhoz chairmen or anybody else working in the brigades, as well as militiamen and OGPU officers. Those arrested might be sent, often without accompanying documents or explanation, not only to the local jail or militia post but also to the raion soviet. Prosecutors worked frantically trying to reduce this chaos to quasi-legal form, so that there was at least a file for each person under arrest. "There have been cases when people have literally 'caught' the prosecutor at a meeting at 11 or 12 at night to [draw up the documents] on cases which have to be sent [to Smolensk] that same night."[39]

There were some reports that other peasants were indifferent to the kulaks' fate or even applauded it. Bedniaks were said to be the initiators of dekulakization in some cases and active participants in others. There were villages that not only passed resolutions calling for the kulaks' expropriation and deportation but also petitioned for the death penalty to be applied to them. An observer in the Western oblast saw no signs of pity for the kulaks, only occasional sympathy for their children.[40]

But there are many more reports of sympathy with the kulaks. In a few cases, whole villages petitioned for the release of their kulaks. The OGPU reported that in one village a majority of peasants voted against exile for the local kulaks "since they had not been ill-treated by them." In another village, bedniaks "passed a resolution 'to reestablish the rights of the liquidated kulaks.'" A kolkhoz in Moscow oblast refused to accept the property of the dekulakized peasants, explaining that "they didn't want things that were not theirs and not won by their own labor." "Who are these kulak exploiters?" wrote a peasant to a local newspaper early in 1930. "We have none like that in the village any more, only honest toilers and otkhodniks who have struggled to improve their farms and situation."[41]

Sometimes villagers put up active resistance to the kulak deportations. In Vikulovskii raion in the Urals, a crowd gathered as the kulaks were being deported and shouted "We won't let you deport the kulaks, down with the Communists, beat them the dogs." Having freed one kulak, the crowd set off to take revenge for the arrests on the rural soviet chairman, but he had prudently gone into hiding.[42]

More often, villagers wept as the kulaks were taken away. "In Briansk okrug when an echelon with 200 exiled kulaks, including priests, went through Bolva station, the priests sang a religious funeral song 'On the sea wave,' which called forth pity in the watchers gathered at the station, some of whom wept. . . ." At a village gathering in Manuilovo, young kulaks played such plaintive songs on the accordion that they "forced all the young people to weep." In another village, bedniaks organized a formal farewell for the kulak going into exile. Ceremonial public farewells (*provody*) accompanied by vodka, comparable to those held in earlier times on the departure of Army recruits, were also reported in the Urals.[43]

Many peasants clearly saw dekulakization as part of a broader assault on the village. "By arrests and deportations of kulaks, the Communists are trying to scare the rest, so that . . . all the peasants join collective farms." Many said that once the kulaks had been disposed of, it would be the turn of the middle peasants or the whole peasant community.[44]

The Drive Against Religion

The antireligious campaign had reached the villages in some places even before the New Year, especially in regions adjacent to cities. There were a number of reports of churches being closed or taken over for "temporary grain storage" after the 1929 harvest. In a factory village in Vladimir oblast, "the lads" organized an anti-Christmas carnival procession through the village at the end of the year, and then gathered on the porch of a church, where a service was in progress, and started to pound on the door with rocks.[45]

But the campaign against religion in the countryside really got into its stride in January 1930, with dekulakization and the collectivization drive. It was unclear who, if anyone gave the order for this campaign; clearly a great deal of what happened was the result of local initiative. As one provincial observer put it, "Our Kaluga was announced to be a district of total (*sploshnaia*) collectivization, and total closing of churches began."[46]

In the closing of churches, as in the signing up of villagers for kolkhoz membership, Communists generally insisted on preserving democratic forms. It was important that the local population should pass a resolution asking that the church be closed. But such a resolution was even more difficult to get by fair means than the resolution in favor of collectivization, so the means by which it was often obtained were often foul. In one village in the Urals, for example, collectivizers tried without success to get the village meeting to agree to the closing of the church. Then they tried a new tack.

> The zealous organizers went round house by house to ask each household separately, and by dint of threatening to levy enormous taxes for the church forced everyone to sign. At the same time, they evicted the church *starosta* (elder) and confiscated everything he owned. Local hooligans broke 17 windows in the church, and when the church people came to the soviet to complain they answered: "You have a God, complain to him, let him look after you, but we will charge you for those broken windows. The next day . . . hooligans broke several more windows. And they turned the priests into martyrs. They took the cross from the local priest, and called the religious women into the soviet, threatened them with taxes. . . .[47]

Priests were widely treated as the equivalents of kulaks, as were rabbis, pastors, mullahs, and other ministers of religion; and many were arrested, "dekulakized," and deported along with the kulaks in the first months of 1930. An activist in the Militant Godless League complained that the collectivization brigades were not consulting his organization: "They make completely unwarranted arrests and deportations [of priests], and then send us in: 'Go and calm down the masses that have been upset by our actions.'" Some priests were also roughed up by local hooligans, as in the case in the Urals when "three hooligans burst into the house of the local priest at 12

o'clock at night, and under the pretext of the struggle against religion conducted a pogrom in the residence, beating up the priest and his wife."[48]

The result of all this was widespread closure of a substantial proportion—perhaps even the majority—of working churches in rural areas in just
a few weeks at the height of the dekulakization and collectivization drives.
For example, Spas Demensk raion of the Western oblast, with a population
of about 50,000, had eleven churches. All but two closed at this time; and a
report a few months later indicated that even in the two remaining churches
services could not be held because the priests were gone and church property had been confiscated.[49]

The League of the Godless (*bezbozhniki*) had little to do with starting
the antireligious movement. While its leaders were in some ways exhilarated
by seeing a mass movement take off so unexpectedly, they were also alarmed.
At the end of January, the leaders were already expressing concern at the lack
of preparation and tact shown in the closing of churches and taking down of
church bells, the adverse impact on tempos of collectivization, and, of course,
the fact that it was all happening without any direction from the league. At a
meeting of the league in March, Iaroslavskii stated that "Before us, staring
us in the face, is an enormous antireligious movement coming from below.
We must say straight out that in an organizational sense we do not encom-
pass that movement. . . . For example, the closing of churches and the taking
down of churchbells happened without any participation of the League of
the Militant Godless."[50]

Most observers pointed to Komsomol activists as the most frequent initiators of such actions. The reports usually do not indicate clearly whether
the young men involved were local or came from outside the village; but
some were certainly outsiders, sent out to the countryside by their Komsomol
groups in the town to help with collectivization. The carnivalesque fervor
with which they launched their attacks on the churches, the zest with which
they committed acts of sacrilege and blasphemy, and the outrage with which
these were greeted by older villagers constitute one of the most dramatic
episodes of the whole collectivization process.

In the village of Novouspenskoe in the Western oblast, a Komsomol
member named Vasilii Smirnov, his brother Sergei, and cronies in various
stages of intoxication turned the closing of the local church into an im-
promptu theatrical performance. Smirnov and his friends took the key from
the church watchman on the pretext that they had to make an inventory of
property in the church.

> "Arriving at the church, the Smirnovs and Bokov lighted candles, dressed up in
> priests' vestments and held dances in the church. When they came out on to the
> street, they wandered through the village in priests' vestments with a lighted
> censer in their hands, accompanied by the sound of church bells. Smirnov said:
> 'Let them consider us hooligans, but the priests have gone round doing this for
> three hundred years and nothing happened to them, so we have acted com-
> pletely correctly.'" The group then went down to the basement of the church,
> where they noticed the tombs of the old landowning family of the locality, the

Zhidkovs, and broke them open. "Observing that the deceased had been embalmed, they lifted the [corpse of the] wife of the former estate-owner out of the coffin and made it stand up, and moreover poked it in the stomach with a stick. . . ."[51]

After they had finished with the Zhidkovs, the Smirnov brothers organized a dance for young villagers in the church; and there were similar reports from other villages in the Western oblast whose churches were closed. In one case, a report noted that the young people of the village had voted to close the church and hold a dance in the building, but among the older peasants "some women wept at such an event." In a village in Kursk oblast, the secretary of the raion soviet closed the church and seized all its valuables, and then "dressed up the horses in crowns and vestments and in this manner rode with the kolkhozniks to the [raion soviet] and held a meeting."[52]

The public destruction of icons, church plate, and other valuables taken from the church was a specialty of Komsomol brigades. Icons were often thrown on a bonfire in the village square and burned, à la Gorlovka. One case was cited where the Komsomols took the icons to the local fair and set up a mock execution, shooting at the icons and then hanging labels on them announcing that "We, the *udarnik* (shockworker) brigade, shot such and such a saint for such and such an offense." In another similar case, the saints portrayed in the confiscated icons were formally sentenced to death by the firing squad "for opposition to kolkhoz construction"—then the sentence was carried out by shooting the icons.[53]

Many collectivizers took the attitude that once peasants had joined the kolkhoz, they were not allowed to keep icons in their houses, or go to church. The new kolkhozniks were often ordered to bring the icons from their houses and hand them over. Sometimes they were publicly burnt in the village square, sometimes broken up so that the silver icon covers could be taken "for the industrialization drive."[54] In one village, a member of the Young Pioneers, the Soviet youth organization for the under-fifteen age group, proposed at a village meeting that all inhabitants of the village including the local priest should give up their icons. Eight cartloads of icons were accordingly collected, and later thrown on a bonfire in the market square on market day. This caused great outrage in the village. At a subsequent village assembly, when one peasant "expressed the thought that we are for God," he received "thunderous applause."[55]

The effect of all this was to produce an unprecedented level of demonstrative peasant support for the churches and their priests and to add a powerful symbolic dimension to the peasants' resistance to collectivization. Peasant women, accompanied by the priest, often followed the collectivizers around the village wailing and weeping and sometimes chanting parts of the Orthodox liturgy. In Spas Demensk raion, in protest against the closing of churches, "a group of perhaps 300 women organized a procession singing 'Christ is Risen.'"[56]

After watching Komsomol members parade around the village wearing the vestments of a priest they had just dekulakized, peasants who had signed up for the kolkhoz often tried to withdraw their signatures. In the village of Karel, where all the peasants had joined the kolkhoz, everything fell apart when a Komsomol teacher made a speech calling for the closing of the church: "The women gathered, and the speaker barely escaped lynching (*samosud*)." In another village, the priest was arrested during the organization of the kolkhoz and the whole process was disrupted by protests: "The women gathered and started shouting. They broke up the [collectivization] meeting, crying: 'We will not go away until you give up the priest.' And they had to let the priest go."[57]

In one village in the Western oblast, all 200 households resigned from the kolkhoz after local activists took down the icons in the church and "chopped them up on the spot with an axe in order to separate out the metal parts for recycling." In the Central Volga region, indignation about the drive against religion led to "openly anti-Soviet demonstrations" in many regions. In Siberia, where 90 percent of church bells were taken down and 250 churches closed in the first quarter of 1930, a member of the local branch of the Militant Godless reported that "a savage class war" had erupted over the issue of religion. But even the Godless had become frightened by their temerity. The same reporter noted that no sooner were churches closed down than "church candles light up of their own accord, you can hear the chanting of prayers at night, and even Communists are afraid to go past those churches."[58]

Struggle

The collectivization drive of the winter of 1930 was the beginning of a bitter struggle between the state and the peasants that lasted more than three years. Violent resistance was not the peasants' typical weapon, especially in central Russia. Passive resistance was the dominant form, but it was passive resistance carried to a high degree—including refusal to sow, which jeopardized the peasants' survival as well as the success of the state's plans. The regime's first response to peasant resistance was conciliatory ("Dizzy with Success," March 1930). But it did not abandon the objective of collectivization, and soon reverted to policies of harsh repression and economic extortion. By the end of 1932, peasant agriculture was more than 60 percent collectivized—and the grain-producing areas of the country were on the verge of a famine that marked the climax of the struggle over collectivization.

Dizzy with Success

At the beginning of March 1930, Stalin published an article entitled "Dizzy with Success," which denounced the "excesses" of local officials and their violation of the voluntary principle of collectivization, especially in areas of non-Russian population in the Soviet Union (that is, the peripheries were most of the violent resistance was concentrated). Stalin said that some regional authorities had widely forced the pace of collectivization. They had compelled peasants to join instead of persuading them, and in collectivizing all the peasants' property including cows, pigs, and chickens, they had gone too far. In fact, Stalin stated, the fully collectivized *kommuna* was not the right form of the kolkhoz to aim for. The objective should be the artel form, where peasants kept a cow, a vegetable plot, and small animals for their own household purposes.[59]

Stalin did not publicly repudiate the antireligious campaign, though he made a contemptuous reference to "'revolutionaries' who *begin* the business of organizing the [kolkhoz] by taking down the bells from the churches." But a directive went out from the Central Committee at about the same time condemning the forcible closing of churches without the consent of the population, which "pours water into the mill of counterrevolutionaries and has nothing in common with the policy of our party."[60]

The reason for this abrupt retreat seems to have been that the party leaders panicked in February when they heard news of the angry reactions of peasants in a number of areas including Ukraine, Kazakhstan, Siberia, and the Central Black Earth oblast. The situation looked extremely dangerous, they explained a few months later in a secret letter to regional party organizations.

> If measures had not been taken immediately against distortions of the party line, we would now have a broad wave of insurrectionist peasant uprisings, a good half of our "grass-roots" cadres would have been slaughtered by the peasants, the sowing would have been ruined, kolkhoz construction would have been destroyed, and our internal and external security would have been threatened.[61]

If this in retrospect looks like an exaggeration of the danger, it was an understandable one. The party leaders had a lot of explaining to do to local party organizations, having made them the scapegoat for failures that were in large part the leadership's own responsibility. "Dizzy with Success" was a blatant betrayal of local Communist cadres, and many reacted angrily. The article "simply dumbfounded local workers," reported an observer in the Western oblast. "Some of them to this day still assert that the article of Stalin appeared at the wrong time, that is, they say 'Everything was going well, then Stalin's article came out and spoiled everything.'" After reading Stalin's article, one party secretary in the Volga region "went out on a drinking bout 'from grief' and in his distress tore up comrade Stalin's portrait."[62]

Peasants, of course, reacted to "Dizzy with Success" in a different way. For many of them, it was a green light for withdrawing from the kolkhoz. In the next few weeks, literally millions of peasants withdrew their signatures from the list of kolkhoz members: Overnight, villages that had been "90 percent collectivized" on paper became ordinary villages again, although with a considerably reduced number of draught and domestic animals. Nationally, the proportion of peasant households registered as collectivized dropped from 57 percent on March 1 to 28 percent two months later; in the Central Black Earth oblast, the drop was from 83 percent to 18 percent.[63]

Departure from the kolkhoz turned out to be not such a simple matter, however. The first problem was recovery of the peasants' animals, if they had been taken by the kolkhoz. Confiscation of property was often in practice ir-reversible. In some cases, collectivized animals had died of neglect or been sold; in others, the kolkhoz or individual in whose charge they were was unwilling to return them. As one Communist district official said plaintively at a local party conference, "we recognize that we committed excesses, we say unanimously that we recognize the mistakes, but that doesn't change the fact for a muzhik who had a foal and a horse, that we sold the foal" and there was no getting it back.[64] In addition, a great many animals had been slaughtered by the peasants themselves, in protest against collectivization; and a peasant without a horse or a cow was unlikely to survive as an independent farmer.

The second problem for the peasant who had joined and then quit the kolkhoz was recovering his land. The mir had collapsed under the impact of collectivization and could no longer adjudicate questions of land allocation. It was now up to the local rural soviet or the kolkhoz itself—the power of the two institutions and their relationship with each other was still unclear—to decide which part of the village land should constitute a peasant's allot-ment. But of course the kolkhoz was interested in keeping the best part of the village lands for itself. Peasants who withdrew were not able simply to reclaim the strips or blocks of land they had previously cultivated. They got a new allocation, generally worse than the old one, and in many cases with such delay that in practice it proved virtually impossible to resign from the kolkhoz before the 1930 spring sowing. Often they were deprived of access to pastureland and water by the kolkhoz.[65]

It soon became clear that the state would not willingly accept peasants' withdrawal from the kolkhoz, despite "Dizzy with Success," and that the proclaimed voluntary principle was largely fraudulent. On a tour of inspec-tion of the southern grain-producing regions at the end of March, Molotov told the North Caucasus kraikom that it was quite appropriate to prevent peasants from leaving the kolkhoz until the spring sowing had been com-pleted. Of course, this contradicted the Central Committee's endorsement of the voluntary principle to some extent, Molotov acknowledged, but the party's tactics were "to maneuver" so as to consolidate the kolkhoz and, above all, establish its status as the new "master" in the village by planting as much as possible of the village lands.[66]

The regime's real intentions were also revealed in the continuing expro-priations, arrests, and deportations of kulaks. Stalin's discussion of "ex-cesses" in March had not included any comment on dekulakization. He did mention a few months later that it was wrong to expropriate seredniaks, but his stance on kulaks remained immovable: "We have put up with these bloodsuckers, spiders, and vampires long enough," he told kolkhozniks on April 25. In the spring of 1931, there was a new wave of dekulakization throughout the country, even larger than the one the previous year. The vil-lages of the agriculturally poor non-Black Earth belt, which had hitherto often escaped dekulakization (perhaps because there were no real kulaks to expropriate), now found it was their turn; and the grain-growing regions that had suffered most the first time got a second dose.[67]

All this had the desired effect. Only 26 percent of peasant households participated as kolkhoz members in the spring sowing of 1930, and the number of households collectivized rose only gradually through the year. But between January and March 1931—the time of the second wave of dekulakizations—the figures rose sharply from under 30 percent to 42 percent. Over half the peasant households of the Soviet Union were collectivized by the end of the 1931 sowing, and more than 60 percent by the end of the harvest season.[68]

Peasant Resistance

While many peasant disturbances (*volneniia*) were reported in response to collectivization in the first months of 1930, the worst violence occurred in regions on the periphery such as Kazakhstan, Siberia, the mountainous regions of the North Caucasus, and Cossack areas in the south of Russia and the Ukraine. In the central Russian provinces disturbances were mainly on a relatively small scale. In the Tambov area, there were some armed uprisings by bands of "former Antonovites," that is, person who had participated in the 1921 revolt in that area. But this was not the norm in European Russia. Most of the reported disturbances were short-lived affairs in which local peasants—sometimes as many as a few hundred, sometimes a smaller number—gathered outside the rural soviet or the raion center to protest specific acts such as church closings or dekulakizations.[69]

One of the most boisterous of these events took place in a village in the Astrakhan region on February 22. A drunken crowd of several hundred people, armed with clubs, pitchforks and axes, and urged on by the ringing of the church bells, laid siege to the building of the rural soviet building, where members of the dekulakization commission had barricaded themselves in. Six Communists were killed or wounded in the ensuing mêlée. In a village in the Briansk region, three or four hundred peasants attacked the Komsomol activists who were taking down the church bells, beat them, and drove them out of the village. When district and regional officials came to the village to investigate, the crowd attacked them with staves and pitchforks.[70]

Women were often prominent in the demonstrations against collectivization. The party leaders seem to have been worried about this, particularly in connection with the wave of "women's revolts" (*bab'i bunty*) in the North Caucasus in February; but it is not clear that they were right in concluding that women were more hostile to collectivization than their menfolk. Vociferous protests by women often seemed to be an expression of the general feelings of the village community—but a form of expression that was less likely than others to provoke the authorities into violent punitive responses. The men agreed with their wives about the kolkhoz, one observer concluded;

they just thought it was safer to stay in the background while their wives did the protesting ("Make a fuss, Matrena, nothing will happen to you."). Officials were unlikely to arrest women, even when fifty of them broke up a meeting by shouting: "Down with the collective farms! Give the speaker a thrashing! Bring back the Tsar!" Old women, in particular, could take outrageous liberties, like the seventy-year-old who disrupted the skhod when she "came forward and began to dance and sing anti-kolkhoz chastushki."[71]

Innumerable individual acts of violence were committed against collectivizers who were caught alone. There were many incidents when a peasant or group of peasants lay in wait for a "25,000-er" on a dark night, set fire to the kolkhoz chairman's izba, or hid behind the barn to take a potshot at a soviet official. In a Siberian village, peasants savagely attacked a teacher who was a Soviet activist, "hit[ting] him several times with axes and saying as they did so: 'Take this for grain, take this for the church, take this for the commune (*kommuniia*).'" Sometimes women also attacked collectivizers, although, unlike men, they rarely acted alone. In the Western oblast, women "seized the chairman of the rural soviet and dropped snow into his pants." In Dagestan, "an enraged crowd of women cry[ing] 'Down with the kolkhoz' . . . attacked the agronomist and beat him up" and then went on to wreak havoc in the office of the soviet.[72]

Slaughter of livestock by peasants was one of the most widespread forms of protest, devastating in its economic consequences. In the Central Black Earth oblast, 25 percent of cattle, 53 percent of pigs, 55 percent of sheep, and 40 percent of chickens were slaughtered in the first three months of 1930. When they could, peasants were getting a cash return for their livestock: State slaughterhouse and procurements agencies for meat and hides had more traffic than they could handle all over Russia; and in the North Caucasus, where the insurance payment for the loss of a horse exceeded the market price, many were slaughtering and collecting insurance. But there is no doubt that a lot of the slaughter was pure protest, accompanied by wild days of feasting as a kind of farewell to the old life. When asked why they had slaughtered a horse or a cow, the peasants had two standard explanations that were surely examples of peasant cunning rather than (as officials often thought) peasant naiveté: "The state will give us everything we need, now that we are kolkhozniks," and "There will be no need for draft animals on the kolkhoz—we will have tractors."[73]

Other forms of resistance were passive. Even in these first months of collectivization, the peasants were showing the apathy, inertia, and spirit of dependency that were to be so evident in subsequent decades of Soviet collective farming. A Moscow official returning from an inspection tour of the provinces in March was struck by the peasants' apparent expectation that in the kolkhoz everything would be done for them. They were besieging the kolkhoz chairmen, he said, with insistent requests for flour, milk, boots, and other commodities. In one kolkhoz, a chairmen who was being mercilessly harrassed by kolkhozniks demanding that he give them milk and butter "jumped out the window and ran away."[74]

In his memoirs, General Grigorenko (himself of peasant origin) provides an interesting description of a Ukrainian steppe village, Arkhangelka, that he visited as a party organizer in summer of 1930. Although it was the height of the harvest season, the village seemed dead.

> Eight men worked one thresher for one shift daily. The remaining workers—men, women, and young people—sat around or lay in the shade. When I tried to start conversations people replied slowly and with total indifference.
>
> If I told them that the grain was falling from the wheat stalks and perishing, they would reply, "Of course, it will perish." . . . The people were so repulsed by the forced collectivization of farms that they were consumed by apathy.[75]

Many peasants expressed resistance to collectivization by lodging legal appeals and writing petitions. Mainly they wrote to the oblast centers or to Moscow, since they assumed that they were unlikely to get justice at the raion level. An enormous number of complaints and appeals were lodged by peasants against actions of the collectivization and dekulakization brigades. The greatest number were complaints against dekulakization. In Siberia, for example, more than 35,000 petitions protesting against unjustified dekulak-ization or deprivation of voting rights had been submitted by June 1, 1930, and almost 50 percent were found to be justified. In the Central Black Earth oblast, according to incomplete data, state prosecutors upheld more than 30,000 similar petititions from seredniak households protesting that they had been unjustly dekulakized.[76]

The Rumor Mill

Peasant rumor firmly labelled collectivization as "a second serfdom." But the rumors were rarely a direct incitement to revolt; more typically, they dwelt on the possibility of war, relayed news about international condemna-tion of the antireligious campaign and collectivization, and held out the hope that foreigners would miraculously come to the rescue of the insulted and injured Russian peasantry. "In the spring there will be war." "Soon there will be war. The peasants do not want to fight and will not fight, the Red Army men will refuse to go into the trenches, and then Soviet power will fall." There will be "a massacre of Communists when Soviet power falls, like that of St. Bartholomew's Night."[77]

These rumors were clearly derived from the peasants' reading and rein-terpretation of Soviet newspapers. The threat of foreign attack had been a more or less constant theme in the newspapers ever since the 1927 war scare. More recently, the Soviet press had given sarcastic but basically accurate coverage of critical international reactions to the Mennonite affair (Soviet obstruction of the German colonists' desire to emigrate, partly in protest against collectivization); and they also reported the Pope's strongly phrased appeal for an end to religious persecution in the Soviet Union in January 1930.

In the rumors in the villages of the Western oblast, with a relatively significant Catholic minority, the Pope was a heroic figure and potential savior. "The Pope of Rome has interceded for us"; "The Pope of Rome has announced war against the Bolsheviks." Similar rumors circulated in other parts of the country for more than a year after the Pope's appeal. In the southern Urals, Orthodox peasants were saying in the spring of 1931 "that the Roman Pope defends believers, demanding in return from them that they give the strongest rebuff to the kolkhoz movement." In a village in Moscow oblast, only 40 kilometers from the industrial center of Orekhovo-Zuevo, peasants said that "The troops of the Roman Pope are marching in Moscow to the sound of drum-beats."[78]

If rescue did not come from the Pope, perhaps other members of the international community would intervene. "The whole world is for us," "The whole world is against Soviet power," said the more optimistic peasants. There were "stubborn rumors" in the Western oblast that an English ship had rescued hundreds of people who had been banished to Solovki as class enemies "as an act of mercy to those insulted by fate in the USSR." In the Don Cossack region, a priest reassured his congregation that "the Christ-loving military forces will attack from America." In the Urals, there was even a rumor that the *workers* of America (a frequent subject of discussion in Soviet newspapers), had heard "the wails of the injured peasantry" and written to Stalin expressing indignation at collectivization and the closing of churches.[79]

There was a flurry of rumors concerning the Soviet campaign to collect metal and other scrap (called *util'syryë*, a grating Soviet neologism) for industrial and export purposes. Even by Soviet standards, this campaign was bizarre. In 1929-30, a real obsession with recycling seemed to grip schools, youth groups, and voluntary societies, all of whom were competing to bring in record-breaking hauls of scrap. The League of Militant Atheists, for example, sent its members a list of recyclable materials to gather that included tin cans, old shoes, cherry pits, corks, rope, scraps of rubber, and human hair. Collectivizers who took down church bells or broke up icons often justified it in terms of the recycling campaign ("Metal for the industrialization drive!").[80]

Violation, dehumanization, and exploitation were the dominant emotions associated with the rumors about *util'syryë*. Apart from the melting down of church bells and icon covers, hair was the most popular subject of rumors. It was said that women's plaits were to be cut off for scrap and exported to China; that the beards of Old Believers would be cut off and "sent abroad in exchange for tractors."[81] In a particularly strange twist, the *util'syryë* metaphor seems to have appealed to the violators as well as the violated: As noted earlier in this chapter, there were occasions when collectivizers really did cut off plaits "to buy a tractor" or pull clumps of hair out of beards "for recycling".

The idea of collectivization as a second serfdom was a staple of rumors in the early 1930s. "A man who joins the kolkhoz goes into slavery, as under serfdom." The initials VKP, a common way of referring to the Soviet Communist Party (*Vsesoiuznaia kommunisticheskaia partiia*), really stood for "the second serfdom" (*vtoroe krepostnoe pravo*). The legal term for serfdom, *krepostnoe pravo*, was sometimes used, as in the two examples above, but more often peasants talked about collectivization as a reimposition of barshchina, the serf's labor obligation to his master. "They are driving people forcibly into the collective farms and introducing barshchina"; "In the kolkhoz there will be barshchina; 25,000 workers are coming as masters."[82]

The themes and judgements of the rumors were echoed in angry letters against collectivization that peasants in the Western oblast sent to newspapers and Soviet institutions. "It is hard for the 'dark peasant' to understand what is going on in the countryside now," wrote Prokofii Maksimovich Kiselev, of the village of Zavidovka. Take the new labor obligations (*guzhpovinnost'*), for example. "One may think either that it is forced labor for the peasant because he lives under Soviet power, because they ride on the muzhik's back now as they rode on him before. Or it is that the old serfdom is still alive and kicking[?]." "The kolkhoz is just like barshchina," wrote another peasant. "It lacks only the whip."[83]

It is not true that peasants are joining the kolkhoz voluntarily, wrote Ivan Chugunkov, a bedniak. "You are driving them into the kolkhoz by force. For example I will take my own Iushkovskii rural soviet: a brigade of Red Army men came in, that brigade seized control of all populated centers, and you think that they organized a kolkhoz, no they didn't, the batrak and bedniak spoke against that enterprise and said we don't want barshchina, we don't want serfdom."[84]

The collectivization idea is no good, wrote Ignat Rubtsov of the village of Bordashevka. The supposed "bedniak aktiv" is just "half a dozen ne'er-do-wells and drunkards capable of anything." Anyone who worked hard is now a kulak, wrote another peasant, "but those who got drunk and wandered around idly [are] in power [and] take the last thread from him for the kolkhoz."[85] It would be better to drop the whole stupid idea of collectivization, wrote a peasant writing anonymously. Things are ten times worse than they were under the tsar—better to give the peasants free trade and give them shoes, and "let the young people have their fun (*guliane*), why have you shut us up in the village, you can't even go to the village, we are sitting like wild goats in a cage."[86]

Famine

The famine of 1932–33 was an outcome of the regime's struggle with the peasantry over the compulsory grain procurements quotas associated with collectivization. This was not only the way it looks to most historians but also the way it looked to the peasants, who blamed the Soviet government for this famine even more strongly than they had blamed it for the Volga famine of 1921–22 (in connection with requisitions) or blamed its Imperial predecessor for the famine of 1891 (in connection with high taxes and grain exports). While the 1932–33 famine was an egregious case, some degree of government responsibility—and popular perception of government responsibility—are more the norm than the exception in the modern history of famine. As Amartya Sen has pointed out, famines are rarely the result of droughts or ruined harvests alone, and they rarely occur because of an absolute deficit of food supplies in the country.[87]

The section that follows deals mainly with three aspects of the 1932–33 famine. The first is the struggle over procurements and its connection with peasant resistance to collectivization. The second is the way that struggle was represented and interpreted by peasants, on the one hand, and the regime, on the other. The third is the savage repression of the peasantry in the first months of 1933, when the famine was at its height.[88]

Struggle Over Procurements

One way of explaining the famine is to say that the regime put the compulsory grain procurements quotas too high. But this begs the question of what the "real" ceiling for grain procurements and how it could be known. The 1932 harvest was only the third since collectivization, and the state was still trying to find out just how much it could extract from the peasants under the new order. The peasants, for their part, were doing their best to find out what was the lowest level of deliveries they could get away with—if necessary, by lowering total production.

When the government set procurements quotas, the guesswork started with the size of the future harvest. But that was only the beginning. Once the year's quotas were announced, the standard response—starting with the peasants at kolkhoz level, but going upwards through the administrative hierarchy from rural soviet to raion to oblast and even republic—was an attempt to haggle. Each kolkhoz, raion, and oblast was likely to try to show that for a series of objective reasons, its particular quota was impossible to meet. Furthermore, each kolkhoz, raion, and oblast knew that to meet the quotas fully and in timely and efficient fashion this year would only mean that next year the quotas would be larger—or even that the state would come back for an additional collection from this year's harvest.

Peasants habitually exaggerated local difficulties and underestimated the crop. Raion officials knew this, and always dismissed such arguments when talking to kolkhoz chairmen. When they were talking to the oblast, however, they were likely to use the same arguments as the peasants had used to them. Oblast officials in turn would brusquely reject the raions' hard-luck stories, and then turn around and incorporate them in their reports to the republic and to Moscow. Even dedicated Communist administrators were not immune from this inexorable logic. Its operation was inhibited to some extent by the exceptionally harsh measures of coercion, including summary arrest, that superior bodies exerted over inferior ones. But state coercion was not a reliable method of finding out how much grain the kolkhoz, raion, or oblast actually could deliver. Once coercion reached a certain level, it was likely to block the transmission of reliable information from the localities up to Moscow, and thus prevent the government making informed decisions.[89]

From the standpoint of both peasants and the state, the new procurements routine had strong similarities with the traditional taxation ritual. In every village, the tax collector would be told the peasants' standard tale of woe: The crops were blighted, the animals were stricken with disease, the men were absent on otkhod, fires had destroyed barns and izbas, and so on. The official would recognize this as the standard story. At the same time, some of it was probably true. His job was to work out how the village stood in relation to others, and how much it could really afford to pay.

Nevertheless, procurements in the early 1930s had some characteristics that set it apart from normal negotiation routines. In the first place, it was a new practice. There was no backlog of experience to draw on. Moscow and its agents were more likely to misjudge the situation.

In the second place, Moscow was more likely than usual to make irrational judgements because of the pressures of the First Five-Year Plan. On the one hand, the leaders were deeply convinced of the need to maximize procurements and grain exports in order to meet industry's needs. On the other hand, they had developed the habit during the First Five-Year Plan of announcing targets for economic output that were wildly unrealistic. This was no doubt an unfortunate habit even with regard to industry, but it was not potentially fatal, as it was in agriculture. If industrial targets were too high, workers still got wages and rations. If procurements quotas were too high, and ruthlessly enforced, peasants could be left without the food needed to survive the winter or the seed grain needed for the spring planting.

A third distinguishing characteristic of procurements in the early 1930s was that the peasants were angry about collectivization. This expressed itself in a general unwillingness to work on the kolkhoz—what a leader of the Siberian party organization, Sergei Syrtsov, called "the production apathy and production nihilism which appeared in a considerable proportion of the peasantry when they entered the collective farms"—and a specific unwillingness to sow, as long as most of the harvest was to be taken away in state procurements. "They will take the grain anyway," peasants in the Dnepropetrovsk region said in the spring of 1933, refusing to begin sowing even when they had been given an emergency allocation of seed grain. The annual "sowing campaigns" of the early 1930s were tussles between the state, determined to keep up the acreage sown on the kolkhozy and ensure that the crops sown corresponded to the state's procurements need, and the peasants, determined to reduce the acreage devoted to "procurements" crops even if they risked going hungry by doing so.[90]

As had been the case with requisitions during the Civil War, the procurements struggle was most bitter and desperate in the country's major grain-growing regions: Ukraine, the Northern Caucasus, the Central Volga area, and Russia's Central agricultural region, including Tambov and Voronezh oblasts. These same regions, together with Kazakhstan, were the ones hit by famine in 1932–33. The non-Black Earth regions of the north and west had less bitter procurements struggles and did not experience famine in that year.

After a surprisingly successful harvest in 1930, the state raised the level of procurements. But the harvest of 1931 was not as good, especially in Ukraine, which fell far below its quotas for grain delivery. The proportion of the gross yield collected in state procurements was 33 percent in 1931, compared to 27 percent in 1930. In the North Caucasus, a rich agricultural marketing area, the state took 63 percent of the harvest in 1931, compared to 46 percent in 1930.[91] As a result of the poor harvest, and high procurements, the collective farms had very little grain to distribute among kolkhoz members. (The procurements procedures that the state was trying to establish at this time allowed the kolkhoz to take an "advance" of 10–15 percent of the crop for distribution to members immediately at harvest time, then meet its state obligations, and then set aside seed grain. Only after these requirements had been met could the kolkhoz pay its members the remainder of what they were owed in kind for their work during the year. But in the early 1930s, there was often nothing left to distribute, and a share of the 10–15 percent "advance" was all the kolkhoz households ever got.)

This rate of procurements inflicted great hardship on the peasants in many regions, and was universally perceived by them as unjust and extortionate. Not only was the state taking far more of their grain than was considered a marketable surplus in peasant eyes, it was also paying extremely little for what it took. In 1931, state procurements organizations were paying the collective farms five or six rubles per centner (100 kilograms) of rye and seven or eight rubles per centner of wheat, which a Soviet historian describes as well below the cost of production.[92]

Peasants responded to this situation in a number of ways. Some despaired of the kolkhoz and went off on otkhod; others wrote complaints to Stalin;[93] and a large number began pilfering from the kolkhoz. In the spring, groups of kolkhozniks in Western Siberia attacked the kolkhoz barns where the seed grain was stored and seized cows and horses from the collectivized herd. As the crop ripened in the summer of 1932, raids on the kolkhoz fields and group thefts of grain became common in many parts of the country. There were even reports of the holding of village meetings at which the assembled peasants was decided to take the grain before the state could get it. Sometimes the raids were done by "bandits" and "kulaks"— that is, peasants outside the collective farms—but on many occasions they were carried out by the kolkhozniks themselves, who were "stealing" their own crop to prevent the state from stealing it via procurements.[94]

In some places, the peasants were stealing primarily out of hunger; in others, anger appears to have been a major element. There was a wave of stealing other types of kolkhoz property—"spades, wheels, anything"—that sometimes was evidently motivated purely by spite, since the stolen items were found nearby, broken and discarded. In the Central Black Earth oblast in the spring and summer of 1933, there was such an epidemic of theft that kolkhozniks were afraid to leave their izbas unguarded to go out and work in the fields.[95]

The state's response to stealing in the kolkhoz—was the law of August 7, 1932 (Stalin's own work, it is said), a resounding declaration that the kolkhoz crop and everything else belonging to the kolkhoz was state property, "sacred and untouchable," and those who stole it, including kolkhozniks, would pay dearly. The law stated that those who "make attacks on public property [including kolkhoz property] must be regarded as enemies of the people." Persons guilty of stealing grain from the barns, ears of grain from the fields, and cattle were to be sentenced to death by shooting, and all their possessions were to be confiscated.[96]

Peasants were the main objects of prosecution under the law of August 7. In the first quarter of 1933, three out of five of those convicted under the new law were kolkhoz members. The victims included such petty offenders as the adults and children who crept out into the fields before harvesting with scissors and knives and cut the ears of grain, the old kolkhoz watchman who pulled up three potato tubers after going hungry for three days, and the kolkhoznitsa who stole 3 puds of wheat from the kolkhoz storeroom and was sent off for ten years, leaving her three small children "in grave material difficulties." The law of August 7 put considerable emphasis on kulaks as the source of the major threat to socialist property, but peasants had their own interpretation of what it meant. "Now they've got round to the bedniaks and seredniaks," was what they were saying in the villages about the law.[97]

The peasants' mood during the harvest was ugly and desperate. So was the mood of Communists—both those in Moscow, who were bombarding local officials with orders to get procurements quotas in at any price, and those out in the grain-growing regions, who saw or feared what this might mean. On both sides, a confrontational stance hardened.

Kolkhozniks talked about refusing to deliver procurements. There were reports from Ukraine and the Northern Caucasus that "many kolkhozniks spoke at meetings against the grain procurements plans that had been handed to them and refused to go out to work". Officials reported that, despite their hunger, the peasants were harvesting with the same lethargy as they had sown in the spring. At the "Molotov" kolkhoz in the Central Volga, for example, where the sowing had gone on for forty-two days, the harvest also dragged on "into the depths of autumn" and a lot of the crop was lost. Although the state took enormous precautions to prevent the stealing and hiding of grain at all points of the process from standing in the field through harvesting and threshing, the peasants continued to steal, and tried to hide grain from procurements officials. There were attacks on the carts taking grain out of the district, and bridges were wrecked to impede their progress.[98]

When procurements fell short of the targets in the 1932 harvest, as they did most notably in Ukraine, Moscow sent the procurements brigades back again. This happened even in some regions that met their procurements quotas but were then landed with an additional quota, the so-called "counter-plans" (*vstrechnye plany*, also referred to as taking grain *povstrechnomu*). The peasants, of course, protested that they were being cleaned out of their seed grain for next spring as well as the grain the needed for consumption until the next harvest. But they had said that before; it was what peasants always said to procurements officials. The standard state response was that procurements officials were not under any circumstances to take seed grain—even though they must at all costs meet the procurements quotas that had been laid down.

At the end of December 1932, in a paroxysm of rage and frustration at the low procurements, the Politburo sent out instructions that kolkhozy that had not fulfilled procurements quotas were to give up "all the grain they had, *including the so-called seed funds* [my emphasis]".[99] Here one of the vicious circles in the struggle of Communists and peasants over procurements snapped shut. If the peasants could refuse to sow, the state could refuse to leave them the grain to sow with. Then—if the logic was followed to the end—there would be no crop, no harvest, no procurements, and the game would be over.

Perceptions and Representations

How the regime spoke and thought about the famine was worlds apart from how the peasants spoke and thought about it. The regime's representation was known to peasants and sometimes parodied or rebutted by them. The peasants' representation was probably less well known to the regime, for all the OGPU's information-gathering efforts in the countryside, because of the danger and difficulty of transmitting to autocratic leaders information that they do not want to hear. The famine, and the different ways in which it was understood, remained a looming presence throughout the prewar period. This was the episode that crystallized a certain view of the Soviet regime in the mind of the peasantry, and of the peasantry in the minds of the leaders.

The Soviet media did not acknowledge the existence of a famine in the Soviet Union. Instead, in the winter and spring of 1932–33 the newspapers told readers about the disastrous famines and harvest failures that were occurring throughout the rest of the world. "It is not a crisis, it is a catastrophe," trumpeted one headline. This was a story about Poland, where peasants were allegedly reduced to begging for food. "Dying villages" proclaimed another headline—a story about Czechoslovakia. "Catastrophe of agriculture. . . . Hunger despite a good harvest. Rise in peasant revolts." That was in China. "Foreign peasantry in the grip of poverty and ruin." This was the heading of an editorial reporting that farmers in the United States and Canada were on the verge of bankruptcy, and the wheat harvest had failed disastrously in Poland, Slovakia, Transcarpathian Ukraine, Hungary, Rumania, Yugoslavia, and Bulgaria.[100]

In denying the famine, the press was taking its cue from Stalin. In January 1933, Stalin boasted of "the annihilation of begging and pauperism in the countryside," and in February—the very height of the famine—he told an audience of kolkhoz activists that collectivization had saved "at least twenty million bedniaks . . . from ruin and poverty."[101]

How was it, then, that seemingly starving peasants were thronging the railroad stations and begging on the streets of Kharkov and Moscow? It was playacting, the language of Soviet reports suggested, a ploy to gain sympathy. The apparent victims were "trying to *stage a 'famine'*." This constituted "a new maneuver" by kulak sympathizers, who were "*turning on a hunger strike*." The beggars who appeared in Volga towns were "*passing themselves off* as ruined kolkhozniks." Those who tried to flee from Ukraine to Russia were not famine victims but anti-Soviet propagandists, incited by Poland to spread rumors about famine. Hunger was a gambit to evade procurements obligations: For example, one delinquent peasant "starved his family, and *made propaganda* out of it: 'Look at my family, swollen from hunger, and you are demanding seed from me.'"[102]

Along with this almost pathological representation of the famine, Stalin offered a rational if one-sided analysis of its causes. The peasants were staging a go-slow strike (*ital'ianka*), he said. Their unwilling to work in the kolkhoz and meet the state's orders for grain was a form of political protest. Answering the writer Mikhail Sholokhov, who had written to protest against the coercive measures that Communists were taking against starving peasants in his native Kuban, Stalin insisted that Sholokhov was missing the point, namely:

> that the respected tillers of the soil in your raion (and not only your raion!) have conducted an "*ital'ianka*" (sabotage!) and would not have any qualms about leaving the working class and the Red Army without bread. That fact that the sabotage was quiet and overtly innocent (without blood)—that fact does not change the position that the respected tillers of the soil in essence conducted a "quiet" war against Soviet power. A war to starve us out (*voinu na izmor*), comrade Sholokhov. . . .[103]

If it was war on the peasants' side, the implication was that it was war on the regime's side, too. Thus, according to the Ukrainian party leader, Petr Postyshev, compulsory procurements were more than a means of providing the state with grain. They were "a weapon" and "a method of re-education." By forcing kolkhozniks to meet their quotas, the regime was teaching them what socialism and the kolkhoz were all about.[104]

Peasants had heard news of the famine on the grapevine, even in the non-Black Earth provinces such as the Western oblast that were not directly affected. Otkhodniks brought back news of famine in Ukraine that quickly spread through the villages. The silence of the Soviet press about the famine did not go unremarked, and added to the already considerable skepticism with which peasants regarded what they read in the papers or heard from official propagandists. "You tell us that in foreign countries very many people are without work and are beggars and starving," one peasant wrote to President Kalinin a few years later. "But . . . it's the other way round; it's not abroad [it happens] but in the USSR."[105]

From the peasants' standpoint, the state's refusal to give aid to famine areas was a breaking of the social contract between government and people, or perhaps an indication that the state had not so far signed any such contract with kolkhozniks. It was worse than serfdom, because under serfdom a master was supposed to have an obligation to help his serfs in time of need. The rumors circulating in the Central Volga (a region stricken by famine) took for granted that the regime bore total responsibility for the famine, and assumed that it was a product of intention rather than accident. The only question, then, was why the regime had done it.

One school of thought in the villages had it that greed was the state's motive for forcing grain procurements so high and producing the famine. There was a rumor that the famine and the establishment of the Torgsin stores[106] were two parts of a single strategy to extract hidden reserves of gold from the population. Another school of thought, clearly influenced by statements like Postyshev's on procurements as an educational tool, held that the point of the famine was to show peasants that they had better make their peace with collectivization, or to punish them for refusing to work properly in the kolkhoz. The most pungent comment, which was in circulation in villages of Saratov and Penza in 1933, was that the regime's method of "reeducating" peasants was the same as that of Durov, the famous circus performer, who trained animals to obey by starving them.[107]

Repression

The joint plenum of the party's Central Committee and Central Control Commission in January 1933 underscored the leaders' commitment to a ruthless policy of reprisals against the peasantry. For this purpose, Kaganovich announced the creation of a new control institution in the countryside, political departments (*politotdels*) of the MTS. Tens of thousands of urban Communists were to be mobilized for service in the MTS politotdels (a more threatening replay of the 1929 mobilization of the "25,000-ers"). Their tasks were to purge the collective farms of "alien" members, purge the local Communist cadres (especially those "moderates" who claimed that famine was preventing fulfilment of procurements targets), and ensure that the kolkhoz fields would be planted in the spring sowing, especially in the major grain-producing regions—also, at this point, the famine-stricken and in some cases rebellious regions—of the North Caucasus, Lower and Central Volga, and the Central Black Earth oblast.[108]

Savage reprisals were launched in the early months of 1933 against collective farms, mainly in the Ukraine and the North Caucasus, that had failed to meet the procurements obligations. The "black board" of dishonor was created for such cases. When a kolkhoz was put on the black board, which seems to have been close to a collective death sentence, it meant removal of all goods from the local cooperative stores, a total prohibition on trade, the sealing of warehouses containing food grain, and the seizure of seed grain, which was then distributed to surrounding collective farms. If a kolkhoz failed to mend its ways, it was to be dissolved and all its property (including animals and equipment) confiscated. An even more drastic punishment was the deportation to the north of whole collective farms from the North Caucasus.[109]

At the same time, there was a new wave of arrests, deportations, and expulsions from collective farms of "kulaks" and their "associates" (*pod-kulachniki*). This differed from the past waves of dekulakization in several respects. In the first place, most of these "kulaks" had none of the appropriate socio-economic characteristics: they were just peasants whom the state identified as troublemakers. In the second place, most of the victims were kolkhoz members, and the kolkhoz was often required to collaborate in their victimization. In one kolkhoz in the Central Volga, for example, a local official (probably from the MTS politotdel) came in with a list of "kulaks" in the kolkhoz, some of whom were slated for prosecution for unspecified offences, and demanded that the kolkhoz purge itself by expelling them. An "extraordinarily tumultuous" kolkhoz meeting was held, lasting until four in the morning, according to a representative of the Commissariat of Agriculture who was present as an observer. Although a majority of kolkhozniks finally voted to expel the "kulaks," they did so unwillingly, with friends of the accused ("podkulachniki") putting up "stubborn resistance."[110]

As Stalin explained, kulaks had changed their tactics. They no longer waged an open struggle against Soviet power and the kolkhoz, but opposed them furtively, "on the sly (*tikhoi sapoi*)," under the mask of obedience and loyalty.

> They sit right in the kolkhoz, holding positions as storemen, business managers (*zavkhozy*), bookkeepers, secretaries, and so on. They will never say "Down with the kolkhoz." They are "for" the kolkhoz. They are for procurements—but they insist on creating all sorts of unnecessary reserves for animal husbandry, insurance, and so on; [they] insist that the kolkhoz should "distribute 6–10 pounds of grain a day for each working member."

Despite their peaceable demeanor, Stalin stated, these kulaks commit desperate acts of sabotage and destruction, breaking machines, setting fire to barns, and causing the death of horses and other animals. And, above all, they steal. "It is as if they feel with a class instinct that public property is the foundation of the Soviet economy, and it's just that foundation that they have to shake."[111]

Stalin also made some very disenchanted comments on the kolkhoz at this time. Communists should not "idealize" the kolkhoz, "overvalue" it, or "turn [it] into an icon," he warned. The kolkhoz form of organization was "a weapon, only a weapon." That weapon could be used either by the state or against it (as in the recent kolkhoz uprisings in the North Caucasus). Communists should have no scruples about punishing insubordination on the kolkhoz. Any kolkhoz or kolkhoznik who defied Soviet power should be dealt "a crushing blow."[112]

There are no good figures on the extent of repression in the first months of 1933, but it was undoubtedly a serious episode. Even in Leningrad oblast, which as a grain-consuming rather than grain-producing region was not a prime target of repression, and moreover had a party leader (Kirov) who was known for his comparative mildness in implementing collectivization, more than 7,000 peasant households were purged from the kolkhoz as kulaks, arrested and deported—that is, one household in every two collective farms.[113]

Why Soviet purging campaigns had an automatic tendency to excess is easier to understand if we look at the bureaucratic reporting procedures involved. Every MTS politodel in the country had to fill in printed forms headed "Purging of Class-Alien and Anti-Kolkhoz Elements from the Collective Farms. Promotion of New Cadres." For each kolkhoz, the responsible MTS official had to fill in the following numbers: How many kolkhoz officers and rank-and-file kolkhozniks had been purged (*"vychishcheno, sniato"*), and how many had been promoted (*"vydvinuto"*). Clearly the MTS official who wished to excel would want high figures in both columns—exceeding, if possible, any firm or implied target figure, just as he would try to exceed a target for grain procurements or acreage of kolkhoz land sown. In the Central Black Earth oblast, the MTS politotdels were able to report that they had purged 3,677 kolkhoz officers (chairmen, accountants, brigade leaders, stablemen, and others) and fired another 20,000. In addition, they had unmasked, expelled, and arrested almost 11,000 "class alien elements" who had managed to join the collective farms as rank-and-file members.[114]

Putting on the Brakes

The first months of 1933 constituted one of the peaks of repression in a highly repressive decade. The burden on the state's resources of such high-intensity coercion soon made itself felt. Indeed, even in 1932 the problems of resettling such huge numbers of deportees had led the government to try—apparently in vain—to stem the flow of deportations from central Russia.[115]

In May 1933, a secret instruction signed by Stalin and Molotov and sent to party, government, police, and judicial officials around the country called a halt to mass repression. It stated that "as a result of our successes in the countryside. . . , *we no longer need the mass repressions* which, as is well known, have injured not only kulaks but also independent peasants and part of the kolkhoz population." Other than in exceptional circumstances, it was time to stop using such forms of control as mass deportations and "sharp forms of repression in the countryside."[116]

The secret instructions gave a memorable picture of the wild repressions and arrests practiced by Communist officials as they attempted to cope with the pressures from above and below. Provincial authorities repeatedly peti-tioned Moscow for approval to deport more peasants, the instruction stated. "There are applications for the immediate deportation . . . of about 100,000 families [awaiting confirmation] by the Central Committee and Sovnar-kom." "Disorderly arrests" were occurring on a mass scale.

> Kolkhoz chairmen and members of kolkhoz boards are making arrests. Rural soviet chairmen and secretaries of [party] cells are making arrests. Raion and krai plenipotentiaries are making arrests. Everyone who feels like it is making arrests, though, to tell the truth, they have no authority to do so. It is not surprising that, with the practice of arrest so chaotic, those bodies which actu-ally have the right to make arrests, including the organs of OGPU and espe-cially the militia, lose their sense of proportion and often arrest people without any grounds, acting on the rule: "Arrest first, and then find out what the prob-lem is."[117]

Noting that such methods of work "have outlived their time," the Cen-tral Committee and Sovnarkom ordered that "mass deportations of peasants cease immediately." No more than 12,000 more peasant households should be deported from their oblasts. The privilege of making arrests should be confined to officials of the procuracy, the OGPU, and the militia. Only persons charged with major offences such as counterrevolution, terrorism, wrecking, banditism, and murder should be imprisoned before trial; and the OGPU must obtain preliminary authorization from the procuracy before making arrests, except in broadly defined political cases (terrorism, causing explosions, arson, espionage, desertion, political banditism, and opposition-ist political activity).[118]

According to the secret instruction, there were currently 800,000 per-sons confined in prisons (not including those in labor camps and labor colo-nies) in the USSR.[119] This number must be halved within two months to ease prison overcrowding. Lesser offenders should be released. Others should be sent to OGPU labor camps or, in the case of kulaks sentenced to three to five years' imprisonment, be sent together with their families to special settle-ments for deported kulaks.[120]

The May instruction seems to have been successful in stopping large-scale deportation and forced resettlement of peasants. There were no subse-quent peasant deportations on a similar scale in the 1930s, although the technique was revived in the 1940s with the wartime deportations of whole ethnic groups as well as the deportation of large groups of people from the newly acquired Baltic States and the territory that had formerly been eastern Poland. As for arbitrary arrests, this was a phenomenon that certainly did not disappear from the countryside at any point in the decade. But the May instruction produced some abatement, and it is likely that the volume of "disorderly" arrests in the villages by nonaccredited persons never again reached the heights of the wild early years of collectivization.

3

Exodus

For millions of peasants, the experience of collectivization was associated with departure from the village rather than entry into the kolkhoz. For every thirty peasants who became kolkhozniks in the years 1929–32, ten peasants gave up peasant agriculture and became wage earners. For some, this meant going to work on state farms, but for the majority it meant leaving the countryside. The rate of rural-urban migration reached unprecedented heights at the beginning of the 1930s. More than two and a half million peasants moved from village to town in 1930, compared with about a million a year in the late 1920s. Four million moved in 1931. All twenty of the Soviet Union's largest cities grew rapidly in this period; and six of them—the rapidly expanding industrial cities of Sverdlovsk and Perm in the Urals, Stalingrad and Gorky (Nizhny Novgorod) on the Volga, Stalino (Iuzovka) in the Donbass, and Novosibirsk in Siberia—doubled or triped their population in the years 1929–32. The population of Moscow—the Soviet Union's capital and largest city—almost doubled, jumping from 2 million to 3.7 million (a 181 percent increase). The next largest cities of the empire, Leningrad, Baku, and Kharkov, grew almost as dramatically in size.[1]

Over the period 1928–32, the total transfer of population from village to town was in the range of 12 million. This great outflow of population from the countryside was partly coerced and partly voluntary. Some peasants were forcibly deported from the village in connection with dekulakization; and of these, about half ended up as industrial wage earners. Other peasants fled the village out of fear of being dekulakized or hatred of the kolkhoz. Still others left because the great expansion of industry associated with the

First Five-Year Plan had created new employment opportunities in the towns.[2]

Communist theorists in the 1920s generally assumed that the country-side was overpopulated—one respected economist, a specialist on otkhod, put the "surplus" rural population at 10 million; other estimates ranged from 5 million to as high as 30 million[3]—and that rapid industrialization would draw this surplus rural population into the urban labor force. All the same, nobody seems to have anticipated an exodus of the dimensions and sudden-ness as that which occurred during the First Five-Year Plan.

It is impossible to understand the impact of collectivization on the Rus-sian village without taking this exodus into account. The number of peasant households in the Soviet Union dropped from 26 million in 1929 to 19 million in 1937.[4] For the village, such a huge outflow of population inevita-bly meant demoralization, even had the kolkhoz system proved less exploit-ative and more appealing. Men left in greater numbers than women; and of the men, it was the young, strong, and energetic who were the most likely to go. Many of those who remained had lost a husband to the exodus, or grown sons who should have provided support in old age.

The exodus had the paradoxical effect of simultaneously diminishing the likelihood of active resistance to collectivization and removing most of the kolkhoz's supporters from the village. The departure of so many young males from Russian villages removed the potential leaders of armed upris-ing; moreover, the very existence of jobs outside the village took the edge off peasants' anger and despair. Yet at the same time, the exodus took away a large proportion of the village's "Soviet elements": the young rural Komsomols, who stayed around long enough to assist in the closing of the church and burning of icons before going off to school or to work at Mag-nitogorsk; the Red Army veterans, many of whom were sent off to other parts of the country as organizers and administrators; the industrial otkhod-niks and village craftsmen, who were likely to go away and work in industry. The peasant who had taken the progressive, modern, urban-oriented, Soviet position in the 1920s was the same peasant who was likely to respond to the opportunities outside the village at the beginning of the 1930s. The most stalwart early supporters of the kolkhoz, as well as its most passionate oppo-nents, had often departed permanently from the village by 1932.

As for those peasants who remained in the village, they showed many signs of demoralization and trauma that seemed related to the mass depar-tures as well as collectivization itself. No doubt there are situations in which a peasantry can maintain self-respect and a sense of the worth of their work and way of life even in the face of high out-migration (Ireland being a case in point), but such instances are surely few. The demoralization of the Rus-sian peasantry in the 1930s seems closely comparable to that of the peasants of southern Italy in the 1950s, a period when high emigration and a sense of economic exploitation combined to devalue peasant life in the eyes of the peasants themselves.[5] After collectivization, it became almost axiomatic that the "good life" was to be found only outside the village, and the brightest of the peasant children were bound to leave as soon as they were old enough. It was also widely believed in the countryside, though not necessarily admitted, that "The clever ones left the collective farms long ago; all that remain are the fools."[6]

Modes of Departure

For the 12 million or so peasants who left the village during the First Five-Year Plan, there were a number of different modes of departure. The most traumatic and terrifying of these was departure under OGPU guard, either as a convict or a deportee, as a result of dekulakization. Then there was panic-stricken flight by peasants who were afraid of being dekulakized or, in 1932, who were fleeing famine. A third mode of departure was the "normal" one of going on otkhod to earn money outside the village and not returning. Sometimes the transition from peasant to permanent wage earner was abrupt; sometimes it was spread out over years. The peasants who took this route had a range of motives for departure. Some left out of disgust with collectivization; others left because jobs had opened in the towns and at new construction sites. For many of the departing peasants, undoubtedly, these two motives were inextricably combined.

In the dekulakization campaign at the beginning of 1930, kulaks were divided into different categories according to the degree of danger they were supposed to represent to society. The worst were the first-category kulaks who were to be sent to labor camps or, in the case of "the most virulent counter-revolutionary elements," shot. The families of first-category kulaks were to be deported. Molotov's commission set 60,000 persons as the approximate number of first-category kulaks who should be sent to camps. Second-category kulaks were deported by the OGPU together with their families for resettlement in the North, Siberia, the Urals, and Kazakhstan. The Molotov commission recommended that 150,000 households should be deported.[7]

Lesser categories of kulaks were to be expropriated (that is, all their property was to be confiscated and they were to be evicted from their houses), along with the first and second categories. But they were not required to leave the raion, and local authorities were meant to help them resettle on inferior land. In addition to the official categories, an unofficial category of "self-dekulakizing" kulaks quickly emerged. These were peasants who were on the list for dekulakization, or feared that they were, and disposed of their assets and fled before the authorities got round to expropriating them. This was illegal, incidentally: According to a government decree of February 1, 1930, kulak households were forbidden to sell their property and leave the district.[8]

While it was the initial wave of dekulakization in 1930 that made the most dramatic impact, the second wave in 1931 was almost twice as large (a quarter of a million households, according to a recent report from the former Soviet Union), and the expropriation and deportation of households continued in 1932 and the first months of 1933. Local and regional authorities flung themselves to the task with a will, disregarding central attempts to slow the pace and cries of anguish from overburdened officials in the receiving areas. It is clear that the Molotov commissions's "targets" were far exceeded, at least as far as deportations were concerned. Recent archival discoveries have raised the number of households believed to have been dekulakized and deported in 1930 and 1931 to 381,000. According to a memo to Stalin from Genrikh Iagoda, the head of the OGPU, 1.4 million persons had been deported and resettled in the Urals, Siberia, Kazakhstan, and the Northern krai as of January 1932. Although deportations continued for another 18 months at a reduced rate, Iagoda's figure probably represents close to the peak of resettled deportees, given the high death rate in transit and during resettlement. When a count was taken at the beginning of 1935, a year and a half after the end of kulak deportations, almost 1.2 million deported kulaks and family members were living in their places of resettlement.[9]

About 60 percent of the deported kulaks ended up working in industry, where their situation after the first few years was not very different from that of other (free) workers, except that the deportees were not allowed to leave the region where they had been settled. Some 640,000 deported kulaks and family members were working in industry at the beginning of 1935, constituting a distinctive corps in the huge army of peasants (more than 10 million) that entered the wage-earning labor force in the first half of the 1930s.[10]

After decades of near silence about experience of the deported kulaks, memoirs and oral histories have begun to appear. One of the most remarkable is the memoir of Ivan Tvardovskii, brother of the Soviet poet Aleksandr Tvardovskii. Their father, Trifon Tvardovskii, was the blacksmith in a village in the Western oblast. Aleksandr had already gone off to school in Smolensk and was in the process of joining the Communist Party and making a name for himself as a "proletarian poet" at the time of collectivization. In the spring of 1930, a heavy individual tax was laid on the family, and the father disappeared on otkhod to the Donbass. A year later, after a frantic and fruitless journey to the Volga, the Black Sea, and the Donbass by Ivan and his eldest brother, Konstantin, the family was dekulakized, and all the family members who were home were taken to the raion center for deportation. They were joined there by Konstantin, who had been in prison in Smolensk (presumably for nonpayment of the individual tax), and Trifon, taken into custody on his return from the Donbass. Aleksandr, who may or may not have known what was happening to his family, kept his distance and came through relatively unscathed, although living the next five years under a shadow, knowing that at any moment the shameful secret that his father was a dekulakized kulak might be discovered and his career ruined.

After dekulakization, the Tvardovskii family was packed into a freight train with other deportees and sent to the Urals, where several years passed in unsettled wanderings, unsuccessful attempts to return to the Smolensk region, and the constant struggle to survive and maintain contact among deported family members. They kept in touch with their native village, where a friendly neighbor acted as a kind of *poste restante* for the deported Tvardovskiis, but after a few years had to accept that they would not be able to return. Then their attention turned to the struggle to obtain passports and urban residence permits so as to establish a firmer foundation for their new lives as urban wage earners. Finally, with varying degrees of bitterness against the regime and Aleksandr, who by the mid-'30s was a bright rising star in Soviet literature, they grudgingly settled into a new existence as workers and urban dwellers.[11]

Many peasants who were not dekulakized, or who were dekulakized (expropriated) but not deported, fled from the village in fear of meeting these fates. Out of the total number of peasants that were officially dekulakized in the years 1930–32 (estimated at about 600,000 households), probably around half were deported. Of the residue, an unknown number were shot or sent to gulag, and the rest, evicted from their homes and stripped of their possessions, were left to fend for themselves. In theory, these third-category kulaks were meant to be resettled by local authorities on inferior land within the raion, but in practice this scarcely ever happened. The majority fled from the countryside and found work in the towns. With them went members of the quarter of a million peasant households that were described as "self-dekulakized", meaning they sold their assets and fled before the state had had time to expropriate them. Several million peasants—men, women, and children—fled the village in this way.[12]

The records that remain of such flights are fragmentary and incomplete. The Smolensk Archive provides brief glimpses of a number of cases. A peasant named Balashev had worked in industry before 1921 but returned to work on the land in the 1920s. He prospered, but in 1931 this earned him the individual "fixed quota" obligation that was both onerous in itself and dangerous, since a "fixed-quota" peasant was the nearest thing to a kulak left in the village. As soon as he was put in the "fixed-quota" category, he left the village and returned to the life of an industrial worker. In the village of Shetinino, "the kulak Gorenskii sold his house, his smithy, his property, and everything he had, cut down his trees, and went away to Gzhatsk, where he bought a house, installed his family in it, and himself went on to Moscow." Lokshina, a miller's widow, departed to work in a Moscow leather plant in 1932 after being deprived of voting rights. In Komarichskii raion, four millers abandoned their mills and fled.[13]

Sometimes we get a glimpse of the process and mechanism of departure in these fragments. Kulaks living in the Pokrovshchina settlement in the Western oblast had a meeting and decided, "There is only one thing left for us to do—leave this place and get away as quickly as possible, while we are not yet under arrest." In the Stavropol region, an official reported on March 1, 1930 that "kulak families are loading their property on to carts at night . . . and carrying it off in an unknown direction." It was desirable, but not essential, for those departing to have documents identifying them as something other than kulaks. Petro Shcherbakov, of the village of Vertnoe in the Western oblast, was dekulakized but managed to bribe the rural soviet chairman with a sewing machine to get a document identifying him as a "middle peasant"; the two of them sat up all night drinking and then Shcherbakov left the village for ever. A group of dekulakized peasants from Mordovia had no such luck with papers, but fellow villagers had established a *zemliachestvo* (informal network of people from the same village or district) at an auto plant in Moscow, and they managed to get jobs there and living space in the plant's hostel.[14]

From the writer Mikhail Alekseev's native village, "Vyselki" in Saratov krai, "Bald Mitrofan" ran away to the Kazakh steppe to avoid dekulakization, leaving behind his wife and children. He was not seen again in the village, but according to indirect reports he later became chairman of a "millionaire kolkhoz" in Kazakhstan. Many others left Vyselki around the same time. The village chronicler, Innokentii Danilovich, even made a list of them:

> In Saratov there are about 200—that's not counting their children, who were already born in the city and know Vyselki only from the stories of their fathers and mothers. There are more than 50 in Moscow, 16 in Kiev, 10 in Alma-Ata, 5 in Novosibirsk, 7 in Vorkuta, 11 in Kamchatka, and 10 in Sakhalin.

One of those who departed was Epifan Lesnov, a middle peasant, who was later to work on construction sites and in factories in Moscow and Kiev. As Innokentii Danilovich told the story,

> He took fright at the kolkhoz, nailed the windows shut, put his wife under his arm, and went off to the city. I took a sin on my soul and got him the necessary document in the rural soviet. We drank a half liter together in farewell, and that was that. . . .[15]

For some of those departing, the lure of industry and the town was the most important factor. Rapid expansion of the industrial labor force began in 1929. Throughout the 1920s, industrial jobs had been hard to come by, there had been substantial industrial unemployment, and the trade unions had done their best to keep factories from hiring new arrivals from the village without union cards. The unions were still unenthusiastic about the influx of peasants in 1929, especially in view of the First Five-Year Plan's projection that there would still be half a million unemployed even at the end of the plan period (1932). By the beginning of 1930, however, the labor exchanges were having difficulty supplying industry with enough workers, even though there were still over half a million registered unemployed; and there were periodic acute alarms about labor shortages in the expanding sectors of industry throughout the first half of the year.[16]

From then on until the temporary crisis of 1932, it was a sellers' market for labor. Peasants leaving the village—four out of five of whom were of working age (16–59 years)—had no trouble finding work because of the abundance of unskilled jobs in industry, construction, state trade, and food preparation. Most of them went on their own, often with no very clear idea of whether they were otkhodniks who would return after a time to the village or permanent migrants. Some were recruited by industrial enterprises, who in theory made labor-recruitment (*orgnabor*) contracts with the collective farms to recruit kolkhozniks, but in practice tended to take anyone who showed up at the collection point. (A 1931 report from the central agricultural region noted that of 22,000 peasants recruited in one raion for work in the Donbass mines, "a quite considerable proportion" turned out to members of kulak families.) The total number of wage and salary earners in the Soviet Union doubled in this period, with 16–17 million new jobs being created. At least 10 million of the new wage earners were peasants.[17]

It is impossible to estimate exactly how much the departing peasants were influenced by the "pull" of industry and how much by the "push" of collectivization. There can be no doubt that once industrial jobs opened again after the hiatus of revolution, civil war, and NEP, many peasants would have left the villages to go and work in the towns under any circumstances. When jobs were available in the towns, many young and poor peasants had always left in search of opportunity and a better life. Such is the path described in the memoir of N. P. Sapozhnikov, a peasant from a poor Cossack family in the Urals who became an outstanding steelworker at Magnitogorsk. Sapozhnikov graduated from the sixth and final grade of the local school at the end of the 1920s:

> At that point, my education ended: the eight-year school was in the city and there was no money to go there. At that time rumors reached our *stanitsa* that an iron foundry would be built on Magnitnaia mountain. . . . The rumor that the biggest plant in the world would be built at Magnitnaia mountain excited everyone, old and young. It was said that huge numbers of people were going there. We, my cousin and I, decided to go too.[18]

Of course, we have no means of knowing whether Sapozhnikov had other reasons for departing than those he chose to recall in his memoir, which was published in a volume celebrating Soviet industrialization. His motives may well have been mixed, as many peoples' were. It was possible for a young peasant whose family was in trouble as a result of collectivization to leave the village both because of family problems and because of his own urge to go to the city. It was also possible for the son of a dekulakized peasant who fled the village and found refuge in the factory to "reinvent" his departure along Sapozhnikov's lines, and believe his invention.

Among those departing for the towns were peasants who were relatively well disposed to collectivization. This may seem paradoxical, but it was a natural consequence of the fact that the minority of villagers who in the 1920s had an urban, Soviet orientation were likely both to support the kolkhoz and to welcome the new opportunities for urban employment. In this "love it and leave it" group were many otkhodniks and village craftsmen (blacksmiths, carpenters, builders), who were likely to end up as urban industrial workers, and young peasants in the Komsomol orbit who dispersed in many different directions (education, military service, industry). Many of the former Red Army men who were such a visible presence in the precollectivization era also disappeared from the village in the early 1930s, presumably into urban industry or the expanding bureaucracy.

A snapshot of one departure of a young peasant who was not ill-disposed towards the kolkhoz is presented in Gerasimov's memoir of collectivization in Spas na peskakh. Passing through the village of Makrushino one day in 1930, Gerasimov chanced upon a curious scene: A cow, in process of being collectivized, was being led away by the horn by a young man from the kolkhoz while the peasant woman who was its former owner held on to its tail and shouted that she would not give it up. The woman's husband stood by silently observing the scene:

> He didn't want to get involved. Although he had joined the kolkhoz, the labor recruiter who came from the city had already signed him up for an important construction site for the First Five-Year Plan—he had the advance and the agreement in his pocket. He wasn't responsible for his wife. What can you do with these women? It's well known—darkness, lack of consciousness, nothing but rural idiocy.[19]

There were real kolkhoz enthusiasts among the departers, too. Nikolai Miniaev, an eighteen-year-old peasant from Moscow oblast, was a passionate supporter of the kolkhoz who quarrelled with his father on account of it. As a result of the quarrel, the village seemed too small to contain the two of them—so the son, the kolkhoz enthusiast, departed.

> In 1929 I had to wage a big "war" with my father, who did not want to join the kolkhoz. . . . I left him. I began to live with my friend, a Komsomol, Ivan Klimov. Soon Klimov and I went away to Baku, and I went to work at a ship building plant. The Komomsol organization mobilized me into the commercial fleet of the Caspian basin. There I worked on a ship as a sailor of the second class.

In the meantime, Miniaev Sr. joined the kolkhoz. After a few years, Nikolai returned and married a village girl, but in 1935 he was poised to leave again. It was not that he was any less of a kolkhoz enthusiast than before; it was just that both he and his wife had seven years' schooling, which meant that like every other young Soviet enthusiast of the 1930s they had to leave to continue their education. She planned to become an actress. He was aiming to be an engineer.[20]

The writer Mikhail Alekseev presents another case of an enthusiast's departure, this one associated with ambition for a career in Soviet service. Mishka Zelenov, secretary of both the Komsomol and the party cell in the writer's native village of Vyselki in Saratov krai at the beginning of the 1930s, was "the biggest activist in the village." He was one of the original organizers of the kolkhoz, and he was the person responsible for taking down the bells from the local church. According to the villagers' version of events, "In the worst time, Mishka went off to the city, you know, he got frightened by the difficulties."

Zelenov, of course, had a different version of the story. "I got promoted (*menia vydvinuli*)," he would say. He ended up in a senior administrative post in the city of Saratov, returning periodically to the village to recall the heroic struggle of collectivization and the early days of the kolkhoz.[21]

In July 1932, many speakers at the Third Ukrainian Party Conference reported that because of hunger peasants from Ukrainian villages were fleeing to Moscow, Leningrad, the North Caucasus, and Ukraine in search of food and livelihood. A socialist émigré journal carried a report that "the countryside is starving in the southeast. The railway stations of the Ukraine, the Don, the Northern Caucasus and other most abundant in the past grain-growing regions are now crowded with hordes of hungry peasants from the neighboring villages, who are begging passengers to give 'a crust of bread.'. . ."[22]

There was already a substantial peasant-refugee population roaming the countryside: In 1933, President Kalinin received a pathetic letter from peasants who had been expelled from collective farms in the Central Agricultural region in 1932 and "had been turned into tramps, roaming the whole Soviet Union." Having wandered to Siberia, Central Asia, the Northern Caucasus, and even the Far East, "many have now returned to their home districts, and now we have no strength and nothing to eat." About 40,000 peasants fled from the famine-stricken region of Saratov and Kuibyshev in 1932–33 and took refuge in Gavrilovka raion in Tambov oblast. They were more fortunate than many other wanderers: According to a report in 1937, they had acquired land and horses as independent peasants and were making a good living as carters.[23]

In Kazakhstan, departure took a particularly dramatic form. In 1932, an entire population of Kazakh herdsmen—"at least two million," according to a recent Soviet account—picked up their tents, mounted their horses, and left the collective farms in which they had been settled. Some went across the Chinese border. Others took their herds to the Volga provinces of Russia. Still others had no clear destination. "Enormous crowds" of Kazakhs thronged the railroad stations and cities of Kazakhstan, and the city of Karaganda was said to be "literally surrounded by rings of nomads on the move (*otkochev-shchiki*)."[24]

Many Ukrainian peasants went to the Donbass to work in the mines. But some were unable to travel, like the peasant grandfather of a Soviet journalist, Iurii Chernichenko. Chernichenko's cousin told him the story:

> We lived in the Donbass at that time, in Stalino. In that year fifteen relatives came to us. You know it is terrible to remember that time: [they were] swollen up, starving. . . . Father asked the aunts why they didn't bring the old man. Aunt Varia said "He was in very poor health, he wouldn't have made it. . . ." "But you made it—he could have made it." We started to collect as much food as we

could and send parcels. But grandfather was too weak to go to the post office and we sent the parcels to his sister-in-law Stepanida, who took them and fed her own family. All of her family remained alive, but grandfather died.[25]

Communists, too, were in flight from the stricken countryside. About 30,000 Communists decamped from the Northern Caucasus at the height of the famine there, and in Kazakhstan half of all party members disappeared from their posts.[26] In Mikhail Alekseev's memoir/novel of a Saratov village, *Drachuny*, when the last grain procurements brigades left his Volga village in the fall of 1932—having cleaned out the last supplies of grain in a "counter-plan"—and winter settled on the countryside, the village seemed to be totally forgotten, abandoned to its fate by the outside world. Among those who departed was the writer's father, the chairman of the rural Soviet, recently separated from his wife. He got a job in the raion center and went to live with another woman there.[27]

Soviet urban migration figures show a surplus of arrivals over departures for 1932 of 2.7 million—less than the record 4.1 million in 1931, but higher than the previous record of 1930. Months before the effective introduction of passports and urban registration in 1933, however, rail travel was forbidden except for those with special authorization, and the authorities were trying to prevent peasants from coming in to the big towns and expelling the destitute. Hundreds of thousands of peasants were taken into custody at railroad stations and sent back to their villages.[28]

In addition to the various urban destinations, peasants leaving the village and/or the kolkhoz had another option, namely to go and work as a hired hand at a state farm (sovkhoz). The regime's plans for the modernization of agriculture included a major expansion of state farming as well as the creation of collective farms. The state farms' geographical distribution reflected that of the prerevolutionary commercial farms whose lands they partially inherited, being concentrated largely in the Volga region, the North Caucasus, Western Siberia, Ukraine, and the Crimea.

Between August 1929 and August 1930, the number of persons employed on state farms increased from 663,000 to 1,100,000, and by August 1931 it stood at more than 2 million. The high point was reached in August 1932, when almost 2.7 million were working in state farms. Only 44 percent of these were permanent workers, however; and while the number of permanent workers declined only slightly over the next five years, the total number including temporary employees dropped sharply. In 1937, there were only 1.2 million sovkhoz workers (66 percent of whom were permanent). It is evident that peasants had used the state farm as a temporary refuge against famine, much as homeless children would use the orphanages in winter. When the crisis passed, many of those who had gone to work in the sovkhoz went back to the village and resumed work as kolkhozniks.[29]

Unlike peasants, laborers on state farms received the desirable social classification of "proletarian" (as batraks had done in the 1920s). But this was one of the few advantages of working on a state farm in the early

1930s—and its main practical consequence, preferential access to secondary and higher education for one's children, was at best of secondary importance to most rural people. The sovkhoz was not attractive to peasants in the early 1930s because conditions were bad and pay was low. Working at a state farm generally meant living in hastily constructed temporary accommodation of the most primitive type, barracks or mudhuts (*zemlianki*). The typical sovkhoz dormitory of the early 1930s had no heating, no cooking facilities, no running water, and no bathhouse. The workers ate poorly in a communal dining room that was often lacking the barest necessities like spoons and bowls. Until 1933, sovkhoz workers were forbidden to keep animals or culti-vate a private plot. For peasants in the prewar period, the sovkhoz option as no more desirable, and probably less, than being forced by need to work for the local kulak as a batrak in earlier times.[30]

Regulating Departure

Internal passports had been abolished at the time of the revolution. In the 1920s, the government made only perfunctory efforts to control or monitor peasant departure,[31] which was regulated primarily by the shortage of jobs in the towns and the trade unions' efforts to enforce closed-shop practices on state industry. To be sure, the trade unions raised the alarm about "peasanti-zation" of the industrial labor force when peasant departures surged upward in 1929, for that was when unemployment was still high and the impact of the First Five-Year Plan industrial expansion had still to be felt. The party leadership was worried, too, because surveys indicated that those leaving the village and taking industrial jobs were not bedniaks, as in the past, but pros-perous peasants and kulaks who saw no future for themselves in agricul-ture.[32]

Nevertheless, the leaders did not take any serious steps to halt the flow, and within a few months the balance of supply and demand had changed. By the summer of 1930, many expanding industrial enterprises were experi-encing acute labor shortages, and the labor exchanges were unable to meet their demands. In a panic, senior labor officials wondered what forms of co-ercion and inducement might persuade peasants to leave the countryside and go to work in industry in sufficient numbers. Ironically, in the light of later developments, they were afraid that collectivization might dry up the supply of peasant recruits to industry. As one labor official gloomily re-marked to his colleagues in January 1930,

> Life in the countryside is beginning to improve, and there will no longer be the incentive to go and earn money in the town that existed up to now. There won't be that overwhelming need that drove many [peasants] to go to the town for wages.[33]

The main reason for this anxiety was that the new collective farms were energetically trying to assert their right to control the movement of their members (as the mir had done in the decades after Emancipation) and, in addition, take a cut from any wages earned outside the kolkhoz. Labor officials reported a lot of opposition from kolkhoz boards when members of the kolkhoz tried to go on otkhod in 1929–30. Industrial enterprises found that their recruiters in the village were often rebuffed by kolkhoz officers ("When we tell them it's wrong, that they are disrupting construction [of socialist industry], they reply that they have their own construction to do"), or forced to make substantial payments to the kolkhoz before it would authorize the departure of its members.[34]

The clash of interests between collective farms, which wanted to hold on to their members, and industrial enterprises, which wanted to recruit them to work in industry, was reproduced at the level of high politics. For the first year and a half after the initial collectivization drive at the beginning of 1930, the powerful industrial bureaucracy (headed by Politburo member Sergo Ordzhonikidze) urged the priority of industry's needs during the crucial years of the First Five-Year Plan, while the government agency in charge of collectivized agriculture (Kolkhoz Center, headed by Ia. A. Iakovlev) argued for the interests of the collective farms.[35]

Despite the heavy outflow of peasants from the villages to the towns and industrial construction sites over the past two years, industry continued to suffer acute labor shortages because there was no effective mechanism in place to match labor supply (coming mainly from the central Russian countryside) with industrial demand (experienced primarily by the new enterprises and industrial construction sites in distant parts of the Soviet Union). The Soviet industrialists felt that the success of the First Five-Year Plan was imperilled by the labor shortages.

The party leaders accepted the industrialists' analysis of the situation, and for the time being greatly underestimated the dimensions of the existing out-migration from the villages since collectivization. It was no longer reasonable to expect a spontaneous outflow (*samotëk*) of labor from the countryside, Stalin told a meeting of Soviet industrialists in June 1931. With the success of collectivization in abolishing rural poverty, the traditional "flight of the muzhik from village to town" had become a thing of the past.[36] (When the rural-urban migration figures were calculated at the end of the year, they would show that the surplus of urban arrivals over urban departures stood at an all-time high: four million for 1931.)

The decision that came out of the June meeting represented a victory for the interests of industry over those of collectivized agriculture. The government decree on otkhod issued on June 30, 1931 was a response to the industrialists' pleas for legislation that would clearly state that the kolkhoz had no right to inhibit the departure of its members to work in industry, and was in fact expected to facilitate it. According to the decree, the kolkhoz was not allowed to take a cut from the industrial wages of its members. Kolkhozniks who went away on otkhod were entitled to an equal share in the harvest with the kolkhoz members who did the harvesting. If a kolkhoz otkhodnik decided to remain in industry as a worker, he did not require kolkhoz permission for this step, and the kolkhoz was not allowed to penalize family members who remained in the village.[37]

The Passport Law

Within eighteen months, the regime was obliged to think again about the desirability of unchecked rural-urban migration. The main reason was that the onset of famine in many of the major grain-producing regions of the Soviet Union and the consequent flight of starving peasants to the towns as winter approached in 1932 produced a crisis. The towns, already drastically overcrowded by the immigration of previous years, could not handle the fresh influx. The rationing system, on which urban residents depended for their survival, threatened to break down entirely. In addition, industry had overextended itself this in the pell-mell expansion of the past three years, and its needs for labor were temporarily glutted.

Three important steps were taken in the winter of 1932–33 to cordon off the towns from the influx of starving peasants and prevent the collapse of the urban rationing and supply systems. The first, a labor discipline decree, was intended to reduce the number of workers receiving rations and ease the pressure on housing. The second was a reorganization of the rationing system to prevent double-dipping and link access to rations directly to employment. The third, the most important and lasting in its impact, was the introduction of internal passports and registration of urban residents, intended to halt the peasant influx into the towns and, at the same time, purge them of socially undesirable and unproductive residents. In addition, as the spring sowing season approached, a new law was introduced restricting peasant departure from the collective farms for work in the towns.

Bread rationing had been introduced in Soviet towns in 1929, and in the next few years most basic food commodities and manufactured goods became rationed. The number of people receiving centralized bread rations rose from 26 million in 1930 to 33 million in 1931 and 40 million in 1932. This meant that the state was supplying seven million more mouths in 1932 than it had done in 1931, an increase that significantly outpaced even that year's 4-million growth in the size of the urban population.[38]

The labor discipline law issued on November 15, 1932 gave enterprise managers not only the right but the duty to fire any worker who took even one day off without permission. The law emphasized that workers dismissed under this law must immediately be evicted from enterprise housing and must also be deprived of their ration cards. A companion measure, taken by the government in early December, reorganized the urban rationing system by putting enterprises directly in charge both of the issue of ration cards and of the delivery of rationed goods to their own employees through the closed distribution network. New cards were issued by enterprise administrations early in the new year, and there were immediate reports that "tens of thousands of hangers-on (*prikhlebateli*)" and "dead souls" had been eliminated from the ration system.[39]

The new law mandating the introduction of internal passports was issued on December 27, 1932. Passports were to be issued to "all citizens of the USSR aged 16 years and over, permanently living in towns and workers' settlements, working on transport, in the state farms, and at new construction sites"—in other words, all urban residents and wage earners, even the lowly sovkhoz workers, but not peasants (regardless of whether they were kolkhozniks or independents). In order to obtain a passport, citizens must be registered (*propisany*) under a new, stricter system as urban residents. The new passports would show the bearer's full name, age, nationality, social position, permanent place of residence, and place of employment.

Simultaneously with the introduction of urban registration, the population of the towns was to be purged. Persons who were not working for the state, studying, or generally "engaged in socially-useful labor" (with the exception of invalids and pensioners) were to be refused registration and expelled from the towns. A special effort was to be made to rid workers' settlements and the new construction sites of "kulaks, criminals, and other anti-social elements hiding there." Persons refused passports had to leave the city within ten days.[40]

The reintroduction of internal passports, long villified as instruments of Tsarist repression, was a dramatic and (to many Communists of the older generation) disconcerting step. Abel Enukidze, secretary of the Central Executive Committee of the All-Union Congress of Soviets, was one of those who clearly found it embarrassing, but he tried to explain that this measure was not as regressive and repressive as it seemed. The government, he said, had no choice but to take measures to reduce "this great, senseless, wasteful flow of people from village to town, and from city to city" of the past eighteen months. He admitted, in an oblique way, that the measure had an antipeasant flavor, saying that it aimed to protect the towns not only from urban idlers and criminals but also from "the touring artist (*gastrolёr*) from the village, who doesn't take kindly to the collectivization of agriculture."[41]

As the Japanese historian Nobuo Shimotomai has pointed out, the mood in the party leadership at this time had become distinctly antikolkhoznik, not just antikulak as in the past. Peasant-bashing—sometimes in the guise of kulak-bashing, sometimes overt—was prominent in the commentaries on the new laws. One newspaper's editorial quoted Lenin's dictum that the peasant worker aspires to give the Soviet state "as little and as poor work as possible and drag from 'it' as much money as possible" in its commentary on the law against worker absenteeism.[42]

Pravda went further in its editorial on the passport law a month later. While grudgingly conceding that there were some admirable new recruits to the labor force, especially "working-class youngsters and kolkhozniks," *Pravda* emphasized that the new construction sites were crawling with "hundreds of persons [who are] declassed and alien in a class sense to the proletariat, who sense the possibility of easy profits and try to corrupt and weaken the iron discipline of socialist labor." In *Pravda*'s picture, the arrival of new peasant workers became a malevolent invasion of kulaks, determined "to live as [they are] accustomed, that it, parasitically, without working."

> Exposed in their "native" villages and raions by progressive kolkhozniks and party and Komsomol members, hundreds and thousands of kulaks and their henchmen . . . strive towards and penetrate the vital centers of our country—the cities, the new construction sites, the workers' settlements.[43]

All this undoubtedly reflected the leaders' rising paranoia about peasants associated with the famine and their denial of it. In a remarkable secret telegram on peasant flight sent to party organizations at about the same time, Stalin and Molotov stated that peasant flight to the towns was definitely not the result of famine. Instead, they claimed, the peasant exodus from the Ukraine was organized by "enemies of Soviet power—SRs and agents of Poland" who wanted to spread anti-Soviet propaganda in Russia and incite peasants in the areas not stricken by famine against Soviet power.[44]

Newspaper commentaries emphasized the connection between the passport law and the law against absenteeism, passed in November 1932, that made it mandatory for industrial enterprises to fire truant workers, remove their ration cards, and evict them from company housing.[45] Once the law against absenteeism had struck at "pseudo-workers who are disorganizing labor discipline and ruining production," the "next logical step" was "to toss out (*vytriakhnut'*) this social trash from the overcrowded cities, to unburden our industrial centers of people who are not essential to any socially-useful labor." Removal of the "scum" would "preserve the housing fund of Soviet industrial centers for the accommodation of the cadres of workers and specialists which the country really needs." It would get rid of kulaks, thieves, speculators, and swindlers, and deal with the problems created by an influx of expropriated peasants, some of whom had become professional speculators in ration cards. "The task of purging, unburdening our cities and new construction sites and workers' settlements of . . . parasitical elements is very important," *Pravda* emphasized. Indeed, it was so important as "a *political* task" that it would be undertaken by the OGPU.[46]

Passportization was begun in Moscow on January 5, 1933, with workers at the ninety leading industrial enterprises issued passports first. Persons not issued passports had to leave the city and were not allowed to settle in any of the other cities where the passport system had been introduced.[47]

The New York Times reported in January that "an exodus on a small scale has already begun from Moscow" in connection with the imminent passportization and cited "a recent inspection at the Moscow electric factory, one of the city's largest plants, showing that of about 5,000 employees 800 were not allowed to receive passports because they were classified as former White Guards, kulaks, disfranchised persons and criminals." A few weeks later, the same paper carried a report from Finland of "wholesale exodus" from Leningrad of persons refused passports: "huge crowds of people are wandering along roads out of the city searching for food and shelter. . . . Some of the deported persons were taken by railway to rural districts a minimum of 60 miles from Leningrad."[48]

According to an apparently well-informed *Sotsialicheskii vestnik* correspondent, the original target for deportations from Moscow alone was half a million, but "the unfortunates doomed to ruin put in motion such forces and raised such a moan that the number of persons being deported is now reduced: from Moscow, for example, they are deporting only 300,000 (!) and they are proposing to deport 800,000 altogether from the big cities! Those deported are doomed to outright hunger and homelessness, since food cards are taken from them, they are not allowed to take their furniture with them and even the amount of clothes that can be taken is limited." In addition to those officially refused registration and required to leave, many people at risk (former kulaks and Nepmen and others deprived of voting rights) apparently left voluntarily once passportization was announced.[49]

The spring of 1933 was marked by a fierce drive to identify and remove "class enemies" from industry and reduce the workforce that had to be paid and supplied with rations. In Baku, where many dekulakized peasants had found work, "a tense struggle for purity of the workers' ranks" began with the passportization process and continued throughout the first half of 1933. Large numbers of "kulaks" were arrested, and the reports hint at strikes and "intentional disorganization of production" by workers.[50]

At the same time, the government was taking measures to prevent starving peasants from leaving the villages. To stop the flight of starving Ukrainian peasants into the Russian Republic, much of which was free of famine, the Soviet Commissar of Transport, A. A. Andreev, issued an order forbidding the sale of railroad tickets in the Ukrainian countryside to anybody without a travel authorization from local authorities, and OGPU guards inspected all trains at the border to detect peasant stowaways. In other regions of the country, too, cordons and security detachments were used to prevent peasant movement. According to a recent Soviet publication, 220,000 fleeing peasants were caught and returned to their villages in the spring of 1933.[51]

In addition, the government hastily passed a new law on otkhod on March 17, 1933 that was much more restrictive. According to the new law, otkhodniks must have the permission of the kolkhoz to depart, and anyone who left or stayed away without permission would be expelled from the kolkhoz and should not expect any payment for labordays already earned. The new law specifically warned "flitters who leave before the sowing and return for the harvest" that they would not share in the annual distribution of grain after the harvest.[52]

Under the Passport Regime

The restrictions on peasant mobility that were imposed in response to the crisis of the winter of 1932–33 stayed on the books long after the crisis was over. The internal passport system remained in effect for the rest of the Soviet era, and it was not until the 1970s that peasants received the automatic right to a passport. Similarly, the rule requiring kolkhozniks to obtain kolkhoz permission before going on otkhod remained in effect; and indeed the 1933 decree on otkhod as a whole was apparently never rescinded, even though its recommendations on expulsion were contradicted in a number of later decrees and policy statements.[53] These restrictions were irksome to peasants. During the national discussions on the new Constitution in 1936, many peasants wrote to say that kolkhozniks should have the right to work where they want to, like workers, and that the kolkhoz should not be permitted to withhold the documents permission for them to depart for work outside the kolkhoz.[54]

In practice, however, the restrictions on peasant mobility were much less onerous than they were in theory. The sole exception to this was in 1933, the first year of the passport regime, when a serious and reasonably successful effort was made to restrict peasant otkhod and migration to towns. From 1934 on, despite the formal restrictions that caused annoyance and inconvenience to kolkhozniks and contributing greatly to their sense of being second-class citizens, it was relatively easy for employable kolkhozniks to depart, either temporarily or permanently, and in some years of industrial labor shortage the government actively encouraged them to do so.

After the crisis of 1933, the urban economy grew steadily throughout the 1930s, with the number of wage and salary earners increasing from 24 million in 1932 to 34 million in 1940. This was not as dramatic as the increase during the First Five-Year Plan, when the size of the employed labor force doubled in about four years, but it was substantial enough to require a constant influx of peasants to sustain it. According to the calculations of a Soviet scholar, close to seven million peasants became wage and salary earners in the period 1935–40. The majority of these were kolkhozniks leaving the village to work in the towns. The urban population grew from 40 million in 1933 to 56 million in 1939, indicating in-migration of similar dimensions.[55]

This was in no way contrary to the regime's intentions. The regime's top priority for most of the 1930s was industrial growth, and industry could only expand by constant recruitment of peasants for the industrial workforce. It might not be in the interests of the collective farms to give up so many of their best workers, but as Stalin had made clear in 1931, where the interests of industry and the interests of the collective farms were in conflict, it was industry that must prevail. Indeed, at the late 1930s, when increased military call-up started to deplete the kolkhoz labor supply, Stalin called on the collective farms to do their duty by industry and supply it with at least a million and a half young kolkhozniks a year. This led the publicity-conscious activists of Shcherbina raion in the Kuban to challenge other raions to a competition to see whose collective farms could supply the most recruits for industry.[56]

There were different ways of making the move. Further education and military service were major routes for young kolkhozniks. For others, otkhod—departure for nonpermanent wage work outside the kolkhoz—was often a stepping stone towards permanent departure. The volume of otkhod from the collective farms was running at about 4 million a year in the latter part of the 1930s, about the same level as it had reached at the end of the 1920s, before the great outflow of the First Five-Year Plan period.[57] Each year many otkhodniks returned to the kolkhoz, but some did not. Sometimes this involved a conscious decision to become a permanent member of the urban labor force, signified, for example, by moving wife and children from village to town. But quite often there was no conscious decision: The otkhodnik simply returned less and less often to the village (and to his wife and family), until finally he stopped coming at all.

There were two ways of leaving the kolkhoz to work for wages outside agriculture. The first was the traditional individual otkhod, in which individual peasants went away of their own volition and found jobs for themselves. Many peasants who went to work in industry and all peasants who went to work in any other sphere used the individual otkhod route. The second was "organized labor recruitment" (*orgnabor*), in which the kolkhoz signed a contract with an industrial enterprise guaranteeing to provide a certain number of peasants to work for the enterprise for a given period of time, in return for which the enterprise promised to provide transport, accommodation, and so on. In practice, the orgnabor method was primarily used to recruit peasants from central Russia to work in industry in remote areas (logging, mining, construction, new enterprises in Siberia and the Urals, and so on). Although the statistics on this topic are meager and confused, it looks as if about half the departures from the village in the latter portion of the 1930s were on orgnabor contracts and the other half were on individual otkhod.[58]

Despite its name, orgnabor was not a highly organized and efficiently planned method of industrial recruitment. After the abolition of the People's Commissariat of Labor in 1933, there was no central governmental authority responsible for labor recruitment and distribution. Although attempts were made at the end of the 1930s to rationalize industry's labor recruitment practices,[59] rational planning was scarcely its hallmark. An economic geographer describes the functioning of orgnabor in the 1930s as follows:

> It was seldom or ever centrally planned or directed and instead of resettling surplus rural population in areas with a deficit of industrial labor, the actual mechanism was anarchic in the extreme. Individual enterprises sent out recruiters who promised the world to potential recruits in villages with severe labor shortages. Recruits sometimes travelled tremendous distances—crossing the paths of others going in the opposite direction. The recruits were untrained village men and did not meet the demand for skilled labor. Much money was spent in paying bonuses at the time of recruitment to peasants who had already collected bonuses from other recruiters. . . .[60]

Industrial enterprises in the well-populated territory of European Russia and much of Ukraine usually had no difficulty attracting labor without any special recruitment procedures. Indeed, they preferred not to recruit through orgnabor, because that meant writing contracts guaranteeing housing, of which no enterprise in the 1930s ever had enough. In 1937, for example, the "Kalinin" plant in Voronezh reported that although it had hired more than a thousand workers that year, it had not signed any orgnabor contracts—and could not legally have done so, since it had no accommodations to offer new workers. In Voronezh, as at the Lipetsk factory that in the same year hired less than 10 percent of its new workers through orgnabor, hiring at the factory gates was by far the easiest option, even though this was somewhat disapproved of and the plant managements had to make excuses for it in their annual reports.[61]

The industrial enterprises that found orgnabor useful were those that were distant from convenient sources of peasant labor supply: the big new industrial projects in the Urals, Siberia and the Far East, logging and mining enterprises in remote parts of the country, and so on. The Donbass mines and metallurgical plants did some orgnabor recruiting in the countryside, just as they had done in central Russian provinces before the Revolution. Indeed, the whole orgnabor procedure was very similar to that of capitalist enterprises in Tsarist times. The recruiters (*verbovshchiki*) distributed bribes, made promises, and told stories of the wonderful life at the mines and factories just as their Tsarist predecessors had done, and the kolkhoz played the role of the old peasant mir.[62]

In theory, the Soviet orgnabor recruiter went to a kolkhoz, discussed with its chairman and board the feasibility of its providing a group of workers for his industrial enterprise, told the kolkhozniks of the conditions of work there, and then worked out a contractual arrangement of mutual benefit to the kolkhoz and the enterprise. If the recruiter was from a mining enterprise, he might offer to supply coal to the kolkhoz, in addition to various technical services and hard-to-get items like nails, glass, and pipes.

In reality, the recruitment process worked somewhat differently. In order to get a foot in the door, the recruiter probably had to bribe both the kolkhoz and the rural soviet chairman. He would rarely bother to work out what mix of industrial goods and services might be useful to the kolkhoz but would simply offer money. In the documents of the central Coal Administration, these cash payments are delicately described as "socialist aid" (*sotspomoshch'*), and the going rate in 1937 was about ten rubles for each kolkhoznik recruited. The recruiters complained, however, that this was now too low to attract the kolkhoz boards, especially if the kolkhozniks were to stay at the mines through the harvest season.[63]

The coal industry recruited 5,145 peasants, just over 4,000 of them from collective farms, in 1937. But hardly any of the recruitment was covered by formal contracts. The recruiters explained that, for all their efforts, the kolkhoz boards "generally refused to conclude contracts . . . which placed them under any sort of obligation."[64]

In some circumstances, orgnabor could be more onerous and coercive than the above account suggests. This was the case when regional authorities drafted peasants for short-term heavy labor in logging camps or urgent construction projects. If it was a logging mobilization, peasants were drafted with their horses, as in the corvée obligation (except that the peasants were paid). It was a considerable burden on the collective farms that was much resented. Moreover, the composition of the workforce on many of these projects conveyed its own message. The northern timber industry, which had almost no permanent labor force, depended for manpower on gulag and the collective farm system in almost equal measure. In 1937, for example, the Ust-Vaengskii mechanized timber processing collective employed 115 locals, 200 convicts from labor colonies, and 103 peasants drafted from Kuibyshev oblast. Similarly, of the 13,000 timber floaters working in the Arkhangel region in the summer of 1939, fewer than a quarter were permanent workers, half were peasant *orgnaborshchiki*, and the rest were convicts.[65]

For the young, leaving the kolkhoz was relatively easy. In the first place, young men called up for military service received a passport at the end of their term, and many chose not to return to the kolkhoz. This was not publicly acknowledged in the Stalin period, or for that matter in the two decades between Stalin's death and the passport reform of the early 1970s. But it was a fact of life that peasants sometimes referred to in their complaints to the authorities: for example, the writer from East Siberia who in a letter to Stalin and Kalinin in 1937 cited as "the best proof" of the miserable state of the collectivized village that "the Red Army man, having served out his term in the [Army], very rarely establishes himself in the kolkhoz; the majority forget everything that smells of the kolkhoz and take to their heels to get into industry and the town."[66]

In the second place, education was a way out of the kolkhoz. This applied not only to the relatively small number of kolkhozniks who were able to go to colleges and technical schools, who automatically received a passport upon graduation and virtually never returned to the kolkhoz.[67] It applied also to some degree to all young kolkhozniks who pursued their education beyond the limits of the local rural school (generally grade four in the early 1930s, rising towards grade seven by the end of the decade). Once a kolkhoz youngster went off to board in the town for grades five through seven, the chances that he or she would return and make their adult life on the kolkhoz were very much diminished.

Even a six-week training course in the raion center for kolkhoz accountants, truck drivers, or tractor operators could provide the enterprising young peasant with a ticket out of the kolkhoz. A plethora of such courses existed in the 1930s, and selection of candidates was one of the important perks of the kolkhoz chairman's office. (There were also courses for kolkhoz chairmen, and reports of chairmen who went off to take them and never came back.) Bookkeeping and accountancy were skills that had an obvious application outside the kolkhoz. In practice, however, the skills of the kolkhoz machine operators—kolkhozniks trained to drive trucks, operate tractors, repair simple machinery, or work with a lathe—seemed to be in even greater demand. The result was that there was an incredibly high turnover of kolkhoz machine operators: no sooner were they trained than they found a wage-paying job at an MTS, sovkhoz, or factory and disappeared.

The phenomenon of the disappearing tractor driver was noted by the People's Commissar for Agriculture, Ia. A. Iakovlev, at a meeting of kolkhoz activists in 1933:

> IAKOVLEV: We have a lot of tractor-driving "flitters" (*letuny*)—today they are here, and tomorrow nobody knows where they are. We checked in a number of MTS where their tractor-drivers are. . . . 30–40 percent are on the books. And where are the rest? . . . This is what the rest did: they studied for a month, got their credentials—"I am a tractor-driver"—and fled away from the village. And you . . . let them get away with it. Isn't that true? How many tractor-drivers have been replaced in the past years? Half or more?
>
> VOICES: . . . More!
>
> IAKOVLEV: More, undoubtedly! In many MTS now they have the same number of people studying to be tractor-drivers as were working as tractor-drivers last year. That means that many MTS have turned into a revolving door: the tractor-driver comes in at one end and goes out the other.[68]

Of course, there was no automatic issue of passports for young kolkhoz mechanizers who got a job in a town, any more than there was for other kolkhoz otkhodniks who decided not to return to the village. But it is clear that once the kolkhoznik had a permanent wage-paying job in the town, regularization of status as an urban resident was not particularly difficult—by no means as formidable a problem, for example, as that of obtaining permanent residence status for present day illegal immigrants to the United States.

The fact that education and training offered a way out of the kolkhoz into urban life was was clearly recognized by peasant parents and children. That is undoubtedly one reason for the high regard for the value of education that was shown by peasants in the 1930s. When peasants were asked to contribute their comments on the draft of the new Soviet Constitution in 1936, they emphasized the importance of educational opportunity and access to secondary and higher schools for young peasants, even though some ruefully acknowledged that the child that got education was lost to the village and would not be a support to parents in their old age.[69]

Frequent topics of complaint from peasants were that the kolkhoz board had refused a kolkhoznik permission to go and take a course for accountants, drivers, tractorists, or whatever; or that it had sent him but refused to pay for it; or that it had refused permission to a graduate of such a course to take a job outside the kolkhoz in which these skills would be used.[70] There were equally heartfelt complaints about kolkhoz boards that refused permission to depart to kolkhozniks who wanted to go away and work in industry. The kolkhoz should not have be allowed to refuse such permission, peasants stated in their letters, because "every toiler has the right to work where he wants. . . . Many kolkhozniks have the desire to work in factories, and they could get good results in their work and improve their lives."[71]

The fact that younger kolkhozniks could and did leave the village in large numbers produced mixed feelings in the older generation. On the one hand, it could lead to anxiety about the future (who would look after them in old age if their children were gone?) and even resentment. On the other hand, the achievements of the younger generation could be a source of pride. It was the second feeling, understandably, that was emphasized by the publicists of the 1930s. A popular gambit of journalists was to have peasants in a given village (kolkhoz) list the names of all their children and fellow villagers who had gone away for further education and become well-paid urban professionals. For example:

Three old men from the village of Novorusanov in Zherdevka raion—Tuchin, Korotkov and Korotin—wondered which of their fellow-villagers are studying in secondary and higher educational institutions and who became a specialist. They counted up . . . that 75 persons are students of higher educational institutions. . . . The son of kolkhoznik Avdeev has become a pilot, Malakhov's son is studying in a civil engineering technicum, Shashin's daughter has become a teacher, and so on. In prerevolutionary times only 40 people got any education, and most of those were from kulak and priestly families.[72]

In a neighboring raion, a similar calculation was made for the village of Nalzhi, which turned out to be the birthplace of more than forty former kolkhozniks and village residents—all under thirty-three years of age—who had become members of the intelligentsia, including nine teachers, two agronomists, three pilots, three accountants, and seven Army officers.[73]

It is hard to tell whether peasants really felt this kind of pride in their departed children, or whether it was something thought up by the journalists. There can be little doubt, however, that they recognized that village life had been devalued in the eyes of the younger generation—and, for that matter, even in their own eyes. Letters written by peasants to Stalin and Kalinin in 1937 clearly express a sense of demoralization and a resentful acceptance of the younger generation's judgement that life was better in the town. One correspondent from Eastern Siberia recalled the good old days of NEP with nostalgia—"when people were interested in living and working as peasants" and villages were full of economic vitality and energy. But now, he continued, all that was changed:

Since the year of collectivization, 1930, all wealth disappeared as if by magic. . . . People work as if they were forced to, the majority are leaving the kolkhozy to go to the city, they are completely not interested in living in the kolkhoz. . . . People go away to the city to industry—they say there things are better (*poriadki luchshe*).[74]

In similar spirit, a correspondent from Kirov oblast wrote to Kalinin:

I read . . . about the achievements of the collective farms, but that's all window-dressing. If you look inside the collective farms, then it will surely be the opposite, and if you look inside the kolkhozniks, they will be thinking something different, and that's just the way it is. What really shows how things are is the way that kolkhozniks are leaving the collective farms. . . . If you count the old population that used to be in the [villages], only 50 percent is still there. That fact demonstrates that people are unwilling to live in the kolkhoz. . . .

But what explains the kolkhozniks' departure from the collective farms? I think it is that the kolkhozy and the kolkhozniks are insulted (*obizheny*) by the government. And this is why: if you compare workers in factories, they live much better than kolkhozniks. If you want to prove that—there are kolkhozniks who left the collective farms two years ago and got jobs at factories and enterprises, and they write that now it has become better to live at the mills and factories than in the kolkhozy. There you know how much you earn every day, they write; you can make 15 rubles and more at the factory; you can buy cloth and other goods too, as much as you want; and they write "I live much better here than in the kolkhoz."

But just let the kolkhoznik try to buy something where *he* lives—you can't buy cloth here and the kolkhozniks go round badly dressed. . . . Now what we have is a pecking order in real life (*zhivaia ochered'*) in which kolkhozniks have missed the boat and you can't get any lower than the village. . . .[75]

4

The Collectivized Village

"The kolkhoz" was still an empty vessel waiting to be filled in 1930. The regime had called for collectivization without indicating exactly what it meant. The main type of kolkhoz in existence in the 1920s—the small kommuna, farming on nonvillage land—was clearly inappropriate as a model. No official guidelines on the structure of the collective farm were distributed until after the initial collectivization assault: indeed, the Model Charter of the Agricultural Artel, signed into law on March 1, 1930, was published in the same issue of *Pravda* as Stalin's "Dizzy with Success." Thus, the Charter could not have served as a guide for collectivizers; rather, it was a summary of what the regime had learned from their recent experiences.

The answers to the question "What is a kolkhoz?" emerged only gradually over time. Some of the answers were given in official pronouncements or government legislation. For example, the question of the kolkhoznik's right to keep a cow was settled by "Dizzy with Success," while the question of the kolkhoznik's right to trade was settled by a decree of May 1932. Other answers emerged from the practice of real life but were never officially announced or formulated as policy (for example, the dominant role of the kolkhoz chairman, or the status of the household as a basic unit in the kolkhoz). Still other answers, such as the 1935 reformulation on the private plot, were presented in a context of conspicuous consultation between the regime and representatives of the peasantry.

Underlying these different processes, there was always a kind of dialogue between government and peasants. In the interactions that took place between the state and the peasants, there were certain constants. The state wanted to take more grain; the peasants wanted to give less. The state usually wanted to maximize collective property (especially land, draught power) while the peasants wanted to minimize it. The state also tended to expand its own sphere of control, for example, by giving detailed sowing plans and instructions relating to the actual agricultural process, while the peasants wanted to minimize state interference.

Of course, "the state" was not really a monolith but a collection of related but distinct interests. The interests of the central party and government leadership (assuming, for the purposes of argument, that *that* was a monolith) were not identical with those of the raion administrations. The interests of the raion administrations were not identical with those of the procurements agents sent from the center, or of the state industrial enterprises that wanted to hire kolkhozniks, not to mention those of the Machine-Tractor Station (MTS) politotdels. This does not even in take into account the conflicts over authority and subordination that raged between 25,000–ers and raion and rural soviet officials at the beginning of the 1930s, or between the raions and the MTS politotdels in 1933–34.

The peasantry, similarly, cannot be regarded as a monolithic actor. There were major regional differences: In the south, for example, issues concerning trade (and hence size of private plots, policy on orchards, etc.) were of prime importance, as was also the case for collective farms providing produce to neighboring large cities; in the less fertile provinces of the central industrial region, the rules governing otkhod and off-farm work generally were much more important. There were differences related to age and gender. Increasingly, there were also differences related to position in the kolkhoz: kolkhoz chairmen had one set of interests (partially those of the kolkhoz vis-à-vis the raion, partially their own personal interests), tractor drivers another, and fieldworkers yet another. The interests of "the kolkhoz" (meaning the village community as well as the kolkhoz as an institution) and individual kolkhozniks were often divergent, notably on the question of otkhod and the availability of manpower for the kolkhoz.

This chapter deals with three important aspects of the process of constructing the kolkhoz in the first half of the 1930s. The first aspect concerns territory and size, and is closely related to the key question of the relationship of the new kolkhoz to the old village and mir. The second has to do with kolkhoz membership, particularly the rights and obligations of members and the extent of the kolkhoz's disciplinary powers over them. The final topic considered is the discussion of principles of kolkhoz organization at the Second Congress of Outstanding Kolkhozniks in 1935, and the new version of the Kolkhoz Charter that the Congress endorsed.

Land

In the summer of 1929, Soviet authorities adopted a new strategy of collectivization, that of attempting to sign up whole villages and peasant land societies for the kolkhoz instead of individual peasant households.[1] This was the basis on which collectivization was carried out in the first tempestuous months of 1930, and in broad outline it remained the basis for the kolkhoz throughout the decade. When the mir was abolished in Russia in the summer of 1930, the kolkhoz was its de facto successor.[2] The kolkhoz of the 1930s, in other words, was a collectivized village.

This was not an easy thing for Communists to acknowledge, however. From their standpoint, "the village" implied small-scale, technologically backward, traditional peasant farming, while "the kolkhoz" belonged by definition to a different world of large-scale, mechanized, socialist agricultural production. Soviet commentators, both contemporary and subsequent, did a remarkable job of obfuscation on the question of the basic unit of collectivization. It was not until 1935 that the village was implicitly recognized as the normal basis of the Soviet kolkhoz.[3]

In the first flush of collectivization, Communists had not only been enamoured of the idea of a larger-than-village kolkhoz, they had also tried to create such a kolkhoz in practice. This was what happened during the brief phase of *gigantomania* in the first years of Soviet collectivization. Gigantomania arose out of the same strange mixture of modernizing intentions, coercive methods, and utopian fantasy that was characteristic of the Cultural Revolution and was expressed dramatically in the collectivizers' onslaught on the village church. The Communists collectivizers assumed that their purpose was the socialist modernization of peasant agriculture. That meant a move from economically irrational, small-scale, traditional farming to the modern, economically rational, large-scale farming that lent itself to mechanization. Regarding "tradition" as a synonym for backwardness, irrationality, and superstition, Soviet Communists had no sympathy for commonsense arguments that it was easier to build on the basis of existing structures. In a favorite phrase of the day, it was a "new world" they wanted to build.

Gigantomania was a term retrospectively applied to the passion of Communist officials and collectivizers in 1929 and 1930 for unrealistically huge collective farms. In these years, regional and district authorities competed to establish giant kolkhozy that extended (on paper) over tens of thousands of hectares—sometimes over whole raions—and included dozens or even hundreds of villages and settlements.[4] The preferred form of collective farm was the one with maximum collectivization, the commune (*kommuna*). In a spirit of utopian fantasy and harebrained scheming, some local authorities planned communes that covered whole raions and hundreds of villages. In one district of the Urals, for example, a visiting agricultural official from Moscow reported in March 1930:

> On the instruction of the raion executive committee, twelve agronomists have been sitting for twenty days composing an operational-production plan for the nonexistent raion commune without leaving their offices or going out into the field. . . .[5]

A similar giant was created, bureaucratically speaking, in Velikie Luki in the Western oblast. Then, when the planners saw that the unwieldy giant was not functioning, they decided to break it up into thirty-two squares, each with an acreage of 2,500 hectares. Each square would correspond to a kolkhoz; and the squares were drawn on a map without any reference to actual villages, settlements, rivers, hills, swamps, or other demographic and topographical characteristics of the land.[6]

It was not only utopian fantasy that led local authorities to try to bypass the village as the basic unit of collectivization. A report from the Western oblast early in 1930 noted that where village kolkhozy were approved by the authorities, they generally elected a competent administrative board (upravlenie) from among their members and oriented themselves quickly to the new tasks. But that situation often did not please the raion authorities, according to the report, because it made the collective farms too independent. Communists were suspicious of the genuinely elected boards of village kolkhozy, no doubt fearing that these would be dominated by the old leadership of the mir and perpetuate traditional patterns. An advantage of giant collective farms, from the Communist point of view, was that their boards were most unlikely to be elected in any meaningful sense by peasants. With a giant kolkhoz, you could just gather your cadres together in a putatively elected board, divide the kolkhoz area into sections, and sent out a board member as manager of each section ("like the bailiffs in the old days [of serfdom]," as the report wryly noted).[7]

The "squares theory" of collectivization was officially repudiated as unrealistic by 1932–33, and critics began to use the pejorative term gigantomania to describe the more fantastic ambitions of regional collectivizers. Few of the many collective farms that had proudly taken the name *Gigant* in the first years of collectivization remained giants in scale in real life. For example, the Gigant kolkhoz in Serdobskii raion, Saratov oblast, was reduced to fewer than 150 households in 1934–35—a typical size for a village (*selo*) in the Central Volga area.[8]

At the Second Congress of Outstanding Kolkhozniks in 1935, the word selo (village) was substituted for the word *selenie* (settlement) in the draft of the new Kolkhoz Charter on the suggestion of delegates who were anxious that no loophole should remain that might allow local authorities to bypass the village. (In the 1930 version of the Charter, the plural *seleniia* [settlements] was used.)[9]

Land Allocation to Independents

The land situation in the villages was immensely complicated in the first half of the 1930s by the fact that not all the peasant households belonged to the kolkhoz. The village was divided into kolkhozniks and *edinolichniki* (independents, noncollectivized peasants), but the relative share of the two groups was constantly changing. In 1933, independents still constituted 35 percent of peasant households in the Russian Republic, though their share dropped to 17 percent in 1935 and 7 percent in 1937.[10] The kolkhoz was the de facto inheritor of the village lands, but the independents also had claims that could not be denied. How was the village land to be divided up between the two groups?

When the village (or a proportion of its households) collectivized at the beginning of the 1930s, the first step was to divide the communal lands on a proportional basis between the kolkhoz and the independent households. Since collectivization was carried out in great haste and the division was assumed to be temporary, this was done in a very rough-and-ready manner by a commission of the rural soviet on which both the kolkhoz and the independents were represented. Sometimes the village fields were divided into two large blocks, one for the kolkhoz and the other for the independent peasants. In other cases, a number of smaller blocks were distributed among the two groups. Since kolkhoz membership fluctuated greatly in the early years, the division often had to be renegotiated each year before the sowing in order to correspond with the proportion of households currently in and out of the kolkhoz.[11]

The resulting confusion is not hard to imagine. Officials frequently changed their minds in mid course and made arbitrary allocations of land to favored households. The rules did not cover all contingencies: If an independent household joined the kolkhoz, its land was supposed to be added to the kolkhoz block, but if a kolkhoz household left the kolkhoz to farm independently (which was not uncommon in the early years), its allotment was not supposed to be taken from kolkhoz lands. A report from Velikie Luki raion in 1933, for example, describes how, after a wildly disorganized division of land by local authorities before the spring sowing, "the kolkhozniks went into the field, but the independents were still camped at the door of the rural soviet and the raion land department in June, not knowing where they were going to sow. Even when they had received land, they were uncertain whether to sow it or not, since maybe in winter that land would be taken away."[12]

To complicate matters further, the independents were still working their plow land in strips in the traditional manner, but the kolkhoz was supposed to have abolished them by mowing down the grass boundaries between strips (*mezhi*) before the first kolkhoz sowing.[13] That was reasonable enough in principle, but the independents' strips were sometimes scattered throughout kolkhoz plowland. If there were many independents in the village, it was often difficult for the kolkhoz to get rid of strips and cultivate the land as an integrated tract. Many collective farms were still reportedly working their land in strips in the mid 1930s.[14]

"Cut-offs"

In the process of collectivization, a considerable amount of land that had previously been village land, cultivated by peasants, was lost to the collective farms, usually because the raion authorities decided to transfer it to state farms (*sovkhozy*, using wage labor) or give it to various organizations and institutions. This meant that peasants were left with a host of grievances about "cut-offs," just as they had been after the Emancipation settlement of the 1860s. There were plaintive petitions to the central agricultural authorities to restore this land. For example, in 1932 the "Red Star" kolkhoz in Western Siberia complained that the raion land department had handed over all its crop land to two state farms, receiving in exchange 200 hectares at a distance of 12 kilometers from the kolkhoz, and a hayfield that was fully 40 kilometers away.[15]

There were many other complaints of similar nature. In one of the more bizarre, involving a kind of round-robin transfer of lands between neighboring collective farms, the kolkhozniks were all ready to begin the spring sowing when "representatives of the raion land department appeared on the territory of the kolkhoz and silently busied themselves with the redivision of the land," refusing to explain or justify their actions. In another case, large numbers of peasants fled from villages in Podolsk raion in 1931 to escape collectivization, abandoning 5,000 hectares that was transferred to local state farms. The next year some of them changed their minds, came back to the villages and joined kolkhozy, and started petitioning for the land to be returned.[16]

During the discussion on the new Constitution in 1936, the NKVD (political police) reported, some peasants in Voronezh oblast made the "counter-revolutionary" suggestion that all land and equipment belonging to state farms ought to be transferred to collective farms.[17]

In February 1937, the government decided to return the cut-offs that had been taken by state farms and other organizations to collective farms in the Moscow, Orenburg, East Siberian, and Western oblasts, as well as other regions and republics of the Soviet Union. In Omsk oblast (Eastern Siberia), this meant that collective farms increased their total acreage by 2.3 million hectares.[18]

Stabilization of Land Tenure

Although the government decreed in September 1932 that collective farms should be guaranteed tenure of the lands they were working, it took several years for the situation to stabilize. As a Central Committee spokesman complained in 1933,

> In every raion, wherever you go, no matter who you talk to, everyone says that up to the present time, despite the fact that the government has prohibited it, our collective farms are expanding and contracting. [Local authorities] are moving land from one kolkhoz to another for some reason that the raion understands, but which is unknown to the kolkhoznik.[19]

At the end of 1935, however, the Central Committee itself added to the confusion by instructing that "extremely small" collective farms in the non-

Black Earth belt should be merged into larger units—of course, "on condition of the strictest observance of the voluntary principle." Local authorities, at least in the Western oblast, understood this as a green light for another major reorganization, guided by rational-planning principles rather than regard for tradition and existing patterns of settlement. A year later, *Pravda* was berating the Western oblast authorities for unnecessarily offending the local peasantry and succumbing to gigantomania by forcibly merging middle-sized as well as small collective farms, sometimes including as many as seventeen or eighteen settlements in the one kolkhoz.[20]

One might suppose that professional surveyors and land organizers (*zemleustroiteli*) would have been key figures in collectivization. But they seem to have played only a peripheral role in the first half of the 1930s. There was no time to do the careful measuring that had accompanied the creation of new collective farms in the 1920s, and the shifting population of the villages and energetic land grabbing being carried out by state farms and other institutions was no doubt a further disincentive. The district land departments did not attempt to provide scientific "land organization" (*zemleustroistvo*) for the collective farms in these years; they just gave "land directives" (*zemleukazaniia*).[21] The peripheral status of the surveyors and land organizers also reflected the fact that their profession was in political disgrace at this time. Many of its members were holdovers from the pre-revolutionary Stolypin reforms who (with the somewhat surprising encouragement of the Soviet government) had continued to help peasants separate from the commune, consolidate their land, and set up as independent small farmers in the 1920s. But this approach was thoroughly discredited by collectivization. The regime staged a show trial of Alexander Chaianov, the distinguished theorist of the family farm, and other agricultural specialists in the early 1930s, and many lesser surveyors and land organizers were arrested as "wreckers."[22]

The surveyors came back into the picture in a big way only in mid 1935, when the government passed a law giving collective farms the right to "eternal use" of their land, with the stipulation that in future these lands might be increased (as the last independents joined the kolkhoz) but under no circumstances diminished. This meant that the exact extent of kolkhoz lands had to be determined, the land surveyed and mapped, and the boundaries marked with posts. More than 80,000 land organizers were urgently needed, according to the People's Commissariat of Agriculture, to rationalize and consolidate the kolkhoz land tracts, resolve boundary disputes, and, where necessary, eliminate strips once and for all. (The land departments currently had not much more than a tenth of that number at their disposal, and the profession was still buffeted by accusations of counterrevolutionary "wrecking." Only a few months earlier, a show trial of land organizers accused of provoking peasant discontent by clumsy "cut-offs" and favoritism to independents had been held in the Volga city of Gorky.)[23]

The surveying of kolkhoz lands and issuing of titles went on all through

1936 and into 1937. There were many difficulties. In the first place, there were not nearly enough surveyors and land organizers to do the job. In the second place, the peasants were often dissatisfied with the results, because they ended up without land they needed or saw as historically theirs.

Peasants from Pskov raion complained that the land organizer who came to their village to divide land among a newly organized kolkhoz and eleven independent households charged them 80 kopeks a head for his services but never set foot in the fields. He simply took a map of the village land and "poked his thumb in [it]" to indicate the divisions between kolkhoz land and the independents' allotments. As a result, spring sowing was held up because nobody knew where to sow. In Andreevka raion in the Western oblast, kolkhozniks were outraged when they were offered land titles that failed to correspond with the traditional boundaries of village land. In one kolkhoz, 40 hectares of the village's best land were allegedly cut off, and the kolkhoz boundary was drawn in such a way that "you have to cross three ravines and a stream" to get from the village to the kolkhoz fields.[24]

In the Western oblast, where the process of issuing titles seems to have more plagued by troubles than elsewhere, almost a thousand complaints about land titles had been received by the oblast land department by the middle of 1937, even though close to a fifth of all collective farms had still to be issued with titles. Cut-offs and the substitution of poor and swampy land were common complaints, as were the loss of private plots adjacent to the peasants' cottages and the allocation of inaccessible land in the fields for private plots. Some collective farms complained that their timbered land had been designated as state forest, which meant they were forbidden to cut it. All of these complaints figured prominently in the Great Purge trials that were held in the Western oblast in the autumn of 1937.[25]

Despite all the vexing problems of land tenure, the prewar Russian kolkhoz was essentially a collectivized village, cultivating more or less the same lands that had previously been cultivated individually under the mir. In 1937, when more than 90 percent of all peasant households were collectivized, the average kolkhoz in the Russian Republic had sixty-seven households (in the Soviet Union as a whole, it was seventy-six households). This average covered wide regional variation because of the different historic patterns of settlement in the fertile south and the infertile non-Black Earth belt. In the northwest region of the country, including the Western oblast, the kolkhoz averaged only thirty-seven households.[26]

Thanks to the arbitrary tinkering with boundaries in the early 1930s, however, there were innumerable instances where the kolkhoz lands did not correspond exactly with those of the old mir. This was a source of constant grievance and complaint, as the collectivized villages that had lost land energetically sought to recover pasturelands and croplands that had been handed over to neighboring villages or state farms, while those that had been beneficiaries sought to preserve their gains. All this contributed to the spirit of acrimony and discord that was so characteristic of the Russian countryside in the 1930s.

Membership

To be a kolkhoznik was more than an occupational description in the 1930s. It meant that you had a special legal status in Soviet society. This is best understood by analogy with estate (*soslovie*) status in Tsarist Russia. If you belonged to the merchant estate, for example, or if you were a state peasant, that status defined legally defined your rights, privileges, and obligations to the state. So it was if you were a kolkhoznik in Stalin's Russia. You had special obligations with respect to taxes and corvée requirements that were not imposed on other groups of citizens. As a kolkhoznik, you were not allowed to own a horse, and you had to request permission to leave the village for outside work. On the other hand, you had the right to a private plot of land that was larger than that allowed any other social group; and you had the right to trade in its produce—a right that was unique to kolkhozniks and "independent" peasants.

All social groups were developing some estate characteristics in the 1930s,[27] but the kolkhoz peasantry was certainly the furthest along the road. For example, the 1937 and 1939 censuses treated kolkhoz membership as a special status that had to be acknowledged in addition to occupation—a requirement that also existed for various outcast statuses such as administrative exiles (*spetsposelentsy*), but for no other category of free citizen. This once again raises the question of the relationship of collectivization to serfdom. But there was a basic difference: Serf status was virtually always a minus, whereas kolkhoznik status could also be a plus. Like serfs, kolkhozniks often did their best to flee the kolkhoz and find work elsewhere. But, unlike serfs, once they had established themselves in other work, they had no special need to conceal or rid themselves of their kolkhoznik status: The Soviet authorities did not catch runaway kolkhozniks and return them to their villages. Within a village context, moreover, loss of kolkhoz status (through expulsion from or disbanding of the kolkhoz) was often a disaster of the first magnitude.

By the mid 1930s, the kolkhoz had emerged as an association of village land users, like its predecessor, the mir. More specifically, it was an association of village land users who received payment from the kolkhoz on the basis of labordays (*trudodni*), which were weighted units reflecting both time worked and the nature of the job. Salaried persons in the village like teachers and agronomists were not usually kolkhoz members after the earliest years, although they had the right to join and had originally been strongly encouraged to do so.[28] This was almost certainly an instinctive response to the rise of an unacknowledged system of Soviet estates (*sosloviia*) in which the estate of state employees had higher status than the estate of kolkhozniks.

The kolkhoz was a cooperative and (in principle) voluntary association in which each member owned a share of the whole. This share (*paevoi vznos*) was initially "bought" when the peasant joining the collective contributed his means of production. If he subsequently left the kolkhoz, he was supposed to get most of his share back in cash (although, needless to say, this was an extremely complicated and chancy procedure in practice), and if he transferred to another kolkhoz, property equal in value to what he had contributed on joining was meant to be transferred to the new kolkhoz.[29]

The Problem of the Dvor

Kolkhoz membership, unlike membership of the mir, was on an individual adult basis, not a household one. This was one of the things Soviet writers liked to boast about, since it gave women equal rights with men for the first time and was expected to destroy traditional patriarchal oppression within the peasant household. The peasant household (*dvor*), it was initially believed, would simply lose its significance as a socio-economic unit in the village. Collectivization "destroys the concept of the peasant dvor", said a senior labor official in 1930. Jurists in the early 1930s assumed that the dvor had lost its standing as a legal entity.[30]

From the peasants' standpoint, however, the household remained the basic unit in the village. Sometimes they were not even aware that membership of the kolkhoz was supposed to be on an individual rather than a household basis, it was reported, or were aware of it but registered their disagreement by allowing only heads of households to vote at kolkhoz general meetings.[31] Indeed, in most of the functions of everyday life, including economic and financial relations with the state, the primacy of the household was untouched, regardless of whether or not jurists recognized it as a legal entity. It was the kolkhoz household, not the individual, that had the private plot and the cow; and it was the household on which state and local taxes and procurement quotas were levied.

The peasants' view prevailed in practice over that of the Communists, and in 1935 this was implicitly recognized when the new Kolkhoz Charter identified the household as the unit of entitlement in its provisions on the private plot and the keeping of domestic animals.[32] Then in 1936 the Stalin Constitution gave definitive recognition to the kolkhoz household (*kolkhoznyi dvor*) as a legal entity whose rights to a private plot were guaranteed. As a result, Soviet jurists had to adjust to the new situation and come up with a definition of the kolkhoz household. That turned out to be surprisingly broad. Any peasant household that contained a kolkhoz member was defined as a "kolkhoz household," entitled to a lower rate of taxation and a larger private plot than an "independent" household. The kolkhoz member did not have to be the head of the household. Other household members could be "independents," sovkhoz workers, or wage earners employed outside agriculture without prejudice to the household's kolkhoz status.[33]

Mixed kolkhoz households were quite common. An inspector for the

Commissariat of Agriculture reported in 1935 on one kolkhoz in the south in which seventy of the "kolkhoz households" had in fact only one kolkhoz member, the others working either as independents in agriculture or as wage earners in the mines or on the railroad. As an example, he cited the Iatskov family, consisting of a mother, the kolkhoz member, and three sons in their twenties who were prosperous independent peasants.[34]

Even the mix between kolkhozniks and independents occurred fairly frequently. In such cases, the kolkhozniks always explained to officials that they had so far been unable to bring the spouse or parent around to their progressive point of view. But in fact they were probably trying to take advantage of a legal loophole: An independent could keep a horse, while a kolkhoznik was entitled to a larger private plot. Of course the effort was not necessarily successful because local officials did not invariably observe legal niceties. If it worked, however, the best arrangement in a mixed household was supposedly for the wife to join the kolkhoz, since convention allowed her to give a larger proportion of her time to the private plot than a man, and the husband (and his horse) to stay outside.[35]

Admission to the Kolkhoz

All "toilers" had the right to join a kolkhoz, and the kolkhoz did not have any clearly articulated right to refuse them. Kulaks and priests and their families, however, were forbidden to join collective farms in the early 1930s. After a few years, this prohibition was lifted first from the children of kulaks and then from kulaks, but village priests and probably their children remained ineligible.[36]

There were special problems surrounding kolkhoz admission in the famine year, 1933, when starving peasants in areas like the Northern Caucasus and Krasnodar *krai* desperately tried to join the collective farms in the spring because they had no seed grain. Their applications swamped the collective farms, which could not possibly admit them all. The local newspaper, perplexed by the dilemma, suggested that those applicants who were "sincere" might be admitted.[37]

By the mid 1930s, the crisis was over and the collective farms were once again expected to admit all eligible applicants. But now that the tide had turned in favor of the kolkhoz and independents were obviously a disappearing species, kolkhozniks were often reluctant to allow independents to join. This was partly because the independents were resented as latecomers who showed up after the old kolkhozniks had done all the hard work, but mainly because they came with empty hands: Animals and inventory had all been sold or confiscated by the taxman, or had perished during the famine. The kolkhozniks had no right to refuse entry to independents, a party spokesman told the Congress of Outstanding Kolkhozniks in February 1935, but they did have the right to make them pay a sum equivalent to the value of any animals that had been sold off during the last two years, as long as they let them spread the payments over a reasonable period. This provision was duly written into the new Kolkhoz Charter approved by the Congress and issued in 1935. Even in 1937, however, there were occasional reports that kolkhozy were unwilling to take in "naked" independents and raion authorities did not think it worth pushing them to do so.[38] But the issue lost its salience as the numbers of independents dwindled towards the end of the decade.

While few peasants were really eager to become kolkhoz members in the early years of collectivization, the situation changed over time. By the second half of the 1930s, it was not uncommon to find peasants angrily protesting against denial of membership or expulsion by the kolkhoz. This was clearly because they perceived advantages in having the status of kolkhoznik. The advantages were basically of two kinds. One set had to do with life within the village and the advantages of being a kolkhoznik rather than an independent: for example, the right to a larger private plot, a lower level of taxation, or access to kolkhoz meadows for grazing. But there were also advantages in retaining the status of a kolkhoznik for persons who were basically working for wages outside the village: for example, support for a family left behind in the village, "insurance" against disability or retirement, and sometimes simply guarantee of respectability (meaning essentially nonkulak status) in the eyes of urban employers. In one case from Kalinin oblast in 1937 or 1938, for instance, an independent peasant named Agafia Zvereva lodged a complaint against the local kolkhoz for refusing to admit her and won a favorable verdict. It turned out, however, that her reason for seeking admission (and the kolkhoz's reason for refusing her application) was that she wanted to work in Leningrad, "for which purpose she needed a document saying that she was a *kolkhoznitsa*."[39]

Expulsion

The kolkhoz had the right to expel members, although the 1935 Charter (par. 8) required that expulsions be approved by a majority vote at a general meeting of the kolkhoz at which at least two-thirds of the kolkhozniks were present. But this was supposed to be a step of last resort, and expelled kolkhozniks had the right to appeal to raion authorities for reinstatement, and were often in fact reinstated. If the rules were followed (something not to be relied on in all cases), it was a complex proceeding. Members of the kolkhoz were theoretically part owners. Even if they left via expulsion rather than of their own free will, the kolkhoz was still supposed to pay them the equivalent in cash of their original investment.[40]

In practice, expulsions occurred frequently. In the first place, kolkhoz chairman and other rural officials often used expulsion as a disciplinary sanction—the equivalent of firing a lazy or troublemaking employee. In the second place, the kolkhozniks themselves were inclined to expel households they felt were not pulling their weight, especially in cases when the kolkhoz was short of labor and absent males refused to return from otkhod. The kolkhoz, in short, inherited from the peasant commune something of the old ethos of collective responsibility (*krugovaia poruka*) and the willingness to punish households that failed to bear their share of the burden.

With regard to expulsions, as with admissions, the 1932–33 famine created an exceptional situation. By the spring, with the only seed grain left in many regions that which the state had recently shipped out to kolkhozy and sovkhozy, kolkhoz membership suddenly became a very important possession. "Expulsion from the kolkhoz is the equivalent of death for the kolkhoznik. If someone is expelled, he weeps and begs them not to expel him," reported an MTS politotdel in the North Caucasus. At the same time, the kolkhozy themselves were close to starvation. There was strong pressure to expel kolkhoz members who were away on otkhod during the spring and summer to prevent them returning in the fall and claiming a share of the harvest. Expulsion was "a weapon in your hands" to be used against "idlers," Ia. A. Iakovlev, the head of the Central Committee's agricultural department, told kolkhoz activists at the beginning of 1933.[41]

Two years later, however, after the expulsion of "hundreds of thousands of kolkhozniks" for disciplinary reasons, Iakovlev was talking in a very different vein. Expulsion should generally be avoided, he told the Second Congress of Oustanding Kolkhozniks in 1935. Kolkhoz chairmen and other officials should not use it as a way of disciplining and punishing recalcitrant or truant kolkhozniks. When it was absolutely necessary to expel a kolkhoz member, this should only be done by decision of the kolkhoz assembly, never on the whim of the kolkhoz chairman or any other rural official. The message was underlined a few months later when the Central Committee's representative, Andrei Zhdanov, delivered a stinging rebuke to the Saratov regional party committee for (among other sins) allowing an epidemic of "groundless expulsions" of kolkhozniks.[42]

For all this, punitive expulsions from collective farms remained very common, otkhodniks and their families (often viewed by the kolkhoz as dependents who had been abandoned by the head of household to be a burden on the kolkhoz) being the main but not the only victims. In one Leningrad oblast kolkhoz, more than a third of all the households had been expelled at one time or another. Although some of those expelled complained to the raion, no action was taken to reinstate them. Others who were expelled lacked the boldness or knowledge of their rights to protest. "I never complained because I thought that was how it was supposed to be," said one peasant in Voronezh oblast who had been expelled after she married a railwayman, even though she continued to live and work in the kolkhoz.[43]

The consequences of expulsion were often severe, especially for those who were not otkhodniks with an outside source of income, since the peasant was generally left without land, a horse, or agricultural equipment. "To expel a kolkhoznik from the kolkhoz means . . . not only to disgrace him in the eyes of the public but also to doom him to a hungry existence," the Central Committee noted in 1938. In some cases, it is true, a peasant expelled from one kolkhoz was able to move to another village and join the kolkhoz there. There was no legal impediment to this, but in practice it seems rarely to have been done unless there were close family members in the new kolkhoz. Women who married peasants from other villages were likely to move their kolkhoz membership to the husband's village, and elderly peasants sometimes moved to the kolkhoz where one of their children lived. In at least one case, a peasant who was chronically at odds with the leadership of his kolkhoz was expelled, moved to his wife's native village, and was able to join the kolkhoz there.[44]

In the winter of 1937–38, during the Great Purges, expulsion from the kolkhoz once again reached epidemic proportions.[45] This provoked a government decree in the spring of 1938 condemning indiscriminate expulsions and forbidding "the carrying out of purges (*chistki*) under any pretext whatsoever" in the kolkhozy. But it was not a significant policy shift. Little more than a year later, a new decree introducing the compulsory minimum of labordays was deploring the presence of "pseudo-kolkhozniks" who wanted the benefits of kolkhoznik status without sharing in the common work of the kolkhoz and recommended that such persons should no longer be considered kolkhoz members.[46]

There was one other way that peasants could lose their status as kolkhoz members. That was by the collapse or disbanding of the entire kolkhoz. In most of the reported cases, this was a result either of a mass exodus as a result of hunger, or of punitive or arbitrary actions by local authorities that were enormously resented by the peasants. Many collective farms collapsed, at least temporarily, during the 1933 famine. There were some collapses under similar, although less extreme circumstances, in the spring of 1937 after the harvest had failed in many regions of the country in 1936.[47]

Examples of mass resignation of kolkhozniks as a collective statement of political protest are extremely rare, but there is at least one in the Smolensk Archive. In this case, the "Village" (*Selo*) kolkhoz, whose very name suggests alienation from Soviet values, became so acutely dissatisfied (for reasons that are not explained) that "in mid July [1934] all the kolkhozniks signed a statement of resignation from the kolkhoz and began to reap the grain as independent farmers (*edinolichniki*)." This provoked the raion leadership into an action that was subsequently sternly condemned by higher authorities: It sent an armed detachment of forty-two persons to the fields where the (former) kolkhozniks were working and attempted to take eight hostages. In the resulting fight, one kolkhoznik was killed and another severely wounded.[48]

The forcible disbanding of a kolkhoz by local authorities, which occurred more frequently than fire fights in the fields, was almost equally disapproved of by those higher up the chain of command. Such actions were usually taken because some locally powerful institution wanted to get its hands on the kolkhoz land or other assets, or as the ultimate measure of punishment when a kolkhoz defied the raion on some significant issue such as sowing plans or appointment of a kolkhoz chairman. In Dnepropetrovsk in 1933, for example, the "Red Dawn" kolkhoz was liquidated by the local rural soviet, evidently as a way of seizing control of the kolkhoz animals. In Kursk in 1937, several collective farms were disbanded against the will of their members because a neighboring sovkhoz wanted their lands.[49]

Some cases of kolkhoz liquidation became notorious in 1937 when the raion leaders responsible were put on show trial for the crime, charged with counterrevolutionary sabotage of collectivization. In these cases, the basic reason for liquidating the kolkhoz was to punish the kolkhozniks for defying the raion authorities, but no doubt some of the assets confiscated found their way into various officials' pockets.

Liquidation of the kolkhoz meant, in effect, liquidation of the whole village economy and complete ruin for the individual kolkhoz households; the kolkhozniks "wept" when they heard the news. When the "New Life" kolkhoz in Iaroslavl oblast was forcibly disbanded in 1936, the raion seized all its property including animals, distributed the land (including private plots) among neighboring collective farms, and slapped the punitive "independent" tax on the former kolkhozniks. The same happened in a case in Kirillovo raion, Leningrad oblast, except that the authorities there overlooked the possibilities of the "independent" tax but confiscated samovars and other personal property in addition to kolkhoz assets.[50]

A Congress and a Charter

Toward the end of 1934, the Central Committee decided that the existing Kolkhoz Charter, hastily published in March 1930, had become outdated and needed to be replaced by a new Charter incorporating the evolution of the kolkhoz in the past four and a half years. For this purpose, it summoned the Second Congress of Outstanding Kolkhozniks, which was supposed to serve as a consultative body that would help to formulate the new Charter. The Congress met in Moscow in February 1935.

In some ways, this Congress was an example of phony political participation, part of the larger phenomenon of "the Potemkin village" discussed in a later chapter. Although delegates were elected by local kolkhozniks, only those "leading" (*peredovye*) collective farms preselected by raion authorities had the right to hold such elections. The Congress was intended to be representative of "outstanding kolkhozniks" (*kolkhozniki-udarniki*), a phrase that suggested peasants who were in good standing with the regime rather than peasants who were respected in the village. The draft Charter under consideration had been prepared by the Central Committee's Agriculture Department without any formal peasant input, and delegates seem to have received copies only on the opening day of the Congress.[51]

Nevertheless, the Second Congress does not completely fit under the rubric of Potemkinism. In contrast to the First Congress of Outstanding Kolkhozniks, a miserable affair held at the height of the 1933 famine that featured mendacious accounts of kolkhoz triumphs by delegates and almost no real exchange of opinion, the Second Congress turned out to be a forum for genuine discussion in which delegates supplied the party leaders with useful information and suggestions based on local experience. The delegates' suggestions even had a slight impact on the final text of the draft Charter, although there was nothing resembling a formal parliamentary process of offering amendments and voting them up or down. But it was not the Western parliamentary model that the Second Congress was following. The Congress is best understood in terms of an eighteenth-century Russian model of state consultation with society, the Legislative Commission called by Catherine the Great in the 1760s, which did not generate legislation or curb the power of the crown, but did provide a forum for the upward transmission of information and the expression of local concerns and (within limits) grievances.

Kolkhoz Activists

The Second Congress was a meeting ground for Communist Party leaders and Central Committee officials, on the one hand, and kolkhoz activists on the other. Stalin was present throughout, and took part in the deliberations of the Congress's editorial commission (which prepared the final text of the Kolkhoz Charter), even though he did not make a formal speech in the plenary session. The government's People's Commissar of Agriculture, Mikhail Chernov, chaired the editorial commission and made the closing speech. But it was Ia. A. Iakovlev, who had recently left the office of People's Commissar to head the Central Committee's agriculture department, who was clearly the key figure in drafting the 1935 Charter and in formulating agricultural policy in general. Iakovlev had acquired genuine expertise on peasant problems in the 1920s, despite his urban Jewish background and prerevolutionary status as a student revolutionary and engineering dropout in St. Petersburg. Evidently more of a believer in consultation and popular input than most Bolsheviks of his generation, he was the longtime editor of *Krest'ianskaia gazeta*, the newspaper to which peasants most frequently addressed their complaints and petitions.[52]

On the peasant side, about a quarter of the 1,433 delegates at the Second Congress were kolkhoz chairmen, and a slightly larger group (27 percent) were brigade leaders. Tractor drivers and combine operators comprised 4 percent, and the rest were rank-and-file kolkhozniks, the great majority of whom were undoubtedly peasant activists who had joined the kolkhoz early and were strongly committed to it. For the Second Congress, as for the first, the instructions to local authorities emphasized the importance of choosing delegates directly involved in kolkhoz production, a stipulation that was presumably intended to prevent the automatic selection of kolkhoz chairmen.[53]

In reporting on the makeup of the Second Congress, the spokesman for its Mandate Commission (Nikolai Ezhov, at this time a relatively humble Central Committee secretary) noted with approval that the proportion of delegates who were Communists had dropped to 27 percent, down from 40 percent at the First Congress in 1933. The reason that Ezhov viewed this so positively was that party leaders wanted the Congress to represent peasant opinion, albeit under controlled conditions, and it was well known that even "progressive" peasants were not usually party members. The same reasoning lay behind Ezhov's approval of the fact that the Second Congress had much weaker ties to the "old" kolkhoz movement than its predecessor. At the First Congress, four-fifths of the delegates had joined collective farms before 1930. At the Second Congress, the corresponding figure was only 40 percent, and a mere 6 percent of delegates were veterans of the kolkhoz movement before 1928.[54]

What the Congress showed, however, was that between the peasant activists of the kolkhoz and ordinary peasants lay an attitudinal gulf. True, there were a few delegates who came with specific "mandates" (*nakazy*) from their fellow kolkhozniks, and two women chairmen of predominantly female collectives spoke with evident sincerity on behalf of "our women".[55] But speaking for the kolkhoz was not yet the same thing as speaking for the village. In many villages, it was only a few years since kolkhozniks—the hard-core members who did not try to resign from the kolkhoz after "Dizzy with Success"—had been an embattled minority. This was still evident in the speeches of delegates to the Second Congress. Many of the delegates seemed confused when the party leaders tried to treat them as representatives of a constituency (the collectivized village), rather than addressing them, according to the precedent set at the First Congress, as fighters for a cause.

No group is so elusive as the kolkhoz activists of the early to middle 1930s. In the first years of collectivization, local village activists—that is, peasants with a real commitment to the Soviet cause and the kolkhoz—were often hidden in the shadow of the outsiders, 25,000-ers and the like, who had come in to organize and manage the kolkhoz. Judging by the sparse biographical information available on delegates to the First Congress, they tended to be former bedniaks and batraks, often with earlier experience as industrial workers, or veterans of the Red Army in the Civil War. Other early activist types that were less well represented at the First Congress were widows who were heads of bedniak households, often roughly treated by the mir, and young male peasants who were members or admirers of the Komsomol. The male activists, although not the widows, were attracted to the world outside the village and had many opportunities to join it in the early 1930s.[56]

At the Second Congress, we encounter a wider variety of activist types. At one end of the spectrum were activists of the old school, peasant veterans in military tunics who ended their speeches with cheers for the Red Army and its leader, Voroshilov. They were often party members who and told blood-curdling tales of their struggles with the local kulaks. A good example of this type was Dmitrii Korchevskii, son of a bedniak, who went away to work in a metallurgical plant in the Donbass and served in the Imperial Army, where he headed a revolutionary committee, before returning to his native village and becoming chairman of the local rural soviet in 1924, and kolkhoz chairman in 1931. According to Korchevskii, local kulaks had plotted to kill him, and he was saved only by the intervention of the GPU (secret police.[57]

At the other end of the spectrum were young peasants who had found their niche in the kolkhoz as tractor drivers and displayed little or nothing of the militant, revolutionary psychology. Some of these were comparatively well educated and probably came from solid middle-peasant families, like Aleksei Solodov from Kharkov oblast, one of whose brothers was a train driver and another a rural teacher. Others were former bedniaks, for example the award-winning tractor driver from Stalingrad, Nikifor Shestopalov, who had been illiterate when he was first singled out for promotion and recalled being mocked and teased by other peasants.[58]

For *Izvestiia*'s series of "literary portraits" of Congress delegates, the writer Vsevolod Ivanov interviewed Trofim Kazhakin from Moscow oblast, who told a story of a hard life—"breaking bricks from the age of 15, and that's the worst work in the world, you get so many illnesses, especially if you want to go back to agriculture and are inclined to melancholy." But as kolkhoz chairman, Kazakhin's life had improved; he had just bought an overcoat for 100 rubles. Konstantin Paustovskii, interviewing a middle-aged kolkhoz chairman from the Kazan region, Andrei Lazarev, had difficulty getting him to say anything about himself as an individual. He had lived almost all his life in the village, and had an old father who still made *lapti* and plaited rope, a wife who was not yet literate, and four children. When pressed, he admitted unwillingly that he had fought at the front during the Civil War, but refused to elaborate.[59]

Among the most articulate and forthcoming of the delegates were a number of the women, who had clearly been picked as models for emulation. One of them was Pasha Angelina, leader of a women's tractor brigade in Ukraine and soon to be a nationally famous Stakhanovite. Another was Ekaterina Kulba, a young milkmaid from Minsk raion, who spoke with feeling about the oppression of women by "landlords and kulaks and even our own husbands" who tried to stop women from speaking at meetings or participating in public life. Like Korchevskii, Kulba was a militant whose experience of fighting the class enemy had left an indelible mark. In this case, the "class enemy" had been entrenched as an official in the rural soviet, and Kulba and her fellow activists had had to write to *Pravda* and alert the MTS politotdel in 1933 before this official was removed and prosecuted.[60]

Issues

Among the major issues discussed at the Second Congress were the size of the private plot, maternity benefits for kolkhoz women, the possibility of admitting kulaks to the kolkhoz, kolkhoz admissions, and expulsions. The party leaders' position on all these questions was demonstratively conciliatory towards the peasantry, indicative of a desire to move away from the confrontational posture associated with collectivization. The kolkhoz activists were a good deal less conciliatory than the leaders, who gently chided them for this. It was a much milder replay of Stalin's tactics with "Dizzy with Success," when the regime suddenly retreated from maximalist objectives and left local officials and collectivizers out on a limb. This retreat was more deftly executed, however. It left some of the delegates puzzled, but there was no sense of mass outrage. The personal accessibility of the leaders during the Congress, the large amount of flattering publicity given to the event in the press, and the many photographs with delegates for which Stalin and other leaders patiently posed, seem to have left a generally favorable impression.

Stalin and the Private Plot

The private plot was one of the most important issues under discussion at the Congress. It was also one of the key points on which the party leaders wanted to demonstrate a conciliatory spirit towards the peasantry. This was not made clear to the delegates in advance, and as a result, intentionally or otherwise, the demonstration was made partly at the delegates' expense.

The draft of the Charter had evidently included the right of kolkhozniks to small private plots whose size would be determined by the People's Commissariat of Agriculture.[61] While the delegates did not generally speak out against private plots, they gave every sign of being unhappy with the idea, both on ideological grounds (since they had fought so hard for the principle of collective cultivation in the past) and for practical reasons (having private plots would distract the kolkhozniks from work on collective fields). Most speakers emphasized the importance of keeping the size of the private plot to a minimum and forbidding the planting of grain crops on the plot.[62] It was not economically rational to spend time on a small private plot rather than a large collective field, said one delegate from Kursk. Women spend too much time working in the yard as it is; besides, the peasants will plant food crops, not flax, which is what is needed locally and by the state.[63]

Timofei Vlasenko, the delegate from Shishkovo, had to admit that the private plot was another issue on which the Congress had forced him to adjust his thinking. Once having accepted the principle, however, he was quick to turn it to his own purposes, which were to give "old" kolkhozniks a permanent edge over other villagers:

> VLASENKO: Let me touch on the question of private plots. Until the Congress I thought that we ought to give the kolkhoznik less land, but I turned out not to be right. . . . In a few days we will begin to work out our own kolkhoz charter on the lines of the Model Charter laid out at the Congress, and then we will make sure that our kolkhozniks have private plots secured forever.
>
> VOICES: But what about the independents (*edinolichniki*)?
>
> VLASENKO: If there is land left in the village itself, we will give it to them; if there is not, they will have to take land further off in the fields. The kolkhozniks will get the best pieces of land. . . .[64]

The debate on private plots that had started in the general session the Congress continued at the meeting of the editorial commission, a body of 170 persons (including Stalin and Chernov, Iakovlev's successor as People's Commissar for Agriculture) elected by the Congress to produce the final version of the Kolkhoz Charter. Its proceedings were not included in the minutes of the Congress, but a Leningrad delegate who was a member of the editorial commission gave the following account:

> There was a particularly large amount of discussion on the second section of the Charter—the part on land. Here it was interesting to notice something. Comrade Chernov [in the chair] asked: "Who wants to speak?" So many hands went up that they didn't know who to let speak first. . . . The big argument was over the size of the private plot. Some people suggested allocating 0.12 hectares for the private plot, others suggested 0.25 hectares. I personally suggested 0.45 hectares. A few said that the [size of] the private plots ought to be determined by the number of people in the household (*po edokam*). Our delegate Kariutina . . . spoke against determing the [size of] the plot according to household size. "Family members are added and subtracted, so that each year you would have to redo the plot," she said. . . .
>
> After he had listened to everyone else, comrade Stalin then expressed his own opinion. "You are all progressive (*peredovye*) people that are gathered here," he said, "and it's very good that you think more of working on the kolkhoz land than on your own plots. But you must not forget that the majority of kolkhozniks want to plant an orchard, cultivate a vegetable garden, or keep bees. The kolkhozniks want to live a decent life, and for that this 0.12 hectares is not enough. We need to allocate a quarter to half a hectare, and even as much as one hectare in some districts.[65]

This intervention of Stalin's in favor of the private plot provided one of the strongest messages that came out of the Congress. In summarizing the work of the editorial committee for the Congress, Chernov reported Stalin's comments at length. Then they were relayed by Iakovlev to the Moscow and Leningrad party organizations. Finally, on March 13, Stalin's remarks to the editorial commission were published in *Pravda*.[66]

In his comments, Stalin was clearly trying to stake out a position of sympathy with ordinary peasants and their desire for a decent life, distancing himself (as in "Dizzy with Success") from those low-level Communist officials and activists who were intolerant of peasant aspirations and prone to commit excesses. If you want to make the kolkhoz work, he said, you have to take into account that the peasants have personal interests as well as collective ones. You have to let them have a reasonable-sized private plot and a few animals. The trouble with you activists, Stalin had the nerve to say, is that "in general you want to squeeze the kolkhoznik. That won't work. It's not right."[67]

Stalin and the Women's Cause

Stalin's other major intervention at the Second Congress had to do with peasant women. This had been a theme of his at the First Congress, too, when he announced that women were "a great force" in the kolkhoz. It is unclear just what motivated this. Sometimes Stalin and other leaders seemed to be making a pitch for women's support because they reasoned that women were an oppressed class in the village (the "surrogate proletariat" argument, as Gregory Massell expresses it). At other times, the leaders seemed to be coming from the opposite direction, attempting to conciliate women because they perceived them to be more deeply offended by collectivization than men were (as is implied by Stalin's reference at the First Congress to "a little misunderstanding . . . about the cow" that had temporarily bedevilled the regime's relationship with peasant women until the issue was cleared up by "Dizzy with Success").[68]

At the Second Congress, Stalin's "women's" theme was maternity benefits for kolkhoz women. The draft Charter presented to the Congress included a provision for support to kolkhoz women in childbearing, but without making any specific promise on the benefit that should be offered. As related by Fedotova, the Leningrad delegate who participated in the editorial commission deliberations,

> Comrade Stalin's attitude to us, kolkhoz women, was very considerate, very sensitive. He listened to all our comments and said a lot about making the lot of kolkhoz women easier. Comrade Stalin did not agree with the idea that some kolkhoz men expressed that women should be freed only for two weeks before giving birth. He said: "In my opinion, the kolkhoznitsa ought to be freed for a month before giving birth and a month after. And they shouldn't be hurt in terms of pay. For those two months they should be paid half of their average earnings.[69]

Chernov gave essentially the same account in his report to the Congress, and his remarks were greeted by "tumultuous applause" from the delegates,[70] although not all of them had been so enthusiastic in their comments during the discussion. The provision was duly included in the Charter. Still, it may be noted that Stalin was not being overly generous by offering two months' maternity leave: One delegate, a woman chairman of a predominantly female kolkhoz, had recommended three months and reported that this was already the rule on her kolkhoz.[71]

The Issue of Kulaks' Return

The draft Charter contained a clause allowing for the admission to collective farms of expropriated kulaks whose subsequent conduct indicated that they had reformed and were no longer enemies of Soviet power. In his opening speech to the Congress, Iakovlev dwelt on this at some length, mentioning the contributions of former kulaks "in various sectors of work, including the Northern forests and the Belomor canal" and warning against policies based on a spirit of "vengeance" (*mest'*).[72] But there was a fuzziness, no doubt intentional, about just which categories of dekulakized peasant Iakovlev had in mind when he talked about kolkhoz admission. Did he mean the gulag ("first category") contingent, as the Belomor reference implies? Or was it the deported ("second category") kulaks whom he had in mind, as several passing references to "deportation" suggest; and if so, was he proposing that they be admitted to kolkhozy in their new place of settlement or allowed to return to their native villages? Or, finally, was he thinking primarily of "third category" kulaks, expropriated but neither deported nor sent to gulag, who remained in the village?

The delegates who addressed the question assumed that he was at least hinting at the possibility that the kulaks who had been forcibly removed from the village via deportation or arrest might be allowed to return. This prospect clearly filled them with horror, although in light of the leadership's position this was expressed somewhat obliquely. Reading between the lines, one senses that these local activists expected nothing but trouble, feuding, and violence in the village to come out of such a volte-face. They were worried about a "spirit of vengeance", certainly—but it was the possible revenge of the dekulakized against the village activists that was on their minds.

"If Soviet power says we have to take the former kulaks, then we take them," said one speaker, a kolkhoz chairman from the north, after indicating his doubts by citing Stalin on the importance of eternal vigilance against class enemies. "But we will be looking keenly to see what kind of man this is." Let's be careful that these former kulaks are really "sheep" and not just "wolves in sheep's clothing," warned another kolkhoz chairman. Several speakers stated they had no objection to deported kulaks who had reformed being allowed to join collective farms—but not *their* collective farms. Let them become kolkhozniks out there, in the distant regions to which they were deported, but "there's no need to send them back to us." This applied particularly to Ukraine, added a nervous Ukrainian kolkhoz chairman. Reformed or not, the dekulakized kulaks would be "especially dangerous" in collective farms that were still shaky and (he implied) not yet recovered from the impact of the famine. "In my opinion, we ought to refrain from letting kulaks who were sent to Solovki join weak collective farms."[73]

The Charter in its edited form retained the rather ambiguous formulation of the original draft. Thus, no formal concession was made to the anxieties expressed by delegates, though Iakovlev picked up one of their phrases later in explaining to the party aktivs of Moscow and Leningrad that "the Model Charter allows . . . (reformed kulaks) to be admitted as members of the artel, of course, with due caution and after a strict check to make sure that *wolves in sheep's clothing* were not getting in on the pretext of being reformed characters. . . ."[74]

Expulsion and Membership Issues

At the First Congress, held in a year when mass flight from the villages in the face of imminent famine had left many collective farms alarmingly short of working hands, government spokesmen and delegates alike had taken a very tough line on expulsion and the kolkhoz's right to demand the return of absent or "idle" members. In 1935, however, the situation was different. Labor shortage on the kolkhoz was no longer an acute problem, arbitrary disciplinary expulsions of kolkhozniks had become a major embarrassment, and the Soviet leaders had had time to reflect that, after all, the real priority was to draw peasants into the kolkhoz, not to push them out.

The draft Charter therefore proposed restricting the right to expel kolkhoz members to the kolkhoz general meeting assembly (implicitly removing this right from kolkhoz and rural soviet chairmen and visiting raion officials) and requiring that any expulsion be approved by two-thirds of the kolkhoz members. Most of the delegates spoke in favor of this and agreed that expulsions had got out of hand, but there was a detectable undertone of concern among them about how kolkhoz leaders would be able to discipline their members and make them go out to work in the fields if the sanction of expulsion were removed.[75] As one delegate confessed after the Congress, it was hard for an old kolkhoz activist to accept such a laissez-faire approach to the obligations of kolkhoz membership.[76]

The admission of new kolkhoz members was a more touchy issue at the Second Congress. In his opening report, Iakovlev reminded his audience that it was the government's aim to enroll all the peasantry in collective farms, not to retain the present division of the village into kolkhozniks and independents. He discerned a tendency on the part of kolkhoz activists to make the independents suffer for their early hostility to the kolkhoz, even if they now wanted to join. Many kolkhoz leaders were "holding up" the admission of independents for so long that they finally gave up the struggle and left the village, Iakovlev said. When independents applied to join, the kolkhozy were demanding that they make immediate entrance payments equivalent to the full value of any animals or equipment they had sold off in the past four or five years to avoid being labelled kulaks. Obviously this was impossible for most independents, who (although Iakovlev did not mention this) were most likely applying to join the kolkhoz because they had been ruined by punitive taxation and procurements. The new Charter permitted collective farms to demand compensation from applicants for membership who had disposed of horses and seed grain in the past two years. If the applicants were unable to raise this sum, however, they should be admitted to the kolkhoz anyway and allowed to repay the debt over a six-year period.[77]

This was a bitter pill for the activist delegates to swallow. After all, they had contributed their horses and equipment to the kolkhoz when they joined. Why should peasants who had earlier sold or slaughtered their animals be allowed to enter with empty hands? Where was the justice of it, if late joiners—those peasants who for years had scoffed at the kolkhoz—were to be allowed in at a cheaper rate than early joiners, the kolkhoz's most staunch supporters? In discussion at the Congress, a number of delegates expressed this distress and proposed various amendments to make admission of new members tougher.[78] "In comrade Iakovlev's report there was much that was hard for us to understand about the Charter," said one kolkhoz chairman from Siberia.

> For example, [take] the fact that an independent peasant joining the kolkhoz will not have to give up minor farm equipment (*melkii inventar'*) to the kolkhoz, keeping it for his individual use on the private plot. Comrades, before my departure we had twenty new kolkhozniks due to join up. If we leave them in possession of small farm equipment, and we count a plow and harrow as belonging to that category, then the old kolkhozniks too will asking for plows and harrows to be returned for their private plots.... If that happens, then... kolkhoz discipline may be destroyed.[79]

When the final version of the Charter emerged from the Congress's editorial commission, some concessions had been made to the delegates' objections: New entrants to the kolkhoz were to have "up to six years" (instead of "six years") to pay, leaving the kolkhoz more discretion to penalize them for past sins. Also, plows and harrows were specifically identified as belonging to the category of major farm equipment—that is, subject to collectivization.[80]

When Timofei Vlasenko, one of the delegates from Leningrad oblast, returned to his village of Shishkovo and reported on the Congress, he was still struggling with this question. He started with a blunt statement of the new official line on admission of new members, which was of considerable relevance to Shishkovo, where thirty households were still outside the kolkhoz:

> Not too long ago one could still hear our kolkhozniks making comments like this: "Why the hell should we let them join when they have nothing." [But] according to the new Charter, we must let them join, and give them six years to pay off the money value of the horse and seeds that they disposed of.

Having said that, however, he switched back on to more familiar rails.

> Many independents . . . have the wrong attitude. [They think:] "Let the kolkhozniks build, and we will watch. When the right time comes, we will sit down to a laden table!"
>   No, comrades, that won't work. We did the work, we toiled night and day, so be so kind as to return to us the property that you disposed of.[81]

The Kolkhoz Charter was published as a set of guidelines that were exemplary, not obligatory. Each kolkhoz was supposed to discuss and modify it according to local conditions, vote on its approval, and register it with the raion land department. Its democratic nature was underlined by the fact that it was not promulgated as a regular government decree, but rather issued as a decision of the Second Congress of Outstanding Kolkhozniks that the highest government and party organs had simply endorsed.[82]

The emphasis on the Charter's democratic and nonobligatory qualities was largely fraudulent. But it was not fraudulent of the party leaders to represent this document as a compromise with the peasantry. The Second Congress and the Charter firmly established the kolkhoz as a village-based institution, combining elements of collective and private agriculture, which could and should accommodate all peasants (except the disgraced kulaks) and not just reflect the activist minority in the village, and would not exercise undue disciplinary powers over its members. These were the most encouraging words that had been directed at the village for many years. The 1935 Charter was the manifesto for what an émigré writer justifiably described as "the kolkhoz NEP," an interlude of conciliation following the confrontational and coercive policies of the collectivization era.[83]

5

A Second Serfdom?

Stalin had a picture of the Soviet kolkhoz as a large-scale, modern, mechanized farm that was economically and socially light years ahead of the backward, small-scale farming of the Russian peasant.[1] This was the image propagated by Soviet publicists and accepted by many outside observers. Reading the Soviet press of the 1930s, it is hard to catch any glimpses of the real Russian village behind the Potemkin facade. This is not only because of the shameless exaggeration and deception that became a standard feature of Soviet writing about agriculture during collectivization, but also because a whole new language was invented to describe peasant farming in its collective guise.

One of the effects of the new language (if not one of its purposes) was to obscure continuities with the past. Who could guess, on the basis of knowledge of Russian peasant farming before collectivization, what real-life institutions and practices lay behind such terms as "laborday" (*trudoden'*), "auditing commission" (*revizionnaia komissiia*), "brigade leader" (*brigadir*), "fulfilment of the sowing plan" (*vypolnenie plana seva*), "capital fund" (*nedelimyi fond*), "mechanizer" (*mekhanizator*), "shockworker" (*udarnik, udarnitsa*), "Stakhanovite" (*stakhanovets, stakhanovka*), "organized labor recruitment" (*orgnabor*), "independent" (*edinolichnik*), not to mention that most clumsy of acronyms, "*trudguzhpovinnost'*" (labor and cartage obligations)?

Peasants gradually came to use the new language, or part of it. Indeed, a new genre of peasant humor seems to have emerged in this connection, as peasants started to sprinkle "Soviet" phrases in everyday speech for ironic effect.[2] All the same, their understanding of the global meaning of collectivization was very different from Stalin's. They saw it less as a leap forward into the future than as a leap backward into the past.

The historical analogy that immediately presented itself was serfdom.[3] It was probably inevitable that this analogy should be used by peasants whose entry into the kolkhoz had been forced. But it also had some real applicability, especially the analogy with barshchina (where the serf's obligations were in labor rather than money). The argument underlying the analogy ran as follows. On the kolkhoz, as on the old master's estate, peasants were obliged to spend at least half their time working in someone else's fields (meaning the kolkhoz fields) essentially without payment. They lived on the produce of their own small plots, but constantly had to struggle for enough time to work on them. As in the days of serfdom, they did not have the right to leave the village for work outside without permission. This implied that kolkhozniks belonged to a special category of second-class citizen, just like serfs. They were obliged to perform corvée obligations to the state. It was not unusual for local officials, kolkhoz chairmen, and brigade leaders to assume the prerogatives of estate owners and their stewards under serfdom, subjecting field peasants to beatings and insults.

The serfdom analogy had force because of the restrictions on mobility introduced with the passport law of 1932, the corvée obligation, and the level of state procurements and prices that the state imposed on collective farms in the 1930s. As long as the state took the greater part of the crops grown on the kolkhoz fields and paid ridiculously low prices for them, most kolkhozniks received almost nothing in cash for their labor on their kolkhoz fields, and the payment in kind fluctuated, sometimes falling below subsistance. This was not literally barshchina, when serfs received no payment for their labor on the masters' fields, but at its worst it was close enough.

In their approach to work on the kolkhoz, peasants displayed many of the characteristics of unfree labor. They worked poorly and unwillingly, going out to the fields late and sneaking away early whenever possible. In the fields, they were likely to start work only when the brigade leader told them to and continue only as long as he watched them. They pilfered anything they could from the kolkhoz, implicitly rejecting the idea that collective property was in any sense theirs rather than the state's. They avoided direct confrontation with their masters but used cunning, deception, and assumed stupidity to avoid obeying instructions. They often displayed what baffled officials described as a "dependent psychology" (*izhdivencheskie nastroeniia*), working only when they were given explicit instructions and expecting the authorities to give them handouts when times were hard.

This last characteristic suggests that serfdom lived on in peasant memory as a more complex phenomenon than their antikolkhoz rhetoric allowed—and perhaps also that their attitudes to the kolkhoz contained similar ambiguities. The peasants' petitions and grievances, as well as their practices, implied that more than one concept of the "good life" was to be found in the kolkhoz-village of the 1930s.

The peasants' demands for the return of horses and the enlargement of private plots and their efforts to increase the time spent working on their plots relative to that spent in the kolkhoz fields suggested one version of the good life, namely small-scale subsistence farming of the type practiced by most peasants during the Soviet New Economic Policy (NEP). But there were also market-oriented peasants—a minority in most regions of Russia, but possibly a dominant type by the late 1930s in the Black Sea hinterland in the south and the truck-gardening areas around big cities such as Moscow and Leningrad—whose implicit notion of the good life had a much more capitalist flavor. These were the peasants who used their private plots to produce for the market and expanded their acreage by illegal buying and leasing of land.[4]

A third version of the good life was a situation in which the state assumed the patriarchal or patron-client responsibilities towards kolkhozniks that (ideally, at any rate) the noble had had towards his serfs. This was implied by the strong indignation expressed in the many peasant complaints against officials who had failed to help kolkhozniks in time of need (harvest failures, loss of a horse, fires, and other natural disasters)—that is, failed to act as the "good master" would have acted under serfdom. It was also, perhaps more unexpectedly, expressed in the peasants' increasingly frequent demands that the state should extend to kolkhozniks benefits like pensions, a limited work day, and a guaranteed minimum wage that were available to urban wage-earners.[5]

Collective and Private Spheres

The term "kolkhoz" (*kollektivnoe khoziaistvo*) stood for collective farm. But what was a collective farm? How much of the peasants' land, animals, farming implements, and everyday life had to be collectivized? There were debates on this subject,[6] but the final resolution came only after a costly practical process of trial and error in the collectivization drive at the beginning of the 1930s. The outcome was that, under Soviet collectivization, peasants lost their allotments in the village fields and their horses (which became kolkhoz property), but kept a cow, pigs, chickens, and their private plots.

The private plot (*priusadebnyi uchastok*) was part of the essential basis of peasant subsistence in the 1930s, since the payment in kind and cash that the kolkhozniks received was unpredictable and generally small. In 1935, Stalin explicitly recognized the dual nature of the kolkhoznik, who was both a collective producer, by virtue of his work on the kolkhoz fields, and an individual farmer, by virtue of his work on his own private plot. Stalin also acknowledged that peasants often had to live off their private plots, because the kolkhoz were not strong enough to support them.[7]

The kolkhoz provided a good share of the peasants' calories but virtually no meat and dairy products. Cereals were the largest single item in the peasant diet, and those came mainly from the kolkhoz. Potatoes were next: In the mid-1930s, the kolkhoz supplied about a third and the private plot two-thirds. Almost all the meat, dairy products, and eggs that the kolkhozniks ate came from their private plots. According to budget studies of kolkhoz households in 1937, kolkhozniks were eating less of many foods than they had done in 1923–24. Consumption of dairy products was not much more than half of the 1923–24 level in 1937, and cereals and meat were also somewhat lower. To compensate, peasants were eating more potatoes.[8]

The private plot was important to peasants not only as a source of food for the household but also as a source of marketable produce. In 1932, peasants (kolkhozniks and independents, and also collective farms) received the right to sell surplus produce at the kolkhoz market.[9] This was in many ways a strange anomaly in a society in which, with regard to all citizens except kolkhozniks and independent peasants, trade of any sort was treated as "speculation," a criminal offense. If the peasants had not been able to trade, however, the state would have been unable to collect from them the very substantial taxes that it levied in the 1930s.

Although the kolkhoz was supposed to supply kolkhozniks with a cash income as well as payments in kind, less than 10 percent of the kolkhoz household's cash income came from the kolkhoz. More than half came from trade and contract sales to the state of produce from the private plot. The share of market trade was modest—in the mid 1930s, budget studies showed that peasants were marketing 17–22 percent of the meat and bacon and 6–7 percent of the dairy products they produced on their private plots (although these figures may not give the full picture of legal and blackmarket trade)—but it seems to have increased rapidly in the late 1930s. Otkhod was also an important source of cash earnings for the kolkhoz household in the 1930s. According to Bergson's calculations, in 1937 Soviet kolkhoz households were earning almost as much from wage work outside the kolkhoz as they were receiving in cash payments for their work on the kolkhoz (including premiums and salaries for kolkhoz chairmen as well as laborday payments).[10]

Obligations

Peasants made payments to the state both in money (taxes) and in kind (procurements). In each case, the kolkhoz had one set of obligations, the individual kolkhoz household another.[11] The major taxes in the 1930s were the agricultural tax, the cultural tax (*kul'tzhilsbor*, introduced in 1931), and local taxes (*samooblozhenie*). The tax burden was substantially heavier than it had been before collectivization, primarily as a result of a big tax hike during the First Five-Year Plan. Taken at face value (as Russian peasants, like noneconomists everywhere, were likely to do), the tax payments collected from peasants increased by more than 500 percent in the period 1929–34, rising from 405 million rubles in 1929–30 (when the only tax levied on peasants was the agricultural tax) to 2,197 million rubles in 1934 (when, in addition to the agricultural tax, the peasants had to pay a new cultural tax as well as buy "voluntary" state bonds (*zaimy*) for an even more substantial sum).[12]

To be sure, this was a period of rapid inflation: Even according to Soviet calculations, the retail price index rose from a base of 100 in 1928 to 536 in 1937, while the American economist Janet Chapman puts the 1937 index considerably higher. But peasants were not so massively affected by retail price rises as urban wage earners. From their standpoint, the tax burden has to be assessed not so much in a context of the declining purchasing power of the ruble as in the context of the sharp reduction of peasant cash earnings that was attendant upon collectivization. After a period in the mid 1930s when the "real" tax burden on kolkhoz households probably declined, there was a new rise in taxes for many in 1939, when assessment of the agricultural tax was changed from a flat rate to a progressive rate that could go as high as 15 percent of cash income from the private plot.[13]

As with taxes, procurements obligations—aptly described by one American economist as "taxation in kind"[14]—bore both on the kolkhoz and on the kolkhoznik. The kolkhoz had to deliver quotas of grain, potatoes, and other produce. Kolkhoz grain procurements constituted a substantially larger proportion of the crop than peasants had marketed before collectivization; and the prices paid by the state have been described by a Soviet historian as "symbolic," "ten to twelve times lower than market prices." The procurement prices were often well under production costs. When the harvest was brought in, state procurements were the first priority. Then came the kolkhoz seed fund, and only after all other obligations had been met was the kolkhoz supposed to divide the remainder among member households on the basis of their work during the year.[15]

The kolkhoz household had the obligation—reminiscent of the obligation of the serf household to the lord in earlier days—to deliver meat, dairy products, eggs, and other produce from the private plot to the state. Under state procurement regulations, first introduced in 1934, every kolkhoz household (and, of course, every "independent" household as well) was required to deliver a quota of meat and milk, even if it did not have pigs or sheep to slaughter or a cow to milk. This was a subject of great peasant resentment and complaint.[16]

Once the state set procurements quotas for the various types of agricultural produce that collective farms and kolkhoz households were required to deliver, that fact in itself obliged kolkhozy and kolkhozniks to cultivate certain crops in certain quantities. But the state was not prepared to leave it at that, fearing that if the peasants' sowing was left unsupervised, they would turn up at harvest time with all sorts of excuses and explanations justifying their failure to deliver the goods the state wanted. Such considerations prompted the notorious "sowing plans," in which the raion land department gave instructions to the collective farms on what crops to plant, and over what acreage.

Even private plots were covered by an annual raion "sowing plan." When the Voronezh land department first applied itself to this task in 1935, it gave detailed instructions to kolkhozniks on the amount of grain, flax, potatoes, cabbages, cucumbers, carrots, beets, beans, and tomatoes they must cultivate on their private plots. This so outraged the kolkhozniks that they threatened to refuse the private plots newly offered by the Kolkhoz Charter rather than accept them under such onerous conditions. The zealous Voronezh officials had in fact gone too far in giving orders on the sowing of cabbages and cucumbers. But the land departments were entitled and required to set sowing plans for private plots with regard to crops such as potatoes where there were state procurements quotas.[17]

Sowing plans were bitterly resented by the kolkhozniks, both because the land department officials were often ignorant of agriculture and because the state's priorities for crops did not necessarily correspond with the peasants'. There were many conflicts between raion authorities and collective farms on this score; and during the Great Purges, when peasants were encouraged to express their grievances against rural officials, this was one of the major sources of complaint. Perhaps in response, the Central Committee made a concession to the collective farms at the end of 1939, allowing them to make their own decisions on which grain crops to sow (albeit within narrow limits) and forbidding the raion to interfere unless the farms' ability to meet procurements targets was jeopardized. What impact this had in practice is not clear, but in any case it did not last long. Soon after the war, the raions recovered their old right to determine kolkhoz sowing plans.[18]

In addition to their tax and procurements obligations to the state, kolkhozniks also bore labor and cartage obligations (*trudguzhpovinnost'*) within the framework of a corvée system established in the early 1930s. The immediate antecedents of this system lay in the Civil War, but in longer perspective it represented a revival of a practice associated with serfdom. All peasants, not just kolkhozniks, bore these labor obligations (from which all wage and salary earners were exempt). But since it was much easier to mobilize kolkhozniks than independent peasants, the real burden tended to fall on the kolkhozniks.

The labor and cartage obligation required peasants to put in six days work a year on the roads, bringing their own or (in the case of kolkhozniks) kolkhoz horses. Women peasants had to perform this obligation from the age of 18 to 40, men from 18 to 45. When the labor obligation was first introduced in 1929, the peasants were to be paid for these services, but the question of payment disappeared from supplementary legislation of 1931 and 1932. Jurists still sometimes argued that peasants *ought* to be paid. But reports indicate that they often and perhaps habitually were not paid. Peasants who did not wish to fulfill their labor obligation could make a cash payment instead, according to a report from Belorussia in 1932. Those who failed to show up for duty were liable for a fine "of up to ten times the cost of the work" for each day missed.[19]

Another corvée obligation, introduced early in 1930, was that in forest areas peasants should provide labor brigades and horses for timber felling and timber rafting in the winter. In this case, the peasants received payment for their labor but not for the use of horses; and those drafted were often absent for weeks or months. It was a heavy obligation on the collective farms, which in many cases tried to ignore or evade instructions to send kolkhozniks to the timber camps. Finally, it should not be forgotten that raion and rural soviet officials were in the habit of regarding kolkhoz labor power and kolkhoz horses as a free resource that they could mobilize at will (see Chapter 8). There was no legal framework for this, but it was nevertheless an important part of the material and psychological burden on the collectivized peasantry in the 1930s.[20]

The Private Plot

The peasant's private plot (*priusadebnyi uchastok*) was basically just the peasant household's yard (*usad'ba*), that is, the land around the hut, including a kitchen garden and perhaps a few fruit trees. Peasants' yards naturally varied in size. But of course the Soviet authorities could not resist regulating this matter and attempting to establish uniformity. At the Second Congress of Outstanding Kolkhozniks, the proper size of the private plot was the subject of one of the most lively debates, with the activists inclined to be less generous than Stalin. The conclusion, which was written into the 1935 Kolkhoz Charter, was that the size of the kolkhoznik's private plot should be in the range of 0.25–0.5 hectares—roughly an acre—in most regions, not counting the area occupied by the peasant's izba.[21]

The yards (private plots) of independent peasants, and later of wage and salary earners living in the village, were also eventually subject to official size specifications: They were supposed to be smaller than the yards of kolkhozniks.[22]

This left local authorities with the formidable task of trimming villagers' yards to the proper size of the private plot to which they were entitled. This was a miserable business involving a great deal of conflict. Since many Communists felt that it would be better if kolkhozniks had no private plots at all, regional and local authorities often tried to cut the norms to the minimum. On the Right Bank of the Volga, for example, the Saratov party committee set the norm as low as 0.1 hectare (for which it was sharply rebuked by Zhdanov in July). Kolkhozniks, on the other hand, pushed hard and sometimes successfully to have the norms raised in their districts.[23]

In the Kiev region, as well as in the Northern Caucasus, problems arose about peasant yards that included orchards and thus exceeded the maximum size. Should local authorities force kolkhozniks to cut down fruit trees until their yards were reduced to the size prescribed for a private plot? The head of the oblast land department counselled local authorities to use their commonsense and avoid needlessly offending peasants: If it was not possible to incorporate the orchard cut-offs in a general kolkhoz orchard, he suggested that the peasants' fruit trees should be left alone.[24] But it was against the nature of Soviet local authorities to use commonsense, and the axe no doubt fell on many cherry trees in the spring of 1935.

The existence of prescribed norms for the size of peasants' private plots also meant that some kolkhozniks were entitled to demand additional land because their yards were too small. These add-ons (*prirezki*) could sometimes be taken from the yards of neighbors who exceeded the norm, but in cases where this was not possible kolkhozniks sometimes ended up with private-plot land that was cut out of the kolkhoz fields. This made the concept of the private plot dangerously elastic from the standpoint of Soviet authorities. Despite the very substantial size difference between the 1–acre private plot and the 20–acre land allotment (*nadel*) that was the norm in European Russia before the revolution,[25] Communist officials always had the uneasy feeling that the private plots of the kolkhozniks might eat away at the kolkhoz fields, gradually getting bigger and bigger, until one day they would metamorphose back into allotments and there would be no collective farming area left.

At the beginning of 1934, the Belorussian party organization was sharply rebuked by the party Central Committee for having allowed kolkhozniks to cultivate private plots so large that they took up a goodly proportion of the kolkhoz fields, and "it got to the point where private plots in actuality turned into the basic farming units." Similar concerns were raised, although without any specific regional reference, in the 1939 decree on the protection of the kolkhoz collective fields from encroachment, which, as already noted, prompted a new round of cut-offs from private plots. The decree stated that "all kinds of illegal add-ons to the private plots" were commonly practiced, including "allotment" (*nadelenie*) of land to kolkhozniks in the kolkhoz fields. When the private-plot land was located in the fields, not around the peasant's house, the private plot tended to "lose the character of a subsidiary economy" and become the basic preoccupation of the kolkhoz household, whose members were sometimes able to live entirely off their plots and stop working in the kolkhoz's collective sphere altogether.[26]

There seems little doubt that peasants would have liked to accomplish a de facto decollectivization by such means. But whether they were actually succeeding in doing this on any significant scale at the end of the 1930s, and if so, in which regions of the country, is not clear on the evidence currently available. It is interesting to note, however, that despite the vigorous cutting down to size of private plots conducted in 1939–40, developments of exactly the kind condemned by the 1939 decree occurred when collective farms were left more or less unsupervised during the Second World War. During the war, as Arutiunian's research shows, there was a general tendency for private plots to expand and kolkhoz fields to shrink. Sometimes the change was quite dramatic, as in the case of the kolkhoz in the Lower Volga region whose chairman distributed more than 30 acres from the kolkhoz fields to each kolkhoz household, in addition to their existing private plots. At the same time, the private plots were increasingly given over to cultivation of cereals, something that had been largely a prerogative of the collective sphere in the 1930s and strongly discouraged if not forbidden on private plots. In 1945, 31 percent of the private plots of kolkhozniks were under grain, compared with 19 percent in 1940.[27]

There were other consequences of private-plot regulation that should be noted. The plot was not private property and could not legally be leased or sold (although in fact such transactions were quite often reported). But the house and other buildings that stood in the midst of the plot *were* private property, and peasants were legally entitled to sell or rent them. This created many complications. In one reported case, a kolkhoznik sold both his house and his yard to another villager, who was not a kolkhoz member. The kolkhoz objected to the whole sale, and revoked the kolkhoznik's right to the plot (that is, his yard), which it allocated to another kolkhoznik. When the would-be seller appealed to the courts, a local court approved the sale of both the house and the yard. But then the kolkhoz in turn appealed, and a higher court ruled that only the sale of the house was valid.[28]

In general, the house remained private property even if its owner moved from the village. But there were exceptional circumstances: If the village had originally been collectivized as a commune rather than an artel, for example, houses had also become collective property. At the end of the 1930s, a Iaroslavl railroad worker named I. I. Berezin, in poor health and close to retirement, tried to recover the village house he had left in 1930, shortly after the organization of a commune-style kolkhoz, of which he was briefly a member. Since that time, the "Searchlight" kolkhoz had become an artel. Berezin argued that since his house would never have been collectivized in the first place in an artel-style kolkhoz, he retained his property rights; but this argument was rejected on the grounds that the Civil Code established a four-year statute of limitations.[29]

The decision to make the household the unit of entitlement for the private plot created an incentive for large peasant households to divide, so that the new households would receive their own plots from the kolkhoz. This was probably one reason—although by no means the only one—for the trend away from large, multigenerational families in the 1930s (see chapter 7). But there were also possibilities for trickery: As a 1939 decree noted, some households pretended to divide in order to claim an additional private plot when in fact they intended to continue to operate as an economic unit.[30]

Tractors and Horses

Collectivization was supposed to bring the tractor and combine harvester to the Russian village, superseding the horse as the basic draft power. But it did not happen quite that way. In the first place, collectivization and famine produced disastrous losses of livestock, particularly horses. In 1928, peasants in the Soviet Union owned 33 million horses. When they joined the kolkhoz, they had to hand over the horses. But at the end of 1932, when about 60 percent of peasant households had joined the kolkhoz, all the collective farms of the Soviet Union had only 12 million horses in their possession. Between January 1929 and January 1934, the total number of horses in all types of Soviet farm dropped from 33 million to 15 million.[31]

Tractors and combine harvesters came to the countryside in the early 1930s. But they did not come in sufficient numbers to compensate for the terrible loss of animal draft power—and, furthermore, they did not come to the village. In the early 1930s, in fact, the villages lost even those tractors and harvesters they had possessed at the time of collectivization under a new policy of centralizing all complex agricultural machinery in Machine-Tractor Stations (MTS) and state farms.[32]

The MTS network, still minimal in June 1930, grew rapidly after the Central Committee resolved in December of that year that the MTS should play the leading role in mechanization and operational direction of collective agriculture. By the end of 1932, there were 2,446 MTS with almost 75,000 tractors, and they were allegedly servicing 50 percent of the sown area of collective farms. While the latter claim should be treated with skepticism, there is no doubt that the MTS became a pivotal institution in the country-side of the 1930s, primarily as centers of agricultural mechanization, but also as centers of political control. For a year in 1933–34, the MTS political department even usurped the raion's place as the dominant administrative entity in the countryside.[33]

Bright boys from the village went to the MTS to learn to operate the new machines, thus acquiring an extravillage connection and skill that in many cases took them off to the towns to seek their fortune within a few years. The tractors and harvesters came into the village for spring plowing and harvest—for which services the collective farms had to make large pay-ments in kind to the MTS. By the end of 1934, the MTS claimed to be ser-vicing 64 percent of the total area sown by collective farms, and by the end of the decade, 94 percent. In reality, however, there were many problems with MTS service. In the non-Black Earth region in particular, a great deal of agricultural work on the kolkhoz was still done with the traditional horse-drawn plow. Even in more fertile agricultural areas, a kolkhoz with sufficient draft power might prefer to get by without MTS help because of its high cost.[34]

Thus it was the horse rather than the tractor that was a really significant element in village life. It could be argued, indeed, that horses became even more important in socioeconomic terms in the 1930s than they had been before. Horses were a major object of contestation. They were usually the only available means of transport and cartage in the countryside, and they were often also the only available draft power for plowing and other agricul-tural tasks. The collective farms needed them desperately; so did the kolkhoz-niks. In addition, rural officials needed kolkhoz horses. The collectivization of horses turned out to be one of the few issues on which the state's position was inflexible. While the 1935 Kolkhoz Charter made concessions to peasant grievances on some issues, notably the private plot, returning horses to household ownership was not even discussed. When kolkhozniks in the Western oblast objected to the Charter on these grounds and asked for their horses back, this demand was characterized as "counter-revolutionary."[35]

The peasant household needed a horse for cartage and marketing, private-plot plowing, and personal transport, as well as for earning money on the side in activities like timber hauling. It was a particularly bitter pill for the kolkhoznik to be deprived of his horse and the right to own one when independent peasants still possessed horses. For a few years, some households managed to get round the problem by having the wife join the kolkhoz and the husband remain an independent and keep his horse, but this was only a short-term solution. Most kolkhozniks had to hire a horse when they needed one for any purpose other than working in the kolkhoz fields. If there were independent peasants with horses in the village, they could hire from them. Otherwise, they had to pay the kolkhoz for the use of the very horses they had once owned—and even then there was no guarantee that the kolkhoz chairman would make one available. After all, there were other people besides ordinary kolkhozniks who needed kolkhoz horses: for example, kolkhoz and rural soviet chairmen, even raion officials, who needed horses to take them about their business.[36]

The denial of horses when kolkhozniks needed them was one of the most frequent causes of complaint against kolkhoz chairmen. As this grievance was conventionally expressed, the kolkhoznik always needed a horse to go to the hospital (which perhaps gives an unduly rosy picture of the availability of healthcare in the countryside) rather than for any of the other equally real but less unassailable reasons for which a horse might be needed—such as going to market, visiting another village, plowing private-plot land, and so on. As one correspondent of *Krest'ianskaia gazeta* from Kalinin oblast wrote indignantly in a complaint against his kolkhoz chairman, he had never once in his three years as a kolkhoz member been allowed to use one of the horses to go to the hospital or bring in firewood. "I personally and many other kolkhozniks have to go to the independent peasant for a horse—it is simply shameful." Another correspondent from Tambov oblast wrote that the only way to get the use of a kolkhoz horse in his kolkhoz was to bribe the chairman with vodka.[37]

The 1935 Kolkhoz Charter stated that "when necessary the kolkhoz board will allocate a few horses from among the stock of collectivized draft animals for carrying out the personal needs of kolkhoz members for a fee." According to a later clarification from the Commissariat of Agriculture, the "personal needs" for which kolkhozniks had to pay included going to market, working on the private plot, or visiting. If the horse was used for transporting firewood or going to the hospital, the kolkhoznik should not have to pay.[38]

The clause on horses was a subject of intense discussion in Leningrad oblast after the publication of the Charter, a local newspaper reported. There was a lot of variation in local practice with regard to horses. In the "Land of Soviets" kolkhoz in Ostrov raion, for example, the kolkhoz board was charging kolkhozniks 5 kopeks a kilometer for using a kolkhoz horse to go to the hospital and 10 kopeks for visiting. But, the newspaper warned, "that is too little, comrades kolkhozniks. . . . That is simply a masked violation of the . . . Charter, an attempt to preserve the old pattern of disorganized free use of the kolkhoz horse." On the other hand, the price of 40–50 rubles a day that was being charged by collective farms just outside Leningrad (and presumably serving the Leningrad city market) was too high, in the opinion of the newspaper. The right price for use of a kolkhoz horse was a few rubles a day, depending on the region.[39]

The authorities' position was that ownership of a horse in any form was incompatible with the status of kolkhoznik. It was wrong if kolkhozniks banded together to buy a horse for their personal use, as was sometimes reported. ("They carry out all kinds of private commissions with this horse, and refuse to work in the kolkhoz.") It was also wrong if a kolkhoznik shared ownership of a horse with independent peasants.[40]

It is clear, nevertheless, that collectivization of horses was not always enforced as stringently as officials desired. Not all collective farms charged kolkhozniks for the use of horses, and some actually allowed the former owners to continue to care for their own collectivized horses. In one case reported in the Western oblast, a kolkhoz with thirty-five housholds and a total of twenty-seven working horses kept the horses in a kolkhoz stable, but left individual households responsible for the care of particular horses and in possession of that horse's equipment (bridles, saddles, etc.). No charge was made for the use of horses by kolkhozniks, and the kolkhoz board put no restrictions on their use. In Viriatino, Tambov oblast, the new kolkhoz initially lost so many horses that they decided that some degree of decollectivization was the only solution. "In order to save the horses and cattle they appointed the former owners of each animal to take care of it. Then each peasant caring for his `own horse' did not overburden it and each fed it from his own private store if there was a lack of provisions in the kolkhoz. This continued for several years until collectivization was accepted."[41]

Work and Pay

Although the kolkhoz was theoretically a cooperative organization of equal partners, its internal structure quickly became stratified. The stratification, based on the type of work performed by kolkhoz members, was something new in the village. Indeed, it is ironic that after all the Bolsheviks' alarm in the 1920s about the possibility of economic differentiation within the peasantry, it was only in the kolkhoz of the 1930s that a clear pattern of differentiation emerged.

It has often been suggested that the Russian peasants' historical experience of the mir fostered egalitarian and cooperative instincts. There is some evidence in favor of this hypotheses in the attitudes and behavior of kolkhozniks after collectivization. In the early 1930s, in particular, the peasants often succumbed to what was known in Soviet discourse as "vulgar egalitarianism" (*uravnilovka*), trying to divide the kolkhoz income equally among the households, with adjustment for family size, rather than calculating the number of labordays earned by each adult kolkhoz member through his work.[42]

But not much was heard of uravnilovka after about the middle of the decade. Instead, there was a noticeable tendency toward increased differentiation of rewards for various types of kolkhoz work, and a determined effort on the part of kolkhoz officeholders and those with special skills (for example, tractor drivers) to improve the situation of the upper strata of kolkhoz society by putting them on wages or salary or giving them a guaranteed minimum cash income.

Two privileged strata emerged in the kolkhoz of the 1930s. The first was the "white-collar" group: the kolkhoz chairman, members of the kolkhoz board, the accountant, the brigade leaders, the business manager (*zavkhoz*), and an evergrowing list of other offices (head of the warehouse, head of the club, head of the reading room, director of the choir, head of the agronomy bureau [*khata-laboratoriia*], mailman, etc.) that the kolkhoz administrators awarded to their relatives and friends. A Soviet scholar has estimated that this group comprised about 5 percent of all kolkhoz members, although this is almost certainly a low estimate, especially by the end of the decade, when the burgeoning of kolkhoz offices had become a major cause of concern at the center. Men made up 75 percent of the white-collar group in 1937, and earned 90 percent of its labordays.[43]

Members of the "white-collar" group were paid in labordays, like other kolkhozniks, despite energetic and sometimes successful efforts of chairmen and accountants to put themselves on salary. But the chairmen, board members, and brigade leaders usually earned much more than other kolkhozniks, not only because their labordays were formally assessed at a higher rate, but also because they were usually credited with working seven days in the week throughout the year. Alhough the formal assessments for white-collar occupations averaged only 1.2 labordays for every day worked in a selective survey conducted by government statisticians in 1937, the senior white-collar workers were being paid for thirty days work in the month, whereas most kolkhozniks worked no more than twenty days in an average month in 1937.[44]

Moreover, members of the white-collar group were freed by convention (although not by law, except in the case of the chairman) from the obligation of working in the fields, and sometimes they managed to get their wives off fieldwork, too. This suggests a parallel between the stratification of the kolkhoz and that of the serf village as described by Steven Hoch, in which the bol'shaks, that is, older men who were heads of households, constituted a comparatively privileged group that provided all the serf functionaries, such as serf managers and overseers, and whose members were free of the obligation to work in the fields.[45]

The second stratum was the skilled "blue-collar" group of machine operators (*mekhanizatory*), including the modern occupations of tractor driver, combine operator, and truck driver (*shofer*), as well as the traditional occupation of blacksmith. Of all kolkhoz members, 7 percent fell into the skilled blue-collar category at the end of the 1930s according to the Soviet historian's estimate,[46] but there was a very high turnover because the majority in the category were young men, many of whom soon used their mechanical skills to get jobs in urban industry. Members of the blue-collar group were also released from fieldwork, as were their wives in some cases, and had their labordays assessed at a higher value than fieldworkers. Because their skills were much in demand in the village, the machine operators often negotiated excellent conditions for themselves, including (illegal) salaries paid with kolkhoz funds: One report from the Tatar Republic in 1938 said that kolkhoz drivers (*shofery*) were making 150, 200, and 300 rubles in cash a month, as well as payment in kind.[47] Moreover, tractor drivers and combine operators had by law a unique privilege that not even the kolkhoz chairmen had attained, namely a minimum income in cash and kind guaranteed by the state (acquired by tractor drivers in 1933) and a wage paid by the state through the MTS (acquired by combine operators in 1935).[48]

Unlike the white-collar group, whose attention was strongly focussed on the perks to be won from kolkhoz office and who were the primary combattants in most feuds and faction fights in the village, the machine operators tended to be outward-oriented. The local MTS rather than the kolkhoz was the center of life for these young men, many of whom were likely to leave the countryside within a few years. They did not usually challenge the older kolkhoz bosses and their perks, and they were not prominent in village feuds and the writing of complaints. The Soviet media idealized the kolkhoz machine operators, but even so it is clear that they really were the young hopefuls of the kolkhoz—the most desirable fiancés for the girls, the kolkhozniks with the best future prospects, and the ones with the most "modern," Soviet outlook.

The third group of kolkhozniks, those who worked in the fields with scythes and sickles and tended the animals, were the *lumpen* of the kolkhoz, possessing neither skills that had currency outside the farm nor access to the perks associated with kolkhoz office. In the summer, at the peak period of agricultural activity, women slightly outnumbered men in the fields in 1937, although they earned fewer labordays. In the winter, when men went on otkhod and women worked at home, men outnumbered women by almost two to one, but the total number of kolkhozniks engaged in kolkhoz work was only half what it was in the summer.[49]

The kolkhoz jobs in which women predominated or were strongly represented—work with livestock (excluding draft animals), work in kolkhoz nurseries, and so on—tended to be poorly paid, especially when they were held by women. A day of work with livestock earned an average 1.3 labordays for men and 1.1 labordays for women. A day of work in the cultural and child-care sphere, which was predominantly female, earned an average of under 1 laborday. For all kolkhoz jobs, a man's average earnings per day worked in 1937 were 1.4 labordays, while a woman's were 1.2 labordays.[50]

Rewards were offered to encourage the best workers among rank-and-file kolkhozniks—the shockworkers (*udarniki* and *udarnitsy*), as they were called in the early 1930s, and Stakhanovites, to use the term for high achievers borrowed from industry in 1935—and within this group, young, unmarried women were particularly favored. This no doubt did a little to redress the balance of privilege within the kolkhoz, but it was a mixed blessing for a rank-and-file kolkhoznitsa to become a Stakhanovite. Norm-busting was strongly disapproved of on the kolkhoz, as in most workplaces, especially if it was done by women; and those rank-and-file kolkhozniks who tried to work longer or more productively in the fields or in the milking shed were likely to be mocked or even assaulted. Another problem with Stakhanovite status was that it was as honor that male authority figures in the kolkhoz (in particular, brigade leaders) could confer on female subordinates. That meant favoritism and malicious gossip were an almost inevitable part of the rewards process.

Organization of Work

The brigade was the basic official work unit on the kolkhoz fields. Early on, many collective farms organized brigades (the *brigady-dvorki*) that really consisted of groups of households working in very much the same way as they had done before collectivization—cultivating the same allotments they had formerly cultivated, using their old crop rotation rather than one determined by the kolkhoz (or by the raion for the kolkhoz), and sometimes even using the same animals and equipment that had belonged to them before they became the property of the kolkhoz. Needless to say, this was viewed as fraudulent collectivization and denounced editorially by *Pravda* on February 16, 1932. It was against the spirit of collectivization for peasant households to work as units.[51]

The brigade was meant to be responsible for a particular section of the kolkhoz fields and to be a permanent, not ad hoc, working group. The brigade was headed by a brigade leader or foreman (*brigadir*) chosen by the kolkhoz board. He was responsible for getting his team to work, seeing that it carried out the tasks allocated by the kolkhoz administration, and registering the work done by each kolkhoznik and the laborday payment due to him or her for the day's work.[52]

Where the brigade system really functioned, organization of field work appears to have been similar to that on a state farm, and probably also to a big estate in the old days of serfdom. According to one contemporary description of a large grain-growing kolkhoz in the south, villagers were awakened by a bell at 5 A.M. and were required to present themselves in front of the administration building an hour later for the day's instructions. The brigade leaders met each evening with the kolkhoz chairman and other kolkhoz officers to plan the next day's work and hear reports from the kolkhoz's outstanding workers. As noted earlier, the bell that summoned kolkhozniks to work was often a church bell, put to new use after the closing of the churches for worship at the beginning of the 1930s.[53]

The work did not always go so smoothly, however, especially in the early years. It took time for the collective farms to organize brigades and persuade the peasants to accept the new style of work. Even in the mid-1930s, many of them still had only the most rudimentary form of labor organization and division of labor. According to a chronicler of two adjoining villages in the Voronezh region, these collective farms had no real brigades or accounting system in 1930 and 1931: Everyone went out to the fields and worked together, and the harvest was distributed among the households in the traditional manner, that is, by family size (*po edokam*), not by work. It was only in 1932 that production brigades and the system of payments by labordays (see below) became part of the official kolkhoz structure.[54]

On smaller collective farms, especially in the non-Black Earth region, the whole brigade system was probably something of a fiction in the 1930s. The average Soviet kolkhoz had only two or three brigades, and one of these would often be a small specialized brigade whose task was to look after the kolkhoz animals.[55] A smaller work unit than the brigade, the link (*zveno*), began to make its appearance in the second half of the 1930s and was recommended for general adoption at the XVIII Party Congress in 1939. But it was not until the postwar period that it acquired real significance.[56]

Getting the peasants out to work in the fields and keeping them working there was a constant struggle for many kolkhoz officers. Brigade leaders and kolkhoz chairmen sometimes had to go around the village in mid-morning knocking on doors to summon the reluctant peasants to work. In the "Red Fir Tree" kolkhoz in the Leningrad area in 1937, only ten or eleven of the twenty-seven adult kolkhoz members went most days, and work in the fields did not start until eleven o'clock in the morning. Fines and other penalties were liberally applied to peasants who failed to show up for work or came late. In the "Gigant" kolkhoz in the Central Volga, eighty-nine kolkhozniks (61 percent of all kolkhoz members) were fined in 1934–35 for these and other offences. In some cases, the fines were quite substantial: Ten to fifteen labordays were subtracted from their yearly earnings.[57]

The kolkhozniks' unwillingness to work on kolkhoz fields was often attributed to their wish to stay home and work on their private plots or some other economic motive. In "Spark of Socialism" kolkhoz in Krasnodar krai in 1938, for example, the peasants reportedly felt it was not worth working because the kolkhoz was not paying them enough, specifically because it was making laborday payments only in kind and not in money. Only a few dozen out of 180 able-bodied kolkhozniks were going out to work: "The rest are loafing around, and some categorically refuse to work altogether on various pretexts—one [says he is] sick, another has his own work to do, others have no boots and jackets. . . ."[58]

A kolkhoz chairman in Iaroslavl oblast found that his entire workforce had succumbed to this malaise after the bad harvest of 1936, and wrote a desperate letter to the newspaper *Krest'ianskaia gazeta* asking what he should do:

At the present time kolkhozniks have given up kolkhoz work and gone to work outside [the kolkhoz] or are working around their houses, and the kolkhoz has still not fulfilled its state obligations for grain and potatoes. Winter preparations for cattle have not been made, the yards have not been repaired, kolkhozniks do not go out [to earn] labordays, brigade-leaders repudiate their responsibilities. . . .[59]

Peasants often cited demoralization as a reason for poor work performance. In their letters to *Krest'ianskaia gazeta* in 1938, kolkhozniks would frequently explain that abusive behavior by kolkhoz chairmen and brigade leaders or some other unfair or corrupt practice of local administrators had removed all their inclination to work. One peasant wrote from Tambov oblast to complain that the wives of the rural soviet chairman and other office-holders were not going to work in the kolkhoz fields, so other peasants saw no reason to go either.[60]

A retired worker living in a village in the same oblast described the following scene:

On the morning of July 12 I went down to the kolkhoz pasture where haymaking should have been in progress and went up to the kolkhoz women sitting there. I asked, "Why are you sitting here?" They answered, "We don't know what to do, there is not one brigade-leader in the pastures." Kolkhoznitsa Anna Vasilevna Bogachkova and others complain that with leadership like this and the fact that the [kolkhoz] board and the brigade-leaders spend their time drinking, people have no desire to go out to work.[61]

The peasants' claim that poor leadership sapped the desire to work nicely combined malice towards the kolkhoz activists (since reiteration of such complaints was likely to get the latter in trouble with higher authorities) with the foot-dragging and evasiveness characteristic of serfs and disgruntled proletarians. Stalin had accused the peasants of using the tactics of the go-slow strike (*ital'ianka*) in 1933, and this characterization of the behavior of many kolkhozniks remained apt throughout the 1930s. Only in rare cases did kolkhozniks use the strike weapon in more overt form. In one exceptional case, kolkhozniks who were engaged in a bitter fight with the raion over the appointment of a kolkhoz chairman seem to have made an explicit threat to go on strike in a letter of complaint to *Krest'ianskaia gazeta* in 1938. Their letter itself is absent from the archive (probably because the newspaper had sent it on to the police), but the file includes an anxious reply from a *Krest'ianskaia gazeta* staffer sympathizing with their grievance but warning them in the most urgent terms not to think of going on strike as a protest.[62]

In the context of this kind of apathy and resentment, an energetic initiative from a Stakhanovite could be truly jarring. No wonder that at the "Red Partisan" kolkhoz in the Western oblast the Stakhanovite D. Kravtsov was set upon by enraged fellow workers when he suggested staying on at the end of the day to finish scything the field. A woman Stakhanovite on a sugarbeet kolkhoz in Kursk oblast encountered a less violent but equally hostile reaction. She and her team had carefully fertilized their allotment with 10 centners of ash and 9 centners of chicken manure in order to obtain a high yield. But then at the last moment the brigade leader switched allotments so that her team got an unfertilized tract that was full of weeds, saying: "You Stakhanovite women are causing trouble for the whole kolkhoz."[63]

Laborday Payments

Since the kolkhoz was a collective enterprise, its members were partners who were supposed to share its income among themselves. The individual share was calculated on the laborday principle—essentially a piecework system whereby peasants were paid according to time worked and the level of skill attached to the task. Field work rated the lowest laborday payments, with ascending scales for livestock tenders, tractor drivers, brigade leaders and, at the top of the scale, kolkhoz chairmen.[64]

The laborday principle was unpopular with peasants, whose idea of equitable distribution was that payments would be made to households, on an equal basis, with differentiation only by size of household. Most collective farms started at the beginning of the 1930s with an egalitarian distribution by household (with adjustment for household size), and there was considerable resistance to transferring to the laborday principle. Despite the firm injunctions of the Kolkhoz Charter, there were reports as late as 1936 and 1937 of collective farms that were still distributing earnings among the households "according to the number of mouths" (*po edokam*). Moreover, even when earnings were calculated on the laborday principle—that is, according to the work performed by every individual kolkhoz member—the payments customarily were made not to the individual but to the household. This was reported in central Russia not just in the 1930s but as late as the 1950s.[65]

The average kolkhoz member earned 197 labordays in 1937, which translates into average household earnings of 438 labordays.[66] But there was considerable variation in the laborday payments that were made to different members of the kolkhoz. In 1937, 21 percent of kolkhozniks earned fewer than 51 labordays, 15 percent earned 51–100, 25 percent earned 101–200, 18 percent earned 201–300, 11 percent earned 301–400, and 9 percent more than 400 labordays.[67]

In the first place, this reflected the different value put on various jobs: A kolkhoz chairman's day was worth more than the average kolkhoznik's (1.75–2.00 labordays, as against 1.3); and, in addition, the chairman was assumed to work every day of the year, whereas the fieldworker was paid only for the days he actually went out into the fields. In 1937, the average kolkhoznik (male and female) in nine regions of the Soviet Union was paid for nineteen days work in the off month of January and twenty days in July, in contrast to the chairman's regular thirty to thirty-one days a month.[68]

In the second place, the difference in earnings reflected the fact that the degree of the kolkhozniks' involvement in kolkhoz work varied greatly. This was a cause of concern for the authorities, who did their best to combat the two major causes of low involvement in kolkhoz work: otkhod in the case of men; and the private plot, in the case of women.

Out of a total of almost 20 million kolkhoz women of working age in the Soviet Union in 1937, 7 million earned fewer than fifty labordays. The reason for this minimal involvement in kolkhoz work was that they could afford to stay home or found it more profitable to work on their private plots. Even the women who earned a reasonable number of labordays often worked for the kolkhoz only at peak periods. In winter, as noted earlier, two male kolkhozniks were engaged in kolkhoz work for every one female.[69]

Despite official exhortations to the contrary, the convention prevailed within the family that if both husband and wife were rank-and-file kolkhozniks, the man spent more time on the kolkhoz fields and the woman on the private plot. In 1939, an attempt was made to force women to work for the kolkhoz through the introduction of a laborday minimum. But the national agricultural newspaper indignantly reported that kolkhozniks in Saratov thought that "if the husband works well, then his wife is permitted not to work at all, because he alone has earned the minimum of labordays both for himself and for his wife. Therefore here the majority of wives of tractor drivers, brigade-leaders and some members of the administration as before do not work in the kolkhoz, and work exclusively in their own private plots. . . ." According to another report, the kolkhoz women who showed up for work for the first time were mocked by other women as "cowardly crows, frightened by a decree."[70]

Laborday payments were made primarily in kind (grain, potatoes, and other foodstuffs) in the 1930s, although in theory the collective farms paid both in kind and in money. It was strictly forbidden to make payments in kind ("advances") to the kolkhozniks before state procurements quotas had been fulfilled after the harvest. Since the quotas were very high, this could leave the collective farms with little grain to distribute in a bad harvest year.

Payments in kind per laborday tended to rise in the course of the 1930s. In 1932, the average Soviet kolkhoz gave 2.3 kilograms of grain per laborday, while in 1937 (the most bountiful harvest of the decade) it was almost 4 kilograms, not including the potatoes, beans, and other foodstuffs that were also distributed on the laborday principle. In 1937, therefore, the average kolkhoz household received 1,636 kilos of grain in laborday payments, or about a kilo a day for each family member. But the problem with laborday payments was that they were capable of wild variation according to the fertility of the region, the success of the harvest, the level of procurements, and the efficiency of the kolkhoz. The "Pugachev" kolkhoz in Bashkiria gave out 8 kilos of grain per laborday in 1937. But the year before, when the harvest failed in many regions, collective farms in Leningrad oblast were giving only a third of a kilogram of grain per laborday.[71]

As to cash payments for labordays, according to official figures the average kolkhoz member received a total payment of 108 rubles for the year in 1932 and 376 rubles in 1937. But once again there was enormous variation from region to region and kolkhoz to kolkhoz. There were many collective farms that paid out no cash at all in laborday payments. This was not only the case in times of temporary economic crisis, for example the non-Black Earth region in 1936. It was also true of some collective farms in fertile agricultural regions in 1937, the year of the bumper harvest. In 1940, 12 percent of all Soviet collective farms gave no cash payment for labordays. In Tambov oblast, it was 26 percent; in Riazan oblast, 41 percent.[72]

The reason that cash payments to kolkhozniks were so small was that the kolkhoz chairmen and boards had other uses for kolkhoz income. The kolkhoz's capital fund (*nedelimyi fond*), intended primarily to finance kolkhoz construction and purchase of animals and agricultural machinery, had a lot of potential uses that were more appealing to many chairmen than routine laborday payments to kolkhozniks. For example, it could be used to pay salaries to kolkhoz chairmen and accountants (see Chapter 7). Or it could be used to hire labor for the kolkhoz, either to meet a genuine labor shortage or to free kolkhoz members for other activities.

According to the Kolkhoz Charter, annual deposits to the capital fund were supposed to be in the range of 10–20 percent of the kolkhoz's money income. Recognizing that in practice this was often exceeded, leaving insufficient funds to distribute cash payments to kolkhoz members for their laborday earnings, the government tried another tack: A 1938 resolution "On incorrect distribution of income in collective farms" required that a minimum of 60 percent of the total money income of the kolkhoz should be used for disbursement in laborday payments to kolkhozniks, and reiterated earlier instructions that no more than 2 percent should be used for "administrative and housekeeping expenses" (primarily cash payments to kolkhoz officers). It is clear, however, that this injunction, like its predecessor, was often ignored.[73]

As collective farms grew more prosperous, particularly in the south, towards the end of the 1930s, reports multiplied of their efforts to free themselves from the cooperative framework and move towards a kind of rural capitalist market in labor.

In addition to the ceaseless efforts of kolkhoz chairmen to get themselves put on salary, other kolkhoz officers and placemen made similar demands to receive a regular money income from the kolkhoz in lieu of the unpredictable payments in kind and cash that were based on a proportional share of kolkhoz production and earnings. Brigade leaders, accountants, stablemen, drivers, and watchmen are among those reported to be receiving regular wages in collective farms in Kuibyshev oblast in 1938. The same demand was reported in Leningrad oblast from rank-and-file kolkhoz members. Kolkhozniks were also trying to make contracts with the kolkhoz to perform specified tasks, rather than have them credited to their laborday account. In one kolkhoz in Leningrad oblast, kolkhozniks working in the stables wanted the kolkhoz to pay them 5 rubles for each barrel of water they brought in. In a prosperous kolkhoz in the Central Volga region, a kolkhoz member bought a pair of oxen and offered to use them for kolkhoz work if the kolkhoz would pay him in cash at the same rate it paid independents.[74]

Although it was forbidden for collective farms to hire outside labor, the practice was common, especially in regions whose proximity to urban markets gave kolkhozniks many opportunities for substantial nonfarm income. A kolkhoz in Leningrad oblast spent 4,500 rubles hiring outsiders for field work in 1936. Another kolkhoz hired outside labor for 6 rubles a day in cash, not counting a sizeable payment in kind, while its own members were receiving only 60 kopeks in cash per laborday. At the "Five-Year Plan" kolkhoz in Kalinin oblast, where hiring was particularly common, half the kolkhozniks were working in local brick and glass factories, and the kolkhoz was hiring independents to do the field work. If the official statistics are to be believed, however, these were exceptional cases. In most regions, the average collective farm hired fewer than ten outsiders in the course of the year to work for three or four days each.[75]

Finally, individual kolkhozniks were hiring surrogates to do their kolkhoz work for them. At the "Stalin" kolkhoz, three kilometers from the oblast center of Ordzhonikidze, the wife of a kolkhoznik named Nikolai Piskachev was sending along her domestic servant to work for her in the kolkhoz fields while she traded on the black market in Ordzhonikidze. In "Budennyi" kolkhoz in Kiev oblast, S. Lymar, a kolkhoznik, hired an independent peasant to do his work in the fields. Lymar paid the independent in cash, and the kolkhoz credited Lymar with the labordays worked.[76]

Peasant Grievances

Many of the peasants' grievances about the kolkhoz, and by implication their aspirations for change, were expressed in their comments and suggestions during the national discussion of the new Soviet Constitution in 1936.[77] In their letters, some peasants—we cannot know what proportion of the whole, since the collections of letters in the archives have evidently been presorted to some extent—expressed extremely negative feelings about the kolkhoz, describing it as a condition of exploitation similar to serfdom. For example, a kolkhoznik from Moscow oblast, who had recently been denied permission to leave his kolkhoz and go and work in industry, penned the following indictment:

> Are the collective farms to remain state slaves? . . . Why do they collect tribute from us? The kolkhoz delivers hay, rye, wheat, oats, potatoes, and other products. It costs more to transport them than they pay for the produce. And they consider it a great achievement, a victory. From kolkhoz members they collect potatoes, [agricultural] tax, self-taxation payments, cultural tax, six days of corvée work, and milk procurements and meat procurements, even if you don't have a cow.
>
> With tears, we all handed over our horse, cart, harrow, and all our equipment. And we get paid labordays.

The proletarian has a house, a cow, chickens, a vegetable garden and so on. But why do we have to pay? Because we are kolkhozniks? . . . Can I consider myself free, if I am counted as a serf (*barskii*)?[78]

From Bashkiria, a peasant correspondent expressed similar attitudes:

Our government now has all the rights that kulaks, landlords, and speculators use to have. For example, bread. The state takes grain at 6 kopeks a kilogram and sells cookies and so on at 75 kopeks. Isn't that pure speculation, isn't it exploitation?[79]

Opinions openly expressed at the public discussions in the collective farms were usually tamer than the above quotations from letters, but there were exceptions that were duly reported to the NKVD, generally involving brief ironic asides like the suggestion by a peasant woman in Voronezh that the paragraph in the Constitution stating that "He who does not work, does not eat" should be rephrased in positive terms, namely "He who works should eat."[80]

The quotas for milk, meat, and other produce that individual kolkhoz households had to deliver from their private plots were an object of great resentment. Peasants frequently pointed out the unfairness of the fact that workers and employees living in the village, who also had plots, did not have to make such deliveries. They wanted the milk and meat procurements from households to be abolished, or at least reduced, because this was a burden that made it "difficult to survive in the kolkhoz, not like in the factory or sovkhoz." Alternatively, workers and employees with plots should be liable for these procurements, too.[81] "The government . . . ought to rescind meat and milk procurements, otherwise the peasant will remain a slave. We've had enough, we're sick of eating chaff."[82]

The strength of this particular grievance was probably related to the fact that 1936 was a year of drought and harvest failure in many parts of the country. Officials analyzing the Constitution discussions among peasants in the Western oblast noted that the "unhealthy moods" (that is, antiregime attitudes) that were often visible were no doubt the result of hunger and fear of famine. This was borne out by the comment of one kolkhoz woman that

Soon there will be a collapse—our youth is all blackened, tormented by hard work, and there is nothing in the fields. We will all go hungry and the independents will eat wheaten bread.[83]

A strong theme in the letters was that the collectivized peasantry was an exploited and underprivileged class in Soviet society. This was usually done by contrasting the peasants' situation with that of urban workers and asking for equal rights—an argument the authorities considered "typically anti-Soviet." The specific areas of discrimination that the peasants emphasized most frequently were pensions and other state benefits that were available to urban wage earners but not to kolkhozniks. In Arch Getty's sample of letters on the Constitution (which includes letters from persons of all social groups), the largest category consisted of letters suggesting that peasants should be guaranteed the same state benefits, especially pensions, as were available to urban workers.[84]

> In what way are we kolkhozniks worse than workers? But if we become invalids the new Constitution says that the state will not give us any help. This Constitution is only good for workers. As for us peasants, they'll drive us before the lash again, only twice as hard as in past years.[85]

The great majority of writers on this theme treated it as self-evident that the state should provide pensions for elderly or invalid citizens, including (or perhaps especially) kolkhozniks. Only a few took the more traditional peasant view that support of aged and infirm parents was the responsibility of their children, who should be forced by the state to pay if they had gone off to work in the city ("Garnish a third of their wages," suggested one kolkhoznik).[86]

"When will the boundary between town and countryside be wiped away?" asked peasants in the Western oblast, at least in the paraphrase of officials reporting on the Constitution discussion. But this phrase, at first sight merely a quaint echo of a lively theoretical debate among Marxist intellectuals a few years earlier, clearly had a quite concrete meaning for peasants, namely that "the collectivized population" should have the same advantages as the wage and salary earners. "Why don't they introduce the eight–hour day in the kolkhoz?" many peasants asked (another "typically anti-Soviet" question). Many peasant letters on the Constitution proposed that, in addition to old-age and invalid pensions and the eight–hour day, the state should offer kolkhozniks one free day a week, like workers, and annual paid vacations. Double pay for overtime would also be a good idea, suggested one advocate of the eight–hour day: Why should urban wage-earners have this privilege when kolkhozniks have to work "12 hours a day and sometimes 27 hours [*sic*]"? If the kolkhozniks had had more leisure, one correspondent wrote, they would have been able to take a more active part in discussing the new Constitution.[87]

Kolkhozniks who expressed such ideas almost invariably disregarded the fact that as members of a cooperative they were paid on a different basis from wage earners. Most wrote as if kolkhozniks were on a kind of state dole, and argued that it should be converted into a living wage. "No matter how well they say the kolkhoznik lives, the kolkhoznik's labor is the cheapest all the same." The income of kolkhozniks should be raised to the level of urban workers and employees, writers suggested.[88]

Those few peasants who paid any attention to the formal aspect of the question considered that the kolkhoz's cooperative structure should be abandoned and the kolkhozniks turned into state employees. If kolkhozniks received regular wages, they would not be vulnerable to the risk of a poor harvest, one kolkhoznik wrote. This might have sounded like a suggestion that kolkhozy be turned into sovkhozy, but that was not what peasants wanted in the mid 1930s, when conditions in the sovkhoz were bad and sovkhoz workers were not allowed to keep livestock and private plots. Underlining the point, one advocate of state wages for kolkhozniks invented a new name for the institution he had in mind—"government farms" (*gos-khozy*).[89]

Regardless of how it was achieved, it was beyond dispute for many kolkhozniks that the state had welfare obligations towards its peasants. "The state ought to feed and clothe us," one peasant stated simply.[90]

6

On the Margins

While kolkhozniks whose primary occupation was agriculture occupied the central place in the village, they were not its only inhabitants. In the first place, there were the independent peasants who remained outside the kolkhoz (*edinolichniki*). Independents were a short-lived phenomenon, historically speaking. But as long as they existed, they constituted an alternative peasant "estate" with different rights and obligations from kolkhozniks. This provided kolkhozniks with a basis of comparison for assessing their own situation, and also offered a spectrum of possibilities for manipulation and evasion of kolkhoz rules, especially in cases where the same household contained both kolkhozniks and independents. The great distinguishing characteristic of independents was that, unlike kolkhozniks, they were allowed to own a horse.

In the second place, there were kolkhozniks who were not primarily employed in agriculture but worked at various crafts. In general, the economic structure of the kolkhoz was not encouraging to craftsmen, and many traditional village crafts withered in the 1930s. The village miller had usually been deported as a kulak; the village blacksmith had often left to work in the town. The smiths that remained had an anomalous and often prickly relationship with the kolkhoz.

Khutor dwellers, who might formally be kolkhoz members while participating only minimally in any collectivized agriculture, were another marginal group. Their isolation from the village made any close connection with kolkhoz life difficult. It was not until the end of the 1930s that a serious effort was made to shore up this weakness in the kolkhoz structure and local authorities were ordered to organize the physical relocation of khutor dwellers and provide them with housing in the village.

The village of the 1930s contained many peasants who worked for wages all or part of the time, were often kolkhoz members, but retained only a minimal connection with kolkhoz agriculture. The wage earners can be divided into two groups: those who lived permanently in the village and worked at a neighboring state farm or other enterprise, and the otkhodniks who worked and lived outside the village for various lengths of time.

Otkhodniks were important for two reasons. The first was that their wages were an essential supplement to kolkhoz earnings for many kolkhoz households. The second was that they were peasants with a foot in two worlds, the village and the town. They provided much of the information on which other kolkhozniks formed their view of the outside world. It must surely have been primarily through their eyes that peasants acquired the comparative sense that led them to assert so often and so bitterly that since collectivization peasants had become second-class citizens.

Independents

In 1932, 39 percent of peasants in the Soviet Union were still uncollectivized. By 1937, it was only 7 percent, and the total number of independent peasants had shrunk to 7.5 million workers and dependents (the workers dividing more or less equally into men and women, in contrast to kolkhozniks engaged in agriculture, of whom 63 percent were women).[1] Thus we are dealing with a vanishing species, under pressure from punitive taxation and various other forms of official discrimination. Throughout the decade, a steady stream of independent households was flowing out of the countryside as well as into collective farms and state farms. After 1938, when a new law forced independents to give up their horses, only a few old or eccentric peasants remained outside the kolkhoz. Nevertheless, as late as 1935–36 the independent was still a real factor in the social and economic equation of the village.

As we know, the great advantage that the independent peasant had over the kolkhoznik was that the independent had the right to own a horse. Thus independents tended to become the village haulers and carters, taking produce to markets, hiring out the horse and cart to kolkhozniks to go to markets or do business in the raion center, hiring out the horse so kolkhozniks could plow their private plots, and so on.[2] This entrepreneurial, market- and service-oriented profile was one that good Communists were bound to dislike. But of course Communists would have disapproved of independent peasants regardless of their occupation. It was a group that contained kulaks! A group that spoke against the kolkhoz and poisoned the minds of kolkhozniks! All the same, the independents with their horses and carts served a useful function in the countryside. When they finally left the scene, even good Communists had some pragmatic reasons to miss them.

At the beginning of the 1930s, most independents had undoubtedly been engaged in peasant agriculture. But agriculture was the most difficult of all rural occupations for them to survive in, and by 1938 only a small proportion of the remaining independents were cultivating land. The reason was that those who cultivated land had the same obligations as kolkhozy and kolkhozniks to accept sowing plans laid down by the raion land department and to meet procurements quotas.

Among the independent households in the early 1930s were those of the so-called "fixed-quota" group (*tverdozadantsy*), relatively prosperous peasant cultivators who were given high sowing plans and procurements quotas and a special pejorative label to remind them that they were perilously close to being categorized as kulaks. Such peasants tended either to leave the village or seek safety and anonymity in the kolkhoz, and we hear no more of them after 1933.

Independent peasants became notorious for committing the strange offense of "refusing to sow." That meant that they would rather leave their allotments uncultivated and support themselves by carting or black-market trade than become part of the compulsory procurements system. In one village in the Western oblast in 1936 or 1937, only five out of twenty-two independent households were engaged in agriculture; and when local agricultural authorities tried to allocate land to them, more than half refused to take it because of procurements.[3]

In Omsk oblast, where independents constituted about 5 percent of the peasant population, almost all the independents refused to sow in the spring of 1935, claiming that they had no seed, because they were unwilling to accept the independents' sowing plans that the raion was handing down for the first time. Some went to work in a state farm. Others hastily joined the kolkhoz. A few families reportedly packed all their belongings into carts and left the village in search of a new place of residence where there were no sowing plans. In addition, a large number of men disappeared abruptly from the villages:

> The most common method of sabotage in a number of raions was the departure of the men "without leaving an address." Just before the sowing they sold the horse and the head of the household "departed for an unknown destination." In one village in Ikonn[ikovskii] raion all 17 independents sold their horses just before the sowing and went away, leaving their wives and children there. The wives said that they did not know where the men had gone and they could not sow because they had no horse. (In place of the horse the husbands had bought a cow.)[4]

Since the state's objective was to "squeeze" the independent peasant until there was nothing more to get out of him, they were often given plans and quotas that were not only unrealistically high but intentionally so. Independents who failed to meet these targets were liable to severe punishment. In Iaroslavl oblast in 1936, for example, the independent peasant Anna Avdeevna Bazanova was fined 400 rubles by the people's court for not carrying out her sowing plan, and "the rural policeman then sold property of citizen Bazanova up to the sum of 400 rubles in the state store." But Bazanova got off relatively lightly: In such circumstances, independents were often simply "dekulakized" (that is, had all their property confiscated by local authorities) and/or thrown in prison. In Siberia in 1936, criminal charges were brought against seven independent peasants who had failed to deliver their quota of 980 centners of grain. Six of the seven, described as "anti-Soviet kulaks" in the report, received prison sentences of three to ten years, and the seventh got the death sentence.[5]

There was always the possibility, however, that local land departments would be too busy or too careless to give sowing plans and set procurements quotas for all the independent households. Kolkhozniks often complained that this was so, especially with regard to the private-plot procurements of milk and meat to which both independent and kolkhoz households were liable. A 1938 report from Pliusskii raion in Leningrad oblast stated:

> Out of 500 independent households counted in the raion, only 244 farms are carrying out any state obligations. Dozens of independent households have never yet been given state obligations for delivery of potatoes, meat, and milk. Out of 66 households drawn into milk deliveries, only 46 farms are giving produce, and the remaining 20 evade it. . . . Out of 244 farms receiving quotas, only 4 are delivering grain. . . .[6]

Taxation was a major burden on independents. They were liable to the same taxes as kolkhozniks (see above, pp. 131–32), except that where kolkhozniks had a flat rate, the charges on independents, theoretically on a sliding scale, were in practice often determined quite arbitrarily and with punitive intent by local authorities. In addition, special one-time taxes were levied on independents in 1932, 1933, and 1934. This tax raised 166–170 million rubles in 1932 and 1933; and the punitive quality of its application is suggested by the fact that in 1933 the revenue actually collected from independents (not counting the 548 million rubles they paid that year in regular agricultural taxes) was more than five times the amount projected in the annual financial plan. In 1934, the one-time tax raised 331 million rubles, a sum equal to 60 percent of the sum collected from *all* peasants (independents and kolkhozniks) on the agricultural tax.[7]

There were occasional complaints that independents had been taxed less heavily than kolkhozniks in particular regions (for example, Western Siberia in 1933); and, given the essentially arbitrary basis of taxation of independents, this was always a possibility. In general, however, the typical independent household in the early 1930s found itself presented each year with a staggering, impossible tax bill. For a year or so, the household might struggle to pay by selling off a horse, a cow, or other assets, hoping that this sign of cooperation would deflect the state's wrath. But finally the message would get through that the tax bills were always going to be staggering and impossible, and the independent would give up, either joining the kolkhoz (which explains why late-joining households usually came in with empty hands) or leaving the countryside.[8]

The relationship of independent peasants with kolkhozniks and the kolkhoz was necessarily multifaceted. The independents' houses and yards were often side by side with those of the kolkhozniks, and the two groups were likely to be linked by a network of family ties. In the mid-1930s, moreover, it was not uncommon for the one household to contain both a kolkhoz member and an independent, usually the husband. If an independent cultivated an allotment of land, it was generally cut out of the kolkhoz (village) fields and would in due course revert to the kolkhoz. (There was no "eternal title" issued to the lands of independents.) If a kolkhoznik was expelled from kolkhoz membership and remained in the village, he automatically became an independent.

In the early 1930s, when the kolkhozniks and independent peasants often formed opposing camps in the village of more or less equal size, hostility between the two groups was common. This is recalled by an émigré memoirist from a peasant family who witnessed the early years of the kolkhoz in his village. The independents, he said,

> were annoyed that certain privileges were granted to the kolkhozniks, and ridiculed them at every opportunity. They tried to use every failure of the young kolkhoz as an opening for their jibes. The kolkhozniks were not slow to retort, usually with a warning: "He who laughs last, laughs best! They'll strangle you with taxes and you'll have to join us anyway—and your eyes won't be dry either!"[9]

In this particular village, there had been no initial enthusiasm for the kolkhoz, except among the village children; the core group of kolkhoz households had joined the kolkhoz not out of conviction but only because they were afraid of being dekulakized. All the same, once they had joined and found themselves the object of malicious jibes from the independents, these new kolkhozniks started to develop a definite kolkhoz patriotism. "The success of kolkhoz affairs became a matter of honor and self-respect for each member," wrote the émigré memoirist.[10] (The same point, needless to say, has been made repeatedly by Soviet historians, but one is more inclined to suspect that their testimony on the point is biased.)

Wariness, hostility, and above all a sense of separateness is conveyed in a exchange between kolkhozniks and independents in a non-Black Earth village in 1930 reported by a visiting journalist. The newspaper had sent a photographer to take pictures of the kolkhoz activists. In this kolkhoz, however, the activists were a drab group of middle-aged soldiers' widows all dressed in black, and the photographer wanted to bring in some young peasant women from independent households to brighten up the picture. But the kolkhoz chairman, herself a widow, would have none of it:

> "No, we don't agree. Some of them didn't join the kolkhoz or else joined and then signed out again; we don't want to be photographed with them. Photograph them separately if you want to."
> And all her old activists, "*likbezovki*" as they were called in the village [because of their work in literacy (*likbez*) classes], warmly supported their chairman:

"We don't agree. We don't want it. Let them be photographed separately."
And then the "independent" women started making a commotion.

"Akh, what fine ladies they became when they joined the kolkhoz. People
come to them from the city in a carriage to take their pictures—you don't dare
go near them now!" they said angrily, spitting loudly as was the local custom.

The upshot was that the kolkhoz activists stalked away in dudgeon, putting an end to the photo session.[11]

The unwillingness to admit new applicants to the kolkhoz who came
with empty hands that was widely reported in the mid-1930s owed something to this developing spirit of kolkhoz identity and patriotism, as well as
to the obvious economic motives. Children were particularly likely to take
such partisanship to heart, of course, and some of the "Pavlik Morozovs" of
the 1930s—adolescents who publicly denounced their parents (see Chapter
9)—were children of independents who had become patriots of the kolkhoz
along with their schoolmates. In 1935, for example, a seventh-grader named
Serezha Fadeev went to the headmaster of his school and informed him that
his father and another independent peasant had twice sneaked out into the
fields at night and dug up 80 puds of potatoes they had buried there. Young
Fadeev had apparently been deeply mortified by the fact that his family and
one other household were the only ones that still remained outside the
kolkhoz.[12]

As numbers of independents dwindled, however, there are fewer reports
of two-camp hostility between them and the kolkhozniks, and more reports
of the complex net of economic interrelationships that had sprung up, based
on the different rights and restrictions of the two groups. Many of these
economic relationships had to do with the independents' horses, which
might be hired out by kolkhozniks for going to market or plowing the private plot. Others had to do with the hiring of labor. When collective farms
hired outside labor, as they frequently did in the latter part of the 1930s,
independents were often the people that were hired.[13]

In 1938, some kolkhozniks from Ivanovo oblast wrote to *Krest'ianskaia
gazeta* to complain that the independents in their village had made an agreement with the kolkhoz of a neighboring village to mow their hay meadow in
exchange for some of the hay. That was unfair, the kolkhozniks thought.
After all, these were "our independents," not theirs. Moreover, many of
them were married to kolkhozniks and were thus legally members of kolkhoz
households, which meant that their procurements quotas for milk and meat
were lower than independents' quotas would have been. It was not right that
they should be able to get a good deal on procurements *and* be allowed to
hire themselves out mowing hay in another kolkhoz, which was forbidden to
kolkhozniks. (*Krest'ianskaia gazeta* did not try to resolve this complex issue
of fairness. It firmly informed the kolkhozniks that it was illegal for anyone to
hire himself out for a percentage of the crop.)[14]

By the last years of the decade, independents in most regions had been
thoroughly marginalized. Most households were small and poor, and a fair
number consisted just of elderly couples whose children had gone to the city.

Local officials started to treat them contemptuously rather than vindictively, as in the past. In Oboian raion of Kursk oblast, which had more than a thousand independent households left in 1938, the raion authorities described them dismissively as "inveterate" and "incorrigible" and called them "Hindus" (*indusy*). ("Communist Shatokhin, an official in the Oboianskii finance department, calls independents '*indusy*' even in official documents."[15])

To be an independent became an eccentric position, earning mockery in the village, embarrassing to one's children. The writer Mikhail Alekseev relates a story similar to that of Serezha Fadeev that occurred in his native village in Saratov krai. Spiridon Podiforovich Solovei, the last remaining independent in the village, was nicknamed "the museum-piece" (*muzeinyi eksponat*) by other peasants for his stubborn refusal to join the kolkhoz despite threats, cajoling, punitive taxation, and finally, in 1938, confiscation of his horse. Both his sons quarreled with him over the issue. The elder left the village. The younger, Vanka, became so deeply alienated and distressed by his father's stance that in 1945 in desperation he finally burned down the family house. Having confessed to the deed, he was sent off to a colony for juvenile delinquents. His father, a broken man, left the village forever the next day.[16]

The coup de grâce for most independents (though not for Spiridon Podiforovich) was the law introduced in the summer of 1938 that imposed a special tax of 275 to 500 rubles on the horses of independent peasants. The only way to avoid paying the tax—or having your horse confiscated because you were unable to pay—was to join a kolkhoz and hand over the horse.[17] That was what most of the remaining independents did, thus ending their brief chapter in history.

Craftsmen

Crafts production in the village was adversely affected by collectivization in the extreme. Craftsmen of all kinds—millers, carpenters, pottery makers, tailors, shoemakers, blacksmiths—were automatic suspects for dekulakization. They had a product that they sold or a facility they hired; in some cases, they had ties to entrepreneurial middlemen who distributed their products. Many observers were astonished to see how quickly and apparently thoroughly the practice of rural crafts collapsed. Collectivization wiped out many of the old craft villages specializing in a particular trade, for example, lacemaking or shoemaking. Many craftsmen left the village and joined artisan cooperatives in the towns: As an émigré journal reported in 1930, "everyone who was linked with the town and had any kind of artisan skills (carpenters, smiths, coopers, saddlemakers and others) tried to move to the city. . . ."[18]

Other peasants simply stopped working at their crafts, either because they could no longer get the raw materials or because cultivating the private plot in order to feed themselves had become the first priority. As we will see in a later chapter, peasants even stopped making clothes and other products for themselves.

Even after the first traumatic impact was past, crafts remained weak because the kolkhoz structure created many impediments. Kolkhozniks were not forbidden to sell craft items of their own making at the kolkhoz market, but it was clearly discouraged. Moreover, work on crafts did not earn them kolkhoz labordays. As for independents, to engage in crafts only added to the sense that they were all speculators under the skin. In one village in Leningrad oblast, independents were accused of "sabotaging procurements" by making tapers, for which they were earning 12–15 rubles a day (meaning that they should have been growing food to fill state procurements quotas).[19]

In 1933, a rural soviet chairman and a kolkhoz chairman from the Vologda region, long famous for crafts, wrote a letter to the Russian government deploring the situation and explaining its dynamics. The countryside needs goods like boxes for salting cucumbers, they pointed out, but they are nowhere to be found because peasant craftsmen are no longer making them. Rope making, for example, had formerly been a specialty of the two villages. But they had dropped the craft, and rope was now unobtainable in the region. The famous Vologda lacemaking craft was still alive, although its continuation depended on the goodwill of kolkhoz chairmen who were prepared to release the female lacemakers from work in the fields. But sometimes, according to the writers, a good lacemaker with the capacity to earn valuable foreign currency for the state by making goods for export had to spent her whole time working in the fields or tending kolkhoz livestock. Why have crafts been dropped? Because collective farms regard them as a secondary activity and do not pay labordays for craft work.

> In the . . . village of Pestovo, which is now the "Truth of the North" kolkhoz, there are feltmakers whose mastery of their trade is something to marvel at. But [even] a master craftsman like that [has to] go out into the fields and work one or one and a half labordays. The laborday now weighs a lot in the scale—that's your bread and potato and meat. If he goes out and makes a felt backing for a horse's yoke, there's not the same reward.[20]

Two crafts that the village could not easily do without were those of the blacksmith and the miller. But these were both problematical figures in the countryside of the 1930s, and both were in short supply. Since they had generally been reasonably prosperous in the 1920s, a large number of them had either been dekulakized or had left the village fearing dekulakization. (Blacksmiths seem to have been more prone to leave for jobs in industry, millers to be dekulakized.) Those that remained were in a special position: useful if not indispensable because of their skills, socially suspect (especially millers), often in an anomalous relationship to the kolkhoz, and still in a position, no matter what rules and regulations surrounded them, to become more prosperous than other peasants.

The blacksmith was a particularly odd character. Traditionally a somewhat intimidating presence, thought to have knowledge of the black arts, he often continued to be associated with some kind of sinister power. In one raion in the Western oblast, three blacksmiths and one carpenter were

among the eleven "oppositionists" (former SRs and religious activists as well
as Party opposition sympathizers) that the party was keeping under surveil-
lance in the countryside in 1936.[21] It was also often alleged that village
(kolkhoz) blacksmiths were former kulaks.[22]

It was not even clear what the proper relationship of blacksmith to
kolkhoz should be after collectivization. The 1930 kolkhoz Charter did not
indicate that village smithies should be collectivized, nor did it indicate the
contrary. The only official guidance was an instruction from the Commissariat of Agriculture of July 3, 1934 stating that if the blacksmith joined the
kolkhoz, his smithy might be collectivized—but only if he agreed and the
kolkhoz wanted it. But it is not at all clear that this was the norm in the first
half of the 1930s. The situation of M. P. Stepanov, a blacksmith who wrote
to *Krest'ianskaia gazeta* for advice in 1935, may have been more typical.
Stepanov had joined the kolkhoz in 1931, but his smithy and tools of trade
remained his own property. The kolkhoz took responsibility for providing
him with raw material, and evidently paid him in labordays for his work for
the kolkhoz. Now, however, the kolkhoz wanted to collectivize his smithy
and machinery, and he wanted to know if they had the right to do this.[23]

Krest'ianskaia gazeta did not know the answer—the 1935 Kolkhoz
Charter, just issued, had once again failed to clarify the question of blacksmiths—and wrote to the Commissariat of Agriculture for a ruling. But it
turned out that the Commissariat was also confused. A deputy Commissar
(A. I. Muralov) drafted an instruction saying that smithies should *not* be collectivized; if the kolkhoz wanted to own the village smithy, it should buy it
from the blacksmith. But the Commissar himself, Mikhail Chernov, dis-
agreed. He drafted his own instruction, which stated that when blacksmiths
joined the kolkhoz, their smithies and equipment (except small tools)
should be collectivized, and sent it over to Ia. A. Iakovlev at the Central
Committee for confirmation.[24]

It is not clear how this issue was formally resolved, though a 1938 report from Leningrad oblast suggested that blacksmiths were unwilling to
join the kolkhoz because that would mean collectivization of their smithies
and equipment. What is clear is that blacksmiths continued to operate under
a variety of agreements with collective farms, and those kolkhozy that had a
smithy—fewer than 40 percent in 1936—considered themselves lucky.
Blacksmiths are "the most forgotten, the most uncontrolled people in the
kolkhoz," commented a writer on agricultural problems in 1938, adding
that how their relationship with the kolkhoz was structured and how they
got paid were usually a complete mystery to the raion authorities.[25]

When the blacksmith was a kolkhoz member, which was presumably the
normal situation by the end of the decade, he was supposed to be paid in
labordays for the work he did for the kolkhoz. But what about the work he
did for individual kolkhozniks? This was a major part of the smith's activity,
and it had to be paid for in cash. "They mend spades, do tinplating of samovars, make knives, . . . turning the kolkhoz smithy into a private commercial

enterprise." Kolkhozniks often complained that the blacksmiths were profiteering by charging high prices for these services.[26]

As for the blacksmith's work for the kolkhoz, the same problem arose here in the second half of the 1930s as with respect to kolkhoz chairmen, accountants, and others with special skills: Blacksmiths wanted to be paid at fixed rates and put on salary rather than being paid in labordays. There were many reports of kolkhoz blacksmiths who were either fully on salary (250 rubles a month, in one case cited from Novosibirsk) or else working for labordays plus an additional money stipend.[27]

The complaints about the blacksmith's "greed" in charging high prices to the kolkhoz or to individual kolkhozniks were matched by similar complaints against other skilled craftsmen. For example, a carpenter named Zaitsev, evidently much in demand in Rybinsk raion, tried to charge a kolkhoz 4,930 rubles (expressed as 1,000 labordays at a rate of 4.93 rubles per laborday) for work on a vegetable storehouse that took only 100 days, and finally agreed on 3,235 rubles. Then he started to build an orphanage for the kolkhoz, but after working for a few days, broke the contract and went off and did private work. Zaitsev had no respect for kolkhozniks: He called them layabouts (*bezdel'niki*) who "don't deserve to get paid your labordays."[28]

Millers were an even more suspect group than blacksmiths and carpenters—so suspect that there was an acute shortage of qualified and acceptable persons to run mills throughout the 1930s. A spokesman for the Central Committee of the Millers' Union reported early in 1935 that there were still many class enemies in the small mills, such as those operated by kolkhozy. In the "Krasnyi Perekop" kolkhoz in the Crimea, for example, the kolkhoz miller was a man who had formerly had his own mill (evidently in another village) and been dekulakized. Many villages had lost their mills during collectivization as a result of the dekulakization of millers. A 1936 survey of collective farms found that only 25 percent had mills in operation.[29]

It is clear, in fact, that it was very difficult in the 1930s to find an experienced miller who had *not* been dekulakized. This may be one reason why kolkhoz millers usually seem to have been hired outsiders rather than kolkhoz members. In Nabelye village in Leningrad oblast, the kolkhoz hired the former lessee of the mill to run it when he showed up again in 1934, he had been dekulakized and then probably served time in prison or camp. When he was arrested a few years later on charges of cheating the kolkhoz, the kolkhoz hired another former kulak to run the mill.[30]

In Kozelsk raion in the Western oblast, the raikom sent out a certain Baryshev to repair the Pliusskii turbine mill, property of the Western Milling Trust, which provided four neighboring collective farms with electricity. Baryshev got the mill working again, and the trust appointed him to direct it. But then the raikom received information that Baryshev was "a kulak, perhaps even dekulakized," and held up the appointment while it investigated further. It turned out that Baryshev was the son of a former estate manager, himself a former owner of a mill, and "in any case . . . a class-alien element." So the raikom decided he should be fired, regardless of the fact that there was no other "miller-specialist" available in the raion and four collective farms were likely to have their electricity cut off as a result.[31]

There was a critical shortage of millers and working mills, both small and large, in the countryside throughout the 1930s. Peasants were constantly complaining about the enormous waits at the few mills that were working (not to mention the bribes that had to be paid to the miller to get to the front of the line), and the newspapers frequently reported disapprovingly that in such and such a raion not a single mill was operating at the height of the harvest season.[32]

In the second half of the 1930s, statements deploring the collapse of craft industries, especially "folk" industries that had potential for export, appeared with increasing frequency in the press. It was a sign of the times that the traditional work of Orel lacemakers, embroiderers, and glassmakers was put on display in the Orel pavilion at the much-touted All-Union Agricultural Show in Moscow at the end of the decade.[33]

The old craft village, renamed a "craft kolkhoz" (*promyslovyi kolkhoz*, or *promkolkhoz*), reemerged after a period of dispersal and disintegration in the early 1930s.[34] Some already had a net income of a million rubles, a Moscow newspaper boasted at the end of 1936. Those cited in Moscow oblast included a pottery promkolkhoz, "Path to Socialism," in Ramenki, which had netted 630,000 rubles.[35] These claims, however, should be treated skeptically. In reality, the promkolkhozy (except those involved in primary industries like fishing, mining, logging, and hunting) seem to have remained relatively marginal phenomena.[36]

Around the same time (1936), great enthusiasm was expressed in the press about the income-generating possibilities of kolkhoz craft workshops. A number of kolkhozy in Moscow oblast were making guitars, balalaikas, mandolins, and other musical instruments; one of them had cleared 4,500 rubles in seven months of operation. Lacemakers were back in business, now (as publicists did not fail to remark) earning money for the kolkhoz instead of for the capitalist middleman. At the "New Path" kolkhoz in 1936, 100 kolkhoz women were producing 6–8 meters of lace a day and earning up to 10 rubles. How the lacemakers' earnings were divided between the actual lacemakers and the kolkhoz is not recorded. But in the case of a carpentry workshop in the "Truth" kolkhoz in Vereia raion, Moscow oblast, the kolkhoz put 80 percent of the net profits into its capital fund and distributed 20 percent to the carpenters—a ratio that the old capitalist middleman would not have despised.[37]

The problem, of course, was distribution. It was clearly no accident that so many of the newly flourishing promkolkhozy were in Moscow oblast, with the country's largest commercial center readily accessible. In order to make one of these enterprises go, you had to find a state or cooperative buyer that wanted the goods and could use or distribute them. This was a daunting problem even in Moscow, but out in the provinces it was often virtually impossible to find a legal distributor. When the kolkhozniks of Usadishche village wanted to revive their old craft of producing spades for the local markets of Pskov, Ostrov, and Porkhov, they could find no wholesaler to buy them.[38]

Of course, that is not to say that there were no blackmarket possibilities. Although the old Dubovka coopers' village on the Upper Volga was still in business as a craft kolkhoz in 1933, a critic noted that you would rarely find their produce on the kolkhoz market at Dubovka, but "almost every day speculators come in to collect goods for dispatch to Saratov or Stalingrad."[39] Undoubtedly the collective farms in the Moscow region were often engaged in similar business dealings. Sometimes one has the impression that providing cover for blackmarket manufacturing was becoming almost the raison d'être of collective farms in Moscow oblast by the last years of the decade. This tendency, however, was also noticed by the judicial authorities, and there was a series of prosecutions of kolkhozy that had left the path of honest craft production and started making deals with urban conmen (*zhuliki*). In one such case, a kolkhoz in the Moscow oblast allowed an urban entrepreneur, a total outsider, to organize a workshop on its premises to produce maps and other school supplies. In another, this time in Ramenki south of Moscow, a kolkhoz was used as a front for blackmarket manufacturing of haberdashery goods.[40]

Khutor Dwellers

Khutors, the individual enclosed farms separate from villages whose establishment had been encouraged by the prerevolutionary Stolypin reforms, were still quite common in certain parts of the Soviet Union, notably in the west (Russia's Western oblast, Belorussia, parts of Ukraine) and Siberia. The khutor dwellers were sometimes nominal members of collective farms and sometimes not. At the beginning of 1939, the total number of khutors (collectivized and uncollectivized) was almost a million.[41]

In the west and northwest, most khutor dwellers were "collectivized" in the first half of the 1930s, and some collective farms even consisted largely of khutors. What this meant in practice is unclear, but it seems likely that in these cases the kolkhoz was often a facade for individual farming. In Leningrad oblast, where there were many collectivized khutors, a party spokesman noted vaguely in 1934 that "something would have to be done" to make the khutor-based kolkhozy more effective as a collective form of land use.

At the end of 1935, the Central committee's decree on the non-Black Earth belt noted that the khutor form of land tenure made collectivization essentially meaningless, and suggested that regional authorities should give material support to khutor dwellers who wished to move into villages. But this recommendation was issued mildly, without either the threats or the promise of extra budgetary allocations that were usually needed to get a real response in the provinces, and progress was slow. One raion in Leningrad oblast reported that the resettlement of khutor dwellers was "on the agenda"—

but this turned out to mean in practice that one (and only one) khutor-based kolkhoz had started building a village and relocating the households from their outlying homesteads.[42]

The decree on the non-Black Earth belt had also instructed the authorities to merge collective farms based on very small settlements (five to ten households), which often included khutors. In attempting to implement this, the Western oblast authorities went too far, sometimes merging a large number of small settlements in the one kolkhoz. This was later criticized as a new manifestation of gigantomania, and most of the mergers had to be rescinded. The experience clearly discouraged officials in the Western oblast from further efforts to solve the problem of khutors.[43]

In Siberia, by contrast, most khutors remained uncollectivized up to and perhaps beyond the mid 1930s. In 1934, only 14 percent of khutor households in Western Siberia belonged to collective farms. In the taiga of Eastern Siberia, some predominantly khutor districts were reported in the same year to be almost untouched by collectivization. It was said that the small, scattered khutor settlements provided refuge for "many kulaks and individual peasants who did not want to join the kolkhoz or had fled there from other regions."[44]

At the beginning of 1937, the Politburo decided to begin moving khutor dwellers in Kalinin (formerly Tver) and Leningrad oblasts and in Belorussia into villages. This resettlement program, which was supposed to involve 26,000 households, seems to have foundered in the confusion of the Great Purges.[45]

The real action on khutors occurred only after May 1939, when the Central Committee decided that khutors were no longer to exist within the kolkhoz framework, and that all "collectivized" khutor households in the northern and western regions of the country were to be relocated in villages by September 1, 1940. These decision affected 666,000 khutor households, the majority of them in Ukraine, Belorussia, and Smolensk oblast. A plan was developed to create or radically reshape 5,500 kolkhoz villages to accommodate the former khutor dwellers. This was a big, expensive operation, and it was interrupted by the outbreak of war before completion. By the summer of 1941, however, it appears that most of the kolkhoz khutor dwellers, as well as some households that were not collectivized, had been resettled in villages.[46]

Otkhodniks and Other Wage Earners

In the first years of collectivization, wage work outside the kolkhoz was a controversial issue because the kolkhoz felt it had a right to part of the wages of its members. When the issue was argued in the central government labor agency in January 1930, speakers reported that "a pitched battle" was going on between wage earners and the rest of the village: "The peasants say if you join the kolkhoz, give us 50–75 percent of your wages." Kolkhoz Center proposed a more moderate cut of 30–40 percent, and even labor officials thought that the kolkhoz might take 15–20 percent of its members' outside earnings. But the government's decision on otkhod in 1931 did not allow the kolkhoz to take any part of its members' outside earnings, which remained fully the property of the wage earner throughout the 1930s.[47]

Whether kolkhozniks required the permission of the kolkhoz to go away on otkhod or take paid employment outside the kolkhoz was also a matter of controversy in the early years. This was resolved in favor of the kolkhoz by a government decree of March 1933. Henceforth, the formal procedure for otkhod required kolkhozniks to obtain permission to depart from the kolkhoz and then, like independent peasants, apply to the rural soviet for a passport. The passport was valid only for three months, but it could be renewed at the place of work without the need for further applications to the kolkhoz and rural soviet.[48]

As we have already seen, it was easier for kolkhozniks to depart on otkhod, or even to depart permanently, at almost all times in the 1930s than the provisions of the 1933 decree would imply. This was because in almost all circumstances the regime gave priority to industry's needs—including a freely flowing labor supply—over the needs of agriculture. Although the 1931 decree on otkhod represented an effort to assert state control over peasant labor through a system of contracts between industrial enterprises and collective farms, this system, known as orgnabor, proved difficult to operate and by no means eliminated the possibility of individual otkhod. In the first place, it was usually not difficult (for a price) to get kolkhoz permission to depart and a passport from the rural soviet. In the second place, it was not unknown for kolkhozniks to depart even without permission and a passport. Despite the existence of laws that threatened state enterprises with stern penalties if they ever hired a kolkhoznik who showed up at the factory gate without kolkhoz permission and a passport, enterprises often systematically violated these rules.[49]

The wage-earning group of kolkhozniks (of which otkhodniks constituted two-thirds) was involved in a variety of activities: working in towns and industrial construction sites, working on state farms and Machine-Tractor Stations (MTS), serving terms as contract laborers in logging camps and mines, holding white-collar jobs in the rural soviet or the raion, and so on. Some (the registered otkhodniks) were absent from the kolkhoz with its permission. Others were working as part of a labor-recruitment (orgnabor) contract that the kolkhoz had made with an industrial enterprise or trust. A considerable number were working locally for wages, for which formal permission from the kolkhoz was not required. There were also episodes of acute economic crisis when virtually the entire working population of a kolkhoz fled to earn money elsewhere.

What most of the wage-earning kolkhozniks had in common was the belief that by working outside the kolkhoz without resigning their kolkhoz membership they were maximizing their advantages. The outside job gave them a predictable income in cash and (for those who had permanent jobs and joined trade unions) the possibility of pensions and other benefits. The kolkhoz membership provided the family with grain and potatoes (assuming that the wife worked labordays in the kolkhoz) and a private plot that was larger than the plot allowed to nonkolkhoz households.

The "maximization of advantages" attitude was clearly seen in the reactions of some otkhodniks when the government tightened up on kolkhoz membership and introduced the laborday minimum in 1939:

> A member of the Stalskii kolkhoz came in haste from the city of Tbilisi. He arrived safely in the village of Tokhchar . . . in the republic of Dagestan, showed up in the office of the Stalskii kolkhoz, and announced that he "had come to work off the prescribed minimum—60 labordays—and after that would return to his previous job." The board came to an agreement with the visitor. It was agreed that he should repair the mill, for which they would register 60 labordays in his workbook. The next day, that "artisan" hired five persons, and they finished the repair of the mill in two days.[50]

In the central industrial region, most otkhodniks were working for urban state enterprises, usually in industry. In the more commercially oriented south, the entrepreneurial otkhodnik was a more prominent figure. Lakskii raion in Dagestan seems to have been a particularly favorable environment. According to a 1939 newspaper report,

> More than 50 kolkhozniks from Lakskii raion in Dagestan live in the city of Stalinabad. They all have documents saying that they are members of a kolkhoz. Each of them has a craft workshop and an income in the tens of thousands, but they pay only 20–40 rubles agricultural tax more than the kolkhozniks who are their fellow villagers working in the kolkhoz.[51]

In most cases, the wage-earning kolkhoznik belonged to a kolkhoz household that cultivated its private plot; usually the wife of the wage earner worked in the kolkhoz fields as well. But this was not always the case. Sometimes the otkhodnik took his whole family to town. He was legally entitled to rent his dwelling but not his private plot (even when the "plot" was his yard). According to a 1939 government decree, however, it often happened

> that the kolkhoznik's private plot becomes effectively the private property of the kolkhoz household, at the disposal not of the kolkhoz but of the kolkhoznik at his own discretion: he leases it and retains the private plot for his own use regardless of the fact that he does not work in the kolkhoz.[52]

The wage earners, particularly the otkhodniks, were distinctive among peasants for their concern about legal rights. The whole question of their rights and obligations was complex as a result of their dual status as kolkhozniks and wage earners. Kolkhozy and local authorities frequently ignored or misunderstood the law, and the law itself was not always clear or free of contradictions. So the wage-earning kolkhozniks were kept busy lodging complaints, writing to *Krest'ianskaia gazeta* for rulings on tricky questions, and probably also bringing legal suits. In their complaints, better written than the majority of peasant letters, they presented themselves as law-abiding citizens in a society governed by written law. Principles of natural justice and customary law were rarely if ever invoked.

A large number of their problems had to do with liability for taxes and procurements. From Iaroslavl oblast, a kolkhoz member with a white-collar job and a wife who worked in the kolkhoz wrote to *Krest'ianskaia gazeta* to ask whether local authorities were correct in counting his household as liable for the agricultural tax and procurement obligations. His view was that the household was not liable because it was headed by a salary earner. A similar inquiry came from the secretary of a rural soviet in the Tatar Republic whose wife continued to work in the kolkhoz. (*Krest'ianskaia gazeta*'s consultants gave them two different readings of the law: the Iaroslavl writer was told that liability was indeed determined by the occupation of the head of the household, while the inquirer from the Tatar Republic was told that a household was liable for agricultural tax as long as any member of it was engaged in agriculture.)[53]

In the real world, of course, the kolkhoz wage earners' concern with law and procedures also involved an interest in knowing how to manipulate them. A kolkhoznik from a Voronezh kolkhoz wrote to *Krest'ianskaia gazeta* with the following story. Two of his fellow kolkhozniks applied for permission to go off on otkhod and work in a sugar plant. The kolkhoz was unwilling to grant permission, but the raikom secretary intervened, presumably because the sugar plant was short of labor, and the two got permission and passports. After only a few weeks, however, both returned home to the kolkhoz and got employment in the local MTS. In the opinion of the letter writer, the whole sugar-plant episode was a ruse "to get the passports and letters of authorization" and thus have freedom of movement.[54]

Relations between the kolkhoz and its absent or wage-earning members were often less than cordial. Other kolkhozniks tended to resent the fact that the otkhodniks and their families were getting the benefits of kolkhoz membership without making enough of a contribution to the kolkhoz. The kolkhoz sometimes refused members the right to go away on otkhod, tried to force absent members to return, or punished otkhodniks by expelling their wives and aged parents. These actions were almost always locally initiated, not the result of instructions from above; and they were strongly reminiscent of similar actions against otkhodniks in the prerevolutionary village.[55] Expelled otkhodniks often had to be reinstated after they appealed successfully to raion authorities. In general, it was not the regime but the collective farms themselves that wanted to discipline and control their wage-earning members.

The attitude of the kolkhoz towards departure of its members tended to be most negative when all the profit from outside work went to the individual and none to the kolkhoz. But the kolkhoz had various ways of making departure a paying proposition. With regard to individual otkhodniks, the usual practice was to require a bribe from the would-be otkhodnik to the kolkhoz chairman and perhaps board members as well before the necessary permission was granted.

> In order to get permission to go on *otkhod* you have to get a passport, for which it is necessary to have a paper (*spravka*) [from the kolkhoz], and to get that paper you have to pay in vodka—"drink to the wedding," as the kolkhozniks like

to say—by entertaining three or four members of the [kolkhoz] board and officials of the rural soviet.

"If a bedniak asks for a paper to go on *otkhod*," a group of self-styled "bedniak" kolkhozniks from Kursk oblast complained in 1938, "[the kolkhoz chairman] will not give it because there is nothing to extract from him."[56]

Contractual arrangements to supply labor from the kolkhoz to industrial enterprises (orgnabor) could be even more profitable.

> The recruiter goes in . . . to recruit carpenters, and the kolkhoz board says: give us 12 rubles and we will give you carpenters. The recruiter starts bargaining, and then the kolkhoz asks 7 rubles a day. If the recruiter refuses to make a deal, he goes away without getting anyone.

Kolkhoz chairmen could also turn a profit out of orgnabor by playing off one enterprise's recruiter against another, accepting "advances" from several different organizations simultaneously.[57]

In practice, however, the kolkhoz's right to refuse permission seems to have been quite circumscribed. True, the kolkhoz was allowed to refuse permission for departure, at least temporarily, if there was a shortage of working hands, and kolkhozniks did not have the formal right to leave without permission on their own initiative. But what about the many cases when they *did* leave without permission? The crucial issue was whether the kolkhoz then had the right to use the only sanction available to it, namely expulsion. In the innumerable contested cases of expulsion on these grounds, higher authorities almost always decided against the kolkhoz in the mid-1930s. As the head of the Pereslavl raion land department ruled in a 1938 case, "otkhod may not in any circumstance serve as the reason for expulsion from [kolkhoz] membership, all the more if the family members remain in the kolkhoz."[58]

All the same, expulsions of this kind were commonplace. A typical case was that of the otkhodnik in Kalinin oblast who was expelled after refusing to obey the kolkhoz's order that he give up his factory job and return to the kolkhoz. His wife and parents, who remained working in the kolkhoz, were subsequently subjected to harrassment by kolkhoz officers. The expelled otkhodnik then wrote letters complaining about his and his family's treatment.[59]

Kolkhoz chairmen and other officers often put the argument for control over otkhod in economic terms—both absolute need for labor and the fact that the kolkhoz's assessments for procurements, labor obligations, etc. were based on the number of members on the books, not the number currently in situ. A complaint written late in 1939, probably by a kolkhoz chairman, makes their position sound extremely reasonable. The writer's kolkhoz had so many members away on otkhod that it had been unable to perform its labor obligations for roadwork: as a result, it was fined 2,400 rubles, which it was naturally unable to pay. He argued that it was not fair that the kolkhoz otkhodniks should be allowed to stay away as long as they liked, thus both increasing the financial burden on the kolkhoz and getting out of paying their proper share. For example,

> in 1937 G. I. Kharlamov, a kolkhoznik of our kolkhoz, and his wife submitted a request to the kolkhoz board for permission to go to earn money on the side. The general meeting allowed Kharlamov to go for work on the side up to 1 May 1938. But Kharlamov did not return to the kolkhoz to work after that time was up and even took his wife away to work in the flax plant. The same sort of thing happens in other collective farms. It is all done with the aim of avoiding payment for compulsory deliveries and taxes. His old parents remained in the kolkhoz. The household is taxed with taxes and procurements like a kolkhoznik's household. He lives with his parents [in the village] and goes to work at the flax plant . . .[60]

The accountant of the "Red Perekop" kolkhoz had similar concerns. He wrote to *Krest'ianskaia gazeta* asking what to do about otkhodniks who have been gone from the kolkhoz for extended period, working in factories and mines and on the railroads, and will not come back. "In our kolkhoz there are 62 such people, the majority of whom have not worked in the kolkhoz for four or five years. Therefore according to the [kolkhoz] register the number of kolkhozniks and their families is very great, but in fact very few are working." The kolkhoz administration wanted to expel them, but feared that they were legally unable to do so.[61]

Members of the families of otkhodniks who remained in the village while the otkhodnik was absent were often targets of reprisal by the kolkhoz administration. In one case, the kolkhoz chairman confiscated "seven puds of millet and pork because the husband of Beresneva [a kolkhoz member] is an otkhodnik and does not return to the kolkhoz," and also took her daughter's overcoat, causing the child to miss five days of school. When a kolkhoznik named Kazakov left the "Red Banner" kolkhoz in the Western oblast to work in a factory, his son and daughter were expelled from the kolkhoz, as a result of which the son "threw himself in despair under a train." Another kolkhoz in the same oblast expelled a sixty-year-old woman who had worked ninety-two labordays because her two daughters had left without permission to work at a flax plant. The "Red Valley" kolkhoz expelled the wife and brother of Andrei Maslov, who had gone to work on the railways, after Maslov ignored the kolkhoz chairman's instruction that he return to work on the kolkhoz.[62]

It was not just kolkhoz officers who believed that otkhodniks ought to be brought under kolkhoz discipline. Many and perhaps most rank-and-file kolkhozniks had the same opinion. When peasants in the Western oblast were introduced to the new Kolkhoz Charter in 1935 and asked to comment, officials reporting their discussions noted that there was "a big desire to write something into the Charter limiting otkhod." They reported, too, that because of an acute labor shortage in the region's collective farms, a number of resolutions had been passed at kolkhoz general meetings ordering otkhodniks to return for summer work under threat of the expulsion of their families from the kolkhoz.[63]

In the kolkhoz, as in the serf and post-Emancipation village, the burden of collective responsibility for taxes and obligations—the famous *krugovaia poruka*—was keenly felt. The sense that the otkhodniks were taking unfair advantage and deserting their fellow kolkhozniks was well conveyed by a peasant from Krasnodar, who contrasted his own virtuous conduct with their selfishness:

> I, Skvortsov, have been in the kolkhoz since 1930 and was not a flitter (*letun*), bore all the hardships and deprivations, and did not permit myself to go away as an otkhodnik and earn big money, thus showing myself to be an exemplary builder of kolkhoz life.[64]

A similar sense of grievance against otkhodniks who continued to enjoy the privileges of kolkhozniks was expressed in a letter from "Red Toiler" kolkhoz in Sverdlovsk oblast asking if the kolkhoz could expel fifteen households. Although members of these households were working fulltime in the timber industry, they continued to exercise their right to graze their cows in the kolkhoz "which is very unpleasant for good honest members of the artel."[65]

In the "Lenin" kolkhoz in Kursk oblast, a group of kolkhozniks blew the whistle on otkhodniks who, without kolkhoz permission, had ceased to work in the kolkhoz and taken jobs in the raion.

> The [kolkhoz] chairman took no action. But we began to send signals to the raion, not waiting for the chairman and the kolkhoz,[66] and gave a list of the people who went away without permission to the raikom.[67]

From the "Pushkin" kolkhoz (formerly named "Death to Capital") in Voronezh oblast, a kolkhoznik wrote to complain about unauthorized otkhod. First one kolkhoznik had taken a white-collar job at the local MTS without asking permission, and now five or six more were intending to do the same. At a general meeting of the kolkhoz, the assembled kolkhozniks had voted not to allow spontaneous departures and to insist that all organizations employing them cease to do so. The kolkhoz board sent off this resolution to the organizations concerned and got the raikom secretary to intercede with their directors on the kolkhoz's behalf. But this had so far produced no results. The kolkhoz really needed some of these people urgently, the letter writer emphasized, because they knew how to repair some agricultural equipment that was essential for the harvest. If they didn't come back, everybody's earnings for the year were going to be hurt.[68]

Punitive expulsions of otkhodniks might also have other kinds of motivation. Some complainants alleged that they had been expelled because of longstanding feuds they had had with the clique of peasants running the kolkhoz. An otkhodnik named A. Kukushkin claimed he was expelled from membership of the "Red Plowman" kolkhoz in Kalinin oblast in 1938 for this reason. Kukushkin, a party member since the 1920s, had been a worker by occupation until collectivization, although he continued to live in the native village and cultivated an allotment with family labor. He became one of the early leaders of the kolkhoz, and in this capacity was responsible for putting eight prosperous households in the village on the "fixed-quota" list. These households had since joined the kolkhoz; in fact, they had won control of it and were now taking their revenge on former enemies. Not content with expelling Kukushkin from the kolkhoz, they had immediately levied the independent tax on him, claiming that he sold meat at the bazaar. (This was true, Kukushkin admitted, although he had not sold as much as they claimed.) The tax was levied not once but twice, first 384 rubles and then 107 rubles. "In order to pay all that tax, I would have to destroy the farm, sell the cow and the house—that's all I have."[69]

It was not always the case, however, that the kolkhozy treated their Communist otkhodniks so badly. Some saw them as assets—brokers between the village and the outside world—who could be used to help fellow villagers find jobs in the town, give character references, legitimize complaints, or represent the kolkhoz's position in conflicts with other organizations. When collective farms found themselves in dispute with the raion over an unpopular kolkhoz chairman, a common event in the mid to late 1930s, they sometimes tried to resolve it by nominating one of "their" Communists, that is, one who worked outside the village but whose family belonged to the kolkhoz. In one case in the Western oblast in 1936, for example, a kolkhoz whose economy had suffered under an incompetent chairman elected as its new chairman Semen Mitroshin, a Communist from the village who worked at the local cement factory. In a similar case in Iaroslavl, the "Women's Labor" kolkhoz asked V. E. Sysoev, a Communist from the village who had a good white-collar job in the raion, to come back and serve as kolkhoz chairman. The strategy here was clearly to force the raion to withdraw its own (unacceptable) candidate for chairman by offering an alternative that was acceptable both to the raion and to the village.[70]

To sum up: If we compare the level of otkhod in the late 1930s to that of the 1920s or early 1900s, we find that it was running at a higher level than it had been in the 1920s, despite an outflow of more than ten million peasants at the beginning of the 1930s that should have mopped up most of the surplus rural population according to most calculations. Otkhod levels in the late 1930s did not equal those of the prewar decades, however, even though part of the difference was made up by an increase in neighborhood wage working by village resident kolkhoz members. In the third quarter of the 1930s, about one in every four kolkhoz households in the Soviet Union contained an otkhodnik, and about one in every three contained a wage earner.[71]

Nevertheless, the level of otkhod was down substantially in the latter part of the 1930s, compared to the immediate prerevolutionary decades. One possible hypothesis, which must await investigation by an economic historian, is that the financial burden on the peasants was less in the late

1930s than it had been twenty to twenty-five years earlier. Be that as it may, the burden was still considerable. Since cash earnings from the kolkhoz were small and unreliable, outside cash earnings were essential to any peasant household that was unable to make enough selling private-plot produce on the market to pay its taxes—which means a substantial proportion of all households. Even in a bumper agricultural year like 1937, the total cash income of all Soviet kolkhozniks from the kolkhoz barely exceeded their cash income from wage work outside the kolkhoz.[72]

Other peasants still resented the otkhodniks, as they had done under serfdom and in the post-Emancipation decades, feeling that they were shirking their share of communal (collective) obligations. This is one of the strongest indications we have that the kolkhoz was indeed functioning as the successor to the mir and its principle of shared responsibility, even if it was the punitive and envious expression of that principle that was more in evidence—as it perhaps always had been—than the mutual support that was supposed to be its corollary.

It is worth emphasizing that an astonishingly large proportion of all kolkhozniks spent little or no time working for the kolkhoz. Out of 36 million male and female kolkhozniks of working age (sixteen to fifty-nine years), according to an investigation conducted by the State Planning Commission in 1937, more than 13 million—37 percent—were essentially non-contributing members who earned fewer than fifty-one labordays (that is, worked for the kolkhoz no more than about forty-five days in the year), and almost 5 million of these earned no labordays at all. Otkhodniks, numbering 4 million, and kolkhozniks who lived in the village but were wage workers outside the kolkhoz (2.3 million) accounted for perhaps half of the noncontributors, the rest being women working on the family's private plot. Using data from the suppressed 1937 census, it can be calculated that the noncontributing group (earning fewer than fifty-one labordays per year) comprised 42 percent of all female kolkhoz members of working age and 30 percent of males.[73]

A selective survey of collective farms in ten regions conducted in the same year reinforces the impression that a large proportion of kolkhozniks were occupied with something other than working for the kolkhoz. In the winter months, the survey shows that the average kolkhoz household (whose size is not indicated) had only one working member in the sixteen to fifty-nine age group. Only for a few months in the summer did the average household provide two working members. In some individual regions, moreover, the degree of involvement in kolkhoz work was much lower. In Kiev and Voronezh oblasts, for example, the average *household*—men, women, and children—provided only about 260 days work per year for the kolkhoz.[74]

In May 1939, alarmed by widely reported shortages of manpower in the collective farms, and of kolkhozy that were spending all their cash income hiring labor from outside, several meetings of party leaders with obkom and raikom secretaries were held in the Central Committee to find out what the problem was. Speaker after speaker described how large numbers of kolkhozniks—a third or more in many places—found it possible to support themselves by something other than kolkhoz laborday earnings. In the south, kolkhozniks were often making a good living by marketing produce from their private plots. In the central industrial region, the nonworking kolkhozniks were generally wage workers in industry who had left their families in the village; but in some cases, as the Moscow obkom secretary reported, they were wage earners who were supplementing their wages by renting out their private plots in the kolkhoz to kolkhozniks and independent peasants.[75]

The laborday minimum enacted at the May 1939 plenum, which was the outcome of the discussion cited above, was the first serious effort to limit the outside wage-earning capacity of kolkhozniks since the introduction of passports and restrictions on otkhod at the beginning of 1933.[76] The outbreak of war makes it difficult to judge how much impact this measure had. As long as money remuneration of kolkhozniks remained very low, they had a strong incentive to seek outside sources of income. This situation did not significantly change until the dramatic rise in cash income of kolkhozniks in the Khrushchev period, which seems to have made the widespread practice of otkhod a thing of the past.

7

Power

Soviet rule in the countryside was coercive, arbitrary, and often brutal. But, as had historically been the case in Russia, officials were spread thin over a wide area. That meant from the standpoint of peasants, neglect by Soviet power was as characteristic as coercion, and perhaps sometimes even as much resented. At the beginning of the 1930s, a great flood of urbanites swept in to the countryside to organize collectivization, followed by a smaller wave of Communist troubleshooters sent out to the (MTS) politotdels in 1933 to cope with famine-associated unrest. But the great majority of these outsiders went home to the towns within a few years. In normal times, the Communist presence in the village was still very much a matter of the season. Each year many Communists came on various official missions for the procurements campaign in the autumn, and a somewhat smaller number appeared in the spring in connection with the sowing campaign. But very few spent the winter with the peasants.[1]

The average rural raion in the USSR, with a population of 40,000–50,000 in the middle of the 1930s, had about 100 paid officials, 40 of them working in the raion center and 60 out in the rural soviets.[2] In the hierarchy of raion officials, the top man was the first secretary of the raion party committee (raikom), and the chairman of the raion soviet executive committee (RIK) ranked second. From the peasants' standpoint, the other key official was the head of the land department of the raion soviet (*raizo*). Organized at the end of 1934, the raion land departments took over many of the discipline and control functions formerly exercised by the MTS politotdels. Their responsibilities included the approval and removal of kolkhoz chairmen and the setting of sowing plans for individual collective farms.

"The raion" was a resonant phrase in the village (as in "The raion ordered," "You will answer to the raion for this"), and raion leaders often cut a swaggering figure on their rare visits out to the collective farms. The privilege of going to the raion center to take a course in animal husbandry, say, was coveted by peasants, and getting a job in the raion constituted a major step up in the world. Still, by most other standards, "the raion" was not much of a cultural center. Consider, to take a particularly dreary example, the town of Griazovets (population 8,400), center of Griazovets raion (population 90,000) in the Vologda region, which in 1932 could boast a railway station, twenty-one buildings with running water, one lodging house with thirty beds, one pharmacy, and a town fire brigade consisting of three horse-drawn carts.[3]

Four out of five raion administrations in the Soviet Union in the mid-1930s had telephonic connection with the oblast, and the raions in turn could reach about two-thirds of their rural soviets by telephone—that is, if the telephones were working, which at any given time they most likely were not. Very few collective farms had telephones in the 1930s: If the raion wanted to communicate with them, it had to summon the chairman to the raion center or send out a raion official (usually in a horse-drawn cart or on horseback).[4]

The rural soviet (*sel'skii sovet*, shortened to *sel'sovet*) was an administrative unit whose territory had an average of about 2,000 inhabitants in the mid-1930s. It might have jurisdiction over three or ten collective farms, depending on the region, and there were about twenty rural soviets in the average raion. Historically, the *selo* from which the term was derived signified a village with a church (as opposed to a churchless village, *derevnia*). But in the 1930s the selo might well have lost its church, although it had not gained very much in return from Soviet power. The rural soviet was essentially a tax-collecting organization until 1937, when the function of collecting state taxes (although not local "self-taxation" levies) was shifted to the raion. In the summation of one observer, its work "consisted of the chairman . . . running around the countryside collecting taxes and self-taxation, forcing people to go out for wood, [and] seeing that the compulsory labor obligations were carried out." Starting in 1933, the soviet also had the function of issuing passports to peasants departing for work outside the village.[5]

The rural soviet of the mid-1930s had a salaried chairman and secretary, along with a small budget (amounting to up to half the chairman's salary per month) which the chairman could use for hiring additional personnel, generally an untrained village policeman and general gofer, the *sel'skii ispolnitel'*. In the 1930s, the chairman was paid 100–200 rubles a month, depending on the size of the rural district, and the secretary 80–160 rubles. This was enough to live on, in contrast to the miserly 20 rubles a month that a rural soviet chairman had received in 1926–27; and of course the very fact of receiving a regular salary boosted the status of the office. All the same, the status of a rural soviet chairman does not seem to have been very different from that of a kolkhoz chairman, judging by the frequent reports of personnel switches between these two positions. Like kolkhoz chairmen, the rural soviet chairmen usually came from the local peasantry—often members of one of the collective farms in their jurisdiction, with family members who were working kolkhozniks.[6]

One of the most remarkable things about Soviet rule in the countryside in the mid-1930s was the weakness of the Communist Party presence. There were few Communists in rural areas after the first years of collectivization, and the number steadily declined for most of the decade.[7]

The peak year for rural party membership was 1932. This was the culmination of a four-year period of unprecedented party recruitment in the countryside that more than doubled the number of Communists attached to rural primary party organizations. On January 1, 1933, there were close to 900,000 rural party members (just under a quarter of the party's total membership); and two-thirds of the rural members were attached to party organizations in the kolkhoz.[8]

From 1933, however, numbers declined rapidly. Rural organizations were particularly hard hit by the purges of party membership in 1933. Many rural organizations lost a quarter to a third of their membership in 1933, a phenomenon that must have been connected to the large-scale arrests of rural officials at the same period for "liberalism" in their dealings with the peasantry. In the Northern Caucasus in 1933, wracked by famine and Cossack uprisings, 26,000 Communists were expelled in the course of the formal party purge and another 13,000 were expelled for specific errors, including deserting their posts and fleeing from the area—in all, approximately half the total membership of the regional party organization. Nationwide, almost one in four kolkhoz chairmen and rural soviet chairmen who were party members were expelled in 1933, and the attrition rate for ordinary kolkhozniks was even higher. A new round of party purges in 1934 did even more damage, removing a full third of the remaining members of all rural party organizations, and almost 40 percent of those in kolkhoz cells. The party purges of 1935–36 brought further losses to rural party organizations, although not on the same scale as the two previous years. Thanks to a moratorium on party recruitment imposed in 1933, no new members came in to replace those that were expelled until close to the end of the decade.[9]

By the beginning of 1937, the number of Communists in rural party organizations had dropped below 400,000, with the number in kolkhoz cells below 200,000. Communists who were peasants by occupation now constituted a smaller proportion of all party members than they had done in 1927 (11 percent, as against 14 percent), and even in absolute terms their number (205,000 in 1937) was not much higher.[10] Belyi raion in the Western oblast had a mere 239 party members and candidates in 1937, according to one source.[11]

Several consequences followed from draining of party membership. In the first place, there were not enough Communists available to fill all the major offices in the raion center, let alone the rural soviets and the collective farms. Only one in five kolkhoz chairmen in the Soviet Union was a Communist in 1938, down from one in two in the early 1930s and almost one in three at the beginning of 1936. The picture for rural soviet chairmen was even worse: Fewer than one in five were Communists in January 1936.[12]

In the second place, there were probably more *former* Communists than Communists in the countryside in the second half of the 1930s. The kolkhoz that did not have a resident party member might well have a former member, often aggrieved by his expulsion and the loss of opportunity it involved. This probably accounts in part for the surprisingly high degree of attentiveness to politics in the village (see Chapter 11) and the "oppositionist moods" (rarely if ever associated with any organized party opposition) that were frequently reported in the countryside.

In contrast to the situation in the 1920s, the Komsomol did not take up the slack in the 1930s. With the exception of the untypical First Five-Year Plan period, Komsomol members seem not to have been prominent in any part of the rural power structure. Hardly any kolkhoz chairmen were Komsomols (4-5 percent in 1936), and the same is true of MTS directors and their assistants. The reason, undoubtedly, is that the young peasants who were seriously interested in the Komsomol were usually also seriously interested in leaving the countryside. Although the Komsomol formally became a mass-membership organization for adolescents in 1935, a change that was supposed to increase its influence among nonproletarian youth, this was scarcely reflected in the countryside: Total rural membership in 1938 was only 36 percent higher than it had been in 1927, when the Komsomol was still a selective, elite organization.[13]

Rural Officials

From the peasants' standpoint, the whole apparatus of state administration hanging over the kolkhoz was there to get things from them. "The rural soviet people and the Komsomols only know how to do one thing—go round the villages and squeeze out taxes," villagers in the Western oblast complained in 1935.[14] The peasants' sense of exploitation was accentuated by the fact that their new "masters"—from the raion to the rural soviet— often exercised their power in an arbitrary as well as brutal manner, and seemed to treat kolkhoz property as their own. "Arbitrariness" (*proizvol*) in the exercise of power, coupled with "lack of respect" for the peasants in words and deeds, were major objects of peasant grievance and complaints.

Rural officials' disregard for legal formalities was notorious. Most of them lacked the sense that it was important to follow legal forms and procedures, and party policies in the 1930s scarcely encouraged them to develop it. The legal and judicial framework had been distorted and compromised by being used for political and coercive purposes. Local cadres were both victimizers and victims in this process.

Confusion over property rights exacerbated the general problems of the legal system. Was "collective property" really the property of the state, as the harsh sanctions against stealing it of the law of August 7, 1932 implied, or was it the property of a collective farm, that is, of a specific community of kolkhozniks? The expropriation of kulaks had set a bad precedent whose memory lingered throughout the decade. When an official stripped a peasant household of all its property (as happened not infrequently in contexts of extortion as well as punishment), he usually called it "dekulakization," even years after that campaign was supposedly finished.

Extortionate and arbitrary as the officials often were, they themselves were almost equally vulnerable to arbitrary punishment by their superiors. The situation of all officeholders in the countryside was precarious throughout the decade. Extraordinarily high rates of turnover prevailed, and officials who were fired for failing to meet ("sabotaging") procurements or some other infraction were also at risk of losing their party membership or facing criminal charges. Probably the worst period was 1932–33, the years of famine. So many rural officeholders—especially kolkhoz chairmen—were arrested at this time for "sabotaging procurements" that in 1935 the government took the extraordinary step of ordering a general annulment of such convictions and release of prisoners, on the grounds that "their crimes were not linked with any venal motives and were in the great majority of cases the result of incorrect understanding by those convicted of their official duties. . . ."[15]

Higher-level (raion) officials do not seem to have been beneficiaries of this measure, probably because they were less likely to be held criminally responsible for procurements failures. Nevertheless, they too were often fired or abruptly transferred. According to a Leningrad oblast report, a third of all raion instructors and more than a fifth of all rural soviet chairmen in the oblast were removed from their jobs in the first half of 1936. In one raion, two-thirds of all rural soviet chairmen were fired or transferred.[16]

Extortion

There were frequent complaints that funds collected from the peasantry as taxes or loan subscriptions ended up in the pockets of officials. Kolkhoz chairmen sometimes felt obliged to make gifts to raion officials "so as to have protection in the raion." A major cause of peasant complaint against rural soviet chairmen was arbitrary confiscation of animals and other property under the pretext that taxes were owed: Until April 1937, this was not actually illegal, reflecting the frontier mores of rural administration in the immediate aftermath of collectivization and dekulakization. The issuing of passports was another lucrative line of work for rural soviet officials, since it generally seems to have been accompanied by a bribe, or at least a gift of a bottle of vodka. In one case, a rural soviet chairman in Saratov confiscated an accordion won as a prize by a Stakhanovite tractor brigade (since then he "sits at home for days at a time playing the accordion").[17]

Even within the boundaries of the law, the new masters had some power to command the peasants' labor. Under the corvée laws introduced at the beginning of the 1930s, collective farms and independent peasant households were required to provide unpaid labor for the state a set number of days a year, and also to bring along their own horses. In practice, their labor obligations were often interpreted much more broadly than the law allowed. Local authorities treated the collective farms as vassals, showing no respect for their autonomy or property rights. "Everyone pushes the peasants around as they please (*dergaiut krest'ian, komu ne len'*), and whenever it takes their fancy."[18]

Local officials often used the collective farms as a convenient source of labor for all kinds of tasks and campaigns. If the raion or the rural soviet needed labor for a construction or repair project, they called on a nearby kolkhoz to provide it—often without payment. Equally problematic was the assumption of all rural authorities that kolkhoz property was state property, available for their use whenever they required it. Horses were the most frequent target, but any kolkhoz property—from carts to vacant huts in the village—might be a target. "They give orders to the kolkhoz, and without asking, send so many kolkhoz horses and machines to this place and that place. They take horses from the kolkhoz for trips by the raion bosses, they take a house, a buggy. They force the collective farms to take on themselves payment for persons who do not work in the kolkhoz and do not have a direct relation to kolkhoz production."[19]

Such behavior was not only illegal and much resented by the kolkhozniks, it also often caused great hardship:

> Our kolkhoz is not large, it consists altogether of 20 households, it has 14 head of draft power, moreover it was organized not long ago—in the fall of 1934. Every second day (that is at best) and more often every day comrade Krupkin, chairman of the rural soviet, takes from the kolkhoz both draft power and horses for construction of the school, for making his own personal rounds, and even for the coop people (*kooperatory*) to make their rounds. . . .[20]

The kolkhoz bank account was another convenient resource for raion agencies that ran out of funds, and sometimes kolkhoz land was treated in a similar high-handed manner. On one occasion, the Bezhitsa city soviet decided to liquidate a neighboring kolkhoz entirely so that it could give its lands to the "Red Profintern" factory. This meant that the kolkhozniks lost all their collective property, including 400 puds of wheat, horses, and inventory worth 37,000 rubles, and the beneficiaries celebrated with a banquet in the city costing 2,300 rubles.[21]

In addition to practicing extortion against collective farms, rural officials also practiced it against specific peasant households and individual kolkhozniks. It is evident that bribery, traditionally characteristic of Russian lower officialdom, remained so in the 1930s. Some forms were strongly rooted in tradition, for example, offerings of vodka and farm produce to visiting officials ("You only had to slaughter a calf or a pig, and [the rural soviet chairman] would immediately come and take without payment four or five kilos of meat"). Others, such as confiscation of peasant property, had their immediate antecedents in the practices of dekulakization at the beginning of the 1930s, but had been adapted to be of more direct benefit to the confiscating official (as in the case of the rural soviet chairman who took twenty-two horses from peasants who failed to meet state procurement obligations, and was later seen riding round the district on one of them).[22]

Internal passports and permissions to leave on otkhod were sold (that is, issued after receipt of a bribe) on an almost routine basis, as were attestations of social origin from the rural soviet ("X is from a bedniak family with no black marks on his record," "Y [really the daughter of a priest] comes from a hardworking family of seredniaks"). In one police report from the Western oblast in 1934, we read that a kulak, Petr Shcherbakov, bribed the local rural soviet chairman, Ignatov, with a sewing machine in order to get the documents allowing him to depart to work in the Ukraine, and Ignatov obligingly categorized him as a seredniak by social position.[23]

Discipline and Punishment

The range of punishments available to officials in dealing with recalcitrant individual peasants was as follows: beatings, fines, arrest, confiscation of livestock or other property, expropriation, and expulsion from the kolkhoz. In cases of collective disobedience, officials might liquidate the whole kolkhoz, which in effect meant collective expropriation, sometimes involving the forcible incorporation of the former kolkhoz into a state farm and the overnight transformation of the kolkhozniks into landless agricultural laborers. Most of these methods were either of dubious legality or unquestionably illegal.[24]

Arrests and fines were the most commonly used and overused; hence the regular stream of instructions from Moscow reiterating that the right to arrest was limited to police and NKVD (although in practice all officials used it against peasants); and forbidding officials to practice "arbitrary and illegal levying of fines" on the population; and the 1935 abrogation, similar to that applied to rural officials (see p. 178), of many sentences imposed on kolkhozniks in the early 1930s.[25] In a secret instruction of May 1933, Stalin and Molotov noted:

> It is evident that many disorderly arrests in the countryside still continue to exist in the practice of our officials. Chairmen of collective farms and member of kolkhoz boards make arrests. Chairmen of rural soviets and secretaries of [party] cells make arrests. Raion and krai agents make arrests. Everybody and his brother makes arrests, although, to tell the truth, they have no right to do so. . . . [26]

Moscow also warned repeatedly against expulsions from the kolkhoz (since they had the effect of turning collectivized peasants back into independents), and had a still more negative attitude to the liquidation of collective farms or their forced incorporation into state farms. But it is likely that officials quite often used the threat to liquidate a delinquent kolkhoz for disciplinary purposes.[27]

Men, Women, and Office

Rural officials at the raion and rural soviet level were usually male, poorly educated, and of peasant background. They often came to administrative work after serving in the Red Army or finishing their two-year term of military service. Officials at the raion level were usually Communists, while those at the rural soviet level usually were not. Either way, their records generally had some black marks. The party members were likely to have received party reprimands and suspensions and even prison terms for offenses ranging from "sabotage of procurements" to misappropriation of funds, while the non-party people were even more likely to have served time in prison and had often joined and been expelled from the party at some earlier point.

Take, for example, a group of officials in Krasnogorsk raion in the Western oblast in 1937, consisting of the raikom secretary, the chairman of the raion soviet, three heads of departments in the raion, and one rural soviet chairman. All but one were born between 1899 and 1901, of Russian parents, in villages that were either in the Western oblast or close to its borders. They were from reasonably prosperous peasant families (one, the head of the raion land department, was the son of a former "fixed-quota" peasant) and had three or four years schooling in the village. The rural soviet chairman had been prosecuted three times in the past decade for job-related offences and hooliganism and served two short prison terms. One of the raion officials had also come close to serving a prison term for failure to meet grain procurements quotas. The exception in the group was its senior man, the raikom secretary, who was Jewish and came from a town in the oblast. He was a graduate of higher party school (that is, he had something approaching a secondary education). Presumably he had been drafted for work in the countryside in the early 1930s and remained there.[28]

The poor representation of women among rural officials at any level was not the fault of the regime, which gave strong and consistent support for the promotion of women to positions of authority in the countryside. Stalin made many overtures to peasant women, starting with his statement in 1933 that women were "a great force" in the kolkhoz and should be encouraged to take positions of responsibility and continuing with his intervention on the question of maternity leave for kolkhoz women at the Second Congress of Outstanding Kolkhozniks in 1935 (where, as an unmistakeable statement of political intent rather than as a reflection of the real world, almost a third of the delegates were women). Stalin also emphasized again and again the importance of liberating peasant women from the oppression of the patriarchal family, and made many public appearances with Stakhanovites such as the champion beet grower, Maria Demchenko, and the tractorist, Pasha Angelina.[29]

President Mikhail Kalinin, the member of the party leadership most closely associated with peasant questions, was tireless in his advocacy of the promotion of peasant women.[30]

Indeed, one could almost say that the regime was biased against men and in favor of women in its dealings with the village in the 1930s, for the negative stereotypes such as that of the kulak were all male, while the positive stereotypes such as that of the peasant Stakhanovite tended to be female. This made sense in terms of the locus of power in the village: Men were powerful, therefore more of a threat; women were powerless, therefore nonthreatening and possibly even, as an exploited group, cooptable. But there were also practical considerations. A 1935 resolution of the Central Committee noted that, as women constituted a majority of the kolkhoz labor force in much of the non-Black Earth belt, it was necessary to follow an aggressive policy of promoting women into positions of authority in these regions.[31]

Yet it was notoriously difficult for women to hold positions of authority in the countryside. The main reason was that peasants, men and women alike, disapproved of it, and local officials generally shared their feelings. Whenever a woman served as chairman of a kolkhoz or rural soviet, malicious gossip and rumors were likely to fly, focusing often on her sex life or the favors she was allegedly dispensing to her male relatives.[32] Moreover, the representation of women in rural salaried office does not seem to have increased in the course of the decade, as might have been expected given the high level of government encouragement, but instead tended to decline—another reflection of the withdrawal of the central government's presence from the countryside. In 1934, Maria Shaburova, a prominent national figure in women's affairs who later became People's Commissar for Social Security, expressed frustration and disappointment about the downward trend in promotion of women in the countryside. Many women had been appointed to such positions in the early 1930s, she said, but now those gains were being wiped out. In the Western oblast, for example, the number of women chairmen of rural soviets had dropped from 206 to 58. In Georgia and Armenia, there had been fifty women holding this office in 1931, but now all but four had been removed. In 1936, only 7 percent of rural soviet chairmen and less than 3 percent of kolkhoz chairmen were women.[33]

A similar point was made in 1937 by a group of women in Ostrov raion, Pskov oblast, who wrote to the local newspaper to complain that there was not a single woman chairman of a rural soviet in the raion, and only two women kolkhoz chairmen. True, there were some women on the raion soviet executive committee, but they were just there for decoration, excluded from all the real work and "invited only for the sake of appearances to plenary meetings." They blamed the former raion leaders (victims of the Great Purges, who had just been put on show trial as "enemies of the people") for having "tried in every possible way to remove women from leading work, to keep them hidden in obscurity," called for energetic promotion of women to positions of authority from now on, and even suggested some candidates by name.[34]

Many of the women who held office in the early 1930s were poor widows who had often at some point worked as batraks for kulaks in the 1920s. Agrippina Gorodnicheva, for example, lived in a village in Moscow oblast with her husband until he died in the early 1920s. Unable to cope with the farm alone, she went off to Moscow and worked as a domestic servant for seven years. When collectivization began, nearly 50, she returned to her village and became an active supporter of the kolkhoz. As of 1933, she was chairman of the kolkhoz auditing commission and deputy chairman of the rural soviet. "Aunt Varia," a central figure in a Soviet journalist's account of collectivization in Spas na Peskakh, a small village in the non-Black Earth region, was a First World War widow who was active in the local Committee of the Poor during the Civil War and became the first chairman of the kolkhoz at the beginning of the 1930s. By the middle of the decade, however, village men had taken over the kolkhoz leadership and Aunt Varia retired to the sidelines.[35]

Leadership Style

Within the raion, and from the viewpoint of the local peasants, the raion leaders were towering figures. It is not surprising that some developed an inflated sense of their own importance and even encouraged a local "cult of personality." In this, they were Stalin's true disciples, no doubt, but they were also lineal descendants of those inept, ignorant, and self-aggrandizing Russian provincial officials satirized in Saltykov-Shchedrin's nineteenth-century chronicles of the town of Glupov, *A History of One Town*. Raion leaders of this kind required marked deference and flattery (*podkhalimstvo*) from their subordinates:

> The raikom secretary, Povarov, and the raion soviet chairman, Gorshkov, were unchangingly dignified as "Vasilich" and "Efimich". "Hurrah for Efimych!"—more than one meeting led by Gorshkov was conducted under that banner. . . .

They were also liable to outbursts of temper to intimidate subordinates:

> The chairman of one of the rural soviets related: "At the meeting of rural soviet chairmen, when Gorshkov lost his temper, he struck the table with his hand so hard that the telephone receiver flew to the floor. We took over that example and carried it into the rural soviets. . . . It was bad to be in [conflict] with Gorshkov: if you criticized him, he would pluck you like a chicken: you would get seed later than the other rural soviets [and other penalties]. . . ."[36]

Macho bullying was not an administrative style to apologize for in the 1930s. Decisiveness and a firm hand were highly valued. The Civil War "command" model was generally considered exemplary by Communist cadres themselves, and in many circumstances cadres in the countryside carried guns. Theirs was a harsh, frontier world where bandits—often dekulakized peasants hiding in the forest—were likely to take potshots at officials while sullen peasants looked the other way. Officials could often exercise frontier justice, throwing recalcitrant peasants into prison without formalities. But they themselves were also liable to severe punishment from their superiors, including terms in prison or labor camp, if they failed to meet sowing or procurements quotas.

In an official's contacts with his superiors, one of the most important things he had to demonstrate was that he was tough and knew how to give orders and get them obeyed:

> On 2nd August Sokolov, chairman of the rural soviet, and Kubyshkin, the raion soviet chairman, came out to the kolkhoz settlement. Chairman Patrikeev wanted to show that he knows how to discipline [his people]—and at that moment he ran into a kolkhoznitsa, Olga Kostina, on the street and began to curse her out roundly, [saying] why don't you go to work. But Kostina has two little children, one of them breast-feeding and the second two years old.[37]

Given the pressures on these officials, it is not surprising that we encounter instances where the macho, bullying style went over into almost demented hysteria. Take the case of Belousov, a raikom secretary in the Western oblast whose behavior produced so many complaints that the oblast sent an instructor to investigate. He reported as follows:

> Belousov is extraordinarily rude, especially with the chairmen of rural soviets; he curses them out like a completely crazed man, especially in the mornings (his head aches after drinking), shouts, curses and angrily pulls at the telephone and smashes it to smithereens—every week the electricians have to repair it. The population has formed the opinion that he is a psychopath and approaches him very warily, preferring to go away empty-handed than listen to his cursing. It is sufficient to cite one other fact. Last year during sowing at the Budennyi kolkhoz . . . he was drunk, threw himself on the chairman of that kolkhoz, took aim at him with his revolver, and shouted: "I will shoot you mother-. . . (*sic*) and so on." The kolkhoz chairman fell ill after that incident.

Belousov's immediate superior, receiving this report, admitted that Belousov tended to be rude, but pleaded extenuating circumstances. It was not drinking that made Belousov act that way, he explained; it was "psycho-neurasthenia," for which Belousov had received special medical treatment two years earlier.[38]

Peasants wrote endless letters of complaint against officials who bullied, insulted, and threatened them, or were habitually drunk. When they had the opportunity, as they did in the 1937 show trials, to make such charges in public, they did so at length and with pathos.[39] Yet there is a formal quality to these complaints about abusive and bullying behavior; only rarely does one sense the genuine outrage that often seems to be associated with stories of theft or arbitrary confiscation of property by officials. When officials got drunk, swore, and knocked peasants around, these were appropriate things for peasants to complain about to higher authorities—especially if they had other grievances against those officials in question. All the same, there was some sense that bullying was the officials' métier, just as complaining was the peasants'.

In terms of the conventions governing the interactions of Russian peasants and officials, it was possible—perhaps even expected or required—for an episode of outrageous bullying of peasants by officials to be followed immediately by revelry in which both officials and peasants joined. Naturally this was not something that either officials or peasants were likely to report to higher authorities, so accounts of such behavior are hard to come by. We can catch an echo in the bewildered report in a provincial newspaper of the strange conduct of a procurements brigade, which punctuated its fierce and threatening interrogation of delinquent peasants with outbursts of "wild dancing" to the music of the accordion.[40]

What must have been going on becomes clearer when we read the memoirs of Arvo Tuominen, a Finnish Communist who in 1934 accompanied a procurements brigade charged with collecting an extra 8,000 tons of grain from a raion in Tula oblast. At each kolkhoz, the five brigade members, all "with Mausers dangling from their belts," would call a general meeting and browbeat the kolkhozniks until they voted their acceptance of the additional quota. One kolkhoz was particularly recalcitrant, and the brigade finally arrested the chairman and other ringleaders, dumping them in the truck and telling them they would be charged with "grain speculation." The kolkhozniks still refused to vote for the extra quota.

> Finally, after midnight, an old man said, "This won't get any better. They'll just come again tomorrow and the day after, until no one is left."
>
> Maslov [leader of the procurements brigade] immediately ordered another show of hands, and this time he got a slight majority, just enough to suffice. While the minutes of the meeting were being recorded [by candlelight], the bitter lament of the old man was etched in my memory: "You could at least have brought along enough kerosene so that we could see to sign this robbery resolution!"
>
> . . . Then followed the most astonishing scene of all. When the robbery resolution had been signed, the leader of the theft asked whether anyone had an accordion so that there could be dancing. And behold! An accordion was produced, the unarrested kolkhozniks formed a circle, one began to play the accordion, others clapped their hands in rhythm, and in the center of the circle some kolkhozniks and the politruk and the GPU men danced the hopak. . . ."[41]

Kolkhoz Chairmen

The kolkhoz chairman was the person crucial to the success of the kolkhoz. He was the one who had to direct the work, manage the community, and mediate between the kolkhozniks and the raion. Yet for all its importance, the office of kolkhoz chairman was not even mentioned in the first Kolkhoz Charter, hastily issued in March 1930. That Charter spoke only of a governing board (*upravlenie*) elected by the assembly of kolkhoz members. This may have expressed an ideological quirk of the Stalinist leadership, namely the belief that Stalin and Molotov evidently held in the late 1920s that collective farms should not depend too much on the charismatic leadership of one energetic central figure, the kolkhoz chairman. On the other hand, it may simply have reflected uneasiness about the fact that urban outsiders—reminiscent in their administrative approach, some said, of the old bailiffs under serfdom—were currently organizing and directing many collective farms. By 1935, in any case, the new version of the Kolkhoz Charter explicitly recognized that the kolkhoz board was led by a chairman elected at the general meeting of kolkhozniks.[42]

The kolkhoz chairman occupied an intermediate position between kolkhozniks and the rural power structure. On the one hand, he (or, much less frequently, she) could boss the peasants and exploit them economically in much the same way as his superiors could. On the other hand, his position was different from that of his superiors at the raion level in that they were salaried officials and he was paid by lafrom labordays, that is, treated like a kolkhoznik (albeit a well-remunerated one). There were also differences depending on whether the chairman was an outsider or insider. When he was an outsider to the village or locality, someone "sent in from the raion," his position was closer to that of the salaried rural soviet chairman. When he was a local, a member of the village community, his position was closer to that of the other peasants, and his status and functions more closely resembled those of the old village starosta.

In statements by peasants, we can find evidence for both views of the kolkhoz chairmen—one of "them" and one of "us." At a 1937 show trial, for example, peasant witnesses harshly criticized a kolkhoz chairman, along with the local MTS director, for forcing the kolkhoz to adopt a bad crop rotation. Obviously this chairman was being cast as one of "them." But another kolkhoz chairman (one of the relatively few women in this position) cast herself as one of "us" in her testimony at the trial, speaking angrily about the impossible sowing plans "they" had sent down from the raion.[43]

Outsiders and Locals

In the first years of collectivization, kolkhoz chairmen were often outsiders—worker 25,000-ers, Communists sent out from the city—rather than members of the village community. This was especially true in the major grain-growing regions: In the North Caucasus in 1930, for example, two-fifths of kolkhoz chairmen were 25,000-ers. But by the mid-1930s, urban outsiders were becoming a rarity, and the great majority of kolkhoz chairmen were local peasants.[44] While there was no direct precedent in village experience for the "outsider" chairmen, "local" kolkhoz chairmen belonged to a long historical line of appointed or elected village leaders—serf managers and overseers, volost and communal elders—whose jobs were not only managerial and disciplinary but also required them to act as brokers between the village and outside authorities.

To be sure, there was still a degree of local variation. At a conference of kolkhoz chairmen early in 1935, one speaker reported that more than 90 percent of chairmen in Kursk raion in the Central Agricultural region were locals, while another regretted that in Kiev raion, which was still painfully recovering from the devastating effects of the famine, there were as yet "practically no locals among the kolkhoz chairmen." Three years later, a survey of Melitopol raion in the southern Ukraine showed that 76 percent of incumbent kolkhoz chairmen came from within the particular village, and another 7 percent came from other villages in the area.[45]

We get an unusual glimpse of the "outsider" chairman in the transitional period from an unpublicized informal meeting of kolkhoz chairmen held in the People's Commissariat of Agriculture in April 1935. Of the twenty or more participants from the collective farms, drawn from different areas of the country, almost all were "outsider" chairmen—dedicated and committed Communist cadres who had spent the past five years as professional trouble-shooters, moving from one collapsing kolkhoz to another and experiencing all the hardships of life in the countryside during collectivization and famine.

The chairman of the "Kirov" kolkhoz in Vinnitsa oblast in the Ukraine, Frantsuzov, had a background that was typical for the group:

> I have worked for two years in this kolkhoz. I myself am a worker; I was working in industry and came to [a job in] Antonievskii raion only in 1930. From there I was sent in 1931 to a kolkhoz of that same raion, a kolkhoz that was lagging behind. I worked there for eight months while the kolkhoz got on its feet. . . . After that, they sent me off again to a raion job, but in 1933 I went to the "Big Tuzy" kolkhoz, where the whole board had been fired for sabotaging kolkhoz work. . . ."[46]

Other speakers gave a similar description of the job of "outsider" chairman as that of an itinerant trouble-shooter. It was only for the past two years, one speaker said, that outsider chairmen had been staying put for any length of time in the one kolkhoz: "Before that, if you didn't make the rounds of five collective farms as chairman, what kind of chairman were you—you had to be a real softy (*miakish' kakoi-to*)."[47]

Several speakers distinguished themselves explicitly from the home-grown insider chairmen, whom they referred to as "locals" (*mestnye*). Although outsiders themselves, the speakers had no objections on principle to local chairmen. In some respects, they thought that there were advantages for a chairman in being local, notably the fact that the local chairman would have his own livestock and private plot and would therefore be able to feed himself. One speaker, who had gone through the famine year in Kiev oblast as an "outsider" chairman, made this point poignantly:

> The conditions for a chairman, in particular one who is coming into the raion from outside, who is not at home there, are very difficult. Take 1933, when I came to the kolkhoz—for a whole year I literally went hungry. . . . There was no grain, nothing was given to me in advance. Now things are fine—I received [grain] for [my] work in the kolkhoz, I have some grain, if they transfer me to

another kolkhoz I have a reserve. But think of the situation when a chairman is sent to the locality from Moscow and has to wait for the new harvest. . . .[48]

Those who had been in the field took it for granted that an outsider chairman coming into a new job would have to commandeer some livestock from the kolkhozniks in order to survive economically. Although this was generally not an issue to be raised in polite society, even off the record, the Kiev chairman was provoked into doing so by the naive questions of a bureaucrat from the Commissariat, who seemed to think that cows grew on trees, or at least were miraculously produced by resolutions written in Moscow.

QUESTION: Do you have a cow?

ANSWER: No I don't have my own cow, [though] I commandeered one sucking pig.

QUESTION: Why don't you have a cow?

ANSWER: You probably don't have one either.

QUESTION: You are a kolkhoz chairman.

ANSWER: I didn't take a heifer, for that you need to have at least 1,000–1,500 rubles. When I came to the kolkhoz, there was one cow and one ox, so even if I had wanted to take one, I couldn't have. . . .

QUESTION: So you don't mean to stay long. . . .[49]

Outsider chairmen rarely stayed long in the job. But then, neither did local chairmen. The extraordinarily high turnover of kolkhoz chairmen was deplored again and again by central authorities, but without result. As of January 1936, 37 percent of all Soviet kolkhoz chairmen and their deputies had been in that particular job for less than a year, and only 18 percent had held the office for three years or more. And that was a comparatively peaceful period for the countryside: Turnover was even greater in the tumultuous years of the early 1930s or the Great Purges of 1937–38.[50]

There were a great many reasons for turnover of kolkhoz chairmen. One was their vulnerability to scapegoating if the kolkhoz failed to meet its procurements quotas. In one fourteen-month period in the middle of the 1930s, 73 percent of all kolkhoz chairmen in Kirov (Viatka) province were fired from their jobs and in addition faced criminal charges for "economic sabotage" (two-thirds of them were convicted). A Communist chairman from Belyi raion in the Western oblast, threatened with charges for squandering 4,000 rubles, noted bitterly that he was the seventh chairman of his kolkhoz, and it looked as if he was going to be the seventh who ended up in jail—as if "all the kolkhoz chairmen were knaves and thieves, and I among them." In other cases, however, firing was less of a major event than might appear: "I have been working here in Belyi since 1932," said the head of the local MTS on the same occasion, "and each year they remove me from my job, and each year they reinstate me."[51]

According to Ia. A. Iakovlev, the party's senior agricultural official, this was one of the ways that raion leaders tried to get themselves off the hook:

For any raion leader, removing kolkhoz chairman from their job is equivalent to showing one's mettle as a good manager. If you ask such a "manager" why the sowing or the harvest or grain procurements are in a mess, he always has a ready answer proving that he has been energetic and active: "We did our bit, we removed such and such a number of chairmen."[52]

As the "kolkhoz democracy" movement gained momentum around the middle of the decade, moreover, kolkhoz chairmen—now locals in most cases—were increasingly likely to be forced out of office by their fellow kolkhozniks. They were also vulnerable to denunciation, a technique that was widely and successfully used by peasants wishing to get rid of an unpopular chairman.

If we look carefully at the report written by a party investigator after one such denunciation, we can see another reason for high turnover, namely the difficulty of finding suitable candidates for the chairman's job. The object of the denunciation, Vasilkov, was a former Communist and raion official who had been expelled from the party and fired from his raion job after a scandal (he had probably been caught stealing). No doubt his friends in the raion thought that he had better sit out the storm in his native village, and appointed him kolkhoz chairman there. But it was not an ideal choice: Vasilkov owed child support payments to his first wife, who was still living in the village, and his father, who also lived there, caused him embarrassment by refusing to join the kolkhoz. There were two Communists in the village who should have been alternative candidates for leadership, but neither came up to scratch, one being literate but of poor social background, the other of good bedniak origins but "feeble and without initiative." As for the three kolkhoz brigade leaders who had led the anti-Vasilkov drive, they did not inspire confidence either: The first had been convicted of buying stolen goods, the second had recently been convicted of assault, and the third was always drunk. The kolkhozniks had just picked a new chairman, the investigator reported, and he was satisfactory in all respects except that, instead of being a working kolkhoznik, he was a wage earner at a local factory.[53]

As has already been noted, women rarely held the job of kolkhoz chairman in the second half of the 1930s. There were some impressive and articulate women chairmen at the Second Congress of Outstanding Kolkhozniks in 1935: for example, Maremiana Kariutina, a self-confident, tough-minded fifty-six-year-old delegate who had been chairman of a kolkhoz in Leningrad oblast since 1929; and Aleksandra Levchenkova, a young woman with cropped hair and decided opinions, who was a kolkhoz chairman in Voronezh oblast. (In both cases, the workforce of the kolkhoz was largely female because the men had all gone off on otkhod or had become urban workers.) But these women were exceptional: Female kolkhoz chairmen were even more unusual than female chairmen of rural soviets. There were 7,000 of them nationwide at the beginning of 1935, and that may have been the highest figure of the decade.[54]

A more typical representative of the group than Kariutina and Levchenkova was probably Appolonova, a kolkhoz chairman in the Western oblast whose troubles were the subject of an investigation by an oblast inspector in 1936. Appolonova's main problem was that she was being undermined by a young kolkhoznik who had recently returned to the village after graduating from a Soviet party school and obviously thought himself better fitted for the job. The investigator found that Appolonova was doing her best as chairman, and was not (as her opponent charged) unduly favoring her brother and his family, but suffered from having very little education: "An energetic woman, . . . a widow with four children, she fights strongly for the cause, but the kolkhoz is going to pieces."[55]

The relatively few women who held positions of authority in the kolkhoz were usually lower down the ladder than chairman (heads of livestock farms, leaders of livestock brigades, or link leaders). Aunt Varia, the early kolkhoz chairman at Spas na Peskakh who was sidelined by the mid-1930s, ended up as a humble link leader, and it is not unlikely that a similar fate awaited Appolonova.[56]

Chairman's Pay and Perks

According to the rules, a kolkhoz chairman was a member of a kolkhoz who should be paid, like other kolkhozniks, on the basis of labordays—that is, a share of the kolkhoz earnings that was proportional to the number of labordays accumulated. It went against the principle of cooperative endeavor for a kolkhoz to pay salaries to any of its members; indeed, the kolkhoz was not allowed to pay salaries or wages to anyone (although exceptions could be made for agronomists and other technical specialists hired by the kolkhoz).[57]

While kolkhoz chairmen were supposed to be paid on the laborday principle, this did not mean that they were to be paid the same as an ordinary kolkhoznik. Labordays represented not just time worked but also the value of the work performed. A chairman's work was supposed to be assessed at the rate of 2 labordays per day worked in large collective farms and 1.75 labordays per day worked in smaller ones. But the best part of this was that every day of the year counted as a working day for the kolkhoz chairman. An ordinary kolkhoznik was lucky if he averaged a third of the chairman's 50–60 labordays a month.[58]

The rules about membership and payment in labordays were difficult to apply to "outsider" chairmen. The earliest of the outsiders, the 25,000-ers, were specifically exempt from the requirement that all kolkhoz chairmen must be kolkhoz members; and they were paid salaries in cash, rather than being wholly dependent on labordays. Later "outsider" chairmen were not formally given these special conditions, but they often managed to approximate them in practice. The outsider chairman was essentially "a hired worker in the kolkhoz," in the words of one such chairman, who "established a monthly salary and a bread ration for himself" immediately on his appointment and declined to go through the formality of applying for membership. ("When kolkhozniks suggested that he ought to join the kolkhoz, Ivanov answered indifferently, 'I'm with you temporarily, there is no point in joining.'")[59]

Most outsider chairmen joined the kolkhoz, even though it was a pure formality. But most of them were also paid salaries, or at least a monthly cash stipend in addition to their laborday earnings in kind and cash. The exact situation varied from region to region in the mid-1930s, but the common feature was that the local obkom or kraikom decided the rules, and the kolkhoz provided the cash. Local chairmen, it appears, were usually paid in labordays, like other kolkhozniks.[60]

At the 1935 meeting of kolkhoz chairmen, Mikhail Chernov, Iakovlev's successor as People's Commissar for Agriculture, expressed himself strongly in support of the laborday principle of payment, using the argument that the kolkhoz chairman should feel that his economic fortunes were inseparable from those of the kolkhoz. He rejected the notion of a guaranteed minimum for chairmen, such as tractorists already received. He did bow to reality, however, by conceding that kolkhoz chairmen might be paid a stipend of 50 to 150 rubles a month in addition to their regular laborday payments.[61]

While the number of outsider chairmen declined over the next few years, the number of local chairmen who managed to get themselves put on salary evidently increased. From the standpoint of local kolkhoz chairmen—not to mention other kolkhoz officeholders such as accountants and brigade leaders—it was much better to be on salary (albeit paid out of kolkhoz funds) than to receive payment in labordays, because the regular salary protected one against disaster in case of a bad harvest. There was also the status question, since to be paid in labordays indicated membership of the kolkhoznik "estate," whereas to be paid a salary meant that one belonged to the higher "estate" of cadres.

The suggestion that kolkhoz officeholders should be salaried surfaced several times in the press in 1936–37. Advocates of the salary argued, in the first place, that kolkhoz chairmen ought to be treated like other managers (receiving salary, days off, annual paid vacation, and so on), and, in the second place, that the salary or something like it was already common practice, regardless of the law.[62]

In the fall of 1937, several oblast administrations passed resolutions on their own authorizing regular cash payments to kolkhoz chairmen of up to 250 rubles a month, in addition to their laborday earnings. This provoked an angry response from Moscow. Early in 1938, the party Central Committee "and comrade Stalin personally" intervened to point out to one of the erring oblasts that they were following a "politically incorrect line" and forced it to repudiate its earlier decision.[63]

Confusion reigned for the next few years. In Kalinin oblast, one of those that had been slapped down by Stalin for authorizing cash payments to kolkhoz chairmen, land department officials refused to approve anything but a straight laborday payment. In Sverdlovsk oblast, on the other hand, officials believed the government had recently *authorized* cash payments to chairmen in some secret resolution. When they asked *Krest'ianskaia gazeta* for confirmation, the newspaper could only reply that "as far as we know" no such resolution existed.[64]

The issue was resolved only in 1940–41, and then a roundabout way, by a series of government decrees relating to different regions of the country that authorized monthly cash payments to kolkhoz chairmen. The payments, ranging from 25 to 400 rubles a month depending on the kolkhoz's money income, were a supplement to the chairman's laborday earnings in kind. Although there was still some room for ambiguity (what if kolkhoz income fluctuated wildly from year to year?) this seems to have been the basis for the postwar pattern whereby kolkhoz chairmen received a salary as well as laborday payments.[65]

Regardless of whether the kolkhoz chairman received a regular cash supplement, he certainly had privileged access to the kolkhoz's money income. As noted earlier, ordinary kolkhozniks in many regions of the country received very little payment in money for their labor in the 1930s; almost all of what they were paid was in kind. Nevertheless, the kolkhoz did have a money income from its sale of agricultural produce to the state as well as market sales. Much of this went into a kolkhoz savings account (*nedelimyi fond*) that was supposed to be used for building, puchases of agricultural equipment, and other similar collective needs. According to the Kolkhoz Charter, up to 2 percent of it could be spent on "administrative-economic expenses" (primarily personnel expenses: paying agronomists and surveyors for their services, hiring craftsmen or extra hands for the harvest, and so on). Ingenious chairmen often found ways of turning both the kolkhoz savings account and the 2 percent allocated for administrative needs to their own personal advantage.

It was the "2 percent" (often, in practice, more than 2 percent) that was widely used to pay money supplements to the chairman, and sometimes to other kolkhoz officers as well. The savings account seems to have been tapped by chairmen most commonly for the purpose of building themselves a new house. The writer Mikhail Alekseev described how this practice worked in his native village in the Saratov region, where so many kolkhoz chairmen had built new houses that a section of the village had become known as *Predsedatelevka* ("Chairmen's Row"). As the peasant narrator in Alekseev's story recounts:

> They change them, the chairman that is, every two or three years, sometimes every year. Of course, that's not long to put kolkhoz affairs in order, but it's quite long enough to gear up your own household economy—steal yourself a prettier little house than ours, breed some ducks or geese, plant an orchard, get a Simmenthal cow, a sheep, a pair of hogs. . . . They may remove him from his position, but what does he care, the chairman that is—he has improved his family's economic position, and on top of that has an excuse not to do fieldwork in the future (arguing that "the former chairman's title does not allow it").[66]

Permanent freedom from field work was another important perk of the chairman's office. According to the official regulations, chairmen currently in office might be released from field work, unless the kolkhoz was very small,[67] but there was no official suggestion that former chairman shared this privilege. There was a long-standing village tradition in Russia of releasing senior members of the community from field work, however, and many former chairmen clearly invoked it. In addition, the privilege of release from field work was often extended to the chairman's family, as well as to kolkhoz officers such as accountants and brigade leaders and their family members. According to one peasant complainant from East Siberia, the presence of this "mass of non-working people such as chairmen, accountants, brigade leaders and so on" was one of the worst things about the kolkhoz, compared to the precollectivization village. Field-working kolkhozniks were particularly inclined to complain when the privilege was extended to the wives and daughters of kolkhoz and rural soviet chairmen and other officeholders.[68]

The kolkhoz chairmen who acted like "little tsars of the kolkhoz" called themselves "the boss" (*khoziain*) and treated the kolkhoz as as their private patrimonial estate (*votchina*). They disposed of kolkhoz property as if it were their own and were frequent targets of complaint from other peasants. Among the offences frequently cited were selling kolkhoz produce and property on the market and keeping the proceeds to themselves, expanding their private plots, monopolizing the use of kolkhoz horses and trucks, and favoring their relatives by releasing them from fieldwork, sending them off to training courses in the raion, and so on.[69]

It caused great offence when chairmen underlined their difference in status from ordinary kolkhozniks. Peasants in a Krasnodar kolkhoz deeply resented it when an unpopular kolkhoz chairman, "driving around in the [kolkhoz] truck, overtook kolkhozniks who were walking but did not order the driver to stop and forbade him to take them in the car. . . ."[70] When the chairman and other board members of the "Politotdel" kolkhoz in the Western oblast, along with their wives, celebrated Revolution Day apart from other kolkhozniks and in more luxurious style, a bitter drunken fight broke out between the two groups.[71] In a Stalingrad kolkhoz, peasants found the behavior of one chairman—an outsider to the village, "sent by the raikom"—absolutely intolerable, not just because he stole from the kolkhoz but also because he "refuses to talk to kolkhozniks" and "clearly despises them."[72]

A Tambov kolkhoznik writing to *Krest'ianskaia gazeta* complained about the behavior of the kolkhoz chairman as follows:

> There are a lot of outrageous things that make the kolkhozniks feel indignant and say we are not masters, we are batraks. Our business, they say, is just to work; the kolkhoz chairman, comrade Avidov, is the only one who has control over kolkhoz assets.

The kolkhozniks had lost all interest in working because of Avidov's attitude, the writer claimed. Avidov's favorite saying was "I am the master (*Ia-khoziain*)." But this was wrong, in the writer's opinion: "The Kolkhoz Charter says that the kolkhozniks are the masters."[73]

"Kolkhoz Democracy"

Peasants did not necessarily covet the position of kolkhoz chairman. They might view it, as they had viewed the old mir offices, as more of a burden than a privilege.[74] In addition, many hoped in the early years that the kolkhoz would prove to be an ephemeral phenomenon. As the years passed, however, the solid peasants of the village became more involved with the kolkhoz and more interested in leading it. The possibilities for individual and family economic gain through incumbency (much greater than in the mir) became more obvious. Peasants began to covet their neighbor's offices in the kolkhoz, and wrote many self-interested denunciations of incumbent officeholders to prove it.

Still, there is no doubt that there were disadvantages to being a kolkhoz chairman. The chairman ran a much higher risk than rank-and-file kolkhozniks of facing criminal charges for "sabotaging procurements" and receiving a substantial prison term. Even in the latter half of the 1930s, when the risk was less and the economic opportunities greater, negative notes can still be picked up occasionally: sometimes a kind of stubborn refusal to cooperate ("You Communists wanted this kolkhoz; you run it and make it work"); sometimes a sense that the task of being chairman and meeting the state's unreasonable demands was just too formidable. Send us "a firm and stalwart party man," pleaded kolkhozniks in Belyi raion, overwhelmed by the kolkhoz's economic problems, in a petition to the Western oblast land department in the summer of 1937.[75]

One of the kolkhoz chairman's main functions was to act as broker between the village and the raion authorities. To play that role successfully, he needed acceptance on both sides: If the village "elected" him, he needed raion approval; if the raion "appointed" him, he need the approval of the village. This was not fundamentally different from the situation on Prince Gagarin's Manuilovo estate a century earlier, where the serf manager (*burmistr*) was "elected by and from the local peasants and approved by Gagarin."[76]

The first version of the Kolkhoz Charter (1930) provided for election of the kolkhoz board (not the kolkhoz chairman, since that office was not mentioned in the first Charter) by a general assembly of kolkhoz members. A reminder of the importance of observing "the elective principle" (*vybornost'*) in selection of kolkhoz boards was contained in a government directive of June 25, 1932 "On revolutionary legality."[77]

The revised Kolkhoz Charter of 1935 mentioned the office of chairman for the first time, stipulating that, like the board members, the chairman should be elected by the general assembly of kolkhozniks. Did this mean that the practice of de facto appointment of kolkhoz chairmen should cease? Ia. A. Iakovlev, addressing the Second Congress of Outstanding Kolkhozniks (a large proportion of whose members were kolkhoz chairmen who undoubtedly owed their position to de facto appointment rather than real election), did not go so far. The collective farms had reached the stage where they needed "permanent leading cadres," chairmen who "genuinely know their fields," rather than visiting firemen, Iakovlev said. Moreover, it was important that the chairman establish the habit of holding genuine kolkhoz meetings, attended not just by a handful of activists but by the majority of kolkhozniks. Iakovlev was clearly recommending a larger dose of democracy in the practice of kolkhoz leadership. But he was not suggesting that the raion authorities should abdicate responsibility for selecting chairmen, or that kolkhozniks should be encouraged to challenge the raion's choices.[78]

"Kolkhoz democracy," meaning greater input from kolkhozniks in the business of selecting and dismissing chairmen, emerged as an issue (although as yet unnamed) in 1935 and gained strength for several years thereafter. This emergence of the issue undoubtedly reflected the existence of conflicts at the local level. But it is notable that some Soviet newspapers picked up this story early and followed it assiduously, leading one to suspect that there may have been some backstage politics involved as well.[79] With the advent of the Great Purges in 1937, the cause of "kolkhoz democracy"—always implicitly critical of interfering officials, especially those at the raion level— profited from the regime's general endorsement of agin-the-bosses populism at this time.

Frequent and widespread reports of conflicts over the selection and dismissal of kolkhoz chairmen are to be found in the press of 1936, as well as in the Smolensk Archive files of that year. The press reportings of such conflicts were increasingly likely to favor the kolkhozniks ("prevented from exercising their democratic rights") over the raion authorities ("violating the Kolkhoz Charter" by appointing and firing kolkhoz chairmen without consulting the kolkhozniks). One report said kolkhozniks had "elected their own kolkhoznik as chairman of the kolkhoz" but the raion refused to accept their choice. It insisted on "forcibly imposing an outsider whom the kolkhozniks do not want" as chairman, provoking the kolkhozniks to stop going out to work in the fields. The report blamed this on the raion's intransigeance, not the peasants'. In another case, raion officials who had forced a kolkhoz to accept two unpopular chairmen in a row without any pretense of consultation were severely reprimanded by a government investigative commission.[80]

Party instructors investigating similar conflicts over selection and removal of chairmen in the Western oblast appeared to have an open mind as to whether the fault lay with the raion or with the kolkhozniks, according to materials in the Smolensk Archive. The investigators were critical of raion authorities if they had ignored peasants' complaints about unpopular chairmen, failed to consult kolkhozniks in advance about candidates for kolkhoz office, or imposed a candidate who turned out to be incompetent or corrupt, implicitly allowing the kolkhozniks something like a right of veto over the raion's appointments. On the other hand, the investigators were likely to support the raion if the kolkhozniks (or a group of them) were pushing a candidate they deemed undesirable, for example, as occurred more than once, a kolkhoz member who was just out of prison.[81]

The term "kolkhoz democracy," which inevitably injected an antiraion and prokolkhoznik bias into the evaluation of any conflict, seems to have entered the discussion in 1937. This seems to have been an outgrowth of the recent public discussions of the new Constitution rather than a response to any specific policy pronouncement on kolkhoz chairmen. One of *Izvestiia's* peasant correspondents invoked the Constitution and its provision for secret ballot when he wrote to complain about the chairman of his kolkhoz, a certain Fedosov, whom the local MTS had forced the kolkhozniks to accept:

> [They] sent him down [as candidate] with the intention that he had to go through, that is, be elected chairman, justifying it with the argument that the politotdel knows better, meaning he has to be elected. Well, of course, they elected him. And what was the result of such elections[?] But if they had voted on comrade Fedosov by secret ballot, then probably the kolkhozniks would not have elected comrade Fedosov because nobody knew him, [nobody knew] what kind of man he was and what kind of manager [*khoziain*], or whether he could direct such a big enterprise....[82]

In April 1937, one provincial newspaper published a survey of letters from kolkhozniks focussing on the violation of kolkhoz democracy by raion officials. In some of the cases cited, the problem was unwanted initiatives from the raion:

> When kolkhozniks began to discuss candidates for the chairmanship at the annual meeting of the kolkhoz "Greetings to October," the head of the raion land department, Boiko, who was present at the meeting, proposed a certain Nikitenko. The kolkhozniks tried to object; they said that they did not know Nikitenko, that he was not even a member of the kolkhoz. Boiko then raised his voice: "I am head of the raion land department, I am in charge of the collective farms, and you have to obey me. And the fact that Nikitenko is not a member of your kolkhoz is a mere triviality—we can make him a kolkhoznik in two seconds."

In other cases, it was the kolkhozniks who took the initiative—for example, by voting to remove a chairman "for prodigal spending of collective funds and a rude attitude to kolkhozniks" and electing a new chairman—but the raion refused to ratify their decision.[83]

In the show trials held in many raions in the fall of 1937, peasant witnesses recounted many stories of how local officials had overridden the wishes of kolkhozniks with regard to selection and removal of kolkhoz chairmen, and the press accounts of the trials reproduced their tone of outrage:

> Ask any kolkhoznik of the "Krasnyi Bitiug" kolkhoz why they elected Zazdravnykh chairman and they will answer: "But we didn't elect him, Kordin [the rural soviet chairman] appointed him. We protested, we did not want to take him, but they forced us to."[84]

The newspaper *Krest'ianskaia gazeta* responded very sympathetically throughout 1938 to complaints of this kind in its (unpublished) correspondence with peasants, and often wrote strong letters to raion authorities rebuking them on the basis of information in the complaints. In a letter to the Krasnodar kraikom secretary, for example, *Krest'ianskaia gazeta*'s staffer wrote:

> We consider that the head of the raion land department violated the principle of kolkhoz democracy, making it possible for worthless leaders to destroy the kolkhoz, despite signals from the kolkhozniks.[85]

The newspaper's peasant correspondents also became more aggressive in stating their complaints. When the raion tried to make the "Molotov" kolkhoz in Voroshilovograd krai accept its nominee as chairman, the kolkhozniks reacted (as they told *Krest'ianskaia gazeta*) with righteous indignation. "Who elects the [kolkhoz] board—you or us?" they challenged the raion officials. "Who is master in the kolkhoz?"[86]

This, of course, was the period of the Great Purges, when "signals from below" about abuses at raion and oblast level had to be taken seriously. It was undoubtedly a high point of peasant influence on the appointment and removal of kolkhoz chairmen; and "kolkhoz democracy" turned out to be more of a temporary condition than a permanent redefinition of the relationship between the raion and the kolkhoz.[87] While it lasted, all the same, at least some kolkhozniks took full advantage. Seven kolkhoz chairman had recently been fired "by the kolkhozniks themselves," a disgruntled raion prosecutor complained at a closed party meeting in March 1937; one might assume from the form that it was a proper raion-initiated action, he added, but in fact all the raion official did was "write up the protocol" the way the kolkhozniks told them to.[88]

Impact of the Great Purges

In the countryside, as in Moscow, the Great Purges were dramatized in show trials. But the trials held in rural raion centers in 1937 had a different message from the Moscow trials. Both were trials of counterrevolutionary "enemies of the people," former leaders of the party. But in the rural show trials, "enemies of the people" meant "enemies of the peasantry." The men indicted in the rural show trials were former raion bosses, along with a selection of lesser officeholders such as rural soviet and kolkhoz chairmen, who were accused of mistreating the peasantry, violating the rights of kolkhozniks under the Kolkhoz Charter, and being responsible for disastrous failures of kolkhoz agriculture.[89]

These "enemies" were not products of fantasy. They were the peasants' real-life enemies (or at least a theatrical representation of them)—those same "little Tsars" of the raion, extortionate rural soviet chairmen, and sadistic kolkhoz chairmen described earlier in this chapter, who figured so often in peasants' complaints to higher authorities.

Of course, the show trials were not exact representations of the reality of the Great Purges in the countryside. In real life, bosses fell victim to the purges, but not necessarily the bad bosses. Nor were bosses the only real-life victims. Ordinary kolkhozniks were at risk, although to a much lesser extent than officeholders and Communists. Former kulaks and their relatives were (as always) at risk, presumably on the principle of rounding up the usual suspects. A whole category of rural victims—social marginals with criminal records, illegally returned exiles, underground religious activists—was swept up and in many cases executed during the Great Purges without publicity.

For all this, the Great Purges in the countryside in 1937–38 were a lesser event than the Great Purges in the towns. "Who was there to arrest? The poor women who did the weaving? Everything was quite peaceful there." This is how A. N. Iakovlev, ideologist of former President Mikhail Gorbachev's *perestroika*, recalled the impact of the Great Purges in the small village on the Volga where he grew up. Yet a few sentences later Iakovlev remarks that his father (who was probably a rural officeholder of some kind) "avoided arrest during the purges of 1937 only because an army buddy tipped him off that local authorities were after him." It is not that there was no terror in the countryside during 1937–38, it is rather that there was no *particular* terror. The countryside had experienced many episodes of repression since the onset of collectivization, some of them much more dangerous to ordinary peasants. Perhaps it was not the first time that Iakovlev's father had been in danger of arrest. In any case, he knew what to do: He "hid and waited for the wave of arrests to end," and a few days later the whole episode was over.[90]

Officeholders at Risk

Waves of repression were transmitted down through the bureaucratic hierarchy, leaving cadres at all levels frightened and demoralized. Obkoms that had been purged turned round and purged the raikoms subordinate to them, and the raikoms passed on the same treatment to their subordinate cadres in the village (that is, chairmen of rural soviets and collective farms). This is how the process of the Great Purges was described in an internal Central Committee memo written in the second half of 1938, when the momentum of the terror was already faltering. Rural cadres were in a state of panic, the memo reported. The number of party members registered in rural organizations (including those in raion centers) had dropped by 62,000 (12 percent) between January 1, 1937 and July 1, 1938. In Novosibirsk oblast, where 5,000 collective farms were now left without even a single Communist, kolkhoz chairmen reportedly "consider themselves doomed to find themselves on the bench of the accused, and then in prison." The chairman of one kolkhoz "told his wife to prepare hard bread (*sukhari*) so that he could take it with him if he went to prison."[91]

Also at risk, although to a somewhat lesser extent, were those kolkhoz chairmen who were not party members. The increased rate of turnover of chairmen and other kolkhoz officers in 1937–38 suggests that the purges had considerable impact even here. At the end of 1937, 40–50 percent of kolkhoz chairmen, brigade leaders, and heads of kolkhoz commercial farms and 35 percent of kolkhoz accountants and bookkeepers had been on the job for less than a year. In 1938, 54 percent of kolkhoz chairmen had held the job for less than one year, compared with 30 percent in 1934.[92] Of course, these figures on job turnover cannot be mechanically translated into arrests and prison sentences. Arrest was by no means an inevitable concomitant of removal from office, any more than it was necessarily the prelude to a long incarceration. It is unlikely that more than a small proportion of rural officeholders who lost their jobs in 1937–38 ended up in gulag.

Sometimes chairmen of rural soviets and collective farms fell victim to the Great Purges because their patrons in the raion leadership had been arrested. In one raion in Kursk oblast, the head of the raion land department was arrested as an enemy of the people. This official had recently fired the chairman of the "Red Dawn" kolkhoz in response to complaints about the chairman's behavior from several kolkhozniks, who were viewed as his protégés. After the official's arrest, the kolkhozniks who had complained were discredited, and two of them were arrested (one on a charge of counterrevolutionary agitation, the other as a "socially-harmful element").[93]

The process by which low-level cadres were drawn into the Great Purges when their patrons fell is illustrated in the show trials that took place in many raions in the fall of 1937. In these trials, a group of raion leaders— almost invariably including the raikom secretary and chairman of the raion soviet, together with a selection of other top officials such as department heads of the raion soviet—would be indicted on charges of mistreating kolkhozniks and wrecking of kolkhoz agriculture. A small number of lower-level personnel, chairmen of rural soviets and collective farms, would be included in the indictment as catspaws of the enemies of the people in the raion leadership. These low-level cadres usually got off with lighter sentences and were sometimes convicted of ordinary, not "counter-revolutionary," crimes.[94]

Another way in which low-level cadres (kolkhoz chairmen and accountants, rural soviet chairmen) might fall victim to the purges was if they were associated with economic disasters, for example, the complete collapse of a kolkhoz, or an egregious failure to meet procurements quotas. A report from Siberia published in the fall of 1938 described the following incident:

> At the end of July, the head of the Soltonskii raion land department, Koshkarov, made a farewell speech to a group of accountants going out to the collective farms. "It is your duty not only to investigate the kolkhoz [finances] thoroughly . . . but also to do everything you can to uncover enemies of the people. We will judge the quality of the work you do by whether you find enemies of the people in the collective farms, and how many. . . ." Somebody asked the speaker: "How do we find enemies?" Koshkarov was quick with his reply. "You are accountants; you look with a pencil in your hands in the course of checking the figures. If, say, the kolkhoz grain sowing or grain harvest fell short of the Plan, or there was a shortfall from livestock losses, translate it all into market value, and if the figure is high, find the enemy!"[95]

Rural officeholders might also get caught up in the purges through denunciation from below. Complaints were surging up from the villages about officials and officeholders of all kinds, especially kolkhoz chairmen and rural soviet chairmen. The newspaper *Krest'ianskaia gazeta* received so many denunciations of local officials in 1938 that such letters were classified under a separate heading: "Abuse of power and wrecking." It is difficult to be sure if the upsurge of complaints preceded or followed the central signals legitimizing and encouraging complaints against bosses. As early as April 1937, the head of *Krest'ianskaia gazeta*'s letters department wrote to inform the Western obkom of the flood of complaints it had received from kolkhozniks about abusive treatment and violation of rights by officials in the oblast.[96]

Such complaints and denunciations were routinely investigated; in 1937–38, as can be seen from archival reports, the investigations quite often led to removal from office and, in some cases, arrest and criminal prosecution.[97] Such denunciations—or indictments modelled upon them—formed the basis of the raion show trials in the fall of 1937.

Echoes in the Kolkhoz

With rural officials at risk, and feeling obliged to show special vigilance, it was inevitable that something of the atmosphere of the Great Purges would reach down into the kolkhoz. Criticism of officeholders by rank-and-file kolkhozniks was a particularly sensitive issue at this time; and those who were criticized tended to hit back with invective from the lexicon of the Great Purges, to the bewilderment of their victims. One kolkhoznik from Krasnodar wrote to complain about this to *Krest'ianskaia gazeta* in 1938:

> [The kolkhoz chairman] began to shut off the discussion, making accusations against everyone who spoke, and said to me "You are supporting a counter-revolutionary grouping." . . . Please help me. Why does he call me a supporter of a counter-revolutionary grouping? How could I be a counter-revolutionary (*Kakoi ia kontr-revoliutsioner*)? . . .[98]

Similarly, another kolkhoznik wrote in to complain that the kolkhoz chairman had responded to his criticism in the wall newspaper by a savage counterattack, also posted on the wall, using "bad slanderous words" such as "butcher, Fascist, Trotskyite, renegade, hanger-on (*palach, fashist, trotskist, otshchepenets, prishebenets*)."[99]

One peasant letter to *Krest'ianskaia gazeta* in 1938 described a kolkhoz chairman—no doubt always an abusive, hard-drinking, and bullying one—who seemed to have gone over the edge in the climate of intense suspicion about "wreckers," "saboteurs," and "terrorists" that developed at this.

> Not a day passes without chairman Patrikeev cursing out one of the kolkhozniks, calling each one a wrecker [and saying] I will drive you out of the kolkhoz and put you in prison . . .
>   Once, Patrikeev drove out into the field and hurled abuse at a kolkhoz brigade-leader, a member of the board [saying], "You Jew-breed (*evreiskaia*

poroda), wrecker, I will expel you from the kolkhoz and put you in prison.". . . . [On another occasion, he] threw himself on some kolkhozniks—Nik. Andrievskii, a member of the kolkhoz board, Dmitrii Shashkin and others [who] were bringing in grain from the field to the granary. He called them wreckers. Then he went to the house of the chairman of the kolkhoz auditing commission, Iakov Lezhepekov, demanded wine from Lezhepekov, and began to mumble: "All the same I will put you in jail, you wreckers. . . ."[100]

There were occasional reports that officials trying to show vigilance had arrested innocent kolkhozniks on trumped-up charges of "counter-revolutionary crimes."[101] But probably expulsion from the kolkhoz, rather than arrest, was the more common fate of rank-and-file kolkhozniks touched by the purges. In Altai krai alone, according to one report, almost 2,000 households were expelled from collective farms in the first half of 1938. Of course, expulsion was an endemic problem in the collective farms. But here we seem to be dealing with real "purges" (*chistki*) of collective farms, following the model of early 1933, when many kolkhozy purged themselves of "kulak elements" under the guidance of the new MTS politotdels. In the 1937–38 version, "links with enemies [of the people]" and kulak connections were both cited as grounds for expulsion. In one kolkhoz, fourteen households were expelled (in the presence of raion representatives) as "kulaks" and "alien elements." In another kolkhoz, four households were expelled simultaneously on the grounds that they were "dangerous," two being specifically identified as "enemies of the people."[102]

In April 1938, the Central Committee condemned "groundless expulsions" from collective farms, noting that some local officials had been encouraging collective farms to expel "socially-alien elements," and forbade the conduct of purges "under any pretext whatsoever" in collective farms.[103]

Anybody with a skeleton in his closet, whether officeholder or ordinary kolkhoznik, was vulnerable in times of high political tension such as the Great Purges. For example, a peasant who had been in trouble before from allegations that his aunt was of noble family and her son a former SR found that he had to answer the allegations all over again in 1937. A Communist kolkhoz chairman, in trouble for failing to provide a horse when ordered to do so by local military authorities, was also charged with concealing his social origins and socializing with class enemies, and was expelled from the party. There were a number of reported instances in which a peasant family that had lost one or more members to deportation in the early 1930s lost another to the Great Purges: For example, a report on a man under investigation in Smolensk oblast in 1938 noted that "two brothers . . . were dekulakized and exiled in 1930 [and] a third brother was arrested in 1937 by organs of the NKVD under article 58 [for counterrevolutionary crimes]."[104]

Roundup of Marginals

An extraordinary and little-known aspect of the Great Purges in the countryside and town was the operation to round up and eliminate tens of thousands of social marginals in the second half of 1937. Stalin signed a secret order for this operation on July 2, 1937, instructing all regional party organizations to round up "former kulaks and criminals, exiled at an earlier time out of various oblasts into the northern and Siberian regions, and then returned after serving out their terms of exile to their own oblasts." These people had become "the chief instigators of all kinds of anti-Soviet and diversionist crimes, both in the collective farms and state farms, and on the railroads and in some other branches of industry," the instruction stated. The most "actively dangerous" troublemakers should be arrested and shot immediately. The rest should be arrested and deported or sent to gulag.[105]

Little is known about the context of this order, which itself has only recently been discovered in secret former-Soviet archives. While it reflects the familiar Soviet paranoia about kulaks, it also has a ring of something more familiar in a German Nazi context than a Soviet Communist one, namely the notion that a prerequisite for social betterment was to rid the society of its unclean, deviant, and marginal members.

Ezhov's follow-up instructions, issued on July 30, gave target figures for the number to be executed and deported in each oblast and krai, based on estimates received from them of the size of the relevant local population. The totals for the Soviet Union as a whole came to 70,000 slated for immediate execution without trial, and 186,500 to be deported. The former figure included 10,000 prisoners already in gulag who were to be shot. While Ezhov did his best to clarify the social categories targeted by this operation, there seems to be a muffled note of puzzlement in his commentary, as if he were not totally certain just what Stalin had in mind. Ezhov's categories were as follows:

"Former kulaks, earlier repressed, who are in hiding from repression or have escaped from camps, exile, and labor settlements"

"Church people (*tserkovniki*) and sectarians who have been repressed in the past"

Persons who were participants in armed uprisings against Soviet power or former members of anti-Bolshevik political parties

Common criminals who had served terms of imprisonment, "repeat offenders who are part of the professional criminal world (horse thieves, cattle-rustlers, robbers, thieves, etc.)."

Little information has so far come to light on the implementation of these instructions. Its effect on the gulag population is probably discernable in the sharp increase in the number of convicts in Soviet labor camps classified as "socially harmful and socially dangerous elements" in the period between January 1937 and January 1939 (from 106,000 to 286,000). A report on "the kulak operation" in Orenburg oblast states that 3,290 persons had been arrested, of whom 2,108 were "kulaks" and 1,182 "counter-revolutionaries"; and that, as of September 16, 1937, 1,650 had already been sentenced to death. This is probably the same operation as the one Stalin and Ezhov ordered in July, since the executions were ordered by the same special troikas, and the number of executions corresponds closely to Orenburg's target figure of 1,500. Outside of highly classified archives, the information on this episode is only fragmentary. It may explain, for example, one puzzling case in the *Krest'ianskaia gazeta* files in which, despite the fact that a peasant's complaint against a kolkhoz chairman had been vindicated and led to criminal prosecution, the investigation report noted that the complainant had been "arrested by the NKVD in 1937 as a socially-harmful element" after having been identified as a habitual thief with a criminal record.[106]

With the exception of the "kulak operation," we have no reliable way of quantifying the impact of the Great Purges on kolkhoz officeholders and ordinary kolkhozniks. Indeed, even if full data were available on rural arrests, convictions, firings, and expulsions, it would be a conceptual challenge to determine which of them should be categorized as "normal" and which "Great Purge-related." The countryside was used to a very high incidence of such events; and ever since collectivization, the line between criminal and political offences had been hopelessly blurred.

For the urban population, or a part of it, the Great Purges were a singular, cataclysmic event that left an indelible mark on memory. But this does not seem to have been the case for the rural population. On the scale of peasant trauma, the terror of 1937–38 paled in comparison with collectivization and dekulakization in the early 1930s. On the scale of peasant suffering, the famine of 1932–33 and even the hunger of 1936–37 were more terrible episodes; and the bumper harvest of 1937 probably did a lot to counterbalance the impact of the 1937–38 waves of repression in the countryside. The available sources give no indication that "the year 1937" ever possessed the sinister resonance for peasants that it had for the urban, educated population. In peasant memory, it shrunk into insignificance compared with collectivization, famine, and the Second World War.

8

Culture

Religion

The assault on religion in the village that accompanied collectivization took a heavy toll. At least half of the churches that had been working at the end of the 1929 were closed by 1933, according to one estimate by a Western observer. The number of priests and other ministers of religion in the USSR recorded by the census dropped from 79,000 in 1926 to 31,000 in 1937. To be sure, these figures cover considerable regional variation, of which we have so far little information. In Stalingrad oblast, according to one source, there were only 300 Orthodox churches functioning at the beginning of 1936, compared with over 2,000 in 1929. But in the Western oblast in 1937 there were 852 working places of worship, including Catholic churches and synagogues.[1]

What this meant in terms of the peasants' religious faith or even their religious observance is, of course, another question. Reliable information on the subject is hard to come by. The 1937 census, unlike those of 1926 and 1939, included a question about religious belief. The question made people extremely nervous, and some believers decided not to declare themselves. Nevertheless, an impressive 57 percent of the population aged 16 and over (56 million persons, including 42 million Orthodox) identified themselves as believers. As might be expected, believers tended to be older and less literate than nonbelievers. Only 45 percent of people in their twenties said they were believers, while 78 percent of those in their fifties made the same statement.[2]

The large-scale closing of churches and the disappearance of priests made it very difficult for peasants to observe religious rites. To find a priest to conduct a wedding, christening, or funeral, peasants might have to bring one in from a distant village. That usually meant finding a horse to carry him—no easy matter in the 1930s, since the great majority of horses were kolkhoz property. Not surprisingly, there are many reports of dramatic decline in religious observance in the countryside in the 1930s. A survey of kolkhozniks in the Central Black Earth oblast in 1934 found that in the 25–39 age group, 38 percent of women and 10 percent of men were still carrying out religious rituals, but in the age group sixteen to twenty-four, only 12 percent of women and 1 percent of men were doing so. In one village in Tver oblast, only 35 percent of marriages were celebrated with religious rites in the 1930s, as against 88 percent in the 1920s.[3]

In the absence of priests and working churches, believers were often forced to change their religious practices if they did not abandon them altogether. This happened even among Orthodox believers, despite the church's history of rigid adherence to established rituals. More and more religious believers were doing without priests because they had no choice, reported a writer for the League of the Godless. Orthodox laymen were becoming "self-ordained" priests (*samosviaty*) and conducting services and rites. In the village of Pavlovka in Dnepropetrovsk oblast, where the church was closed and there was no priest, prayers and religious rites were conducted by a former member of the church council in his house. The Soviet writer Mikhail Alekseev recalls that, for want of a church in his native village in the Central Volga region, his aunt Agafa and other old peasant women used to gather in Agafa's hut on Sundays and conduct religious ceremonies. In a village in Kiev oblast, a peasant woman who was directing the liturgy and prayers— "moreover, [she] does all this dressed up in clerical vestments."[4]

In these circumstances, it is not surprising to hear that the old distinction between Orthodox and Old Believers was losing its meaning in some places. Some observers also thought that the sects were gaining at the expense of Orthodoxy. Delegates to the Second Congress of Militant Atheists in 1930 reported a burgeoning of sectarian organizations, some of them headed by former Orthodox priests whose churches had just been closed, and said that in the collective farms "they say that the priests are bad but the sectarians are good," and put up "sectarian slogans" instead of Communist ones.[5]

Writing in 1937, F. Putintsev, the Godless League's ranking expert on the sects, said that peasants who remained believers tended to turn from Orthodoxy to the sects, which had been less vulnerable to the persecution of the early 1930s because of their lower visibility and degree of institutionalization. According to Putintsev, sectarians were often able to manipulate state policies for their own ends. For example,

[they] willingly agitated for the closing of [Orthodox] churches and gave their signatures to statements about the closing of churches, but in place of one

closed church they tried to open one or several sectarian prayer "clubs" at home. Now these sectarian "clubs," existing in many villages and towns, are trying to unite and transfer to the position of officially registered sectarian communities and groups.[6]

Certainly Protestant and other sects were holding up well on the evidence of the 1937 census. All Christian sects had a total of almost a million adherents, which was not very much lower than their reported membership in the late 1920s. The Protestant sects, with more than 450,000 members in 1937, stood out among religious confessions, as in the past, because of their highly literate membership and strong following among young people.[7]

But the less cerebral Orthodox sects had devoted followings, too. A report from the Western oblast in 1936 noted ten different sectarian persuasions with more than 6,000 adherents in the oblast. The available evidence is fragmentary and discontinuous, since the sects usually tried to stay discreetly out of sight of any possible informant of the state (and of historians). But in their rare moments of visibility, such as the sudden upsurge of religious activity associated with the new Constitution, urban observers were startled by the rich variety of sectarian belief in the countryside: "'shakers', 'leapers', evangelicals, all kinds of 'saints'," as a journalist in Iaroslavl reported in some bemusement.[8]

Although the 1939 census, in contrast to that of 1937, did not include a question about religious belief, it nevertheless provided another occasion for "sightings" of practicing believers by state agents. This time a number of sects had decided to refuse to answer any questions put by the census-takers, evidently in token of a broader repudiation of state authority. Such refusals were reported from many different regions and involved such disparate groups as Fedorovites in Voronezh and Baptists in the Volga region. According to one report in the archives of the census bureau, two Old Believer sisters in the village of Klimovo, Moscow oblast, "gave only their last name; and to the question about [who was] the head of the household answered that God was the head of their household."[9]

Religious Holidays

Although it was the hope and intention of Communists that peasants would stop celebrating religious holidays once they had been raised to a higher cultural level by collectivization, this hope was disappointed in the 1930s. The old holidays continued to be celebrated in the countryside, as well as a few new revolutionary ones. In most instances, however, these "old" holidays were pagan rather than Christian in nature, although Soviet commentators rarely made the distinction. The peasants' adherence to pre-Christian holidays such as the Paraskeva Fridays (associated with a pagan fertility rite) and Ivan Kupalo's Day seems to have been particularly tenacious. This seems to support the suggestion of the ethnographers Stephen and Ethel Dunn (based on postwar studies of central Russia) that the longterm effect of the Soviet assault on religion was to strip away much of the Orthodox veneer that had covered the pre-Christian religion of the Russian peasantry, leaving most of the basic folk rituals and beliefs intact.[10]

Some observers had the impression that kolkhozniks were actually celebrating more religious holidays then peasants had done in the past. They are "now 'resurrecting' even such 'holidays' of whose existence few people remembered even in the best times for the church," wrote a correspondent for a Leningrad paper in 1938. "In some of our raions, such 'holidays' number up to 180 a year. . . ."[11] Since the essence of a holiday was not going out to work in the fields, this proliferation of observance looks less like piety than a form of resistance.

The most bothersome celebrations, from the standpoint of Soviet authorities, were those that took place in the summer months when, according to the logic of the agricultural calendar, peasants should have been working intensively. Instead, the kolkhozniks tended to take off days at a time to go drinking at local fairs. The sequence of religious holidays in July that included the (pre-Christian) Ivan Kupalo (Ivan's Day) (on July 7) and Peter's Day (*petrov den'*) on July 12 caused particular concern because it interfered with the mowing and hay gathering. Peter's Day was celebrated "in the majority of collective farms," according to reports from different regions, even though it was likely to hold up the haymowing. In one rural soviet in Leningrad oblast in 1938 "kolkhozniks absented themselves at the height of the hay gathering for 299 man-days" because of religious holidays; and in Sverdlovsk oblast, peasants in one kolkhoz "did not work for several days, drinking in connection with the holiday of Peter and Paul, when each day needed to be used for harvesting the hay."[12]

> Three days ago dozens of kolkhozniks celebrated [Paraskeva] "Friday."[13] And during that time the scythed hay lay not picked up. Then there was rain two days in a row. And the day after came "Ivan" [Ivan's Day] and once again dozens of collective farms in Skrypovskii, Kosonogovskii, Slavkovskii, Solinskii, and other rural soviets were taken time off at the fairs. Many collective farms had a lot of hay spoiled over that time.
>
> A big harvest is waiting for the kolkhozy to reap. But ahead lies a long series of holidays and the fairs that accompany them. In Slavkovskii raion, 85 fairs have been arranged, and almost all the fairs fall in summertime.[14]

Not all Communists and Soviet officials were prepared to pick a fight with the local peasants about the fairs, however. "What do the fairs matter!" one raion official was quoted as saying. "That's just a standard thing here!" On holidays and fair days, not only would the peasants stop work but the village's "Soviet" institutions—the kolkhoz administration and the club— would also shut down, according to one report. Indeed, rural Communists would probably go to the fair themselves:

> The Lebedevs, husband and wife, are party members. Both swear that they do not believe in God. But on "Trinity Day" and "Paraskeva Friday," and also on "Ivan's Day," they dress up in their best clothes and go off to the fair, just the same as the backward kolkhozniks.[15]

In areas where kolkhozy were expected to provide manpower for logging work in the winter, there were also complaints about the celebration of
winter holidays like Epiphany (*kreshchen'e*). In one kolkhoz of the Northern
krai in 1936, for example, the kolkhoz chairman and accountant were said
to have "organized a drinking party in honor of 'Epiphany'" instead of making sure that the kolkhozniks fulfilled their timber procurements quotas."
Moreover, the kolkhoz chairman, "knowing that they were preparing for the
'holiday' in the kolkhoz, deserted from the timber procurements himself on
14 January. . . ." In a kolkhoz in Leningrad oblast, the celebration of
Epiphany had a particularly impudent, antiauthoritarian flavor, since the
main entertainment consisted of sleigh rides using the kolkhoz horses. One
kolkhoz brigade leader "took out a pedigreed mare without permission of
the stablemen and with drunken panache seated his dekulakized relatives in a
sleigh and drove them around the village."[16]

The heavy drinking that was an important part of any village celebration
provided the occasion and excuse for a variety of antisocial and anti-Soviet
behavior. The "Third International" kolkhoz in Omsk oblast, for example,
was said to have spent 30,000 rubles on drink for a three-day binge associated with a religious holiday in 1939. Fires and fistfights were commonplace
during such celebrations, but in addition there was frequent drunken singing
of chastushki mocking the Communists, and occasionally physical attacks and
even murders of unpopular "Soviet" types in the village, such as Stakhanovites
and peasant newspaper correspondents (*sel'kory*). In one raion in Moscow
oblast, seven tractor drivers, prize-winning milkmaids, and other activists
were murdered on religious holidays in one year, while in another raion there
were twenty-two fires on religious holidays during the year.[17]

The calendar of religious holidays could also be used to tweak the tail of
the regime in another way, namely to justify peasant resistance to the much-
resented instructions from the raion on the proper time for sowing, haymowing, harvest, and so on. A whole range of folk wisdom was cited by
kolkhozniks on this subject: for example, that cattle might not be driven to
pasture before St. George's Day (Egor's Day) on the sixth of May, that hay
might be scythed only from St. Peter's Day on July 12, that winter crops
might be sown only from the Alena's Day on July 3, and so on. In 1938,
peasants in some regions were "still insisting on beginning the plowing on
the day of Jeremy the Harnesser, starting to sow flax on Alena's Day, and
starting to sow buckwheat on the day of Akulina-Grechishnitsa."[18] Whether
all of this actually represented the continuation of old traditions or was the
product of more recent invention is difficult to determine. But one suspects, at
any rate, that the ancient lore came particularly strongly to the peasants' minds
when they received unwelcome orders from the raion land department.

Types of Believer in the Village

A rare glimpse of the attitudes of individual peasants to religion in the late
1930s is provided by a League of the Godless agitator, G. Sornov, who went

to villages in the Tula, Riazan and Moscow oblasts giving readings from the newspaper *Bezbozhnik* and conducting discussions about religion.[19] Sornov was a native of a Tula village now working in Moscow; his atheist propaganda was evidently a part-time, volunteer activity. As a propagandist, he was surely unusual in his openness and accessibility: He liked to spend hours relaxing with "local hunters, fishermen, storytellers (*skazochniki*)" as well as kolkhoz activists during his visits to the village, and he was happy to have believers and even church activists come to his meetings.

One of the devotees of the church he describes, E. I. Morosanova of the "Maxim Gorky" kolkhoz, was

> an active fighter for clerical interests, [who] runs around the villages getting sig-natures of believers in support of various priestly petitions. Since she has decided that there is absolutely no danger in attending the readings [of *Bezbozhnik*], she speaks here too as a passionate churchwoman. For example, when I read articles unmasking the role of priests in the imperialist war, Morosanova goes wild in defense of the priests: the priests, she says, prayed not for the victory of their governments but for the reconciliation of the hearts of the leaders, so that they would end the bloodshed. . . .

In contrast to Morosanova, Grigorii Koloskov, head of a parish council in Riazan oblast, would "only attend 'select' readings where 5–7 persons gather and firm believers are in the majority." He spoke only on certain sub-jects, usually to respond to Sornov's "exposure" of miracles and particular church beliefs. For example, he would say:

> *Bezbozhnik* is wrong to assert that christening water has no holy properties and that there are no devils. F. Koloskov saw the virgin in holy water; and M. Titov, an atheist, met the devil and repented, has become a believer. . . .

One of Sornov's fellow villagers, A. Fedin, had been deeply religious for fifty out of his fifty-three years—the local priest always used to cite him as an example of piety, and he said he "used to feel nauseated at the very words 'disbelief in God'." But now he was wavering in his faith, and had many doubts and questions that he wanted to talk about. For example: "If there is no God, where does the world come from? Who created man? Where does life on earth come from?"

In the "Proletarian Path" kolkhoz, M. G. Khodakov, aged seventy-three, long ago had become privately convinced that there was no God as a result of his observation of human misery and degradation. His special inter-est was finding out the history of the church's successful exploitation of human suffering, but he was not interested in hearing about the misdeeds and corruption of individual priests—a staple of Soviet godless propaganda. In contrast, G. F. Andreev from "First of August" kolkhoz, was "ready to lis-ten for days on end to stories of greedy, profitseeking, spiritually bankrupt priests." This was because of a traumatic personal experience in the past:

> When he paid for his wedding, Andreev did not pay off a debt of a ruble that his grandfather had owed the priest. For that, the priest, Mitrofan, forced Andreev

to wait seven hours for his wedding.(!) It was in the depths of a winter night, in a snowstorm, that the priest let them go. The wedding party got lost and spent the night in a ravine, and everybody was frozen. Forty years after the event, Taras Fedorov cannot forgot the priest's mockery. . . .

I. V. Zharov had been a peasant "seeker," testing various religious groups including Baptists and Evangelicals to see which faith was best. Now he considered himself an atheist and his particular interest lay in reading about sectarians and hearing scientific exposés of Biblical stories. But he was discriminating in his critique of religion. For example, he always objected to the argument against the literal truth of the Bible that science had disproved its claim that the world is 7,000 years old. According to Zharov, this was based on a misreading of the Bible (time in the first days of Creation was not the same as time now), and he always got up and said so at Sornov's meetings if the subject was raised.

Modus Vivendi

The state's agents in the countryside were supposed to be the sworn enemies of religious superstition. These agents were few and poorly educated, however, and often differed little in their culture from the rest of the peasantry. Rural Communists (that beleaguered group!) were constantly explaining to party purge commissions why the priest had been seen coming to their house, why their mother-in-law had been buried with religious rites, and why they had got drunk with the rest of the village on the local saint's day. (The standard justification was to blame the womenfolk, who were taken to be the licensed representatives of superstition and ignorance even in a Soviet household.)[20]

For a number of years after the savage onslaught against religion of 1929–30 and its abrupt halt, the state's policy towards rural priests and believers was relatively tolerant. Village churches that had been closed were not reopened, but further closings and harrassment of believers were not encouraged. In 1936, when the young Komsomol leaders included the usual militant paragraph about "struggle against religion" in their policy statement, Stalin made them change it to a mild suggestion that the Komsomol should "patiently explain to young people the harmfulness of superstition." In the new spirit of the times, an obkom secretary instructed his subordinates "not to hurt the feelings of believers" and "definitely not to allow any irresponsible pranks (*vykhodki*) in relation to believers. . . ." The League of Militant Godless fell on hard days, and its leader, Emelian Iaroslavskii, complained to the Central Committee in 1937 that people just dismissed its work and "look at me like some kind of eccentric, to be still working away at something everyone else has given up long ago."[21]

Some rural Communists, to be sure, remained nervous about the church, especially its potential as a source of agitation against the kolkhoz. For example, a correspondent from Gorky oblast wrote to *Antireligioznik* to complain about the disruptive activity of the local priest and an aggressive believer, "Mother Maria," in the "Red Hills" kolkhoz:

> "Mother" conducts religious conversations with the women. . . . There are many non-collectivized peasants in the village. They do not join the kolkhoz out of "fear of God." "Mother" calls the [kolkhoz] club "the devil's home." Hearing her old wives' tales, three girls—Nadia Tiumina, Tania Shumilkina and Varia Petrunina—stopped going out with the other young people and declared themselves to be "nuns". . . .[22]

But there are also many reports of local officials and kolkhoz chairmen who had found a comfortable *modus vivendi* with local church people, tolerating, for example, the zealous women kolkhoz members who "run around the village for the signatures of believers on various priestly petitions." In Moscow oblast, one kolkhoz chairman "gave the deacon Komarov a document saying he is an activist (*obshchestvennyi rabotnik*) and organized a 'choral circle' of young people. In fact, the 'choral circle' was used for singing in the church. . . ."[23]

Priests did not have the right to join the kolkhoz even after their civil rights were restored by the 1936 Constitution; even their children were apparently barred from kolkhoz membership right up to the end of the 1930s. But some collective farms—it is not clear how many—ignored the ban and treated the priest as a full member of the village community. According to Iaroslavskii (who may have been exaggerating), "a large number" of kolkhoz chairmen simultaneously held the office of church starosta. There were cases when kolkhoz chairmen detailed kolkhozniks to do free repair work on the church or made kolkhoz horses available to local priests to make their rounds of the parish. In one instance, a rural soviet chairman got the priest to help him collect subscriptions from the peasants to the state loan, and then, in recognition of his services, "blithely put the priest's name on the board of honor!"[24]

The chairman of Sukhomlinsk raion soviet in Sverdlovsk oblast allegedly went so far as to appoint a priest when a vacancy occurred in his district, sending a polite notification of his action to the bishop. In Tatar villages in the Upper Volga, it was reported that kolkhozniks not only earned labordays preparing firewood for the mosques but had even tried to have the mullahs put on the kolkhoz budgets and paid in labordays. A suggestion on the same lines came from Sverdlovsk during the 1936 discussion of the new Constitution: "To take the church into the kolkhoz administration; the kolkhoz will get all the income of the church and the priest, and the priest will earn labordays in the kolkhoz by working at his profession."[25]

The favors between local rural officials and priests went both ways. Priests sometimes lent money to officials to help them meet their payroll. In one case in the Western oblast, the priest of Kolodets village had a horse and was always willing to lend it to kolkhozniks or the local teacher when they needed to go into town. He was on the most cordial personal terms with the village's Soviet activists—the people's judge, the doctor, the teacher, and the kolkhoz chairman and brigade leaders. "Is it any wonder after that that some Kolodets Communists . . . invited the priest over at Easter?" the local paper enquired plaintively.[26]

Hopes and Fears

Crosscurrents of peasant hopes and fears about religion intersected in the second half of the 1930s. On the one hand, there was hope that the state would definitively repudiate its persecution of the church (as it in fact did a few years later, after the outbreak of the Second World War). This was associated primarily with the promise of religious tolerance contained in the new Constitution of 1936. On the other hand, there was fear of a new outbreak of persecution. This was both a response to the Great Purges and part of a broader unease related to the threat of war and expressed in a new wave of apocalyptic rumors.

In 1936–37, signs of a "revitalization of church people and believers" (*ozhivlenie tserkovnikov i veruiushchikh*) in the countryside were widely noted in the Soviet press. This revitalization seems to have been a response to two external stimuli: the new Constitution of the Soviet Union, subject of a national discussion in 1936, and the population census conducted in January 1937. The new Constitution was a major encouragement to believers because it guaranteed freedom of religion and restored civil rights to priests. The census aroused their excitement because of the inclusion of a question on religious belief, which suggested to some peasants that a basic shift in the regime's attitude might be taking place.[27]

Peasants were aware of the new Constitution because of their participation in the public discussion organized around it. Many took the clause on religious tolerance as a green light to petition for the reopening of their village church.

> In the village of Krasnopole, the priest has started campaigning among some of the backward kolkhozniks so to be returned "to service" in that village. In the village of Taromskoe, a group of Baptists began to gather signatures for a request that they be given special premises for meetings.[28]

Petitioners were sent to Moscow or the oblast center to convey peasant pleas for the reopening of churches. One such petition had 700 signatures. Peasants also wrote to newspapers and the government asking that churches be reopened in connection with the new Constitution.[29]

Some rumors going round the countryside gave an optimistically edited version of the Constitution's statement on religion:

> A kolkhoznik returning from military training found icons in the family home for the first time since 1917. When he asked his son for an explanation, he was told: "According to the new Constitution, every house has to have its icons— that's what the boys in the village say."[30]

Priests and believers were quick to spread the word that the Constitution had given the state's imprimatur to religion, and it was no longer necessary to be ashamed of being a believer. On the strength of this, "one pastor opened a kind of club in his prayer house, with a choral circle and small library for young people." There were many reports that priests were becoming more visible and assertive in village affairs.

> In many places, priests have begun to go to meetings (parents' meetings, kolkhoz meetings, etc.) and have become frequent attenders at reading rooms, libraries, seminars, and lectures. In Khvatovka village, Arzamas raion, the priest asked to be invited to meetings of the rural soviet.

The most frequent reports on these lines were of priests offering to work as cultural organizers and heads of kolkhoz clubs and libraries. "In view of the fact that I am now equal in rights according to the Stalin Constitution, please give me work as head of a [kolkhoz] club," wrote one priest to the raion authorities.[31]

This was the period when the push for "kolkhoz democracy" was at its height, and many collective farms were in the process of reelecting their officers. Although, as already noted, priests did not formally have the right to belong to the kolkhoz, at least some did, and were even elected to offices by the kolkhozniks. There are reports at this time of the election of priests and psalm readers as kolkhoz chairmen, deputy chairmen, and chairmen of kolkhoz auditing commissions (although such elections were generally quickly annulled by the raion authorities).[32]

There were elections, too, in the church itself. In one rural soviet in the Urals, the church council decided to hold its own elections by secret ballot in 1937. In Gorky krai, the raion soviet received eleven requests to sanction church elections (for starostas and councils). Probably this was simply the churchmen's response to hearing so much about soviet elections and kolkhoz democracy. But Communists were puzzled and suspicious at this odd behavior, wondering what the religious people were up to. Obviously it was some kind of ploy on the part of the religious party, one provincial newspaper commented, but just what kind of ploy had yet to be discovered.[33]

When the revitalization of religion started to impinge on politics, as it did during the 1937 elections for the Supreme Soviet,[34] the predictable crackdown followed. Along with mass arrests of churchmen and sectarians went a wave of paranoia about antiregime conspiracies hidden behind the mask of religion. A Leningrad newspaper reported, for example, that "A spy, wearing a false beard and posing as a religious mendicant, came over the frontier. He was caught when someone realized the beard was false and pulled it off."[35]

The Great Purges generated many kinds of fear. On the one hand, there was the Communists' fear of religious conspiracy and subversion. On the other hand, there was the believers' fear, reawakened at every time of social tension, that the end of the world was at hand. As the Soviet press gave its daily reports of the imminent danger of war and the unmasking of fresh traitors, spies, and saboteurs' acts of treachery, conspiracy, and espionage, peasants translated this as a message that the future held yet more suffering and turmoil.

> The rumor went from izba to izba. Two nimble old women quickly ducked into the house, furtively looked round, sat down on a bench as if unwillingly. Then they heaved heavy sighs and, in response to questions, said: "Misfortune hangs over us, women! The Day of Judgement draws near. War and famine have begun. . . . Pray!"
>
> This example is not unique in Mginskii raion. Church people have started going more and more frequently to the houses of kolkhozniks to spread their anti-Soviet talk and threaten those who do not go to church with "The Last Judgement."[36]

Prophecies of famine, rumors of imminent war, and other unspecified "anti-Soviet" rumors (probably predictions of the collapse of the Soviet regime) proliferated. Wandering holy men and women distributed mysterious "letters from Heaven" and "letters from Jerusalem" warning of the coming apocalypse. In the Pskov region, a frontier zone where all citizens including peasants were issued passports, peasants refused for several months to accept the passports or sign any official documents. They said that wandering monks and "Holy Fools" had told them that the end of the world and the coming of Antichrist were imminent and advised them to refuse all contact with the state.[37]

As so often in Russia, the language of religion in the countryside had distinct antiregime overtones.[38] Antichrist and the state remained linked in the imagination of the Russian peasant, as they had been two centuries earlier after the great schism. If the Communist regime attached political significance to every manifestation of popular religious belief, this was not only a reflection of the party's obsessions and paranoia, but also caught something of the reality of rural Russia.

Everyday Life

For all the backwardness of the Russian village in the decade after collectivization, some of the basic objects of everyday life including peasant clothing underwent a striking transformation from traditional to modern in the 1930s. It was perhaps not so much that peasants had crossed a psychological Rubicon as that the crafts on which traditional patterns of peasant life depended had disappeared around the time of collectivization.

There were two main practical reasons for the abrupt collapse of peasant crafts at the beginning of the 1930s. The first was dekulakization: Peasant craftsmen, often among the village's more prosperous citizens, were particularly vulnerable to being labelled kulaks. In addition to those who were dekulakized and deported, many others left the countryside in 1929–30 to avoid such a fate. The second reason was the inhospitable climate for craft production in the countryside after collectivization. The kolkhoznik did not earn labordays by working at a craft, nor did he feed himself, as he might by cultivating his private plot. Often, crops like flax and hemp that provided the raw material for many crafts were no longer planted: The collective farms stressed grain production above all, and the kolkhozniks could not afford the space on their own small plots for flax and hemp. The private plot was likely to be wholly given over to food production. As for the "independent" peasant who continued to practice a craft, he was at risk of being accused of showing capitalist tendencies (by trading) or sabotaging procurements (by not concentrating on agriculture), and was liable to punitive taxation on his craft income.[39]

"Without me there will be no beekeeper [in the kolkhoz] and the production of felt boots (*valenki*) will cease," wrote Ivan Makarov, a peasant in Moscow oblast, petitioning the Commissariat of Agriculture in February 1933 to reverse the kolkhoz's decision to expel him as a kulak.[40] The Commissariat did not respond, and no doubt Makarov went off to find a job in Moscow, and the kolkhozniks went without honey and new valenki. They may also have started buying sugar or rubber boots at the local coop store— if, of course, these goods could be obtained there. For all the statistics on increased delivery of manufactured goods to the countryside proudly cited by Soviet historians, it is clear that supply to the rural trade network was extremely irregular. Scarcity was the norm, both in the sphere of traditional craft goods and modern manufactured ones.

Thus there was surely an element of choice in the substitution of urban material culture for that of the village. This could suggest (as Soviet historians of the pre-*glasnost'* era tirelessly asserted) that peasants were assimilating modern, "Soviet" values. But it could also be a reflection of the malaise or demoralization that is evident in many aspects of life in the postcollectivization village—an erosion of confidence in traditional customs related to the peasants' sense of violation, abandonment, and second-class citizenship in Soviet society.

Material Culture

In many areas of Russia, peasant women were still spinning and weaving their own cloth at the end of the 1920s, and *lapti* (bast sandals) were still standard footwear in the villages. In Riazan oblast, for example, ethnographers report that village-made lapti were worn and domestic weaving was common. Until the early 1930s outer clothing was still largely made of homespun cloth and sewn by tailors, who might be local, from a specialized tailors' village in the region, or itinerant. To be sure, members of the younger generation were developing a taste for urban dress and fashions in the 1920s, especially in non-Black Earth provinces like Tver with many urban otkhodniks. But, like other urban customs such as divorce, lipstick, Komsomol membership, and atheism, this was something that the majority of villagers saw as a provocative repudiation of accepted norms, a sign of the postwar and Soviet corruption of mores.[41]

This changed quickly after collectivization. Domestic weaving was sharply reduced. Specialized tailors' villages disappeared, along with those devoted to other crafts, such as the famous bootmaking village of Kimry. Itinerant tailors and other traveling craftsmen and peddlars came under suspicion as potential rumormongers, liable to inflame peasants against the kolkhoz, and were often arrested or chased away by local authorities.[42]

In Riazan, sweaters and skirts like those worn in the town replaced the traditional homespun skirts (*ponevye*) for younger women. Many also abandoned the old hairstyle of two plaits under a headdress and put their hair up; the most daring—Stakhanovite tractor drivers and the like—cut it short. Lapti went out of popular use in many regions (although in Tambov oblast, peasants were still wearing them for reaping in the 1950s). While older women in the village remained more traditional in dress, men of all ages almost completely abandoned the old village dress for an urban jacket and cap. The old "dirty" clothes—lapti, the homespun coat (*zipun*), the coarse burlap *deriuga*—had disappeared, a kolkhoznik from Kursk oblast reported in 1935, "Now we wear factory-made clothing."[43]

One of the craft industries that collapsed most dramatically around the time of collectivization was the making of samogon. This had been the rural growth industry of the 1920s, but of course it required that the peasants have surplus grain or potatoes and access to sugar. The kolkhoz structure and the high level of state procurements made domestic distilling much less viable in the 1930s. Indeed, it seems to have disappeared almost completely, to judge by the paucity of references in archival as well as published sources. Peasants must have "lost the art" of making samogon, one observer hazarded.[44]

When peasants drank (which was certainly less often than they would have liked), they usually drank state-produced vodka bought in the local co-op. The state, having discarded the impulses towards temperance manifested in the 1920s, was not averse to providing peasants with vodka in the 1930s, since this was a powerful generator of state revenue. In practice, however, vodka was in short supply, at least through the first half of the decade, and there is little doubt that absolute consumption must have declined sharply compared to the late 1920s. There were also fewer places to drink in the countryside, outside of the peasants' own izbas, since most taverns, being private enterprises, had been closed.[45]

A few large items of modern factory production started to make their appearance in the village in the course of the 1930s. Tractors and combine-harvesters, the quintessential modern industrial goods associated with collectivization, came first, albeit in small numbers. But within a few years almost all these machines were removed from the collective farms and transferred to regional Machine-Tractor Stations, although they were operated by kolkozniks and used on kolkhoz fields.

In terms of our earlier model, the tractor was a factory-made substitute for a vanishing homegrown commodity—the horse, a major casualty of the collectivization and famine years. Also substituting for horses, which remained a deficit good throughout the 1930s, were trucks, which the larger and more prosperous collective farms started acquiring in the latter half of the decade. It was news in Moscow oblast in 1935 when the collective farms in one rural soviet clubbed together to acquire a 1.5–ton truck, repaired the road and appointed a driver. In 1937, however, hundreds of trucks were sold to collective farms, especially in prosperous agricultural areas like Krasnodar, Dnepropetrovsk, and the Crimea.[46]

It is hard to find reliable data for comparing the village standard of living in the 1930s to that of the 1920s. At the most basic level, there was clearly less to eat and drink in the village after collectivization. There were glaring gaps in the customary fabric of life caused by human flight and deportation and the closing of familiar institutions, from churches to taverns to mills.

With regard to public health and medical facilities, the picture was gloomy. Despite the frequent occurrence of "trips to the hospital" in peasant rhetoric ("I needed the horse to take my wife to the hospital"), such trips cannot have happened very often because rural medical facilities were few and far between. In 1932, there was about one hospital bed in rural areas per thousand of population, although by 1937 the ratio had risen to about 1.6 per thousand. In 1937, according to the census, a rural population of 110 million was served by fewer than 12,000 physicians, 54,000 feldshers (paramedics) and midwives, and fewer than 7,000 pharmacists. Soviet efforts to persuade urban-trained physicians to practice in rural areas or even raion centers were mostly unavailing, and official ambivalence about feldshers seems to have been an impediment to the expansion of the feldsher network in the prewar period. The field of rural medicine was left largely to the traditional wise women, *znakharki*, in the 1930s, a historian of Russian public health concludes.[47]

Although it is sometimes argued that peasants were hostile to modern medicine and had more trust in the znakharki, the inadequacy of rural medical care was nevertheless a subject of complaint in peasant letters on the 1936 Constitution. Complaints focussed particularly on the fact that this was yet another instance in which the urban population was privileged vis-à-vis peasants, and on the cost of prescriptions and medical care. Many letters described the pathetic plight of widows and children who had to go without medical treatment because they could not afford it. "Before, in earlier years, we used to go to the hospital for free," complained one kolkhoznik. "Now you pay 50 or 70 kopeks just for a dose of quinine water, and if you need ointment, they charge a ruble."[48]

In many villages, collectivization actually brought economic and technical retrogression because of the removal of human resources. A native son revisiting his remote village in the Viatka region in the mid-1930s found that lack of kerosene had forced the peasants to revert to using birch splinters (*luchiny*) for light. The Saratov village where the writer Mikhail Alekseev grew up was electrified for a few years in the 1920s, when a powerline was brought in and run through a turbine at the local water mill. It lost electric-

ity when the miller was dekulakized in 1929 and did not recover it until the
end of the 1950s. In general, electricity was a benefit of modern civilization
that reached most villages in the Soviet Union only in the Khrushchev era.
Only one out of every twenty-five collective farms had electricity on the eve
of the Second World War, and even in 1950 the proportion was not quite
one in six.[49]

Broken Families

The village was a demoralized place after collectivization. The reasons for
this were as much demographic as political. There had been a huge outflow
of population, taking away the young and ambitious, and in many regions
taking away the men as well. According to the 1937 census, women outnumbered men by a factor of almost two-to-one in the working (*samodeiatel'noe*)
population of agricultural collective farms in the Soviet Union (18 million
females to 10 million males).[50]

"How many . . . single women (*bobylki*), abandoned by their husbands
at the beginning of the 1930s, I . . . met in the villages," wrote Evgenii
Gerasimov, chronicler of the village he calls Spas na Peskakh in the non-
Black Earth region of Russia. "Pulling a cluster of half-orphaned children
[at their heels], they carried the collective farms on their own backs."[51]

Aunt Varia, one of the central figures in Gerasimov's real-life story, was
the first chairman of the kolkhoz in Spas na Peskakh. She had been a widow
during the First World War. With a group of women in similar straits
(known as "the widows"), she dominated the kolkhoz aktiv at the beginning of the 1930s. Aunt Varia had a grown son, but in 1929 he and his wife
left the village to work in factories in the city, vanishing almost completely
from her life. For ten years, Aunt Varia brought up their young son, along
with an orphaned niece and two grandnieces.[52]

A second figure in Gerasimov's tale, Babka Mania, was briefly glimpsed
by him in 1930, as she despairingly resisted the the collectivization of her
cow while her husband, Filia, looked on in silence. Filia left the village that
same year and was not heard of again (with the exception of one chance
meeting with a fellow villager in Central Asia) for thirty-five years. Then,
after an adventurous life involving much travelling and two other marriages,
he came back to the village and moved back in with Babka Mania.[53]

A third story was related to Gerasimov by a man he met fishing in the
river near Spas na Peskakh. The man was a native of the village, but he had
left in 1930, like so many others, and was now a Muscovite. Although he
had remained married to his village wife, he lived apart from his wife and
children for seventeen years after collectivization.

> Everyone's family life was turned upside down then. After all, how could you
> take the family when there was nothing at the construction site except founda-
> tion pits, and the uncultivated taiga all around? Later I could have taken them.
> At Kuznetskstroi, they promised me a room in the family barracks, but by that
> time life had begun to settle down in the kolkhoz and my wife had bought a cow

again. And they had given me credentials and a ticket to Moscow to take foremen's courses—well, how could I refuse?

I studied for a year in Moscow and stayed there to work. [Then] I went to the village and summoned my wife: "We will live in the capital, they are giving a room." "And how about the farm?" she asks. "To hell with it, I say, what kind of farm have you—one cow." "And the izba?" "We will sell everything." "No, she says, I know how people live in the town. Here you have your own potatoes, your own milk, and there everything is for money." So up to the war I had not persuaded her. . . . [54]

Just as there were many broken and incomplete families in the village, so there were also many orphans—children without one or both parents who had been left to fend for themselves. The same term, *besprizornye*, was used for them as for the better-known homeless children of the 1920s who formed gangs in the cities and rode the railroads, hobo style. But this was a second cohort of homeless children, formed by collectivization and out-migration, dekulakization, and the famine.

A special category of orphans in the early 1930s were those from the families of kulaks who had been left behind when their parents were deported or fled. These constituted an enormous problem for the village, not just materially but also morally.

A young child's parents are arrested. He goes along the street crying. . . . Everyone is sorry for him, but nobody can make up his mind to adopt him, or take him into his home: "After all, he is the son of a kulak . . . There might be unpleasant consequences."

The author of this bold article on the plight of kulaks' children was Nadezhda Krupskaia, Lenin's widow, who was a senior official in the education ministry in 1929. There are firsthand reports that confirm her observations. In an autobiographical novel published in the 1960s, a Soviet writer describes how his peasant parents quarrelled over the issue: His father, a Communist kolkhoz chairman, said kulaks' children must be treated as class enemies, but his wife could not reconcile herself to it.[55]

As Krupskaia pointed out, officially encouraged mistreatment of "kulaks' children" was all the more outrageous and irrational in that many of them were actually adopted or foster children, taken in to work as batraks, shepherds, and nannies. The advantage of relying on adopted child labor was not just that it was cheap but also that it created no dangerous record of hiring nonfamily labor (a prime kulak trait). In the later part of the 1920s, ironically, the state had strongly encouraged such adoptions by peasants and artisans in order to empty the orphanages.[56]

Sometimes the village had to deal with various manifestations of the problem of kulaks' children for many years. In one village in Briansk raion, four children of a kulak deported with his family to the Urals returned to the village after the death of both their parents in exile. The kolkhoz took the orphans in, the eldest being an able-bodied young man and the two teenagers, aged sixteen and thirteen, also being capable of working in the kolkhoz. But then the siblings started asking for the return of the family izba, now the property of the kolkhoz chairman. Their request was firmly and repeatedly turned down by the local authorities, even after a representative of the Western obkom, responding to a petition from the three youngest children, interceded on their behalf.[57]

In earlier times, we are told, the village commune acknowledged a responsibility to look after orphans who had been left unprotected, although peasant custom decreed that the responsibility lay with the extended family. It is not surprising to find that the struggling collective farms in famine areas in 1933 were unable to act in the same way, and that cities in the Ukraine and the North Caucasus experienced an influx of "homeless, sick, and starving children" from the countryside.[58] What is perhaps more noteworthy, since it suggests continuing demoralization and disintegration of the community, is that the villages were still systematically repudiating any responsibility for their orphans several years later.

"The village is one of the main 'suppliers' of homeless children . . . ," an education official said at a meeting on this problem in 1935. "The rural soviets immediately send children whose parents have died to the town or the nearest orphanage (*detdom*). Absolutely nothing is done to help the child locally. . . . " The head of the Leningrad city education department said that 70 percent of the orphans in institutions under his jurisdiction came from the village.[59]

In 1936, a new law on homeless children placed the responsibility for appointing guardians and arranging placement of orphans on the chairmen of the rural soviets, warning them against allowing orphans to take up a life of vagrancy. The same law instructed the collective farms to give high priority to supporting orphans and children in temporary distress in the kolkhoz, offering to reimburse 30 rubles out of every 100 rubles spent on orphans from central funds.[60]

Despite these instructions, a year later the Western obkom had to remind raion and rural authorities that they were still failing in their duty by orphans and children of kolkhozniks in acute need, including children of single mothers. Such children were being pushed into a life of vagrancy and degeneracy, the obkom said. Rural soviets and collective farms must take responsibility for these children, and not "refuse to look after [them] . . . on the obviously incorrect and un-Soviet grounds that 'They are not local children; they come from somewhere else'." The obkom warned that all children found vagrant and homeless would be returned to their original place of residence, and the rural authorities responsible for letting them fall into vagrancy and homelessness would be prosecuted.[61]

Marriage and Divorce

As is already clear, the peasant family was in considerable disarray in the 1930s. Since the collective farms were not required to make detailed reports on family structure and ethnographers and sociologists were effectively banned from the Russian village for more than twenty years after collectivization, good data are very scarce. It is clear, however, that mean family size dropped significantly. At the end of the 1920s, the mean peasant family consisted of about five persons. A decade later, the mean as calculated by Soviet historians ranged between 3.9 persons and 4.4 persons. This is interpreted by Soviet ethnographers to mean that the nuclear family was finally and decisively replacing the old extended family.[62] No doubt the kolkhoz structure did encourage fission of large extended families by virtue of the rules pertaining to private plots. All the same, it seems unwise to leap to the conclusion that the Russian village family of the 1930s was necessarily nuclear just because it was small, since impressionistic evidence tends to suggest the contrary. Aunt Varia's grab bag family—a widow living with a grandson and niece (who in the course of time acquired two daughters but no husband)—was by no means uncommon.

The rural birthrate fell dramatically in the 1930s, according to Soviet statistics. In 1913, the rural birthrate, at forty-nine births per thousand of population, was way above the urban rate of thirty per thousand. It dropped somewhat in the 1920s, and then plummeted in the 1930s. By 1935, the rural birthrate was down to thirty-two per thousand of population, which is approximately where it stayed for the rest of the decade. As of 1940, there was no significant difference between the rural birthrate (thirty-two per thousand) and the urban birthrate (thirty-one per thousand).[63]

Statistics on fertility show the same general pattern, although in this case the time frame is more elastic. As far as the rural population of European Russia is concerned, the marked drop in the fertility rate that Western demographers associate with modernization was manifest in a few provinces as early as the 1897 census, in just over half the provinces by the time of the 1926 census, and in all provinces by 1940.[64]

Although there are no reliable statistics on rural divorce in the 1930s, divorce among young peasants was evidently not uncommon, particularly in areas within reach of a big city. "In our villages, young men still often get drunk and still often get married and [then] divorced," a young Stakhanovite peasant commented disapprovingly in the mid-1930s.[65] An example of such behavior was the following:

> On May 16th, kolkhoznik M. S. Matiukhin, taking an accordion and a few lads from his brigade . . . , went to seek the hand of Pasha Pekarnikova. The table at Pasha's house was laden with wine and snacks. Glasses clinked. Everyone had a lot to drink. The intoxicated young men went back to their homes, but the impatient fiancé Matiukhin stayed to spend the night with Pasha. He left early in the morning and was never seen again.[66]

In many reports of courting and marriage customs, the shortage of young men in the villages comes through strongly as the major determinant of practice. A report on the "Molotov" kolkhoz in Rybnoe raion, near the border between Moscow and Riazan oblasts, provides a striking example. This was an area where the groom's family had traditionally paid bride-price (*kladka*), compensating the bride's family for the loss of her labor and gaining rights to her reproductive capacity. Dowries were uncommon in central

Russia, but where they existed, they remained the wife's inalienable property and did not constitute a payment to the groom's family. In a reversal of traditional norms, according to the report, the parents of young women were paying a substantial money "dowry" (*pridanoe*)—in effect, a groom-price—to get husbands for their daughters.[67]

> A young kolkhoznik, Kuzma Kiriushin, got the conceited idea that he is the best of all possible fiancés and took a dowry of 1,000 rubles from the parents of his fiancée, Marfa Katomina. Marfa's parents tried to protest. There were long negotiations with Kuzma Kiriushkin's parents. Kuzma Kiriushkin posed an "ultimatum": "Either you give me a dowry of 1,000 [rubles], or I will not marry your daughter."

In some instances, to make matters worse, the grooms, having taken the money, were not living up to their obligations.

> This year a young kolkhoznik, Vasilii Oblezov, married Niura Romashkina. He took a dowry of 700 rubles, and in addition Niura's parents gave presents to all the relatives of the bridegroom. . . . Niura and Vasilii got married. Niura lived for two months with her husband and then came home to her parents. Oblezov had driven her out. Niura's life was ruined. But Vasilii Oblezov, having got such a high price for himself, is thinking of getting married again and earning himself another effortless 700 rubles. . . .
>
> A kolkhoznik, Kuzma Gusev, married a kolkhoznitsa, Niura Morozova. He took a dowry of 700 rubles. After living with Niura for a year and a half, he drove her out and married another girl, once again taking a dowry of 500 rubles.

Although social commentators naturally deplored exploitative behavior of this kind, the prevailing "Soviet" attitude to divorce in the villages was not indiscriminately critical. While the 1930s were indeed a period of "great retreat" from revolutionary values on family questions, as Nicholas Timasheff argued, this was very much an urban phenomenon. Peasant women were still praised for liberating themselves from tyrannical husbands and fathers and asserting their status as independent workers in the kolkhoz with a status equal to men's. Even divorce was not too high a price to pay. At the highly ritualized national meetings of Stakhanovites, peasant women often told stories of the battles they had had with unenlightened husbands, sometimes ending in raised consciousness and sometimes in divorce: and the party leaders present applauded them. The following autobiographical account by a twenty-eight–year old kolkhoznitsa from Moscow oblast is typical for a "progressive" Soviet peasant woman in the 1930s:

> I defied my husband and began to work as a member of the rural soviet, and as soon as the collective farms were announced, I joined the kolkhoz at once. . . . My husband became absolutely like a wild animal. I couldn't live with him, I had to take action through the soviet and divorced him.[68]

Such divorces, however, were surely less common in the villages of the 1930s than divorce—or, more likely, desertion—initiated by the husband. Like Babka Mania in Gerasimov's story, many peasant women found themselves in an ambiguous situation: neither effectively married nor formally divorced, with an absent husband working somewhere in the towns or industrial construction sites who might or might not at some point choose to return. These wives could not remarry (unlike their husbands), but undoubtedly some had extramarital relationships. From the fragmentary and scattered data on sexual behavior in the village in the 1930s, it seems almost certain that the peasant community was no longer capable of imposing as strong sanctions against pre- and extramarital sex as it had formerly done. Note, for example, the letter from a kolkhoznitsa from the Western oblast deploring the fact that "in the villages girls are losing their honor at a young age" to boys who later disappear, "which is why a reduction of legal marriages is occurring in the Soviet countryside."[69]

Single mothers in the kolkhoz were a sufficiently important category to be noted in the legislation on homeless children. One such young woman— admittedly, an uncharacteristically self-confident and educated one—recalled that, when she returned from the big city in 1930 and joined the kolkhoz as an unmarried, pregnant eighteen–year-old, the village women "gave me dirty looks, and wouldn't put me to work anywhere." Five years later, however, she had become kolkhoz accountant and was a candidate member of the party, so "they take account of me."[70]

The minutes of a village discussion of the draft abortion law of 1936, published in a Leningrad newspaper as part of the general nationwide discussion of the government's proposal to outlaw abortion and restrict divorce, provide an unusual insight into the attitudes of peasant women on such matters.[71] The women of the "Great Path" kolkhoz in Leningrad oblast were generally against abortion, which from their point of view was primarily an urban phenomenon. They thought abortions were dangerous ("A person can die from abortions"). They thought they encouraged male promiscuity ("If a man has no children, he will take up with one woman today, another tomorrow"). In addition, they had a firm belief that what they had suffered, others ought to suffer also: "Our mothers gave birth, we gave birth, and the young women ought to give birth." "I bore 9 children and survived it. Let others do no less."

True, there were some dissident interjections, evidently from the young.

VOICE FROM THE CORNER: But how can you get an education if you have children?

ANSWER FROM A NEIGHBOR: Sweetheart, for the time being you've got to keep your tail down (*poprigladit' khvostik*). . . .

WOMAN IN RED KERCHIEF [regretfully]: And I was just wanting to have an abortion.

INTERJECTION OF NEIGHBOR: No, now you can give birth to a kolkhoznik. (Laughter)

Many of the peasant women argued strongly that those who had abortions should be punished. This was directed mainly at urban women, who were spoken of contemptuously as persons with low morals, and angrily as potential seducers of village men.

ALEKSANDRA IUDINA [an elderly kolkhoznitsa, chair of the meeting]: What punishment should there be for abortions? Let's talk about that.

VOICES: Public shaming (*poritsanie*) is not enough for an illegal abortion.

OLGA ANUFRIEVA: They ought to give more for the first time pregnancy— a 600–ruble fine for them.

TATIANA ELIZAROVA: They ought to send city women to jail and fine village women 300 rubles. Then they wouldn't chase after men.

IUDINA: That means fining them [village women] for the first offence?

VOICES: Yes, yes! People don't have many abortions in the village.

The women expressed a lot of anger against men, particularly unfaithful or absent husbands. The proposals in the draft law to penalize men who had many marriages and punish those who defaulted on child-support payments were greeted with enthusiasm. Furthermore, the women wanted to abolish "free" (unregistered) marriage, since this only encouraged male irresponsibility.

ANNA ZAITSEVA: The husband ought to pay for registering divorce. Marriage should be registered compulsorily, and de facto marriages not recognized. Dissipated men (*rasputniki*) ought to be put in prison. My husband is an agronomist. As well as my children he pays child support also to another woman and now has taken a third wife. For people like that, there's nothing for it but prison.

For this group, indeed, the draft law did not go far enough in punishing errant men. It provided for a registration fee of 50 rubles for a first divorce, 150 for a second, and 300 for a third. But the women of "Great Path" kolkhoz voted to raise this to 200 rubles, 500, and 600 rubles respectively.[72]

Education

The 1930s was a decade of expansion of rural education, paid for by the peasants via a special cultural tax and local "self-taxation" levies. Universal primary education (grades one through four) became mandatory in both urban and rural areas of the Soviet Union from the 1930–31 school year. For rural schools, grade five was to become mandatory for all students from the 1937–38 school year, grade six from the subsequent year, and grade seven from 1939–40. In principle, therefore, all peasant children were receiving at least seven years of schooling at the end of the 1930s, compared with four years at the beginning of the decade.[73]

In practice, the situation was more complicated; but all the same there is no doubt that the number of rural children in primary and secondary school increased greatly in the 1930s. In rural primary schools, the number of pupils rose from 8 to 14 million between 1928–29 and 1932–33, thereafter remaining until the war in the 14–16 million range. In rural secondary school (grades five through seven), the number of pupils more than tripled over the period 1932–33 to 1940–41, reaching almost 7 million. The ratio of rural primary to rural secondary pupils (grades five through seven), which had been 5:1 in 1932–33, shrunk to less than 2:1 by 1940–41. In addition, there were almost a million pupils in rural grades eight through ten in 1940–41, a tenfold increase for the decade.[74]

To be sure, access to education in the Russian countryside was still skewed, as it had been in the 1920s, by the preponderance of overage pupils in the primary grades. In practice, peasant children were both starting and finishing school late. The 12–14 age group, for example, should have been in grades five through seven. But in fact, 53 percent of the twelve to fourteen year olds who were in rural schools in 1937 were still in the primary grades.[75]

The impressive expansion of primary and secondary education in the countryside in the course of the 1930s suggests that peasants were becoming increasingly convinced of the benefits of education. This was undoubtedly related to their perception that education was a ticket out of the kolkhoz for the younger generation.

All the same, many peasants initially resented the laws making primary and then junior secondary education compulsory. In 1930 and 1931, the years of greatest resistance, compulsory primary education was perceived as part of the same pattern of state coercion that produced collectivization. Similar rumors flew around about the school as about the kolkhoz: for example, that pupils would be branded with the mark of Antichrist; that girls weighing 64 kilos would be sent to China; or that their plaits would be cut off and used for scrap.[76]

In the longer term, peasant resentment against compulsory education focused primarily on its cost. The expansion of rural education was financed largely by a new tax—the cultural tax (*kul'tzhilsbor*), introduced in 1931 that placed a heavy burden on the peasantry (fifteen to eighty rubles per household, with the average peasant household paying almost as much in cultural tax as it paid in agricultural tax). On top of this, peasants had to pay for the upkeep of the school and other related expenses out of "self-taxation" (*samooblozhenie*), a form of local taxation of the peasantry that in the 1930s retained not even a vestige of the voluntary principle associated with it in the 1920s and was highly unpopular. Kolkhoz households paid between five and twenty rubles in self-taxation in 1934. Finally, peasants had to pay out of their own pockets for their children's books and writing materials, as well as providing them with clothes and shoes to go to school. [77]

The adult literacy of the rural population also increased in the 1930s, although by no means as spectacularly as Soviet propagandists claimed. According to the census figures, the literacy of the rural population in the

9–49 age group increased from 51 percent in 1926 to 84 percent in 1939. For rural men in the age group, that meant a rise from 67 percent literacy in 1926 to 92 percent in 1939; for rural women, a rise from 35 percent to 77 percent. Now that the suppressed 1937 figures have emerged, the 1939 figures look a little high and should probably be adjusted downwards by 7–8 percent. Even so, the overall increase was impressive—or would have been, had the regime not been claiming 90 percent adult literacy for the Soviet population since 1932.[78]

Problems of the Village School

The welfare of the rural school depended very much on the attitude of the chairmen of the rural soviet. The raion education department was also important, in that it controlled teachers' appointments and determined priorities for school building. But it was the rural soviet that was responsible for collecting and disbursing "self-taxation" funds, providing housing and a vegetable plot for the teachers, heating the schools, and general maintenance of the school buildings. The rural soviet also paid the teacher's salary until 1936, when this responsibility was shifted to the raion education department.[79]

The local collective farms (and their chairmen) could also play a major role in facilitating or impeding rural education. If the kolkhoz chairman were not willing to help with transport for a school that was a substantial distance from the village, children from that kolkhoz were unlikely to be regular attenders. If the children were to get a hot meal at school, the local collective farm(s) would have to provide the wherewithall. If school repairs were to be carried out, that generally meant sending a kolkhoznik carpenter and crediting him with labordays. Finally, if the kolkhoz chairman sent all the twelve or fourteen year olds out to work in the kolkhoz fields, as sometimes happened, they were not going to be sitting in school.[80]

For rural soviet chairmen, schools were a low priority; their main duties were collecting taxes and facilitating procurements. "My work is grain procurements. The school has nothing to do with me," one chairman said testily. This attitude was quite understandable. In the words of another rural soviet chairman, "whatever fuss they make against compulsory primary education and the campaign against illiteracy, all the same, they won't put you in prison for weakness on that front." The national newspaper of the teachers' union, *Za kommunisticheskoe prosveshchenie*, did not often have a good word to say about rural soviet chairmen. But occasionally it discovered a just man: For example, "Comrade Baranov at the rural soviet is a real fighter for the Soviet school. He comes to the school to check the temperature; he did his best about firewood and meals for the children."[81]

In another case reported by the newspaper, the chairman of a rural soviet in Novgorod raion led a community effort to build a junior secondary school so that the local children would not have to go up to 30 kilometers for grades five through seven. The raion refused to authorize the financial allocation for a new school building. But under the leadership of the rural soviet chairman, the peasants of seven small collective farms in the area went ahead on their own. The timber and labor they provided themselves; and for nails, window glass, and other industrial materials they turned to their *shef*— a Novgorod factory whose management and workers were supposed to provide advice and practical help for peasants in this particular village.[82]

One of the most galling things for the peasants was that, despite their very substantial involuntary contributions to education through the cultural tax and "self-taxation," there remained many expenses to do with the school that required further individual or collective financing. Peasants complained that they could not send their children to school because they could not afford the books and writing materials, not to mention the boots and clothing, that were necessary.[83]

Almost all the school success stories reported in the press involved local fund-raising among the peasants, often to the tune of thousands of rubles.[84] This could cause further resentment about the relative shares of rural educational costs being borne by the peasants, on the one hand, and the state, on the other. During local soviet elections in 1934, one kolkhoznik, Pavlov, who had recently been fired as brigade leader, got up at the election meeting and made a scene on the issue of school funding. His kolkhoz, which had apparently already made substantial voluntary contributions to the school earlier, was being asked to pledge more in honor of the election, and this was too much for Pavlov. He attacked the government for pushing all the costs of the schools onto the local population, and compared Soviet policies unfavorably with those of the old Tsarist regime. Despite his intervention, however, the kolkhozniks voted the extra funds.[85]

Teachers

Teachers led a difficult and precarious life in the countryside, as they had done since the revolution and before it. They were dependent on village authorities and villagers for many necessities of life. They were at the mercy of raion education departments, which frequently transferred them abruptly from one school to another, forcing them to abandon whatever fragile material base—a decent hut, a small vegetable plot—they had managed to build. One has the impression (although no hard data are available) that a smaller proportion of teachers than in the 1920s were natives of the village in which they taught, and that a smaller proportion were married to peasants or had close relatives in the village who could support them in hard times. Rationed goods that were supposed to be available at the store were sometimes denied. Salaries were paid irregularly, often late. When the teacher's load was increased by the addition of junior secondary classes to an existing primary school, it might be impossible to get authorization from the raion for the appropriate increase in salary.[86]

What it could mean when local authorities were hostile or indifferent is illustrated by the story of a young male teacher who was sent to a village in Kursk oblast for his first job as head of an elementary school.

> From the beginning I encountered major obstruction on the part of the kolkhoz board and the sovkhoz. It was already winter, and there was no firewood in the school. The children worked in overcoats. Despite my pleas, neither the [kolkhoz] board, nor the rural soviet helped. The kolkhoz board had a similarly irresponsible attitude to the repair of the school. . . . [87]

Female teachers—almost half of all teachers in the countryside[88]—were liable to the predictable kinds of harrassment, especially when they arrived as fresh young graduates of teachers' college. One such episode took place in Kineshma raion, Ivanovo oblast, and concerned a new young teacher, educated in an orphanage from which she had been sent to teacher's college, evidently in her first job. The rural soviet chairman and the secretaries of both the party and Komsomol cell in the village made advances that she rebuffed. This led the chairman to have her fired as a "morally unstable person."[89]

Other embarrassments are also reported. In one village school, housed in what had formerly been the priest's house, the priest retained a room separated from the classroom only by a thin partition. He made it his business to wreck the lessons by praying in a loud voice; moreover, "during lessons the priest would come into class and talk to the pupils on 'godly' themes, and even managed to get the pupils to stand up when he entered the classroom." To add insult to injury, the priest was a subscriber to *Pravda*, while the school's teachers had been unable to obtain subscriptions to either *Pravda* or *Izvestiia*.[90]

The housing provided for the teacher was often inadequate. A rural teacher from Kharkov oblast, for example, wrote to the newspaper to complain that he and his wife, also a teacher, were living in an izba whose thatch roof had rotted through, letting in water when it rained, with no place to keep a cow, and no outhouse. The school's director was living in similar conditions, and the fourth teacher, a woman, had "spent all winter living in the director's kitchen and has now moved to the kitchen of the school." The chairman of the rural soviet not only disclaimed any responsibility for upkeep of these buildings but threatened to fine the teachers for failing to repair them.[91]

In 1934, the writer Fedor Gladkov made a trip to his native village in Kuibyshev (formerly Samara) oblast and reported on the dismal condition of education there.[92] Everywhere he went, he wrote, school buildings were run-down and dilapidated. Some had even been used as grain warehouses during procurements. Chernavka, his native village, had a prosperous kolkhoz, but its leaders had no interest in the school, which in earlier (prerevolutionary) times had flourished.

> Once the schoolhouse in Chernavka the school building was not bad. One of the headmasters of the school had lovingly planted the school plot with many

plants. Next door was the teacher's house. Its whole spacious plot was surrounded by a fence. And now the fence has been broken by wandering animals, the trees and plants have run wild, there is rubbish, mud and tall weeds growing round the buildings. The steps of the porch have rotted. When I called the attention of the kolkhoz leaders to its ruined condition, they answered carelessly: "We have no time to think about that. We have grain procurements and threshing to do now. There are no carpenters. And anyway it's no business of ours—it's the rural soviet that ought to worry about schools."

The school lacked exercise books, pencils, and maps until Gladkov himself supplied them. The teachers were demoralized. "They have no assertiveness, no will to struggle, no authority to fight for the school." They felt at the mercy of the local bosses, any one of whom felt free to tell them off.

> It's an absolute crime when . . . the kolkhoz chairman—drunk, to make matters worse—bursts into the school during classes and gives orders in the classroom like a little tyrant! More than one teacher complained to me of his vulnerability: they have bosses "coming out their ears," starting with the raion soviet and education department and ending with the rural soviet chairman and kolkhoz chairman, and the first thing any of them does is give orders. . . .

Historically, rural teachers had always been vulnerable to the arbitrary actions of local authorities. At the same time, as a group apart from the peasant community, they also had the historical legacy of being perceived as agents or at least associates of the state. After the revolution, this duality continued. In the 1920s, rural teachers were held in suspicion by Communists because many of them had been SRs and came from families of prosperous peasants or priests; during the Cultural Revolution, they were often harrassed and sometimes actually "dekulakized." At the same time, the teacher was heavily involved in the state's educational causes (compulsory primary education and the campaign against illiteracy) by the end of the 1920s and often served as an interpreter if not exactly an advocate of the kolkhoz, with the result that teachers as well as Soviet officials and collectivizers were often victims of assault by angry peasants at this period.[93]

When the first shockwaves of collectivization had passed, rural teachers found themselves once again in the ambiguous position of being peculiarly vulnerable to mistreatment by local officials yet at the same time representatives of Soviet power. The teacher was a central figure in the development of a new "Soviet" culture in the village, from organizing the cultural program on revolutionary holidays to conducting propaganda in favor of toothbrushing and running literacy classes. Many teachers were elected to membership of rural soviets[94]—a largely symbolic position that conveyed their association with Soviet values.

The expansion of rural education in the 1930s brought with it a substantial increase in the number of rural teachers, which more than doubled between 1930 and 1940.[95] Many of these raw, new teachers were barely more literate than their pupils. In 1934, there were 60,000 teachers at the beginning of 1934 who had fewer than seven years general schooling. Even two years later, when the situation had improved somewhat, only about a third of all teachers were graduates of teachers' colleges or training courses. As grades five through seven became more common in the countryside, many primary-school teachers with inadequate qualifications were moved up to teach them.[96]

The press began to build up the status of the older generation of teachers (who had suffered most from the suspicion that they were socially or politically "alien" to Soviet power) and hold them up as a model to the new recruits in the mid-1930s. Several newspapers ran stories on dedicated female teachers who had been teaching in the same village schools for thirty years and knew how to inculcate basic skills and keep order. Andrei Bubnov, the education minister of the Russian Republic, took up the same theme in 1936, emphasizing the role of the prerevolutionary cohort (which in Siberia constituted about a fifth of all teachers) as a model for young teachers. In 1939, the Presidium of Supreme Soviet gave honorific orders and medals to more than 4,000 rural teachers in 1939—although admittedly, teachers were only one in a series of professions so recognized, and by no means the first.[97]

Peasant Attitudes to Education

In both the 1920s and the 1930s, peasants who wrote to the authorities on education often asked for a new school to be built in their district or for state financial support for their children's schooling, notably free meals, writing equipment, and textbooks, and help with clothing. Such requests were fairly standard, and it is difficult to make good comparative assessments of how broadly and strongly such opinions were held in the village.[98]

One indication that peasants were putting a higher valuation on school education after collectivization than they had done before is the rapid expansion of the rural school system. It is true that the government had made primary school compulsory in the early 1930s and declared its commitment to universal primary, and then to universal seven–year, education. But state intentions alone are rarely enough to achieve such changes, especially when most of the costs of educational expansion were being paid directly by the peasants. One must suppose that the schools were probably satisfying peasant needs to a greater extent than they had done before collectivization.[99]

One possible reason for this was that at the beginning of the 1930s, the regime had dropped its former support of progressive educational methods —a bête noire of peasant parents who insistently demanded that their children be taught the basic skills of reading, writing, and arithmetic. The educational reforms of the early 1930s, a decisive repudiation of the educational experimentation of the 1920s, ended the complaints from peasants about the irrelevance of the school curriculum that were so frequent in the previous period. These reforms reinstated not only traditional teaching methods but also to a large degree the traditional school curriculum: In 1934, the Central Committee even warned schools not to burden schoolchildren with too much ideology (Marxist-Leninist theory, resolutions of party congresses) because it was beyond their understanding and bored them.[100]

A more important reason for the shift in attitude, however, was that education had acquired specific practical utility for peasant parents and children. Previously only a minority of urban-oriented peasants had seen education as a way of improving their situation in life. In the 1930s, as a result of the devaluation of the village attendant upon collectivization and the passport restrictions on peasant mobility, virtually all peasants seem to have acquired this perception. Education was a ticket out of the kolkhoz. It was the means of entry into the urban wage-earning classes, a privileged group in peasant eyes, occupying a superior position to their own in Soviet society.

Naturally there were some peasant parents who took a narrow view of self-interest, reasoning that if they let their child stay in school after grade four, he was liable to "go away and forget us," whereas with only four years of education, "he will work in the kolkhoz and earn his bread and will feed me." But most peasant parents either put the welfare of the children first or calculated that a wage-earning child, even if absent from the village, was a better bet for support in old age. The children had a particularly clear view of the connection between education and opportunity. In a rural school in Serpukhov raion, Moscow oblast, for example, all the pupils in grades five through seven wanted to continue their education.[101]

Because it was so important to go on to further schooling outside the village, a large share of all peasant comments about education had to do with impediments to departure or difficulties of access to higher education for peasants. The archives are full of petitions from young kolkhozniks to continue their education, and complaints when the opportunity was denied. In the opinion of one petitioner, the new Soviet Constitution should forbid the kolkhoz to impede the departure of young peasants for further schooling, regardless of whether it needed their labor.[102]

Another common complaint was that secondary technical schools and colleges in towns should be more accessible to peasants, either via admissions quotas (like the ones that had existed for proletarians and their children in the 1920s) or more generous provision of stipends. The state should have preferential quotas so that children of kolkhozniks would be as well represented in higher education as those of other social groups, one correspondent wrote during the discussion on the Constitution. Otherwise, "it means that only children of teachers, doctors, engineers, professors, and so on can go to higher educational institutions."[103]

The utility of education in the collectivized village was not limited to facilitating departure. It was useful for self-advancement within the rural context, too. The kolkhoz had created a structure of rewards for kolkhozniks based on the acquisition of special skills and formal qualifications, the like of which had never existed in the countryside. If a kolkhoznik was sent off to the raion center to take a six–week course in bookkeeping or chicken breeding, that opened the path for promotion from ordinary fieldworker to a higher status and better paying position as kolkhoz bookkeeper or head of the chicken sheds. Thus, there was keen competition among kolkhozniks to take such courses (selection for which was usually the kolkhoz chairman's prerogative). Peasants wrote many letters of complaint about not being selected to take a driving course, or a course in accountancy or animal husbandry. They also wrote in to protest if, after having taken such a course, they were not given the appropriate recognition and skilled job in the kolkhoz or MTS.[104]

Peasant letters of the 1930s convey a strong conviction that education was a *right*. In support of this view, they cited the new Constitution.

"I consider that each citizen, including the kolkhoznik, has the right to education. It says so in the draft of the new Constitution," wrote a young kolkhoznik from Leningrad oblast, indignant that the kolkhoz board had denied him the opportunity to go away to study. "It is written in letters of gold in the Stalin Constitution that every citizen of the Soviet Union has the right to study," asserted a kolkhoznik from Voronezh oblast, angry at having been denied permission to take courses to qualify as a tractor driver or chauffeur.[105]

These were firm statements of values that are clearly "Soviet," not part of the peasant's traditional value system. It was a rare example from the 1930s of wholehearted adoption by most adult peasants of a key component of Soviet ideology, namely the centrality of education as a means of individual self-advancement as well as social betterment.

9

Malice

Malice, anger, and bitterness were rife in the village in the decade after collectivization. It was the state that had initiated collectivization and forced it through against the will of the peasants, and no doubt it was the state and its agents that were the primary objects of peasant resentment. But they were not the only objects, for a great deal of peasant anger was directed against other peasants. Although collectivization was a trauma for the peasantry as a whole, this did not mean that it contributed to peasant or village solidarity. On the contrary, the Russian village (kolkhoz) of the 1930s seems to have been a place in which feuds and dissension flourished and mutual support and solidarity among peasants were a rarity. To be sure, the state would scarcely have welcomed the emergence of a real spirit of collective solidarity on the new collective farms, since that would have raised the possibility of active collective resistance and perhaps revived communal traditions that the state wanted to bury. But there is no sign that the peasants were striving towards village unity and harmony as a balm for the wounds inflicted during collectivization. On the contrary, a spirit of free-floating malice seems to have hovered over the Russian village throughout the 1930s.

A number of circumstances created or intensified discord within the village. The first was the violence and general lawlessness generated by collectivization, expressed in the first half of the decade primarily in banditry, attacks on Soviet officials and sel'kory, and fights between collectivized and noncollectivized peasants, and in the second half of the decade by attacks on Stakhanovites. The second was the ambiguous status of kulaks and peasants who had been dekulakized, which continued to cause problems throughout the prewar period. The third was the intense feuding within many villages, often related to injuries and grievances arising out of collectivization and dekulakization, but also fueled by the desire of competing peasant factions to gain control of kolkhoz offices and patronage. The fourth was the widespread peasant practice of writing complaints and denunciations to the authorities—a habit that had some historical precedent but was also encouraged by the Soviet regime.

Crime and Violence

Banditry, which had died down during the 1920s after flourishing during the Civil War, revived again as a result of collectivization. Expropriated kulaks often led the new bandit groups, which were said to be smaller than those of the Civil War, generally numbering two to five persons. They were armed mainly with revolvers, sawed-off shotguns, and hunting rifles, according to a 1934 police report from the Western oblast, but the average band in this region had only one or two firearms. Collective farms and kolkhoz activists were the main targets of their attacks, which included "savage murders" of kolkhoz leaders and physical assaults on kolkhozniks as well as arson and other forms of destruction of kolkhoz property. In Siberia, where banditry was particularly rife, a 1931 survey indicated that more than 40 percent of collective farms had suffered from such attacks. In the Soviet Union as a whole, according to a kolkhoz census in the spring of 1931, one out of six collective farms had experienced bandit attacks.[1]

Although banditry, being a negative social phenomenon, was not generally given much coverage in the Soviet press, some lively accounts appeared from time to time in a Leningrad newspaper, *Krest'ianskaia pravda*. In one case from a village in Porkhov raion (Leningrad oblast), bandits killed a kolkhoz chairman and severely wounded a raion police inspector. The kolkhoz chairman, a Communist 25,000-er, had heard that suspicious persons were hiding at the home of one of the kolkhozniks. When he went with the police inspector to investigate, he found two armed desperados: M. E. Orekhov, nicknamed "The Devil," no fixed address or occupation, and Filaret Druzhinin, nicknamed "The Priest," son of a former archpriest from the district. Orekhov had five criminal convictions, while Druzhinin was on the run from prison, where he was serving time for robbing a kolkhoz. When the kolkhoz chairman and police inspector appeared, the two bandits opened fire with their rifles and made their escape. Orekhov was caught almost immediately, but it was not for some months that Druzhinin was apprehended at his father's apartment in Leningrad, where police found five revolvers and a large quantity of ammunition.[2]

Another case of banditry, this time from a rural soviet in Kresttsy raion, was reported in the same newspaper a month later. Here the bandits were Aleksei Stolbnev, of no fixed address or occupation, and Vasilev-Lavrentev, described as a "fixed-quota" peasant (*tverdozadanets*), that is, a quasi-kulak in Soviet eyes. The two had been in prison, probably for collectivization-related offenses, but escaped and took refuge with Stolbnev's relatives, Petr and Maria Stolbnev, forging identity documents on official stationery provided by a former rural soviet chairman. Having obtained revolvers and a sawed-off rifle from Petr Stolbnev, who himself had earlier convictions for arson and hooliganism, and ammunition from another fixed-quota peasant, they started terrorizing local cadres:

> For some time it has become dangerous for kolkhoz activists . . . to go out at night, especially to go through the forest. People have been shooting at them from the forest, shooting at the men who exposed class enemies and purged the village of hooligans. Naumov, a Communist, has been attacked. Bliunger, the headmaster of the school, has been shot at twice. Gavrilov, the secretary of the rural soviet, and Ulianov, the veterinarian, were saved from death [only] by chance. . . .[3]

Stolbnev and Vasilev-Lavrentev were early recipients of the death sentence for banditry, which was introduced in the Russian Republic in March 1935 and at least for a short time freely applied. In Moscow oblast, 63 percent of those convicted of banditism in the month after the decree were sentenced to death. The use of the death sentence for banditry seems to have disturbed Soviet jurists, but there are indications that it was very popular with the population—a central legal journal even warned judges against being overly influenced by popular sentiment on the question.[4]

In Gorky krai in 1937, the police reported the liquidation of a long-established bandit group, the Romanov gang, known not only for its armed robberies in Voskresenskii raion but also for arson and murderous attacks on rural activists. The gang was said to be led by kulaks and to include young criminals whose parents were "social aliens" (presumably kulaks, priests, Nepmen, and the like, all of whom held a marginal position in society). This was one of the last reports of the type of banditry involving expropriated kulaks taking revenge against the kolkhoz that was endemic in the first years after collectivization. Thereafter, although banditry continued to plague the countryside, it reverted to more traditional forms of raids and robberies carried out against peasant settlements by outlaws in the forest.[5]

"Hooliganism" also flourished in the countryside in the aftermath of collectivization. This was a new form of disorderly behavior, differing markedly from the boisterously iconoclastic, parent-defying, adolescent hooliganism of the 1920s. The new rural hooliganism was surly, vindictive, anti-Soviet, and as often associated with adults as with adolescents. According to a Soviet legal commentator in the mid-1930s, it was generally connected with opposition to state grain procurements or state orders on sowing, and its manifestations included disruption of kolkhoz meetings and physical attacks on officials.[6] Peasants often committed acts of hooliganism after drinking, which not only lent them courage but enabled them to deny anti-Soviet intention afterwards. In contrast to the old rural hooliganism, which challenged traditional peasant values and tended to be associated with the Komsomol and a pro-Soviet orientation, the new hooliganism seems often to have been a form of peasant resistance to the state stemming from resentment of collectivization.

Threats against kolkhoz leaders, defiant outbursts against procurements, beating up of activists, and disruptive conduct at meetings were characteristic of the behavior that was prosecuted under the heading of hooliganism at this time. A legal journal cites one example from a rural soviet where officials had called a meeting to organize collection of peasants' "voluntary" subscriptions to a state loan. "Hooligans" learned of this meeting "and burst in and raised an uproar, breaking the lamp and driving everyone out"; then they went on to vandalize the kolkhoz office. In another case, violence occurred during the procurements season, when a drunken kolkhoznik burst into the barn where threshing was in progress and "started shooting at the kolkhozniks working there, wounding two of them and disrupting the threshing."[7]

A particularly vivid example of defiant hooliganism was provided by a kolkhoznik named Shchedrov, who

> showed up drunk at work during the time of procurements. Riding drunkenly around on a horse, Shchedrov caught sight of the commission for potato procurements and began to insult them and play the fool. Mounting the horse backwards with his face to the tail, he rode through the village jerking the horse's tail and crying "That's how we ought to deliver procurements."[8]

The villages also suffered from more mundane forms of hooliganism expressive of the general demoralization of the population. In the village of Arshinitsa in the Western oblast, a fourteen-year-old boy, the son of a former fixed-quota peasant who had not joined the kolkhoz, shot a fifteen-year-old girl dead in a random act of hostility with no ascertainable motive. A subsequent investigation by the obkom revealed that Arshinitsa and a neighboring village were notorious for hooliganism. According to a sixty-year-old woman from the Arshinitsa kolkhoz,

> "After sunset, we are already used to locking our doors and windows. You can't plant anything in the garden plots. You can't say a word against the hooligans. . . ."[9]

Strange as it may seem, it appears that in the 1930s, as in the 1920s, there was no regular policeman (or NKVD man) at the village level, and small raion-based militia forces did their best to police the surrounding countryside.[10] No wonder that peasants frequently complained that "crimes go unpunished here in the village" and suggested various ways of remedying the situation: for example, that samosud, the village's old form of popular justice, "should simply be allowed by law." In the discussion of the new Constitution in 1936, some peasants also suggested that rural soviet officers should be given the right to arrest hooligans and thieves on the spot, "otherwise they will hide and never be found."[11] In practice, as is clear from many reports and admonitions, rural soviet and kolkhoz officers often assumed this right even without legal authorization. One of the consequence of the under-policing of the countryside was that every administrative official was liable to become a policeman.

In the first half of the 1930s, hostility between kolkhozniks and the "independents" who remained outside the kolkhoz often led to violence and disorder. There were reports of villages where independents pasted leaflets on the windows of kolkhozniks warning that they would all be murdered. In some areas, kolkhozniks came back from working in the fields to find that personal property had been stolen; moreover, this was not normal theft, but "a more demonstrative kind of stealing in which the stolen objects, destroyed, are found not far away."[12]

Violence against kolkhoz leaders and activists was common in the early 1930s. Kolkhoz and rural soviet chairmen were particularly vulnerable, but teachers and other local "intelligentsia" were also at risk. In one village in the Urals, "a group of drunken kolkhozniks burst into the kolkhoz office with shouts of 'bloodsuckers' and tried to beat up the accountant," and, in a separate incident, an angry kolkhoznik who went to the chairman's home and, finding him absent, beat up the chairman's wife instead. In Kirov oblast in 1934, a teacher was seriously wounded when her house was blown up, allegedly to punish her for being a Soviet activist.[13]

Sel'kory—the volunteer newspaper correspondents whose exposure of local wrongdoing was much resented in the village—were often targets of violence in the early 1930s. A famous case of this kind was the murder of Strigunov, a kolkhoz brigade leader and sel'kor in the Voronezh region who had had a longstanding conflict with the dominant group in the village, which now controlled the kolkhoz. Unsuccessful attempts on his life were made in the winter of 1931 and the autumn of 1932 (when a shot fired through window just missed him), and he was finally killed in the summer of 1933. This led to a major campaign by newspapers and judicial organs for greater protection of sel'kory and harsher punishment of persons who attacked them. In 1932, there were 462 prosecutions of such cases in the Russian Republic; in the first half of 1933 alone, 313 prosecutions were logged.[14]

In the second half of the 1930s, kolkhoz Stakhanovites became frequent objects of attack by other villagers envious of the privileges given to them or resenting their collaboration with the Soviet regime. The Stakhanovite movement, which started in industry in 1935 and was quickly applied in agriculture, involved individual workers or kolkhozniks volunteering to overfulfil their work norms and increase output, and being publicly honored and rewarded by the state for doing so. The increase in output was supposed to be achieved by improving or rationalizing production methods, but in the kolkhoz context it often just meant working harder. In agriculture, the male Stakhanovites were usually tractor drivers or combine operators, while the females—much more prominent in the Stakhanovite movement in the countryside than in its counterpart in the town—were often milkmaids or otherwise involved with the care of kolkhoz livestock.

Stakhanovites were resented as scabs and normbusters in all walks of life, but in the village these sentiments were expressed more violently and frequently. Well-known agricultural Stakhanovites often received beatings or death threats from fellow villagers when they returned from the oblast or national conference at which their achievements were celebated. An obscure village Stakhanovite was physically attacked by another kolkhoznik "because at the end of the working day he suggested finishing the scything of the remaining two hectares of seed clover." Female Stakhanovites were often subjected to abuse and attack, both by other women and by men. In Sychevka raion in the Western oblast, nineteen criminal cases linked with the Stakhanovite movement in agriculture were heard in the summer of 1937. The typical offenses against the Stakhanovites were beatings, insults, harrassment of various kinds, and the spoiling of flax worked on by Stakhanovite teams. The victims were mainly women, the attackers male.[15]

During the Great Purges, a peculiar new category of rural crime made its appearance, namely offences committed against NKVD victims and their families or by persons falsely claiming NKVD connections. One such incident was an attempted rape of a kolkhoznitsa from the Krasnodar region, Elena Suslova, whose husband had recently been arrested as an "enemy of the people." As she described the incident in a semiliterate letter of complaint to the newspaper *Krest'ianskaia gazeta*, her attacker, Pantelei Pavlenko, a former chairman of the soviet,

> drank himself stupid, and at eight o'clock in the evening came to the apartment of Elena Suslova and said: "Come to the soviet, the NKVD summons you." The woman was frightened and asked why. He answered: "You won't come back from there," and on the way he said "Everything is in my hands; I can save you, Suslova." She began to implore him, and he threw himself on her and began to do unspeakable things. Suslova began defending herself and begging him [to stop]. Pavlenko said: "If you are stubborn, it will be worse—we'll throw you in prison. You know they are putting people in prison for nothing now."[16]

In another case, also described in a letter of complaint to *Krest'ianskaia gazeta*, a gang of young peasants—at least one of them with a criminal record—terrorized the village of Malinovka in Saratov oblast for more than a year in 1937–38, claiming that their contacts in the raion NKVD made them invulnerable. Once they broke into the house of a kolkhoznik, Arsentii Vukolov, in broad daylight, demanding food and vodka.

> "If you don't give it to us," they told Vukolov, "we will send in information on you that will get you exiled from Saratov oblast." Furthermore, [they] said that they had friends in the raion leadership, especially one worker in the investigative organ of Arkadak raion.[17]

Shadow of the Kulak

Although the kulaks of the Russian village had been expropriated and in many cases deported or sent to gulag, that was not the last to be heard from them. Their shadow hung over the countryside throughout the 1930s. Dekulakization left behind it an untidy jumble of petitions, legal actions, and property claims whose resolution dragged on for years. Relatives of deported or arrested kulaks, tarred by association, thrashed around trying to free themselves from the taint. A small proportion of former kulaks, expropriated but not arrested or deported, and choosing for whatever reason not to follow the majority course of fleeing to the towns, looked for ways of surviving in the countryside. The "unmasking" of former kulaks who were trying to conceal their old identities became a familiar ritual in collective and state farms as well as in urban workplaces. In the countryside, peasants engaged in internal village feuds learned that no argument impressed Soviet authorities so much as the accusation (whether justified or not) that the opponent had "kulak ties."

If the kulaks (real or imaginary) had gone, a new category of trouble-makers had taken their place: the dekulakized (*raskulachennye*). The existence of former kulaks produced endless legal and administrative problems. Should they be allowed to enter the kolkhoz, if their behavior indicated spiritual regeneration? Should they be allowed to return to the village if they had earlier been deported? Could they be reintegrated into society, and if so, how and where? Despite a prohibition on the return of the deported kulaks to their native villages, a number did return, ready whenever an opportunity presented itself to lay claim to the house that had been confiscated for use as the kolkhoz office or the samovar that had become the property of a kolkhoznik, and others who had settled in nearby towns made periodic visits reminding villagers of these potential claims. Some former kulaks joined kolkhozy in the latter half of the decade, and this was probably legal, although—by a bizarre twist of Soviet administrative logic—its legality was secret. Some even became kolkhoz chairmen, which was not illegal but was deeply disapproved of.

The party leadership appeared uncertain and was probably divided about how to handle the question of former kulaks. Peasants, for their part, seem to have contemplated the potential and actual return of the dekulakized with a very wary eye. This was not so much because of any longstanding hatred of kulaks as because the return of the dispossessed would start a new cycle of recrimination and revenge and raise all kinds of awkward questions about the disposition of confiscated kulak property.

Policy Toward Former Kulaks

State and party policy on kulaks in the 1930s (after the last of the dekulak-ization campaigns in 1932–33) was remarkably incoherent and sometimes self-contradictory. The two big issues were whether deported kulaks and their children could recover full civil rights, including the right of return, and whether former kulaks and their children were eligible to become kolkhoz members.

Deported kulaks legally recovered their civil rights in May 1934—but, as a supplementary decree in January 1935 explained, this did not mean that they had the right to move from their current places of settlement. Thus the apparent concession turned out to be virtually meaningless. The deported kulaks were not allowed to return home, and that prohibition remained in force until the late 1940s or early 1950s (although the children of deported kulaks recovered their freedom of movement in 1938).[18]

It seems, however, that there was a moment when the party leadership (or part of it) really did consider letting the deported kulaks return to their native villages. Iakovlev, head of the agriculture department of the Central Committee, seemed to imply that this was a possibility in his speech to the Second Congress of Kolkhoz Shockworkers in 1935 on the proposed Kolkhoz Charter. But the suggestion was received unenthusiastically by delegates, and it was not publicly raised again.[19]

On the question of the eligibility of former kulaks for kolkhoz membership, the Kolkhoz Charter approved by the Second Congress in March 1935 sought to clarify the issue but only succeeded in confusing it. In this instance, too, Iakovlev seems to have taken a "soft" position, suggesting that former kulaks who had truly mended their ways might be admitted to the kolkhoz. This was the reading of the relevant paragraph of the Charter that he later gave to party activists, but it was in fact not exactly what that paragraph said. The text of the Charter allowed children of kulaks to join collective farms, and it also allowed deported kulaks and their families to join or form kolkhozy in their new places of settlement. What it omitted to say was whether former kulaks who had *not* been deported were allowed to join the kolkhoz in their native village.[20]

In December 1935, some subterranean wave in high party politics produced a new attempt to define and resolve the kulak question. We are told by a Soviet historian that the Central Committee decided to lift the ban on admitting former kulaks to the kolkhoz during the discussions that led to the resolution on collectivized agriculture in the non-Black Earth belt. The Central Committee must also have decided to keep its decision secret from all but a limited circle of Communist officials, for it is not to be found in the published text of the decree and no reference to it appeared in the contemporary press.[21]

In an almost simultaneous development, Stalin and Iakovlev seem to have cooperated in staging a little drama about the redemption of kulaks' children at a conference of Stakhanovite combine operators. One of the delegates, A. G. Tilba from Bashkiria, identified himself as the son of a deported kulak who had worked his way up from being a laborer on a construction site to becoming a record-breaking combine operator on a sovkhoz. Because of his kulak origins, however, local authorities were unwilling to send him to a national Stakhanovite conference despite his achievements, and it required Iakovlev's intervention to get him invited.[22]

As Tilba had finished telling this story, Stalin called out encouragingly from the floor: "A son does not answer for his father." The remark was reported in the press, along with other proceedings of the congress, and the words quickly became part of Soviet folklore. Uncharacteristically, however, the theme was not taken up and developed in the press; there were even some indications of disagreement with the policy of relaxing vigilance against the children of class enemies.[23]

The policy of reconciliation with former class enemies was still in place when the new Stalin Constitution was unveiled in 1936, although there had been discord and uncertainty behind the scenes during the two years of its drafting. The Constitution guaranteed voting and other civil rights to all citizens, including former kulaks. While this had partly been anticipated by earlier legislation, Communists and kulaks alike seem to have seen it as a turning point. In Sychevka raion in the Western oblast, the party secretary called a meeting of rural soviet chairmen and instructed them to destroy all the lists of kulaks, disenfranchised persons, and fixed-quota peasants that survived from the early 1930s. There was still no official announcement that admission of former kulaks to kolkhoz membership was now permissible, but it is clear that the practice was widespread by 1937. Some former kulaks took the Constitution as a sign that it was time to petition for the return of the land and property that had been confiscated from them.[24]

Many peasants participating in the organized nationwide discussion of the new Constitution expressed doubts about the policy of reconciliation with former kulaks. The kulaks are gloating, wrote one kolkhoznik from Gorky krai, because they see this as the beginning of the restoration of the old order. They are waiting to get their revenge on everyone who took part in or profited from the expropriations of 1930. Thus it would be very bad if former kulaks got access to administrative offices, and even allowing them to vote and stand as candidates in soviet elections is premature. Only the kulaks' children, "those young people [who] have already soaked up our values and do not share the opinions of their fathers," are ready for this. It is no good to let the former kulaks and other exploiters vote and stand as candidates, wrote another, because even if they seem to have become reconciled with Soviet power, they are inwardly "full of malice and hatred . . . and undoubtedly, according to their old habit, will start beating the former toiling proletarians, who often even now have not fully become prosperous and among whom there are many illiterate and semiliterate persons, with their bronze tail (*sic*)."[25]

These lingering suspicions burst out once again during the Great Purges, both at local level and in the center. We have already seen that in July 1937 Stalin ordered the roundup and execution of tens of thousands of former kulaks returned from deportation and other "habitual criminals." A few months later, the Sychevka officials who had tried to implement the class reconciliation policy were charged in a local show trial with "favoring kulaks." Everywhere, persons with kulak connections or a kulak past found themselves vulnerable to the new wave of terror, and many former "class enemies" were swept away as "enemies of the people."[26]

Survival Strategies

Most of the kulaks who were expropriated but not deported or imprisoned fled from the villages to the cities. Nevertheless, quite a number of former kulaks remained in the countryside, leading a socially marginal (though occasionally prosperous) existence. Some remained in their native villages; others moved in with relatives in other villages in the neighborhood. Since their animals and equipment had been taken from them and they were not allowed to join collective farms in the first years after collectivization, they had difficulty reestablishing themselves as farmers. The formal provision that "category 3" kulaks should be resettled on inferior land within the raion seems to have had little meaning. In real life, the former kulaks were left to fend for themselves. That meant not only finding a way of making a living but also finding a house in which to live (since their houses were taken by the kolkhoz when they were dekulakized).

What were they to do? In order to survive, the former kulaks were virtually obliged to violate Soviet law in some way, and that is what they regularly did. Some acquired a plot of land, illegally or by devious pretexts, and cultivated it. This could often be done by bribing a rural soviet or kolkhoz chairman, since there was an active (though illegal) business whereby collective farms rented out plots belonging to absent villagers. Squatting on state land was also practiced. In Donetsk oblast in 1935, it was reported that local "kulaks" (presumably, dekulakized peasants) were among those who had illegally taken possession of a plot of state land, built a hut and a barn on it with timber stolen from the state forest, and set about cultivating it. As an indignant report noted, until they were caught these peasants were in the happy situation of paying no taxes and being issued with no sowing plans or procurements quotas.[27]

Some former kulaks resettled in another village and made a living as craftsmen, black market traders, or (in one reported case) as a horse trainer; some used personal connections to move to a new place and join a kolkhoz. To buy a house in the village—let alone to get a private plot—involved all sorts of dubious transactions. In one case, a former "kulak," probably a peasant bootmaker who had been expelled from his own village, settled in a village in a neighboring raion, where he obtained a white-collar job from a Communist patron who was head of the local department of roads. He also set up a bootmaking enterprise employing two hired hands and sold boots and black market clover seed (for 250 rubles a pud) and occasionally vodka. The kolkhoz in his new village gave him a plot of land confiscated from a local peasant (presumably after he had bribed the kolkhoz chairman), and in addition the rural soviet approved his purchase of an orchard.[28]

Many dekulakized kulaks, of course, went to live in towns. But this did not necessarily mean that they were lost from sight. Often the town was quite close, and the departed kulaks made periodic trips back to their native village—generally, in the view of the authorities, upsetting the kolkhozniks or causing some sort of trouble. In an autobiographical novella, Mikhail Alekseev recalls the regular visits to his Saratov village of a group of dekulakized peasants who had relocated to the outskirts of the city of Saratov and were engaged in profitable black market trade. A 1937 newspaper report on a village in the Simferopol district noted that "the kulaks sent out of the village . . . in the period of dekulakization often come to visit," and that the former village mullah had made a return visit too, badmouthing Soviet power in his conversations with the villagers. In the village of Mokhovatka in Voronezh oblast, all the kulaks went off to work in Voronezh and other towns at the time of collectivization, but a few years later a group of them returned secretly one night and beat up one of the kolkhoz organizers, almost killing him.[29]

The dekulakizations of the early 1930s left a host of legal, property, and family complications that dragged on through the decade. Some dekulakized peasants arranged fictitious divorces in order to leave property to their wives, although such cases were viewed skeptically by the authorities. In the Urals, for example, one wife of a deported kulak sued for the return of confiscated marital property on the grounds that she herself was not a peasant but working-class. (The suit was rejected because she had lived and worked as a peasant and kulak's wife for the five years preceding dekulakization.)[30]

In a case that caught the attention of a central legal journal, a kulak's wife suing for return of half their confiscated property used the rhetoric of women's liberation: While conceding that her husband was indeed a kulak, she claimed that for the twenty years of their married life she had essentially been a oppressed laborer (*batrachka*) to her husband, not a fellow exploiter. Another peasant's wife, expelled with her husband from the kolkhoz on the grounds that her late father-in-law had been a trader, also couched her petition to the People's Commissariat of Agriculture in quasi-feminist terms. It was wrong, she argued, for the kolkhoz to have treated her as a mere appendage to her husband: Their cases should have been considered separately. Whatever judgement might be made about her husband's social position, she wrote, she herself came from a family of poor peasants, had never known her father-in-law (who died in 1922), and therefore "could not have been infected by his ideology."[31]

For the deported kulaks, return to the native village was forbidden. This did not mean, however, that none returned. Many kulaks immediately ran away from the places to which they had been sent as deportees or convicts, although if they returned to their native villages they were often caught and sent back again. Among such unsuccessful escapees were several brothers of the poet Aleksandr Tvardovskii. It was also possible for deportees to leave their new place of residence by bribing the rural soviet chairman to authorize their departure as otkhodniks. (According to a recent study, this was the real offence for which Pavlik Morozov, the famous child informer, denounced his father, a rural soviet chairman.)[32]

Paradoxically, the legal ban on return to the native village applied only to deported ("second category") kulaks, not to the "first category" kulaks who had been judged so dangerous that they had to be sent to prison or labor camp. At least some of these returned to their villages after serving three or five years, and were the source of many troubles and conflicts.[33]

It was undoubtedly safer for returnees to live somewhere other than their native villages, where their identities were known to the authorities. This was the course chosen by Piliugin, a peasant from the Donetsk, who returned to the region in 1934 after having been deported by the OGPU a few years earlier for speaking against the kolkhoz. Although the Piliugin family had held on to a private plot in the village, Piliugin decided that it would be more prudent to go elsewhere. He sold his house and plot to a local peasant (an illegal transaction) and went off to another district in the region, where he settled illegally on state land and built himself a house. (Later, being an entrepreneurial type, he sold this house and land to someone else for 400 rubles, and repeated the whole process.)[34]

Other returning kulaks checked in at the village only in order to get the documentation necessary for a new life in the town. In Liubyshe village in the Western oblast, for example, Vasilii Kuzin, a kulak "well known not only in Liubyshe but in all Diaktovo raion" as a big trader and leaser of land, returned in 1935 after five years in exile. His daughter was apparently a kolkhoz activist, and his son was a party member. Kuzin persuaded the rural soviet chairman to reinstate him and his wife as citizens with the right to vote, then successfully applied for a passport and went off to the nearest town.[35]

The situation for former kulaks improved after the Central Committee's unpublicized decision at the end of 1935 to allow reformed kulaks to enter the kolkhoz. But of course that decision also created new problems, one of the most vexing of which concerned the kulaks' former dwellings in the village. These houses, confiscated from kulaks during collectivization, were usually the best in the village. They became the legal property of the kolkhoz (though they were sometimes coveted and seized by superior authorities), and were often used to accommodate kolkhoz offices, clubs, schools, nurseries, or other community enterprises. The houses, although not the plots on which they stood, could be more or less legally sold. When former kulaks were admitted the kolkhoz, the first thing many of them did was try to get back their old houses.

In 1936, reports of the return of houses to former kulaks began to appear regularly in the press. In Borisovka raion of Kursk oblast, for example, at least seventy-five houses were returned to the kulaks who were their former owners in 1936 and the first half of 1937, despite the protests of other villagers; and similar cases were reported elsewhere in the oblast.[36] Probably most of these transactions were actually sales by the kolkhoz to the former owner, although this was rarely stated explicitly in the reports. But there were also cases where peasants who had been dekulakized (some still living in the village, others not) interpreted the new policy line on kulaks to mean that they could appeal for the restitution without payment of property that had been improperly confiscated from them during collectivization.[37]

But such transfers rarely happened without ill feeling and fights, since returning the houses to their former owners meant evicting an incumbent resident. Resentment against the return of kulaks' houses was expressed by peasant witnesses in some of the raion show trials of 1937. In a trial in Kursk raion, for example officials were accused of showing favor to former kulaks who had returned from deportation or labor camp by allowing them to join the kolkhoz and in some cases get their houses back; and two of the allegedly favored kulaks were on trial along with the officials. In a similar trial in Smolensk oblast, peasant witnesses testified to the "enormous damage" done by the former kulaks who were appointed kolkhoz chairmen.[38]

In the same spirit, a peasant correspondent from Kursk oblast wrote indignantly to *Krest'ianskaia gazeta* describing how one enterprising kolkhoz chairman had coped with the harvest failure that in 1936–37 left his kolkhoz close to economic collapse and caused twenty kolkhoz households to flee from the region in search of food and wages. This chairman "began to recruit kulaks into the kolkhoz, telling the kulaks `You pay for the houses and you can come and live and work in the kolkhoz'." In this manner, he sold eight houses with their attached plots to former kulaks—thus providing himself (or, to be more charitable, the kolkhoz) with what was probably the only significant income for the year.[39]

Once former kulaks were admitted to the kolkhoz, the possibility existed that these people, many of whom must have played a dominant role in village life before collectivization, would once again assume positions of leadership. This was clearly not a development that Soviet authorities were likely to welcome. Whether peasants would welcome it is another question, and one not easy to answer. The turn in the mid-1930s towards greater "kolkhoz democracy," that is, giving peasants more of a say in the selection of kolkhoz chairmen, certainly offered the possibility that the power in the village would gravitate back to the old leading families of the village. As far as can be judged on the basis of the available evidence, this indeed happened in some cases. But the watchfulness of the authorities—and perhaps the peasants' own ambivalent attitude to the kulaks' return—seems to have prevented it from becoming a very widespread phenomenon.

Interpreting the evidence on former kulaks and kolkhoz leadership is complicated by the fact that when peasants wrote denunciations and complaints about their kolkhoz chairmen (a subject discussed later in this chapter), they almost invariably called them "kulaks," regardless of their actual social status in the past, because this was a good way of damaging them in the eyes of Soviet authorities. Nevertheless, it is often possible to work out whether the accusation is more or less true or more or less false, and thus draw some conclusions on the actual state of affairs.

It seems to have been highly unusual for a 100 percent kulak—one who, as the head of a household, had been dekulakized in the first or second category and deported or imprisoned—to return to the village and become a kolkhoz chairman in the second half of the 1930s.[40] But there are quite a number of reports of the *sons* of deported kulaks becoming kolkhoz chairmen, and of collective farms with nonkulak chairmen that were alleged nevertheless to be run from behind the scenes by "kulak cliques." In addition, as we shall see later in the chapter, there were peasants who complained that even in the kolkhoz they were still bedniaks, and the prosperous peasants who had always run things in the village were still mistreating them.

For example, in one kolkhoz in Leningrad oblast in 1935, a kulak's son was chairman of the kolkhoz, another son was a brigade leader, and the father, also a kolkhoz member, worked as the kolkhoz swineherd and had recently been rewarded (by his chairman son) with a gift of two pigs. In another kolkhoz, this one in the Western oblast, the chairman was the son of a former starosta who had recently returned to the village after serving time in prison for opposing collectivization. In Tambov oblast, a man who held a series of management positions including kolkhoz chairmanships throughout the 1930s was the son of a prosperous miller and dairy owner who had prudently disposed of his various assets on the eve of collectivization.[41]

To have held an office of rural leadership—volost *starshina* or village starosta—before collectivization was often counted in the 1930s as the equivalent of having been a kulak, and was even sometimes grounds for dekulakization. "Who serves as deputy chairman of the raion soviet? Viktor Davydov—son of the starshina," wrote a sel'kor, clinching his case that the raion leadership was filled with kulak wreckers. In at least one case, the spontaneous reelection of kolkhoz chairmen that occurred in many villages in 1936–38 involved the replacement of an unpopular raion nominee by the kolkhozniks' choice—the former starshina.[42]

Village Feuds

Village society was factious and contentious in the 1930s. Some feuds undoubtedly sprung from family or ethnic rivalries that may have divided villages for generations. But many feuds and grievances arose out of conflicts generated by great public events. First among these were collectivization and dekulakization, episodes that were by their nature divisive and in which some peasants improved their position in the village and many others were deeply injured. But the animosities of the Civil War period were important as well, and even envies and grievances going back to the prewar Stolypin agrarian reforms were not forgotten.

The object of many village feuds in the latter part of the 1930s was to win office in the kolkhoz and thus control kolkhoz assets and patronage. Previously, in the days of the peasant mir, office had not conferred such benefits and had not usually been coveted. But there were drawbacks to holding office under the new order, notably increased vulnerability to arrest. If there was, as it appears, an upsurge of village feuding and faction fighting in the 1930s, this was probably the result both of the collapse of traditional communal structures that promoted village solidarity and unity, and of the new weapons (expulsion from the kolkhoz, denunciation for kulak origin or ties with enemies of the people) that were to hand in the collectivized village.

Settling Scores

K. R. Berdnikov, do you remember what a parasite you were before the revolution, how you exploited the village with your steam windmill. . . . Do you remember how your corn-bin burst with grain when the village was swelling from hunger. . . . Do you remember how in the years of the Civil War you took others' valuables for a bucketful of potatoes and how you swapped a bowl of soup for a whole harness. Do you remember how you burst into the rural soviet and how many poor peasants you put in the basement and beat about the face. . . . Can you count the batraks whose backs were bent for you? . . .

K. F. Petrin, do not hide in the rags of a poor peasant. They are soaked in the blood of Communists whom you betrayed in 1919. . . . In 1919, two Red Army communards were living with you. . . . Cossacks came from the band of Shkuro and Mamontov, and you whistled and waved your hand to them so that they came over . . . and you showed them where the communards were hiding. . . . You thought people had forgotten about that. No, everyone knows it. They know that you are willing to betray any kolkhoznik to the White bastards. . . .[43]

These rousing indictments were posted on the wall in the "Red October" kolkhoz (formerly the village of Novo-Zhivotinnoe) in the Voronezh region in 1931, presumably in connection with the dekulakization of Berdnikov and Petrin. They are rhetorical exercises, giving some local wordsmith the chance to show that he could express militant class consciousness as well as any journalist from *Pravda*. All the same, there surely was real bitterness in Novo-Zhivotinnoe going back to the Civil War. Sometimes the bitterness went back even further. In the late 1930s, a peasant denouncing the dominant clique in his kolkhoz, "Wave of Revolution," recalled not only that the accountant had retreated with Denikin's Army but also that the kolkhoz chairman "had a Stolypin plot of 13 hectares before the revolution."[44]

In the "Red Army" kolkhoz in the Crimea, the longstanding feud between S. F. Rusanov and Fedor Pismennyi was framed (at least by Rusanov's supporters) in terms of conflicting Civil War allegiances. Rusanov, a bedniak, supported the Reds and became a member of the local revolutionary committee. Pismennyi came from a prosperous peasant family that supported the Whites; his brother, allegedly head of a White Army punitive squad, was shot by the Communists in 1921. In the 1920s, Rusanov, the leading Soviet activist in the village, was in constant conflict with local kulaks, including P. L. Kotov, over the leasing of land and exploitation of poor peasants. When collectivization came, Rusanov joined the kolkhoz and became its chairman. But Pismennyi also joined the kolkhoz, and so did other enemies of Rusanov such as Kotov. Pismennyi, "a subtle and cunning man," had friends in the rural soviet, and even managed to get various poor peasants on his side against Rusanov. When the kolkhoz ran into major economic difficulties in 1932, he succeeded in getting Rusanov removed from his position as kolkhoz chairman. The Rusanov camp responded by placing a story on the "Wave of revolution" feud—the story paraphrased above—with the evident intention of discrediting Pismennyi as a kulak.[45]

Collectivization generated new grievances and hostilities. Early joiners of the kolkhoz were sometimes pitted against late joiners; relatives of peasants who had been dekulakized were pitted against peasants who had participated in or benefited from their expropriation; and whistleblowers, especially sel'kory, who had denounced other peasants as kulaks were objects of particular animosity.

In the early days of the "Red Cooperator" kolkhoz in the Western oblast, a young peasant named Borzdov, a Komsomol member, took part in confiscating the property of a prosperous peasant, Merkalov. Merkalov's son, who in the mid-1930s still remained outside the kolkhoz, remembered this with bitterness. His hostility to Borzdov was all the greater because of the latter's visible distinction as a kolkhoz tractor driver. On the Revolution Day holiday in 1934, Merkalov organized a drinking party, to which he invited both Borzdov and another kolkhoznik, Bandurin, who had a history of violence and had served time in prison for assault and battery. Borzdov was then beaten up so severely by Merkalov and Bandurin that he died of his injuries.[46]

There are many similar reports of acts of revenge, sometimes performed years after the event, for injuries inflicted during collectivization and dekulakization. For example, a party official investigating the denunciation of a kolkhoz chairman by a kolkhoznik, Kabankov, concluded that Kabankov's charges were unfounded and his motive was to get revenge on the chairman for the dekulakization and deportation of all four of Kabankov's grandparents. A similar motive—"taking revenge for the dekulakization of his brother"—was attributed to another kolkhoznik who regularly laid complaints against the leaders of his kolkhoz.[47]

While the lines of cleavage associated with collectivization often set family against family, they sometimes ran through families and households. The peasant parents of the writer Nikolai Voronov fought and finally divorced because he was a partisan of the kolkhoz and she was not. In a more extreme case, a peasant woman who belonged to the Evangelical sect and strongly opposed collectivization murdered her activist husband with an axe while he slept, allegedly because he was a kolkhoz activist. Pavlik Morozov, the famous child informer whose story is told later in this chapter, was murdered by family members after denouncing his father. Indeed, murders within families that were divided over collectivization were sufficiently common for jurists to argue about whether or not such cases should be prosecuted as political crimes.[48]

In one Siberian case, tensions over collectivization led to fratricide. I. K. Koval, a peasant activist, was one of the organizers of the kolkhoz in the village of Bazhei. His brother and other relatives also initially joined the kolkhoz, but later they withdrew and encouraged other families to leave as well. In retaliation, the activist had his brother's farm searched for hoarded grain. When hidden grain was found, the brother was disenfranchised and threatened with dekulakization and deportation. Finally, when I. K. Koval and another kolkhoz activist were out in a meadow guarding kolkhoz horses and equipment during the harvest of 1932, his brother and another relative fell on them and beat them both to death.[49]

Where ethnic tensions were added to the conflicts of collectivization, the mix was particularly volatile. The "Dzerzhinskii" kolkhoz in Voronezh oblast, which combined Russian and Ukrainian peasants, was a case in point.

This kolkhoz was organized in 1929 in Tumanovka, once a serf village owned by the Tushnev family, by a group of Red Army men who were outsiders, natives of the Briansk region. Later some Ukrainian settler families moved in from a neighboring village. These three groups—the original Tumanovka peasants, the Briansk contingent, and the Ukrainians—remained distinct and antagonistic, defeating the efforts of a whole series of chairmen to run the kolkhoz effectively. The old inhabitants and the Briansk contingent, both Russian, sometimes joined in abuse of the Ukrainians ("The devil knows who brought you 'khokhols' here"). But they also abused each other:

> From the time when the commune (*kommuna*) was first organized up to the present, hostility has not died down between the old inhabitants of Tumanovka village, from which three families (whose close relatives remain [in the village]) were dekulakized and deported at the time of collectivization, and the new families that came in and organized the commune. Often [it is expressed] in open abuse. The old inhabitants say: "The devil brought you, if it hadn't been for you, there would have been no kolkhoz here," and the new inhabitants say to the old ones: "This isn't [like the old days when] you used to bow and scrape to the landowner Tushnev as if he were God and steal from him whatever you felt like."[50]

Class and Politics in the Village

In theory, collectivization had equalized the peasantry and eliminated the previous class conflicts in the village between kulaks and bedniaks. In practice, the situation was more complicated. In the first place, as discussed in Chapter 5, there was an emerging class differentiation in the kolkhoz between the privileged groups that monopolized kolkhoz offices and held mechanical jobs and the rank-and-file kolkhozniks who worked in the fields. This was mitigated, however, by the frequent turnover of kolkhoz chairmen and the consequent instability of the kolkhoz managerial elite.

In the second place, the old peasant "classes"—part real and part imagined by the Bolsheviks in the 1920s, but permanently imprinted on peasant consciousness by the indisputable fact of dekulakization—lived a restless half-life as ghosts in the collectivized village. It was one of Stalin's unique contributions to Marxist theory to discover that when social classes are destroyed, the class consciousness of their surviving members may become even stronger.[51] This certainly applied to dekulakized kulaks, whose previous relationship to a socio-economic kulak class may have been nonexistent. But it applied also, though in lesser degree, to those peasants whose status as bedniaks was confirmed by their early acceptance of the kolkhoz and appointment to kolkhoz and rural soviet offices.

We have already encountered some of the multiple uses of the term kulak in peasant discourse of the 1930s. The analogous term bedniak occurred less frequently (because it had positive rather than negative overtones and was less useful in denunciations), but nevertheless remained in circulation. It was used mainly to demonstrate loyalty and political credentials, as in kol-

khoznitsa Ekaterina Belova's unintentionally comic preamble to a complaint
to the Commission of Party Control:

> By origin I am the daughter of a poor peasant. . . . I was a *bedniachka* the whole
> time, and even before collectivization I had already attained the level of a below-
> average peasant farmer of the Western oblast.[52]

A rural Communist official was likely to cite his bedniak origins in the
same way and for the same purposes that an urban Communist would
describe himself as a "son of the working class." The lowly social origin
showed that he had had no stake in the old regime, and his upward mobility
into the new elite implied that he was a beneficiary of the revolution and
hence a grateful Soviet patriot.

A second usage of the term is more surprising: There were peasants who
were still writing of themselves as bedniaks in the old literal sense (that is,
poverty-stricken peasants) five or ten years after collectivization, and moreover suggesting that they were being abused and ridiculed by the more
prosperous village families just as they had been before collectivization. In
one letter in 1938, a peasant complained that the kolkhoz chairman, who
came from a prosperous peasant family, despised bedniaks and called them
"wreckers, idlers, and sowers of demoralization."[53]

A group of peasants from the "Hammer and Sickle" kolkhoz in Kursk
oblast wrote to *Krest'ianskaia gazeta* to complain that the kolkhoz chairman, the son of a former starosta, mistreated the bedniaks in the kolkhoz,
especially the Gumnikov family (to which at least three of the letter's five
signatories belonged). The chairman (or possibly his father) had done exactly
the same thing before the revolution, when he "used to insult bedniaks and
drove bedniak orphans [for example, V. Z. Gumnikov] out of their homes."
Now he was continuing on the same course, refusing to give bedniaks (specifically, L. Z. Gumnikov] a horse to go to the hospital when they were sick.
Furthermore, he discriminated against bedniaks by giving permission to go
on otkhod only to those kolkhozniks who could afford to pay a bribe.[54]

Another bedniak group wrote from "Red Dawn" kolkhoz in Leningrad
oblast to complain that kulaks had control of the kolkhoz and were systematically favoring their own.

> Kolkhoz chairman Mikh. Parikhin panders to kulaks and swindlers in everything.
> The former meat trader and owner of a leather factory kulak Timofei Parikhin is
> the chairman's cousin. In the kolkhoz he receives the most desirable and easiest
> work. . . . The former bedniaks Arsenii Maksimov, Miron Golitsyn, and others
> have work only in the summer, and in winter the kolkhoz chairman distributes
> all the work among his in-laws and favorites.[55]

Young peasant activists and sel'kory, although comparatively few in
number, tended to act as lightning rods for trouble in the village. One of
them, Lebusenkov, a rural soviet chairman in the Western oblast, wrote a
frantic letter to the newspaper in 1936 about his persecution by the kulaks.
Lebusenkov was one of only three Communists in the district. His great
enemy in the village was Petrov, the schoolteacher, who had been a prosper-

ous peasant before collectivization and continued to farm as an independent while teaching school. They had been enemies since Lebusenkov informed the authorities that Petrov beat his pupils and Petrov received a reprimand from the raion education department.

Petrov was a man of status and achievement in precollectivization or prerevolutionary terms: Lebusenkov refers to him as a "former tsarist officer," probably meaning that he won a commission while serving during the First World War. But his brother and nephew had become bandits after dekulakization, so Lebusenkov feared for his life: "Petrov said to me straight out: 'I am not going to let you get away alive—mark my words,' and his brother and nephew are bandits and I am afraid. . . ." After the incident with Petrov, Lebusenkov felt obliged to resign his position as rural soviet chairman, but he still feared for his life, especially as he had participated in dekulakization in this same village.

> After all, I am an uneducated person and young, they may outmaneuver me, I understand that, and especially now, when our raikom secretary comrade Bolshunov has gone, who of course would not have handed me over to the mercy of kulaks and scoundrels. . . . I have been on Soviet work for eight years—there were a lot of tensions with the muzhiks at the time of dekulakization, and many people take revenge. . . .[56]

Another sel'kor in a similar situation was Maksimov, a young peasant from Dorogobuzh raion who, after joining the Komsomol in 1932, had read "books of Lenin, Stalin, and Marx Engels" (*sic*) and become convinced of the reality of the concept of class struggle. That had led him to write to the raion prosecutor denouncing the kolkhoz chairman, a former miller named Ermakov, as a kulak who was squandering and stealing kolkhoz assets and had given all the best jobs in the kolkhoz to his family (his mother was in charge of milk deliveries, his son was bookkeeper, his father was kolkhoz watchman, and his wife ran the dairy).

The prosecutor did not react to Maksimov's signal, but the Ermakovs did. Maksimov was swiftly expelled from the kolkhoz. Despite this setback, Maksimov remained in the village and kept harrassing the kolkhoz leadership. He called "secret meetings of the kolkhoz aktiv" in the forest. He "investigated the chairman's stealthy entrance into the kolkhoz warehouse in the dead of night." On this last occasion, Ermakov, realizing he was being spied on, took out a gun and shot at Maksimov. "He has started threatening to murder me and set fire to my house," Maksimov wrote desperately. "What should I do now?"[57]

In Kalinin oblast, a sel'kor was driven out of the kolkhoz by the kolkhoz leaders he had criticized, leaving his sixty-five-year-old mother to take the brunt of their wrath. His mother wrote to *Krest'ianskaia gazeta* to tell the story of her persecution.

> My son Ivan Rumiantsev was a sel'kor for various Soviet newspapers for a long time. By this means he exposed all wrongdoing, hindering the cause of Soviet construction, regardless of persons. But this came to an end.

My son and I joined the newly organized kolkhoz "Victory" in 1930, and he worked there conscientiously until 1936. But recently the [kolkhoz] administration members were wearing down my son and me as well. For that reason my son was obliged to apply for release to go and live in the city of Leningrad, even though I remained here alone. After my son's departure, the kolkhoz administration expelled me, a 65-year-old woman, from the kolkhoz (those are the same people my son exposed). At the same time, that is, the end of 1936, the rural soviet levied a tax of 912 rubles on me, which was against all Soviet laws. They gave me 24 hours to pay. When the time was up, the rural soviet conducted a thorough search in my house, breaking the lock on the barn, and took away property right down to underclothing. . . .[58]

The Spirit of Faction

"A harmful and unprincipled spirit of faction" reigned in the "Lenin Days" kolkhoz in the Western oblast in May 1936, concluded an NKVD investigator. The conflict in "Lenin Days" dated back to collectivization, possibly to antagonism between the three small hamlets that were formed into one kolkhoz. It became acute in 1935, when Denis Dolnichenkov, the leader of one faction, became chairman of the kolkhoz. Seven of the peasants holding office in the kolkhoz were his supporters and presumably his appointees, and he was also supported by two rank-and-file kolkhozniks. The opposing faction was led by Petr Zhuravlev, the kolkhoz quality controller who was classified as an invalid, and consisted of eleven rank-and-file kolkhozniks, including three of his siblings. The remaining kolkhozniks, perhaps eighty adults in all, were nonaligned.

In August 1935, Petr Zhuravlev used his position as quality controller to inform the raion soviet that a lot of grain was left standing in the fields. There was an investigation resulting in the firing of a brigade leader belonging to Dolnichenkov's faction, Mikhail Kharitonenkov.

This was taken as a major provocation by the Dolnichenkov group, which launched a counterattack. Through their machinations, Zhuravlev's brothers, Nikolai and Egor, were both charged with hooliganism, convicted, and sent to prison in August 1935. Two days after their conviction, the Dolnichenkov people staged a faked attempt on Kharitonenkov's life and tried to pin the shooting on Petr Zhuravlev, citing angry threats he had made the evening after his brothers' conviction.

In March 1936, Nikolai Zhuravlev returned to the village after early release from prison. He was courting Ekaterina Ivanova, the niece of one of the kolkhoz's upstanding citizens, Domna Golubeva, an elected deputy to the soviet and outstanding worker who did not belong to either of the two factions. The evening of his return, there was a party at the kolkhoz club. Nikolai walked home with Ekaterina and Domna and was invited to stay the night, Domna giving up her bed to the young lovers and going to sleep in another room. Unfortunately, nobody remembered to warn Domna's simple-minded sister Uliana, who shared her room. Uliana, who had not gone to the club and was sleeping when they returned, woke up, "saw 'something strange' in her sister's bed and started screaming." Then she ran outside, still screaming and arousing the neighbors. Not knowing what was going on, Domna rushed in to the room and attacked Nikolai with a stick. He pushed her away and she fell and hurt her arm.

The Dolnichenkov faction saw a new opportunity to discredit the Zhuravlevs, and accused Nikolai of attempted murder of a rural activist (Domna Golubeva). But this ploy proved unsuccessful. In the words of the NKVD investigator, "the case was dropped when Zhuravlev married Ekaterina Ivanova."[59]

The "Lenin Days" case is unusual in that those involved had obviously become more interested in feuding for its own sake than in achieving any end. More typically, the feuding parties had a clear end in view, namely to get power in the kolkhoz and control its assets and the distribution of jobs. The files of *Krest'ianskaia gazeta* contain many examples of such feuds. Often, two contending factions in the village/kolkhoz seemed to alternate as the dominant group in the kolkhoz, rather like a two-party system in which the raion played the part of the electorate. One faction would have its candidate appointed kolkhoz chairman and distribute the important and desirable jobs, ranging from brigade leader to watchman, among its members. After a while, some kind of trouble would arise—procurements quotas would not be met, a crop of potatoes would rot, too many kolkhozniks would go on otkhod and the kolkhoz would be left short of labor—or else the kolkhoz leaders would become too blatant in siphoning off kolkhoz assets. The opposing faction, seeing its opportunity, would write letters of complaint and denunciation to the authorities, who would investigate and find that indeed there had been stealing and mismanagement. Then the raion would appoint a chairman from the opposing faction, and the cycle would begin again.

In some instances, the contending factions represented different sociopolitical groups in the village. This was the case in the "Red Plowman" kolkhoz in Smolensk (formerly Western) oblast, according to analysts in the raikom consulted by *Krest'ianskaia gazeta*. The "kulak" faction was led by T. I. Shalypin, who in the past had been a fixed-quota peasant. The "Soviet" faction included a brigade leader, Zuev, who had "waged active struggle in the past against the prosperous and kulak section of the village, for which even now many people hate him." Perhaps because of this activist past, Zuev did not hold the office of chairman when his faction was in power. That honor went to one Poliakov, possibly a prosperous peasant in the past, since the raikom (which supported him) did not give him a sociopolitical characterization. The Shalypin-Zuev feud, whose development during the Great Purges is outlined in the next section, had frequently been on the raion leaders' agenda over a period of years, as the head of the complaints desk of the Smolensk land department informed *Krest'ianskaia gazeta* in a long-suffering tone.[60]

Feuds frequently engendered intense bitterness. "Hatred surrounds me for that affair [not further explained]; if I were not the blacksmith, they would long ago have driven me out," wrote a peasant from Krasnodar."[61] The bitterness must partly be explained by the extremely serious damage that feuding parties could inflict on each other. The repertoire directly available to kolkhoz and rural soviet leaders to punish their enemies ranged from everyday discrimination (bad work assignments, refusal to allow use of a kolkhoz horse, withholding of permission to go on otkhod) to major sanctions such as expulsion from the kolkhoz and confiscation of property. With support from the raion, however, it was possible to punish opponents even more severely via criminal prosecutions and prison and gulag sentences: The coercive machinery of Soviet power was easily set in motion from below by a well-aimed denunciation or the right connections in the raion. Reading through the letter files of *Krest'ianskaia gazeta*, one is amazed at the savagery and extent of the devastation that warring kolkhoz factions repeatedly wreaked on each other, either directly or by manipulation of the state's coercive apparatus.

A case in point is the eight-year battle between the leaders of "Proletarian Dawn" kolkhoz in Stalingrad oblast and a kolkhoznik named A. S. Zakharov. It began in 1930, probably in connection with collectivization. Zakharov evidently made a practice of denouncing the sins of the kolkhoz leaders, who enjoyed the patronage of leaders at the raion level, both by speaking out at kolkhoz meetings and by writing letters of complaint to higher authorities. In return, the local bosses made a practice of initiating criminal prosecutions against Zakharov, for what offences we do not know. In the period 1930–1938, Zakharov was under criminal investigation six times, was three times convicted, and served a total of four years in prison. On the occasion of his last arrest, in 1937 or 1938, his family was expelled from the kolkhoz. His wife sold everything they had and went to live in her native village in a neighboring raion. The Zakharovs were fortunate, however, in that their persecutors' protectors in the raion fell victim to the Great Purges. Zakharov was then released from prison and moved to his wife's village, where he was able to join the "Komsomol" kolkhoz.[62]

Denunciation

Denunciation—informing the authorities of the wrongdoing of other citizens —became part of the culture of everyday life in the Russian village in the 1930s. While it is best known in connection with the story of Pavlik Morozov, the child informer, it was not specifically characteristic of adolescents or of Pioneers and Komsomols. Most of those who wrote denunciations were just ordinary peasants, usually adult males, judging by *Krest'ianskaia gazeta*'s mailbox. Unlike Pavlik Morozov, who denounced his father, most of *Krest'ianskaia gazeta*'s correspondents denounced their bosses. Unlike the sel'kory of the 1920s, whose denunciations rested on Soviet, nonvillage values, their judgements were implicitly based on a peasant morality, not a Communist one.

There were a number of possible motives for denunciation. Ideological commitment, as in the case of the mythologized Pavlik and many real sel'kory, was one. The quest for justice in a country whose legal system worked poorly was another. Personal malice and settling scores was a third. In functional terms, the practice of denunciation (which the regime encouraged) can be seen in "top down" terms as a state control mechanism and a means of monitoring public opinion. But there is also a possible "bottom up" interpretation of the function of denunciation: If the state used this practice to control its citizens, individual citizens could also use it for the purpose of manipulating the state.

Pavlik Morozov

The name of Pavlik Morozov was known to all Soviet citizens as that of the boy who informed on his kulak father and was killed by his uncles in revenge in September 1932. Pavlik's motivation was allegedly that of any upstanding young Pioneer of the period, namely that in a situation where family and state loyalties conflicted, he nobly put the interests of the state first. His murder led to a show trial in the Morozovs' village, Gerasimovka in Sverdlovsk oblast, which was reported by local journalists and attracted the attention of the Komsomol Central Committee. At the Soviet Writers' Congress in 1934, the writer Maxim Gorky cited Pavlik Morozov as an example of Soviet heroism, and for decades he was treated as a kind of patron saint of the Pioneers and was eulogized in public monuments, meetings, and inspirational children's books.[63]

When the Pavlik Morozov legend was carefully investigated in the 1970s by a Soviet (later émigré) writer, Iurii Druzhnikov, it turned out that the real situation was rather different—but no less interesting and characteristic of the times. Pavel's father, it turns out, was not a kulak. He was chairman of the rural soviet in a remote village in the northern Urals, still uncollectivized, which was one of the dumping grounds for dekulakized peasants deported from other parts of the country. A few years earlier, Grigorii Morozov had abandoned his wife and children and moved in with a younger woman from the same village. This left a resentful Pavel, at thirteen or fourteen the eldest child, to take over his father's place on the farm as well as coping with an angry (and also, by all accounts, lazy) mother. He was not a Young Pioneer —few peasant children were at that time, let alone in a remote spot like Gerasimovka.

Pavel did not inform on his father for hoarding grain, as is often thought, although he may have got the idea of informing from the schoolteacher's questioning of the children about hidden grain stores in the village. The offense of which he accused his father was that, as rural soviet chairman, he had signed a document attesting that one of the recently arrived kulak deportees was a poor peasant from Gerasimovka who was authorized to leave the village on otkhod. It may have been Pavel's own idea to inform on the father who deserted his family, or he may have been put up to it by his mother or a cousin who wanted to become chairman of the rural soviet himself. The father, in any case, was arrested late in 1931 and disappeared into a labor camp. A few months later, Pavel and a younger brother were found murdered in the forest. Exactly who killed them is unclear, but those accused of the crime included his paternal grandfather and grandmother, a young Morozov cousin, and two of his uncles.[64]

A number of cases of ideologically motivated informing by adolescents were reported around the same time. Some of the informers were praised and rewarded: Serezha Fadeev, for example, got a trip to Artek, the famous Pioneer camp in the Crimea, for telling his headmaster where his father had hidden a store of potatoes.[65] But others shared Pavlik Morozov's fate.

Nikita Senin was a fifteen-year-old Pioneer in the Western oblast. Described as a school activist and hardworking student, Nikita became a sel'kor for the local raion newspaper at the early age of thirteen. (He was also, from age fourteen, the village correspondent for the Sukhinichi metereological station, and no doubt would have lived longer if he had confined his activities to recording information about the weather.) In his letters to the raion newspaper, he uncovered wrongdoing in the rural soviet, the school, and the local post office, headed by a "degenerate" type appropriately named Kulakov, who was also leader of the local Pioneer troop. He denounced Kulakov in a letter to the raion Komsomol committee, saying that the Pioneers in his village considered Kulakov an unfit leader, since he drank and had beaten them. In his capacity as postmaster, Kulakov naturally opened and read all correspondence, so he was aware of Nikita's actions, and threatened him with bad consequences if he continued writing such letters. Finally Kulakov managed to acquire a gun (it cost him 150 rubles). A few days later, he persuaded Nikita to take a bag of mail to the raion center in Kozelsk, lay in wait for him along the road, and killed him.[66]

The peak period for peasant children informing on their relatives and neighbors was the early 1930s. Later, despite the official adulation of Pavlik Morozov, there was less encouragement of this type of action, and even some discouragement.[67] In the Great Purges, children were expected to denounce fathers and mothers arrested as enemies of the people, but only after the fact—they were not actively encouraged to initiate the process by informing against them.

Peasant Letters on Abuses of Power

Whistleblowing was a well-established tradition in Soviet (and, for that matter, pre-Soviet) Russia. Ordinary citizens were encouraged to alert higher authorities to lower-level bureaucratic corruption and incompetence, and writing letters to newspapers was one of the standard ways to do it. The peasant whistleblower who wrote to newspapers acquired the name of sel'kor (rural correspondent) in the 1920s.

The sel'kor was someone who identified with Soviet, progressive values and was critical of rural backwardness and squalor. He lived in the village, but was to some degree an outsider, often a Red Army veteran or a teacher.

Out of a sense of affinity with the new regime and its revolutionary goals, the sel'kor of the 1920s was willing to be "the eyes and ears of Soviet power" in the village, which meant writing letters exposing the various anti-Soviet and reactionary things that went on (kulak domination of the mir and exploitation of bedniaks; corruption and drunkenness of officials; Communists who disgraced the party by beating their wives or christening their children, and so on). Conceptually, these were not the sel'kor's personal grievances but *Soviet* grievances, and the sel'kor was not an informer and traitor to the peasant community but an exceptionally public-spirited and courageous citizen. Of course, peasants did not necessarily see it that way. Known sel'kory were often ostracized and sometimes murdered by fellow villagers.

This militant sel'kor tradition was still flourishing (although with high casualties) during the years of collectivization. But by the mid-1930s it had weakened considerably, perhaps because many of the natural candidates for such a role had left the village. Sel'kory of the classic type became rarer, and newspapers like *Krest'ianskaia gazeta* and *Bednota* no longer kept lists of the names, addresses, and biographical data of "our" sel'kory as they had done in the 1920s. The term was applied increasingly vaguely to anybody who was prepared to get pen and paper and a 20-kopek stamp to send a letter to the newspaper exposing "abuses of power." In 1938, about two out of five letters received by the newspaper fell into the "abuses of power" category and were in effect denunciations of kolkhoz chairmen and other officeholders.[68]

Who was writing these letters? In contrast to the prerevolutionary pattern of peasant petition, almost all the letters came from individuals or small groups, not from peasant communities as a whole.[69] (A kolkhoz that complained collectively was likely to be regarded as seditions by Soviet authorities.) Among the individual letter writers, classic sel'kory and truly public-spirited citizens were a relatively small minority. As already noted, the classic sel'kor—now, in contrast to the 1920s, almost always a Komsomol or Communist—was a vanishing although not yet extinct species. The public-spirited citizens—those who appeared to have no grudge or personal stake but were concerned to correct injustices and make things work better—were usually either older men living in the village, sometimes retired workers, or former villagers, now living in towns or serving in the army, whom peasants had asked to act as their spokesmen. One of the most appealing of these was an elderly peasant who wrote his complaint about abuses on the kolkhoz in the middle of a family letter to his son in the city:

> You go round to the editorial board as I asked you, son, my dear Mitia, and explain everything that I wrote to you and ask them to look into it. This wrecking must be stopped, and then we will be able to live well, but now those kulaks have begun to do things in their kulak way again (*a to oni opiat' kulaki po-kulatski stali delat'*).[70]

The name "pseudo-sel'kory" (*lzhesel'kory*) was applied by the authorities to a rather larger cluster of categories at the other end of the spectrum: malingerers, busybodies, and cranks. The malingerers were people who used their self-proclaimed sel'kor status to justify lack of success or failure to work: for example, the peasant who complained of having been expelled from the kolkhoz because he was a whistleblower, whereas (according to an official investigator) the real reason for his expulsion was that he pretended to be too ill to work and spent every summer day fishing on the river.[71] "They persecute me because I am a sel'kor" was a familiar refrain of those with many reprimands and black marks on their records.

Busybodies were the village gossips (usually male, contrary to stereotype) who picked up every piece of discreditable information, however trivial, and felt bound to pass it on. Their letters usually had some initial focus on an authority figure, usually a kolkhoz chairman or brigade leader, but wandered off into all sorts of extraneous matters like the pilfering of cabbages from somebody's plot. The busybodies often referred to their indefatigable labors in writing dozens of letters each year to newspapers, raion authorities, oblast authorities, the procuracy, the NKVD, and so on.

Letter-writing cranks came in various shades and sizes. Some were paranoid, like the peasant Vorobev from Tambov oblast, who complained that other kolkhozniks refused to talk to him in order to make him sick. "Almost every day he writes letters to organizations, [and] in his letters he calls all the raion leaders enemies of the people," wrote the raion prosecutor to *Krest'ianskaia gazeta*. "I have warned Vorobev about his stupid writing, which wastes a lot of useful time of the investigative organs and other organizations to which he writes complaints. . . ."[72] Another writer of denunciations was discredited when a journalist from an oblast paper went to the village to investigate and found that he was a fantasist with delusions that he was the headmaster of the school as well as an important NKVD operative:

> He goes around all the time telling the kolkhozniks that he worked as "head of an investigative organ" and that if anyone has any complaints, they should pass them on to him and he will set things in motion.[73]

The three largest categories of letter writers may be labelled plaintiffs, petitioners, and politicians.

Plaintiffs were those who thought their legal rights had been infringed in some specific situation and were seeking justice. They seem to be using letter writing as a substitute for or supplement to the courts—something that suggests that the legal system in the countryside worked very poorly[74]—and were inclined to base their arguments more on formal law than natural justice. Plaintiffs were more literate than the majority of letter writers and tended to use a more dispassionate tone. Otkhodniks in conflict with the kolkhoz were particularly prominent in this group.

Petitioners were simple kolkhozniks who saw themselves as powerless victims of local officials and were appealing to powerful people "up there" to right their wrongs. A wrong, in their view, was something that was an offense against justice and custom, whether or not it was against the law. Most petitioners were ordinary fieldworkers in the kolkhoz, lacking educa tion and sophistication. Women were better represented in this group than in the others. The letters of petitioners accused chairmen and brigade leaders of such things as refusing help to kolkhozniks in need; cursing, beating and insulting them; stealing and cheating on laborday payments; favoring relatives and generally dealing unequally with kolkhoz households; and "behaving like a little Tsar" in the kolkhoz.

Petitioners also approached the state's representatives in other contexts, for example, to get help or advice. They did this in person, when possible, as well as in writing. In 1933, for example, the politotdels of the Machine-Tractor Station (MTS) in the Central Black Earth oblast reported that they were receiving fifteen to twenty visits a day from kolkhozniks with questions, requests, and complaints—including, as they noted with surprise, petitions for divorce.[75]

Politicians were letter writers who were rivals of the peasants currently holding the most important offices in the kolkhoz and rural soviet. They wrote complaints in the hope of discrediting and replacing these officeholders, and often became involved in the vicious circles of mutual denunciation and feuding described earlier in this chapter. Generally confident and articulate, they used Soviet jargon like "suppression of criticism" and "counter-revolutionary" and their letters had the smell of denunciations (*donosy*) in the strict sense—that is, letters communicating damaging information on other individuals to the police. In one case from the Western oblast, one village "politician," Shishkov, denounced the rural soviet chairman, Botenkov, as a "socially-alien element." This led to Botenkov's being fired and Shishkov appointed as rural soviet chairman. But Botenkov was also a politician. When Shishkov's wife got drunk at a party and joined in the singing of antiregime chastushki, Botenkov wrote a denunciation to the authorities in the hope of getting Shishkov fired and recovering his old job.[76]

The Uses of Denunciation

The great advantage of writing denunciations, petitions, and complaints in Stalin's Russia was that there was a good chance of getting results. The authorities read such letters from citizens with attention. These were among the few forms of political participation that were available to ordinary citizens; and of the various types of letter writing, denunciation was by far the more powerful tool.

Of course, that did not guarantee a favorable outcome for writers of denunciations and petitions. Even if a higher authority intervened on behalf of a petitioner, the local authorities might ignore its recommendations. As for denunciations, their submission was not free of risk. There are a number of cases in *Krest'ianskaia gazeta*'s files where the investigation sparked by a peasant's letter ended with the writer being arrested by the raion NKVD as a troublemaker, idler, or "socially-alien element."[77] The frequent requests that the writers' names be withheld reflected their justified fear that the raion authorities might take such action to protect themselves and their appointees.

But there was a sporting chance of a successful outcome from writing denunciations. This was not only because the authorities encouraged such communications and responded to them attentively but also because the regime had certain automatic reflexes that the intelligent citizen could use to his advantage. The most important of these was an acute sensitivity on the question of class enemies. If you wanted the state to dispose of your enemy in the village, you called him a kulak.

It became standard practice in the 1930s for participants in village feuds or power struggles to denounce their opponents as kulaks. In some cases, the allegations had some foundation: that is, the person in question really had built a prosperous farm or business before the Revolution or in the 1920s, or else members of his immediate family really had been dekulakized at the beginning of the 1930s. More often, however, they were extrapolations from trivial biographical facts such as a long-dead uncle who had been a trader, or a mother-in-law's brother who had been dekulakized.

The beauty of the "kulak" allegations was that Soviet officials could be counted on to respond so vigorously. Judging by the behavior of the Western obkom, which we know from the Smolensk Archive, the authorities frequently sent an investigator to the village when such an allegation was made, and these investigators conscientiously plowed their way through the maze of accusation and counteraccusation in an effort to find the elusive truth about who was a kulak and who was not. Reading these multipage reports (which, incidentally, contain some of the most interesting sociological research available on the Russian village of the 1930s), it is hard not to feel that the party, through its obsessive concern about kulaks, had become the peasants' patsy, being jerked and manipulated at will.

The same thought sometimes occurred to the investigators, to whom such denunciations became depressingly familiar. In general, it was imprudent for a Communist investigator or official to dismiss "kulak" denunciations out of hand, because that left the Communist himself vulnerable to accusations that he had kulak sympathies. Occasionally, however, an official would dismiss a "kulak" denunciation impatiently, as in the case of the raion prosecutor who responded to a denunciation forwarded by *Krest'ianskaia gazeta* with the acerbic comment that "Pavlov was never a kulak and in general no kulak groups exist in the village of Meretiak, but what exists is absence of labor discipline and a lack of friendly relations among the kolkhozniks."[78]

An NKVD officer who went out to "Lenin Days" kolkhoz in the Western oblast to investigate a denunciation was similarly skeptical. Noting that the village was locked into a pattern of factional feuding in which each side continually denounced the other for connections with kulaks and merchants, he concluded that the accusations were basically trivial, although not totally without foundation in either case. But the most interesting thing about his report is that, despite this conclusion and his generally favorable judgement of the abilities of the kolkhoz chairman who had been denounced, he still recommended that the chairman be replaced. Because of his family's prerevolutionary background in trade, he explained, the chairman would always be vulnerable to denunciations from rivals in this faction-ridden village, and keeping him in office was just not worth the trouble.[79]

During the Great Purges, a denunciation that mentioned links with "enemies of the people," unidentified visitors, or any meeting that could be construed as conspiratorial was even more successful than the "kulak" denunciation at producing a reflex reaction from the authorities. This was not lost on peasant writers of denunciations, many of whom quickly mastered the discourse of the Great Purges. Towards the end of 1936, someone wrote in to *Krest'ianskaia gazeta* to denounce a kolkhoz chairman named Sukhanov as a "sympathizer with the Trotskyite-Zinovievite bloc"—an accusation that the NKVD judged to be groundless, while reporting that it had led to the unfortunate man and his children being "persecuted" in the village and at school.[80]

"The Trotskyite Ia. K. Korobtsov . . . openly took the path of terror," thundered one of *Krest'ianskaia gazeta*'s correspondents, a kolkhoznik from Kursk oblast, early in 1937.[81] (This turned out to mean that Korobtsov had assaulted a kolkhoz watchman while trying to steal seed grain from the warehouse.) A peasant from Krasnodar, denouncing his kolkhoz board for making laborday payments only in kind and not in money, commented:

> Indeed, as you read in the newspaper . . . about the trial of wreckers, diversionists, proclaimed murderers of our beloved leaders, then you involuntarily wonder if it's not their hands at work here too. . . .[82]

There is nothing further in the letter to suggest that the writer himself took this idea seriously, and that he was interested in making the innuendo more concrete. It was just a gambit to catch the authorities' attention and make them more likely to investigate the financial practices of the kolkhoz leaders.

For village politicians, the Great Purges offered a golden opportunity to dislodge incumbent kolkhoz and rural soviet chairmen by linking them with disgraced "enemies of the people" in the raion leadership. This had the advantage of plausibility, since incumbent low-level officeholders had almost always been appointed by the raion leaders and could often be accurately described as their clients in a patronage network. There are many examples of long-running village feuds that were redefined to suit the new political moment. A sel'kor with an old grudge against the party organizer in his kolkhoz wrote to say that he now understood that his enemy had all along been carrying out "the Trotskyite instructions of the former raikom secretary." Another inveterate feuder added a new dimension to his earlier denunciations of the leaders of his kolkhoz by pointing out that they were protégés of two former raion officials who had recently been unmasked as enemies of the people.[83]

10

The Potemkin Village

Potemkinism

If the typical Russian village of the 1930s was hungry, drab, depopulated, and demoralized, there was another village, happy and prosperous, bustling with people, and enlivened by the cheerful sounds of the accordion and balalaika, that existed in imagination. I call this the Potemkin village, but it meant something more in Soviet life than a facade to impress visiting VIPs. The Potemkin village existed for the benefit of the educated Soviet public—even to some degree for the benefit of peasants. Like other socialist-realist representations of the Stalin period, the image of the New Soviet Village so lovingly created in newspapers, movies, political speeches, and official statistics was not life as it was, but life as good Soviet citizens hoped it was becoming. The Potemkin village was a preview of the coming attractions of socialism.[1]

Many years later, a man of peasant origin who had begun a successful urban career in the 1930s recalled his deep distress when Stalin, discarding the socialist-realist metaphor that Soviet socialism was "under construction," announced in 1936 that the building of socialism was essentially finished.

> I had just returned from my native village in the Viatka region, lost in the depths of the forest, cut off from the world by lack of roads. In the izbas there was mud and cockroaches, and because of the lack of kerosene they had had to go back from lamps to candles. I wouldn't have thought anything of that—after all before us shone the beacon of the bright future, which we were building with our

own hands. Maybe we would still have to labor for another five or ten years, straining all our forces, but we'd get there! And suddenly it turned out that this *was* socialism around me. . . . Never, neither before nor after, have I experienced such disappointment, such grief.[2]

This degree of involvement with the metaphor of socialist realism was rare, if not totally unknown, among peasants still living in the village. From the village standpoint, the Potemkin representation of peasant life was regarded skeptically, and became a standard target of peasant jokes and sarcasm. At the same time, however, Potemkinism had its intermittent rewards for peasants in the real world. Crumbs from the richly laden table of the Potemkin village sometimes fell into peasant laps. *Some* peasants had to have the commodities and amenities that in the Potemkin representation were available to the peasant masses, even if the main mode of entry into the village for such goods was via the peasants' imagination.

The press played a major role in constructing the Potemkin village, as did professional writers, artists, and filmmakers. Published Soviet statistics, appearing in the 1930s under titles such as "Our Achievements" and "Socialist Construction" were dedicated primarily to Potemkin ends. Conferences of Stakhanovite peasants, at which record-breaking tractor drivers and milkmaids dwelt lovingly on the prizes they had received for their work, were part of the same process.

After the writer Fedor Gladkov revisited his native village on the Volga in 1935, he wrote both a Potemkin representation of it and a much less glowing account emphasizing the neglected school and the plight of the teachers.[3] The Potemkin version used one of the favorite tropes of Stalinist socialist realism, the contrast between the miseries of the village in the past and the glories of the kolkhoz in the present/future. Once, Gladkov wrote, there had been "pitiful, beggarly settlements: dirty cottages with rotten roofs, stinking of ordure, unfenced. The streets were bare, dusty, sad, unwelcoming. . . ." Now all was changed (changing).

> You see shrubs planted in front of the houses, orchards, in almost every village now. The izbas are often roofed with iron. . . , white-washed or smoothly spread with clay, as if plastered. The street is being cleaned up and becoming spacious and green, the squares are planted with trees. The windows of the izbas have white curtains, often lace, and there are flowers on the window-sills.

On the walls inside hung "paintings of revolutionary scenes, portraits of the leaders, and photographs," and there was a bookshelf ("The kolkhoznik reads greedily and a great deal") for works such as Stalin's *Problems of Leninism.* Bicycles were commonplace. In general, "the breath of the city can be felt everywhere, even in the appearance and clothes of the kolkhozniks."

The white lace curtains and pot plants on windowsills were standard furnishing in the Potemkin village, and inside there was often a radio or sewing machine on the table and beds on which to sleep. The Potemkin houses were of modern type, divided into rooms, unlike the traditional peasant izbas. The following reports from provincial newspapers are typical of the items that appeared regularly in the press about the transformation of peasant lifestyle. In Voronezh oblast, N. A. Federiakin, a kolkhoznik who was a former bedniak, had built himself such a house with four rooms, an iron roof, and plastered walls; and three other peasants in the same kolkhoz were building themselves "brick houses with three or four spacious rooms." I. D. Baliuk, a kolkhoznik from the Altai, bought "a soft couch, Viennese chairs, and a gramophone" for his home. Vera Pankratova, an outstanding worker in the "Iskra" kolkhoz, actually had a telephone installed in her izba in 1935, according to one report. She was the first (and perhaps the only) peasant in Gorky krai to be so honored.[4]

The Potemkin kolkhoz boasted many new administrative buildings and cultural, educational, and medical facilities. At a "millionaire" sheep-raising kolkhoz in Siberia, for example, there were fifteen public buildings including a seven-year school, a reading room, a library, a maternity home, and a nursery, and the kolkhoz owned three trucks, according to a letter from a proud member of the kolkhoz published in a national newspaper. Potemkinism did not end with the village proper but even extended into the fields. In Stalingrad krai, a prize-winning tractor driver told the Second Congress of Outstanding Kolkhozniks about the cultured surroundings created for those who had to spend the night in the fields at peak periods of agricultural work: "We had a cabin for sixteen people in which each tractor-driver had a separate cot. In the cabin there were a radio, a wind-up gramophone, a clock, and music."[5]

Presumably the report of the Stalingrad tractor driver had some connection to a specific local reality, however fleeting. But more convincing testimony to the fact that the real world, as well as the world of imagination, contained Potemkin phenomena comes from the minutes of an unpublicized, closed meeting on forms of remuneration for kolkhoz chairmen preserved in the archives of the People's Commissariat of Agriculture. A kolkhoz chairman from Vinnitsa oblast, not on salary but paid on the laborday principle, commented wryly that raion authorities had refused to authorize any salaried position in his kolkhoz except that of a musician, whose job—a perfect example of Potemkinism in real life—was to play cheerful tunes to the kolkhozniks as they worked in the beet fields.[6]

Music was important in the Potemkin world. The newspapers often carried small items on the musical activities of kolkhozniks and the supply of musical instruments to rural consumers. In 1933, a photograph captioned "As the prosperity of the kolkhoz masses grows, so does their cultural level" showed a peasant boy playing the violin; he was a pupil at a special musical school for kolkhoz children in Uriupinsk, Lower Volga. Four grand pianos were ordered by rural consumers in the Western oblast in 1937; fifty pianos and fifty sets of band instruments were sold to collective farms in Dnepropetrovsk oblast in the same year; kolkhozniks in Krasnodar acquired more than a hundred sets of band instruments in the first seven months of 1938.[7]

Local party and government organizations had the responsibility of fostering the musical and other cultural inclinations of the peasantry. Thus, in Moscow oblast, always a pacesetter, the party organization announced in 1935 that it planned to organize 100 kolkhoz piano classes, in addition to 3,000 choirs, 4,000 dramatic circles, 500 string ensembles, and 131 raion brass bands. Kolkhozniks were encouraged to form amateur theater groups, painting circles, orchestras, and choirs. For the best participants in these kolkhoz amateur arts circles, there was the possibility of participation in regional and national festivals and competitions (as depicted in the movie *Volga-Volga*).[8]

While folk arts were not neglected in the Potemkin village, the emphasis on high culture was striking. The plans of the Moscow oblast party organization, for example, included the organization of 100 kolkhoz circles for the study of foreign languages. Newspapers reported approvingly on the initiative of kolkhozniks in Moscow oblast and Saratov krai who formed "Pushkin committees" to prepare for the poet's centenary and create "Pushkin corners" in kolkhoz clubs. An even more remarkable high-cultural initiative was taken by the rural soviet in Kursk oblast that in 1936 organized a local conference of "readers of Henri Barbusse."[9]

Sport was another major activity in the Potemkin village. A memorable example of the kolkhoz athlete was provided by a young kolkhoznitsa from the Caucasus, B. Sh. Misostishkhova, who described her achievements as follows at a national conference of Stakhanovites.

> MISOSTISHKHOVA: In my kolkhoz I am a record-holding worker of the kolkhoz fields. But I am not only a record-holding worker of the kolkhoz fields; I am also ready for labor and defense. (Points to her "GTO"[10] and "Voroshilov's Marksman" badges.)
>
> STALIN: How old are you?
>
> MISOSTISHKHOVA: Seventeen. I am also a record-holding mountain climber. I was the first, together with comrade Kalmykov, to climb the highest mountain in Europe, Mt. Elbrus. . . . Now I'm preparing myself for parachute jumping. I haven't done it yet, because I didn't have enough time after storming Mt. Elbrus. But, comrades, I give my word to comrade Voroshilov that in parachute jumping I am also going to be ahead of the men. . . .[11]

In 1936 a spokesman for the sports department of the Komsomol Central Committee told a national Komsomol Congress that there was scarcely a kolkhoz in the country that did not have its group of physical-culture enthusiasts and its sports field (*ploshchadka*) for volleyball and football— pastimes that not long ago had been unknown in the village. (This blatant Potemkinism was a mistake, however, since the hall was full of genuine sports enthusiasts who knew that this claim was not true and shouted angry rebuttals. The claim was nonsense, said one later speaker. "The majority of kolkhozy do not have either physical-culture groups or sports fields.") In the same year, Moscow oblast authorities claimed to have organized almost two thousand sporting events in rural areas.[12]

Such quantitative claims about cultural progress—2,000 sporting events held, 3,000 choirs organized, a hundred thousand students graduated, a million copies of newspapers distributed—were an important part of Potemkinesque "cultural construction" in the Soviet Union. Statistics became a handmaiden of the Potemkin enterprise. Around the time of collectivization, there was a basic change in the function of Soviet statistical handbooks. In the 1920s, the numerous statistical handbooks published were aimed at the Marxist intellectuals (including those in the political leadership) who needed data for sociological, political, and economic analysis. In the 1930s, the relatively few handbooks published were primarily sources of statistical illustration for propagandists and journalists writing about the Potemkin world. Statistics of growth were favored, preferably expressed in terms of percentages from a base of 100, starting with an exceptionally bad year such as 1932. Among the favorite headings for growth statistics on the countryside were education and literacy, the Stakhanovite movement, clubs and cultural circles, sports events, newspaper reading, radios and movie projectors, and supply of consumer goods.[13]

Under this last heading, the statistical handbooks emphasized "cultural" consumer goods: bicycles, motorcycles, sewing machines, pocket watches, alarm clocks, radios, wind-up gramophones, wind instruments (for brass bands), and pianos. In all cases, the statistics showed remarkable increases in production and sales in rural cooperative stores. For example, fifty times as many bicycles and twenty times as many gramophones were sold to rural consumers in 1938 as had been sold in 1933. (In 1933, to be sure, only 5,000 bicycles were available for rural consumers, and no pianos, motorcycles, radios, sewing machines, pocket watches, or alarm clocks at all.)[14] Despite the fact that demand far outstripped supply in the 1930s, these goods were also advertised in journals and provincial newspapers, often with photographs or line drawings of the product.

If the goods sent for sale to rural cooperatives had been equally distributed among Soviet collective farms, every kolkhoz would have acquired one bicycle and one gramophone, with a reasonable chance of getting a sewing machine and a pocket watch as well. One kolkhoz out of six could have had an alarm clock, and one out of a hundred a motorcycle.[15] In the real world, of course, many of these goods were siphoned off before they ever got to the rural cooperative store or sold to a handful of "millionaire" collective farms in the fertile south. But *in principle*, to use a favorite Soviet phrase, they were available to peasants. It was unlikely, but certainly not impossible, that an ordinary kolkhoznik would become the possessor of a watch, a sewing machine, or an iron bedstead.

In additional to the commercial path of acquisition, peasants could also acquire these goods as rewards for outstanding performance on the kolkhoz. This was the kind of prize that was available for kolkhoz udarniks and Stakhanovites. The awards were made on the game-show or lottery principle, that is, without regard to any specific needs or preferences of the winners. This was probably just as well, since the number of kolkhozniks who possessed a *working* motorcycle or watch was undoubtedly smaller by a large factor than the number who could claim to possess those items. Function was not the point of Soviet cultural goods for the countryside. They were symbols of modernity and socialist hope, not utility items.

In the latter half of the decade, the listing of prizes became a regular feature—indeed, one of the *raisons d'être*—of national and regional Stakhanovite conferences. But even before such recitation became a standard formula, peasant delegates at various meetings sometimes spontaneously and proudly mentioned their prizes:

> For my work as a brigade-leader in the past two years, I have received prizes twenty times. I will not list all the prizes. I will just say that I used not to have a hut, but the kolkhoz gave me a hut as a reward. I received a bicycle, a wind-up gramophone, and a watch from the krai [authorities], and a rifle from the raion.[16]

The Potemkin village was related to a larger Potemkin world of huge factories and modern technology that peasants knew mainly from hearsay and the newspapers. The airplane was one of the most powerful symbols of this larger world. Peasants had already started incorporating it in their folklore in the 1920s, but in the 1930s they could sometimes catch a glimpse of the real thing. In one rural soviet in Voronezh oblast, the local Komsomol managed to arrange for an airplane to fly in from the oblast center for one of their events, and felt "extremely proud." In backward Belyi raion, Western oblast, the kolkhozniks actually collected 22,000 rubles to build an airplane that was to be named "Belyi Kolkhoznik." (At last report, they were still waiting for their plane; it seems that local authorities, feeling the gesture was eloquent enough, had taken no concrete steps to turn 22,000 rubles into an airplane.)[17]

It was in the movies that the Potemkin village found its apotheosis. In the second half of the 1930s, several Soviet films portrayed kolkhoz life in bright, primary colors with much singing and dancing—a cross between *Oklahoma!* and the peasant crowd scenes from an opera by Rimsky-Korsakov. *A Rich Bride* (*Bogataia nevesta*), made in Kiev in 1938 by the director Ivan Pyriev (Pyr'ev) with music by the popular songwriter Isaak Dunaevskii, was an immediate success and received a special award from the Supreme Soviet in March 1938.[18] *Tractor-Drivers* (*Traktoristy*) was a follow-up by the same director, with music by the Pokrass brothers. *Volga-Volga* (1938), directed by Grigorii Aleksandrov for Mosfilm with music by Dunaevskii, was in the same genre although not directly focused on the kolkhoz.

Described by a contemporary reviewer as joyful and realistic, "the first really successful film comedy on a kolkhoz theme," *A Rich Bride* was the archetypal boy-meets-girl-meets-tractor film of the 1930s.

The film historian Jay Leyda summarized the plot as follows:

> The "rich bride" of the title is Marina Lukash, outstanding worker on her Ukrainian collective farm. The farm's book-keeper sees her as the best catch to secure his future comfort, and when a handsome tractor-driver threatens to upset his

plans by attracting Marina to himself, the book-keeper juggles the driver's pro-duction figures so that the marriage of such a "shameful" worker to the prize-winning Marina will be obviously a poor match. But love and the inspection sys-tem triumph, all accompanied by songs and dancing that smell of the fields rather than of the state.[19]

To a contemporary Soviet reviewer, Marina's status as an udarnitsa—an outstanding worker, similar to a Stakhanovite—who had earned 400 labor-days for the year deserved special emphasis. Though the courtship of Pavlo Zgara and Marina was a personal matter, he explained, the collective also had a legitimate interest in it.

> "Are you getting married? Congratulations! Well, have you asked what kind of worker he is? How he gets on in his MTS?—whether he is a shockworker, a Stakhanovite or . . . (*sic*) an idler?" asks the brigade leader. . . . Is this a personal matter? No, not only personal. The brigade has an interest in assuring that when she marries, Marina will remain the same outstanding worker she was before.[20]

A permanent Potemkin lifestyle—that is, a way of living that corre-sponded to "Soviet" values and was the way educated urban people hoped peasants would live in the future—was out of the reach of all but a very few collective farms for economic reasons, even if the kolkhozniks had wanted to live that way. Nevertheless, there were Potemkin episodes—the flyover in Voronezh, a winter's experiment with amateur theatricals, the award of a sewing machine to a local Stakhanovite, a burst of enthusiasm for sport when someone acquired a volleyball—in the life of all but the most remote collective farms. These usually occurred as the result of an initiative by an outsider, and tended to collapse when the outsider's attention turned else-where.

Peasants often spoke of Potemkin representations ironically, but their attitude to them—especially to the Hollywood-style movies, full of song and dance and good cheer, set in the Potemkin village—was not always negative. Why not, after all, have a bit of escapist daydreaming in one's life? Aunt Varia, a central figure in Gerasimov's history of Spas na peskakh, reportedly went to see every movie that was shown in her village after the war, when the village acquired a projector for the first time. Sitting up front with the chil-dren, she would watch the Potemkin-village musical comedies and joke, "Well, we'll soon be living the way they show in the movies."[21]

New Soviet Culture

Meetings were the core of the new Soviet culture in the village. Unlike Potemkin goods such as radios and grand pianos, meetings were a part of the kolkhozniks' real everyday life—obligatory, frequent, ritualized, and requiring peasants to acquire a knowledge of Soviet procedural rules and semantic conventions that had previously been unknown. Along with news-paper reading, meetings were collectivization's main contribution to the cul-tural repertoire of the village.

Since the revolution, meetings and public speaking had always been the hook that drew a small minority of peasants into political participation. "When you go back to town, take me with you," pleaded one young peasant boy to a visiting urban Komsomol member. "I want to go to school and become an orator." A speaker at a national congress of soviets, a former batrachka, had similar memories of her own induction into public life:

> "Lobanova loves to go to meetings," the women said of me. And it was true. I took an interest in civic activity and went to all the meetings.[22]

Village activists like Lobanova were often rewarded by being allowed to attend more and more meetings, conferences, and congresses at higher and higher levels. As the level became higher, the trips became longer—first the raion center, then the oblast, and finally, for the lucky few, the Kremlin in Moscow. Meetings were the natural habitat of the activist, and consequently the skills associated with the conduct of meetings were highly prized in this milieu. At the Second Congress of Outstanding Kolkhozniks in Moscow in 1935, most of the sessions were chaired by peasant delegates. Their feelings of responsibility and excitement at chairing a meeting at which hundreds were present and Stalin and other party leaders were sitting beside them on the podium were vividly conveyed in a series of articles and interviews published on the front pages of *Pravda* and *Izvestiia* ("I conducted the meeting with a firm hand," was the self-congratulatory heading of kolkhoznitsa T. P. Shapovalova 's report).[23]

The great majority of peasants did not love going to meetings. They went anyway, since attendance at kolkhoz and rural soviet meetings was expected, and absence was liable to be construed as a political statement. Local officials called numerous meetings, both because they were encouraged to do this by their superiors and because they regarded meetings as their métier and liked to show off their skills. (Periodically, superior officials rebuked their subordinates for excessive indulgence in meetings that gave no concrete results.)

Perhaps, one elderly peasant later suggested to a Soviet sociologist, the culture of meetings that came in with collectivization was the cause of the decline in religious observance in the village.

> With the collective farms, it seemed we had no time left to think about God and praying and fasts: you work during the day, you are running around at home during the evening, and then you realize they're showing a good movie or they're holding a meeting and you have to go. It's only as you are going to sleep that you remember that you didn't say your prayers today. Well, you think, I'll say them tomorrow, and so you put it off.[24]

Regardless of the validity of this causal connection, it is certainly true that, as a result of the widespread closing of churches, and taverns, and other meeting places, the meeting in the kolkhoz club was one of the main occasions outside the work context for peasants to get together.

The most important kolkhoz meeting of the year was the general meeting at which the end-of-the-year production report was presented and elections for the kolkhoz board and chairman were held. Meetings with state procurements agents to discuss delivery quotas might also be held. The elections and procurements meetings could become lively and passionate on occasion, if the kolkhozniks decided to dispute the raion's choice for chairman or wanted to reject the delivery quotas laid on them. But in general the meetings were dull, formal, and stereotyped.

The chairman's report and the auditing commission's report, each interminably long, filled with figures and as much Soviet jargon as the speaker could handle, took up the first part of the meeting. Sometimes the main speaker would be a representative of the raion or the MTS, come to introduce the new nominee for chairman or rebuke the kolkhozniks for their lateness in sowing or the high rate of pilfering during harvest, and in such circumstances the kolkhoz chairman and brigade leaders might be called on for "self-criticism," that is, acknowledgement and apology for past mistakes. The last part of the meeting invariably consisted of formal voting procedures: either the nomination of candidates for the kolkhoz board or the office of chairman, followed by an election by show of hands, or the proposal of motions approving the chairman's report, pledging the kolkhoz's commitment to meet its procurements obligations, and so on. On most occasions, all motions were unanimously and routinely approved.[25]

Speakers from the raion periodically came out to collective farms to give lectures on topics of current interest and recent government and party decisions. In the villages of Omsk oblast in 1939, to cite one of the Potemkin statistics referred to earlier, 13,416 such lectures were held. These lectures were generally very boring, lacking specificity and relevance to the peasants' immediate concerns, as the party's central agitation and propaganda (agit-prop) specialists acknowledged. There was little real exchange between speaker and audience, and the question period was usually short and formal. Raion propagandists particularly liked to talk to kolkhozniks about "the international situation," using terms and placenames that were unfamiliar or incomprehensible to many peasants. (Nevertheless, the popularity of peasant speculation in rumors and chastushki about the *real* international situation indicates that the lectures had some effect, even if it was not exactly the effect intended.)[26]

Soviet anniversaries and revolutionary holidays were also marked by kolkhoz meetings. The main Soviet and revolutionary holidays—Revolution Day (November 7), May Day, International Women's Day (March 8), Day of the Paris Commune (March 18)—had not been celebrated in villages as a rule before collectivization, unless perhaps by some Komsomol enthusiasts without the involvement of the village as a whole. In the kolkhoz, these holidays were routinely marked by formal meetings in the club, along with memorial days for Bloody Sunday (January 9) and the death of Lenin (variously cited as January 21 and 22).[27] The teacher seems to have had the main responsibility here, at least in the early years, when the formal entertainment offered in connection with revolutionary holidays usually involved some kind of performance or recitation by the schoolchildren, and perhaps a short statement on the importance of the occasion by a local official.[28]

In addition to the formal meeting, at least two revolutionary holidays—the Day of the Revolution (November 7), and May Day (May 1)—seem to have been actually celebrated in the villages in the 1930s, though not earlier.

The Revolution Day celebration seems to have been introduced into the villages after collectivization under strong official pressure, and it was anxiously monitored for hooliganism and anti-Soviet outbursts in the early years. Some villages took to it with a will: In the "Red Warrior" kolkhoz in 1931, for example, 100 liters of vodka were purchased with kolkhoz funds, and the drinking went on for five days, from November 6–10. But in other villages the kolkhozniks grumbled because the stores had no vodka. The authorities, of course, emphasized the official part of the program of Revolution Day rather than the drinking afterwards. Indeed, government trading regulations in 1930 prohibited sale of spirits on November 7 and 8, as on January 22 (the anniversary of Bloody Sunday) and May 1 and 2.[29]

Within a few years, however, the custom of celebrating November 7 with a drinking party paid for with kolkhoz funds had clearly became a valued tradition in many places. May 1 was also celebrated: "The kolkhoz will have a dinner," an old kolkhoznik wrote to his son in 1938. "They have made beer and got vodka—a quarter-liter (*chertvertinka*) for each person." Apart from the official program in the club, the form of Soviet celebrations closely resembled that of the religious holidays. Incidents of arson and violence and singing of anti-Soviet chastushki were not uncommon features of revolutionary holidays as well.[30]

The circulation of newspapers in the countryside increased dramatically after collectivization, rising from under 10 million in 1928 to more than 35 million in 1932. In a prosperous Melitopol kolkhoz-village whose reading habits were surveyed in 1936, 412 out of 555 households subscribed to at least one newspaper, and many to two or three. Of course, these are Potemkin statistics. But the newspapers, particularly *Krest'ianskaia gazeta*, had real meaning in peasant lives. Perhaps only a handful of devotees regarded this peasant newspaper with the enthusiasm of the delegate to the Second Congress of Outstanding Kolkhozniks who said it had given him his education. But the tens of thousands of letters that *Krest'ianskaia gazeta* received from peasants each year are testimony to a real relationship between the paper and its subscribers—even if the most important information flow between them went from readers to newspaper rather than vice versa.[31]

Radio seems to have been less important, despite the extensive publicity given to this new medium. Even at the end of the 1930s, only a quarter of all village clubs had their own radio receivers—and the receivers they had were very likely to be out of order. In Moscow oblast in 1935, for example, it was reported that only about one third of the radio receivers there actually worked.[32]

Movies made their first significant impact in the countryside in the 1930s. Peasants usually had to go into the raion center to see them, since there were still relatively few cinemas and projectors in the countryside (13,000 mobile projectors in 1937 and a mere 2,500 cinemas with the equipment to show sound films). The repertoire was small. Western films were no longer imported, and the most successful of the Soviet-made films—in 1939, for example, *Peter the First, Alexander Nevsky,* and *Lenin in October*—circulated in 800–850 copies and were shown over and over again.[33]

Young peasants, in particular, fell in love with the movies. "It is difficult to convey the ecstatic reaction of kolkhoz youth to the movies," said a speaker at the Tenth Komsomol Congress in 1936, describing the success of a film festival in Voronezh oblast attended by thousands of enthusiasts from the collective farms in which 7,000 young and adult kolkhozniks participated. A selective survey of young kolkhozniks (up to twenty-three years of age) conducted in 1938 found that almost all had been to the cinema in the past year, and 37 percent had been sixteen times or more. On average, each had seen four or five of the Soviet Union's top eleven movies, which included *Chapaev* (on the Civil War hero), *A Great Citizen* (a drama of political intrigue inspired by Kirov's assassination), *Childhood of Gorky,* and *A Rich Bride.*[34]

In general, the notion of a "new culture" entering the Soviet village after collectivization has more validity for peasant schoolchildren than for any other cohort in the village. This was the group that responded most enthusiastically to the big crazes of urban Russia in the 1930s: sound movies, sports, parachute jumping, long-distance aviation, and arctic exploration. In one of the most remarkable passages in his fictionalized memoirs of a peasant childhood, Mikhail Alekseev described the zest with which he and his fifteen- and sixteen-year-old peers threw themselves into these "Soviet" enthusiasms in the autumn of 1933, when a new school year began and the famine that had killed half the villagers the previous year could be forcibly banished from consciousness. When the movie *Chapaev* was shown in the raion center, the whole school camped out overnight in the square to see it, and the hero "burst into our souls and conquered them forever." When the ship "Cheliushkin," carrying a team of Soviet polar explorers, was stranded on an ice floe, these village children followed the rescue drama (which was headline news in the Soviet media for weeks) with the same passionate intensity as their urban counterparts:

> We heard about the Cheliushkinites and their rescuers in the field, where we were battling . . . stubborn weeds, and we shouted "Hurrah!" until we were hoarse when the last Cheliushkinite was taken from the ice and carried back . . . to Bol'shaia zemlia. Our joy was so great we did not even feel the itch in our palms, did not feel tiredness, and asked the brigade leader to leave us out in the field for the night.[35]

Celebrity

In terms of representation of peasants and their relationship to the Soviet regime, 1935 was a transitional year. During the first half of the 1930s, the fig-

ure of the kolkhoz activist—resourceful, energetic, tough, consciously committed to Soviet values—was offered as a model for other peasants to emu-
late. Two national conferences of activists or "kolkhoz shockworkers"
(udarniki) were held and widely publicized, as well as many provincial conferences. The second of the national conferences was held in March 1935
for the purpose of discussing the draft of the new Kolkhoz Charter prepared
by the Central Committee's agriculture department and formally endorsing
it on behalf of the peasantry. But there were problems with the activists' as-
signed status as representatives of the peasantry. In the first place, many of
them were kolkhoz chairmen and brigade leaders rather than ordinary kolkhozniks. In the second place, as the Second Congress of Outstanding
Kolkhozniks had demonstrated, the activists' relations with the passive (or
hostile) majority of peasants during collectivization had left a legacy of acrimony which made them reluctant as well as unrepresentative spokesmen for
the majority.

With the rise of the Stakhanovite movement in 1935, the exemplary
figure of the kolkhoz activist was beginning to give way to a new figure, the
peasant celebrity. Whereas the activist lived in a world of power, the celebrity's natural habitat was the Potemkin world of publicity. Whereas the
typical kolkhoz activist was a man, usually a Russian, the typical peasant celebrity was a woman, often a member of a colorful ethnic minority. Although
it was generally necessary to have production achievements in order to become a celebrity, once that hurdle had been cleared the celebrity's basic
occupation (until the moment of fame passed) was attending conferences
and meetings, being photographed, and meeting political leaders. At the
national level, one of the celebrities' main functions was to allow Stalin to
play the wise and caring leader-father with his affectionate peasant daughters.

Although the Second Congress was a substantive meeting with a real
agenda, the Stalin cult, in which peasant celebrities later played a considerable role, was already in evidence. Stalin was half an hour late for the first
meeting of the editorial commission because he was being photographed
with delegates. These photo opportunities were enormously important to
the delegates, as many accounts attest; and those who were able to stand
beside him or see him at close range were invariably moved by the experience.[36] When Stalin came in and took his place on the Presidium for the
third session, the minutes record,

> his appearance is met by thunderous applause which does not die down for a
> long time. The voice of one of the women delegates to the Congress cries:
> "Long live our Leader, the great teacher Stalin!.."[37]

Reporting back to his fellow villagers in Leningrad oblast in a mammoth six-hour question-and-answer session, one of the delegates emphasized the symbolic importance of the fact the Congress meetings had been
held in the Kremlin: "Would that really have been possible earlier [i.e., before the Revolution]? Would they have let us into that palace? Never! This
seemed to strike a chord with his peasant listeners, one of whom, in true

Potemkin spirit, inquired whether Western capitalist countries had been informed of the event. "Were foreign ambassadors present at the congress?" he asked hopefully.[38]

One of the first and most durable of the celebrity peasants, Pasha Angelina, was present at the Congress as a delegate. Although she spoke soberly on matters of substance, she also seized the occasion to pledge that she would plow 1,200 hectares on her tractor. This seems to have been a pioneering effort in the later very competitive field of solemn vows to Stalin on the raising of productivity.[39]

It was with the national adoption of the Stakhanov movement at the end of 1935 that new rituals involving peasants and leaders really blossomed. In industry, where the movement originated, the term "Stakhanovite" was used for workers who overfulfilled their norms by rationalizing the work process. In agriculture, however, there was less emphasis on rationalization, and the term Stakhanovite differed little from its precursor, shockworker (udarnik). Both Stakhanovites and udarniki in agriculture were peasants who were rewarded for producing more and working harder than other peasants. They were given material rewards like sewing machines and dresses, and in addition they received a privilege that was highly coveted, that of being sent to a Stakhanovite conference in the raion or oblast center, or even conceivably in Moscow. In the hierarchy of peasant Stakhanovites, those at the bottom, whose trips and publicity were only local, remained working in the fields and farms, where they were often treated with malice and hostility by other peasants. Those at the top, however, went to national conferences of Stakhanovites in the Kremlin,[40] where the lucky few who were sufficiently appealing or quick-witted were drawn into a magic Potemkin realm where they joked with Stalin and other Politburo members, gave interviews to journalists, and were sent on tour as celebrities.

Conferences and congresses had serious significance in the reward structure of Soviet life and as pageants at which the Soviet state displayed its most deserving and colorful citizens. It is not surprising, therefore, that the extraordinary tactlessness of one local authority in organizing a "congress of idlers," to which the *worst* producers of the kolkhoz were invited, earned a sharp rebuke from the party Central Committee.[41]

The shockworkers and Stakhanovites—along with sundry other "ordinary people" who became media celebrities in the 1930s, such as "hero mothers"—were members of a new Soviet category of celebrated ordinary people (*znatnye liudi*). The two most famous of the peasants in this category were Pasha Angelina and Maria Demchenko. Angelina, born in 1912 to a poor peasant family of Greek descent in Ukraine, joined the kolkhoz with her family in 1928, became a tractor driver the following year, and organized the first women's tractor brigade in the USSR in 1933. Demchenko, born in the same year, was a combine operator on a Ukrainian sugarbeet kolkhoz who initiated the movement of "500-ers" (*piatisotnitsy*) with her pledge to Stalin to gather not less than 500 centners of sugar beet per hectare, almost four times the average yield.[42] These two were clearly women of unusual ability and initiative, both of whom chose to enter the male-dominated mechanical professions. But many other peasant celebrities were simple milkmaids or swineherds, who attributed their success to their tender care for their animal charges and love for Stalin.

When the Stalin cult and Stakhanovite conferences were still young, a Soviet journalist—clearly fascinated by the new ritual, but more observer than participant—sat down and wrote an almost anthropological account of it.

> Applause burst forth, now dying down, now rising with new force, in honor of the leader of the people, comrade Stalin. When everything had quietened down, an excited voice from the depths of the hall suddenly shouted out a welcoming greeting in honor of Stalin in Kazakh. The Stakhanovites rose to their feet; Stalin, together with the party and government leaders, rose too; and for a long time, wordlessly, they passionately applauded each other. . . .
>
> When Sergo Ordzhonikidze brought the evening meeting to a close, thousands of people rose to their feet as one, and cries in honor of Stalin, in honor of our party, filled the high vaults of the hall. As he had done at the morning meeting, Stalin answered the Stakhanovites with enthusiastic applause, and then, with a broad gesture of acknowledgement, bade farewell to the delegates. . . .[43]

The rhetoric and iconography of the Stalin cult owes a lot to these Stakhanovite conferences of the 1930s. It was at these meetings that photographers learned to capture a new image of Stalin: good-humored and fatherly, plainspoken with no airs or pretensions, the human leader mingling easily with his people. In the mid-thirties, before the Great Purges, Stalin often appeared on such occasions in the company of other Politburo men, with whom he was photographed as but the first among equals (the Caucasus contingent, Ordzhonikidze and Mikoian, along with the genial Voroshilov, were the most successful in establishing this atmosphere of relaxed camaraderie). The Politburo men would engage in easy banter with the more confident Stakhanovite peasant girls, and kindly reassure the shy ones. A relationship of trust, warmth, and humor was projected against a background of natural beauty in one of the notable icons of this period, B. Ignatovich's 1936 photograph of Stalin and the Stakhanovite combine operator, Maria Demchenko, entitled "The Flowering Soviet Ukraine."

The Politburo men used the familiar form, *ty*, when speaking to the Stakhanovite peasant women. This was clearly intended to promote a sense of intimacy and informality, although cynics could interpret it in other ways. In the following exchange between Stalin and a nervous female combine operator from Saratov, a familial relationship was strongly suggested:

PETROVA: Comrades, this is my first year working on the combine. I cut 544 hectares and received 2,250 rubles. . . . I'm upset, I can't speak.

STALIN: Speak out bravely, we're all friends here (*zdes' vse svoi*).

PETROVA: Next year I take the obligation to cut 700 hectares. I call to socialist competition all the girls in the Soviet Union. (Applause)

MOLOTOV: You're doing fine, go on.

PETROVA: I'm too upset.

STALIN: Don't worry, don't worry, it's going fine, be brave. . . . You're at home here (*Zdes' svoia sem'ia*).[44]

For a peasant celebrity, the first meeting with Stalin was a moment of immense ritual significance, recounted over and over again. For some, it was a moment of self-revelation:

> When comrade Stalin said that "only kolkhoz life can make labor an honorable affair, only it can give birth to real women heroines in the countryside," I almost cried, because those words were words about my life and the life of millions of women like me. . . . I listened to comrade Stalin, and before me passed my whole life from childhood and up to the very meeting with comrade Stalin. . . . [45]

The stories often have a fairytale quality; indeed, some of the Stakhanovite peasant women were at least as successful in this line as the pseudofolk bards who published epics in praise of Stalin. Take Maria Demchenko's account of the first meeting, delivered at a subsequent Stakhanovite conference:

> So they came out to greet us—comrades Stalin, Molotov, Kaganovich, Voroshilov, Kalinin, Ordzhonokidze, Mikoian. . . .
>
> Comrade Stalin was standing among his assistants smiling, waving his hand to us (like this!) and looking at the kolkhozniks very, very closely and with a kind of special warmth.
>
> When the cheers had quieted down, he looked at me and said: "Well, comrade Demchenko, tell us your story. . . ."
>
> I told him everything. . . .
>
> I was looking at comrade Stalin—at how he was listening, and I could tell by his face that he hadn't missed a single word: now he would smile, then look thoughtful, or nod like this with his head, as if to say, that's right!
>
> After the kolkhoz women he started talking himself. His whole speech, his every word are so engraved on my memory that I'll never forget them. . . .
>
> At the end of his speech he looked at his comrades and said: "Well, what should we do? . . ." They thought for a while and said: "We should give them medals. . . ." My heart almost stopped. "Can it be that we are so fortunate, that not only did we get to see comrade Stalin, not only did we get to talk to him, but we are even receiving an award from him—the highest there is?"

After the medals had been handed out and the photographs taken, Stalin approached Demchenko and, as in a Russian fairytale, pointed her toward her future.

> I said, "Comrade Stalin, I have met my commitment [to get a yield of 500 centners]. I want you to give me a new task." He thought for a second and said: "Do you want to go to college?"
>
> "So much that I can't even put it into words." He turned to his comrades and said: "You know, comrades, Demchenko is going to study. She is going to be an agronomist." Then we said goodbye.[46]

The Stakhanovite conference was an occasion for rhetoric, not substantive discussion, so it is not surprising that this was an important venue for the development of fulsome epithets for Stalin. Peasant women Stakhanovites were the most inventive at this, especially the non-Russians, and some of them became adept at leading the crowd through a cycle of ovations.

Thank you comrade Stalin, our leader, our father, for a happy, merry kolkhoz life!

He, our Stalin, put the steering-wheel of the tractor in our hand. . . . He, the great Stalin, carefully listens to all of us in this meeting, loves us with a great Stalinist love (*tumultous applause*), day and night thinks of our prosperity, of our culture, of our work. . . .

Long live our friend, our teacher, the beloved leader of the world proletariat, comrade Stalin! (*Tumultous applause, rising to an ovation. Shouts of "Hurrah!"*)[47]

The general representational function of the national peasant Stakhanovite meetings was to show a prosperous, democratic Soviet Union and a happy peasantry. The keynote was the slogan taken from Stalin's speech to the meeting of outstanding male and female combine operators on December 1, 1935: "Life has become better and more cheerful (*Zhit' stalo luchshe, veselee*)."[48]

Happiness had various meanings, but one was to have been rescued from the past miseries. When a newspaper asked members of Angelina's tractor brigade (all in their late teens or twenties in 1935) what their mothers had been doing at the same age, they responded with pathetic stories:

Mother worked for thirteen years for hire. Then she married. She was beautiful, but who wants to marry a batrachka? She never learned to read.

At my age (nineteen), mother worked for wages for the landowner. From hard work, mother became ill; she died young, when I was only six.[49]

As peasant women told their own life stories at Stakhanovite conferences, the contrast between past misfortune and present happiness was frequently emphasized.

I used to be a farm hand and became an orphan at the age of four when my father died. I always lived with strangers, worked in misery, and never saw a happy day in my former life. Now I am an exemplary kolkhoznitsa and a highly esteemed person in our district. . . .

I worked hard then, when I was a batrachka, but nobody respected me for that labor, neither my boss nor the neighbors. Only in the kolkhoz did I win respect with my labor. . . .[50]

The recitation of production successes and autobiography were two key components in the standard Stakhanovite conference speech. In the case of female Stakhanovites, especially peasants, there was another important element: the listing of material rewards. As the women gloated about their new possessions, in what would once have been regarded as a spirit of petty-bourgeois acquisitiveness, party leaders often egged them on with jocular interjections and questions.

In 1935 I received a 700-ruble award for my exemplary work. . . . I used the money to buy some furniture. Also, I had a telephone installed in my home. . . . The People's Commissariat of Food Industry gave me 1,000 rubles, and the kolkhoz rewarded me with a house and a cow.

I have been rewarded for excellent work—three times by raion organizations [in Tadzhikistan] and four times by central organizations. I received a bed, a gramophone, and other cultural necessities. I can report to you that I don't live in my old mud hut anymore—I was awarded a European-style house. I live like a civilized person. . . .

Everything I am wearing I got as a prize for good work in the kolkhoz. As well as the dress and shoes, I got a sewing machine in Nalchik. For the harvest, I got a prize of a silk dress worth 250 rubles.[51]

A fourth component in the speeches of peasant women Stakhanovites was the assertion that the kolkhoz had liberated them from exploitation in the patriarchal family, because in the kolkhoz they were independent earners of labordays. This theme had its canonical statement in Stalin's remarks during his meeting with Stakhanovites of the sugarbeet fields in November 1935.[52] In a passage that undoubtedly provided the basic premise for the movie *The Rich Bride*, Stalin recounted what he had been told in a conversation with one of the women delegates to the Second Congress of Outstanding Kolkhozniks:

"Two years ago none of the lads was going to come round and see me at my place. A girl without a dowry! Now I have 500 labordays. And what happens? I've got suitors galore, they say they want to marry me, but I'm still going to look round—I'll pick my own suitors."[53]

Iakovlev related a similar conversation with a kolkhoznitsa:

I asked her whether she was married. She said no. I asked why not. She said: "I haven't found anybody who suits me so far, and I have no need to hurry. I might have had two children and a mother-in-law if I'd got married in 1929, but now I have 600 labordays."[54]

The theme of liberation was particularly popular with women Stakhanovites from ethnic minority groups. The two quotations that follow are from Pasha Angelina and Z. S. Budiagin, an Armenian brigade leader:

In the old days our Greek girls not only didn't know tractors, but were even afraid to go out into the street, to show their face, or to look at a man. In the old days, if a girl went out into the street with her face uncovered, and looked at a man, she would never be able to get married; she was a ruined girl. But now, thanks to our leader and teacher, comrade Stalin, the Greek girls have achieved such a position that we are leaving many men behind. . . .

Comrade Stalin has said very correctly that in the old days women were exploited. It was especially obvious in our Armenian villages, where women were real slaves. Now our female kolkhozniks have become free. Now they sometimes make more money than their husbands. And when you make more money than your husband, how can he exploit you? Then he shuts his mouth.[55]

Many Stakhanovites described conflicts with husbands that had arisen as a result of their liberation in the kolkhoz. Sometimes a lagging husband saw the light, as in the following rather patronizing account:

When I joined the kolkhoz in 1929, I had to struggle not only with backward kolkhozniks but also with someone very close to me—my husband. But I overcame him. My husband has now joined the kolkhoz and is already doing pretty well. In 1935, he became a shockworker, and he has won several awards and received good prizes.[56]

In other cases, such as this one described by a Stakhanovite from Bashkiria, liberation of the wife led to the collapse of the marriage.

They married me off [at sixteen]. I was married against my will, according to the old custom that still survived then. After living with my husband for a year and a half, I separated from him and began to work independently in the kolkhoz. Then I got the opportunity for a good life.[57]

Elections

As a general rule, Soviet elections belonged to the Potemkin world. Until 1937, national congresses of soviets were chosen every two years on the basis of indirect election, open voting, and an electoral system that not only disenfranchised kulaks and other "class enemies" but also heavily weighted the votes of urban workers in comparison with those of peasants.[58] To be sure, rural soviets were directly elected by the rural population, but infrequently (there were only three such elections in the decade—in 1931, 1934, and 1939) and on the basis of lists of candidates prepared in advance. Rural elections were sometimes conducted with panache: In 1934 in Rudnia raion, for example, a band consisting of local accordion, balalaika, violin, and cymbals players was driven around to liven up the election meetings. Up to 1937, however, the democratic facade was so slight that a government decree transferring tax-collection duties from the rural soviet to the raion was able to link this with the rural soviets' new [*sic*] role "as elective organs of Soviet power in the countryside" under the recent Constitution.[59]

The democratic aspect of the republican and national congresses of soviets consisted primarily of the inclusion of a many people from humble walks of life—peasants, workers, women, members of ethnic minorities—as delegates. These were among the celebrated ordinary people of the Stalin era that we have already encountered at Stakhanovite conferences and elsewhere. Indeed, the groups of outstanding kolkhozniks, Stakhanovites, and soviet deputies overlapped to a considerable degree. Among the delegates to the Second Congress of Outstanding Kolkhozniks were a number who had already been delegates to soviet congresses or were members of the Russian or Soviet parliaments: for example, Diomid Sidorov, a Communist kolkhoz chairman from Moscow oblast, and Praskovia Fomina, a nonparty head of a kolkhoz stock farm in the Northern krai, who were both members of the Russian parliament; or Tamara Shapovalova and Marfa Koniaeva, rank-and-file kolkhoz members from Voronezh and Kiev oblasts respectively, both nonparty, who were members of the Soviet parliament. As Shapovalova innocently related, she seemed to be getting elected to everything recently:

In addition to her membership of the Soviet parliament, she was also a member of the Voronezh oblast executive committee, the raion executive committee, and the board of her kolkhoz—and all this, she claimed, without being released from fieldwork obligations on the kolkhoz.[60]

Candidates for soviet elections were selected according to an informal quota system designed to produce a properly balanced ticket, as can be seen in a top-secret memo from a party secretary of the Western oblast to a raion official advising him to pick "seven male and female workers from production (the best of the Stakhanovites), four male and female kolkhozniks, [and] one representative of the intelligentsia" as candidates for the upcoming soviet elections, and to make sure that there were at least three women on the list and that no more than half the candidates were Communists or Komsomol members.[61]

The presence of peasants and exotically dressed tribesmen as delegates to the congresses added color to the obligatory newspaper coverage of proceedings. It also made a wonderful impression on foreigners, as was noted by A. L. Kapustina, a kolkhoznitsa from Leningrad oblast, who in 1935 became a deputy to the Soviet parliament.

> On November 7th, I was in our Leningrad oblast for the holiday. On the tribune I met some foreign workers and talked to them through a translator. I told them . . . that I, in the past a simple, downtrodden, rural woman, am a member of the Soviet government. They were so astonished that they wrote down my address, looked at my ID, saw my badge, and, finally becoming convinced, shook their heads. Yes, comrades, for them it is a miracle, because over there it would be impossible.[62]

This theme, incidentally, provided the basis for one of the big movies of the 1930s, *Member of the Government* (1939), which tells the story of a kolkhoznitsa who becomes a member of parliament.[63]

But all this changed—or so it seemed—with the new Constitution. As early as the beginning of 1935, the party Central Committee had decided to democratize the electoral system, substituting direct for indirect election, introducing voting by secret ballot, and ending the discriminatory weighting of urban against rural votes.[64] Then came the new Constitution (the draft of which was published on June 12, 1936), with its assurance that all citizens of the country had equal rights, and that all could vote and hold elective office, "regardless of race and nationality, religious creed, . . . social origin, property status, and past activity."[65] It was announced early in 1937 that the first direct elections for the Soviet parliament (the Supreme Soviet of the USSR) under the new Constitution would be held later in the year.

These were to be democratic elections, Zhdanov told the party Central Committee at the February-March plenum of 1937. Not only was there to be universal, equal, and direct suffrage, with the vote extended to former class enemies and a uniform representational principle,[66] but in addition, wonderful to relate, more than one candidate could compete for each seat and there were to be no lists (*spiski*) prepared in advance by party organizations. It was not going to be an easy transition, Zhdanov warned. Communists would have to learn to live with competition from candidates who were not party members, and be prepared for the embarrassment of having some Communist candidates rejected by the voters. They would have to drop the mindset associated with years of comfortable behind-the-scenes selection of nominees whose actual election was only a formality.[67]

There were limits, to be sure, to the program of instant democratization that Zhdanov outlined. In the first place, the 1937 elections were only for the Supreme Soviet, not for local soviets.[68] Thus, they did not directly affect the vital interests either of voters or of local soviet officers, whose jobs were not immediately on the line. In the second place, the Communist Party had not repudiated coercion (*nazhim*) in situations where its dictatorship was threatened. Zhdanov emphasized that if the new procedures encouraged demagogic attacks on local soviet officials—if, in short, the whole thing got out of hand—the party would not hesitate to take decisive action.[69]

What lay behind the new policy and how seriously it was intended by the party leaders are questions that have yet to be fully answered. A possible explanation is that there *had* been a genuine impulse towards democratization at an earlier point, but this impulse had disappeared almost completely by the time Zhdanov presented his report to the February-March plenum, and the program went through out of inertia. This plenum, it should be remembered, was the same one at which Molotov, Stalin, and Ezhov made blood-curdling denunciations of wrecking and conspiracy by highly placed Communists, signalling the onset of the Great Purges. If this was indeed an experiment in soviet democracy, it was stillborn.[70]

It was not long before the first signs of trouble appeared. In the Akkodzha kolkhoz in Simferopol oblast, for example, a didactic reading and discussion of the Statute on Elections, organized out in the fields by a local Communist, Kozlov, went seriously awry when peasants decided to have some fun at Kozlov's expense. It began when one member of the field brigade made the following suggestion: "Everything that you have told us here is very interesting, but we would like to see how it works in practice. Couldn't we now hold a trial election?"

This suggestion was seconded by several kolkhozniks, and Kozlov naively agreed to hold a mock election for the rural soviet and its auditing commission. Nine candidates were then nominated for the five positions on the rural soviet, and five for the three positions on the auditing commission. Then the fun began, as kolkhozniks indulged in "the most disgusting abuse" of local activists and officeholders who were among the nominees. "As if in 'jest,' [they] . . . threw mud on the kolkhoz chairman, comrade Mitrikh, a tractor-driver who used to be a batrak. They 'rejected his candidacy.' . . ."

The joke was continued later in the evening at the kolkhoz club, in the presence of the kolkhoz party organizer and a raikom representative. The mock elections were held, and evidently ended in a debacle for the current leadership of the rural soviet. The raikom representative decided to hush it up rather than make an issue of it. But he advised the kolkhoz's Communists "not to organize any more rehearsals of elections."[71]

This incident suggests the kolkhozniks had a low opinion of the activists and Communists and a sardonic view of the Potemkin aspects of Soviet life, rather than a serious view of forthcoming Supreme Soviet elections. But some of the "anti-Soviet" reactions collected by the NKVD suggested a more somber alienation on the part of some rural voters. In Voronezh oblast, some peasants were saying: "It's a pity they shot the Zinovievites. We would have voted for them in the new elections." Some "counter-revolutionary groups" in the same oblast were calling on peasants to boycott Communist candidates and choose "our own people." One said: "Now the elections will be secret, and we can vote for our own people and not for the Communists. The overwhelming majority of the population will not vote for the Communists, and there will be a change of regime." Another, identified as a sometime supporter of Antonov, leader of the 1921 peasant revolt in Tambov, said: "In the soviet elections we must elect non-party people and former kulaks. These people are cleverer than the Communists and do not covet other people's property, but the Communists just plunder the people."[72]

According to many reports, religious believers and priests, newly enfranchised by the 1936 Constitution, were the ones who responded most energetically to the opportunities offered by the new electoral procedure. Priests and pastors were quick to offer their services to local authorities as agitators and popularizers for the new Constitution and the Statute on Elections, holding meetings for this purpose in churches and prayer houses, and even going door to door as Soviet election propagandists.[73] In addition, however, some priests realized that they could run for election themselves, nominated by the parishes they served.

According to instructions issued in the summer of 1937, candidates for election could be nominated by Communist and Komsomol organizations, trade unions, industrial enterprises, collective farms, and a variety of other bodies, including "other legally registered organizations."[74] It seems to have escaped the attention of the drafters that since Soviet law required all religious organizations to register with the state, a literal reading of the decree gave nominating rights to every Orthodox parish in the country. But this did not escape the attention of believers. When an oblast newspaper published a stereotypical "unmasking" article about a priest's son, a reader wrote in to protest that this was completely out of line with the "new, joyful" life prefigured by the Constitution, which guaranteed that "not only a priest's son but also the priest himself has the right to serve even in the highest organs of [Soviet] power."[75]

Reports soon started coming in that that the priests' and believers' zeal in connection with the elections was not purely altruistic. In one raion, Old Believers tried to organize a congress to choose a list of Old Believer candidates for the Supreme Soviet elections. In another, Baptists and an Orthodox sectarian group, the Fedorovites, reportedly decided to contest the election as a bloc and set up election headquarters in a signalman's booth on the railroad. "Jerusalem letters" and pamphlets with lists of Orthodox candidates were circulated. Priests gave sermons explaining that religious organizations had the right to nominate candidates under the Election Statute; in Ukraine, priests in different regions were said to be coordinating their electoral strategy and making "pre-election tours." Parish meetings were held to elect candidates; straw votes were cast in churches to test the popular mood. In one village, when a visiting lecturer on atheism asked the peasants whom they supported in the elections, half the peasants called out "Father Nikolai" while the other half tried to shout them down.[76]

The NKVD reported to Stalin in October that Orthodox activists and sectarians were calling on peasants to vote against Communists and trying to reopen churches and prayer houses without authorization.[77] This interpretation, like the stories published in the press, attributed leadership to "the church people" (*tserkovniki*) and cast the peasants in the role of passive followers. It is possible, however, that in real life the roles were often reversed. Rarely if ever had "church people" led a grass-roots political movement in modern Russian history. On the other hand, there was ample precedent for peasants expressing protest against the state in the guise of religion.[78]

This hypothesis gains support from the report of a rural official in Belyi raion, Western oblast, in June 1937 that "people who didn't go to church twenty years ago are going now." In terms expressive of the bewilderment, anger, and fear that many Communists were feeling at this time, he continued:

> The priests say that the masses have elected them, that "We have a mandate [*zaiavlenie*] from the masses for the opening of the church." I, as rural soviet chairman, haven't seen any such mandates and doubt that they were given. But comrades, it's impossible to go on like this. In the future we will have to . . . find out who the wreckers are and send them to jail.[79]

Such advice was soon heeded. By midsummer, Soviet leaders were really alarmed by the "revitalization" of religion and its possible consequences in the elections. Their first response was to unleash a wave of terror against the Orthodox hierarchy. The NKVD announced the discovery of a number of counterrevolutionary conspiracies headed by churchmen, usually bishops and other prelates in the Orthodox Church who had sent priests as their agents for subversion in the villages. On the heels of this, although with less publicity, went the roundups of humble religious wanderers, sectarians and others in "the kulak operation."[80] Finally, there was more closing of churches and suppression of religious activity at local level. In several districts of the Western oblast, it was later reported, raikom secretaries created special brigades whose sole function was to close churches. In one raion, where a hasty decision was made to close down *all* churches, "the electoral commission got involved in the campaign, and in its reports on the progress of the electoral campaign regularly submitted information on . . . (*sic*) the closing of churches."[81] (Within a few months, however, these actions were judged to be "excesses" and the campaign against the churches was dropped.)

The most striking of the party leadership's reactions was to change the rules for the Supreme Soviet elections in the middle of the election campaign. There were two major changes. First, Orthodox parishes and other religious organizations were firmly excluded from the category of institutions with the right to nominate candidates. A. I. Stetskii, head of the Central Committee's department of agitation and propaganda and one of the main drafters of the new Constitution, explained that the Constitution certainly did *not* give religious organizations the right to nominate candidates in soviet elections. He condemned the church and sectarian groups that had wrongly tried to claim this right for "making fools" of the simple people who supported them. A few months later—too late to be a real contribution to the discussion—the agitprop people thought of a better argument, namely that nomination of soviet electoral candidates by church groups violated the constitutional separation of church and state.[82]

Second, the party leadership abruptly dropped the whole idea of multi-candidates elections for the Supreme Soviet. This extraordinary volte-face evidently occurred at the Central Committee plenum that took place on October 11–12.[83] It was not made public until December, just before the actual elections, when the uncontested candidates in each electoral district were euphemistically referred to as representatives of "the bloc of Communists and non-party people." Presumably, secret instructions on the decision and its implementation were sent to local party organizations immediately after the October plenum. On October 21, in any case, the press was able to report that the first nomination meetings had been held in three Moscow electoral districts, where the uncontested victors had been respectively Stalin, Molotov, and a thirty-four-year-old promoted worker, currently chairman of the Taganka raion soviet, Praskovia Pichugina.[84]

This, of course, meant that the Supreme Soviet elections were back on the old Potemkin track, but at the cost of considerable surliness on the peasants' side and jitteriness on the part of Communist organizers. Thousands of urban workers had to be sent to the countryside as agitators to combat the "counter-revolutionary slander" that was circulating in the villages in connection with the elections.[85]

Even so, the "slander" continued. In Voronezh oblast, Orthodox believers and Baptists agitated against the official candidates for the Supreme Soviet, "even at a kolkhoz meeting" in one case. Nuns distracted kolkhozniks from the election campaign by predicting that the Day of Judgement was at hand. Priests went around the villages advising people that with the secret ballot you could just "cross out the names of all candidates listed in the electoral bulletins and write in other names instead."[86]

In the village of Staryi Oskol, somebody managed to propose as a candidate "a certain Gorozankin, a relative of one of the accomplices in the evil murder of S. M. Kirov," no doubt plunging local officials into panic when the relationship was discovered. In the "Victory" kolkhoz, unknown saboteurs tore down slogans exhorting voters to support "the best people," a current catchphrase for loyal and upstanding citizens who were not formally party members.[87]

When the elections were finally held at the end of the year, "the bloc of Communists and non-party people" had a famous victory, allegedly winning almost 90 million of the 91 million votes cast. Thus, in the Potemkin world, at least, the peasants' confidence in the regime was unshaken. As to the regime's confidence in the peasantry, symbolically indicated by the proportion of seats allotted to peasants in the Supreme Soviet, a Kremlinological analysis comes up with mixed results. Peasants "won" 27 percent of seats in the Supreme Soviet elected at the end of 1937. This was by no means as impressive as their representation at the Extraordinary Congress of Soviets, held at the end of 1936 to ratify the new Constitution, at which 40 percent of delegates were peasants. On the other hand, it was a considerable improvement over their representation in the previous Soviet parliament (TsIK), in which a mere 15 percent of deputies were peasants.[88]

For the minority of peasants who were elected as soviet deputies, won Stakhanovite awards, and were photographed with Stalin at national conferences, the Potemkin village undoubtedly had meaning, for they were its embodiments in the world outside. Of course, their real ties with other peasants tended to diminish sharply as they became celebrities. Even when they were not physically absent from the village, the raion and the local rural officeholders usually became their real social milieu. But many of them left the village after a few years to continue their education. If they ever returned to the countryside, it was as agronomists or MTS administrators (like Maria Demchenko and Pasha Angelina).

For the peasantry as a whole, the Potemkin dimension of life could sometimes be a source of entertainment or even inspiration, but more often it provoked contemptuous indifference, frustration, or anger.

"Dear leaders, you see very blindly," wrote one Siberian peasant to Stalin and Kalinin in 1937.

> You only hear at all kinds of various congresses and meetings some number of people satisfied with everything who are delegates, and also all our press is pulling the wool over your eyes about the kolkhoz village. In fact the picture that can be seen in the kolkhozy is pitiful in every respect, especially if you compare it with the NEP years. . . ."[89]

Another kolkhoznik, this time from Kalinin oblast, concluded a letter to the newspaper describing the situation on the kolkhoz as follows:

> So you see, respected *Krest'ianskaia gazeta*, what awful things are happening on our kolkhoz. And our dear teacher, comrade Stalin, thinks everything is fine and people are absolutely living in Paradise."[90]

While some kolkhozniks might hope that foreign ambassadors had been present at the Second Congress of Outstanding Kolkhozniks to witness the sight of simple peasants chairing meetings in the Kremlin, others brusquely dismissed the whole occasion:

> The Communist top bosses have to have something to do, so now they have thought up a new Charter, created a prosperous life on paper, but that's all just nonsensical ranting (*brekhologiia*).[91]

11

The Mice and the Cat

The "mice" of the chapter title are Russian peasants, whose subaltern strategies in the 1930s are the subject of this book. The "cat" is the predator-boss, the other side of the equation of dominance and subordination. The symbolism of the cat and the mice was used in Russian woodcuts of the late seventeenth and early eighteenth century, where the cat was traditionally identified with Peter the Great. In our story, the cat is often Stalin, the national personification of *vlast'* (power). But there were also many lesser cats. For the peasants, the most important of these were the "little Stalins" of the raion who personified vlast' at the local level.

This chapter deals with two aspects of the relationship of mice and the cat, both associated with representation. The subject of the first section is rumors, especially those concerned with power and politics. Rumor is as much a medium for the expression of popular opinion as for the dissemination of information. In the rumors that circulated in the countryside in the 1930s, Russian peasants tried to interpret national and even international events and, like Kremlinologists, carefully analyzed the pronouncements of the rulers to discern their real meaning and the motives behind them. Needless to say, this Kremlinological approach implied a profound skepticism on the part of the peasants about the truth of anything "they" (the bosses, the party propagandists, the newspapers) said.

In some earlier historical periods, peasant rumors had invoked the myth of "the good Tsar," whose benevolent intentions toward the people were being thwarted by malign officials. We do not hear of many such rumors in the time of Peter the Great, however, and the same is true of the time of Stalin. The rumors that circulated in the countryside in the 1930s are notable not only for the almost complete absence of "naive monarchism" but also for the depth of the popular antagonism towards Stalin they convey.

The second section of the chapter deals with the show trials of former raion officials that took place in many rural districts in the autumn of 1937. These trials, part of the broader phenomenon of the Great Purges, may at first glance seem to belong purely to the sphere of power and its contestation, that is, the world of cats. But the situation was more complicated. Peasant mice were involved at many levels in the raion show trials. They were the primary victims of the officials' alleged crimes of brutality, extortion, and other violations of rights; and they were also the main witnesses called to testify in court against the accused.

The raion show trials were evidently conceived as a play for the "naive monarchist" vote in the countryside. Their message to peasants was that the true Soviet *vlast'* was not the one that peasants encountered in everyday life—as demonstrated by the fact that Stalin, the personification of *vlast'*, was now punishing local officials for their abuses.

But peasants were deaf to this message. No rumors are known to have circulated in the villages concerning Stalin's benevolent intentions or his role in rescuing mice from the predatory behavior of little cats. Instead, the peasant mice seem to have stuck to their view that a cat is a cat, only some cats are bigger and more dangerous than others. The conclusion they drew from the bloody demise of so many cats in 1937, judging by the "conversation of rumors,"[1] was that the regime was in crisis, close to collapse, and war was imminent. As for the raion trials themselves, by refusing to hear the regime's message the peasants turned the trials into a kind of carnival—a time of revelry in which the world is "turned upside down" and the powerless can mock the great with impunity.

Stalin in the Conversation of Rumors

It is difficult to discover what peasants really thought—or rather, what they said when they talked to each other, not addressing themselves to persons in authority, outsiders, or educated people. Almost by definition, most of our sources are either outsiders' reports on peasants or peasants' communications with outsiders. Rumors are the exception to this rule. Fortunately for historians, the Soviet police collected rumors as an index of popular mood and of public response to government measures. That medium of collection no doubt introduced biases into the source, since the NKVD and its predecessors were always primarily interested in the part of the peasants' conversation that dealt with politics and the state; and in the 1930s the rumors and opinions they reported were almost always seditious.

Whether that is a serious distortion of the real situation remains an open question. A Finnish Communist, Arvo Tuominen, who saw something of the Russian countryside in 1934 as a member of a state grain procurements brigade, formed the opinion that peasants never talked about the regime in anything but seditious terms:

> My first impression, which remained lasting, was that everyone was a counter-revolutionary, and that the whole countryside was in full revolt against Moscow and Stalin.[2]

It is possible that this antiregime consensus was at least partly a product of the appearance of Tuominen's procurements brigade in a village. But it is equally possible, as Tuominen suggests, that the conventions of peasant-to-peasant discourse demanded an unswervingly negative assessment of the regime and all its works. This is characteristic of conversation among subalterns in armies, schools, prisons, and other closed institutions, just as it is characteristic of these same subalterns to exhibit positive, civic-minded attitudes when speaking with superiors. Thus, even as we listen in, courtesy of the NKVD, to the private conversations of Russian peasants, the question of what peasants really thought remains to some extent elusive.

Accepting that caveat, we can nevertheless know what thoughts Russian peasants expressed to each other via the medium of rumor in the 1930s. In the field of politics and government, their favorite topics were the likelihood of internal collapse or overthrow of the regime and the possibility and likely consequences of war. They also paid attention to signs of dissension within the party leadership and the impact of pressure from foreign powers on Soviet policy. As to the party's leader, peasants showed a consistently hostile and suspicious attitude to Stalin—even more hostile and suspicious than their attitude to the Soviet regime in general. In the village, as Tuominen remarks, "there were none of those paeans to the great Stalin that one heard in the cities."[3] The prevailing opinion, as expressed in rumors, was that Stalin, as the organizer of collectivization, was the peasants' inveterate enemy: they wished him dead, his regime overthrown, and collectivization undone, even at the cost of war and foreign occupation.

On Collectivization and Famine

Stalin made his debut as a central topic of peasant conversation in March 1930 with his letter, "Dizzy with Success," condemning the excesses of local officials in collectivization. This disingenuous ploy was deeply and predictably offensive to the Communists at local level who had been doing their best to carry out the party's orders. Stalin and the Politburo presumably made the political calculation before publishing the letter that this cost was outweighed by the benefit of the peasants' gratitude. Almost certainly, they were trying to tap the peasants' "naive monarchist" vein.

Peasants undoubtedly took notice that a message had been sent to them. Reports came in from all over the country about peasants' efforts to obtain a copy of a newspaper in which "Dizzy with Success" was published, paying blackmarket prices and circumventing the efforts of some local Communists to stop its distribution (in one district of the Northern krai, "they took newspapers from the peasants who were reading Stalin's article, tore them out of their hands"; elsewhere, all issues of the papers coming into the villages on personal subscription were seized). In the Urals, peasants made special trips into town to get the issue of *Pravda* with Stalin's article—"and it had to be *Pravda*, not the local paper, since they had absolutely no faith in the latter, moreover for an issue of the paper they paid up to 10 rubles." When a copy of the paper was obtained, it was passed around from hand to hand, and read again and again.[4]

Having Stalin's article as a weapon, peasants then did their best to use it against local officials. In one village in the Urals, a group of peasants with the village priest in tow marched around waving the newspaper cuttings of Stalin's article and threatening to sue local authorities for "illegal organization of collective farms." Rumors were quickly disseminated that "Stalin says it is still too early to build collective farms" or "Stalin has ordered all communes and collective farms to be dissolved." In Mishkino in the southern Urals, there was even a rumor that Stalin was coming to defend the kulaks and chastise the bedniaks and kolkhozniks, as a result of which groups of kulaks sat waiting at the railway station for Stalin's arrival.[5]

These last, undoubtedly, were peasants of the famous "naive monarchist" breed. But they were from a remote region, culturally worlds apart from peasants who thought of bringing lawsuits; and reports of similar behavior are few and far between. Most of the reports of peasant reactions suggest that the peasants were eager to make use of Stalin's letter but reserved judgement on the author and his intentions.

The next cluster of peasant conversations about politics comes from the famine years, 1932–33. According to OGPU reports on the Western oblast, peasants were commenting anxiously in the spring of 1932 on the rumors of famine in Ukraine, talking about the possibility of war and revolution (there were rumors that a revolution would start on May 1), and expressing the hope that if war came, the Soviet regime would fall. They believed that the Soviet regime was hiding important information from them (which of course it was), and that what the newspapers and propagandists told them was lies. Among the comments from the villages that the OGPU reported were the following:

> I think there will soon be war, then the kolkhoz will collapse, I will be the first to leave the kolkhoz. They say that the Poles and the Japanese are already making war [against the Soviet Union], only it is being hidden from us.

> Answer me this question, what kind of "Bloody Sunday" will it be on May 1st? In the village, they are saying that on May 1st there will be war, and the Bolsheviks will be slaughtered everywhere.

> I think that if war comes, not a single [peasant] will go to the defence of Soviet power.[6]

The peasants' evaluations of Stalin reported by the OGPU were uniformly negative. One kolkhoznik compared Stalin unfavorably with Lenin:

> Comrade Stalin began to push too high tempos in that respect [collectiviza-
> tion]. . . . Things would have been otherwise had Lenin lived; [he was] a man
> with higher education and much experience of life, but Stalin unfortunately does
> not have that.[7]

An enigmatic anecdote circulating among Western oblast peasants had
to do with Stalin's slogan, "Socialism in one country." The story was that
Stalin went to the Caucasus on vacation; and while he was there, he worked
as a shepherd, since there was nobody else to look after the sheep (a reference to the outflow of population from the villages that accompanied collectivization). Karl Marx came down from the mountain and heard Stalin singing his song, "We are building socialism in one country." Marx asked for
whom was he singing this song. Stalin said, "I am singing the song to my
sheep, that is, the party."[8]

The peasants' skepticism about Stalin and his songs was not alleviated
by his call to kolkhozniks to become prosperous (*zazhitochnye*, the term formerly used for middle peasants who were dangerously close to kulak status)
at the First Congress of Outstanding Kolkhozniks in January 1933. The
reaction the OGPU picked up was sullen and suspicious, fearing a trap.
Once you become prosperous, peasants said, they will expropriate you.[9]

A more intense hostility, directed personally at Stalin and Mikhail Kalinin,
president of the Soviet parliament, was reported from the famine-stricken
Volga in 1932–33. (Kalinin, the only top party leader of peasant origin, had
earlier been regarded as a protector of peasants; but his stock plummeted
around the time of the famine, and from this time on, he became an object
of special malice and mockery in the countryside.) During procurements in
1932, rumors swept around the countryside that the grain was not to be
used to feed the towns and the Red Army (as Soviet officials claimed), but
instead was to be exported. Chastushki and proverbs about the state's export plans made their appearance. The famine was blamed on Stalin, who
"screwed things up" in 1932, and life under Stalin was compared unfavorably with life under Lenin:

> When Lenin lived, they fed us.
> When Stalin came, they tormented us with hunger.[10]

On Kirov's Murder

In the mid-1930s, the Soviet regime was trying hard to improve relations
with the peasantry, as was demonstrated by the conspicuous consultation
with peasants that preceded the publication of the Kolkhoz Charter, the
concessions contained in the Charter, the 1935 amnesty for kolkhozniks
and kolkhoz chairman arrested for economic crimes a few years earlier, the
moves towards forgiveness of kulaks, and the granting to the collective farms
of eternal titles to their land. Stalin personally made a number of conciliatory
and even ingratiating gestures: for example, his insistence on a larger private
plot and his offer of maternity leave at the Second Congress of Outstanding

Kolkhozniks; his warm public appearances with peasant Stakhanovites; and his famous remark that "A son does not answer for his father."

If this aroused positive reactions within the peasantry, our sources do not show them. The reported reactions from peasants tend to be sour and wary, with the peasants looking all gift horses in the mouth and always inclined to put the worst possible interpretation on any action of the regime. Thus, even the granting of eternal titles to kolkhoz land could provoke grumbling that this was a new form of enserfment and the land titles were meant to ensure "eternal enslavement in the kolkhoz," while the 1935 amnesties could be construed in the village as Stalin's attempt to make amends to the low-level officials who were punished for collectivization "excesses."[11]

Judging by materials in the Smolensk Archive, the topic that provoked the strongest reaction in the villages at this period was the murder of Sergei Kirov, the Leningrad party leader, in December 1934. Kirov has been favorably regarded by most scholars, Western as well as Soviet, as a popular leader of moderate, noncoercive instincts who was responsible for the comparatively mild form of collectivization experienced in Leningrad oblast. In the Potemkin representation of peasant life, Kirov's murder called forth an outpouring of popular sorrow and indignation, expressed in the lament "Weeping for Kirov" (*Plach o Kirove*) composed by the folk bard E. P. Krivosheeva.[12]

In real life, the reaction was quite different. The reports diligently collected by party investigators and the NKVD in the Western oblast indicated that Kirov's murder, far from being regretted or deplored, provoked a wave of excitement and malicious satisfaction in the villages. This was not based on any specific objection to Kirov, about whom Western oblast peasants knew little. The peasants were evidently pleased to hear that *any* Communist leader had perished, especially in circumstances that implied the existence of internal conflicts within the leadership, and thus renewed hope that the regime would collapse. The only note of regret in the rumors following Kirov's death was that the man who had been killed was not Stalin.

Chastushki about Kirov's murder sprang up immediately. Almost all those reported in the Western oblast linked Kirov's murder with the suggestion that Stalin might suffer the same fate. One song played off the coincidence that bread rationing was lifted on January 1, 1935, just a few weeks after the murder:

> When Kirov was killed,
> They allowed free trade in bread.
> When Stalin is killed,
> They will disband all the kolkhozy.[13]

A popular final couplet, used in many chastushkas at this time, expressed the basic idea concisely:

> They killed Kirov,   *Ubili Kirova,*
> They'll kill Stalin too. *Ubyiut i Stalina.*[14]

In one version, sung by kolkhoz women who were drinking and revelling on All Souls Night, the couplet acquired a particularly sinister twist:

They (we) killed Kirov,	*Ubili Kirova,*
We'll kill Stalin.	*Ubyëm Stalina.*[15]

The reaction to Kirov's murder was so marked that it must have made a deep impression on all Communists who read the police reports. Assuming that the peasant mood in the Western oblast was not atypical, Stalin obviously had a lot to worry about—including his own assassination, since there seemed to be no shortage of volunteers to carry it out. Many people believe that Stalin's hand was behind the murder of Kirov, although the accusation remains unproven. If so, it must have been quite a shock to him to find such widespread popular support for his project of killing Communist leaders.

Many threatening and rebellious remarks and gestures were reported in connection with the Kirov murder. In one kolkhoz office, a former party member "went up to the portraits of Voroshilov and Ordzhenikidze (*sic*) and cut their faces with a knife, saying that now that Kirov had been dealt with, they should be dealt with too." There were similar reports involving portraits of Stalin. In a few cases, the remarks reported implied that Stalin was somehow involved in the Kirov murder.[16]

In one village, a former Komsomol member, Arkhipov, boasted to a group of kolkhozniks that if he ever got near Stalin, he would kill him, at which several of his audience expressed similar sentiments. A nine-year-old peasant schoolboy said at a meeting of his Pioneer troop: "Down with Soviet power; when I grow up I will kill Stalin." A young kolkhoznik ended an altercation with the local rural soviet chairman, a Communist, with the threat that "You'll get the same thing that Kirov got."[17]

One reason that Kirov's murder became an event of such mythic proportions in the popular mind was that the Communist Party's own response encouraged this. Early in 1935, the Central Committee sent out a top secret letter to local organizations alleging that Kirov's murder was the product of an anti-Soviet conspiracy led by the former leader of the Leningrad party, Grigorii Zinoviev, and other old opponents of Stalin. All party and Komsomol organizations were required to "work through" this letter (that is, read and discuss it and draw practical conclusions), and then scrutinize their membership lists to see if they contained hidden traitors and class enemies.

This produced the usual "unmaskings" and expulsions of party and Komsomol members.[18] In addition, it served as an amplifier for all the antiregime songs and rumors that had been doing the rounds, which were dutifully repeated and deplored at innumerable "self-criticism" meetings. Another incidental effect was to bring Zinoviev's name to the attention of peasants for the first time: From this time on, ten years after the effective end of his political career, he became a prominent figure in the rural conversation of rumors.

Another reason that the Kirov murder had such resonance in the countryside—and resonance of this particular type—was no doubt the presence in the villages of comparatively large numbers of disgruntled *former* Communists and Komsomol members. The overwhelming majority of these were not former oppositionists but simply people who had been expelled from the party in the long sequence of party purges in the years 1933–35, usually for some mundane offense such as embezzlement, bribe taking, habitual drunkenness, or an "economic" offense such as failure to meet procurements quotas. There is no reason to think that most of them were "anti-Soviet" before being dropped from the party, but every reason to expect that they would be after it, since their status and prospects were considerably damaged by expulsion.[19]

As noted in an earlier chapter, there were probably more former Communists than Communists in the countryside in 1935, and many of the seditious remarks reported from collective farms after Kirov's murder were attributed to such people in the police and party reports. This makes sense, since former Communists were likely to be more interested in politics and better informed about party matters than the average peasant, and they were also likely to be angry and disillusioned with the party that had rejected them. But it also lends weight to the hypothesis that peasants were getting their real political education in the 1930s from *former* Communists rather than party propagandists. Of course, the former Communists were not responsible for the peasants' "anti-Soviet" attitudes, which sprang from the experience of collectivization and the famine. But they probably were responsible for teaching peasants how to be anti-Soviet in a Soviet ("politically literate") manner.

On The Shadow of War

I asked for the floor and began to tell the kolkhozniks about the international situation and about the essence of the capitalist encirclement, remarking among other things that you won't find among us a single honest kolkhoznik who would want war, since war brings people enormous miseries and so on. At that moment a kolkhoznik, Ignat Rodchenkov, jumped from his place and cried out, shaking with anger: "To hell with this kind of life! Let there be war! The sooner the better! I'll be the first to go!"[20]

The possibility of a new concerted military attack by foreign powers aimed at wipe out the world's first socialist state had been a nightmare of Soviet leaders since the Civil War. The Soviet press in the 1930s hammered away at the theme of the peace-loving nature of the Soviet Union and the war mongering tendencies discernible in capitalist nations, particularly after the rise of Hitler in Germany and the consolidation of an expansionist militaristic regime in Japan. War was always represented in the media as a disaster for the Soviet Union, particularly if it came prematurely, before the country's industrial buildup was sufficiently advanced. These questions were among the few on which the regime and most educated Soviet citizens saw eye to eye.

But peasants had a different perspective. In the first place, they were bored by the lectures and angered by the demands for money that often went with them. When a visiting propagandist asked peasants on one kolkhoz to contribute to a state loan for strengthening Soviet military might, "a flood of short exclamations" came from the mutinous kolkhozniks ("Why are they talking about a state loan when there is no bread?" "Nobody gives *us* anything!").[21] In the second place, the content of the rumors suggests that many or most peasants did not agree that war would be such a bad thing, if it led to the overthrow of the current regime.

Why do you work, said a troublemaker to kolkhozniks in Perm oblast in October 1938, when "war is coming and soon there will be a change of regime (*perevorot*) [and] we will divide up the land." In Leningrad oblast in 1937 "a 16–year-old boy wandered through the villages with a Bible . . . and called on young people not to go to the cinema or to clubs and Red corners, and to fight against Soviet power, since 'soon the Fascists will start a war'"; and some Christian groups were "spreading provocative rumors with quotations from *The Protocols of the Elders of Zion* to serve Fascist aims in the event of war." The previous winter, the Western obkom noted that Orthodox and sectarian groups tended to praise capitalist and fascist systems and were trying to set up secret insurrectionary organizations "in case of war."[22]

The ill-fated national population census taken in January 1937 provoked some remarkable popular discussions about religion and politics. The big topic of debate was whether the census question about religious belief should be answered honestly by believers. It was widely assumed that those who identified themselves as believers would get on a special list; the question was, would that be good or bad? Obviously bad, said many rumors. Those listed as believers would be branded, arrested, prosecuted, loaded with extra taxes, deported, expelled from collective farms, taken out and shot. But some people drew different conclusions. Assuming that war and a change of regime were likely, they thought it shrewd and prudent to identify oneself as a believer. "It will be good for non-believers under Soviet power, but not for long. After the war it will be good for believers."

In the event of a war, "Poland and Germany will get all the data on non-believers," and will presumably punish them the same way Soviet power punished believers. In the event of an internal coup, similarly, a new government would also be likely to use religious belief as a litmus test for loyalty; thus, one woman listed herself as a believer, telling the census taker that "if there is a new upheaval (*perevorot*), it will be better for her and her children." But those who expected to find themselves under Japanese occupation had better write "non-believer," for rumor had it that "the Japanese will beat those who write themselves down as believers."[23]

Some rumors treated the census question on religion (see pp. 204–6) as a kind of referendum whose results were likely to influence Soviet policy, either directly or as a result of international pressure. This response surely reflects the peasants' interpretation of the organized discussion on the new Constitution in which peasants had just participated. Many people thought that, presented with an overwhelming "yes" vote on religion, the regime would be obliged to reopen the churches.

According to other rumors, the question was not so much a referendum as a potential weapon in international diplomacy, something Soviet diplomats could cite to demonstrate Soviet "respectability" and further the cause of collective security. "The state wants to find out exactly how many religious people there are in our country so as to show foreign governments that we have religious people and that religion in our state is not under restriction, therefore one ought to write down 'Orthodox'." According to others, a "yes" vote would help the international community put pressure on the Soviet government, "because that census will be reviewed by the League of Nations, and the League of Nations will ask comrade Litvinov [the Soviet foreign minister] why we closed the churches when we have many believers."[24]

A similar belief in the efficacy of foreign pressure had been reported earlier by the NKVD with reference to the provision of the new Constitution that returned civil rights to priests: "This change came about as a result of the fact that foreign governments put pressure on the Soviet Union. Soon there will be a total change of regime."[25]

During the Great Purges, the Moscow show trials presented blood-curdling stories of sabotage, conspiracy, and treasonous collaboration with the capitalist foes of the Soviet Union by former party and government leaders, who publicly confessed their crimes. The trials were presumably intended to mobilize popular support behind the regime. At the same time, Stalin seemed to be reaching for some kind of populist alignment with "the little people" against treacherous bosses when he said: "Leaders (*rukovoditeli*) come and go," he said. "Only the people (*narod*) is eternal."[26]

But neither of these approaches had much success in the countryside. If anything, the trial of Zinoviev and Kamenev for complicity in Kirov's murder seems to have had the opposite effect. On the principle that "my enemy's enemy is my friend," sectarians in Leningrad oblast prayed for the soul of Zinoviev and other Old Bolshevik "terrorists" after their execution in the summer of 1936. Similarly, after reading accounts of the second big Moscow trial in January 1937, one anonymous letter writer concluded that since Stalin hated Trotsky, Trotsky must have been an opponent of collectivization and friend of the Russian peasant.[27]

Stalin's declaration of solidarity with "the little people" in October 1937 seems to have made little or no impression in the villages. Indeed, the infrequency of even a perfunctory bow to the Stalin cult is one of the most striking characteristics of the thousands of letters written by peasants to *Krest'ianskaia gazeta* in 1937–38. In marked contrast to the behavior of "Potemkin" peasants on public occasions, peasant letter writers—even peasant petitioners—rarely showered Stalin with praise and gratitude or quoted his words of wisdom. In fact, they generally avoided mentioning him at all.

Of course, there were exceptions such as Stepanida Iaroslavtseva, a fifty-two–year-old kolkhoz activist who wrote to express gratitude to "the leader of the peoples, Great Stalin," for releasing pensioners from state procurements obligations. There were also peasant petitioners who wrote directly to Stalin and Kalinin, although not necessarily in a spirit of adulation. Even on the comparatively few occasions when peasants complimented Stalin in their letters, they tended to do so in a backhanded manner. Thus one peasant correspondent, having started promisingly by quoting the dictum of "our beloved leader of peoples and all progressive humanity, comrade Stalin," that "one ought to hearken to the voice of the masses," went on immediately to complain that the writer's earlier letters to Stalin had been ignored, that is, Stalin had neglected to follow his own advice.[28]

In 1939, when measures for tightening discipline in the kolkhoz were discussed in the Central Committee, Stalin was reportedly anxious about their possible adverse impact on the peasant opinion. But his Politburo colleagues reassured him: "The *narod* has been expecting it for a long time."[29] This unintentionally captures a real aspect of the peasants' attitude to Stalin that comes through in the rumors, namely their very low expectations of him. Stalin probably assumed that the narod had an image of him as the Good but Terrible Tsar, dispenser of justice and rewards as well as punishments. But it is striking how little any such image figures in rumors or other genuine popular sources (as opposed to the pseudopopular, Potemkin type). Memories of collectivization inhibited the development of any "good Tsar" image for Stalin in the countryside during the prewar period (although this may well have changed after the war). If Stalin made overtures or conciliatory gestures, peasants reacted with skepticism and suspicion. If he tightened the screws, they viewed it not as a betrayal, since there was no mutual trust to betray, but as further confirmation of Stalin's well-established status as Peasant Enemy No. 1.

How the Mice Buried the Cat

"How the Mice Buried the Cat" is an old Russian woodcut often thought to depict popular rejoicing at the death of Peter the Great.[30] It shows a group of dancing and celebrating mice accompanying the corpse of a large cat, firmly tied to a stretcher as if to eliminate any danger of last-minute resurrection, on its last journey. This seems an apt metaphor for the extraordinary series of show trials of rural officials that took place in raion centers throughout the Soviet Union in the fall of 1937, at the height of the Great Purges.[31] The cat stands for the defendants in the show trials, former officials now labeled "enemies of the people," who were accused of abuse of power, mistreatment of the peasantry, and systematic violation of the Kolkhoz Charter. The mice, rejoicing at the cats' downfall, were the peasant witnesses on whose testimony the cases against the officials were built.

The raion show trials had similarities with their Moscow counterparts, notably the fact that the defendants were former political leaders (at raion and national levels, respectively) who were accused of counterrevolutionary crimes and identified as "enemies of the people." But there were also important differences. In the Moscow trials, the defendants were Old Bolsheviks with a long history of devotion to the Revolution accused of fantastic, unbelievable crimes against the state involving elaborate conspiracies, terrorism, wrecking, contacts with Trotsky and foreign intelligence agencies. The case against them rested primarily on their own confessions. In the raion trials, by contrast, the defendants were low-level officials facing perfectly plausible charges relating to abuse of the peasantry and mismanagement of agriculture; and the case against them rested primarily not on confessions but on testimony given by kolkhozniks.

Like all show trials, these raion trials were political theater whose dénouement was known in advance, not "normal" judicial proceedings in which the accused might or might not be convicted. But this political theater was much more realistic and down-to-earth than the melodramatic Moscow variety. It was quite easy to believe that the defendants had committed all the acts that were attributed to them: bullying and abusing peasants, forcing them to meet impossible procurements quotas, interfering in peasant agriculture by dictating "unrealistic sowing plans," and so on. The only part of the indictment that really strained credibility was the premise that these acts were criminal in Soviet terms, that they differed in anything other than degree from the customary behavior of local Soviet officials in charge of kolkhoz agriculture and procurements. In short, the raion show trials had something of the old "Dizzy with Success" smell about them: that is, higher authorities responding to problems in the kolkhoz by shifting the blame to local officials.

The Making of Raion Show Trials

Show trials were no novelty in Russia in the 1930s, and raion-level trials would rarely warrant coverage in the national press. In the spring and summer of 1937, however, *Pravda* did report on several raion show trials concerning agriculture and peasant affairs. It seems clear that *Pravda* was offering these cases as a model, implicitly encouraging oblast authorities to organize similar ones in their own rural raions. A month or so after the last of *Pravda*'s reports, raion show trials were held in many parts of the country, all following a roughly similar pattern. The cases were heard by assize sessions of the oblast court, and the oblast newspaper gave them detailed coverage. This continued for a few months and then stopped abruptly. After December 1937, there are no further reports of rural raion show trials of this type.

The quantity, timing, and thematic similarity of the trials seems to exclude the possibility that they were the result of spontaneous local initiative, although undoubtedly local events provided the specific context. In all probability, secret instructions were sent to oblast party committees and NKVD branches about the organization of such trials, and the oblasts selected the particular raions in which they were held.

The first of *Pravda*'s reports concerned a show trial of former party and soviet leaders in Lepel district in Belorussia that was held in March. The accused were charged with illegally confiscating peasant property as payment for tax arrears, despite the recent law forgiving arrears in the light of the exceptionally poor harvest of 1936. According to *Pravda*'s report, the Lepel investigation was sparked by letters of complaint from local peasants, and the Belorussian state prosecutor took action on instructions from Andrei Vyshinskii, state prosecutor of the USSR. Peasant witnesses testified at the trial, which was held at the Lepel municipal theater, and the court reportedly received dozens of letters from peasants grateful for deliverance from their former oppressors.[32]

Three months later, *Pravda* reported a similar show trial from the Shiriaevo district of Odessa oblast in the Ukraine. There, top district officials had been found guilty of "outrageous" treatment of kolkhozniks and routine violations of their rights under the Kolkhoz Charter, including illegal confiscation of peasant property, extortion, nighttime searches (*obyski*), arbitrary exaction of taxes and of subscriptions to state loans, imposition of impossibly high grain procurement quotas in 1936, and "insulting behavior" towards kolkhozniks. These crimes had come to the attention of the party's Central Control Commission, which had instructed the Ukrainian state prosecutor to take action. The main evidence against the accused in the Shiriaevo trial came from peasant witnesses, more than thirty of whom were called to testify.[33]

A few weeks later, *Pravda* reported similar show trials in Novominsk, a Cossack raion in the Azov-Black Sea oblast, and in Danilov raion of Iaroslavl oblast. The Novominsk trial featured severe economic exploitation by local officials that had provoked thousands of peasants to leave the collective farms. In the Danilov trial, the raion leadership was charged with illegally liquidating the "New Life" kolkhoz and confiscating all its property when officials were unable to resolve a dispute with kolkhoz members.[34]

Early in August, *Pravda* elaborated the message of the Shiriaevo and Danilov trials in an editorial warning local officials not to mistreat the peasantry. Raion officials had been condoning all kinds of violations of the rights of kolkhozniks, *Pravda* stated. Officials had disposed arbitrarily of kolkhoz land and property, behaving as if it were "their own private property, their own little patrimonial estate (*votchina*)"; they had even liquidated entire collective farms, as in the Danilov case. This was to forget the golden rule that "kolkhozniks are the masters of their own kolkhoz."[35]

Emerging from all this was a kind of "master plot"[36] on the theme of abuse and exploitation of the collectivized peasantry by Soviet officialdom at the raion level that formed the basis for the thirty-odd show trials held in rural raions of the Soviet Union in September and October of 1937. The master plot may be summarized as follows:

Enemies of the people, linked in a mutual-protection and patronage network, had wormed their way into key positions in the raion and used their official positions to plunder the peasantry mercilessly. Because of the officials' stupidity and ignorance of agriculture, their incessant orders and interference had done great harm to the collective farms. The peasants, outraged and indignant, had done their best to resist unlawful demands. They had brought law suits and written letters of complaint to higher authorities, but these had often been blocked by the mutual-protection ring. Finally, however, the news of the scandalous behavior of local officials got out, and the guilty parties were brought to justice. The simple people—who demanded the severest punishment for their former oppressors—had triumphed over the officials who had cheated and insulted them.

This master plot was basically the creation of *Pravda*'s journalists, probably acting on instructions from the Politburo and the Central Committee's agriculture department. But its application in any specific circumstance was the work of local hands. No doubt the oblast NKVD men had a hand in it, although less than in the Moscow trials, where confessions of the accused were crucial and the "scenarios" were based on an elaborate interweaving of them. Nor should we forget the contribution of journalists on the oblast newspapers, who provided a literary framework (with strong overtones of the nineteenth-century satirist Saltykov-Shchedrin) and whose detailed reporting of the raion show trials is my major source.

But it was peasant letters of complaint and denunciation—the "abuse of power" letters discussed in an earlier chapter—that were almost certainly the main basis on which the raion trials were built. As we have already seen, peasants were inveterate writers of letters of complaint and denunciation of those in immediate authority above them in the 1930s. They wrote to party and government leaders like Stalin and Mikhail Kalinin; they wrote to the highest organs of the Soviet and republican governments; they wrote to provincial party committees, prosecutors' offices, and NKVD branches; they wrote to provincial newspapers; they wrote to central newspapers, especially *Krest'ianskaia gazeta*. They wrote letters and complaints with or without cause, for good reasons and bad; and they generally sent them outside their own raion, to the oblast center or even to Moscow, because of their belief that the bosses in any given raion would back each other up. Such peasant complaints were often triggers for official investigations by oblast or raion authorities of the behavior of kolkhoz leaders and rural soviet chairmen.

While it is not possible to prove that peasant complaints played an important role in all cases, there are mentions of them sparking the investigations that uncovered wrongdoing in a number of the show trials. Local complaints are mentioned as a stimulus to official action in three out of the four "model" trials reported in *Pravda*: In the Lepel case, Vyshinskii's attention was alerted by "complaints from the toilers of Lepel raion"; "complaints from kolkhozniks" are mentioned in the Shiriaevo case; and in Danilov, "letters of *sel'kory*" disclosed the abuses of the raion leadership, which consequently did its best to suppress them.[37]

Similar references to complaints and petitions from the village abound in the raion show trials that took place in the autumn. In the Andreevka trial, for example, peasant witnesses mentioned that they had sent a telegram of complaint to the People's Commissar of Agriculture. In the Shchuche case, the complaint had been sent to the Russian parliament (VTsIK). In the Aleshki case, a rural soviet chairman had forwarded peasant complaints against another official to the Commission of Soviet Control in Moscow.[38]

Format of the Trials

The show trials were indictments of raion leaderships, not individual raion leaders. The standard array of defendants included the top man in the leadership, the former raikom secretary (although he was sometimes indicted in absentia, indicating that he had been arrested and disposed of earlier); the chairman of the raion soviet, who was the second-ranking member of the leadership; the head of the raion land department and some other raion officials whose jobs involved contact with peasants; plus a sprinkling of chairmen of rural soviets and kolkhoz chairmen.

It became standard practice in these trials to indict the raion officials (although not necessarily the rural soviet and kolkhoz chairmen) under article 58 of the Criminal Code (counterrevolutionary crimes).[39] Despite the use of article 58, the charges rarely included anything remotely political. There were no allegations of contacts with foreign intelligence agents or political terrorism and no serious attempts to demonstrate the existence of counterrevolutionary conspiracies. None of the defendants had ever belonged to a party opposition, and even contacts with Trotskyites and other oppositionists scarcely ever figured in the indictments, possibly because few officials at the rural raion level had had the opportunity to meet such exotic creatures.[40]

The defendants in the rural raion trials were strongly encouraged to confess their guilt, as they were in the central Moscow trials. But they were a good deal less cooperative than their Moscow counterparts, especially where charges of counterrevolution were concerned. Solzhenitsyn has given an account of a single raion trial (in Kady, Ivanovo oblast) in which, as he tells the story, a defendant's withdrawal in court of his pretrial confession unhinged the whole proceedings.[41] In the reports of trials available to me (which did not include Kady), reneging on earlier confessions in court was not unusual. It did not have such a devastating effect on proceedings as Solzhenitsyn suggests, however, because the key element in the indictments was not the confession of the accused but the extremely damaging courtroom testimony of peasant witnesses.

In the Aleshki trial (Voronezh oblast), none of the main defendants made a satisfactory confession. While the top-ranking defendant, the former raikom secretary, had admitted to counterrevolutionary crimes under pretrial interrogation, he recanted in court, and from then on maintained that he was guilty only of failing to curb certain over-zealous subordinates who showed poor judgement and offended the local population. The defendant next in seniority, the former chairman of the raion soviet, was similarly recalcitrant, constantly attacking the credibility of the witnesses and asserting that they were venting personal grievances ("Every few minutes he would jump up and announce to the court that the witness was personally antagonistic towards him"). Another defendant, a rural soviet chairman whose outrageous behavior towards peasants had evidently become legendary in the raion, admitted that he might have been guilty of abuse of power, but stubbornly denied that he had ever committed a counterrevolutionary crime.[42]

In the Andreevka trial (Western oblast), the former senior land surveyor for Andreevka raion, K. V. Rumiantsev, engaged in an angry argument with the prosecutor about his role in forcing mergers of small collective farms. To merge or not to merge had been a constant problem for the Western oblast owing to the instability of central policy on the question and the fact that many kolkhozy in the oblast were extremely small. Rumiantsev's patience snapped when the prosecutor asked him to admit that merging was a counterrevolutionary policy intended to inflame the peasantry against Soviet power:

RUMIANTSEV: Not guilty. I didn't know that forced merging was a counter-revolutionary crime.

PROSECUTOR: Did you know you were committing crimes?

RUMIANTSEV: I knew I was carrying out the will of the head of the raion land department and the party committee.[43]

The trials took place in the largest auditorium in the raion center. Peasants were brought in from neighboring collective farms to constitute the audience. They appear to have treated the occasion as a holiday (probably vodka was on sale in the town after if not during the performance), cheering on "their" witnesses as they described the insults and injuries they had all endured, and figuratively at least booing the villains when they attempted to justify their actions.

The reports in local newspapers frequently asserted that peasants had called for death sentences for the accused, even when the prosecutor had not asked for them or the judge had handed down a lesser sentence. This cannot necessarily be taken at face value, since such expressions of vox populi were often stage-managed by Soviet authorities, but it may well have been true in cases of this type, where the peasants knew the defendants and had genuine grievances against them. At any rate, sentences in the autumn trials were certainly more severe than those in the model trials of the spring and summer. Ten years' imprisonment with confiscation of property was the harshest sentence handed down in any of the model trials, while some defendants got off with as little as six months. There were no death sentences either in two trials that took place in August (Borisovka, Kursk oblast, and Andreevka, Western oblast). In the large batch of trials held in September and October, however, it was usual for two or three of the top-ranking defendants to be sentenced to death, and other defendants to receive eight- to ten-year sentences.[44]

In the Andreevka case in the Western oblast, a second hearing was held to impose a stiffer sentence after Stalin's intervention. The circumstances were as follows. The new obkom secretary, Korotchenko, had made the mistake of sending a rather boastful message to Stalin, informing him (before the verdict) of the success of the Andreevka trial in educating the peasantry and raising vigilance. Stalin responded the next day with a curt instruction that all the Andreevka wreckers should be shot. As the court had just brought in a verdict sentencing the defendants only to various terms of imprisonment, the case had to be reheard immediately.[45]

The Charges

Many of the actions for which officials were indicted in the raion trials were not crimes in the ordinary sense. In some cases, officials were clearly scapegoats for economic disasters in the raion. In others, they were held accountable for behavior that was part of their job description or for state policies that were unpopular with the local peasants. Overall, the outstanding common characteristic of the "criminal" behaviors attributed to the defendants was that they were harmful to peasants, especially kolkhozniks, and offended the peasants' sense of fairness and propriety.

Abuse of power was one of the basic categories of accusation, and the charges made by peasant witnesses under this heading were among the most colorful and bitter. Curses, insults, beatings, humiliation, intimidation, and unjustified arrests were described as commonplace in the behavior of rural officials to peasants. In one trial, an eighty–year-old peasant woman related "with tears" how the rural soviet chairman beat her husband and dumped him in a wheelbarrow; her husband died two weeks later as result of his injuries. Another witness described how a raion official once made four kolkhoz brigade leaders climb on the stove and stay there, guarded by the local policeman, for four hours. "When people asked the kolkhoz chairman . . . why he countenanced this, he said 'What could I do? After all, [he] was the boss, he could have made me get onto the stove too.'"[46]

The wild behavior of Radchuk, a rural soviet chairman, was described by many peasant witnesses in the Novgorod raion trial. Radchuk's specialty was physical assault and forced entry (connected with various forms of extortion) into the homes of kolkhozniks. One witness described how Radchuk began breaking down the door of her house.

> "Now," he cried, "I'll chop down the door with an axe, you just watch." I took fright, jumped out the window, and ran to the post office to telephone my husband in Novgorod. But when he came home, Radchuk had already gone, and the door was broken down with an axe.[47]

The imposition of arbitrary fines and money levies (sometimes described as "taxation" or "contributions to state loans") by local authorities was a frequent subject of complaint. In Shiriaevo, for example, it was said that "a night brigade" had been organized for the purpose, descending on peasants at dead of night to conduct house searches and take inventories of property that might be seized. From the standpoint of peasant witnesses, this was extortion regardless of whether the money went to the state or to individual officials, but they frequently implied that the latter was the case. It was alleged that in Aleshki, Kochetov had imposed fines on kolkhoz members totalling 60,000 rubles in 1935 and 1936: "He imposed the fines on any pretext and at his own discretion—for not showing up for work, for not attending literacy classes, for 'impolite language,' for not having dogs tied up. . . ."[48]

The raion soviet chairman, Seminikhin, indicted in the same trial, was reportedly even more creative in his fund-raising from the population.

> In 1936, 200 kolkhozniks recruited for construction work went off from Aleshki to the Far East. They were already on the point of boarding the train when three militiamen appeared, read out a long list of names and took all those on the list off under guard to the raion soviet and the offices of the chairman.
>
> "Aha, tax delinquents!" Seminikhin greeted them. "You thought you could get away? Pay up and look lively about it. Pay up, or I won't let you out of the office and will not permit you to get on the train. And I'll take your suitcases."
>
> He posted a militaman at the door and gave the order to let out only those who showed a receipt for payment.
>
> In this manner, the raion soviet chairman "squeezed" 700 rubles of their last savings from the kolkhozniks.[49]

In many areas, kolkhozniks had extremely little money to take, so the main form of extortion was seizure of property. There were many and varied accounts of rural soviet and raion officials behaving "as if in their own little kingdoms" and "exacting tribute from the population." One country chairman took 4 or 5 kilograms of meat from each calf or pig slaughtered, plus vodka whenever he visited the village. A second "opened unlimited 'free credit' for himself on products [at the local store]. On occasion, he even roused the manager of the store from his bed at night, demanding immediate issue of vodka and snacks for himself. And when he needed potatoes, he simply sent to the nearest kolkhoz for them with an accompanying note to the person in charge of stores." Kolkhoz chairman were accused of treating kolkhoz property as if it were their own private property, selling buildings and (illegally) leasing land on their own initiative and pocketing the profits.[50]

In one raion, the soviet chairman had established a so-called "auxiliary farm" of the raion soviet containing thirty sheds, ten cows, seven horses, and other items commandeered from various parts of the raion, feeding his herd with feed taken from the kolkhozy. He was particularly successful in raising pigs, selling pork at the local peasant market as well as earning 1,500 rubles by selling pigs to the state procurement agency. The ironic comment going the rounds among the peasants was, "The raion soviet has built up a real kulak farm!"[51]

A more malign variant of extortion than regular, small-scale "tribute" was to strip a kolkhoznik of *all* his possessions in one swoop. In one case cited in the Shchuche trial, a rural soviet chairman, coveting the flourishing kitchen garden of a kolkhoznik, "abruptly dekulakized him and took away all his property." When he discovered that the victim's wife had managed to sell some small household items before he could confiscate them, "he took away the money and behaved so abusively that she was reduced to a state where she was sent to a psychiatric hospital."[52]

Another common charge was that the officials and officeholders had expelled kolkhozniks from the kolkhoz without due process, and in some cases liquidated whole kolkhozy. Almost twenty witnesses from the "Path to Socialism" kolkhoz (Voronezh oblast) testified that they had been unjustly expelled from the kolkhoz. Among them was Matrena Okuneva, who said:

> They expelled me from the kolkhoz because I married a worker on the railways, although I continued to live in Lipiagovka and work in the kolkhoz. I never complained, because I thought that's how it was supposed to be. Soon after that Kachkin and Kabanov [kolkhoz chairman and party organizer respectively] appeared in my yard and demanded that I go to weed the beets. I refused because I considered myself expelled from the kolkhoz. Then Kachkin said that the raion would fine me 50 rubles. . . . They took a man's jacket from me, and Kabanov said: "Be grateful to us, we could have burned [your house] down, only we took pity on the neighbors."[53]

Other expulsion cases cited seem essentially to have been cases of unauthorized departure of kolkhozniks who were on the brink of starvation because of the harvest failure of 1936. In the Ostrov trial (Pskov oblast), for example, witnesses stated that more than a thousand households had left collective farms in the raion in 1935–36 because they could not survive on the meager amount of grain the kolkhoz was giving them.[54] In the Nerekhta trial (Iaroslavl oblast), peasants blamed the raion leadership for "mass expulsions and forced departures from the collective farms" at the same period. These witnesses clearly felt that the raion bosses, like the old estate owners in the time of serfdom, owed it to their peasants to help them in time of trouble. For example, they related with indignation how

> after there was a fire in a kolkhoz and sixteen houses burned down, [the kolkhoz chairman] appealed to accused Begalov [chairman of the raion soviet] for help, saying that otherwise the kolkhozniks would all leave. In answer to the request, the accused Begalov said: "To hell with them, let them go." As a result, twenty households left the kolkhoz.[55]

The liquidation of an entire kolkhoz was one of the most heinous crimes that raion officials could commit in the slate of indictments in the 1937 raion show trials. In the case of the "New Life" kolkhoz in Danilov (one of those initially publicized in *Pravda*), raion officials had confiscated all the kolkhoz's property and animals—and then, adding insult to injury, demanded that the former kolkhozniks immediately pay the heavy tax that was levied on independent peasants. When the "Forward" kolkhoz in Kirillovo was liquidated, its land was distributed among neighboring collective farms in what was officially described as a "voluntary renunciation." The raion authorities went on to confiscate the kolkhoz's horses, agricultural equipment, stock of seed potatoes, and other collective property. From the standpoint of the kolkhozniks, who had owned this same property as individual households before collectivization, the liquidation of the kolkhoz must have seemed a second and definitive seizure of their assets. No wonder that, as witnesses related, the Kirillovo peasants wept when their kolkhoz was dissolved.[56]

Only one of the reported instances of kolkhoz liquidation comes from the fertile Black Earth belt of the country, and it occurred several years earlier than the non-Black Earth liquidations. Witnesses at the 1937 trial in Ivnia raion, Kursk oblast, stated that in 1933—during the famine—the "Lenin" kolkhoz was liquidated by order of the local Machine-Trarctor Station (MTS) and its lands given to the neighboring sovkhoz, despite the fact that twenty-eight out of thirty-one households voted against it. As a result of the transfer, the peasants were reduced overnight to the status of landless agricultural laborers.[57]

In both the Danilov and Kirillovo cases, conflict between local officials and kolkhozniks preceded the liquidation of the kolkhoz. In Kirillovo, it was a violent confrontation over the 1936 spring sowing plan, which the kolkhoz general assembly refused to accept, to the outrage of the rural soviet chairman who was present at the meeting; and the report of the Kirillovo trial implies that liquidation of the kolkhoz was essentially a punitive response by local authorities to the peasants' insubordination. In the report of the Danilov trial, however, there are suggestions that the raion leadership may have had more venal motives for liquidation, perhaps wanting to get hold of kolkhoz property for their own use or that of their friends.

Agricultural disasters figured prominently in the indictments. There was nothing new about blaming Soviet rural officials for harvest failures. The accusations made against officials in the raion trials of 1937 differed from earlier charges in one important respect, however. The officials were not being blamed for failing to meet state grain procurements targets, as had frequently happened in the early 1930s. This time, they were being blamed for failing to meet the *peasants'* needs—that is, allowing so little grain to be distributed among kolkhoz households after the harvest that the kolkhozniks were brought to the brink of starvation.

Most charges of this kind related to the exceptionally bad harvest of 1936, whose consequences had been felt most acutely in the spring and summer of 1937 before the next harvest came in.[58] In the Krasnogvardeisk trial, a kolkhoz chairman, Alekseev, admitted that he had brought the kolkhoz to economic ruin, and described how he had reacted:

> In 1936 the kolkhozniks received zero payments per laborday [that is, no grain was distributed after the harvest]. When I saw it all, I decided to run away from the kolkhoz. I told the chairman of the raion soviet, Gornov. He said: "Get away as fast as you can."

Alekseev took this friendly advice, but not fast enough (probably because he made the mistake of trying to take his house with him, using kolkhoz horses). He was arrested, together with Gornov, by the NKVD.[59]

In Ostrov raion, as a result of the 1936 harvest failure, kolkhoz earnings dropped by 20–50 percent, it was reported at the Ostrov trial. But because state grain procurements took precedence over peasant needs, many collective farms cut their payments in kind to members much more drastically. This was treated as a crime in the 1937 trials. The indicted officials were held responsible for the departure of large numbers of hungry kolkhozniks who went to work for wages in the towns or the state farms in order to survive.[60]

At a number of trials, peasant witnesses charged that the raion authorities had caused hardship to kolkhozniks and damaged agricultural productivity by their inept agricultural instructions. "Unrealistic sowing plans" figured prominently in these complaints; and, despite the fact that it was part of the raion land departments' duty to give orders to the collective farms about what crops to sow and where and when to sow them, the rhetorical conventions of the trials allowed peasant witnesses to speak of such instructions with undisguised resentment and contempt. In the Krasnogvardeisk trial, the testimony of a peasant from "Thirteen Years of the Red Army" kolkhoz was reported to have "left an enormous impression on all present at the court. . . ."

> [The witness] talked about how kolkhozniks tried to protest against wrecking plans and went specially to Manninen, [head of] the raion land department. With contemptuous effrontery, that enemy of the people announced to the kolkhozniks: "If you go to the oblast to complain about our plans, we will add more."[61]

Many instances of agriculturally illiterate instructions given by the raion and the MTS were cited by peasant witnesses. One kolkhoz, for example, was ordered to turn water-meadow and shrubbed area into plowland, which left no pasture for cattle. In another kolkhoz, the raion's sowing instructions were predicated on the false assumption that its hayfields covered more than 200 hectares, which according to the peasants was double their actual extent ("Under the heading of hayfield, the wreckers included pastureland for cattle, quicksands, and the private plots of kolkhozniks").[62]

Another kind of agricultural disaster that figured prominently in a few raion trials was large-scale loss of livestock. In the trial in Shchuche raion (Voronezh oblast), which lost almost a thousand horses in the first half of 1937, this was attributed to lack of fodder associated with the 1936 harvest failure, compounded by an epidemic that started in a Shchuche horse-breeding state farm and spread rapidly throughout the raion. The defendants in Shchuche were charged with gross negligence in the livestock losses, not intentional malice.[63]

In two other cases (the Kresttsy and Sychevka trials), officials in raions with heavy livestock losses were accused of intentionally infecting animals with diseases. The director of the Sychevka sovkhoz (a former member of the Social-Revolutionary Party) was charged with leading a conspiracy to destroy the farm's livestock, using the prevailing unsanitary conditions as a cover for infecting 80 percent of the animals with diseases. Then, it was alleged, the Sychevka raion veterinarian had done his bit to spread the epidemic throughout the country by sending animals from the infected herd to be shown at the All-Union Agricultural Show in Moscow.[64]

A somewhat similar accusation was made against raion leaders in the Porkhov trial, although in this case the actual sabotage had allegedly been carried out by peasants—an "independent" acting at the behest of the raikom secretary, and a former kulak, recently returned from exile and working as a kolkhoz stablehand, acting on his own in a spirit of revenge.[65]

Favoritism towards former kulaks was raised as an issue in some show trials. These trials provide interesting insights on the variety of problems associated with the return of kulaks and the secret decision to allow them to join collective farms.[66] Conflicts over the kulaks' confiscated property were particularly prominent. Officials who had helped the former kulaks in any way were always said to have been bribed, and the fact that it had been state policy in 1936 to reintegrate kulaks was never mentioned. Peasant witnesses at the trials complained that kulaks had managed to get houses and horses back, that they had been given good jobs in the collective farms, and that, once admitted to the kolkhoz, they had taken revenge on peasants who were Soviet activists.

In the Borisovka trial (Kursk oblast), the prosecutor claimed that in 1936 and the first half of 1937, 75 houses were returned to the kulaks who were their former owners, and 134 kulaks had their voting rights restored. Witnesses found this all the more offensive since the party secretary, Fedosov, had behaved so brutally towards ordinary peasants in the raion: "Everything was taken from the population down to their socks, but they [the raion party leaders] returned to the kulaks the property that had been legally confiscated from them." Moreover, witnesses claimed, when kolkhozniks complained to the raikom secretary about the concessions being made to former kulaks, he "oriented those present at the meeting towards reconciliation with the class enemies." (This was reported as if it were a clear violation of party policy in 1936.)[67]

Kursk was not the only place where this happened. At the trial in Sychevka (Western oblast), two senior raion officials were charged with distorting party policy on kulaks by announcing that it was time to forget about the whole idea of class enemies and make appointments on the basis of merit, not class origin. In addition to instructing rural soviet chairmen to destroy all the existing lists of kulaks and other disenfranchised persons, they had selected several former kulaks to be kolkhoz chairmen, as well as giving the village co-ops into the charge of former traders and appointing the son of a landowner as director of the school. This was said to have outraged village opinion. Witnesses stated the kulaks who became kolkhoz chairmen did enormous damage, persecuting Stakhanovites and destroying horses.[68]

"Suppression of kolkhoz democracy" was one of the standard charges brought against raion officials in the raion show trials of 1937. According to the conventions governing these trials, the raion was virtually always at fault when there was a conflict between it and the kolkhozniks over selection or dismissal of a kolkhoz chairman. Peasant witnesses and state prosecutors alike spoke as if kolkhozniks unquestionably had full powers in this matter. In the Kazachkin trial (Saratov krai), for example, the raion authorities were charged with overriding the protests of kolkhozniks and forcing them to accept a former raion official as kolkhoz chairman. When the appointee then robbed the kolkhoz of its assets, it proved that the kolkhozniks had been right all along.[69]

There were allegations that raion and rural soviet officials had applied extreme measures of coercion in conflicts with kolkhozniks over kolkhoz chairmen. The liquidation of the "New Life" kolkhoz in Danilov raion was one example. In another case,

> witnesses I. N. Goltsev and V. A. Mishin related how, when they and other kolkhozniks got up at the general meeting in the "First of May" kolkhoz and criticized the work of the [kolkhoz] board, demanding that the kolkhoz chairman be fired for failure to carry out his duties, the chairman of the rural soviet, Kochetov, disbanded the meeting. Four of the most active kolkhozniks, including the two witnesses, were arrested on the basis of his provocative and false statement.[70]

Virtuous Peasants and Evil Bosses

In the master plot of the raion trials, evil bosses exploited and abused, and kolkhozniks were their victims. There was scarcely any shading of the black-and-white contrast between peasants and their bosses (from kolkhoz chairman to raikom secretary), and no indication that it was possible to cross the great divide between them. One finds the same rhetorical convention in peasant letters to *Krest'ianskaia gazeta*: the bosses (including kolkhoz chairmen and sometimes even brigade leaders) are "they"; the kolkhozniks, "we." In real life, of course, the dichotomy between rulers and ruled in the Soviet countryside in the second half of the 1930s was much more complex, because kolkhoz chairmen were generally local peasants and the office of chairman was often an object of fierce competition among village factions. But such nuances were never acknowledged in the trials, for the drama hinged on the confrontation between the virtuous peasants on the witness stand and the evil officials in the dock.

Usually the peasant witnesses played the main role in establishing this framework. But there were a few exceptions. For example, in the Shchuche trial, which is unusual in the context of raion trials for the defendants' willingness to participate in their own indictment, two defendants gave the following answers when the prosecutor asked why they did not try to recruit peasants and workers into their anti-Soviet activities:

> SEDNEV (sugar plant director): Undoubtedly if they [the workers] had known that I was a Trotskyite wrecker, they would have torn me limb from limb. . . .

POLIANSKII (MTS director): Well, if I had even hinted of wrecking, they [the peasants] would have beaten me up if I was lucky, but more likely would simply have killed me. . . .[71]

The peasant testimony at the trials presented many vivid images of the local bosses taunting peasants and revelling in their own power.

So you appealed to VTsIK [i.e., the Russian parliament in Moscow]! But we are the people in power here. I do what I want.

I am a Communist and you don't belong to the party. However much you complain about me, you won't be believed.

You should have shot the bastard; you wouldn't have got into any trouble for it (*comment of a raion official to a subordinate who had beaten a peasant*).

If five people croak, that will teach you how to work, you idle bastards (*a raion official's remark to kolkhozniks during the 1933 famine*).

Grain has to be given to the horses. The kolkhozniks can survive without grain.[72]

Reports of the trials stressed the "deep hatred" with which peasants spoke of their former oppressors in courtroom testimony. Before and during the trials, newspapers reported, resolutions and petitions came in from neighboring collective farms demanding the death sentence for the accused, who were referred to with such epithets as "contemptible swine" and "rotten bastards." The halls where the trials were held were always described as packed, with the audience listening intently, full of indignation against the accused.

Each evening, crowds of kolkhozniks gather near the school. . . . During the trial, as many as fifty statements indicating new facts of abuse and illegality performed by Seminikhin, Kolykhmatov and the others were personally handed by citizens to the oblast prosecutor, who is attending the trial.[73]

In one of the most dramatic confrontations reported in the press, a peasant witness, Natalia Latysheva, turned on the former leaders of Novgorod raion as soon as she took the stand.

LATYSHEVA: Comrade judges! Are these really human beings? They are ogres, swine. (*Movement in the hall, cries of approval, confusion on the bench of the accused.*)

CHAIRMAN: Witness, it is facts that are asked of you.

LATYSHEVA: Forgive me, comrade judges, but when I saw those swine, I couldn't contain myself. And it is a fact that they are scoundrels! . . . There they sit, damn them. The kolkhozniks will never forgive them for what they did.[74]

In Latysheva's story, as in those of many other peasant witnesses in the trials, the raion's interference in agriculture—for example, in the giving of sowing plans—was completely unjustified and stupid, since the raion officials were totally incompetent. On Latysheva's kolkhoz, for example, the raion had tried to discourage the peasants from developing a stud farm and forced them to grow unprofitable and inappropriate crops. But the kolkhozniks were not to be browbeaten.

> LATYSHEVA: We did not give up. We decided to breed trotters. And we did—those enemies of the collective farms did not break our spirit. To the astonishment of all, we built up a horse farm, and now we have 21 horses of pure Orel stock. (*Spontaneous applause breaks out in the hall, cries of "Good for you!" and "Well done!" are heard.*)
>
> CHAIRMAN: Witness, have you anything more to add?
>
> LATYSHEVA: I have. (*The peasant woman turns to the accused, and stands face to face with the enemies of the people. . . .*) All the same, our side won, not yours. We were victorious![75]

"*Our side won!*" It would be tempting to end the story on this note of populist triumph. But had the peasants really won a significant victory over their oppressors? In the woodcut, "How the Mice Buried the Cat," the mice are rejoicing that the cat is dead, not celebrating their achievement in killing him. In the 1937 trials, similarly, the peasants could scarcely claim to have "killed the cat" themselves: the raion officials whose downfall they celebrated were not overthrown by local peasant revolts but swept away in a political storm that blew from Moscow. At most, the peasants could feel themselves to be participants in the event, since they not only gave testimony at the trials but had also written many complaints and denunciations of officials earlier. But it could also be argued that their participation was just that of bystanders gathered to watch a public hanging.

The 1937 trials removed one cohort of rural officials, probably including many whose abusive behavior and corruption were notorious. But they did not alter the basic power relationships in the countryside, abolish collective farms, or even significantly change the features of kolkhoz life that peasants found most oppressive. To be sure, kolkhozniks were increasing their influence over the selection and removal of kolkhoz chairmen in the second half of the 1930s, but this trend started before the trials and was not a result of them. Government decrees were issued in 1938 that were designed to protect kolkhoz members, especially otkhodniks and their families, from arbitrary expulsion, restrict the ability of a kolkhoz chairman to monopolize control of kolkhoz assets and use them for his personal benefit, and increase the cash payments to kolkhozniks for their labordays. In 1939, another decree restricted (at least formally) the powers of raion officials to set kolkhoz sowing plans.[76]

Much more striking, however, is the state's subsequent reversion to more coercive, controlling policies vis-à-vis the kolkhoz. The most important example, the 1939 decree that required all kolkhoz members to work a minimum number of labordays, not only greatly increased the severity of kolkhoz discipline but also in effect cancelled the previous year's decree limiting expulsions of kolkhoz members. This same decree recommended that the kolkhozniks's private plots be cut back so as to force them to work more on the kolkhoz lands; and accordingly, all private plots were remeasured by government surveyors, and half of all kolkhoz households lost land. In addition, a new tax was introduced on peasants' orchards; kolkhozniks were forbidden to cut hay from kolkhoz fields for their cows; meat and grain procurements quotas went up; and the average payment in kind per laborday consequently fell, with no balancing increase in cash payments.[77]

These developments no doubt saddened kolkhozniks, but there is no reason to think they surprised them. Latysheva and others peasant witnesses surely knew that they were taking part in political theater rather than a political revolution when they criticized former officials so harshly. In letters to *Krest'ianskaia gazeta* in 1938 and early 1939, we find no indications that peasants had recently suffered a terrible disappointment when the state had reneged on the implicit promises of the 1937 trials. The trials did not remain in the consciousness of Russian peasants as a milestone or turning point; the new exactions were just business as usual—even if bad business—from the peasants' standpoint.

But perhaps, after all, it is not the aftermath of the event that matters so much as the event itself. The trials may be seen as a Soviet version of carnival—a people's festival (licensed, admittedly, by the state) where, for a day, the world is turned upside down, revellers celebrate in gaudy costumes, distinctions of rank are forgotten, mockery and humiliation of the proud are permitted.[78] But the point about carnival is that it lasts only for a day or a week. After that, the proprieties and distinctions are restored, perhaps even reaffirmed. Real power relations are untouched. Carnival is not revolution.

Nevertheless, carnivals sometimes get out of hand. This is what Solzhenitsyn thinks happened with the 1937 raion trials; and although his picture, based only on a single example, is somewhat skewed, he may be right about this. In Kady, according to Solzhenitsyn's account, the proceedings in the courtroom got out of control and degenerated into a melée.[79] This could well have happened in other cases; it is an outcome that, for obvious reasons, would not be reported in the oblast newspapers, which are my main sources. Certainly the wave of raion show trials died down as quickly as it had arisen: By December 1937 the whole episode was over. The pattern is consistent with a central decision to halt raion show trials of this type.

It had been a bold, even dangerous, notion to have show trials in which real grievances against the state's agents and policies were aired, and the defendants and their accusers (the peasant witnesses) were real, local people who knew each other. The format of the Moscow trials, by contrast, was much more manageable, despite the problems associated with reliance on confession. In the Moscow trials, the mighty were humbled, but in an unreal, impersonal way and in a setting that was full of mystery and exoticism (spies, foreigners, conspiracies, acts of sabotage, strange journeys). They were accused of sinister crimes, but—with the exception of the "wrecking" charges (causing industrial accidents, putting glass splinters in the butter, and so on)—these were crimes against the Communist Party and the state rather than crimes against the common people.

Such boldness suggests that Stalin, or someone working for him, believed the show trials would reap political benefits. The intention was presumably to tap a populist vein of envy and hostility towards those with privilege and power: *Stalin is giving the Communist big bosses what they so richly deserve—good for Stalin!* As a political ploy, it could be regarded as an extension of the "Dizzy with Success" tactic of 1930, when Stalin tried to shift the blame for collectivization to those local officials who committed "excesses."

There is a clear indication that such an appeal was contemplated in *Pravda*'s reporting on one of the "model" trials (Danilov, in Iaroslavl oblast). At the end of the trial, the newspaper noted, peasants of Danilov raion had written to Stalin telling him of their gratitude to him for protecting them from their enemies and restoring their kolkhoz (which their enemies, the raion leaders, had disbanded).[80] Here, spelled out in *Pravda*, was the perfect "good Tsar" representation, in which Stalin, all-knowing and merciful, has heard of the injustices done to his humble people by evil boyars and officials and come to deliver them from their misery.

The trouble with this appealing fairytale was that peasants did not believe it. Even given our knowledge of their reticence about praising Stalin in other contexts, such as letters of complaint and petition, it is remarkable to observe how consistently the "Tsar-deliverer" representation was rejected by peasant witnesses in the trials. Ignoring *Pravda*'s hint, the witnesses in raion trials did *not* credit Stalin with bringing corrupt lower officials to justice. They did *not* report that he had responded to their letters of complaint or attribute to him any guiding role, and in their testimony they steadfastly avoided "naive monarchist" formulations such as "If Stalin had only known what was going on. . . ." They did *not* send him letters of gratitude for delivering them from their former oppressors (or, if they did, the papers did not report that). In fact, in all the thousands of words published from and on the trials in local papers, there are virtually no references to Stalin at all.

Once again, we are impressed with the stubbornness of Russian peasants' hostility to Stalin on account of collectivization. No doubt they were happy to see their oppressors humiliated in 1937—to throw metaphorical stones at the former officials on the ducking stool. There was the same malicious satisfaction as was expressed in the old woodcut, "How the Mice Buried the Cat," or in the chastushki and comments about Kirov's death. What was totally lacking, however, was any inclination on the peasants' part to share this satisfaction with Stalin, to acknowledge him as a friend because he claimed to have the same enemies. If it was a cause of malicious satisfaction to see raion officials in dock or to hear of Kirov's death, how much greater would have been the pleasure of learning of Stalin's fall? In the words of the chastushka, "They killed Kirov, We'll kill Stalin" (*Ubili Kirova, Ubyëm Stalina*)."[81]

Could it be, then, that Latysheva's "*Our side won!*" was not so far from the mark after all? Were the mice at the cat's funeral really dancing to Stalin's tune? Or was that their own subversive ditty, *Ubili Kirova*, that they were singing?

Afterword

This book has dealt with the prewar experience of the Soviet kolkhoz. For much of the 1930s, peasants were still adjusting to the initial trauma of collectivization. Their perception of collectivization as a second serfdom no doubt became less acute in the course of the decade, but it did not disappear, and neither did the peasants' serf-like, indifferent approach to work in the kolkhoz fields. The main reason for this was that the kolkhoz continued to be a vehicle for state economic exploitation because of high compulsory procurements quotas, for which the state paid extremely low prices.

In other areas, Russian peasants had more success in molding the kolkhoz to their needs. The notable exception was horse ownership, on which the state absolutely refused to budge. But the kolkhozniks had their private plots and cows; they were not significantly impeded (at least by the state) if they wanted to work for wages outside the kolkhoz; and a significant proportion of them were retaining kolkhoz membership despite doing very little work for the kolkhoz. The Machine-Tractor Station (MTS) politotdels had gone by the middle of the decade, as were most of the outsider chairmen who typified the early years. While the kolkhoz was under the authority of the raion, whose de facto powers included the appointment of chairmen, an increasing proportion of kolkhoz chairmen were locals, and in some respects the village (kolkhoz) seemed to be successfully reasserting control over its internal affairs.

I have suggested that three separate strains of peasant aspiration can be identified in the 1930s. "Traditionalist" peasants wanted to be left alone with their horse and cow to be subsistence cultivators, within a communal framework that tended to inhibit economic differentiation. "Entrepreneurs" wanted not just to subsist but also to sell for a profit on the market, have the opportunity to buy and lease land, and become prosperous, on the Stolypin model. "Welfare-state kolkhozniks" wanted the state to act like a good master, providing pensions and other kinds of social welfare that would eliminate the risk of being wiped out in a bad year. Of these three strains, traditionalist aspirations seemed to become weaker in the course of the decade, while the entrepreneurial and welfare-state aspirations probably became stronger.

This does not imply that peasants had accepted the kolkhoz as a permanent fact of life. That they had *not* done so is indicated by the persistent rumors throughout the 1930s that war was coming and then the kolkhoz would be dismantled. And indeed, when war did come in 1941, many peasants in the occupied areas of Ukraine and southern Russia initially welcomed the invaders, or at least were prepared to tolerate them, because of the hope that they would dismantle the kolkhoz. Attitudes changed only after it became evident that the Germans had no such intention.[1]

Since collectivization was a state project whose aim was modernization as well as exploitation, it would be logical to expect that one result would be to draw the village into a closer political and cultural relationship with the town—to incorporate the Russian village into the emerging Soviet nation. Certainly the 1930s were the years in which a sense of Soviet nationhood became broadly disseminated in the urban population. But the rural population seems to have been remarkably unaffected by this process (with the exception of young peasants who expected to leave the village and make their lives in the towns).

More newspapers were read in the villages than before, and more peasant children were in school for a longer time. But there was no significant road and railroad building to link the village more closely to the town; and the industrialization drive did not bring electricity to the village but, on the contrary, often left peasants without kerosene to light their lamps. The peasants' standard of living and rates of consumption dropped sharply with collectivization and did not reach the pre-1929 level again in the prewar period. Moreover, peasants felt that collectivization had made them second-class citizens. It is perhaps not surprising, therefore, that the rumors of war that circulated continually in the countryside displayed such a notable lack of patriotism, either Soviet or Russian, and that kolkhozniks' hopes of emancipation by the invading Germans so closely resembled the serfs' hopes of Napoleon in 1812. If a metamorphosis of "peasants into Soviets" ever occurred in Russia, it did not do so before the Second World War.[2]

World War II brought new suffering to the peasantry, which bore the brunt of the Soviet Union's huge casualties. The war greatly increased the demographic imbalance in the villages. The shortage of males in the village already evident in the 1930s was greatly exacerbated. At the beginning of 1946, a quarter of all able-bodied kolkhozniks in the Russian Republic were men, and three-quarters women; and in 1950, men still constituted only a third of able-bodied kolkhozniks. The shortage of men was the result not just of wartime casualties but also of the decision of survivors not to return to the kolkhoz after the war. Whereas two-thirds of the men in the Soviet armed forces were called up from the kolkhoz, only half of the survivors returned to the kolkhoz after demobilization. The population flow from countryside to town continued after the war, despite the continuing existence of passport regulations. In the years 1950–54, nine million rural inhabitants moved permanently to towns. The rural share of total population continued its inexorable decline, dropping below the 50 percent mark in 1961.[3]

Just as peasants in the occupied areas had initially hoped the Germans would abolish collective farms, so as the war drew to an end peasants throughout the country started to talk about the big changes that would surely come with peace. The increased tolerance of religion during the war, symbolized at the level of high politics by the state's concordat with the Orthodox Church in 1943 and at local level by a cautious reemergence of "underground" religious activity into the light, no doubt encouraged such hopes. During the war, the kolkhozniks' private plots had expanded at the expense of the collective land in many kolkhozy, and some peasant entrepreneurs had made big profits by selling food to hungry townspeople on the black market. It was widely expected that after the war the regime would abolish or at least substantially modify the kolkhoz.[4]

The kolkhozniks' hopes of postwar relaxation were dashed by a government decree of September 19, 1946, "On measures to liquidate breaches of the kolkhoz statute," which ordered those who had appropriated collective land to return it and prescribed various measures for tightening kolkhoz discipline.[5] Procurements and taxes rose to a higher level than ever before, and the currency reform of 1947 wiped out the savings of peasants in the wartime entrepreneurial group. At the end of the 1940s, collectivization (and expropriation of kulaks) was carried out in the Baltic states and other newly acquired territories, which constituted a reaffirmation of the kolkhoz's status as a key institution in the Soviet structure. The period between the end of the war and Stalin's death in 1953 was the harshest the peasants had endured since the early 1930s.

In 1950, the regime made an important break with the past when it decided to amalgamate the existing collective farms into much larger units. The number of collective farms dropped from 250,000 in 1949 to 124,000 in 1950, and continued to decline thereafter—to 69,000 in 1958 and 36,000 in 1965. By the mid-1960s, the average kolkhoz contained more than 400 households, compared with about 80 before the reform. This meant that the village was no longer in any sense self-governing or a significant economic unit. In addition, the new collective farms were so large that they required professional management. In 1955, in an interesting throwback to the first years of collectivization, a campaign was launched for 30,000 volunteers—the "30,000-ers"—to go to the countryside as kolkhoz chairmen.[6]

Amalgamation confirmed a trend visible since the end of the war towards strong kolkhoz chairmen, often outsiders. Many of the men sent out as kolkhoz chairmen in the postwar years were army veterans and Communist party members. These new chairmen were different from their predecessors of the late 1930s and wartime period. A kolkhoz chairman of this type "brought from the war strictness and discipline. He decided to overcome the savage devastation with a desperate attack, as he had recently taken enemy entrenchments. His ears sometimes became deaf to the innumerable human complaints and requests which he could in no way satisfy. The word 'give' became the most frequent in his lexicon."[7]

While the behavior of kolkhoz chairmen became less harsh in the post-Stalin era, the shift towards "career" chairmen—professional managers, authoritarian in their relationship to the peasants and generally distant from them—turned out to be permanent. These new chairmen, closer by temperament and background to the officials in the raion than to the peasants, took all the responsibility on the kolkhoz and made all the decisions. There was now little to distinguish them from sovkhoz directors (who had already been salaried managers in the 1930s), just as there was increasingly little to distinguish the enlarged collective farms from state farms.

The managerial style of the kolkhoz chairmen and state-farm directors, two Western observers in the 1960s noted, had similarities to that of landowners and estate managers in the old days, and the peasants' behavior to them, similarly, had much in common with the serf. "Judging by the actions of one elderly sovkhoz member we met in the street . . . , the lower ranks were also practiced at submissiveness. Spying the director, this old muzhik halted abruptly, jerked off his hat and held it to his chest, bowing with the short repeated jerks of a humble peasant of imperial times."[8]

In the judgement of these observers, the kolkhozniks still performed their work on the kolkhoz as if it were barshchina:

> The collective farm "serf" discharges his labor obligation to the "master" carelessly, grudgingly. He refuses to concern himself with the fertility of the "collective" land. It is not his. He does not see the public weeds, nor the rust on the collective machinery, nor the private cow that grazes just inside the collective cornfield. He steals from the collective or habitually turns a blind eye when his fellows do so. . . .[9]

Kolkhoz chairmen of the new breed could also be compared with Soviet industrial managers. They were the entrepreneurs and wheeler-dealers of the rural scene. Like their industrial counterparts running "company towns" in the Soviet provinces, the kolkhoz and sovkhoz chairmen were masters of their own small fiefdoms, cultivating contacts in the raion and beyond, and making ingenious deals with kolkhoz produce to ensure that the kolkhoz got its rightful share of fertilizer and was not saddled with too heavy procurements quotas. As a Soviet journalist commented in the 1960s,

> Almost all the material and social authority of the village-farm society is concentrated in his hands, and he is compelled to use it, primarily, to solve his production problems. He is the dominant force, the "businessman" who makes everything go. . . .[10]

Other policy changes of the post-Stalin period were even more important for the evolution of the kolkhoz in the last four decades of the Soviet regime. After the harsh exactions of the late Stalin period, there was a consensus among party leaders in the post-Stalin era that the burden on the peasantry must be eased. It was indeed eased substantially, first under Khrushchev and then under Brezhnev. The result was a dramatic improvement in the lives of the Russian peasant in the last quarter century of the Soviet regime.

In the late 1950s and early 1960s, Khrushchev raised procurements prices on agricultural goods by a factor of five. The average income of kolkhozniks from kolkhoz work (in cash and kind) rose by 311 percent in real terms in the period 1953–67. This meant that increasingly it was earnings from the kolkhoz rather than earnings from the private plot that were the kolkhozniks' main support. At the same time, the cash component of earnings from the kolkhoz, which had been negligible for many kolkhozniks in the 1930s, grew significantly, so that by the mid-1960s the kolkhozniks were receiving the bulk of their earnings from the kolkhoz in cash rather than in kind.[11]

Khrushchev tried to have a quid pro quo for this increase in income from the kolkhoz by reducing the permissible size of the private plot and penalizing kolkhozniks who failed to work a sufficient amount of time on kolkhoz land. But these measures were rescinded after his fall. Under Brezhnev, the private plot, although no longer the key element in peasant survival as it had been in the 1930s, was still important to the peasant household and the economy as a whole, producing a third of all livestock products and a tenth of all crops in the latter part of the 1970s, and still occupied a third of the peasants' time.[12]

Peasants had always dreamed of a situation in which they would be safe from the risk of ruin as a result of harvest failure. During the 1936 discussion on the Constitution, peasants suggested that a number of welfare benefits available to urban wage earners be extended to kolkhozniks, and some mentioned the idea of guaranteed minimum wage. The fulfilment of the kolkhozniks' old "welfare-state" aspirations came in the 1960s.

In the first place, the kolkhozniks got state old-age pensions in 1964. Initially, these were substantially less generous than those for urban wage earners, but in 1968 the retirement age for kolkhozniks was lowered to 60 for men and 55 for women, bringing it in line with those in the urban sector, and kolkhoz pensions were raised. State-backed health insurance for all kolkhozniks followed in 1970, although, like pensions, it was not as generous for kolkhozniks as for urban workers.[13]

In the second place, a guaranteed minimum wage for all kolkhozniks was introduced in 1966. The wage, calculated on the basis of payment for similar work on state farms, was the same for kolkhozniks on a kolkhoz that was an economic disaster as it was for those whose kolkhoz was an outstanding producer.[14]

Not surprisingly, the wages (monthly earnings) of kolkhozniks were still

way below those of urban workers, the average monthly wage of a kolkhoznik in 1971 being 78 rubles, compared with 126 rubles in the urban
sector. The disparity was much less, however, if earnings in kind were calculated as well as cash income. Moreover, rural incomes rose much more substantially over the period 1950–1976 than urban incomes. According to
Gertrude Schroeder's calculation, the average wage (cash and kind) of agricultural workers more than tripled in this period, while that of nonagricultural workers only doubled. In 1950, the average agricultural income was
56 percent of the average income outside of agriculture. In 1976, it was 88
percent.[15]

If the 1960s was the decade in which rural income and economic well-
being took a jump upwards, it was in the 1970s that the village finally
started catching up in cultural terms. There was a striking increase in the
educational level of the rural population in the 1970s and '80s. In 1970,
only 318 per thousand of the rural population aged ten years and over had
secondary education, compared with 530 per thousand of the urban population. By 1989, the comparable figures were 588 per thousand for the rural
population and 666 for the urban.[16]

Television reached the countryside in a big way in the 1970s, with the
result that by 1980 there were 71 TV sets for each 100 rural households,
compared with 91 sets per 100 in the towns. At the same date, about 6 out
of 10 rural households also possessed refrigerators and washing machines;
and even cars were beginning to reach the rural population in significant
numbers by the second half of the 1970s.[17]

Despite these manifold improvements, the village still lagged far behind
the town in many respects. While most villages got electricity in the 1960s,
and almost 60 percent of rural homes had gas by 1976, few rural inhabitants
had indoor plumbing, hot water, baths, or telephones, and many still had to
pump their water from wells in the street and carry it home in pails. A survey
of rural housing in Novosibirsk oblast (Western Siberia) in 1977 found that
only a fifth had running water, a tenth indoor plumbing, and 4 percent telephones. Rural roads also remained in a parlous condition. In 1976, only
9 percent of rural settlements in the Soviet Union were located on paved
roads. Village streets "were still the typically wide and rutted thoroughfares
of old Russia, and the sidewalks were paths in the dirt at the side of the
road."[18]

Remnants of the kolkhozniks' old "second-class citizenship" survived
into the 1970s and even the 1980s. When the third Kolkhoz Charter was
promulgated in 1969, kolkhozniks were still not allowed to own horses and
not automatically entitled to passports. There was a debate in the late 1970s
about whether it was time to let kolkhozniks own horses. But horses were
still scarce commodities in Russia (*plus ça change . . .*), and old-guard politicians still felt that the private ownership of a "means of production" was
totally incompatible with socialist agriculture. In 1982, the government
relaxed the rules and allowed sovkhoz workers and all other rural residents

except kolkhozniks to own horses. Incredibly, the formal prohibition on horse ownership by kolkhozniks seems to have survived right up to the collapse of the Soviet Union in 1991, although it was no longer strictly enforced in the last decade.[19]

The regime also had difficulty in solving the passport issue, although its record here was not quite as pitiful as on the horse. By the 1970s, Soviet political leaders recognized that the second-class civil status for kolkhozniks associated with the lack of an automatic right to a passport was inappropriate. But they were afraid that lifting the formal impediment to departure from the countryside would increase the already alarming rate of out-migration. On the eve of the Second World War, despite the great out-migration of the 1930s, two-thirds of the Soviet population was still rural. In 1959, the rural share of total population had dropped to 52 percent (an absolute figure of 109 million). By 1970, it was down to 44 percent (106 million), and by the end of the decade it was only 38 percent (under 100 million).[20]

One would think the politicians might have drawn the obvious conclusion that the passport law was not inhibiting departure in any significant respect. Instead, they thought how much worse it might have been if peasants had actually been given passports. When a new passport law was issued in 1974, they managed to fudge the issue of peasant entitlement. Within a few years, however, rationality prevailed. By 1980, peasants had passports, and the historic inequity of rights established in 1933 was finally abolished.[21]

By the end of the Brezhnev period, most historic inequities had been redressed. The rural population was living better than it had ever done and probably working less than ever as well. It had shrunk from two-thirds of the population in 1939 to one-third a half century later; and the kolkhoz population had shrunk even further, numbering only 39 million in 1979 (15 percent of the total population; under 40 percent of the rural population). This was the result not only of rural-urban migration but also of the transfer of kolkhozniks into state farms, now a much more attractive option than in the 1930s, and generally better paying.[22]

Signs of entrepreneurialism in the aging peasant population were all but invisible, although the kolkhoz chairmen were energetic Soviet-type entrepreneurs (fixers rather than innovators). But signs of the welfare state were everywhere in evidence. The kolkhozniks had achieved their long-sought goal of almost total risk avoidance. The state had been pouring investment into agriculture—in a way that surely had Stalin, not to mention the old Bolshevik Marxists of the 1920s, turning in his grave—with virtually no effect. The low productivity of Soviet agriculture was a byword.

It is little wonder, then, that when the call finally came for peasants to leave the shackles of the kolkhoz and strike out for the brave new world of independent capitalist farming, the response was a dull silence. With an aging population and the security afforded by guaranteed minimum wage, pensions, and health insurance, it is not surprising that kolkhozniks viewed the changes of the late Soviet era and early post-Soviet era with misgivings, often looking to their kolkhoz chairmen for leadership and guidance about how to act in the new situation.

"We wept when they drove us into the kolkhoz in 1949, and now we will weep when they start driving us out of the kolkhoz," said Lithuanian peasants in 1990. Suddenly the kolkhoz seemed very attractive, even in the Baltic states, with a peasantry only forty years separated from the old, independent farming traditions, let alone Russia, separated by almost sixty years, or more than two generations. The young don't want to leave, a rural mechanic in Lithuania told a perplexed Russian journalist, because they don't care about making money and they don't want to work; the old don't want to leave because there's no point, they are just waiting to retire and get their pensions.[23]

In Russia, there were reports of hostility to entrepreneurs who tried to leave or came in as independent farmers, almost reminiscent of the old hostility in the mir to "separators." "Those with a conscience won't sell." "We're accustomed to the collective farm." "We're not going to bury anyone who leaves the collective farm. He's not going to get a coffin from collective farm timber."[24]

The kolkhoz outlasted the Soviet system that produced it (although the future will show for how long); and the "serf" mentality of kolkhozniks survived after the state coercion that generated it had been replaced by state handouts. An endless stream of migrating peasants took their foot-dragging work habits and disdain for the concept of state (collective) property with them to the towns. When the Soviet Union finally reached the end of its road, the kolkhoz and its problems might have been a synecdoche for Soviet society as a whole: no longer dangerous, as it was in the past; no longer brutally governed by ruthless and frightened bosses; but inert, heavy, passively resistant to change—a society whose members were for the most part contemptuous of any notion of public good, suspicious of energetic or successful neighbors, endlessly aggrieved at what "they" (the bosses) were doing, but virtually immovable in their determination not to do anything themselves.

On Bibliography
and Sources

Published secondary sources on the Russian countryside in the 1930s are comparatively few and often not of the highest quality. As far as Soviet scholarship is concerned, the 1930s were the most sensitive years for historians to write about, and collectivization and its outcome were the touchiest of subjects. As for Western scholarship, virtually nothing has been written about the village after collectivization. This undoubtedly reflects the difficulty of working with inadequate and unreliable published sources, the inaccessibility (until very recent times) of Soviet archives, and the fact that the Russian countryside itself was essentially inaccessible to Westerners even for purposes of tourism, let alone fieldwork, for more than half a century after collectivization.

The major Soviet monographs on the kolkhoz in the 1930s are M. A. Vyltsan's *Zavershaiushchii etap sozdaniia kolkhoznogo stroia (1935–1937 gg.)* (Moscow, 1978) and *Sovetskaia derevnia nakanune Velikoi Otechestvennoi voiny (1938–41 gg.)* (Moscow, 1970). On the kolkhoz in the first half of the 1930s, there are two useful articles by I. E. Zelenin: "Kolkhoznoe stroitel'stvo v SSSR v 1931–1932 gg." *Istoriia SSSR*, 1960 no. 6, and "Kolkhozy i sel'skoe khoziaistvo SSSR v 1933–1935 gg.," ibid., 1964 no. 5. On dekulakization, the standard work is N. A. Ivnitskii, *Klassovaia bor'ba v derevne i likvidatsiia kulachestva kak klassa (1929–1932 gg.)* (Moscow, 1972). On kolkhoz population and rural–urban migration, works include M. A. Vyltsan's "Trudovye resursy kolkhozov v dovoennye gody (1935–1940 gg.)," *Voprosy istorii*, 1973 no. 2, and Iu. V. Arutiunian, "Kollektivizatsiia sel'skogo khoziaistva i vysvobozhdenie rabochei sily dlia promyshlennosti," in *Formirovanie i razvitie sovetskogo rabochego klassa (1917–61 gg.)* (Moscow, 1964). Regional studies of the peasantry are often more illuminating than those published in the center: for example, N. Ia. Gushchin, *Sibirskaia derevnia na puti k sotsializmu* (Novosibirsk, 1973) and (with E. V. Kosheleva and V. G. Charushin), *Krest'ianstvo zapadnoi Sibiri v dovoennye gody (1935–1941)* (Novosibirsk, 1975).

In contrast to the 1920s, a very rich period for ethnographic and sociological work on the Russian village, such studies were almost totally lacking in the 1930s. Two exceptions are K. M. Shuvaev, *Staraia i novaia derevnia. Materialy issledovaniia s. Novo-Zhivotinnogo i der. Mokhovatki Berezovskogo raiona, Voronezhskoi oblasti, za 1901 i 1907, 1926 i 1937 g.* (Moscow, 1937) and A. E. Arina, G. G. Kotov and K. V. Loseva, *Sotsial'no-ekonomicheskie izmeneniia v derevne. Melitopol'skii raion (1885–1938)* (Moscow, 1939). Additions to this literature in the post-Stalin period include *The Village of Viriatino. An Ethnographic Study of a Russian Village from before the Revolution to the Present*, Sula Benet, ed. (New York, 1970), and L. A. Anokhina and M. N. Shmeleva, *Kul'tura i byt kolkhoznikov Kalininskoi oblasti* (Moscow, 1964), as well as articles on various regions published in the journal *Sovetskaia etnografiia* in the 1960s.

There are a number of useful documentary publications, notably the series of regional volumes on collectivization, generally covering the period 1927–1937, that appeared in the 1970s. The titles usually follow a standard form: for example, *Kollektivizatsiia sel'skogo khoziaistva v Tsentral'no-Chernozemnoi oblasti (1927–1937 gg.)* (Voronezh, 1978). For a more detailed discussion of this source, complete with annotated bibliography, see Lynne Viola, "Guide to Document Series on Collectivization," in Sheila Fitzpatrick and Lynne Viola, eds., *A Researcher's Guide to Sources on Soviet Social History in the 1930s* (Armonk, N.Y., 1990). Another essential source for any student of the peasantry is the two-volume collection of Soviet and Russian laws and directives on the kolkhoz for the period from the late 1920s to the late 1950s, *Istoriia kolkhoznogo prava* (Moscow, 1958–59).

From about 1988 on, it became possible for Soviet (later, post-Soviet) scholars to publish hitherto secret materials from the archives on sensitive subjects such as dekulakization and the 1932–33 famine, although the volume of such publication is still (as of January 1993) comparatively small. Works include *Dokumenty svidetel'stvuiut. Iz istorii derevni nakanune i v khode kollektivizatsii 1927–1932 gg.*, V. P. Danilov and N. A. Ivnitskii, eds. (Moscow, 1989); I. E. Zelenin, "O nekotorykh 'belykh piatnakh' zavershaiushchego etapa sploshnoi kollektivizatsii," *Istoriia SSSR*, 1989 no. 2; V. V. Kondrashin, "Golod 1932–1933 godov v derevniakh Povolzh'ia," *Voprosy istorii*, 1991 no. 6; and N. V. Teptsov. "Pravda o raskulachivanii (Dokumental'nyi ocherk)," *Kentavr*, March-April 1992.

Western scholarship focuses mainly on collectivization and the famine. Notable works include R. W. Davies's *The Socialist Offensive. the Collectivisation of Soviet Agriculture, 1929–1930* (Cambridge, Mass., 1980) and *The Soviet Collective Farm, 1929–1930* (Cambridge, Mass., 1980); Moshe

Lewin's *Russian Peasants and Soviet Power: A Study of Collectivization* (London, 1968) and some essays in his book *The Making of the Soviet System* (New York, 1985); Lynne Viola's *Best Sons of the Fatherland. Workers in the Vanguard of Soviet Collectivization* (Oxford, 1987) and her articles "'Bab'i Bunty' and Peasant Women's Protest during Collectivization," *Russian Review* 45:1 (1986) and "The Peasant Nightmare: Visions of Apocalypse in the Soviet Countryside," *Journal of Modern History* 62:4 (1990); Robert Conquest's *The Harvest of Sorrow. Soviet Collectivization and the Terror-Famine* (Oxford, 1986) and the three volumes of *Commission on the Ukraine Famine. Report to Congress* (Washington, 1988) prepared by James Mace and his colleagues.

For the post-famine period, the picture is much bleaker. There is an important article by Roberta Manning based on data from the Smolensk Archive, "Government in the Soviet Countryside in the Stalinist Thirties: The Case of Belyi Raion in 1937," published in *The Carl Beck Papers in Russian and East European Studies*, no. 301 (1984). A valuable collection of essays edited by James R. Millar, *The Soviet Rural Community* (Urbana, Ill., 1971) includes much of interest on the 1930s, particularly Jerry F. Hough's article, "The Changing Nature of the Kolkhoz Chairman." There is no history of Soviet agricultural policy in the prewar period, although one aspect of it is covered in Robert F. Miller's *One Hundred Thousand Tractors. The MTS and the Development of Controls in Soviet Agriculture* (Cambridge, Mass., 1970). The pioneering work by the economist Naum Jasny, *The Socialized Agriculture of the USSR* (Stanford, 1949) has been superseded only by Stephan Merl's work in German. Sergei Maslov's *Kolkhoznaia Rossiia* (Prague, 1937) is a valuable description of the functioning of the early Soviet kolkhoz, evidently based on firsthand observation.

Some of the most important Western work comes from European and Japanese scholars. Stephan Merl's *Bauern unter Stalin. Die Formierung des Kolchossystems 1930–1941* (Berlin, 1990) is the best study of the organization and economics of Soviet agriculture in the 1930s. A companion volume *Sozialer Aufstieg im sowjetischen Kolchossystem der 30er Jahre? Uber das Schicksal der bauerlichen Parteimitglieder, Dorfsowjetvorsitzenden, Posteninhaber in Kolchosen, Mechanisatoren und Stachanowleute* (Berlin, 1990), deals with questions of social mobility and social differentiation. The Japanese historian Nobuo Shimotomai has published two articles in English, "A Note on the Kuban Affair (1932–1933). The Crisis of Kolkhoz Agriculture in the North Caucasus," *Acta Slavica Iaponica* 1 (1983), and the appealingly titled "Springtime for the *Politotdel*: Local Party Organization in Crisis," *Acta Slavica Iaponica* IV (1986). Mention should also be made of Nicholas Werth's *La Vie Quotidienne des Paysans Russes de la Révolution à la Collectivisation (1917–1939)* (Paris, 1984), although this book's major contribution is its historical-anthropological description of the Russian village in the 1920s.

With regard to primary published sources, the 1930s presents a challenge to historians. In the years 1929–1933, almost all the good sources of the 1920s either ceased publication or suffered a remarkable decline in the quality and quantity of information. Since this question is examined in detail in Fitzpatrick and Viola, *A Researcher's Guide to Sources on Soviet Social History in the 1930s*, I will discuss it only briefly here. The basic problem is that the severe censorship and self-censorship of the Stalin period not only prevented the publication of information on agricultural failings and peasant grievances but also encouraged the publication of boastful and misleading accounts of agricultural achievements and peasant satisfaction. For this reason, the primary published sources tend to tell us a great deal about the Potemkin village but not much about the real one.

Journals of the 1930s are often disappointing. It is possible to plow through a whole year of the journal *Sotsialisticheskaia rekonstruktsiia sel'skogo khoziaistva* without sighting an actual peasant. *Molodoi kolkhoznik* is one of the very few journals that contains interesting material for the social historian—but it lasted little more than a year. For historians of the peasantry, as for all social historians, the best journal sources tend to be law journals, especially those such as *Sovetskaia iustitsiia* that deal more with cases and implementation problems than legal theory. A useful survey of this genre of source is Peter H. Solomon's "Legal Journals and Soviet Social History," in Fitzpatrick and Viola, *A Researcher's Guide*.

Statistical handbooks of the 1930s (in contrast to those of the 1920s) belong much more to the Potemkin world of publicity than the workaday world of routine government data collection. The general statistical handbooks published in 1934, 1935, and 1936 under the title *Sovetskoe stroitel'stvo SSSR. Statisticheskii ezhegodnik* are among the better examples, but the next and last volume in the series, *Sovetskoe stroitel'stvo Soiuza SSR (1933–1938 gg. Statisticheskii sbornik* (Moscow-Leningrad, 1939), is woefully inadequate. For a fuller discussion, see S. G. Wheatcroft, "Statistical Sources for the Study of Soviet Social History in the Prewar Period," in Fitzpatrick and Viola, A *Researcher's Guide*.

Of the statistical publications that deal specifically with agriculture, *Sel'skoe khoziaistvo SSSR. Ezhegodnik 1935* (Moscow 1936) and *Sel'skoe khoziaistvo SSSR. Statisticheskii spravochnik* (Moscow, 1939) concentrate almost exclusively on the economic and technological aspects, while *Kolkhozy vo vtoroi stalinskoi piatiletke. Statisticheskii spravochnik* (Moscow, 1939) is almost total Potemkinism. A more useful collection of kolkhoz statistics, *Proizvoditel'nost' i ispol'zovanie truda v kolkhozakh vo vtoroi piatiletke*, I. V. Sautin, ed. (Moscow-Leningrad, 1939), has the defect of providing virtually no information on the selection criteria for the 1937 survey of 430 collective farms in ten regions of the Soviet Union from which its data are drawn. A more extreme example of the same problem is the 1938 survey of kolkhoz youth published in *Sotsial'nyi oblik kolkhoznoi molodezhi po materialam sotsiologicheskikh obsledovanii 1938 i 1969 gg.* (Moscow, 1976), based on a small sample of young kolkhozniks selected, one can only assume, on the basis of their above-average prosperity and cultural level.

A very important recent addition to the body of published statistical data is the 1937 census, long suppressed because of the unwelcome information on population losses it conveyed. Although the figures are not final tabulations of the 1937 census returns, they are still a lot more useful than the meager (and probably inflated) 1939 census data on which scholars have previously relied. The 1937 census data are now available in *Vsesoiuznaia perepis' naseleniia 1937 g. Kratkie itogi* (Moscow, 1991) and, with a helpful commentary, in Iu. A. Poliakov, V. B. Zhiromskaia, I. N. Kiselev, "Polveka molchaniia (Vsesoiuznaia perepis' naseleniia 1937 g.)," *Sotsiologicheskie issledovaniia*, 1990 nos. 6 and 7.

In the future, if former-Soviet archives remain open to Western scholars, social historians may decide to work largely from archival rather than published sources. But I did not have that option when I started the research on this book, so I decided to try to break through the Potemkin barrier by a strategy of massive newspaper reading. While there is much to be gleaned from the central press, particularly *Pravda, Izvestiia*, the agricultural newspaper *Sotsialisticheskoe zemledelie*, and the peasant newspaper *Krest'ianskaia gazeta*, the best newspaper sources in the 1930s come from the provinces. The oblast newspapers I have cited most often in this book are the following: *Gor'kovskaia kommuna* (Gorky), *Kommuna* (Voronezh), *Kommunist* (Saratov), *Krasnaia Tatariia* (Kazan), *Krasnoe znamia* (Tomsk), *Krasnyi Krym* (Simferopol), *Kurskaia pravda* (Kursk), *Molot* (Rostov on Don), *Rabochii krai* (Ivanovo), *Rabochii put'* (Smolensk), *Severnyi rabochii* (Iaroslavl), *Sovetskaia Sibir'* (Novosibirsk), *Sotsialisticheskii Donbass* (Stalino), *Tambovskaia pravda* (Tambov), *Tikhookeanskaia zvezda* (Khabarovsk), *Ural'skii rabochii* (Sverdlovsk), and *Zvezda* (Dnepropetrovsk). Special mention should be made of a Leningrad newspaper specializing in rural affairs, *Krest'ianskaia pravda*, which is a godsend for the researcher on the peasantry up to about 1938, when its quality declined.

The single largest problem that confronts a historian of the peasantry in the 1930s is that almost all sources, published or archival, persistently ignore peasants and the village. Even given the regime's preoccupation with output, the single-minded focus on production and procurement is remarkable. More information is available about kolkhoz livestock than about kolkhoz households: The human factor is notably absent. The problem is compounded by the fact that there are very few published memoirs about village life in the 1930s. The memoir genre was somewhat suspect during the Stalin period; but even in recent years, when many memoirs of the Stalin period were published, almost none of them were about the countryside. This reflects the fact that educated Russian society had extremely little contact with the village at this time.

Among the small numbers of memoirs available, the best are Ivan Tvardovskii's "Stranitsy perezhitogo," *Iunost'*, 1988 no. 3, written by a peasant (the brother of the poet Aleksandr) whose family was dekulakized and deported, and E. Gerasimov's "Puteshchestvie v Spas na Peskakh," *Novyi mir*,

1967 no. 12, an account of a struggling kolkhoz/village by a journalist whose newspaper had "adopted" it in the 1930s. Fedor Belov's *The History of a Soviet Collective Farm* (New York, 1955) is a postwar émigré memoir by a former kolkhoz chairman in Ukraine. Memoirs that contain significant episodes of contact with the village include Petro G. Grigorenko, *Memoirs* (New York, 1982), Arvo Tuominen, *The Bells of the Kremlin* (Hanover/London, 1983), *Soviet Youth. Twelve Komsomol Histories,* N. K. Novak-Deker, ed. (Munich: Institut fur Erforschung der UdSSR, Series 1 no. 51, 1959), and Victor Kravchenko, *I Chose Freedom* (New York, 1946). Maurice Hindus's *Red Bread* (London, 1931) describes a visit to the author's native village in Ukraine during collectivization. There are several memoirs by peasant celebrities of the Stalin period including one by a kolkhoz chairman, Fedor Dubkovetskii's *Na putiakh k kommunizmu. Zapiski zachinatelia kolkhoznogo dvizheniia na Ukraine* (Moscow, 1951).

Soviet literary works on the village include some that are either disguised memoirs or disguised histories drawing on firsthand knowledge: for example, Mikhail Alekseev's novel *Drachuny* (Moscow, 1982), which includes a remarkable account of the 1932–33 famine in the author's native village in the Central Volga region; the same author's novella "Khleb—imia sushchestvitel'noe" (written in 1961–63; published in M. Alekseev, *Vishnevyi omut. Kariukha. Khleb—imia sushchestvitel'noe* [Moscow, 1981]), which chronicles the fate of the inhabitants of the village described in *Drachuny* up to the Second World War; Boris Mozhaev's collectivization novel, *Muzhiki i baby* (Moscow, 1988); N. Skromnyi's "Perelom," *Sever*, 1986 nos. 10–12 (about kulak deportations); and Sergei Antonov's "Ovrag," *Druzhba narodov*, 1988 nos. 1–2.

There are obviously problems about using literary works, including fictionalized memoirs and fictionalized histories, as historical sources. But it should be pointed out that in the early 1960s, and again in the second half of the 1980s, this was the favored Soviet genre for rewriting the history of the Stalin period. The Soviet public looked to belles-lêttres to reveal the truth about the past; and literary works in this genre were held accountable for any lapses in historical accuracy. For example, the first serial publication of Mozhaev's *Muzhiki i baby* included an afterword with archival footnotes (*Don*, 1987 no. 3, 96–106)! (This did not stop Mozhaev being criticized in a scholarly historical journal as a bad historian: see V. P. Danilov's comments in *Voprosy istorii*, 1988 no. 3, 22.)

Soviet archives, including classified materials, were in the process of opening up to Western scholars while I was researching and writing this book. Some archives, such as the Central Party Archive, became available to me only after I had completed the first draft of the manuscript. Therefore I will not attempt to give a comprehensive account of the holdings of former Soviet archives. But a few general remarks are in order before I proceed to a description of the main archival sources used in this book.

The great bulk of material preserved in Soviet archives consists of the records of state and party bureaucracies. The type and nature of information passed up the bureaucratic chain always reflects the climate in which bureaucracies operate. In the Stalin period, the climate was very oppressive, and messengers bearing bad news really were in danger of being shot. For that reason, self-censorship in Soviet bureaucratic documents is sometimes almost as severe as the formal censorship governing published materials. By 1937–38, even Central Committee and Politburo files seem to be quite heavily self-censored. The more coercive the Stalinist regime became, the more difficult it became for the leaders to get reliable information through normal bureaucratic channels.

This situation forced the leaders to look for or create other sources of information. The first alternative source consisted of regular secret police (GPU, OGPU, NKVD) reports, and ad hoc reports by special investigators outside police channels. Such investigations were prompted by egregious failures of policy implementation ("excesses"), complaints and denunciations from the population, and scandals of all types. These are wonderful sources for the social historian, but they have their own built-in bias: These channels existed specifically for the purpose of transmitting bad news. A special investigator who concluded that the problem was caused by inefficiency and inexperience might well be suspected of participating in a cover-up; an NKVD man who habitually reported good news from the countryside (improved morale in the villages, better leadership, more identification with the kolkhoz) was likely to be told that he was in the wrong line of business. The business of policemen and special investigators was to dig up dirt.

The second alternative channel of information consisted of petitions, complaints, and denunciations sent to the authorities by individual citizens. These were actively encouraged in the Stalin period; and peasants as well as urban dwellers sent them in enormous numbers to all kinds of institutions—party committees, prosecutors' offices, newspapers, government agencies, the NKVD—as well as to political leaders, particularly Stalin and Kalinin. Many such letters are preserved in the archives of the institutions to which they were sent (one such archival collection is discussed in detail below). These virtually untapped sources should yield a great deal to social historians in the future.

The main archives and archival collections (fondy) that I used in this book are listed below. Since my footnotes identify material from former Soviet archives only by number (fond, opis', delo, and list), I have provided information on institutional provenance here. With the exception of the Smolensk Archive, which is located in this country and available on microfilm from the US National Archives, and the Urals state archive, GASO, which is located in Ekaterinburg (formerly Sverdlovsk), all the archives listed are in Moscow.

Smolensk Archive

Part of the archive of the Western oblast party committee, this is a World War II trophy, seized first by the Germans and then by the Americans: For more on its history and contents, see J. Arch Getty, "Guide to the Smolensk Archive," in Fitzpatrick and Viola, *A Researcher's Guide*. In addition to party materials, the archive contains material sent to the obkom from other institutions, for example, NKVD reports and peasant letters of complaint forward by newspapers. Among the files that were particularly useful to me in this study were those on collectivization "excesses" in 1930, NKVD reports, and reports from obkom instructors sent to the villages to investigate complaints. It should be noted that the Western oblast is not the ideal region for a historian of the Russian peasantry as a whole, being characterized by infertile soil, small collective farms, the greatest incidence of khutor tenure in Russia, a high rate of otkhod, and comparative insignificance as an agricultural producer.

RTsKhIDNI

Russian Center for the Preservation and Study of Documents of Contemporary History, formerly *TsPA* (Central Party Archive of the Institute of Marxism-Leninism under the Central Committee of the CPSU).

This became accessible to me only at the very end of my work on the book, and my investigation of its files was necessarily cursory. The collections that I consulted and cite in the book are f. 5, op. 4 (agricultural department of the Central Committee); f. 17 (Central Committee of CPSU), op. 2 (plenums), op. 3 (Politburo), and op. 7 (statistical dept.); f. 112 (politotdels of MTS); f. 78 (personal archive of M. I. Kalinin); f. 77 (personal archive of A. A. Zhdanov); f. 89 (personal archive of Em. Iaroslavskii).

GASO

State Archive of Sverdlovsk (now Ekaterinburg) Oblast.

The materials I used in a short research visit were from both the open and formerly classified files of the executive committee of the Sverdlovsk oblast soviet (f. 88, f. 88-r, f. 88/52), and from the archives of the Urals oblast court (f. 1148).

TsGAOR

Central State Archive of the October Revolution and Socialist Construction of the USSR, now renamed *GARF* (State Archive of the Russian Federation).

This was not a major archive for the present study, but collections cited include f. 374, op. 9 (People's Commissariat of Workers' and Peasants' Inspection of USSR, agricultural inspectorate); f. 5407 (League of Militant Atheists); f. 5451 (Central Council of Trade Unions); f. 5515, op. 1 (People's Commissariat of Labor; minutes of collegium meetings); f. 3316 (All-Union Executive Committee of the Congress of Soviets [TsIK]), op. 34

and 39 (petitions and complaints files), and op. 41 (letters on the 1936 Constitution).

TsGANKh

Central State Archive of the National Economy of the USSR, now renamed *RGAE* (Russian State Archive of the Economy).

The main collections used were f. 7486 (People's Commissariat of Agriculture of the USSR), especially op. 19 (Secretariat); and f. 396, op. 10 and 11 (the newspaper *Krest'ianskaia gazeta*, letters to the editor, 1938 and 1939). The larger of these two inventories, op. 10, contains about 160 files of letters, classified by oblast and partially by subject-matter. The files I have used from op. 10 come from the following regions: Cheliabinsk oblast (d. 149), Gorky krai (d. 23), Iaroslavl oblast (dd. 160–62), Ivanovo oblast (d. 34), Kalinin oblast (d. 39), Krasnodar krai (dd. 64–67), Kursk oblast (dd. 81, 86–88), Saratov krai (d. 121), Smolensk oblast (d. 129), Sverdlovsk oblast (d. 122), Stalingrad oblast (d. 137), Tambov oblast (dd. 141– 43), Tatar republic (d. 145), and Voronezh oblast (dd. 15, 19).

Krest'ianskaia gazeta

Since the *Krest'ianskaia gazeta* archive was the single most important source for this book, it deserves more than a passing mention. The first nine inventories contain a large and rich collection of peasant letters from the 1920s. For the 1930s, letters of all years but 1938 and 1939 have been lost (and the 1939 collection is very small because the paper was closed in the early spring). The great majority of these letters, which are handwritten and almost invariably signed, come from villagers, mainly kolkhozniks. Many signatories seem to be composing and writing their own letters, judging by the vernacular style and mistakes of spelling and grammar, but a minority (20–30 percent) are written neatly in fairly correct Soviet Russian. The latter usually come from kolkhoz accountants or teachers, but some are from rank-and-file kolkhozniks who may have been using a better-educated villager as a scribe.

These letters were not primarily intended for publication, and very few were in fact published. They were sent in the expectation of getting a practical response, namely information about the rights and obligations of kolkhozniks and the kolkhoz, and the correction of injustices by state intervention and the punishment of wrongdoers. The newspaper had a whole department whose staffers' functions were to answer queries, give advice, forward complaints and denunciations to the appropriate authorities (oblast and raion party committees and soviets, the procuracy, the NKVD), and keep tabs on them to ensure that they took appropriate action.

There are basically two categories of letters in the *Krest'ianskaia gazeta* archive. The first consists of requests for information and legal rulings, the second of complaints and denunciations. The letters seeking information deal mainly with tax questions, rights and procedure on such questions as private plot, work obligations, expulsion from the kolkhoz, and payment of labordays. For example: Can the kolkhoz force otkhodniks to return and take part in the kolkhoz's agricultural work? When a blacksmith joins kolkhoz, are his smithy and work tools collectivized? Should an independent peasant household consisting of two old parents and a wage-earning son have to pay agricultural tax and local taxes?

The taxation enquiries generally come from ordinary peasant households. The other letters in this general category are often written by kolkhoz chairmen or kolkhoz accountants. These letters, and the answers supplied by *Krest'ianskaia gazeta* (sometimes after consultation with the People's Commissariat of Agriculture), are an extremely valuable source of information on how the laws relating to the kolkhoz were actually applied, and the ways in which they were commonly flouted.

The second category of letter consists of complaints and denunciations against local officials and kolkhoz chairmen and brigade leaders. These are separately filed in *Krest'ianskaia gazeta*'s archive for 1938–39 under the heading "Abuse of power and wrecking" (*zloupotreblenie vlasti i vreditel'stvo*), and in 1938 constitute an estimated 30–40 percent of all letters to the newspaper. Unfortunately, given the absence from *Krest'ianskaia gazeta*'s archive of letters from earlier years, there is necessarily a degree of uncertainty about whether peasants were such energetic complainers and denouncers *before* the Great Purges of 1937–38 as they were during them. But such letters were certainly not unique to 1938, although they may well have been less numerous: The Smolensk Archive, for example, contains a number of letters from Western oblast peasants forwarded to the obkom by *Krest'ianskaia gazeta* for investigation and action in 1935 and 1936. The majority of "Abuse of power" letters were written by ordinary (nonofficeholding) peasants about peasants who were officeholders in the kolkhoz or rural soviet. The kolkhoz chairman was the most frequent victim of denunciation.

Abbreviations of Frequently Cited Titles

Alekseev (1981)   Mikhail Alekseev, "Khleb—imia sushchestvitel'noe," in *Vishnevyi omut. Kariukha. Khleb—imia sushchestvitel'noe* (Moscow, 1981)
Alekseev (1982)   Mikhail Alekseev, *Drachuny* (Moscow, 1982)
Anokhina (1964)   L. A. Anokhina and M. N. Shmeleva, *Kul'tura i byt kolkhoznikov Kalininskoi oblasti* (Moscow, 1964)
AR   Antireligioznik
Arina (1939)   A. E. Arina, G. G. Kotov and K. V. Loseva, *Sotsial'no-ekonomicheskie izmeneniia v derevne. Melitopol'skii raion (1885–1938)* (Moscow, 1939)
Danilov (1977)   V. P. Danilov, *Sovetskaia dokolkhoznaia derevnia: naselenie, zemlepol'zovanie, khoziaistvo* (Moscow, 1977)
Danilov (1979)   V. P. Danilov, *Sovetskaia dokolkhoznaia derevnia: sotsial'naia struktura, sotsial'nye otnosheniia* (Moscow, 1979)
Davies (1980a)   R. W. Davies, *The Socialist Offensive. The Collectivisation of Soviet Agriculture, 1929–1930* (Cambridge, Mass., 1980)
Davies (1980b)   R. W. Davies, *The Soviet Collective Farm, 1929–1930* (Cambridge, Mass., 1980).
Diachenko (1978)   V. P. Diachenko, *Istoriia finansov SSSR* (Moscow, 1978)
DIu   Derevenskii iurist
GASO   Gosudarstvennyi arkhiv Sverdlovskoi oblasti
Gerasimov (1967)   E. Gerasimov, "Puteshestvie v Spas na Peskakh," *Novyi mir*, 1967 no. 12
Geroini   Geroini sotsialisticheskogo truda (Moscow, 1936)
GK   Gor'kovskaia kommuna (Gorky)
Gushchin (1975)   N. Ia. Gushchin, E. V. Kosheleva, V. G. Charushin, *Krest'ianstvo zapadnoi sibiri v dovoennye gody (1935–1941)* (Novosibirsk, 1975)
Gushchin (1973)   *Sibirskaia derevnia na puti k sotsializmu* (Novosibirsk, 1973)

IKP Istoriia kolkhoznogo prava, 2 vols. (Moscow, 1958–59)

IndSSSR (1971) *Industrializatsiia SSSR 1933–1937 gg. Dokumenty i materialy* (Moscow, 1971)

ISK Istoriia sovetskogo krest'ianstva, 5 vols. (Moscow, 1986–)

ISSSR Istoriia SSSR

Izmeneniia (1979) *Izmeneniia sotsial'noi struktury sovetskogo obshchestva 1921—seredina 30-kh godov* (Moscow, 1979)

Izv Izvestiia

KG Krest'ianskaia gazeta

KolSK Kollektivizatsiia sel'skogo khoziaistva na Severnom Kavkaze (1927–1937 gg.) (Krasnodar, 1972)

KolSP Kollektivizatsiia sel'skogo khoziaistva v Srednem Povolzh'e (1927–1937 gg.) (Kuibyshev, 1970)

KolSZ Kollektivizatsiia sel'skogo khoziaistva v severo- zapadnom raione (1927–1937 gg.) (Leningrad, 1970)

KolTsChO Kollektivizatsiia sel'skogo khoziaistva v Tsentral'no-Chernozemnoi oblasti (1927–1937 gg.) (Voronezh, 1978)

KP Komsomol'skaia pravda

KPSSvR Kommunisticheskaia partiia Sovetskogo Soiuza v rezoliutsiiakh i resheniiakh syezdov, konferentsii i plenumov TsK (1898–1970), 8th ed., 15 vols. (Moscow, 1970–1984)

KrK Krasnyi Krym (Simferopol)

KrP Krest'ianskaia pravda (Leningrad)

KultStroi (1956) *Kul'turnoe stroitel'stvo SSSR. Statisticheskii sbornik* (Moscow, 1956)

KurPr Kurskaia pravda (Kursk)

Millar (1971) James R. Millar, ed., *The Soviet Rural Community* (Urbana, 1971)

MKG Moskovskaia kolkhoznaia gazeta

MKrG Moskovskaia krest'ianskaia gazeta

Mozhaev (1988) Boris Mozhaev, "Istoriia sela Berkhova, pisannaia Petrom Afanasevichem Bulkinym," in his *Nado li vspominat' staroe?* (Moscow, 1988)

NarKhoz (1932) *Narodnoe khoziaistvo SSSR. Statisticheskii spravochnik 1932* (Moscow-Leningrad, 1932)

NarKhoz (1972) *Narodnoe khoziaistvo SSSR 1922–1972 gg. Iubileinyi statisticheskii ezhegodnik* (Moscow, 1972)

NR Neizvestnaia Rossiia XX veka. Arkhivy. Pis'ma, memuary (Moscow, 1992)

Ostrovskii (1967) V. B. Ostrovskii, *Kolkhoznoe krest'ianstvo SSSR. Politika partii v derevne i ee sotsial'no- ekonomicheskie rezul'taty* (Saratov, 1967)

PIT Proizvoditel'nost' i ispol'zovanie truda v kolkhozakh vo vtoroi piatiletke (Moscow-Leningrad, 1939)

Pr Pravda

PVSKU Pervyi Vsesoiuznyi syezd kolkhoznikov-udarnikov peredovykh kolkhozov, 15–19 fevralia 1933 g. Stenograficheskii otchet (Moscow-Leningrad, 1933)

Poliakov (1990) Iu. A. Poliakov, V. B. Zhiromskaia, I. N. Kiselev, "Polveka molchaniia (Vsesoiuznaia perepis' naseleniia 1937 g.), *Sotsiologicheskie issledovaniia*, 1990 no. 7

RP Rabochaia put' (Smolensk)

RPPKhoz Resheniia partii i pravitel'stva po khoziaistvennym voprosam, 2 vols. (Moscow, 1967)

RTsKhIDNI   Rossiiskii tsentr khraneniia i izucheniia dokumentov noveishei istorii (formerly Tsentral'nyi partiinyi arkhiv KPSS)

SA   Smolensk Archive

SDK   *Spravochnik derenskogo kommunista* (Moscow, 1936)

SE   *Sovetskaia etnografiia*

SevR   *Severnyi rabochii* (Iaroslavl)

SG   *Sovetskoe gosudarstvo*

SGP   *Sovetskoe gosudarstvo i pravo*

Shuvaev (1937)   K. M. Shuvaev, *Staraia i novaia derevnia. Materialy issledovaniia c. Novo-Zhivotinnogo i der. Mokhovatki Berezovskogo raiona, Voronezhskoi oblasti, za 1901 i 1907, 1926 i 1937 g.* (Moscow, 1937)

SIu   *Sovetskaia iustitsiia*

SotsStroi (1934–36)   *Sotsialisticheskoe stroitel'stvo SSSR. Statisticheskii ezhegodnik* (Moscow, 1934, 1935, 1936)

SotsStroi (1939)   *Sotsialisticheskoe stroitel'stvo Soiuza SSR (1933–1938 gg.). Statisticheskii sbornik* (Moscow-Leningrad, 1939)

SovYouth   *Soviet Youth. Twelve Komsomol Histories*, ed. N. K. Novak-Deker (Munich: Institut fur Erforschung der UdSSR, Series 1 no. 51, 1959)

Stalin, *Soch.*   I. V. Stalin, *Sochineniia*, vols. 1–13 (Moscow) and 1(14)–3(16), ed. Robert H. McNeal (Stanford)

SU RSFSR   *Sobranie uzakonenii i rasporiazhenii rabochego i krest'ianskogo pravitel'stva RSFSR*

SV   *Sotsialisticheskii vestnik*

SR   *Slavic Review*

SZ   *Sotsialisticheskoe zemledelie*

SZ SSSR   *Sobranie zakonov i rasporiazhenii raboche-krest'ianskogo pravitel'stva SSSR* (from 1938, *Sobranie postanovlenii i rasporiazhenii pravitel'stva S.S.S.R.*)

Trud (1936)   *Trud v SSSR. Statisticheskii spravochnik* (Moscow, 1936)

TsGANKh   Tsentral'nyi gosudarstvennyi arkhiv narodnogo khoziaistva SSSR

TsGAOR   Tsentral'nyi gosudarstvennyi arkhiv Oktiabr'skoi revoliutsii i sotsialisticheskogo stroitel'stva SSSR

Viriatino   *The Village of Viriatino. An Ethnographic Study of a Russian Village from Before the Revolution to the Present*, trans. and ed. Sula Benet (New York, 1970)

VVSKU   *Vtoroi vsesoiuznyi syezd kolkhoznikov-udarnikov. 11–17 fevralia 1935 g. Stenograficheskii otchet* (Moscow, 1935)

Vyltsan(1978)   M. A. Vyltsan, *Zavershaiushchii etap sozdaniia kolkhoznogo stroia (1935–1937 gg.)* (Moscow, 1978)

Vyltsan (1970)   M. A. Vyltsan, *Sovetskaia derevnia nakanune Velikoi Otechestvennoi voiny (1938–41 gg.)* (Moscow, 1970)

VI   *Voprosy istorii*

ZKP   *Za kommunisticheskoe prosveshchenie*

Zv   *Zvezda* (Dnepropetrovsk)

Notes

Introduction

1. The term "subaltern" and the concept of subalternity were introduced into peasant studies by Dr. Ranajit Guha and his colleagues: see *Selected Subaltern Studies*, Ranajit Guha and Gayatri Chakravorty Spivak, eds. (New York, 1988), 35 and *passim*.

2. At this point, my approach diverges from that of James C. Scott, *Domination and the Arts of Resistance. Hidden Transcripts* (New Haven, 1990).

3. James C. Scott, *Weapons of the Weak. Everyday Forms of Peasant Resistance* (New Haven, 1985). See also Steven L. Hoch, *Serfdom and Social Control in Russia* (Chicago, 1986), ch. 5; and George M. Frederickson and Christopher Lasch, "Resistance to Slavery," in Ann J. Lane, ed., *The Debate over Slavery* (Urbana, Ill., 1971), 223–44.

4. See Anand A. Yang, "A Conversation of Rumors: The Language of Popular Mentalités in 19th-Century Colonial India," *Journal of Social History*, Spring 1987.

5. On the connection between religion and political protest in the Rusian countryside, see Stephen P. and Ethel Dunn, *The Peasants of Central Russia* (New York, 1967), 104–5. The classic work on religion and resistance to the state in Russia is Michael Cherniavsky, "Old Believers and the New Religion," in Cherniavsky, ed., *The Structure of Russian History: Interpretive Essays* (New York, 1970), 140–188.

6. On "moral economy," see E. P. Thompson, "The Moral Economy of the English Crowd in the Eighteenth Century," *Past and Present* 50 (1971), 76–136; and James C. Scott, *The Moral Economy of the Peasant* (New Haven, 1976); and, for an application to Russian circumstances, Orlando Figes, *Peasant Russia, Civil War. The Volga Countryside in Revolution (1917–1921)* (Oxford, 1989), ch. 3. On "limited good," see George M. Foster, "Peasant Society and the Image of Limited Good," *American Anthropologist* 67:2 (1965) 293–315.

7. Samuel L. Popkin, *The Rational Peasant. The Political Economy of Rural Society in Vietnam* (Berkeley, 1979).

8. On hidden and public transcripts, see Scott, *Domination*, 4–5 and *passim*.

9. On *bol'shaks*, see Stephen L. Hoch, *Serfdom and Social Control in Russia* (Chicago, 1986), 129–32.

10. Western scholars such as Moshe Lewin, *Russian Peasants and Soviet Power* (London, 1968), and Teodor Shanin, *The Awkward Class* (Oxford, 1972) have strongly contested the Soviet belief that the village was split along class lines in the 1920s. On the class question, they are surely right; but they miss the point that it was probably the high level of factiousness and hostility in the village that led Soviet Marxists to believe they wre observing class struggle.

11. For a recent ethnographic work in this spirit, see M. M. Gromyko, *Traditsionnye normy povedeniia i formy obshcheniia russkikh krest'ian XIX v.* (Moscow, 1986).

12. Robert Redfield, *Tepoztlan: A Mexican Village* (Chicago, 1930); and Oscar Lewis, *Tepoztlan Restudied* (Urbana, 1951); Joseph Lopreato, *Peasants No More. Social Class and Social Change in an Underdeveloped Society* (San Francisco, 1967).

13. Speech to XX Party Congress (1956), in *The Anti-Stalin Campaign and International Communism. A Selection of Documents* (New York, 1956), 77.

14. See Daniel Field, *Rebels in the Name of the Tsar* (Boston, 1976).

Chapter 1

1. *Itogi vsesoiuznoi perepisi naseleniia 1959 g. SSSR. Svodnyi tom* (Moscow, 1962), 13 (population of territory of Russian Empire incorporated into the Soviet Union); *Vsesoiuznaia perepis' naseleniia 17 dekabria 1926 g. Kratkie svodki* (Moscow, 1928) 5:xiv, 2–7 (literacy of population aged eight years and over in 1926).

2. Vl. Plandunovskii, *Narodnaia perepis'* (St. Petersburg, 1898), 339–40 and Appendix 1; *Entsiklopedicheskii slovar'* (St. Petersburg: Brokgauz, Efron, 1895), 26a:693.

3. On the ethnic composition of Russia in 1917, see *VI*, no. 6, 41–44 (1980).

4. The Black Earth belt, so-called because of its characteristic soil, rich in humus content, is a broad belt running across Ukraine and European Russia, bounded in the south by the Black and Caspian seas and in the north by an imaginary line connecting Kiev in the Ukraine, Tula in central Russia, Kazan on the Volga, and Perm in the Urals.

5. See Field, *Rebels in the Name of the Tsar* (Boston, 1976), and Allan K. Wildman, "The Defining Moment: Land Charters as the Foundation of the Post-Emancipation Agrarian Settlement in Russia, 1861–63," paper presented to Fourth Midwest Russian History Workshop, Chicago, October 1992.

6. *Istoricheskie zapiski* 94:70–71 (1974).

7. Decree on land of 26 October 1917 (old style), *RPPKhoz* 1:15–17.

8. See Danilov (1977), 106–7, and *ISSSR*, no. 1, 37–84 (1981) (on fate of separators in 1917); and Iu. Larin in *Bol'shevik*, no. 22, 46 (1927) (on kulak expropriations). For doubts on the reality of dekulakization, see Teodor Shanin, *The Awkward Class* (Oxford, 1972), 145–52.

9. On requisitions and the Volga famine, see Orlando Figes, *Peasant Russia, Civil War* (Oxford, 1989), 267–73.

10. Iu. A. Poliakov, *Perekhod k NEPu i sovetskoe krest'ianstvo* (Moscow, 1967), 100; Shanin, *The Awkward Class*, 153–54.

11. Data and estimates from Iu. A. Poliakov, *Sovetskaia strana posle okonchaniia grazhdanskoi voiny: territoriia i naselenie* (Moscow, 1986), 120 and 146–48; Frank Lorimer, *The Population of the Soviet Union* (Geneva, 1946), 29–30; *Vsesoiuznaia perepis' naseleniia* 5:2–5.

12. Danilov (1977), 298; Poliakov, *Perekhod*, 377.

13. Danilov (1977), 107, 115, 139–43, 171.

14. *Istoricheskie zapiski* 94:71–72, 110 (1974); *Otkhod sel'skogo naseleniia na zarabotki v SSSR v 1926–27 g.* (Moscow, 1929), ll.

15. N. Rosnitskii, *Litso derevnia po materialam obsledovaniia 28 volostei i 32,730 krest'ianskikh khoziaistv Penzenskoi gubernii* (Moscow-Leningrad, 1926), 13; *Trezvost' i kul'tura*, no. 19, 3 (1929).

16. R. W. Davies, *The Development of the Soviet Budgetary System* (Cambridge, 1958), 68, 114–15, and 117; Iu. Larin, *Voprosy krest'ianskogo khoziaistva* (Moscow, 1923), 117–18; M. Ia. Fenomenov, *Sovremennaia derevnia* (Leningrad-Moscow, 1925), 1:202.

17. *RTsKhIDNI*, fond 17, opis' 7, delo 315, list 58; *Sotsial'nyi i natsional'nyi sostav VKP(b). Itogi vsesoiuznoi partiinoi perepisi 1927 g.* (Moscow-Leningrad, 1928), 80, 87, 89.

18. Dorothy Atkinson, *The End of the Russian Land Commune, 1905–1930* (Stanford, 1983), 299–300; E. H. Carr, *The Foundations of a Planned Economy 1926–1929* (London, 1971), 2:251; M. Golubykh, *Ocherki glukhoi derevni* (Moscow-Leningrad, 1926), 10–12; Shanin, *Awkward Class*, 194.

19. *Bol'shevik*, no. 9, 79–80 (1928).

20. A. M. Selishchev, *Iazyk revoliutsionnoi epokhi*, 2d ed. (Moscow, 1928), 215; Ia. Shafir, *Gazeta i derevnia*, 2d ed. (Moscow, 1924), 100–101.

21. G. I. Okulova, ed., *Zametki o derevnia (iz derevenskoi praktiki studentov AKVO* (Moscow, 1927), 34; A. M. Bolshakov, *Derevnia, 1917–1927* (Moscow, 1927), 425; Golubykh, *Ocherki glukhoi derevni*, 73.

22. Bolshakov, *Derevnia*, 423–25; Fenomenov, *Sovremennaia derevnia* 2:38–39, 95–96.

23. Stalin, *Soch.* 7:334 and 337. Note that the term "Communist," officially adopted in 1918, was used interchangeably with "Bolshevik" in the 1920s.

24. L. S. Sosnovskii, in *Derevnia pri NEP'e. Kogo schitat' kulakom, kto—truzhenikom. Chto govoriat ob etom krest'iane?* (Moscow, 1924), 7. The quantitative estimate is from *Izmeneniia sotsial'noi struktury sovetskogo obshchestva oktiabr' 1917–1920* (Moscow, 1976), 226. For two views on the rate of kulak survival, differentiated by region, see *Bol'shevik*, no. 22, 40–60 (1927), and no. 12, 43 (1929).

25. See Terry Cox, *Peasants, Class and Capitalism. The Rural Research of L. N. Kritsman and his School* (Oxford, 1986) and Susan G. Solomon, *The Soviet Agrarian Debate* (Boulder, Colo., 1977).

26. *Izmeneniia*, 222–27.

27. *Plenum Sibirskogo Kraevogo Komiteta VKP(b) 3–7 marta 1928 goda. Stenograficheskii otchet* (Moscow, Novosibirsk), 1, 21.

28. For elaboration of this point, see Sheila Fitzpatrick, "The Problem of Class Identity in NEP Society," in *Russia in the Era of NEP*, Sheila Fitzpatrick, Alexander Rabinowitch, and Richard Stites, eds. (Bloomington, 1991), 12–33.

29. Danilov (1979), 309–21; Carr, *Foundations* 2:278–80.

30. *Kommunist*, no. 5, 80 (1990); see also Bolshakov, *Derevnia*, 426.

31. *Derevnia pri NEP'e*, 19; see also ibid., 38–39.

32. *Derevnia pri NEP'e*, 53–54, 29–30, 75–76, and *passim*.

33. For examples, see *Istoriko-bytovye ekspeditsii 1949–1950. Materialy k voprosu rassloeniia krest'ianstvo i formirovanie proletariata v Rossii kontsa XIX—nachala XX veka*, A. M. Panfilova, ed. (Moscow, 1953), 158.

34. A. Gagarin, *Khoziaistvo, zhizn', i nastroenie derevnia* (Moscow-Leningrad, 1925), 41.

35. V. A. Kozlov, *Kul'turnaia revoliutsiia i krest'ianstvo 1921–1927* (Moscow, 1983), 105.

36. *Dekrety sovetskoi vlasti* (Moscow, 1957–59), 1:371–73, 210–11, 247–49, 237–39; 2:553.

37. Anokhina (1964), 267; Peter Kenez, *The Birth of the Propaganda State* (Cambridge, 1985), 173.

38. *Molodaia gvardiia*, no. 8, 104 (1925); *Komsomol v derevnie. Ocherki*, V. G. Bogoraz-Tan, ed. (Moscow-Leningrad, 1926), 9, 115; Neil B. Weissman, "Rural Crime in Tsarist Russia: The question of Hooliganism, 1905–1914," SR 37(2): 228–40 (1978); V. G. Tan-Bogoraz, *Staryi i novyi byt* (Leningrad, 1924), 18.

39. *Dekrety* 2:561; *KPSSvR* 2:469–72, 481; *KPSSvR* 3:84–85.

40. See E. H. Carr, *Socialism in One Country* (London, 1964), 1:38–46.

41. Gregory L. Freeze, *The Parish Clergy in 19th Century Russia. Crisis, Reform, Counter-Reform* (Princeton, 1983), 453; Nicholas Werth, *La Vie Quotidienne des Paysans Russes de la Révolution à la Collectivisation (1917–1939)* (Paris, 1984), 188–89; Gagarin, *Khoziaistvo*, 84.

42. *Shkola i uchitel'stvo Sibiri 20-e—nachalo 30-kh godov* (Novosibirsk, 1978), 37–42; Golubykh, *Ocherki*, 53–55; N. Brykin, *V novom derevne* (Leningrad, 1925), 22–23, 100–104.

43. L. I. Emeliakh, *Krest'iane i tserkov' nakanune Oktiabria* (Leningrad 1976), 48–51.

44. Ia. Iakovlev, *Nasha derevnia. Novoe v starom i staroe v novom*, 3d ed. (Moscow-Leningrad, 1925), 120 and 123; *Obnovlenaia derevnia. Sbornik*, V. G. Bogoraz-Tan, ed., (Leningrad, 1925), 118; Anokhina (1964), 269; Ia. Iakovlev, *Derevnia, kak ona est' (Ocherki Nikol'skoi volosti)*, 3rd ed. (Moscow, 1924), 98; *Trezvost' i kul'tura*, no. 24, back page (1929).

45. V. A. Murin, *Byt i nravy derevenskoi molodezhi* ([Moscow?], 1926), 37, 96; Iakovlev, *Derevnia*, 97; Maurice Hindus, *Red Bread* (London, 1931), 48–49, 184–85, 195–96.

46. Iakovlev, *Derevnia*, 98; Iakovlev, *Nasha derevnia*, 120; Rosnitskii, *Litso*, 115–16.

47. Shafir, *Gazeta*, 114–115.

48. Anokhina (1964), 145; Hindus, *Red Bread*, 59–60; *Ocherki byta derevenskoi molodezhi* (Moscow, 1924), 19–20.

49. *Ocherki byta*, 10–12.

50. Tan-Bogoraz, *Staryi i novyi byt*, 18; Selishchev, *Iazyk*, 215.

51. For a detailed account of the crisis of 1927–29, see M. Lewin, *Russian Peasants and Soviet Power* (London, 1968).

52. Stalin, *Soch.* 11:4–5.

53. *Moskovskie novosti*, 12 July 1987, 9. For Siberian examples, see Eikhe's report in *Za chetkuiu klassovuiu liniiu. Sbornik* (Novosibirsk, 1929), 37–38.

54. *TsGAOR*, f. 374, op. 9, d. 418, l. 6.

55. Stalin, *Soch.* 11:4–5.

56. *Soch.* 11:88.

57. *NarKhoz* (1932), 130–31.

58. *Sto sorok besed s Molotovym. Iz dnevnika F. Chueva* (Moscow, 1991), 280–81.

59. On the communes of the 1920s, See Robert G. Wesson, *Soviet Communes* (New Brunswick, 1963). On Churikov, see *Voinstvuiushcheee bezbozhie v SSSR za 15 let*, M. Enisherlov et al., eds. (Moscow, 1932), 149–50, and *Bezbozhnik*, no. 23, 14 (1929).

60. *SA*, WKP 261:5–6; *SA*, WKP 260:267; *Bednota*, 6 Nov. 1929, 4.

61. Davies (1980), 112.

62. Cited P. G. Chernopitskii, *Na velikom perelome. Sel'skie sovety Dona v period podgotovki i provedeniia massovoi kollektivizatsii (1928–1931 gg.)* (Rostov, 1965), 101, 91–92.

63. *KolSK*, 150; *Istoriia kollektivizatsii sel'skogo khoziaistva Urala (1927– 1937)* (Perm, 1983), 73.

64. *Sudebnaia praktika*, no. 1, 12 (1931).

65. *SA*, WKP 260:31.

66. *AR*, no. 2, 56 (1930); *Istoriia kollektivizatsii sel'skogo khoziaistva Urala*, 74; *Bol'shevik*, no. 9, 79–80 (1928). For an overview of the elections, see Carr, *Foundations* 2:274–89.

67. Iu. S. Kukushkin, *Sel'skie sovety i klassovaia bor'ba v derevne (1921–1932 gg.)* (Moscow, 1968), 225; *SA*, WKP 261, 38–9; *Moskovski novosti*, 12 Jul 1987, 9; Gushchin (1973), 201.

68. *SA*, WKP 162:31–32; *Bednota*, 10 Oct. 1929, 4, and 31 Oct. 1929, 4.

69. *Bednota*, 10 Oct. 1929, 4; Chernopitskii, 37, 40; *Bednota*, 25 Oct. 1929, 4 (and see also ibid., 30 Nov. 1929, 4).

70. *Bednota*, 29 Oct. 1929, 4; *Istoriia kollektivizatsii sel'skogo khoziaistva Gruzinskoi SSR* (Tbilisi, 1970), 237.

71. *ISKKS*, 319.

72. *SA*, WKP 261:32.

73. Cited in Davies (1980a), 148.

74. Ibid., 133, 151.

75. Dorothy Atkinson, *The End of the Russian Land Commune* (Stanford, 1983), 356.

76. The new strategy was articulated at a kolkhoz conference held in July 1929. See Atkinson, *Land Commune*, 356.

77. Kukushin, *Sel'skie sovety*, 227–28; P. Voshchanov, "'Kulaki'," *KP*, 8 Sep. 1989. See also Lynne Viola, "The Campaign to Eliminate the Kulak as a Class, Winter 1929–1930: A Reevaluation of the Legislation," *SR* 45(3):503–24 (1986).

78. Cited in Davies (1980a), 138.

79. *Nasha gazeta*, 4 Jul 1929, 1. For conspiracies unmasked by the OGPU, see *Bednota*, 2 Oct. 1929, 4; 10 Oct. 1929, 4, and 15 Oct. 1929, 4; *Nasha gazeta*, 12 Nov. 1929, 4.

80. *AR*, no. 2, 19–21 (1930); *Nasha gazeta*, 24 Dec. 1929, 2; *TsGAOR*, f. 5407, op. 1, d. 47, ll. 65 and 69.

81. Lynne Viola's excellent article on this theme, "The Peasant Nightmare: Visions of Apocalypse in the Soviet Countryside," *Journal of Modern History* 62(4): 747–70 (1990), appeared after this section of the book had been written.

82. *Ianvarskii obyedinennyi plenum MK i MKK, 6–10 ianvaria 1930 g.* (Moscow, 1930), 40; *KolSZ*, 163; *SA*, WKP 434:214.

83. *SA*, WKP 434:214; *KolSZ*, 223.

84. *Nasha gazeta*, 31 Jan. 1928, 1.

85. *SA*, WKP 261:104.

86. *TsGAOR*, f. 5407, op. 1, d. 47, l. 83; *KolSK*, 179.

87. *SA*, WKP 434:161.

88. *Kolkhoznik*, no. 3, 3 (1935).

89. *Ianvarskii*, 40, and *KolSK*, 179; *AR*, no. 8–9, 26 (1930); *SA*, WKP 434: 214.

Chapter 2

1. *Desiataia Ural'skaia oblastnaia konferentsiia V. K. P. (b.)*, bull. 2 (Sverdlovsk, 1930), 18; citation from *TsGANKh*, f. 7446, op. 10, d. 178, l. 161, in author's afterword to novel of Boris Mozhaev, "Muzhiki i baby," *Don* (Rostov), no. 3, 104 (1987).

2. *RP*, 29 Jan. 1930, 1.

3. *GASO*, f. 1148, op. 148 r/2, d. 65, l. 39.

4. *SA*, WKP 260:7; Oblastnoi Komitet VKP (b) A[vtonomnoi] T[atarskoi] SSR. *Stenograficheskii otchet XV oblastnoi partiinoi konferentsii (5–15 iiunia 1930 g.)* (Kazan, 1930), 120; A. N. Malafeev, *Istoriia tsenoobrazovaniia v SSSR (1917–1961 gg.)* (Moscow, 1964), 147–49; *KolSZ*, 174; P. N. Sharova, *Kollektivizatsiia sel'skogo khoziaistva v Tsentral'no-Chernozemnoi oblasti (1928–1932 gg.)*, (Voronezh, 1963), 155, 164.

5. *Nauchnyi rabotnik*, no. 5–6, 72 (1930).

6. *SA*, WKP 261:74, and *KolSZ*, 162.

7. *TsGAOR*, f. 5451, op. 15, d. 33, l. 99.

8. Cited P. G. Chernopitskii, *Na velikom perelome* (Rostov, 1965), 156.

9. *GASO*, f. 1148, op. 148 r/2, d. 65, l. 39. See also *TsGAOR*, f. 374, op. 9, d. 418, l. 79; *KolSK*, 224.

10. Note that Voronezh, Kursk, Orel, and Tambov provinces were joined in the Central Black Earth oblast (TsChO) from 1928 to 1934.

11. *SA*, WKP 151:194; WKP 260:21; WKP 261:32–33; Sharova, *Kollektivizatsiia*, 153; *TsGAOR*, f. 374, op. 9, d. 418, l. 79; *GASO*, f. 1148, op. 148 r/2, d. 65, l. 38; *KolTsChO*, 131.

12. *SA*, WKP 261:32–33, 102; *TsGAOR*, f. 374, op. 9, d. 418, ll. 78, 79.

13. *GASO*, f. 88/r, op. 1a, d. 57, l. 28.

14. *TsGAOR*, f. 374, op. 9, d. 418, l. 5.

15. *GASO*, f. 1148, op. 148 r/2, d. 65, l. 38; *SA*, WKP 151:194; *GASO*, f. 1148, op. 148 r/2, d. 65, l. 39.

16. *GASO*, f. 1148, op. 148 r/2, d. 65, l. 38; *Desiataia Ural'skaia*, bull. 6, 14–15.

17. *GASO*, f. 1148, op. 148 r/2, d. 65, l. 37; *SA*, WKP 261:69.

18. *TsGANKh*, f. 7486, op. 19, d. 61, l. 2; *GASO*, f. 1148, op. 148 r/2, d. 65, l. 39.

19. *GASO*, f. 1148, op. 148 r/2, d. 65, ll. 37–38.

20. Davies (1980a), 267, 270; *TsGAOR*, f. 5451, op. 14, d. 13, ll. 32–36.

21. Kukushkin, *Sel'skie sovety*, 229.

22. Stalin, *Soch.* 12:166–70; *SA*, WKP 260:24.

23. *TsGAOR*, f. 374, op. 9, d. 418, l. 89.

24. N. V. Teptsov, "OGPU protiv krest'ian (Dokumental'naia istoriia stalinskogo genotsida)," unpub. ms. (1991), 8, 10; *TsGANKh*, f. 9414, op. 1, d. 1944, ll. 13–14.

25. N. A. Ivnitskii, in *ISSSR*, no. 3, 43 (1989).

26. Teptsov, "OGPU protiv kresti'ian," 15.

27. *SA*, WKP 260:18 and 20; *GASO*, f. 1148, op. 148 r/2, d. 65, ll. 37–8; *GASO*, f. 88, op. 1, d. 62, l. 180.

28. *GASO*, f. 88-r, op. 1, d. 54, l. 196.

29. Ibid. f. 88, op. 1, d. 62, l. 180, and f. 1148, op. 148 r/2, d. 65, l. 39.

30. *SA*, WKP 260:29.

31. *SA*, WKP 260:43, 161.

32. *TsGAOR*, f. 374, op. 9, d. 418, l. 5. See also *GASO*, f. 1148, op. 148 r/2, d. 65, l. 37.

33. Oblastnoi Komitet, 130.

34. *SA*, WKP 260:10–11, 31, 36–37. Similar examples from the Urals are in *GASO*, f. 88-r, op. 1, d. 54, l. 9, and f. 1148, op. 148 r/2, d. 65, l. 39.

35. *GASO*, f. 88, op. 1, d. 62, l. 126.

36. An exception, from the Tatar Republic, is cited in *TsGAOR*, f. 374, op. 9, d. 418, l. 78.

37. *KolSZ*, 163–64.

38. *SA*, WKP 260:30; Oblastnoi Komitet, 129, 237; ibid., 183; *SA*, WKP 260:19.

39. *SA*, WKP 260:30, 31, and 45.

40. *SA*, WKP 260:12–13; *SA*, WKP 260:34; *SA*, WKP 260:37.

41. *GASO*, f. 88, op. 1, d. 62, ll. 171, 177; *SA*, WKP 260:41; *GASO*, f. 88/r, op. 1a, d. 57, l. 30; *TsGAOR*, f. 374, op. 9, d. 418, l. 63; *SA*, WKP 260:24–25.

42. *GASO*, f. 88/r, op. 1a, d. 57, l. 54.

43. *SA*, WKP 260:24–25 and 42; , WKP 261:73; *GASO*, f. 1148, op. 148 r/2, d. 65, l. 40.

44. *SA*, WKP 260:27 and 16; *GASO*, f. 88/r, op. 1a, d. 57, l. 53.

45. *Bednota*, 10 Nov. 1929, 4; *TsGAOR*, f. 5407, op. 1, d. 47, l. 73; *TsGAOR*, f. 5407, op. 1, d. 47, l. 72.

46. *TsGAOR*, f. 5407, op. 1, d. 47, l. 65.

47. *GASO*, f. 88/r, op. 1a, d. 57, l. 30.

48. *TsGAOR*, f. 5407, op. 1, d. 47, l. 76, and d. 49, ll. 36, 16; *GASO*, f. 88/r, op. 1a, d. 57, l. 43.

49. *SA*, WKP 261:70–71.

50. *TsGAOR*, f. 5407, op. 1, d. 44, ll. 83–84; ibid., d. 47, ll. 7–8, 17.

51. *SA*, WKP 261:69–70.

52. *SA*, WKP 260:43 and 6; *TsGAOR*, f. 374, op. 9, d. 418, l. 7.

53. *GASO*, f. 88/r, op. 1a, d. 57, l. 30; *SA*, WKP 151, 194, and WKP 261:70–71.

54. *GASO*, f. 88/r, op. 1a, d. 57, l. 43; *SA*, WKP 260:6.

55. *SA*, WKP 261:70–71.

56. *SA*, WKP 151:194.

57. *SA*, WKP 260:6 and 146; *AR*, no. 3, 125 (1930).

58. *SA*, WKP 261:70–71; *TsGAOR*, f. 5407, op. 1, d. 44, l. 84.

59. "Golovokruzhenie ot uspekhov," published *Pr*, 2 Mar. 1930, in Stalin, *Soch.* 12:191–99. See also *Soch.* 12:208–9.

60. Stalin, *Soch.* 12:199; undated Central Committee resolution, "Nemedlenno likvidirovat' iskrivleniia politiki partii," in *KP*, 15 Mar. 1930, 1.

61. Cited in Teptsov, "OGPU protiv krest'ian," 20–21.

62. *SA*, WKP 261:74; Oblastnoi Komitet, 124; *TsGAOR*, f. 374, op. 9, d. 418, 70.

63. Davies (1980a), 442–43.

64. Oblastnoi Komitet, 198.

65. For a detailed discussion of these problems, see Davies (1980a), ch. 6.

66. Quoted Chernopitskii, *Na velikom perelome*, 124–25.

67. Stalin, *Soch.* 12:225; Davies (1980a), 379; Teptsov in *Kentavr*, March-April 1992, 50–55; Robert Conquest, *The Harvest of Sorrow* (Oxford, 1986), 123.

68. *ISSSR*, no. 6, 23 (1960).

69. Teptsov, "OGPU," 20–21; Sharova, *Kollektivizatsiia*, 155. A recent estimate puts the number of peasant disturbances in the first two and a half months of 1930 at over two thousand, with perhaps 700,000 peasants involved: *ISSSR*, no. 3, 44 (1989).

70. *Ocherki istorii astrakhanskoi partiinoi organizatsii* (Volgograd, 1971), 348; *SA*, WKP 261:47; *SA*, WKP 151:194.

71. Teptsov, "OGPU," 18; *SA*, WKP 261:70; *KolSZ*, 162. See also Lynne Viola, "'Bab'i Bunty* and Peasant Women's Protest During Collectivization," *Russian Review* 45(1):23–42 (1986).

72. *AR*, no. 8–9, 24 (1930); *SA*, WKP 261:71–72; *TsGAOR*, f. 374, op. 9, d. 418, l. 79.

73. Sharova, *Kollektivizatsiia*, 156; *Nasha gazeta*, 17 Dec. 1929, 2, and 21 Dec. 1929, 4; *KolSK*, 225–26; *Viriatino*, 180.

74. *TsGANKh*, f. 7486, op. 19, d. 61, l. 5.

75. Petro G. Grigorenko, *Memoirs* (New York, 1982), 39.

76. *GASO*, f. 88/r, op. 1a, d. 57, l. 60; Gushchin (1973), 293–94; Sharova, *Kollektivizatsiia*, 166.

77. *SA*, WKP 261:71; *GASO*, f. 88/r, op. 1a, d. 57, l. 53; ibid. With regard to the rumor about the St. Bartholomew's massacre, the reporting official commented that the historical reference indicated that "someone from the city bourgeoisie is helping the kulaks with their agitation."

78. *SA*, WKP 261:71; *SA*, WKP 151:194; *Voinstvuiushchee bezbozhie*, 135.

79. *SA*, WKP 261:71 and 16; *KolSK*, 283; *GASO*, f. 88/r, op. 1a, d. 57, ll. 59–60.

80. *TsGAOR*, f. 5407, op. 1, d. 44, l. 93.

81. *Ianvarskii obyedinennyi plenum*, 40; *Narodnoe prosveshchenie*, no. 7–8, 8 (1930); *AR*, no. 8–9, 26 (1930); and see above, pp. 52–53.

82. *AR*, no. 4, 97 (1930); W. H. Chamberlin, *Russia's Iron Age* (London, 1935), 79; *SA*, WKP 434:214; *SA*, WKP 151:194.

83. *SA*, WKP 261:80; *SA*, WKP 434:163.

84. *SA*, WKP 261:101.

85. *SA*, WKP 261:79 102.

86. *SA*, WKP 261:94–95.

87. See Amartya Sen, *Poverty and Famines* (Oxford, 1981) and David Arnold, *Famine. Social Crisis and Historical Change* (Oxford, 1988).

88. Quantitative assessments of the impact of the famine are complicated, and we will not have reliable estimates under demographers come to grips with the new data that has come to light in connection with the opening of Soviet archives. Recent Soviet scholarly estimates, based on archival data, are in the range of three to four million excess deaths in 1933 (see V. V. Tsaplin in *VI*, no. 4, 175–81 [1989] and E. A. Osokina in *ISSSR*, no. 5, 18–26 [1881]), but these are certainly not the last words on the subject. There is general agreement that Ukraine suffered the greatest losses, and that Kazakhstan, the North Caucasus, Central and Lower Volga,

and the Central Black Earth oblast were severely affected. But detailed demographic studies of the impact of the famine by region have not yet been done.

89. For good examples of this process of information blocking, see the case of Terekhov, a party secretary in the Ukraine who was punished for his unsuccessful attempt to tell Stalin that there really was a famine there, recounted in *Commission on the Ukraine Famine. Report to Congress* (Washington, 1988) 1:xv, and the similar story told by Sheboldaev, head of the North Caucasus party organization, in *Molot*, 23 Jan. 1934, 2.

90. Quoted from *Bolshevik*, 15 Mar. 1930, 48, in Davies (1980a), 300; *ISSSR*, no. 2, 15 (1985). For similar comments from the North Caucasus, see *Molot* (Rostov), 28 Mar. 1933, 2.

91. N. Shimotomai, "A Note on the Kuban Affair (1932–1933). The Crisis of Kolkhoz Agriculture in the North Caucasus," *Acta Slavica Iaponica* 1 (1983), 40–41.

92. *ISK* 2:428–29 (n. 147).

93. *ISSSR*, no. 6, 27 (1960).

94. Gushchin (1973), 443; *SIu*, no. 16, 6 (1933); *SG*, no. 5, 35–36 (1933).

95. *SIu*, no. 25–26, 7 (1932); *RTsKhIDNI*, f. 112, op. 26, d. 21, ll. 56 and 154.

96. Stalin, *Soch.* 13:392 (n. 61); *SZ SSSR*, no. 62, art. 360 (1932).

97. *SIu*, no. 28, 8 (1935); *SIu*, no. 13, 6–7 (1934) *SIu*, no. 19, 12 (1935); *SG*, no. 5, 33 (1933).

98. *ISSSR*, no. 2, 15 (1989) (for a similar report by the OGPU in the Western oblast, see *SA*, WKP 166:797); *TsGANKh*, f. 7486, op. 19, d. 229, l. 130; *Molot*, 12 Mar. 1933, 1; *VI*, no. 6, 180 (1991).

99. *ISSSR*, no. 2, 14 (1989). But note that, having taken the seed grain in the fall, the state had to give it back (in the form of "seed loans") in the spring.

100. *SZ*, 12 Nov. 1932, 4; 16 Nov. 1932, 4; 17 Dec. 1932, 4; 28 Nov. 1932, 1.

101. Stalin, *Soch.* 13:196 and 247.

102. *Molot*, 10 Mar. 1933, 1; *ISSSR*, no. 6, 27 (1960); *ISSSR*, no. 3, 46 (1989). The emphasis is mine.

103. Quoted by N. S. Khrushchev in *Pr*, 10 Mar. 1963, 2.

104. *Izv*, 22 June 1933, 3.

105. *SA*, WKP 166:327; *Kommunist*, no. 1, 100 (1990).

106. The Torgsin stores of the early 1930s, forerunners of the later *valiuta* stores, sold deficit goods for gold, silver, and foreign currency only.

107. V. V. Kondrashin, "Golod 1932–1933 godov v derevniakh Povolzh'ia," *VI*, no. 6, 180 (1991).

108. For a detailed discussion, see Nobuo Shimotomai, "Springtime for the *Politotdel*: Local Party Organization in Crisis," *Acta Slavica Iaponica* IV:1–34 (1986).

109. On the "black board," see *Rabochii* (Minsk), 5 Jan. 1933, 1, and *Molot*, 14 Mar. 1933, 1, and 6 May 1933, 2. On collective deportations, see *Molot*, 28 Mar. 1933, 1; *ISSSR*, no. 2, 11 (1989); Shimotomai, "Note," 47–48.

110. *TsGANKh*, f. 7486, op. 19, d. 229, l. 131.

111. Stalin, as cited by L. Kaganovich in *Bol'shevik*, no. 1–2, 17 (1933); Stalin, *Soch.* 13:229–30, 207–8.

112. *Bol'shevik*, no. 1–2, 18 (1933), *Soch.* 13:226–28; quotation from Iu. A. Moshkov, *Zernovaia problema v gody sploshnoi kollektivizatsii sel'skogo khoziaistva SSSR (1929–1932)* (Moscow, 1966), 217.

113. *Biulleten' obyedinennoi V oblastnoi i III gorodskoi Leningradskoi konferentsii VKP(b)* (Leningrad, 1934) 5:32–33.

114. *RTsKhIDNI*, f. 112, op. 26, d. 21, ll. 254–55. There were 15,800 kolkhozy in TsChO in 1933, according to *SotsStroi* (1935), 318–19.

115. See Gushchin (1973), 441, and *GASO*, f. 88, op. 1, d. 64, ll. 27, 29.

116. *SA*, WKP 178:134–35 (my emphasis).

117. Ibid., 134.

118. Ibid., 135.

119. This figure evidently does not include those in labor camps, of whom there were 334,300 at the beginning of 1933 and 510,307 a year later: V. Zemskov, in *Argumenty i fakty*, no. 45, 6 (1989); *Sotsiologicheskie issledovaniia*, no. 6, 11 (1991).

120. *SA*, WKP 178:135 and 138.

Chapter 3

1. A. I. Vdovin and V. Z. Drobizhev, *Rost rabochego klassa SSR 1917–1940 gg.* (Moscow, 1976), 127; *Trud* (1936), 7; *SotsStroi* (1934), 356–57.

2. For a more detailed discussion of this phenomenon and its quantitative dimensions, see Sheila Fitzpatrick, "The Great Departure: Rural-Urban Migration, 1929–33," in William G. Rosenberg and Lewis Siegelbaum, ed., *Social Dimensions of Soviet Industrialization* (Bloomington, 1992), 15–40.

3. *Istoricheskie zapiski* 94:63 (1974).

4. *NarKhoz* (1932), 130; *SotsStroi* (1939), 85.

5. See Lopreato, *Peasants No More* (San Francisco, 1967).

6. *KrP*, 2 Sep. 1937, 2 (remark of a rural official, quoted with indignation by a kolkhoznik).

7. Teptsov, "OGPU protiv krest'ian," unpub. ms. (1991), 8; Davies (1980a), 247–51.

8. *Dokumenty svidetel'stvuiut* (Moscow, 1989), 330.

9. Figures from Danilov in *SR* 50(1):152 (1991); Ivnitskii in *ISSSR*, no. 3, 44 (1989).

10. N. A. Ivnitskii, *Klassovaia bor'ba v derevne i likvidatsiia kulachestva kak klassa (1929–1932 gg.)* (Moscow, 1972), 326. For a fictionalized account of debates on industrial versus agricultural resettlement, see N. Skromnyi, "Perelom," *Sever*, no. 10, 52–64 (1986). On the kulaks as industrial workers, see John Scott, *Behind the Urals* (Bloomington, 1973), 29–30, 85; John D. Littlepage, *In Search of Soviet Gold* (New York, 1938), 80.

11. Ivan Tvardovskii, "Stranitsy perezhitogo," *Iunost'*, no. 3, 10–30 (1988). See also Skromnyi, "Perelom," and publications by A. Dzhapakov in *Trud*, 10 Jan. 1990, and P. Voshchanov in *KP*, 8 Sep. 1989.

12. For the sources on which these estimates are based, see note 9, above.

13. *SA*, WKP 416:64; *SA*, WKP 151:561; *SA*, WKP 416:74; *SA*, WKP 260:27.

14. *SA*, WKP 260:25; *KolSK*, 274; *SA*, WKP 416:180; *Trud*, 14 Jul 1933, 4.

15. Alekseev (1981), 436, 435, 443.

16. *TsGAOR*, f. 5515, op. 1, d. 224, ll. 112–13; *Itogi vypolneniia pervogo piatiletnego plana razivitiia narodnogo khoziaistva SSSR* (Moscow, 1933), 174.

17. *Trud* (1936), 8; *Sessiia TsIK Soiuza SSSR 6 sozyva. Stenograficheskii otchet i postanovleniia 22–28 dekabria 1931 g.* (Moscow, 1931), bull. 17, 9; *SotsStroi* (1935), 474–75; A. I. Vdovin and V. Z. Drobizhev, *Rost rabochego klassa SSSR* (Moscow, 1976), 109; *Itogi vypolneniia*, 174.

18. *Byli industrial'nye* (Moscow, 1973), 280.

19. Gerasimov (1967), 63–64.

20. *Molodoi kolkhoznik*, no. 1, n.p. (1935).

21. Alekseev (1981), 440–41.

22. *The Black Deeds of the Kremlin. A White Book*, vol. 2. *The Great Famine in the Ukraine in 1932–33* (Detroit, 1955), 455–56, 470, 562; *SV*, no. 10–11, 23 (1932).

23. *RTsKhIDNI*, f. 78 op. 1, d. 456, l. 54; *SZ*, 11 Sep. 1937, 3.

24. *ISSSR*, no. 2, 3 (1989); *VIII kazakstanskaia kraevaia konferentsiia VKP(b) 8–16 ianvaria 1934 g. Stenograficheskii otchet* (Alma-Ata, 1935), 46, 159, 226–29, 235. See also *Shestoi plenum Kazakhskogo Kraevogo Komiteta VKP(b). 10–16 iiulia 1933 g. Stenograficheskii otchet* (Alma-Ata, 1936), 149, 260.

25. *Literaturnaia gazeta*, no. 15, 10 (1988). On flight to the Donbass, see also *Commission on the Ukraine Famine*, 1:242, 253.

26. *Molot*, 23 Jan. 1934, 2; *VIII kazakstanskaia*, 159.

27. Alekseev (1982), 258–63, 273–4, 290.

28. *Trud* (1936), 7; *Black Deeds*, 465–66.

29. I. E. Zelenin, *Zernovye sovkhozy SSSR (1933–1941 gg.)* (Moscow, 1966), 42; idem., *Sovkhozy SSSR v gody dovoennykh piatiletok 1928–1941* (Moscow, 1982), 48, 104.

30. Zelenin, *Sovkhozy*, 203, 207–78, 215. In 1932, permanent workers on the state farm (excluding white-collar, technical, and administrative personnel) earned an average of 68 rubles a month, while temporary workers earned an average of 52 rubles. In 1935, the corresponding figures were 119 rubles and 84 rubles. This may be compared with the average coal miner's wage in 1935 of 213 rubles: *Trud* (1936), 270, 110.

31. Olga A. Narkiewicz, *The Making of the Soviet State Apparatus* (Manchester, 1970), 109–10.

32. *Istoricheskie zapiski* 94:112 (1974); *TsGAOR*, f. 5515, op. 13. d. 14, ll. 122–23, 163; *TsGAOR*, f. 5515, op. 1, d. 146, ll. 11, 102.

33. *TsGAOR*, f. 5515, op. 1, d. 235, ll. 24. For a more detailed discussion of this question, see Fitzpatrick, "The Great Departure."

34. *TsGAOR*, f. 5515, op. 1, d. 235, ll. 22–23.

35. These conflicts are described in detail in A. M. Panfilova, *Formirovanie rabochego klassa SSSR v gody pervoi piatiletki* (Moscow, 1964).

36. Stalin, *Soch.* 13:53.

37. Solomon M. Schwarz, *Labor in the Soviet Union* (New York, 1951), 56–57.

38. A. N. Malafeev, *Istoriia tsenooobrazovaniia v SSSR* (Moscow, 1964), 138.

39. *SZ SSSR*, no. 78, art. 475 (1932); *Trud*, 5 Dec. 1932, 1; ibid., 6 Jan. 1933, 2; ibid., 9 Jan. 1933, 1.

40. *SZ SSSR*, no. 84, arts. 516 and 517 (1932). See also *SZ SSSR*, no. 11, arts. 60 and 61, and no. 46, art. 273 (1933). An exception to the rule on peasants was that those living within a 100-kilometer radius of Moscow and Leningrad or in frontier zones were issued passports (see *KrP*, 23 May 1935, 4).

41. *Tret'ia sessiia TsIK Soiuza SSR VI sozyva. Stenograficheskii otchet. 23–30 ianvaria 1933 g.* (Moscow, 1933), Bull. 24, 6–8.

42. *Trud*, 17 Nov. 1932, 1; Shimotomai, "Springtime for the *Politotdel*," *Acta Slavica Iaponica* 4:26 (1986).

43. *Pr*, 28 Dec. 1932, 1.

44. *ISSSR*, no. 3, 46 (1989).

45. *SZ SSSR*, no. 78, art. 475 (1932).

46. *Trud*, 29 Dec. 1932, 2; *Pr*, 28 Dec. 1932, 1.

47. *Trud*, 2 Jan. 1933, 2.

48. *The New York Times*, 22 Jan. 1933, 15; ibid., 5 Feb. 1933, 1.

49. *SV*, no. 8, 16 (1933). *ibid.*, no. 3, 16 (1933).

50. *VII syezd kommunisticheskikh organizatsii Zakavkaz'ia. Stenograficheskii otchet* (Tiflis, 1934), 159–60. For examples from other cities, see *Istoriia industriali-zatsii Nizhegorodskogo-Gor'kovskogo kraia (1926–1941 gg.)* (Gorky, 1968), 276, and *Trud*, 6 Jan. 1933, 2.

51. *Black Deeds*, 466; *Molodoi Kommunist*, no. 4, 85 (1988).

52. *Pr*, 20 Mar. 1933, 2.

53. See pp. 115–16, 124–25, and 168–69.

54. *TsGAOR*, f. 3316, op. 41, d. 107, l. 61; *TsGAOR*, f. 3316, op. 41, d. 81, l. 49.

55. *Izmeneniia sotsial'noi struktury sovetskogo obshchestva 1921-seredina 30-kh godov* (Moscow, 1979), 194, 196; M. Ia. Sonin, *Vosproizvodstvo rabochei sily v SSSR i balans truda* (Moscow, 1959), 143.

56. Stalin, *Soch.* 1(14):362–63; *SZ*, 30 Mar. 1939, 3.

57. *VI*, no. 2, 24 (1973).

58. Ibid.; Sonin, *Vosproizvodstvo*, 182.

59. *IKP* 2:46–48; *SZ SSSR*, no. 49, art. 397 (1939).

60. Ann C. Helgeson, "Soviet Internal Migration and its Regulation since Stalin: The Controlled and the Uncontrollable," Ph.D. diss. (Berkeley, 1978), 167.

61. *Istoriia industrializatsii Tsentral'no-chernozemnogo raiona (1933–1941 gg.)* (Kursk, 1972) 2, 282–83; 288–89. See also *IndSSSR* (1971), 282–83, 288–89, 414, 445–46 and 489–90.

62. In the Donbass in 1937, about 30 percent of new workers in the mines and 40 percent in the metallurgical plants were brought in by the enterprises' orgnabor recruiters: *Istoriia rabochikh Donbassa* (Kiev, 1981) 1:248–49. On recruitment to the Donbass mines in the 1870s and '80s, see *Istoriko-bytovye ekspeditsii 1951–1953. Materialy po istorii proletariata i krest'ianstva Rossii kontsa XIX—nachacha XX veka*, A. M. Pankratova, ed. (Moscow, 1955), 71.

63. *IndSSSR* (1971), 486–90.

64. Ibid., 486–87; *TsGAOR*, f. 5515, op. 1, d. 235, l. 22.

65. *Istoriia industrializatsii Tsentral'no-chernozemnogo raiona*, 445–46; *Rabochie severo-zapada RSFSR v period stroitel'stva sotsializma* (Leningrad, 1979), 12–13.

66. *Kommunist*, no. 1, 98 (1990). See also Victor Zaslavsky and Yuri Luryi, "The Passport System in the USSR and Changes in Soviet Society," *Soviet Union/ Union soviétique* 6, pt. 2 (1979), 141.

67. Zaslavsky and Luryi, "The Passport System," 141.

68. *PVSKU*, 113. On this phenomenon, see also Iu. S. Borisov, *Podgotovka proizvodstvennykh kadrov sel'skogo khoziaistva SSSR v rekonstruktivnyi period* (Moscow, 1960), 275, and Iu. V. Arutiunian in *Formirovanie i razvitie sovetskogo rabochego klassa (1917–1961 gg.)* (Moscow, 1964), 111.

69. See pp. 231–32.

70. *TsGAOR*, f. 3316, op. 41, d. 107, ll. 69–70; *TsGANKh*, f. 396, op. 10, d. 15, l. 19; *ibid.*, d. 23, l. 4.

71. *TsGAOR*, f. 3316, op. 41, d. 107, l. 61.

72. *Kommuna*, 3 Feb. 1937, 3.

73. Ibid.

74. "Pis'ma iz derevni. God 1937-i," *Kommunist*, no. 1, 98 (1990).
75. Ibid., 101–2.

Chapter 4

1. I will treat the village (*selo*) and the peasant land commune (*obshchina* or *mir*) as roughly equivalent territorial units, though this involves a necessary element of simplification. There were about 110,000 land communes within the territory of the Russian Republic in 1917. During the 1920s, the official unit of registration was the "land society" (*zemel'noe obshchestvo*), a category that included peasant land communes (some of which were divided up into two or three parts, with the encouragement of Soviet land authorities, in the 1920s) as well as smaller associations of land users. The number of registered land societies in the Russian Republic in 1928 was 319,000. The number of collective farms in the same territory in 1940 was 167,000. Data from Danilov (1977), 97, and Iu. V. Arutiunian, *Sovetskoe krest'ianstvo v gody Velikoi Otechestvennoi voiny* (Moscow, 1963) 386.

2. Strictly speaking, it was the land society, the mir's counterpart in Soviet law, that was abolished by decree of the government of the Russian Republic in July 1930. *IKP* 1:306–7.

3. See par. 1 of the 1935 Kolkhoz Charter in *RPPKhoz* 2:519, which defines the population of the kolkhoz as "the toiling peasants of the village (*selo*) of . . . in . . . raion." The words "*stanitsa, derevnia, khutor, kishlak, aul,*" are given in parentheses after *selo*.

4. See Davies (1980b), 34–55.
5. *TsGANKh*, f. 7486, op. 19, d. 61, l. 6.
6. *SA*, WKP 151:193–94.
7. *TsGANKh*, f. 7486, op. 19, d. 61, l. 7; *SA*, WKP 151:115–16.
8. *SZu*, no. 25, 3 (1933); *SZu*, no. 1, 1 (1933); *SDK*, 453.
9. *VVSKU*, 226. For the wording of the 1930 Charter, see *IKP* 1:172.
10. *Izmeneniia sotsial'noi struktury* (1979), 243.
11. N. V. Bochkov, P. N. Pershin, M. A. Snegirev, V. F. Sharapov, *Istoriia zemel'nykh otnoshenii i zemleustroistva* (Moscow, 1956), 172–73, 190.
12. *Leninskii put'* (Velikie Luki), 2 July 1933, 3. See also *Kommuna*, 17 July 1933, 3; *KolSP*, 560.
13. See par. 2 of the 1930 and 1935 Kolkhoz Charters: *IKP* 1:173, and *RPPKhoz* 2:519.
14. Vyltsan (1978), 46; *KrP*, 4 Oct. 1936, 1.
15. *TsGANKh*, f. 7486, op. 19, d. 257, l. 58.
16. *TsGANKh*, f. 7486, op. 19, d. 257, ll. 220–21; ibid., d. 259, l. 166. See also ibid., d. 257, ll. 21 and 55; and ibid., d. 229, ll. 223–24.
17. *NR*, 276.
18. *SZ SSSR*, no. 16, arts. 49–58 (1937); Gushchin (1973), 366.
19. *Materialy pervogo vsesoiuznogo syezda kolkhoznikov-udarnikov peredovykh kolkhozov. 15–19 fevralia 1933 g.* (Moscow, 1933), 113.
20. *SZ SSSR*, no. 65, art. 520 (1935); *SA*, WKP 390:348, 352–59, and 368–69; *Pr*, 16 May 1936, 3.
21. Gushchin (1975), 17.
22. *SZu*, no. 1–2, 4 (1935); *TsGANKh*, f. 7486, op. 19, d. 257, ll. 166 ff.; *ISSSR*, no. 3, 52 (1989).

23. *IKP* 1:458–60; Bochkov, 211–12; *TsGANKh*, f. 7486, op. 19, d. 412, l. 42; *Sotsialisticheskoe zemleustroistvo*, no. 6–7, 2 (1935).

24. *KrP*, 15 Apr 1935, 3; *RP*, 5 Sep. 1937, 3; *RP*, 8 Sep. 1937, 4.

25. *RP*, 5 Aug. 1937, 1. On the trials, see pp. 301–2.

26. Vyltsan (1978), 63.

27. For elaboration of this argument, see Sheila Fitzpatrick, "Ascribing Class: The Construction of Social Identity in Soviet Russia," *Journal of Modern History* 65(4): 745–70 (1993).

28. See, for example, *Na putiakh k novoi shkole*, no. 2, 76 (1930); *TsGAOR*, f. 5451, op. 14, d. 11, l. 183; *KrP*, 27 Feb. 1935, 2.

29. For explication of these issues, see *TsGANKh*, f. 396, op. 10, d. 39, ll. 466 and 492; ibid., op. 11, d. 44, ll. 74 and 76.

30. *TsGAOR*, f. 5515, op. 1, d. 235, l. 28; *SIu*, no. 12, 22 (1937).

31. *SA*, WKP 390:339–40, 342.

32. *RPPKhoz* 2:520. But note that in the draft presented to the Second Congress of Outstanding Kolkhozniks, it was evidently not the household that was entitled to a private plot of specified dimensions but the individual kolkhoz member. Several delegates commented on the impractibility of this: *VVKSU*, 69.

33. *SIu*, no. 20, 14 (1937).

34. *TsGANKh*, f. 7386, op. 19, d. 410, l. 2.

35. *SGP*, no. 4, 54–55 (1939).

36. See pp. 113, 211.

37. *Molot*, 4 Apr. 1933, 2.

38. *RPPKhoz* 2:524; *SZ*, 14 Nov. 1937, 3.

39. *RRPKhoz* 2:524; *TsGANKh*, f. 396, op. 10, d. 39, l. 492.

40. *TsGANKh*, f, 396, op. 11, d. 44, l. 76.

41. *KolSK*, 567; Ia. A. Iakovlev, *Voprosy organizatsii sotsialisticheskogo sel'skogo khoziaistva* (Moscow, 1933), 47–48. For a complaint from an otkhodnik to whom the kolkhoz refused to give the grain earned with his 130 labordays, see *SZ*, 16 Nov. 1932, 3.

42. *SDK*, 168–69; *Pr*, 12 July 1935, 4.

43. *Kommuna*, 2 Sep. 1937, 3.

44. *KPSSvR* 5:315; *TsGANKh*, f. 396, op. 10, d. 34, l. 326; ibid., d. 137, ll. 50–54.

45. See p. 201.

46. *SGP*, no. 2, 29 (1940); *RPPKhoz* 2:650–52; *KPSSvR* 5:398–404.

47. See Chapter 11.

48. *SA*, WKP 178:60.

49. *TsGANKh*, f. 7486, op. 19, d. 257, ll. 184–88; *KurPr*, 2 Oct. 1937, 1, and ibid., 16 Oct. 1937, 4.

50. *KrK*, 2 Aug. 1937, 2; *KrP*, 20 Oct. 1937, 3.

51. On the organization of the Congress, see Vyltsan (1978), 25 and 28, and *SZ*, 31 Jan. 1935, 1. Note that whole process was very rushed: There was only a month between the Politburo's order to hold the Congress (following the instructions of the Central Committee's November plenum) and the opening day of the Congress; and the party leaders involved must have been enormously distracted by the intervening crisis of the assassination of Sergei Kirov, the Leningrad party leader, in December. For a detailed description of the process of electing delegates to the Congress, see *KrP*, 3 Feb. 1935, 4.

52. For the full list of participants and a stenographic report of proceedings of

the Congress, see *VVSKU*. Iakov Arkadevich Iakovlev (né Epshtein), 1896–1938, is an interesting and somewhat puzzling figure in the politics of the 1920s and 1930s who still awaits his biographer. While working in the Central Committee apparat in the 1920s, Iakovlev wrote two valuable sociological studies on the Russian village since the revolution, *Derevnia, kak ona est'* (1923) and *Nasha derevnia* (1924). He became People's Commissar for Agriculture and head of Kolkhoz Center in 1929, holding the former office until 1934, and was thus the man directly in charge of agriculture during the worst excesses of collectivization. Yet his writings and speeches on peasant questions, both before and after this period, are notable for their pragmatism and common sense. Moreover, as chief editor of *Krest'ianskaia gazeta*, he must be held at least partly responsible for that newspaper's unusual responsiveness to peasant concerns (manifest not in what it published, but in how it handled peasant complaints (see pp. 329–30), often acting as a behind-the-scenes advocate for victims of injustice and mistreatment by officials. For biographical data, see *Bol'shaia sovetskaia entskilopediia*, 1st ed. (Moscow, 1931) 65:463; *ibid.*, 3rd ed. (Moscow, 1978) 30:486; *Deiateli SSSR i revolutsionnogo dvizheniia Rossii. Entsiklopedicheskii slovar' 'Granat'* (Moscow, 1989) 2:276–78; *VI*, no. 5, 213–20 (1975); and Zhores Medvedev, *Soviet Agriculture* (New York, 1987), 115.

53. *VVSKU*, 186–87; Vyltsan (1978), 25; *KG*, 4 Feb. 1933, 4.

54. *VVSKU*, 185–87; *PVSKU*, 317.

55. For these *nakazy*, which were essentially questions about taxation and the proper way to handle issues such as otkhod and the incorporation of khutor-dwellers in the kolkhoz, see *KrP*, 3 Feb. 1935, 4, and *KrP*, 5 Feb. 1935, 3. For the women chairmen's remarks, see *VVSKU*, 49, 182.

56. For biographical data on First Congress delegates, see *PVSKU*, 166, 205, and 256, and *Izv*, 17 Feb. 1933, 2. On widows as supporters of the kolkhoz in the non-Black Earth belt, see Anokhina (1964), 32 and 273, and Gerasimov (1967).

57. From a "literary portrait" of Korchevskii by Nikolai Aseev, *Izv*, 17 Feb. 1935, 5. This was one of a series of portraits of delegates by well-known writers commissioned by the newspaper during the Congress. For other veterans, see *VVSKU*, 73–74, 213.

58. *Izv*, 17 Feb. 1935, 5 (portrait of Solodov by V. Lidin); *Izv*, 12 Feb. 1935, 1, and *VVSKU*, 198 (Shestopalov).

59. *Izv*, 17 Feb. 1935, 1.

60. On Angelina, see *Bol'shaia sovetskaia entsiklopediia*, 2d ed., 2:383, and *VVSKU*, 102; on Kulba, see *VVSKU*, 197. On other women delegates, see *VVSKU*, 124 and 215, and below, pp. 189–90.

61. *VVSKU*, 48, 69.

62. Ibid., 93, 102, 118, 194, and 213.

63. Ibid., 75–76.

64. *KrP*, 28 Feb. 1935, 2.

65. *KrP*, 27 Feb. 1935, 2.

66. *VVSKU*, 227; *SDK*, 159–60; *Pr*, 13 Mar. 1935.

67. Stalin, *Soch.* 1 (14), 53–54.

68. Stalin, *Soch.* 13, 252–53; Gregory Massell, *The Surrogate Proletariat. Moslem Women and Revolutionary Strategy in Soviet Central Asia, 1919–1929* (Princeton, 1974).

69. *KrP*, 27 Feb. 1935, 2.

70. *VVSKU*, 230.

71. Ibid., 49.

72. Ibid., 19.
73. Ibid., 213, 130, 81–82, and 177. See also ibid., 60.
74. *SDK,* 167 (my emphasis).
75. *VVSKU,* 19–20, 44, 76, 120, 162.
76. *KrP,* 28 Feb. 1935, 2.
77. *VVSKU,* 17–18.
78. *VVSKU,* 48, 68, 130, 176, 215.
79. Ibid., 85.
80. Ibid., 230, 228.
81. *KrP,* 28 Feb. 1935, 2.
82. Its full title was "Primernyi ustav sel'skokhoziaistvennoi arteli, priniatyi II Vsesoiuznym syezdom kolkhoznikov-udarnikov i utverzhdennyi Sovetom Narodnykh Komissarov Soiuza SSR i Tsentral'nym Komitetom VKP(b)"—that is, a model charter that had been "passed" by the Second Congress and "confirmed" by Sovnarkom and the party Central Committee. The text is in *RPPKhoz* 2:519–29.
83. The term, "the kolkhoz NEP," was first used in Sergei Maslov, *Kolkhoznaia Rossiia* (Prague, 1937), ch. 8.

Chapter 5

1. Stalin, *Soch.* 1(14):108.
2. A good example of this is the first-person narrative in Mozhaev (1988).
3. See, for example, *SA,* WKP 261:80 and 101; *SA,* WKP 434 and 164.
4. On peasants of this type, see the report of a party official from the Rostovon-Don area at a closed meeting of the Central Committee in May 1939: *RTsKhIDNI,* f. 5, op. 4, d. 18, ll. 5–6.
5. This interpretation owes a good deal to Steven Hoch's comments on an earlier draft of the manuscript.
6. See M. Lewin, *Russian Peasants and Soviet Power* (London, 1968), 109–12, for a discussion of the three basic kolkhoz forms (TOZ, artel and *kommuna*) identified in the 1920s.
7. Stalin, *Soch.* 1 (14):53–54; *SDK,* 159. On the dual nature of the kolkhoznik, see Jerzy F. Karcz in Millar (1971), 54–56.
8. Vyltsan (1978), 200, 202, 208.
9. *RPPKhoz* 2:388–89.
10. Vyltsan (1978), 203–4; Gushchin (1975), 175; Abram Bergson, *The Real National Income of Soviet Russia since 1928* (Cambridge, Mass., 1961).
11. Sometimes kolkhozy paid all the individual household taxes out of kolkhoz funds, but this was frowned upon. See, for example, *SA,* WKP 390:319.
12. Data on state budgetary receipts for 1929/30–1937 from V. P. Diachenko (1978), 285, and *IndSSSR* (1971), 58–60, 75, 88–89, 103, 119–20, 126, 134–35, 140. On state bonds, see Franklyn D. Holzman, *Soviet Taxation* (Cambridge, Mass., 1955), 202–4. Although subscription to the bonds was theoretically voluntary, heavy pressure was actually brought to bear by local authorities, and there were many reports of (illegal) punishments such as refusal of private plots and laborday payments being levied on those who failed to contribute. *SA,* WKP 183:20.
13. Holzman, *Soviet Taxation,* 192–99, 252–59; Janet Chapman, *Real Wages in Soviet Russia since 1928* (Cambridge, Mass., 1963), 157; Davies, *Soviet Budgetary System,* 282–83.
14. Holzman, *Soviet Taxation,* 159 and *passim.*

15. V. Danilov in *Kommunist*, no. 16, 37 (1987). For a discussion of the procurements system and its significance, see the excellent article by Moshe Lewin, "'Taking Grain': Soviet Policies of Agricultural Procurements before the War" in *The Making of the Soviet System* (New York, 1985), 165–70.

16. E.g., *TsGANKh*, f. 396, op. 10, d. 160, l. 414. See also below, p. 149.

17. *TsGANKh*, f. 7486, op. 19, d. 410, ll. 44–46; *IKP* 1:449.

18. For conflicts over sowing plans, see below, pp. 305–6; and Merle Fainsod, *Smolensk under Soviet Rule* (Cambridge, Mass., 1958), 267. For the CC resolution of 28 Dec. 1939, see *IKP* 2:127–28.

19. *IKP* 1:329; *SIu*, no. 23, 18–19 (1931); *SIu*, no. 27, 5 (1934); *Rabochii* (Minsk), 29 Mar. 1932, 2.

20. On evasion, see *SIu*, no. 27, 19–20 (1934), and *Krasnoe znamia* (Tomsk), 12 Dec. 1936, 3. On commandeering of kolkhoz labor and horses by local officials, see below, pp. 179, 193.

21. *RPPkhoz* 2:520.

22. As of 1935, the private plots of independents were meant to be about 10 percent smaller than those of kolkhozniks in the same district. In 1939, the norm for independents was lowered to 0.1–0.2 hectares, while that for wage- and salary-earners resident in the village were set at a maximum of 0.15 hectares (including the area occupied by the house). *Za industrializatsiiu*, 16 Mar. 1935, 2; *RPPKhoz* 2:711; *Vazhneishie resheniia po sel'skomu khoziaistvu za 1938–1946 gg.* (Moscow, 1948), 136–37.

23. *Pr*, 12 July 1935, 4–5; *Iz istorii partiinykh organizatsii Urala (1917–1967)* (Perm, 1967), 142; *SA*, WKP 186:62–63.

24. *TsGANKh*, f. 7486, op. 19, d. 410, ll. 1–2, 75.

25. Figure for circa 1910 from Iu. Larin, *Ekonomika dosovetskoi derevni* (Moscow-Leningrad, 1926), 115–16.

26. *Rabochii*, 16 Jan. 1934, 7; *RPPKhoz* 2:707–13.

27. Iu. V. Arutiunian, *Sovetskoe krest'ianstvo v gody Velikoi Otechestvennoi Voiny* (Moscow, 1963), 344–46.

28. *SIu*, no. 24, 4 (1935); *KrP*, 11 Sep. 1936, 2.

29. *TsGANKh*, f. 396, op. 10, d. 160, ll. 130–31.

30. *RPPKhoz* 2:708.

31. *NarKhoz* (1932), 188–89, and *ISSSR*, no. 6, 36 (1960); *Narodnoe khoziaistvo SSSR v 1960 godu. Statisticheskii ezhegodnik* (Moscow, 1961), 448.

32. *ISSSR*, no. 6, 20 (1960); *Sel'skoe khoziaistvo SSSR. Statisticheskii sbornik* (Moscow, 1960), 58.

33. Robert F. Miller, *One Hundred Thousand Tractors* (Cambridge, Mass., 1970), 36–43. On the MTS politotdel, see below, p. 174.

34. Figures from Miller, *Tractors*, 50; Fedor Belov, *The History of a Soviet Collective Farm* (New York, 1955), 16.

35. *SA*, WKP 186:62–63.

36. *SGP*, no. 4, 54–55; Vyltsan (1970), 53–54; Vyltsan (1978), 38.

37. *TsGANKh*, f. 396, op. 10, d. 39, l. 276; ibid, d. 142, l. 71.

38. *RRPKhoz* 2:520; *Trud*, 9 May 1935, 1.

39. *KrP*, 6 Apr. 1935, 2–3.

40. Ibid., 6 Apr. 1935, 3, and 14 July 1936, 3.

41. *SA*, WKP 355:280–81; *Viriatino*, 180. See also *SA*, WKP 390:252 and 259–60.

42. See, for example, *VVSKU*, 31.

43. Vyltsan (1970), 56; Stephan Merl, "Social Mobility in the Countryside," unpublished paper (1988), 9, 14; *PIT*, 85–123 (Table 60). For a list of the offices categorized as part of the kolkhoz's "administrative and service apparat" in 1933, see *DIu*, no. 1 (inside front cover) (1934).

44. *PIT*, 83, 85–123. The survey, whose representativeness is difficult to judge, covered 370 collective farms in nine regions of the Soviet Union.

45. Hoch, *Serfdom and Social Control in Russia* (Chicago, 1986), 126–32, 135.

46. Vyltsan (1970), 144.

47. *SZ*, 4 July 1938, 3.

48. Vyltsan (1978), 116–17.

49. *PIT*, 98, 111, 104, 117.

50. *PIT*, 97, 110, 123.

51. N. N. Anisimov, I. S. Shakhov, K. O. Sofronkov, I. Ageev, M. Plastun, D. Davydov, eds., *Brigadnaia sistema organizatsii truda v kolkhozakh* (Moscow-Leningrad, 2d ed., 1932), 52.

52. *RPPKhoz* 2:380–82; *SDK*, 156.

53. Maslov, *Kolkhoznaia Rossiia*, 210–13.

54. Shuvaev (1937), 61. See also *SA*, WKP 390:252 and 259–60.

55. Gushchin (1973), 25–26; Naum Jasny, *The Socialized Agriculture of the USSR* (Stanford, 1949), 335–36; *SIu*, no. 1, 26 (1938).

56. *Sotsialisticheskaia rekonstruktsiia sel'skogo khoziaistva*, no. 9, 8 (1939); Jasny, *Socialized Agriculture*, 336–37.

57. *Molot*, 16 Mar. 1933, 1; *KrP*, 5 Aug. 1937, 3; *KrP*, 3 Mar. 1935, 2; *MKrG*, 18 Dec. 1936, 2; *SDK*, 453.

58. *TsGANKh*, f. 396, op. 10, d. 65, l. 286.

59. Ibid., d. 161, l. 372.

60. Ibid., d. 143, l. 25.

61. Ibid., d. 142, l. 72.

62. Ibid., d. 65, l. 471.

63. *SA*, WKP 386:370; *TsGANKh*, f. 396, op. 10, d. 87, unpg.

64. *Sovetskoe krest'ianstvo. Kratkii ocherk istorii (1917–1970)* 2d ed. (Moscow, 1973), 278; *Kollektivizatsiia sel'skogo khoziaistva tsentral'nogo promyshlennogo raiona (1927–1937 gg.)* (Riazan, 1971), 513; Vyltsan (1978), 116.

65. *Molot*, 2 Jan. 1934, 1; *KrP*, 6 Sep. 1936, 1; *Krasnaia Bashkiriia*, 11 Aug. 1937, 3; *SA*, WKP 390:252 and 259–60 (number of mouths); *Viriatino*, 251, and Stephen P. and Ethel Dunn, *The Peasants of Central Russia*, (New York, 1967), 47–48 (payment to household).

66. *VI*, no. 2, 24, 27 (1973).

67. Vyltsan (1978), 101.

68. *PIT*, 83, 85, 91; and see below, pp. 190–93.

69. Poliakov (1990), 53; *IndSSSR* (1971), 514.

70. *SZ*, 17 Aug. 1939, 2. See also *SZ*, 6 Jan. 1939, 2.

71. Ostrovskii (1967), 57; *Sovetskoe krest'ianstvo*, 328; *Krasnaia Bashkiriia*, 11 Aug. 1937, 3; *KrP*, 24 Aug. 1937, 2; *KrP*, 26 Aug. 1937, 2; *KrP*, 27 Aug. 1937, 2.

72. *Sovetskoe krest'ianstvo*, 328; *KrP*, 23 Mar. 1935, 2; *KrP*, 1 Sep. 1937, 2; *RPPKhoz* 2:646; Ostrovskii (1967), 58.

73. *RPPKhoz* 2:525 and 648. For examples of violations, see *SDK*, 166; *SA*, WKP 390:253.

74. *SZ*, 28 May 1938, 3; *KrP*, 28 June 1937, 3; *SZ*, 28 May 1938, 3.

75. *KrP*, 6 Sep. 1936, 1; *KrP*, 24 Aug. 1937, 2; *KrP*, 27 Aug. 1937, 2; *SZ*, 8 July 1938, 3; *PIT*, 125.

76. *Sotsialisticheskaia rekonstruktsiia sel'skogo khoziaistva*, no. 9, 8 (1938); *SZ*, 2 Feb. 1939, 3.

77. Close to half a million meetings were held throughout the country, in collective farms and other enterprises, in the fall of 1936; and hundreds of thousands of comments and amendments to the draft of the Constitution were submitted in oral and written form: see *Stroitel'stvo sovetskogo gosudarstva. Sbornik statei k 70–letiiu E. B. Genkinoi* (Moscow, 1972), 76, and *ISSSR*, no. 6, 122 (1976). On the discussion on the Constitution, see J. Arch Getty, "State and Society under Stalin: Constitutions and elections in the 1930s," *SR* 50(1):23–28 (1991).

78. *TsGAOR*, f. 3316, op. 41, d. 107, ll. 69–70.

79. *TsGAOR*, f. 3316, op. 41, d. 107, l. 69.

80. *NR*, 276.

81. *TsGAOR*, f. 3316, op. 41, d. 107, l. 77. See also ibid., d. 193, l. 107; *SA*, WKP 500:127, 183–84.

82. *SA*, WKP 500:127.

83. *SA*, WKP 500:184.

84. *SA*, WKP 500:127; *SR* 50:(1), 25. In Getty's sample of 2,627 letters from citizens of Leningrad oblast and 474 letters from Smolensk (Western) oblast (from *TsGAOR*, f. 3316, op. 41, dd. 127–29), 32 percent of the Leningrad letters and 22 percent of those from Smolensk fell into this category ("Guaranteed insurance, vacation, pension benefits to peasants as to workers").

85. *NR*, 272–73 (NKVD report of comment in Constitution discussion by peasant in Ivanovo oblast).

86. For the majority view (state obligation), see *TsGAOR*, f. 3316, op. 41, d. 81, ll. 74 and 121; ibid., d. 82, ll. 45, 73; ibid., d. 83, ll. 2, 79, 112; ibid., d. 107, ll. 8 and 73; *SA*, WKP 500:126. For the minority view, see *TsGAOR*, f. 3316, op. 41, d. 82, l. 37.

87. *SA*, WKP 500:126; *TsGAOR*, f. 3316, op. 41, d. 81, ll. 58–59; ibid., l. 55; *SA*, WKP 500:126 and 184. See also *TsGAOR*, f. 3316, op. 41, d. 81, ll. 60, 72, and 74; ibid., d. 107, ll. 7, 8, and 26–27.

88. *SA*, WKP 500:127.

89. *NR*, 276. Note that the speaker was careful to avoid the term "state farms" (sovkhozy), despite the fact that here too wages were paid. Clearly the peasants did not want to give up their private plots, live in cold barracks and eat in filthy communal dining-rooms, as in the state farms of the early 1930s.

90. *SA*, WKP 500:125.

Chapter 6

1. *Izmeneniia* (1979), 243; Poliakov (1990), 53.

2. On independents' occupations, see *SZ*, 21 Aug. 1938, 2.

3. *RP*, 29 Sep. 1937, 2.

4. *SIu*, no. 19, 5–6 (1935).

5. *TsGANKh*, f. 396, op. 10, d. 162, l. 398; *Sovetskaia Sibir'*, 2 Oct. 1936, 3.

6. *KrP*, 12 Sep. 1938, 3. See also ibid., 1 Sep. 1937, 2.

7. Diachenko, (1978), 286; *IndSSSR* (1971), 29, 60, 89.

8. Gushchin (1973), 350–51. On independents and taxes, see also *TsGANKh*, f. 396, op. 10, d. 162, l. 43; *SA*, WKP 362:32–33 and 37.

9. *SovYouth*, 189.

10. Ibid.

11. Gerasimov (1967), 75.

12. *KrP*, 23 Apr. 1935, 4.

13. *Molot*, 1 Apr. 1933, 3; Gushchin (1975), 22 and 45; *KrP*, 24 Aug. 1937, 2, and 27 Aug. 1937, 2.

14. *TsGANKh*. f. 396, op. 10, d. 34, ll. 432–33.

15. *SZ*, 14 Nov. 1937, 3.

16. Alekseev (1981), 403–7.

17. Vyltsan (1970), 54–56.

18. *Biulleten' oppozitsii*, no. 11 (May 1930), 25 (report on Uzbekistan). On the collapse of crafts and artisan industry during the First Five-Year Plan, see Sheila Fitzpatrick, "After NEP: The Fate of NEP Entrepreneurs, Small Traders, and Artisans in the 'Socialist Russia' of the 1930s," *Russian History/Histoire russe* 13, no. 2–3 (1986), 209–20.

19. *KrP*, 12 Apr. 1935, 3.

20. *KG*, 8 Dec. 1933, 3.

21. *SA*, WKP 500:133–36.

22. *Molot*, 15 Mar. 1933, 2; *KrK*, 18 Feb. 1933, 2; *SZ*, 3 Dec. 1932, 2.

23. *TsGANKh*, f. 7486, op. 19, d. 412, l. 91.

24. Ibid., ll. 86–89.

25. *KrP*, 18 Nov. 1938, 4; Vyltsan (1978), 179; *SZ*, 9 June 1938, 2.

26. *TsGANKh*, f. 396, op. 10, d. 39, l. 13; *SZ*, 9 June 1938, 2; *Molot*, 28 June 1933, 2.

27. *SZ*, 9 June 1938, 2; *KrP*, 27 July 1935, 3; *SZ*, 12 May 1938, 3; *TsGANKh*, f. 396, op. 10, d. 129, unpg.

28. *TsGANKh*, f. 396, op. 10, d. 160, l. 23.

29. *Trud*, 2 Jan. 1935, 2; *KrK*, 18 Feb. 1933, 2; Vyltsan (1978), 179. See also *SA*, WKP 362:371.

30. *KrP*, 10 July 1938.

31. *SA*, WKP 176:123 and 145.

32. *TsGANKh*, f. 396, op. 10, d. 66, l. 368; *KrP*, 2 Sep. 1938, 3; *KurPr*, 15 Aug. 1937, 2.

33. *SZ*, 16 Oct. 1938, 3; *SZ*, 30 Sep. 1938, 3; *SZ*, 29 May 1938, 2.

34. See A. Budarev, *Melkaia promyshlennost' na putiakh sotsialisticheskogo pereustroistva* (Moscow, 1931).

35. *MKrG*, 17 Dec. 1936, 3.

36. Promkolkhozy had 645,000 members in 1935 according to Adam Kaufman, *Small-Scale Industry in the Soviet Union* (New York, 1962), 43. Of these, 76 percent were in smithies (metal shops), fishing, milling, and logging artels. The number of members of promkolkhozy shown by the 1937 census is 507,000 (not including dependent family members): Poliakov (1990), 53.

37. *MKrG*, 6 Sep. 1936, 4; ibid., 2 Sep. 1936, 4; ibid., 17 Dec. 1936, 3.

38. *KrP*, 6 July 1938, 3.

39. K. V. Vasilevskii, *Promkooperatsiia SSSR ot pervoi piatiletki ko vtoroi* (Moscow-Leningrad, 1933), 47.

40. *Rabochaia Moskva*, 11 Nov. 1938, 2; ibid., 21 Dec. 1938, 4.

41. Vyltsan (1970), 44

42. *Biulleten' obyedinennoi V oblastnoi i III gorodskoi Leningradskoi konferentsii VKP(b)* (Leningrad, 1934), no. 5, 31–32; *SobrZak*, no. 65, art. 520 (1935); *KrP*, 5 Dec. 1935, 3. See also *SA*, WKP 390:347; *RP*, 27 Sep. 1937, 2.

43. See above, pp. 108–9.

44. Gushchin (1973), 349–50.

45. *RTsKhIDNI*, f. 17, op. 3, d. 983, ll. 142–47.

46. *RPPKhoz* 2:711; Ostrovskii (1967), 174–75; Vyltsan (1970), 46–47; *SZ*, 24 Aug. 1939, 1, and 17 Sep. 1939, 4. The decree referred specifically to Smolensk (formerly Western), Kalinin and Leningrad oblasts in the Russian Republic, Belorussia, and Ukraine.

47. *TsGAOR*, f. 5515, op. 1, d. 235, ll. 21–32. On the decree of 30 June 1931 on otkhod, see above, pp. 91–92.

48. *IKP* 1:416; *SIu*, no. 17, 22 (1934); ibid., no. 18, 23 (1934); *DIu*, no. 23, 10 (1934).

49. See, for example, *KrP*, 29 May 1935, 4, and above, p. 98.

50. *SZ*, 20 June 1939, 4.

51. Ibid., 29 Aug. 1939, 2.

52. *KPSSvR* 5:399.

53. *TsGANKh*, f. 396, op. 10, d. 162, l. 302; ibid., d. 145, l. 116.

54. *TsGANKh*, f. 396, op. 10, d. 15, l. 50.

55. See Jeffrey Burds, "The Social Control of Peasant Labor in Russia: The Response of Village Communities to Labor Migration in the Central Industrial Region, 1861–1905," in Esther Kingston-Mann and Timothy Mixter, ed., *Peasant Economy, Culture, and Politics, 1800–1921* (Princeton, 1991), 52–100.

56. *TsGANKh*, f. 396, op. 10, d. 143, l. 97; ibid., d. 87, unpg.

57. Quotation from *TsGAOR*, f. 5515, op. 1, d. 235, l. 22; *IndSSSR* (1971), 486–87; *Kommuna*, 28 Aug. 1937, 4.

58. *TsGANKh*, f. 396, op. 10, d. 160, l. 142. For other relevant rulings from Iaroslavl authorities, see ibid., ll. 5 and 136.

59. *TsGANKh*, f. 396, op. 10, d. 39, l. 271. See also *SevR*, 18 July 1935, 2; *KolSP*, 509–10.

60. *TsGANKh*, f. 396, op. 10, d. 39, ll. 306–7.

61. Ibid., d. 160, l. 151. See also l. 144 for a temporizing response from the oblast land department.

62. *Kommuna*, 12 Jan. 1937, 3; *SA*, WKP 390:343–44.

63. *SA*, WKP 186:62–63.

64. *TsGANKh*, f. 396, op. 10, d. 65, l. 103.

65. Ibid., d. 122, unpg.

66. "Kolkhoz" in this context presumably means a resolution of the kolkhoz general meeting.

67. *TsGANKh*, f. 396, op. 10, d. 88, unpg.

68. Ibid., d. 15, l. 51.

69. Ibid., d. 39, ll. 265–69. After *KG* sent this letter on to the local party raikom, Kukushkin was reinstated in kolkhoz membership.

70. *SA*, WKP 386:l. 83; *TsGANKh*, f. 396, op. 10, d. 161, l. 221.

71. *VI*, no. 2, 22 (1973); *IndSSR* (1971), 513–14.

72. Bergson, 118.

73. Poliakov (1990), 53; *IndSSR* (1971), 513–14.

74. *PIT*, xi, 85–123.

75. *RTsKhIDNI*, f. 5, op. 4, d. 18, ll. 5–111.

76. On the laborday minimum, see above, p. 146.

Chapter 7

1. On Soviet and Russian undergovernment, see Roberta Manning, "Government in the Soviet Countryside in the Stalinist thirties: The Case of Belyi Raion in

1937," *The Carl Beck Papers in Russian and East European Studies*, no. 301 (1984), and S. Frederick Starr, *Decentralization and Self-Government in Russia 1830–1870* (Princeton, 1972).

2. Calculated from *SotsStroi* (1936) 548–49, and *Trud* (1936), 30–31. MTS personnel are not included. A rural raion is defined as one headed by a raion executive committee (RIK), as distinct from a city soviet.

3. Data from *Statisticheskii sbornik po Severnomu kraiu za 1929–1933 gg.* (Archangel, 1934), 33, 213, 214, 217.

4. *SotsStroi* (1936), 505; Manning, 31.

5. *SotsStroi* (1936), 548–9; *SZ SSSR*, no. 42, art. 358 (1935), and no. 22, art. 85 (1937); *3 sessiia Ts. I. K. SSSR 6 sozyva. Stenograficheskii otchet* (Moscow, 1933), bull. 19, 21.

6. *SotsStroi* (1936), 548–9, and *Trud* (1936), 30–31; *SZ SSSR*, no. 66, art. 397 (1937); E. H. Carr, *The Foundations of a Planned Economy* (London, 1971) 2:251; Shuvaev (1937), 52.

7. This was first pointed out in Daniel Thorniley, *The Rise and Fall of the Soviet Rural Communist Party, 1927–1939* (Basingstoke, UK, 1988).

8. *RTsKhIDNI*, f. 17, op. 7, d. 315, l. 58. Rural Communists were classified as members of the following types of party organization: kolkhoz, MTS, sovkhoz, or territorial.

9. *RTsKhIDNI*, f. 17, op. 7, d. 309, l. 140; *Molot*, 23 Jan. 1934, 2; Thorniley, *Rise and Fall*, 143–4.

10. *RTsKhIDNI*, f. 17, op. 7, d. 315 ll. 55, 58. Note that the *RTsKhIDNI* file's figure on rural party membership in 1937 does not include the 118,000 persons who belonged to "institutions from the raion centers" (*sic*), a category of rural party organization not listed for earlier years.

11. Manning, "Government," 8. According to another source, Smolensk (formerly Western) oblast as a whole had 5,651 rural party members as of 1 Jan. 1938: *RTsKhIDNI*, f. 17, op. 7, d. 315, l. 30.

12. Jerry F. Hough, "The Changing Nature of the Kolkhoz Chairman," in Millar (1971), 105; Vyltsan (1978), 234; *SSSR strana sotsializma. Statisticheskii sbornik* (Moscow, 1936), 93.

13. *Trud* (1936), 326; Vyltsan (1978), 232; Thorniley, *Rise and Fall*, 20.

14. *SA*, WKP 415:128.

15. *SZ SSSR*, no. 44, art 365 (1935); *SIu*, no. 16, 15 (1936).

16. *KrP*, 15 Sep. 1936, 4.

17. *Molot*, 15 Apr. 1937, 3; Diachenko, (1978) 318; *Kommunist* (Saratov), 2 Sep. 1937, 2.

18. *SZ*, 16 Nov. 1932, 2; *SIu*, no. 27, 5 (1937).

19. *SA*, WKP 190:185; *SZ*, 16 Nov. 1932, 2 and *SIu*, no. 19, 7 (1934); *SZ*, 16 Nov. 1932, 2.

20. *SA*, WKP 190:185. For similar complaints, see *TsGANKh*, f. 396, op. 10, d. 122.

21. *SevR*, 22 Sep. 1937, 2. See also *SZ SSSR*, no. 65, art. 520 (1935); *SZ*, 15 June 1939, 1; *SZ*, 29 Aug. 1938, 3.

22. *Kommuna*, 4 Oct. 1937, 2; *SA*, WKP 190:222.

23. *KurPr*, 23 Aug. 1937, 4, and 30 Aug. 1937, 4; *SA*, WKP 178:160.

24. See ch. 11, below, for many examples.

25. *SIu*, no. 27, 1 (1935); ibid., no. 15, 20 (1935).

26. *SA*, WKP 178:134.

27. See the example in Arvo Tuominen, *The Bells of the Kremlin* (Hanover/London, 1983), 118.

28. Data from *RP*, 29 Aug. 1937, 1. These officials were defendants in a show trial (see below, Chapter 11), but that does not necessarily make them unrepresentative.

29. Stalin, *Soch.* 13:251–52; 1(14):74–77; *VVSKU*, 184 and 186. See also chs. 9 and 11.

30. *KrP*, 27 Mar. 1935, 4, and *MKrP*, 26 Sep. 1936, 2.

31. *SZ SSSR*, no. 65, art. 520 (1935).

32. *SA*, WKP 166:722; *SA*, WKP 355:286–81; *TsGANKh*, f. 396, op. 10, d. 129, unpg.

33. *4 sessiia TsIK Soiuza SSR 6 sozyva. Stenograficheskii otchet* (Moscow, 1934), bull. 24, 10–11; P. M. Chirkov, *Reshenie zhenskogo voprosa v SSSR (1917–1937 gg.)* (Moscow, 1978), 178; G. N. Serebrennikov, *The Position of Women in the U.S.S.R.* (London, 1937), 107.

34. *KrP*, 29 Aug. 1937, 2.

35. *Zhenshchiny v sel'sovetakh* (Moscow, 1934) 16; Gerasimov (1967). See also memoirs by E. Bushmanova in *Zhenshchiny Urala v revoliutsii i trude* (Sverdlovsk, 1963) and P. O. Degtiareva in *Rabotnitsa*, no. 7, 5 (1935).

36. *SZ*, 26 July 1937, 2.

37. *TsGANKh*, f. 396, op. 10, d. 145, ll. 310–11.

38. *SA*, WKP 386:135–45.

39. For complaints, see pp. 256–69; for show trials, see Ch. 11.

40. *Kommunist* (Saratov), 2 Sep. 1937, 2.

41. Tuominen, *The Bells of the Kremlin*, 117–123.

42. *IKP* 1:175; *Sto sorok besed s Molotovym*, 280–81; *RPPKhoz* 2:529.

43. *KrP*, 26 Aug. 1937, 2; *KrP*, 2 Sep. 1937, 2.

44. Lynne Viola, *The Best Sons of the Fatherland* (Oxford, 1987), 118. The "peasantization" of kolkhoz chairman in the 1930s was first deduced from party membership data by Jerry F. Hough in Millar (1971), 104–106.

45. *TsGANKh*, f. 7486, op. 19, d. 399, ll. 24, 65–66; Arina (1939), 215.

46. *TsGANKh*, f. 7486, op. 19, d. 399, l. 44.

47. Ibid., l. 66.

48. Ibid., l. 65.

49. Ibid., ll. 65–66.

50. *SZ*, 16 Nov. 1932, 2; *SZ SSSR*, no. 65, art. 520 (1935); *Spravochnik partiinogo rabotnika* (Moscow, 1936), 450–51; *Trud* (1936), 27. On turnover in 1937–38, see below, pp. 198–99.

51. *SIu*, no. 15, 20 (1935); *SA*, WKP 111:6, and 11.

52. *VVSKU*, 28.

53. *SA*, WKP 386:79–83.

54. *VVSKU*, 60–61, 49, 33. In the January 1937, the population census counted 5,997 women kolkhoz chairmen: *Vsesoiuznaia perepis' naseleniia 1937 g. Kratkie itogi* (Moscow, 1991), 142, 155.

55. *SA*, WKP 355:286–81.

56. Gerasimov (1967), 73. In 1936, 16 percent of managers of kolkhoz livestock farms, 22 percent of the leaders of livestock brigades, and two-thirds of the link leaders were women. See G. N. Serebrennikov, *The Position of Women in the U.S.S.R.*, (London, 1937), 107.

57. *IKP* 1:431–3.

58. Resolution of the Commissariat of Agriculture of 28 Feburary 1933, cited by a Commissariat spokesman at the 1935 meeting on chairmen's pay: *TsGANKh*, f. 7486, op. 19, d. 399, ll. 2–3. On very small kolkhozy (twenty to thirty households), the chairman was to be paid at the same rate as a brigade leader, but with an additional ten labordays a month.

59. Viola, *Best Sons,* 56–57 and 182; *DIu,* no. 8 inside front cover (1934); *KrP,* 20 Sep. 1938, 3.

60. *TsGANKh,* f. 7486, op. 19, d. 399, ll. 23–5, 44, 65, 106. 118–23, 153, 158–59.

61. Ibid., ll. 170–73.

62. *KrP,* 10 Oct. 1936, 2; *KrP,* 16 Nov. 1937, 3.

63. *KurPr,* 30 Sep. 1937, 1 (Kursk oblast), *TsGANKh,* f. 396, op. 10, d. 39, l. 2 (Kalinin oblast), and *Kommuna* (Voronezh), 8 Sep. 1937, 1 (Voronezh oblast); *TsGANKh,* f. 396, op. 10, d. 39, l. 59; *IKP* 2, 42–44.

64. *TsGANKh,* f. 396, op. 10, d. 39, l. 5; *ibid.,* d. 122, unpg.; ibid., d. 39, l. 57.

65. The basic decree, dated 21 April 1940, grants this as a privilege for "the eastern regions of the USSR" (*SZ SSSR,* no. 11, art. 271 [1940]). A decree acceding to the request of Moscow and Smolensk oblasts to share this privilege was issued on 5 June 1940, and other oblasts were included in ten subsquent decrees between July 1940 and March 1941. For a complete list, see *Vazhneishie resheniia* (1948), 288.

66. Alekseev (1981), 347. See also *TsGANKh,* f. 396, op. 10, d. 65, l. 288, and ibid. d. 86, unpg.

67. *TSGANKh,* f. 7486, op. 19, d. 399, l. 176.

68. *Kommunist,* no. 1, 98 (1990); *SA,* WJP 203:17.

69. *KrP,* 8 Apr. 1935, 3; *KrP,* 18 July 1937, 1; *KrP,* 20 Aug. 1937, 3; *TsGANKh,* f. 396, op. 10, d. 87, unpg.; *RP,* 29 July 1937, 2; *SA,* WKP 203:17.

70. *TsGANKh,* f. 396, op. 10, d. 65, l. 463.

71. *SA,* WKP 351:139.

72. *TsGANKh,* f. 396, op. 10, d. 137, l. 80.

73. Ibid., d. 142, ll. 215–16.

74. Boris Mironov, in Ben Eklof and Stephen Frank, ed., *The World of the Russian Peasant: Post-Emancipation Culture and Society,* 14.

75. *SA,* WKP 362:214–15.

76. Rodney Bohac, "Everyday Forms of Resistance: Serf Opposition to Gentry Exactions, 1800–1861," in Esther Kingston-Mann and Timothy Mixter, eds., *Peasant Economy Culture and Politics* (Princeton, 1991), 239.

77. *IKP* 1:222.

78. *RPPKhoz* 2:528–29; *VVSKU,* 28–30.

79. The Leningrad newspaper, *Krest'ianskaia pravda,* whose editorial policy was generally liberal, is the prime case in point. See, e.g., *KrP,* 1 Feb. 1935, 3; *KrP,* 2 Dec. 1935, 4.

80. *SIu,* no. 8, 7 (1936); *Sotsialisticheskii Donbass,* 10 Dec. 1936, 2.

81. See, for example, *SA,* WKP 362:25; *SA,* WKP 386:79–83, 100–103; *SA,* WKP 390:21–22.

82. *SA,* WKP 203:39–42.

83. *Molot,* 15 Apr. 1937, 3. Similar reports are in *KrP,* 20 Aug. 1937, 3; *Kommunist* (Saratov), 14 Sep. 1937, 3; *SevR,* 5 Apr. 1937, 1.

84. *Kommuna,* 4 Oct. 1937, 2.

85. *TsGANKh,* f. 396, op. 10, d. 65, l. 238.

86. *SZ*, 11 July 1938, 3.

87. See, for example, Alekseev (1981), 355.

88. *SA*, WKP 111, 10.

89. See below, p. 300.

90. *Washington Post*, 16 Aug. 1991, A38.

91. *RTsKhIDNI*, f. 17, op. 7, d. 315, 1. 23, 14–15.

92. Vyltsan (1978), 114–16; Gregory Guroff and Fred V. Carstensen, eds., *Entrepreneurship in Imperial Russia and the Soviet Union* (Princeton, 1983), 263.

93. *TsGANKh*, f. 396, op. 10, d. 88, unpg.

94. On the trials, see below, Chapter 11.

95. *SZ*, 21 Sep. 1938, 3.

96. *SA*, WKP 203:163. On denunciations, see Chapter 9.

97. For cases where the object of denunciation was punished, see *TsGANKh*, f. 396, op. 10, d. 121, 52–55; ibid., d. 142, 1. 729; ibid., d. 161, 1. 53. For a case where the complaint backfired and the complainant was punished, see ibid., d. 64, 1. 165. For a case where both sides suffered (the complainant being arrested, the objects of his complaint being fired), see ibid., d. 143, 1. 325.

98. Ibid., d. 65, 1. 46.

99. Ibid., d. 87, unpg. All these words were familiar terms of abuse in the language of Marxist-Leninist polemics of the 1920s and 1930s.

100. Ibid., d. 145, ll. 310–11.

101. *SZ*, 3 Feb. 1938, 3.

102. *SZ*, 21 Sep 1938, 3; *SZ*, 4 Sep. 1938, 2. On the 1933 purges, see above, p. 77.

103. *RPPKhoz* 2:650–52; N. Dugin, in *Na boevom postu*, 27 Dec. 1989, 3. According to Dugin's figures, over the period 1937–39 the number of prisoners in the "socially harmful and socially dangerous" category almost tripled (rising from 103,513 to 285,831), while the number of prisoners in all political categories (counterrevolution, treason, espionage, etc.) more than quadrupled (from 118,393 to 503,166). The number of prisoners in all criminal categories dropped from 421,687 to 417,552 over the same period.

104. *SA*, WKP 111:22; *SA*, WKP 321:291; *TsGANKh*, f. 396, op. 10, d. 129, unpg.

105. *Trud*, 4 June 1992, 1: publication of documents from ultrasecret "Special files" (*osobye papki*) currently in the hands of President Eltsin's commission for declassifying of archives.

106. Gulag data from N. Dugin, in *Na boevom postu*, 27 Dec. 1989, 3; Orenburg data from Teptsov, "OGPU protiv krest'ian," 35, and *Trud*, 4 June 1992, 4; individual example from *TsGANKh*, f. 396, op. 10, d., 143, ll. 211–13.

Chapter 8

1. John Sheldon Curtiss, *The Russian Church and the Soviet State* (Gloucester, Mass., 1965), 267; *Vsesoiuznaia perepis' naseleniia 1926 goda* vol. 34 (Moscow, 1930), 97, and Poliakov (1990), 53; *TsGAOR*, f. 5407, op. 1, d. 106. 1. 97; *SA*, WKP 500:294.

2. Data from Poliakov (1990), 69. On reactions to the census question on religion, see below, pp. 294–95.

3. *Molodezh' SSSR. Statisticheskii sbornik* (Moscow, 1936), 286; Anokhina (1964), 281.

4. *AR*, no. 6, 3 (1939); Alekseev (1981), 378–79; 3. See also *KrK*, 12 July 1937, p. 2.

5. *AR*, no. 6, 4 (1939); *TsGAOR*, f. 5407, op. 1, d. 44, l. 83; ibid., f. 5407, op. 1, d. 47, l. 100; *AR*, no. 5, 119 (1930).

6. *AR*, no. 6, 14 (1937).

7. Some 88 percent of Protestants aged sixteen years and over were literate, compared with 67 percent of Catholics, and 57 of Orthodox believers. Poliakov (1990), 69.

8. *SA*, WKP 500:294; *SevR*, 10 Sep. 1937, 3. On the flourishing of sects in the 1930s, see William C. Fletcher, *The Russian Orthodox Church Underground, 1917–1970* (London, 1971), ch. 4.

9. *Materialy k serii "Narody Sovetskogo Soiuza". Perepis' 1939 g. Dokumental'nye istochniki Tsentral'nogo Gosudarstvennogo Arkhiva Narodnogo Khoziaistva (TsGANKh) SSSR* (Moscow, 1990), 4:732–34.

10. Stephen P. and Ethel Dunn, *The Peasants of Central Russia* (New York, 1967), 94–110. See also Millar (1971), 370.

11. *KrP*, 26 Dec. 1938, 2. See also *AR*, no. 5 (1939); *Viriatino*, 273.

12. *KrP*, 18 July 1935, 1; *AR*, no. 5, 39 (1939).

13. The feastday of "Paraskeva Piatnitsa" was on Nov. 10, but throughout the year, before major feasts, twelve other Fridays were also celebrated in her honor: see Linda J. Ivanits, *Russian Folk Belief* (Armonk, N.Y., 1989), 33–34.

14. *KrP*, 26 July 1937, 2.

15. *SE*, 1958 no. 4, 115; *KrP*, 26 July 1937, 2.

16. *AR*, no. 1, 55 (1937).

17. *AR*, no. 5, 40 (1939); *SA*, WKP 355:36–39.

18. *AR*, no. 5, 40 (1939). All dates of feastdays are given according to the new calendar.

19. The account and all quotations that follow are taken from *AR*, no. 11, 54–55 (1937).

20. See, for example, *SA*, WKP 412:32, 33.

21. *RTsKhIDNI*, f. 89, op. 4, d. 66, l. 73; *SA*, WKP 500:293; *RTsKhIDNI*, f. 17, op. 2, d. 612, l. 10.

22. *AR*, no. 7, 10 (1937).

23. *AR*, no. 11, 55 (1939); *SIu*, no. 12, 9 (1935).

24. *AR*, no. 10, 54 (1939) and *TsGANKh*, f. 396, op. 10, d. 34, l. 313 (priests' rights); *RTsKhIDNI*, f. 17, op. 2, d. 612, l. 10 (Iaroslavskii); *SIu*, no. 12, 40 (1939); *Sotsialisticheskaia Osetiia*, 6 Aug. 1937, 2; E. Pramnek, *Otchetnyi doklad V gorodskoi oblastnoi partiinoi konferentsii o rabote obkoma VKP(b)* (Gorky, 1937), 22; *GK*, 28 July 1937, 3.

25. *AR*, no. 8, 3 (1937); *AR*, no. 6, 2 (1939); *TsGAOR*, f. 3316, op. 41, d. 107, l. 83.

26. *GK*, 28 July 1937, 3 and *KrP*, 17 Sep. 1937, 3; *RP*, 4 Aug. 1937, 2.

27. On the Constitution, see pp. 280–85; on the response to the 1937 census, see pp. 294–95.

28. *Zv*, 23 Mar. 1937, 3. See also *KrP*, 5 Aug. 1937, 2.

29. *TsGANKh*, f. 396, op. 10, d. 145, l. 286–87; *AR*, no. 9, 12–13 (1937); *TsGAOR*, f. 3316, op. 41, d. 84, l. 72; *SA*, WKP 500:183; TsGAOR, f. 3316, op. 41, d. 84, l. 72. It should be noted that the authorities also received many letters in connection with the discussion of the new Constitution arguing that priests should *not* recover voting rights. See, for example, TsGAOR, f. 3316, op. 41, d. 107, l. 11.

30. *Profsoiuzy SSSR*, no. 5–6, 16–19 (1938).

31. Quotations from *KrP*, 22 July 1937, 2; *GK*, 28 July 1937, 3; Pramnek, 23. See also *AR*, no. 11, 9 (1937); *Profsoiuzy SSSR*, 1938 no. 5–6, 16–19; *RP*, 4 Aug. 1937, 2.

32. *AR*, no. 8, 12 (1937); *AR*, no. 11, 9 (1937); *Kommuna*, 22 Nov. 1937, 2; *GK*, 28 July 1937, 3.

33. *KrP*, 20 June 1937, 3; *GK*, 28 July 1937, 3.

34. See below, pp. 282–83.

35. *KrP*, 9 Aug. 1937, 4.

36. *KrP*, 22 July 1937, 2.

37. *SevR*, 3 Aug. 1937, 2; *SevR*, 10 Sep. 1937, 3; *Krasnaia Bashkiriia*, 29 July 1937, 2; *KrP*, 2 Aug. 1937, 2–3; *KrP*, 20 June 1937, 3; *KrP*, 2 Aug. 1937, 2–3. For more discussion of these rumors, see Chapter 11.

38. See Dunn, *Peasants*, 104–5.

39. Boris Mozhaev, "Muzhiki i baby," *Don*, no. 3, 68 (1987); *KG*, 8 Dec. 1933, 3; *KrP*, 12 Apr. 1935, 3. See also Fitzpatrick, "After NEP," *Russian History/ Histoire russe* 13 (2–3):209–20 (1986).

40. *TsGANKh*, f. 7486, op. 19, d. 259, unpg.

41. *SE*, no. 5, 106–8 (1966); Anokhina (1964), 144–46.

42. *SE*, no. 5, 107 (1965); *Viriatino*, 231. On peddlars, see *Sudebnaia praktika RSFSR*, no. 16, 9 (1931), and *SIu*, no. 10, back page (1932).

43. *SE*, no. 5, 107 (1965); *Viriatino*, 237–38; *VVSKU*, 74–75.

44. *SA*, WKP 166:737.

45. According to official statistics, consumption of state-produced vodka stood at 3.6 liters per head of population per year in 1936, compared to 8.1 liters before the war. State production of vodka (excluding export and industrial uses) was about 320–330 million liters a year in 1935, compared with about 432 million liters in 1913, but output was rising. Later figures are not available. *Spravochnik po syr'ëvoi baze spirtovoi promyshlennosti Narkompishcheproma SSSR* (Moscow, 1934), 4; *Spravochnik po syr'ëvoi baze spirtovoi promyshlennosti Narkompishcheproma SSSR* (Moscow, 1936), 3–4; A. I. Mikoian, *Pishchevaia industriia Sovetskogo Soiuza* ([Moscow?], 1939), 88. On the low level of village drinking in the "bad times" before the war, see Mozhaev (1988), 482.

46. *KrP*, 18 Apr. 1935, 3; *KrK*, 16 Oct. 1937, 4; *Krasnaia Bashkiriia*, 15 Aug. 1937, 4; *SZ*, 12 Aug. 1938, 4; *Zv*, 5 Oct. 1937, 4.

47. *SotsStroi* (1939), 133; *Vsesoiuznaia perepis' naseleniia 1937 g.*, 61, 157; Samuel C. Ramer, in Susan Gross Solomon and John F. Hutchinson, ed., *Health and Society in Revolutionary Russia* (Bloomington, 1990), 135–39.

48. *TsGAOR*, f. 3316, op. 41, d. 81, l. 74; ibid., d. 82, l. 84; ibid., d. 107, ll. 26–27 and 78; *SA*, WKP 500:126; *TsGAOR*, f. 3316, op. 41, d. 107, l. 81.

49. N. L. Rogalina, *Kollektivizatsiia: Uroki proidennogo puti* (Moscow, 1989), 198; Alekseev (1981), 398–403; *ISK* 3:113; *NarKhoz* (1972), 116. See also Tuominen, 117–123.

50. Poliakov (1990), 53. On the preponderance of women, see also *VVSKU*, 49, 61; *SZ SSSR*, no. 65, art. 520 (1935); *Zhenshchina v kolkhozakh—bol'shaia sila* (Voronezh, 1934), 70 and 59.

51. Gerasimov (1967), 64.

52. Ibid., 79–80.

53. Ibid., 64.

54. Ibid., 66–67.

55. *Na putiakh k novoi shkole*, no. 4–5, 15 (1930); Nikolai Voronov, "Iunost' v Zheleznodol'ske," *Novyi mir*, no. 11, 42 (1968).

56. *Na putiakh k novoi shkole*, no. 4–5, 15 (1930). On policy, see E. H. Carr, *Socialism in One Country*, 1:35–36, and Jennie A. Stevens, "Children of the Revolution: Soviet Russia's Homeless Children (*Besprizorniki*) in the 1920s," *Russian History/Histoire russe* 9, pts. 2–3 (1982), 259–61.

57. *SA*, WKP 355:125–132, 181.

58. Christine D. Worobec, *Peasant Russia. Family and Community in the Post-Emancipation Period* (Princeton, 1991), 70–74 (on pre-rev.); *Molot*, 26 Apr. 1933, 3 and 30 June 1933, 2; *SV*, no. 12, 15 (1933); *Sbornik tsirkuliarov i razyiasnenii Narodnogo Komissariata Iustitsii RSFSR deistvuiushchikh na 1 maia 1934* (Moscow, 1934), 169 (on famine).

59. *ZKP*, 12 July 1935, 3.

60. *KPSSvR* 5:206–11; Vyltsan (1978), 206.

61. *SA*, WKP 500:13.

62. *ISK* 3:114; Vyltsan (1970), 25; *SE*, no. 3, 19 (1956).

63. R. I. Sifman, *Dinamika rozhdaemosti v SSSR* (Moscow, 1974), 48; Vyltsan (1970), 141–42.

64. Ansley Coale, Barbara A. Anderson, and Erna Härm, *Human Fertility in Russia since the Nineteenth Century* (Princeton, 1979), 42–43. The main indices they use are "overall fertility," defined as the number of births occurring to women aged fifteen to fifty, relative to the number of births to women in this age group in the prolific sizeable population for which there are reliable statistics, and "marital fertility," restricting the groups to women aged fifteen to fifty who are currently married (11).

65. *KP*, 9 Dec. 1935, 3.

66. *Molodoi kolkhoznik*, no. 4, 2–3 (1935).

67. Ibid. On bride-price and dowry before the revolution, see Worobec, *Peasant Russia*, 63–64, 156–58, and Steven L. Hoch, *Serfdom and Social Control in Russia* (Chicago, 1986), 95–105.

68. Nicholas S. Timasheff, *The Great Retreat* (New York, 1946); *Novyi mir*, no. 8, 261 (1935). On Stakhanovites and divorce, see below, p. 279.

69. *TsGAOR*, f. 3316, op. 41, d. 82, l. 22. See also *SE*, no. 3, 22–23 (1956).

70. *Novyi mir*, no. 8, 261 (1935).

71. *KrP*, 4 June 1936, 2.

72. The draft law was published in *Pr*, 26 May 1936. The final version, dated 27 June, which retained the same scale of payments for divorce as the draft, is in *SZ SSSR*, no. 34, art. 309 (1936).

73. For the relevant government decrees and party resolutions, see *Narodnoe obrazovanie v SSSR. Obshcheobrazovatel'naia shkola. Sbornik dokumentov 1917–1973 gg.* (Moscow, 1974), 42, 109–113, 115–16.

74. *KultStroi* (1956), 122–23.

75. Poliakov (1990), 67. "Schooling" here applies to all educational institutions, from primary to tertiary level.

76. *Za vseobshchee obuchenie*, no. 4, 10 (1931); *ZKP*, 8 Jan. 1931, 1; *Narodnoe prosveshchenie*, 1930 no. 7–8, 20. See also Sheila Fitzpatrick, *Education and Social Mobility in the Soviet Union, 1921–1934* (Cambridge, 1979), 161–63.

77. Diachenko (1978), 285; R. W. Davies, *The Development of the Soviet Budgetary System* (Cambridge, 1958), 225; *IndSSSR* (1971), 58, 60; *ZKP*, 1 June 1934, 1.

78. 1926 and 1939 figures *Itogi Vsesoiuznoi perepisi naseleniia 1959 goda. SSSR (Svodnyi tom)* (Moscow, 1962), 88; 1937 data from Poliakov (1990), 65–66; 1932 claim in *Itogi vypoleniia piatiletnego plana razvitiia narodnogo khoziaistva SSSR* (Moscow, 1933), 222. Unfortunately, the 1937 census literacy figures do not include urban-rural breakdown. For the total urban and rural population aged nine to forty-nine, the 1937 census found 75 percent literacy (86 percent of men, 65 percent of women).

79. Diachenko (1978), 319.

80. *ZKP*, 20 Dec. 1935, 3; *ZKP*, 4 Nov. 1934.

81. *ZKP*, 4 Nov. 1934; *Za vsobshchee obuchenie*, no. 4, 11 (1931); *ZKP*, 18 Jan. 1934, 2.

82. *ZKP*, 21 Sep. 1937, 3.

83. *TsGAOR*, f. 3316, op. 41, d. 107, l. 77. The author, a kolkhoznik from Kharkov oblast writing in 1936 or 1937, claimed that the cost of books for four children in school (grades I to VII) was 80 rubles a year. See also, ibid., d. 84, l. 74.

84. See, for example, *ZKP*, 18 Jan. 1934, 2; *TsGANKh*, f. 7486, op. 19, d. 412, l. 38.

85. *ZKP*, 3 Dec. 1934, 3.

86. Ibid., 18 Sep. 1935, 2; 24 Nov. 1935, 3; 6 Dec. 1935, 3.

87. Ibid., 6 Dec. 1935, 3.

88. Women comprised 48 percent of rural teachers and 67 percent of urban teachers in 1937, according to the census: *Vsesoiuznaia perepis' naseleniia 1937 g.*, 145, 158.

89. *ZKP*, 8 Oct. 1934, 3.

90. Ibid., 14 July 1935, 2.

91. Ibid., 16 Aug. 1935, 3.

92. F. Gladkov, "O sel'skoi shkole," *ZKP*, 24 Nov. 1935, 3. For another report by Gladkov on the same trip, written in very different terms, see below, p. 263.

93. *Narodnoe prosveshchenie*, 1930 no. 6, 16–17; ibid., 1930 no. 7–8, 8–10.

94. *ZKP*, 4 Dec. 1934, 4.

95. *KultStroi* (1956), 84–85. Note that these official figures—340,000 rural teachers in the Soviet Union in 1930–31 and 842,000 in 1940–41—may be too low. The number of persons declaring themselves to be teachers in the 1937 census was over 100,000 more than the official figure for 1936–37: Poliakov (1990), 57; *KultStroi* (1956), 80–81.

96. *Kommunisticheskoe prosveshchenie*, no. 1, 99 (1935); ibid., no. 6, 87 (1934).

97. *KrP*, 6 Sep. 1936, 3 and *ZKP*, 18 Jan. 1934, 2; *Kommunisticheskoe prosveshchenie*, no. 5–6, 33–34 (1936); V. F. Klochko, *Kul'turnoe stroitel'stvo v sovetskoi derevne v gody piatiletki (1933–1937)* (Moscow, 1956), 68.

98. For such complaints in the 1930s, see *TsGAOR*, f. 3316, op. 41, d. 81, l. 74; ibid., d. 107, l. 78. On peasant attitudes to education in the 1920s, see A. M. Bolshakov, *Derevnia, 1917–1927*, (Moscow, 1927) 238–39, 246, 426; and Fitzpatrick, *Education*, 171–72.

99. On questions of peasant demands and their satisfaction in a prerevolutionary context, see Ben Eklof, *Russian Peasant Schools. Officialdom, Village Culture, and Popular Pedagogy, 1861–1914* (Berkeley, 1990), 475–82 and *passim*.

100. *Narodnoe obrazovanie*, 165–66. For peasant complaints about progressive methods, see *Krest'iane o sovetskoi vlasti* (Moscow-Leningrad, 1929), 156–57, 164–65, 166–67, 178–79, and 182–85, and Fitzpatrick, *Education*, 19–25, 136–57; on the reforms of the 1930s, see Fitzpatrick, *Education*, 220–33.

101. *TsGAOR*, f. 3316, op. 41, d. 107, l. 45; *ZKP*, 18 Jan. 1934, 2.

102. *TsGAOR*, f. 3316, op. 41, d. 107, l. 30.

103. Ibid., l. 52.

104. See, for example, *TsGANKh*, f. 396, op. 10, d. 15, l. 19; ibid., d. 23, ll. 4, 74; ibid., d. 81, ll. 25, 56, 91.

105. *KrP*, 6 Sep. 1936, 3; *TsGANKh*, f. 396, op. 10, d. 15, l. 19.

Chapter 9

1. Gushchin (1973), 432; *ISSSR*, no. 6, 31 (note) (1960); *SIu*, no. 15, 17 (1936); *SA*, WKP 351:87–88.

2. *KrP*, 4 Feb. 1935, 4, and 2 Apr. 1935, 3.

3. *KrP*, 4 Mar. 1935, 3.

4. *SIu*, no. 13, 10 (1935); no. 14, 2, 7(1935); no. 15, 17–18 (1936). See also *KrP*, 27 Mar. 1935, 4, and 28 Mar. 1935, 4.

5. *GK*, 14 July 1937, 3; *Zv*, 9 Aug. 1937, 4.

6. *SIu*, no. 2, 17 (1934).

7. Ibid. See also *SG*, no. 4, 66 (1933).

8. Ibid., no. 4. 67 (1933).

9. *SA*, WKP 415:128.

10. See Roberta Manning, "Government in the Soviet Countryside in the Stalinist Thirties," *The Carl Beck Papers in Russian and East European Studies*, no. 301 (1984), 16; Neil Weissman, "Policing the NEP Countryside," in *Russia in the Era of NEP*, Sheila Fitzpatrick, Alexander Rabinowitch, and Richard Stites, eds. (Bloomington, 1991), 174–91. In the 1930s, as in the 1920s, the *sel'skie ispolniteli*, elected at rural soviet level, had few powers and were usually inactive.

11. *SA*, WKP 500:127; *TsGAOR*, f. 3316, op. 41, d. 107, l. 55. See also ibid., d. 84, l. 89; ibid., d. 107, ll. 9, and 31.

12. *SIu*, no. 16, 4 (1933); *TsGAOR*, f. 5451, op. 15, d. 33, l. 100; *SG*, no. 5, 27 (1933).

13. *SA*, WKP 351:28; *GASO*, f. 1148, op. 148 r/2, d. 65, l. 42; *RTsKhIDNI*, f. 5, op. 4, d. 1, l. 37.

14. *KG*, 21 Nov. 1933, 3; 26 Nov. 1933, 3; 28 Nov. 1933, 3; 30 Nov. 1933, 4; 11 Dec. 1933, 2.

15. *TsGANKh*, f. 396, op. 10, d. 145, l. 286; *SA*, WKP 386:369–70; *SIu*, no. 3, 5 (1936); *SA*, WKP 190:195–96.

16. *TsGANKh*, f. 396, op. 10, d. 66, l. 180.

17. Ibid., d. 121, ll. 53–55.

18. *SZ SSSR*, no. 33, art. 257 (1934), and no. 7, art. 57 (1935); I. Ia. Trifonov, *Likvidatsiia ekspluatatorskikh klassov v SSSR* (Moscow, 1975), 389–91. Note that, despite the restriction on mobility, deported kulaks were called up for military service in World War II. Trifonov (391), gave 1947 as the date when restrictions on the mobility of former kulaks were lifted. More recently, V. N. Zemskov has published a secret resolution of the Council of Ministers of the USSR of 13 Aug. 1954 ("O sniatii ogranichenii po spetsposeleniiu s bysvshikh kulakov i drugikh lits") that suggests a later date (*Sotsiologicheskie issledovaniia*, no. 1, 10 [1991]).

19. *VVSKU*, 19, and see above, pp. 123–24.

20. *SDK*, 167; *IKP* 1, 429. Kulaks' children (in contrast to kulaks) had never been formally excluded from kolkhoz membership, so there was no moment when

they were formally readmitted. But their claim to the right of membership was strengthened by the March 1933 decree returning voting rights to kulaks' children who showed no antisocial tendencies (*SZ SSSR*, no. 21, art. 117 [1933]) and the statement on eligibility for membership in the 1935 Model Charter of the Agricultural Artel (*IKP* 1:429), which explicitly included such children of *lishentsy* and exiled kulaks as were "engaged in socially-useful work and work with good conscience."

21. Vyltsan (1978), 251; *SZ SSSR*, no. 65, art. 520 (1935).

22. *KP*, 2 Dec. 1935, 2.

23. See, for example, *KP*, 28 Dec. 1935, 1.

24. *ISSSR*, no. 6, 117, 119, 126 (1976) (controversy in drafting Constitution); *RP*, 16 Oct. 1937, 2 (Sychevka); *SZ*, 28 Dec. 1937, 3; *KurPr*, 26 Aug. 1937, 3; ibid., 29 Aug. 1937, 3; ibid., 2 Sep. 1937, 3; ibid., 14 Oct. 1937, 4; *RP*, 16 Oct 1937, 2 (kolkhoz membership); *Stroitel'stvo sovetskogo gosudarstva*, 77 (petitions).

25. *TsGAOR*, f. 3316, op. 41, d. 107, l. 58; ibid., l. 12. According to one Soviet historian who has analyzed the 6,369 comments on this article of the Constitution systematized by the Presidium of the Executive Committee of the Russian Congress of Soviets, the majority were against returning voting rights to kulaks and priests; and Arch Getty found a similar tendency in his sample of letters on the Constitution from Leningrad and Western oblasts (*ISSSR*, no. 6, 125–26 [1976]; *SR* 50(1):25 [1991]).

26. *RP*, 16 Oct. 1937, 2; and see above, pp. 198, 201.

27. *SIu*, no. 32, 1 (1935); *TsGANKH*, f. 7486, op. 19, d. 412, l. 30.

28. *TsGANKH*, f. 396, op. 10, d. 161, l. 473; ibid., d. 19, l. 25; *KrP*, 2 June 1935, 2.

29. Alekseev (1981), 435–36; *KrK*, 17 Sep 1937, 2; Shuvaev (1937), 48.

30. *GASO*, f. 88, op. 1, d. 62, l. 95; *SA*, WKP 260:24–25.

31. *SIu*, no. 1, 18 (1933); *TsGANKH*, f. 7486, op. 19, d. 259, unpg. While the second writer may have been a bedniachka by origin, the style and content of the letter strongly suggest that she had received at least a secondary education.

32. *SG*, no. 5, 32–37 (1933); *Molot*, 23 Jan 1934, 2; *SIu*, no. 22, 11 (1933); *Iunost'*, no. 3, 11–30 (1988) (Tvardovskii); Iurii Druzhnikov, *Voznesenie Pavlika Morozova* (London, 1988), 30–54.

33. *SIu*, no. 17, 22 (1934).

34. *SIu*, no. 32, 1 (1935).

35. *SA*, WKP 386:80.

36. *KrK*, 17 Sep. 1937, 2; *KrP*, 2 Sep. 1936, 3; *KurPr*, 26 Aug. 1937, 3; ibid., 29 Aug. 1937, 3; ibid., 2 Sep. 1937, 3; ibid., 14 Oct. 1937, 4; *SZ*, 28 Dec. 1937, 2.

37. *TsGANKH*, f. 396, op. 10, d. 160, l. 64; ibid., d. 162, l. 160. In at least one of these two cases, the raion had rejected the appeal.

38. *KurPr*, 14 Oct. 1937, 4; *RP*, 16 Oct. 1937, 2.

39. *KurPr*, 14 Oct. 1937, 4; *TsGANKH*, f. 396, op. 10, d. 86, unpg. (letter from sel'kor Verovoika, 27 March 1938).

40. The nearest case I have come across (*KurPr*, 14 Oct. 1937, 4) is that of a previously "repressed" peasant who returned to the village, was admitted to kolkhoz membership, and immediately became a brigade leader.

41. Examples cited from *KrP*, 8 Apr. 1935, 3; *RP*, 29 July 1937, 2; *TsGANKH*, f. 396, op. 10, d. 143, l. 216. See also *SZ*, 4 Nov. 1932, 1; *Molot*, 21 Apr. 1933, 1; *Krasnaia Bashkiriia*, 14 May 1938, 2; *SIu*, no. 12, 9 (1935); *KrP*, 28 Feb. 1935 2; *TsGANKH*, f. 396, op. 10, d. 86, unpg. (letter from Verovoika, 27 March 1938).

42. *KG*, 21 Nov. 1933, 3; *TsGANKh*, f. 396, op. 10, d. 87, unpg. (complaint from "Serp i molot" kolkhoz, Sovetskii raion); ibid., d. 145, ll. 495–96.

43. Shuvaev (1937), 43–45.

44. *TsGANKh*, f. 396, op. 10, d. 86, unpg.

45. *KrK*, 1 Feb. 1933, 2.

46. *SA*, WKP 415:13.

47. *TsGANKh*, f. 396, op. 10, d. 87, unpg.; ibid., d. 129, unpg. (case of Ilia Mitronov).

48. *Novyi mir*, no. 11, 41–56 (1968); *AR*, no. 8–9, 24 (1930); *SIu*, no. 3, 23 (1932).

49. *SIu*, no. 3, 23–24 (1932).

50. *TsGANKh*, f. 396, op. 10, d. 19, ll. 195–96, 200.

51. For elaboration of this point, see Sheila Fitzpatrick, "L'Usage bolchévique de la Classe," *Actes de la Recherche en Sciences Sociales* 85:78–79 (1990).

52. *SA*, WKP 190:26.

53. *TsGANKh*, f. 396, op. 10, d. 19, l. 24.

54. Ibid., d. 87, unpg.

55. *KrP*, 22 Feb. 1935, 3.

56. *SA*, WKP 386:144–47.

57. *SA*, WKP 190:131–32.

58. *TsGANKh*, f. 396, op. 10, d. 39, l. 477.

59. *SA*, WKP 500:76–77.

60. *TsGANKh*, f. 396, op. 10, d. 129, unpg.

61. Ibid., d. 65, l. 245.

62. Ibid., d. 137, ll. 50–60.

63. For basic Soviet accounts of the Pavlik Morozov story, see *Bol'shaia sovetskaia entsiklopediia* (3rd ed., Moscow, 1974) 16:580, and *Zori sovetskoi pionerii. Ocherki po istorii pionerskoi organizatsii (1917–1941)* (Moscow, 1972), 72.

64. Iurii Druzhnikov, *Voznesenie Pavlika Morozova* (London, 1988), 10, 20, 30–55.

65. *KrP*, 23 Apr. 1935, 4. For other examples, see Robert Conquest, *The Harvest of Sorrow* (Oxford, 1986), 295; *Zori sovetskoi pionerii*, 72–73; *Molodoi kolkhoznik*, no. 6, 10–11 (1935).

66. *SIu*, no. 9, 15–18 (1935).

67. See, for example, the editorial rebuke to a would-be denouncer of his father in *Krasnaia Tatariia*, 5 Apr. 1938, 2.

68. See "On Bibliography and Sources" for a description of these files.

69. There were some exceptions to this rule during dekulakization, when a few villages sent communal petitions in support of a dekulakized peasant: *GASO*, f. 88 (1), op. 1, d. 62, ll. 171, 177.

70. Ibid., d. 161, l. 473. Despite this guileless appeal, the writer was not lacking in resource. He had already sent a letter to the local newspaper, and planned to lodge a complaint against the kolkhoz chairman with the People's Court if the complaint to *Krest'ianskaia gazeta* got no response.

71. Ibid., d. 65, ll. 265–68.

72. Ibid., d. 143, l. 311.

73. *KrK*, 15 Sep. 1937, 2.

74. On the very heavy workload of a raion judge, see Manning, "Government," 14–16.

75. *RTsKhIDNI*, f. 112, op. 26, d. 21, ll. 128–29.

76. *SA*, WKP 355:29.

77. *TsGANKh*, f. 396, op. 10, d. 64, l. 165; ibid., d. 143, l. 211.

78. Ibid., d. 145, l. 448.

79. *SA*, WKP 500:76–77.

80. *SA*, WKP 239:28.

81. *TsGANKh*, f. 396, op. 10, d. 87, unpg.

82. Ibid., d. 66, l. 7.

83. Ibid., d. 142, l. 670; ibid., d. 129, unpg. (letter of T. I. Shalypin).

Chapter 10

1. For a more extended discussion of this question, see "Becoming Cultured: Socialist Realism and the Representation of Privilege and Taste" in Sheila Fitzpatrick, *The Cultural Front. Power and Culture in Revolutionary Russia* (Ithaca, 1992), 216–37.

2. Rogalina, *Kollektivizatsiia: Uroki proidennogo puti* (Moscow, 1989), 198.

3. *Pr*, 16 Sep. 1935, 3. For the other version, see p. 228.

4. *SZ*, 2 Jan. 1938, 2; *Kommuna*, 8 July 1936, 4; *KrP*, 1 Apr. 1935, 4.

5. *SZ*, 2 Jan. 1938, 2; *VVSKU*, 70.

6. *TsGANKh*, f. 7486, op. 19, d. 399, l. 79.

7. *KG*, 21 Nov. 1933, 3; *RP*, 16 Aug. 1937, 4; *Zv*, 5 Oct. 1937, 4; *SZ*, 12 Aug. 1938, 4.

8. *ZKP*, 18 Dec. 1935, 2; *Kul'turnaia zhizn' v SSSR 1928–1941. Khronika* (Moscow, 1976), 504, 514, 620–21 (festival listings).

9. *ZKP*, 18 Dec. 1935, 2; *Kul'turnaia zhizn'*, 493, 530, 523. Barbusse, the noted French writer and Soviet sympathizer, author of the antiwar novel, *Le Feu* and a biography of Stalin, was one of the contributors to a Potemkin volume about the Soviet Union, *Glazami inostrantsev: Inostrannye pisateli o Sovetskom Soiuze*, ed. M. Zhivov (Moscow, 1932).

10. "*Gotov k trudu i oborone*" (Ready for labor and defense)—the Soviet equivalent of a Scout badge.

11. *Geroini*, 71.

12. *Desiatyi syezd Vsesoiuznogo Leninskogo Kommunisticheskogo Soiuza Molodezhi 11–12 aprelia 1936 g. Stenograficheskii otchet* (Moscow, 1936), 1, 288; 2, 118; A. P. Veselov, *Bor'ba Kommunisticheskoi partii za provedenie kul'turnoi revoliutsii v derevne v gody kollektivizatsii* (Leningrad, 1978), 106.

13. Handbooks of the late 1930s such as *Sotsialisticheskoe stroitel'stvo Soiuza SSR (1933–1938 gg.). Statisticheskii sbornik* (Moscow-Leningrad, 1939) and *SSSR strana sotsializma. Statisticheskii sbornik* (Moscow, 1936) reflect these trends most clearly.

14. *Sotsstroi* (1939), 143.

15. Calculated from ibid., 85, 143.

16. *VVSKU*, 70 (Shestopalov, tractordriver).

17. *Desiatyi syezd VLKSM*, 1, 271–72; *SA*, WKP 203:188.

18. *SZ*, 24 Mar. 1938, 1.

19. Jay Leyda, *Kino* (London, 1960), 342.

20. *SZ*, 26 Mar. 1938, 4.

21. Gerasimov (1967), 78.

22. V. G. Tan-Bogoraz, *Obnovlennaia derevnia. Sbornik* (Leningrad, 1925), 8; *Rabotnitsa*, no. 5–6, 16 (1935) (Lobanova quotation).

23. *Izv*, 16 Feb. 1935, 1.

24. Anokhina (1964), 281.

25. This description draws on Alexander Yanov's, "A Collective Farm Meeting," based on observations in the 1960s, in *International Journal of Sociology* 6(2–3): 13–15 (1976).

26. Gushchin (1975), 194–95; *SDK*, 484. For an angry outburst after a speech on the international situation, see p. 293.

27. Peter Kenez, *Birth of the Propaganda State*, (Cambridge, 1985), 138; *Zori sovetskoi pionerii*, 74; *ISK* 2:391.

28. See *SA*, WKP 166:767–8

29. *SA*, WKP 166:774, 737; *GASO*, f. 88, op. 1, d. 66, l. 20.

30. *TsGANKh*, f. 396, op. 10, d. 161, l. 473.

31. *KultStroi* (1956), 300, 322; Arina (1939), 215; *VVSKU*, 213.

32. Vyltsan (1970), 24; *ZKP*, 14 Oct. 1935, 3.

33. *KultStroi* (1956), 300–1; *SotsStroi* (1939), 129 and 130.

34. *Desiatyi syezd VLKSM*, 1:277; *Sotsial'nyi oblik kolkhoznoi molodezhi po materialam sotsiologicheskikh obsledovanii 1938 i 1969 gg.* (Moscow, 1976), 23–24. Note that the sample is clearly biased towards prosperous collective farms.

35. Alekseev (1982), 312–14.

36. *KrP*, 27 Feb. 1935, 2; *VVSKU*, 209; Fedor Dubkovetskii, *Na putiakh k kommunizmu. Zapiski zachinatelia kolkhoznogo dvizheniia na Ukraine* (Moscow, 1951), 41–44.

37. *VVSKU*, 78.

38. *KrP*, 28 Feb. 1935, 2.

39. *VVSKU*, 61; *KrP*, 27 Feb. 1935, 2; *Geroini*, 48.

40. National conferences of this type included meetings of women "500-ers" in sugarbeet production (November 1935), outstanding male and female combine operators (December 1935), outstanding grain harvesters (tractor drivers and threshers) (December 1935), male and female kolkhozniks of Tadzhikistan and Turkmenistan (December 1935), male and female kolkhozniks of Uzbekistan, Kazakhstan, and Karakalpakia (December 1935), leading workers in animal husbandry (February 1936), and flax and hemp producers (March 1936). *ISK* 2:349, 351; Vyltsan (1978), 121–30.

41. *Spravochnik partiinogo rabotnika* (Moscow, 1935) 9:192–3.

42. See their biographies in *Bol'shaia sovetskaia entsiklopediia* (2nd ed.).

43. *KrP*, 16 Nov. 1935, 3. This article, devoted entirely to description of ritual and thus a real oddity in terms of contemporary journalistic convention, was published unsigned.

44. *Geroini*, 44–45.

45. Ibid., 40.

46. Ibid., 36–38.

47. Ibid., 98, 75, 72.

48. Stalin, *Soch.* 1 (14):106.

49. *KP*, 9 Dec. 1935, 3.

50. *Geroini*, 128–29, 40.

51. Ibid., 101–2, 129, 54–55.

52. See Stalin, *Soch.* 1(14):74–76.

53. Stalin, *Soch.* 1(14):75–76.

54. *VVSKU*, 34.

55. *Geroini*, 53, 57.

56. Ibid., 92–93.

57. Ibid., 87.

58. See E. H. Carr, *The Bolshevik Revolution, 1917–1923* (London, 1966), 1:153–54; *Sovetskoe gosudarstvo i pravo v period stroitel'stva sotsializma (1921–1935 gg.)* (Moscow, 1968), 2, 217–18. The RSFSR had a complicated system in which the weighting is hard to assess exactly. In the other republics, the weighting was a straightforward 5:1 in favor of the towns.

59. Vyltsan (1970), 192; *ZKP*, 21 Nov. 1934, 2; *SZ SSSR*, no. 22, art. 85 (1937).

60. Data on delegates from *Pr*, 12 Feb. 1935, 2, and 15 Feb. 1935, 1–2; and *Izv*, 12 Feb. 1935, 1, and 16 Feb. 1935, 1 (Shapovalova). The Russian and Soviet parliaments, renamed Supreme Soviets in 1937, were earlier known by the acronyms VTsIK and TsIK (All-Russian/All-Union Executive Committee of the Congress of Soviets).

61. *SA*, WKP 191:32.

62. *Geroini*, 162–63.

63. See *SZ*, 18 Nov. 1938, 4, for a report of a meeting of the film's director and scriptwriter with a group of celebrity kolkhozniks to check on the verisimilitude of the scenario.

64. Kabanov, *ISSSR*, no. 6, 117 (1976); *KP*, 8 Feb. 1935, 2; *7 Syezd Sovetov. Stenograficheskii otchet* (Moscow, 1935), bull. 17, 41.

65. *Istoriia sovetskoi konstitutsii (v dokumentakh) 1917–1956* (Moscow, 1957), 726.

66. Each electoral district would elect one deputy and represent a population of 300,000. Decree of 9 July 1937 on elections to the Supreme Soviet of the USSR, *SZ SSSR*, no. 43, art. 182 (1937).

67. *Trud*, 11 Mar. 1937, 1–2 (Zhdanov's speech to CC plenum); *KPSSvR* 5:286–87 (CC resolution).

68. Local (oblast, raion, city and rural) soviet elections took place for the first time under the new Constitution in December 1939. E. M. Kozhevnikov, *Istoricheskii opyt KPSS po rukovodstvu Sovetskim gosudarstvom (1936–1941)* (Moscow, 1977), 95–96.

69. *Trud*, 11 Mar. 1937, 1–2.

70. For a different view, see J. Arch Getty, "State and Society under Stalin: Constitutions and Elections in the 1930s," *SR* 50(1):18–35 (1991). The minutes of the plenum convey the strong impression that Central Committee members were so apprehensive about what was to come in later reports (Molotov, Ezhov, and Stalin on wrecking) and so preoccupied about their personal survival that they paid no attention whatsoever to Zhdanov's speech on the elections. The chairman had to call on people by name to get any discussion, and even the top party leaders (with the exception of Zhdanov himself) seemed confused about the subject. "What elections?" interjected Stalin distractedly at one point. Speakers had difficulty remembering whether the elections were to be single- or multicandidate, despite Zhdanov's patient explanations. Kalinin, chairman of the Soviet parliament, disclaimed knowledge of the new electoral procedures, noting that if people expected his office to issue detailed instructions they were going to be disappointed. One speaker, moreover, associated the democratic impulse with Radek, now a discredited "enemy of the people." *RTsKhIDNI*, f. 17, op. 2, d. 612, ll. 4–40, esp. 8, 10, 18, 24, 34.

71. *KrK*, 3 Aug. 1937, 3.

72. *NR*, 276–78.

73. *Profsoiuzy SSSR*, no. 5–6, 16–19 (May, 1938); *Kommuna*, 11 Oct. 1937, 2, and 22 Nov. 1937, 2.

74. *SZ SSSR*, no. 43, art. 182 (1937); *RP*, 3 Jul 1937, 1–2, and 26 Sep. 1937, 2. Collective farms were not originally listed among the nominating institutions, but subsequent clarification of the decree's intent included them.

75. *Zv*, 23 Mar. 1937, 3. This anonymous letter to the editor was not published as such; it was quoted (ostensibly with disapproval) in the body of an article on anti-religious propaganda.

76. *KrP*, 2 Aug. 1937, 2–3; *Kommuna*, 22 Nov. 1937, 2; *Profsoiuzy SSSR*, no. 5–6, 16–19 (1938); *AR*, no. 8, 2 (1937); *Kommuna*, 22 Nov. 1937, 2; *SevR*, 10 Sep. 1937, 3. See also *KrP*, 20 Jun. 1937, 3; *SO*, 6 Aug. 1937, 2; *Kommuna*, 21 Aug. 1937, 1.

77. *NR*, 278.

78. On religion as a means of popular protest in Russia, see Ethel Dunn in Millar (1971), 374.

79. *SA*, WKP 111:74.

80. On conspiracies, see *Bezbozhnik*, no. 7, 8 (July. 1937). On arrests, see *NR*, 278–79, and above, pp. 201–3.

81. *RP*, 4 Dec. 1937, 2. See also *KurPr*, 2 Nov. 1937, 2.

82. *RP*, 10 Sep. 1937, 2; *Kommuna*, 22 Nov. 1937, 2.

83. See Getty, "State and Society," 31.

84. *RP*, 21 Oct. 1937, 1; *Pr*, 12 Nov. 1937, 3.

85. *RP*, 28 Sep. 1937, 1.

86. *Kommuna*, 12 Nov. 1937, 1, and 22 Nov. 1937, 2.

87. *KurPr*, 2 Nov. 1937, 2; *Kommuna*, 27 Nov. 1937, 1.

88. Kozhevnikov, 88; *Rabochii klass v upravlenii gosudarstvom* (*1926–1937 gg.*) (Moscow, 1968), 97–98.

89. *Kommunist*, no. 1, 98 (1990).

90. *TsGANKh*, f. 396, op. 10, d. 39, l. 276.

91. *SA*, WKP 186:61.

Chapter 11

1. See Anand A. Yang, "A Conversation of Rumors: The Language of Popular Mentalités in 19th-Century Colonial India," *Journal of Social History*, Spring 1987.

2. Arvo Tuominen, *The Bells of the Kremlin* (Hanover/London, 1983), 113.

3. Ibid.

4. *TsGAOR*, f. 374, op. 9, d. 418, l. 70; *GASO*, f. 88/r, op. 1a, d. 57, ll. 59–60.

5. *TsGAOR*, f. 374, op. 9, d. 418, 70; *GASO*, f. 88/r, op. 1a, d. 57, ll. 59–60; *SA*, WKP 151:194; *GASO*, f. 88/r, op. 1a, d. 57, l. 30.

6. *SA*, WKP 166:178, 180, and 184.

7. Ibid., 216. This report comes from a non-Russian (Jewish?) kolkhoz.

8. Ibid., 399.

9. Ibid.

10. *VI*, no. 6, 180 (1991).

11. *KolTsChO*, 278–79; Mozhaev (1988), 478.

12. The lament was published in *Pr*, 1 Dec. 1936. See Frank J. Miller, *Folklore for Stalin. Russian Folklore and Pseudo-Folklore of the Stalin era* (Armonk, N.Y., 1990), 11.

13. *SA*, WKP 415:22 ("*Kogda Kirova ubili/Torgovliu khlebnuiu otkryli/Kogda Stalina ubyiut/Vse kolkhozy razvedut*"). A variant is "*Kogda Kirova ubili/Po pudu soli dali/Kogda Stalina ubyiut/Po dva puda nam dadut*" (ibid., 6)

14. Different variants are in *SA*, WKP 352:132, and *SA*, WKP 237:39.

15. *SA*, WKP 355:33 (my emphasis).

16. *SA*, WKP 352:115; *SA*, WKP 355:48, 51, and 57.

17. *SA*, WKP 415:22, and 19.

18. See *SA*, WKP 415 for materials on discussions of the Central Committee's secret letter in Komsomol organizations.

19. On the expulsions, see p. 176.

20. *SA*, WKP 362:240 (NKVD report from Belyi raion, 16 July 1937).

21. Ibid., 240.

22. *TsGANKh*, f. 396, op. 11, d. 44, l. 64; *KrP*, 2 Aug. 1937, 2–3; *SA*, WKP 500:296. The Western obkom does not seem to have taken these "insurrectionary" organizations seriously.

23. Poliakov (1990), 68.

24. Poliakov (1990), 68.

25. *NR*, 277.

26. Stalin, *Soch.*, 1 (14):254.

27. *KrP*, 2 Aug. 1937, 2–3; *SA*, WKP 415:142.

28. *TsGANKh*, f. 396, op. 10, d. 162, l. 222; ibid., d. 88, unpg. (letter from I. A. Koshkin et al.). For examples of peasant letters to Stalin, see above, pp. 101–2 and 285.

29. Dmitrii Volkogonov, "Triumf i tragediia," *Oktiabr'*, no. 11, 105 (1988).

30. *Lubok/The Lubok*, comp. Yu. Ovsyannikov (Moscow, 1968), 11–14. This interpretation is disputed in *SR* 50(3):560–62 (1991).

31. The following account is based on local newspaper reports of thirty raion show trials held in eleven oblasts and krais of the Russian Republic, plus two trials in Ukraine and one in Belorussia. The total number of such trials is unknown, but on the basis of this sample it can be estimated that they were held in at least 3 percent of Russia's rural raions.

32. *Pr*, 9 Mar. 1937, 6; 10 Mar. 1937, 6; 11 Mar. 1937, 6; 12 Mar. 1937, 6.

33. Reports on the Shiriaevo trial appeared in *Pr*, 15 June 1937, 4; 16 June 1937, 4; 17 June 1937, 6; 18 June 1937, 6; and 19 June 1937, 6; *SZ*, 18 June 1937, 4, and 21 July 1937, 1; and also in some provincial papers.

34. *Pr*, 2 July 1937, 6; 5 July 1937, 5 (Novominsk case); 15 July 1937, 1; 29 July 1937, 6; 30 July 1937, 6; and 31 July 1937, 6 (Danilov case).

35. *Pr*, 3 Aug. 1937, 1.

36. I have borrowed this term from Katerina Clark, *The Soviet Novel. History as Ritual* (Chicago, 1981), 5–15.

37. *Pr*, 9 Mar. 1937, 6; 16 June 1937, 4; 30 July 1937, 6.

38. *RP*, 8 Sep. 1937, 4; *Kommuna*, 6 Oct. 1937, 2, and 1 Sep. 1937, 4.

39. But note that this was not part of *Pravda*'s original message, presumably because the concept of "enemies of the people" and the use of article 58 had broadened immensely in the months between March 1937 (when *Pravda* reported the first "model" case) and late August, when the wave of raion show trials began. In the Lepel trial in March, the accused were indicted under article 196 of the Belorussian Criminal Code (violation of Soviet law and abuse of power), and in the Danilov trial in June they were accused of destruction of socialist property under the law of 7 August 1932. *Pravda* did not record the specific article of the Criminal

Code used in the Novominsk and Shiriaevo cases, but probably would have done so had it been article 58.

40. One defendant admitted he had known a Trotskyite in Moscow in 1928, just after graduating from party school. Another had allowed a former Trotskyite, the director of the local veterinerary school, to escape arrest by going into hiding. *Kommuna*, 3 Oct. 1937, 2; ibid., 3 Sep. 1937, 3.

41. A. I. Solzhenitsyn, *The Gulag Archipelago* (New York, 1973), 1–2:419–31. The Kady story, which Solzhenitsyn probably heard in gulag from one of the defendants, is told very much from the defendants' point of view, emphasizing that they were innocent scapegoats who fell victim to factional politics at the oblast level.

42. *Kommuna*, 29 Aug. 1937, 4; 3 Sep. 1937, 3; 4 Sep. 1937, 4. For other similar denials and protestations, see *KurPr*, 29 Aug. 1937, 3; *SevR*, 30 July 1937, 4.

43. *RP*, 5 Sep. 1937, 3.

44. Sentences were reported for ten of the trials and can be deduced for an eleventh: see *KP*, 29 Aug. 1937, 3; *KP*, 2 Sep. 1937, 2; *KP*, 20 Oct. 1937, 3; *KurPr*, 4 Sep. 1937, 2; *KurPr*, 4 Sep. 1937, 2; *RP*, 29 Aug. 1937, 3; *RP*, 18 Oct. 1937, 2; *Kommuna*, 6 Sep. 1937, 4; *Kommuna*, 6 Oct. 1937, 2; *MKG*, 3 Nov. 1937, 4

45. See coded telegrams from Stalin's personal archive (currently held in the so-called "Presidential" or "Kremlin" Archive) recently published in *Izv*, 10 June 1992, 7 (I am indebted to Arch Getty for informing me of this publication); and the report in *RP*, 2 Sep. 1937, 1.

46. *Kommuna*, 30 Aug. 1937, 4; ibid., 4 Sep. 1937, 4.

47. *KrP*, 3 Sep. 1937, 2.

48. *SZ*, 21 July 1937, 1; *SIu*, no. 20, 22 (1937).

49. *SIu*, no. 20, 24 (1937).

50. *Kommuna*, 28 Sep. 1937, 2; *SIu*, no. 20, 22 (1937); *KrP*, 17 Aug. 1937, 4.

51. *SIu*, no. 20, 24 (1937); *Kommuna*, 4 Sep. 1937, 4.

52. *Kommuna*, 28 Sep. 1937, 2.

53. *Kommuna*, 2 Sep. 1937, 3.

54. *KrP*, 28 Aug. 1937, 1.

55. *SevR*, 22 Sep. 1937, 2.

56. *SZ*, 26 July 1937, 2; *KrP*, 20 Oct. 1937, 3.

57. *KurPr*, 2 Oct. 1937, 1; 16 Oct. 1937, 4.

58. An exception was the Nerekhta trial, in which a raion soviet chairman was accused of mistreating peasants during the *1933* famine. *SevR*, 22 Sep. 1937, 2.

59. *MKG*, 5 Oct. 1937, 2.

60. Ibid., 28 Aug. 1937, 1.

61. Ibid., 2 Sep. 1937, 2.

62. Ibid., 26 Aug. 1937, 2, and 2 Sep. 1937, 2.

63. *Kommuna*, 28 Sep. 1937, 1–2, and 3 Oct. 1937, 2.

64. *KrP*, 28 Oct. 1937, 4; *RP*, 12 Sep. 1937, 2; 16 Oct. 1937, 1 and 2. Roberta Manning's "The Case of the Miffed Milkmaid" gives a fascinating account, drawn from the Smolensk Archive, of the events in Sychevka leading up to the show trial.

65. *KrP*, 30 July 1937, 2–3.

66. See above, p. 240.

67. *SZ*, 26 July 1937, 2, and 28 Dec. 1937, 3; *KurPr*, 26 Aug. 1937, 3; 23 Aug. 1937, 4; 29 Aug. 1937, 3; 2 Sep. 1937, 3; 14 Oct. 1937, 4.

68. *RP*, 16 Oct. 1937, 2.

69. *Kommunist* (Saratov), 14 Sep. 1937, 3.

70. *SevR*, 30 July 1937, 4; *Kommuna*, 4 Sep. 1937, 4.

71. *Kommuna*, 3 Oct. 1937, 2.

72. *Kommuna*, 6 Oct. 1937, 2; *KrP*, 27 Aug. 1937, 2; *Kommuna*, 28 Sep. 1937, 2; *SevR*, 22 Sep. 1937, 2; *KrP*, 2 Sep. 1937, 2.

73. *KrP*, 2 Sep. 1937, 2; *KrP*, 26 Aug. 1937, 2; *Kommuna*, 4 Sep. 1937, 4. See also *Zv*, 20 Sep. 1937, 1.

74. *KrP*, 3 Sep. 1937, 2.

75. Ibid.

76. *KPSSvR* 5, 313–20; *IKP* 2:127–28.

77. *KPSSvR* 5:398–404; Alec Nove, *An Economic History of the U.S.S.R.* (London, 1972), 257–58.

78. On carnival, see Natalie Zemon Davis, "The Reasons of Misrule," in her *Society and Culture in Early Modern France* (Stanford, 1975); Peter Burke, *Popular Culture in Early Modern Europe* (London, 1978), ch. 7.

79. Solzhenitsyn, 419–31. In Kady, according to the account told to Solzhenitsyn, the defendants denounced the trial as an NKVD set-up, defending themselves so bravely that the crowd was completely won over.

80. *Pr*, 31 July 1937, 6.

81. *SA*, WKP 355:33.

Afterword

1. See Alexander Dallin, *German Rule in Russia, 1941–1945. A Study of Occupation Policies* (London, 1957), esp. 370–71; Alec Nove, in Susan J. Linz, ed., *The Impact of World War II on the Soviet Union* (Totowa, N.J., 1985), 77–78.

2. For an analysis of the incorporation of peasants into the French nation in the nineteenth century, see Eugen Weber, *Peasants into Frenchmen* (Stanford, 1976).

3. *ISSSR*, no. 5, 130 (1982); Sheila Fitzpatrick, "*War and Society* in Soviet Context: Soviet Labor Before, During and After World War II," *International Working-class and Labor History* 35:45 (1989); M. Ia. Sonin, *Vosproizvodstvo rabochei sily v SSSR i balans truda* (Moscow, 1959), 144 and 148; *NarKhoz* (1972), 9.

4. On popular expectations, see "Ukradennaia pobeda" (interview with G. A. Bordiugov), *KP*, 5 May 1990, 2; on religion, see William C. Fletcher, *The Russian Orthodox Church Underground* (London, 1971), 152–62; on developments within the kolkhoz, see the decree of 19 Sep. 1946, *SZ SSSR*, no. 13, art. 254 (1946).

5. *SZ SSSR*, no. 13, art. 254 (1946).

6. Jerry Hough, "The Changing Nature of the Kolkhoz Chairman," in Millar (1971), 109–11; Arthur E. Adams and Jan S. Adams, *Men versus Systems. Agriculture in the USSR, Poland and Czechoslovakia* (New York, 1971), 22.

7. Quoted from *Sovetskaia Rossiia*, 6 Feb. 1968, 1, by Hough, "Changing Nature," 106–107.

8. Adams, *Men versus Systems*, 55.

9. Adams, *Men versus Systems*, 30. For a similar comment on the kolkhoz of the 1970s, see Roy D. and Betty A. Laird, "The Soviet Farm Manager as an Entrepreneur," in Gregory Guroff, *Entrepreneurship in Imperial Russia and the Soviet Union* (Princeton, 1983), 258–59.

10. Alexander Yanov, quoted in Adams, *Men versus Systems*, 31. On the entrepreneurial nature of the modern kolkhoz chairman, see Laird, "The Soviet Farm Manager," 258–83.

11. David W. Bronson and Constance B. Krueger, "The Revolution in Soviet Farm Household Income, 1953–1967," in Millar (1971), 223.

12. Maggs, in Millar (1971), 155; Laird, "The Soviet Farm Manager," 278–81.

13. *SZ SSSR*, no. 29, art. 340 (1964); F. J. M. Feldbrugge, ed., *Encyclopedia of Soviet Law* (Leiden, 1973) 2:366–67. Before the creation of an All-Union Health Insurance Fund by the 1970 act, the kolkhozy had been supposed to provide sickness, old age, and disability benefits to members at their own discretion and out of their own funds. See the 1935 Charter, par. 11 (*RPPKhoz* 2:524–25).

14. Zhores A. Medvedev, *Soviet Agriculture* (New York, 1987), 347.

15. Feldbrugge, ed., *Encyclopedia of Soviet Law* 2:366; Gertrude E. Schroeder, "Rural Living Standards in the Soviet Union," in Robert C. Stuart, ed., *The Soviet Rural Economy* (Totowa, N.J., 1983), 243. The category "agricultural workers" covers kolkhozniks and sovkhoz farm workers.

16. Michael Ryan, *Contemporary Soviet Society: A Statistical Handbook* (Aldershot, Hants., 1990), 135. For a good overview of sociocultural changes in the Soviet Union since the 1950s, see Moshe Lewin, *The Gorbachev Phenomenon: A Historical Interpretation* (Berkeley, 1988), part 1.

17. Schroeder, "Rural Living Standards," 247–49.

18. *NarKhoz* (1972), 116; Schroeder, "Rural Living Standards," 250, 254; Adams, *Men versus Systems*, 93.

19. Medvedev, *Soviet Agriculture*, 381–82.

20. Ryan, *Contemporary Soviet Society*, 19.

21. Victor Zaslavsky and Yuri Luryi, "The Passport System in the USSR and Changes in Soviet Society," *Soviet Union/Union soviétique* 6(2):137–44 (1979); Medvedev, *Soviet Agriculture*, 323. Note that the rate of out-migration noticeably declined in the subsequent decade. Between 1979 and 1989, the rural population dropped in absolute terms only by one million (Ryan, *Contemporary Soviet Society*, 19).

22. *Itogi vsesoiuznoi perepisi naseleniia 1959 goda. SSSR (Svodnyi tom)* (Moscow, 1962), 13; Ryan, *Contemporary Soviet Society*, 19; *Itogi vsesoiuznoi perepisi naseleniia 1979 g.* 7 (Moscow, 1990), 6. Between 1950 and 1980, the number of state farm workers more than tripled and the number of kolkhozniks halved (Schroeder, "Rural Living Standards," 247–49).

23. *Ogonek*, no. 38, 8 (1990).

24. *The New York Times*, 17 Feb. 1992, 1; *Current Digest of the Soviet Press*, no. 18, 8 (1992).

Index